SPORTS MARKETING

Sports Marketing: A Strategic Perspective is the most authoritative, comprehensive, and engaging introduction to sports marketing currently available. It is the only introductory textbook on this subject to adopt a strategic approach, explaining clearly how every element of the marketing process should be designed and managed, from goal-setting and planning to implementation and control.

Covering all the key topics in the sports marketing curriculum, including consumer behavior, market research, promotions, products, pricing, sponsorship, business ethics, technology, and e-marketing, the book introduces core theory and concepts, explains best practice, and surveys the rapidly changing international sports business environment. Chapters contains extensive real-world case studies and biographies of key industry figures, and challenging review exercises encourage the reader to reflect critically on their own knowledge and professional practice.

Now in a fully revised and updated sixth edition, *Sports Marketing: A Strategic Perspective* includes expanded coverage of social and digital media, analytics, and ethical issues, as well as a greater number of international articles and examples. In a new feature, successful sports marketers reflect on their careers and how they progressed in the sports marketing industry.

It is an essential foundation for any sports marketing or sports business course, and an invaluable reference for any sports marketing practitioner looking to improve their professional practice.

A companion Web site offers additional resources for instructors and students, including an instructor's guide, test questions, presentation slides, and useful weblinks.

Matthew D. Shank is President of the Virginia Foundation of Independent Colleges (VFIC), USA and President Emeritus of Marymount University, USA.

Mark R. Lyberger is Associate Professor of Sport Administration and Director of the Center for Sport and Recreation Development at Kent State University, USA.

6th edition

SPORTS MARKETING

A STRATEGIC PERSPECTIVE

MATTHEW D. SHANK AND
MARK R. LYBERGER

Routledge
Taylor & Francis Group

LONDON AND NEW YORK

Sixth edition published 2022
by Routledge
2 Park Square, Milton Park, Abingdon, Oxon, OX14 4RN

and by Routledge
605 Third Avenue, New York, NY 10158

Routledge is an imprint of the Taylor & Francis Group, an informa business

Every effort has been made to contact copyright-holders. Please advise the publisher of any errors or omissions, and these will be corrected in subsequent editions.

First edition published by Pearson 1998

Fifth edition published by Routledge 2015

British Library Cataloguing-in-Publication Data
A catalogue record for this book is available from the British Library

Library of Congress Cataloging-in-Publication Data
Names: Shank, Matthew D., author. | Lyberger, Mark R., author.
Title: Sports marketing : a strategic perspective / Matthew D. Shank and
   Mark R. Lyberger.
Description: 6th edition. | Abingdon, Oxon ; New York, NY : Routledge,
   2022. | Includes bibliographical references and index. Identifiers: LCCN
   2021025078 | ISBN 9780367141646 (hardback) | ISBN 9780367141653
   (paperback) | ISBN 9780429030673 (ebook)
Subjects: LCSH: Sports—United States—Marketing. | Sports—Economic
   aspects—United States.
Classification: LCC GV716 .S42 2022 | DDC 796.068/8—dc23
LC record available at https://lccn.loc.gov/2021025078

ISBN: 978-0-367-14164-6 (hbk)
ISBN: 978-0-367-14165-3 (pbk)
ISBN: 978-0-429-03067-3 (ebk)

DOI: 10.4324/9780429030673

Typeset in Stone Serif, Avenir, and Rockwell
by Apex CoVantage, LLC

Access the companion Web site: www.routledge.com/cw/shank

Contents

Illustrations

Ads

Figures

Infographics

Photos

Web captures

PART I

Contingency framework for strategic sports marketing

1 Emergence of sports marketing

After completing this chapter, you should be able to:

- Define sports marketing and discuss how the sports industry is related to the entertainment industry.
- Describe a marketing orientation and its relationship to the sports industry.
- Examine the growth of the sports industry.
- Discuss the simplified model of the consumer–supplier relationship in the sports industry.
- Explain the different types of sports consumers.
- Identify historical trends and significant impacts of sport marketing practices.
- Define sports products and discuss the various types of sports products.
- Understand the different producers and intermediaries in the simplified model of the consumer–supplier relationship in the sports industry.
- Discuss the elements in the sports marketing mix.
- Explain the exchange process and why it is important to sports marketers.
- Outline the elements of the strategic sports marketing process.

Mary is a typical "soccer mom." At the moment, she is trying to determine how to persuade the local dry cleaner to provide uniforms for her daughter's Catholic Youth Organization soccer team.

George is the president of the regional Chamber of Commerce. The ten-year plan for the metropolitan area calls for developing four new sporting events that will draw local support while providing national visibility for this growing metropolitan area.

DOI: 10.4324/9780429030673-2

Sam is an events coordinator for a 10K road race, which is an annual fundraiser for fighting lung disease. He is faced with the difficult task of trying to determine how much to charge for the event to maximize participation and proceeds for charity.

Ramiz is the athletic director for State University. In recent years, the men's basketball team has done well in postseason play; therefore, ESPN has offered to broadcast several games this season. Unfortunately, three of the games will have to be played at 10 p.m. local time to accommodate the broadcaster's schedule. Ramiz is concerned about the effect this will have on season ticket holders because two of the games are on weeknights. He knows that the last athletic director was fired because the local fans and boosters believed that he was not sensitive to their concerns.

Susie works for a sports marketing agency that is representing a professional sport franchise. The franchise is planning to expand its international market presence. She is challenged with establishing relationships in a new environment that hosts a unique set of cultural values and customs.

What is sports marketing?

The American Marketing Association defines *marketing* as "the activity, set of institutions, and processes for creating, communicating, delivering, and exchanging offerings that have value for customers, clients, partners, and society at large."[1] Sport and entertainment have been defined in a variety of ways; however, most definitions include terms such as *indulgent, divergence,* and/or *engagement* for valued outcomes of *enjoyment, pleasure,* or *amusement.* Although sport may often consist of a more competitive nature, both sport and entertainment are inclusive of retaining diverse exchange platforms. These diverse platforms provide a variety of engagement opportunities and yet, uniquely, are composed of an array of outcomes that are distinctly similar.

Sports marketing is the specific application of marketing principles and processes to sport products and to the marketing of non-sports products through association with sport. The sports industry is experiencing tremendous growth, and sports marketing plays an important role in this dynamic industry. Many people mistakenly think of sports marketing as promotions or sports agents saying, "Show me the money." As the opening examples illustrate, sports marketing is more complex and dynamic, yet interesting because of the unique nature of the sports industry.

Mary, the soccer mom, is trying to secure a sponsorship; that is, she needs to convince the local dry cleaner that they will enjoy a benefit by associating their service (dry cleaning) with a kids' soccer team.

As president of the Chamber of Commerce, George needs to determine which sports products will best satisfy his local consumers' needs for sports entertainment while marketing the city to a larger and remote audience.

In marketing terms, Sam is trying to decide on the best pricing strategy for his sporting event; Ramiz is faced with the challenge of balancing the needs of two market segments for his team's products; and Susie, the sport marketer, is seeking to persuade international populations of the relevance of diversifying their sport culture. As you can see, each marketing challenge is complex and requires careful planning.

To succeed in sports marketing one needs to understand both the sports industry and the specific application of marketing principles and processes to sports contexts. In the next section, we introduce you to the sports industry. Throughout this book, we continue to elaborate on ways in which the unique characteristics of this industry complicate and call for unique strategic marketing decisions. After discussing the sports industry, we review basic marketing principles and processes with an emphasis on how these principles and processes must be adapted to the sports context.

Understanding the sports industry

Historical development of sports marketing in (North) America

The evolution of sports marketing strategies to meet the needs and wants of the consumer continues to be a priority of practitioners worldwide. Today's realm of sports marketing and sponsorship, though a more dramatically effective and a much more diverse platform, is vaguely similar to what many identify as its origin, 776 BCE, when the ancient Olympic Games began. Marketers for the ancient Olympic Games were no amateurs; these perceptive businessmen realized early on that an affiliation with a popular athlete could produce a potentially lucrative relationship.[2] Throughout history, sport in some form has existed and, though the common-day term of *sports marketing* had not yet emerged, the process of utilizing marketing and promotion strategies to enhance delivery and production has been evident.

The roots of sports marketing in North America can be traced back to the 1850s and 1860s when many businesses, recognizing the popularity of sport, attempted to create linkages to enhance commercial opportunities by marketing through sport. Two events of this era in particular, one collegiate and one professional, illustrate the use of marketing through sport and helped lay a foundation for utilization of sport as a service medium in North America.

In 1852, a railroad official, together with a group of local businessmen, believed that they could garner enough interest in the marketing and staging of the event to produce economic and commercial profits. The end result was the first intercollegiate match between Harvard University and Yale University – a two-mile rowing contest. This event took place at a quiet summer resort called Center Harbor on Lake Winnipesaukee, New Hampshire. The result demonstrated that the entrepreneurs were able to create a positive economic impact on the region, enhancing rail traffic, hotel occupancy, and revenue for the host city.

The second event is tied to the late 1850s and early 1860s and the commercialization of the new sport of baseball. Tobacco companies partnered with professional baseball leagues and began using photographs of the teams to help sell their products and services. These companies made baseball cards with pictures of the teams and players and then inserted them into cigarette packets to boost and enhance brand loyalties. Though the strategies of distribution have been altered over the years – that is, transition from the use of cigarettes, to bubblegum, to today's independent packages – these strategies laid the foundation for a new industry: the memorabilia and card collecting/trading market that exists today.

North American sport experienced a variety of popularity struggles in the late 1800s and early 1900s. A demand for reform arose and threatened sport at a variety of levels. In 1906, with the assistance of President Theodore Roosevelt, efforts were made to transform the image of sport. Strategies and regulations were implemented to enhance the safety and appeal of the game. Rules, regulations, and the control of lurking controversies, such as the controversy distinguishing the amateur and professional status of athletes, became a primary emphasis of sport organizations.

Although the early 1920s were a period of relative calm in American society, the country was intrigued by the newest technology of the day, the radio. Marketers, sports administrators, and broadcasters alike sought to integrate sports utilizing this medium, a medium at the time that many believed symbolized a coming age of enlightenment. No other medium has changed the everyday lives of Americans as quickly and irrevocably as radio.[3] In 1921, the first American baseball broadcast occurred from Forbes Field. Though this broadcast was deemed a success, marketers of the era struggled to transcend executives' opinions, because some believed that the broadcasts would have a negative impact upon attendance and demand.

In the 1930s and 1940s sports organizations utilized radio to enhance team revenue streams. Innovative marketers began relying on the radio to get their message across to the common man. In 1936, this same forum was used as a marketing and public relations campaign to pronounce the success of Jessie Owens and his Olympic debut.

Radio provided the impetus to solidify the era of patronage; however, the invention that soon followed remains to this day the most significant communication medium that has influenced and aided the development of sports. Who knew what sportscaster Bill Stern questioned and introduced in 1939 would enhance the growth and development of sports marketing practices for decades? The display platform, the television, though airing two mediocre baseball teams battling for fourth place, provided an incredibly formidable and profitable union between sport and the American public. The television provided a means for sports organizations to expand their market presence and presented a unique opportunity for marketers to engage their publics. The notion of a "picture being worth a thousand words" became a reality with the invention and its intervention and presentation of sports.

Executives such as Bill Veeck became innovators of sports marketing, utilizing radio and in-game promotional strategies to further market their teams. Owners, players, broadcasters, and fans recognized the variety of impacts television would have on the presentation of sports. In fact, television giant CBS dropped its Sunday afternoon public service emphasis to provide for a 12-week professional football broadcast.

American consumers in the 1950s loved and demanded sports. Participation trends and fan demand steadily increased. Sports became a symbol of changing times in the United States. On April 15, 1947, Jackie Robinson broke the color barrier in baseball. The importance of this event in helping the civil rights movement in the United States is evident, but it also proved the social power of sports in American culture and the impact that could be made utilizing sports as a communication medium. By including minorities in sports, the market grew. Cultural acceptance, along with media presence provided the American public with a means to link personalities and audiences.

This prominence led to the identity era of the 1960s. Chuck Taylor/Converse, Muhammad Ali/adidas/Champion, Jim Brown/NFL, Mickey Mantle/Major League Baseball, Arnold Palmer/PGA and Arnie's Army, to name a few, all became marketable entities. Marketers began to utilize sport to establish linkages with consumer publics. Endorsements and sponsorships evolved. Representation through agents became the norm for those who had prominence. For example, sport marketing giant International Management Group (IMG) founder Mark McCormack and golf great Arnold Palmer instituted a legendary handshake deal that lasted more than 40 years.

The 1970s included several evolutionary events in sports marketing. Consumer demand for sport continued to rise, while existing and emerging commercial entities such as Nike, adidas, Puma, and others fought to snatch up endorsement opportunities. Sponsorships of products by athletes continued to emerge as a trend of the decade. In fact, the first corporate sponsorship of a stadium venue occurred in Buffalo in 1973 – Rich Stadium. Buffalo-based Rich Products agreed to pay $37.5 million, $1.5 million per year over 25 years.[4]

In the 1970s athletes, too, began to stake a presence. Athletes such as Joe Namath became sex symbols, and advertisers began to realize that athletes could add a unique element to any product in the context of an endorsement campaign (e.g., Jack Nicklaus, Muhammad Ali, Mario Andretti, to name a few). This was further demonstrated at the end of the decade when Coke utilized Pittsburgh Steelers tackle "Mean" Joe Greene to star in one of the most acclaimed advertisements ever.

Throughout the 1970s mergers, acquisitions, and governmental ramifications were prominent. Title IX gave women additional access to participate in sports. Advertising laws that forced the tobacco industry off the TV airways freed funding for alternative marketing and advertising strategies. These tobacco companies could avert the law by developing sponsorship arrangements, thus affording the growth of events such as Virginia Slims Tennis and the NASCAR Winston Cup.

Television markets were further expanded due to cable offerings that afforded network growth. Television began bringing teams from across the country into the spotlight. A health craze swept the nation, further complementing commercial and consumer ties to sport. Entrepreneurs grasped new opportunities, with Ted Turner developing and marketing a superstation in 1976 and Bill Rasmussen introducing ESPN, the first true 24-hour sports broadcasting network in 1979.

In the 1980s salaries skyrocketed and leagues saw a need to remain competitive. Increased competition created a variety of economic and financial issues. Emphasis on television revenues became a priority. Money from media contracts became important to a team's bottom line and its ability to recruit and pay top players. Miracle workers such as NFL Commissioner Pete Rozelle and Olympics marketing and television guru Richard Pound continued to develop and enhance sponsorship and media contracts as they related to sport. Professionals such as Rozelle of the NFL, Peter Ueberroth of NBC, and Pound of the IOC had a significant impact on the explosion of so-called strategic alliances as a result of external competitive pressures such as globalism of economies and constantly advancing technologies.[5]

The 1980s represented the "me" decade in sports. Sporting goods were tailored to be aligned with specific sports. With the likes of Larry Bird, Magic Johnson, Joe Montana, and the introduction to Michael Jordan, fans continued through the turnstiles, disregarding the negative influences and impacts of skyrocketing salaries, agents, greed among teams and players, drug use by athletes, and free agency. Despite or because of the greed, sports grew in popularity and became a more desirable marketing platform.

Sport sponsorship began to see double-digit growth. Sponsor dollars were abundant and even mediocre athletes began signing contracts to endorse or wear their products.[6] The expansion of sponsorship as a communication medium was greatly influenced by the emergence of sports leagues and corporate involvement during the 1970s and 1980s. However, this growth did not come without resistance. Resistance by broadcasters, event managers, and consumers alike focused on the intrusion of corporate America into this restricted arena.

Many corporate CEOs became involved with sponsorship for unsubstantiated reasons; that is, they favored a sports activity or they chose to intermingle with famous sports celebrities. Exposure through affiliation was achieved, but without justification of the return on investment. Marketing strategies varied considerably due to the limited channels of exposure, but objectives were to align corporate endorsers to enhance the linkages and exposure of the events. This growth created a corporate reliance that would create many future marketing implications.

During the Michael Jordan era of the 1990s, television had become the driving force behind almost every league, including the NFL, NBA, NHL, MLB, NCAA, and NASCAR. In fact, the majority of teams and sport organizations became reliant upon these television revenues. Increased revenue streams offered opportunities for expansion. Organizations, such as the NHL, expanded to regions in the South, whereas others, such as the NBA, began to focus beyond the Americas. Sponsorship continued to enhance the dollar pool and rose at a double-digit pace. Salaries continued to skyrocket, and leagues expanded to take advantage of untapped markets. Most fans wanted to be loyal; however, struggles such as the 1994 MLB strike had a severe impact on its popularity and adversely impacted consumer loyalty. Strategies became more focused and began to emphasize the transfer of unique connotations inherent in the property and brand image.

Although the modern world of mega-million-dollar sponsorships had begun, marketers questioned the cluttered environment. The driving force behind the game and its growth had become clouded. Prior to the 1990s, management's use of sponsorship was often criticized for the cavalier and often frivolous approaches undertaken.[7] During this era sponsorship became entrenched as a legitimate corporate marketing tool. It saw an unprecedented double-digit growth and that had a significant impact on image, value, recognition, and method of delivery.

In recent years, sport marketing has continued to grow but at a more moderate pace and not without restriction or limitations. PricewaterhouseCoopers (PwC) in their 2018 Sports Outlook estimated that the sports market in North America will grow at a compound annual rate of 3 percent across the four segments analyzed, from $69.1 billion in 2017 to $80.3 billion in 2022. The relative growth of the four revenue segments from 2017 to projected 2022 numbers include media rights (4.5 percent), sponsorship (3.8 percent), gate revenues (2.2 percent), and merchandising (1.2 percent).[8]

Beyond North America, demand through technology has created an international platform, a platform encompassing numerous cultural variances. Today's athletes are a global commodity. In today's sports marketing environment, much more is at stake than free agency, new stadiums, and escalating player salaries. Today, organizations seek to provide resources directly to an individual, authority, or body to enable the latter to pursue some activity in return for benefits contemplated in terms of the sports market strategy, and which can be expressed in terms of corporate, marketing, or media objectives.[9]

For every Nike or LeBron success, there are at least as many ineffective sports marketing strategies that cost millions of dollars. Many athletes today capitalize on their image more than their athletic prowess. From athletes in their primes to athletes who have made lasting impressions, endorsement deals do not necessarily end when a professional career is over. Professional athletes are aware of the effect their image has on endorsement dollars, and most are not willing, nor ready, to give up a share of endorsements. If today's players had Babe Ruth's devil-may-care attitude, they would likely never see the kinds of endorsement dollars the more polished, public images today are garnering.[10]

Today's sport marketer recognizes that image influences the bottom line. The most prolific athletes are not always the most celebrated, and the most celebrated are often not the most gifted athletes. However, in today's environment all are under the microscope of intense media attention. Because of today's growing media and social network influences, it is crucial for sports marketers to recognize consumer need and define the "why" as it relates to sports marketing applications. Defining the "why" is crucial to its successful interpretation. Today's sports marketers must find ways to break through the clutter and present new and better sports promotions, products, ideas, pricing structures, and ways to distribute the action to the fans.

Sport as entertainment

Webster's defines **sport** as "a source of diversion or a physical activity engaged in for pleasure."[11] Sport takes us away from our daily routine and gives us pleasure. Interestingly, *entertainment* is also defined as something diverting or engaging. Regardless of whether we are watching a new movie, listening to a concert, or attending an equally stirring performance by Messi, we are being entertained.

Most consumers view movies, plays, theater, opera, or concerts as closely related forms of entertainment. Yet, for many of us, sport is different. One important way in which sport differs from other common entertainment forms is that sport is spontaneous. A play has a script and a concert has a program, but the action that entertains us in sport is spontaneous and uncontrolled by those who participate in the event. When we go to a comedic movie, we expect to laugh, and when we go to a horror movie, we expect nail-biting entertainment. But the emotions we may feel when watching a sporting event are hard to determine. If it is a close contest and our team wins, we may feel excitement and joy. But if it is a boring event and our team loses, the entertainment *benefit* we receive is quite different. Because of its spontaneous nature, sport producers face a host of challenges that differ from those faced by most entertainment providers.

Nonetheless, successful sports organizations realize the threat of competition from other forms of entertainment. They have broadened the scope of their businesses, seeing themselves as providing "sporttainment." The emphasis on promotional events and stadium attractions that surround athletic events is evidence of this emerging entertainment orientation. Consider the NBA All-Star Game. What used to be a simple competition between the best players of the Western Conference and the best players of the Eastern Conference has turned into an entertainment extravaganza. The event (not just a game anymore) lasts for days and includes slam-dunk contests, a celebrity and rookie game, concerts, a three-point shooting competition, and plenty of other events designed to promote the NBA.[12] In 1982, the league created a separate division, NBA Entertainment, to focus on NBA-centered TV and movie programming. NBA TV has created and produced original programming, including shows like *Finding Giannis, What If: Draft Stories,* and *NBA TV Finals Film*

Room. The line between sport and entertainment has certainly become blurred, if not indistinguishable. Sport venues, athletes, and competition all must have strong entertainment elements and appeal or they will ultimately fail, no matter how successful the team's performance.

Of course, one of the most highly visible and long-lasting examples of "sporttainment" is World Wrestling Entertainment, better known as the WWE. The WWE has managed to build a billion-dollar empire across decades, posting a record revenue of $930 million in fiscal year 2018. Interestingly, a large portion of the jump in revenue was based on international events, specifically in Saudi Arabia.[13] Vince McMahon, WWE founder and chairman, continues to be a driving force behind the WWE, with some calling him the P.T. Barnum of our time.

The sports entertainment phenomenon is also sweeping the globe, and as organizations begin to recognize the value of sport as entertainment in this global environment, it is important for sports marketers to understand *why* consumers are attracted. Defining what consumer needs are and how those needs relate to the global environment will further complement the marketing exchange process we will discuss later.

Organizations that have not recognized how sport and entertainment relate are said to suffer from marketing myopia. Coined long ago by Theodore Levitt, **marketing myopia** is described as the practice of defining a business in terms of goods and services rather than in terms of the benefits sought by customers. Sports organizations can eliminate marketing myopia by focusing on meeting the needs of consumers rather than on producing and selling sports products and services.

A marketing orientation

The emphasis on satisfying consumers' wants and needs is everywhere in today's marketplace, regardless of the industry. Most successful organizations concentrate on understanding the consumer and providing a product that meets consumers' needs while achieving the organization's objectives. This way of doing business is called a **marketing orientation**.

Marketing-oriented organizations practice the marketing concept that organizational goals and objectives will be reached if customer needs are satisfied. Organizations employing a marketing orientation focus on understanding customer preferences and meeting these preferences through the coordinated use of marketing. An organization is marketing oriented when it engages in the following activities:[14]

- ***Intelligence generation*** – analyzing and anticipating consumer demand, monitoring the external environment, and coordinating the data collected;
- ***Intelligence dissemination*** – sharing the information gathered in the intelligence stage; and

- ***Responsiveness*** – acting on the information gathered to make market decisions such as designing new products and services and developing promotions that appeal to consumers.

Using the previous criteria (intelligence gathering, intelligence dissemination, and responsiveness), think about a local college or professional team in your area and their level of marketing orientation and their success. Today's college and professional franchises are making great strides in using a data-informed approach or sports analytics for everything from player personnel decisions to fan promotions. Table 1.1 shows the rankings of best markets for minor-league sports in the United States that have long been known for their market-orientated approach.

Table 1.1 Best Markets for Minor League Sports

Year	Market
2005	Rochester, New York
2007	Fort Wayne, Indiana
2009	Hershey-Harrisburg, Pennsylvania
2011	Hershey-Harrisburg, Pennsylvania
2013	Toledo, Ohio
2015	Quad Cities (Illinois-Iowa)
2017	Des Moines, Iowa
2019	Grand Rapids-Comstock Park, Michigan

Source: D. Broughton. (2019, September 23). "Grand Rapids: Built to Last." *Sports Business Journal.* www.sportsbusinessdaily.com/Journal/Issues/2019/09/23/In-Depth.aspx

Growth of the sports industry

Sport has long been one of the most important and universal institutions in our society. It is estimated that the global sports industry reached a value of nearly $490 billion in 2019 and is predicted to grow to $614 billion by 2022.[15] This growth includes both spectator and participation market segments, which we will discuss later in chapter.

With this growth, the industry has become increasingly complex with respect to conventional and new media distribution fronts. Like it or not, sports are a huge part of our culture, and we have access 24 hours a day. This is leading to a new brand of "superfan" obsessed with sport and their team or, as the following YouTube video illustrates, their tribe (www.youtube.com/watch?v=aY6GTSDYDRo).[16]

We know that the size and scope of the sport industry is growing, but how can we measure this growth? Let us look at the industry in terms of attendance, media coverage, employment, and the global market.

Attendance

While we have discussed the growth of the sports industry overall, one trend to follow closely is the recent decline in attendance for almost every professional sport league in the United States. MLB was at an all-time high in average attendance when it peaked at 32,785 in 2007. The average was at 30,517 in 2015 before declining for 4 straight years, with a 1.4 percent drop in 2019 for an average attendance of approximately 28,300. NFL attendance in 2018 was down 2 percent from the previous year, with an average of 67,100 fans per game, the lowest since 2011.[17]

According to preliminary NCAA numbers for 2019, Football Bowl Subdivision (FBS) college football attendance was down for the seventh time in the last eight seasons, reaching its lowest average mark in 22 years. The average of 41,856 fans per game for the 129 FBS teams in 2018 was the lowest figure since 1996. That's 1 year after the average per-school decline was the largest in 34 years.[18] The drop in football attendance is less of a story these days, but the question remains about how to curb this trend.

The NHL has enjoyed stable attendance over the last decades with attendance at the conclusion of the 2018 season averaging 17,456 fans. Compare this with an average attendance of 17,446 in 2017, and there has been very little deviation over the years. However, the 2019 season saw a slight decrease, with an average of 17,377 fans, and this could be a growing trend. Like other sports, the NHL is continuing to invest in the game experience to keep fans coming to the arenas.[19]

The NBA seems to be bucking the downward attendance trend experience by the other major professional sports leagues in the United States, with 5 years of consecutive increases. The league broke its attendance record in 2018–2019 with 22 million fans attending NBA games and an average attendance per game of 17,987.[20]

Major League Soccer (MLS), which had its inaugural season in 1996, has seen tremendous growth over the life of the league. However, even the MLS has seen slight declines in attendance over the past few years. Since the low point of attendance in the late 1990s (average attendance around 15,000), the league's average attendance has grown to roughly 22,000 consistent with the growing popularity of soccer in the United States.[21]

Media coverage

Although millions of Americans attend sporting events each year, even more consume sports on network and cable television, listen to sports on the radio, or stream their favorite game. For example, the 2019 Super Bowl featuring the Los Angeles Rams and New England Patriots was watched by an estimated 98.2 million viewers, with an estimated 67 percent of all households with televisions in use tuned in to the game. Although these are staggering numbers, viewership was at an 11-year low.[22]

Today in the United States 119 million people own at least one TV, and the numbers continue to increase. According to Nielsen's television data, an average of 19.8 million viewers watched the 2018 Winter Olympics from South Korea during prime time.[23] Contrast this with the always more popular Summer Games. For example, the 2016 Games in Rio averaged about 28 million viewers in the United States per evening. While viewership of both Summer and Winter Games are down, there is still an incredible number of total viewers.

ESPN, the original sports-only network launched in 1979, reached record consumption of its core television business in 2011 and 2012. On television and across digital platforms, ESPN was able to secure a series of healthy financial agreements with the NFL, NCAA, Wimbledon, Pac-12, and Indy 500. With its long-term and wide-ranging pact with its largest distributor, Comcast, ESPN was able to marry compelling content with evolving technology, notably WatchESPN. In addition, ESPN aired a significantly higher number of regular season and college bowl games. The wide variety of ESPN programs serves the sports fan wherever they are in the world. However, a big question remains for all sports media companies, including ESPN: Can they continue to grow revenue in the face of shrinking paid cable subscribers and more people than ever streaming content?[24]

ESPN+, the company's direct-to-consumer streaming service that launched in April 2018, is growing quickly and now has more than 2 million subscribers (as of February 2019). The number of more traditional cable subscriptions, however, is down around 2 million, from 88 million in 2017 to 86 million in 2018. The iconic sports channel has lost about 14 million subscribers over the past 7 years and will need to adjust to a new business model and new ways to be profitable.[25]

Again, even with these shifts in consumption behavior, the media market for sports is still massive. Consider that the U.S. sports media market in 2019 was worth $22.42 billion, a number that is expected to grow over the next several years.[26] In addition, in May 2018 the U.S. Supreme Court lifted the federal ban on sports betting, and this will most certainly drive even greater interest in sports media as people will be even more engaged in the outcomes of sporting events.[27]

The huge demand for sports broadcasting has led to the introduction of more sport-specific channels. Sport networks such as the MLB Network, Fuel TV, Fox College Sports, the Outdoor Channel, and the SEC Network have emerged because of consumer demand. Presently, worldwide there are in excess of 300 sport channels. This practice of "narrowcasting," reaching very specific audiences, continues to be important in the sports media landscape.

What sports remain most popular to watch? Well, in a recent U.S. survey, football is, and remains, king. The numbers remain very consistent since 2014 when nearly 40 percent indicated football was their favorite sport to watch. In 2018, about the same percentage say football is their favorite with the numbers being about the same for men and women. This is about the same percentage (39 percent) of people who *combined* indicated baseball, basketball, soccer, hockey, or auto racing was their favorite sport.[28]

Web Capture 1.1

The growth of sports information on the World Wide Web

Credit: Sports Business Journal

URL: www.sportsbusinessjournal.com/Daily.aspx

Employment

Another way to explore the size of the sports industry is to look at the number of people the industry employs. Data from the Bureau of Labor Statistics (BLS) estimates that there are 3 million jobs within 524 occupations that are directly related to or dependent on the sports industry. In addition to the United States, the United Kingdom employs some 987,000 people in its $23.8 billion a year sports industry.[29]

Consider all the jobs that are created because of sports-related activities such as building and staffing a new stadium. Sports jobs are plentiful, and include but are not limited to event suppliers, event management and marketing, sports media, sport sales, sports sponsorship, athlete services, sports commissions, sports lawyers, manufacturers and distribution, facilities and facility suppliers, teams, leagues, college athletics, and finance.

The number of people working directly and indirectly in sports will continue to grow as the sports industry grows. Sports marketing creates a diverse workforce, ranging from the players who create the competition to the photographers who shoot the action (see Appendix A for a discussion of careers in sports marketing).

Global markets

Not only is the sports industry growing in the United States, but it is also expanding globally. As the following article on international sports marketing discusses, the NBA is a premier example of a powerful global sports organization that continues to grow in emerging markets: www.cnbc.com/2019/01/18/nba-steps-up-its-global-plans-to-take-basketball-to-new-markets.html.

The structure of the sports industry

The structure of the sports industry can be discussed from a number of perspectives. For example, we can look at the industry from an organizational perspective; that is, we can understand some things about the sports industry by studying the different types of organizations that populate it, such as local recreation commissions, national youth sports leagues, intercollegiate athletic programs, professional teams, and sanctioning bodies. These organizations use sports marketing to help them achieve their various organizational goals. For example, agencies such as the United States Olympic Committee (USOC) use marketing to secure the funding necessary to train and enter American athletes into the Olympic Games and Pan American games.

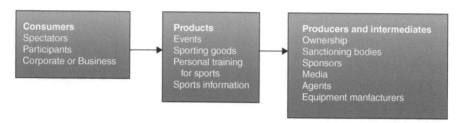

Consumers
Spectators
Participants
Corporate or Business

Products
Events
Sporting goods
Personal training
for sports
Sports information

Producers and intermediates
Ownership
Sanctioning bodies
Sponsors
Media
Agents
Equipment manfacturers

Figure 1.1
Simplified model of the consumer–supplier relationship in the sports industry

Ad 1.1
E-sports blurring the line between spectator and participant
*Source:*www.nea.gg

The traditional organizational perspective, however, is not as helpful to potential sports marketers as a consumer perspective. When we examine the structure of the sports industry from a consumer perspective, the complexity of this industry and its challenge to sports marketers becomes obvious. Figure 1.1 shows a **simplified model of the consumer-supplier relationship**.

The sports industry consists of three major elements: consumers of sport, the sports products that they consume, and the suppliers of the sports product. In the next sections, we explore each of these elements in greater detail.

The consumers of sport

The sports industry exists to satisfy the needs of three distinct types of consumers: spectators, participants, and sponsors.

The spectator as consumer

If the sporting event is the heart of the sports industry, then the spectator is the blood that keeps it pumping. **Spectators** are consumers who derive their benefits (in different forms) from the observation of the event. The sports industry, as we know it, would not exist without spectators. Spectators observe the sporting event in two broad ways: they attend the event or they experience the event via a particular type of media (i.e., radio, television, streaming).

As Figure 1.2 illustrates, the two broad types of consumers are individual consumers and corporate consumers. Collectively, this creates four distinct consumer groups. Individuals can attend events in person by purchasing single-event tickets or series (season) tickets. Not only do individuals attend sporting events, but so, too, do corporate employees representing their firms and entertaining their current and prospective clients. Today, stadium luxury boxes and conference rooms are designed specifically with the corporate consumer in mind. Many corporate consumers can purchase special blocs of tickets to sporting events. At times, tension may exist between the needs of corporate consumers and individual consumers. Many believe that corporate consumers, able to pay large sums of money for their tickets, are pushing out the individual consumer and raising ticket prices.

Both individual spectators and corporations can also watch the event via a media source. The corporate consumer in this case is not purchasing the event for its own viewing, but rather acting as an intermediary to bring the spectacle to the end-user groups or audience. For example, CBS (the corporate consumer) purchases the right to televise the Masters Golf Tournament. CBS then controls how and when the event is experienced by millions of individual spectators who comprise the television audience.

Historically, the focus of the sports industry and sports marketers was on the spectator attending the event. The needs of the consumer at the event were catered to first, with little emphasis on the viewing or listening audience. Due to the growth of media influence and the power of the corporate consumer, the focus has changed to pleasing the media broadcasting the sporting event to spectators in remote locations on their own personal devices.

According to PwC's Sports Outlook, media rights or the fees paid to show sports on TV, the Internet, and other distribution channels will remain the

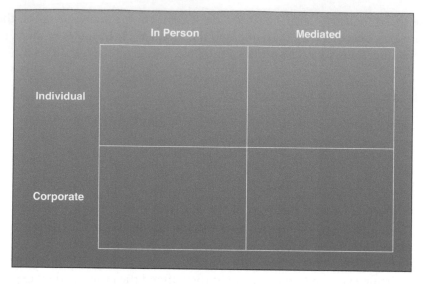

Figure 1.2
Individual versus corporate consumer

largest piece of total sports revenues in North America. Media rights are esti-mated to reach $23.8 billion in revenue in 2022, representing 30 percent of all sports revenues. These dollars are greater than those generated from gate rev-enues, sponsorships, licensing, and merchandise sales, along with other major forms of revenue.[30]

Identifying and understanding the different types of spectator consumption is a key consideration for sports marketers when designing a marketing strategy.

The participant as consumer

In addition to watching sports, more people are becoming active **partici-pants** in a variety of sports at a number of competitive levels. Figure 1.3 shows trends in participation in sports and fitness activities over a period of five years. The figure shows two broad classifications of sports participants: those who participate in unorganized sports and those who participate in organized sports. As the number of participants grows, the need for sports marketing expertise in these areas also increases.

Unorganized sport participants/organized sport participants

Amateur
Youth recreational instructional
Youth recreational elite
Schools
Intercollegiate
Professional
Minor/secondary
Major

Total Participation Rate by Activity Category

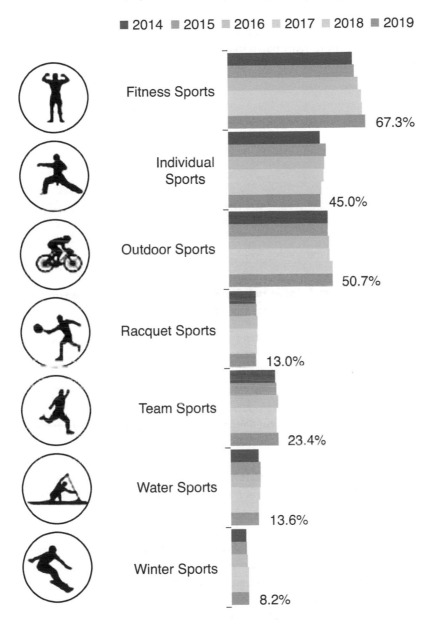

Figure 1.3
Trends in sports participation: 2014–2019

Source: Sport & Fitness Industry Association. (2020). "Sports, fitness, and leisure activities topline participation report." www.sfia.org/reports/802_2020-Sports%2C-Fitness%2C-and-Leisure-Activities-Topline-Participation-Report

Unorganized sports are the sporting activities people engage in that are not sanctioned or controlled by some external authority. Kids playing a pickup game of basketball, teenagers skateboarding, or people playing street roller hockey, as well as fitness runners, walkers, and bikers, are only a few of the types of sporting activities that millions of people participate in each day. The number of people who participate in unorganized sports is difficult to estimate, but as the following article illustrates, it is impacted by a variety of external factors.

ARTICLE 1.1

CONSUMER FITNESS SURVEY FINDS POST COVID-19, BILLIONS IN SPEND WILL BE LOST OR REALLOCATED IN MASSIVE INDUSTRY TRANSFORMATION

Harrison Co. Proprietary Research helps at-risk fitness club industry identify consumers most likely to change their fitness routines, and what it can do to keep them

The U.S. fitness industry will be radically recast post-COVID-19, as billions of dollars in consumer spending is shifted to at-home fitness options at the expense of the health club industry. That was among the findings of an exclusive consumer survey by Harrison Co., a consumer-focused investment bank.

"Before COVID-19, both health clubs and home fitness had been enjoying steady growth driven by a number of trends that pointed to a continued upward trajectory"

The survey, conducted in April 2020 of approximately 1,000 fitness club users, was released in a research report today, "*COVID-19 Fitness Survey.*" The proprietary data reflects that $10 billion annually could leave the club sector, much of it for home fitness options, reflecting changing consumer sentiment surrounding health club safety and cleanliness.

"The difficult economic circumstances currently faced by gyms and health clubs will not disappear once the crisis ends," said Paul Byrne, a partner at Harrison Co. "Once stay-at-home guidelines are lifted, consumers will continue to work out at home in numbers far beyond anything we saw prior to the crisis."

Other key takeaways and areas of exploration of the report include:

- 34% of gym exercisers have or plan to cancel their gym memberships after COVID-19 and more than 20 million gym memberships could be cancelled due to COVID-19;

- As a result of the coronavirus, 40% of respondents exercised at home for the first time;
- More than 38,000 clubs and studios have presently shut down because of the virus. Clubs will have to adhere to increased cleanliness and safety protocols in order to successfully reopen and maintain member trust;
- At least 500,000 fitness club employees have been furloughed as a result of the club shutdowns; and
- Despite having the impact to financially devastate the health club industry, 37% of all survey participants indicated they would work out more after COVID-19, and over 50% of them said they are motivated to do so by a renewed appreciation for their health and well-being.

"Before COVID-19, both health clubs and home fitness had been enjoying steady growth driven by a number of trends that pointed to a continued upward trajectory," Byrne said. "The pandemic has clearly accelerated working out from home. Post-COVID, fitness companies will have to respond to the recasting of the competitive landscape by utilizing the convenient, compelling, and immersive strategy of streaming."

For equipment makers, the report also noted that winners in the at-home sector extend beyond Peloton and other direct-to-consumer suppliers. Manufacturers such as Inspire and Bowflex, as well as specialty retailers such as Precor Home Fitness, have experienced significant year-over-year increases. In many cases, demand has outstripped supply.

Source: Businesswire. (2020, May 26). "Consumer fitness survey finds post COVID-19, billions in spend will be lost or reallocated in massive industry transformation." www.businesswire.com/news/home/20200526005202/en/Consumer-Fitness-Survey-Finds-Post-COVID-19-Billions

The size of the market for unorganized sports is huge, and there are many opportunities for sports marketers to serve the needs of these consumers. The market for organized sports is also massive, particularly when we examine the numbers in youth sports.

Organized sporting events refer to sporting competitions that are sanctioned and controlled by an authority such as a league, association, or **sanctioning body**. There are two types of participants in organized events: amateur and professional.

Amateur sporting events are sporting competitions for athletes who do not receive compensation for playing the sport. Amateur competitions include recreational youth sports at the instructional and elite (also known as "select") levels, high school sports controlled at the state level through leagues, intercollegiate sports (NCAA Division I-III, NAIA, and NJCAA), Olympics, and adult community-based recreational sports. **Professional sports** for athletes who do receive compensation are also commonly classified by minor league or major league status.

ARTICLE 1.2
CAREER SPOTLIGHT

Louise Waxler, Executive Director, McLean Youth Soccer

1. **What is your career background?** I became involved in sports in a professional capacity in 1985, specifically managing events. The skills required for event management helped to guide me into learning the operational elements of managing a sports organization. I took on the task of managing a youth soccer tournament that grew to be one of the top 10 events in the United States providing elite competition in the sport of soccer. What I thought would be a 1- to 2-year position actually lasted 20 years. During those years, I continued to follow my passion for the game and had the opportunity to host the United States Women's National Team in 1994 and prior to the 1995 Women's World Cup held in Sweden. The players on that team drove my passion to even greater heights, and several have become lifelong friends.

2. **How did you get to where you are today?** Through my involvement with youth sports, I was offered a position with the Washington Freedom of the Women's United Soccer League, the first professional women's league in the world. My role with the team was escalated from managing youth events to working at RFK Stadium in Washington, D.C. managing the game-day operations of a professional franchise. It was John Hendricks, founder of Discovery Communications, who gave me this opportunity and launched my career to a level that I could have never imagined.

3. **What is your role as executive director for McLean Youth Soccer (MYS)?** To lead a successful and evolving organization and help ensure that it remains one of the premier youth soccer programs in the Commonwealth of Virginia and the country. The key facets of the job are to manage all employees, volunteers, and contract labor staff; administer the directives and policies of the board of directors; help develop and implement MYS's business, financial, and strategic plans; develop and implement an effective infrastructure for MYS and its programs; administer MYS programs and tournaments; and represent the club locally and nationally in the youth soccer arena.

4. **How does marketing play a role in MYS?** Having the ability to attract players to the club via advertising, cross-marketing with other sports, social media outlets, financial aid programs for need-based players, flexible payment arrangements, quality and well-established coaching staff, and well-versed management staff to operate the club in a professional manner. All of these facets attract potential sponsors/partners/players and elevate the profile of the organization in the community, as well as on a national level.

5. **What are the main challenges facing youth sports today?** Instant gratification, early specialization, and unrealistic expectations from parents. These factors put tremendous stress on players to be overachievers. The love of the game should be the primary reason for kids to participate in sports, not parental pressure. John O'Sullivan, founder of Changing the Game Project, states that the top challenges in youth sports are parents who won't let the game belong to kids; athletes need to *own* their decisions, both good

and bad; coaches who fail to respect the kids and the sport and ignore the massive impact they have on athletes' lives; and youth sports organizations that serve adults, not kids.

6. **Why do you think youth sports are so important?** Sport has the unique ability to effect transformation/change and unite people in an enjoyable, unobtrusive, and sustainable manner. Sport is a vehicle that transcends all boundaries – race, gender, class, and religion. It also has the unique ability to uplift our communities, because through sport we are able to keep our youth off the streets, each one has the opportunity of uncovering or developing some other talent or skill, and we are able to create a sense of pride and belonging. We have to ensure that the benefits of sport filter down to everyone, not just the elite.

7. **What advice would you give to students who want to pursue a career in the sports industry?** Be certain that you are prepared to handle the challenges that accompany the business. You must have a love for sports but also be business-savvy. Sponsorship and marketing are vital aspects of the sports industry as they often "pay the bills and salaries" of professional athletes. Determine if you prefer to work in the nonprofit versus for-profit sector, as the responsibilities are vastly different. Jump in with both feet, look forward, never backwards, and give it your all!

The sponsor as consumer

Other, equally important consumers in sports marketing are the many business organizations that choose to sponsor sports. In **sports sponsorship**, the consumer (in most cases a business) is exchanging money or product for the right to associate its name or product with a sports entity (e.g., events, team, league), creating a commercial competitive advantage for both parties. The decision to sponsor a sport is complex. The sponsor must not only decide on what sport(s) to sponsor, but must also consider what level of competition (recreational through professional) to sponsor. They must choose whether to sponsor events, teams, leagues, or individual athletes.

Although sponsorship decisions are difficult, sponsorship is growing in popularity for a variety of reasons. As Pope discusses in his excellent review of current sponsorship thought and practices,[31] sponsorship can help achieve corporate objectives (e.g., public awareness, corporate image building, and community involvement), marketing objectives (e.g., reaching target markets, brand positioning, and increasing sales), media objectives (e.g., generate awareness, enhance ad campaigns, and generate publicity), and personal objectives (management interest).

Global sports sponsorship spending is expected grow to $65 billion in 2019 and is anticipated to reach over $89 billion by the end of 2024 (see Figure 1.4).[32] Sponsorship spending in North America is projected to reach a record $24.2 billion in 2019, and sports will continue to be the leading category, with 70 percent of the North America sponsorship market.[33]

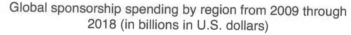
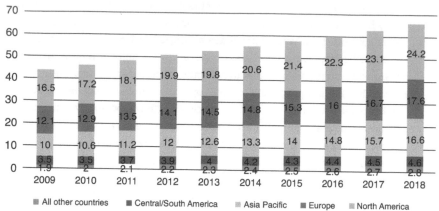

Figure 1.4
Global sponsorship spending by region: 2009–2018

Source: A. Guttman. (November 26, 2019). "Statista, global sponsorship spending from 2007 to 2018." www.statista.com/statistics/196864/global-sponsorship-spending-since-2007/

Projections for future growth are highly dependent upon the unprecedented recognition at the highest levels of corporations that sponsorship is a potential answer to the challenge of how to build attention, support, and loyalty for brands in an environment that is otherwise hostile and exhausted by the quantity of marketing communications.

The sports product

Perhaps the most difficult conceptual issue for sports marketers is trying to understand the nature of the sports product. Just what is the sports product that participants, spectators, and sponsors consume? A **sports product** is a good, a service, or any combination of the two that is designed to provide benefits to a sports spectator, participant, or sponsor.

Goods and services

Goods are defined as tangible, physical products that offer benefits to consumers. Sporting goods include equipment, apparel, and shoes. We expect sporting goods retailers to sell tangible products such as tennis balls, racquets, hockey equipment, exercise equipment, and so on. By contrast, **services** are defined as intangible, nonphysical products. A competitive sporting event (i.e., the game itself) or an ice-skating lesson are examples of sport services.

Sports marketers sell their products based on the **benefits** the products offer to consumers. In fact, products can be described as "bundles of benefits."

Whether as participants, spectators, or sponsors, sports products are purchased based on the benefits consumers derive. Ski Industry America, a trade association interested in marketing the sport of snowshoeing, understands the benefit idea and suggests that the benefits offered to sports participants by this sports product include great exercise, little athletic skill, and low cost (compared with skiing). It is no wonder snowshoeing has recently emerged as one of the nation's fastest-growing winter sports.[34]

Spectators are also purchasing benefits when they attend or watch sporting events. For example, the 2018 World Cup final between France and Croatia attracted more than 1 billion viewers, according to FIFA, the game's governing body.[35] The game provides consumers with benefits such as entertainment, ability to socialize with friends and other fans, and feelings of identification with their country's teams and athletes.

Sponsors also purchase benefits when associating their name and brand with sports venues. The benefits that organizations often receive from naming rights include enhanced image, more awareness, and increased sales of their products. For example, Scotiabank paid a record-setting $800 million for the naming rights to the building that houses Toronto's Maple Leafs and Raptors. Under terms of the deal, the bank will pay a reported $40 million a year for 20 years to rename the building known as the Air Canada Centre to the Scotiabank Arena.[36]

Different types of sports products

Sports products can be classified into four categories: sporting events, sporting goods, sports training, and sports information. Let us take a more in-depth look at each of these sports products.

Sporting events

The primary or core product of the sports industry is the **sporting event**. By primary product, we are referring to the competition, which is needed to produce all the related products in the sports industry. Without the game there would be no licensed merchandise, collectibles, stadium concessions, and so on. You may have thought of sports marketing as being important for only professional sporting events, but, as is evident by the increased number of media outlets and broadcasts, the marketing of collegiate sporting events and even high school sporting events is becoming more common.

Historically, a large distinction was made between amateur and professional sporting events. Today, that line is becoming more blurred. For example, the Olympic Games, once considered the bastion of amateur sports, is allowing professional athletes to participate for their countries. Most notably, the rosters of the Dream Teams of U.S. Basketball fame and the U.S. Hockey team are almost exclusively professional athletes. This has been met with some criticism. Critics say that they would rather give the true amateur athletes their chance to "go for the gold." Of course, there has been a raging debate for the last several years on the virtues of paying college athletes who are amateurs but seen as professionals given the dollar amounts at stake for their colleges and universities.[37]

Athletes   Athletes are participants who engage in organized training to develop skills in particular sports. Athletes who perform in competition or exhibitions can also be thought of as sports products. Neymar, Rory McIlroy, and Megan Rapinoe are thought of as "bundles of benefits" that can satisfy consumers of sport both on and off the court.

One athlete to achieve this "superproduct" status is the billion-dollar phenomenon named Eldrick "Tiger" Woods. Tiger seemed to have it all. He was handsome, charming, young, multiethnic, and, most important, talented. Tiger's sponsors certainly thought he was worth a large investment. However, poor choices and inappropriate behavior attracted controversy that has required the likes of Nike, Buick, NetJets, and American Express to rethink their level of affiliation, impacting Tiger's multimillion-dollar sponsorship deals. Some sponsors, including Nike, stuck by Woods, whereas others (e.g., Taylor-Made, Bridgestone Golf, and Monster Energy) signed on with Woods when there was an opening. These new sponsors and those that continued to support Woods have been handsomely rewarded with his amazing comeback, culminating with his victory at the 2019 Masters.[38]

Sports marketers must realize that the "bundle of benefits" that accompanies an athlete varies from person to person and has affiliated risk. The benefits associated with Rose Lavelle (U.S. Women's Soccer) are different from those associated with Steph Curry or golfer Jordan Spieth. Regardless of the nature of the benefits, and as discussed earlier in the chapter, many of today's athletes are not thinking of themselves as athletes but as entertainers.

Arena or event venue   A final sports product that is associated with the sporting event is the site of the event, typically an arena or stadium. Today, the stadium is much more than a place to go watch the game. It is an entertainment complex that may include restaurants, bars, picnic areas, and luxury boxes. Today's teams are not only trying to create more visually appealing buildings, but they are interested in making attending the game an all-encompassing entertainment experience. In fact, stadium seating is becoming a "product" of its own.

For example, some of the following changes already seen at today's venues will soon become the norm. Features such as free Wi-Fi, mobile apps, fantasy stats on video boards, TVs in seats and bathrooms, customizable instant replays, bars overlooking fields, holograms on the field instead of players, and improved access are not the wave of the future but are now commonplace. According to TeamWorks Media cofounder and CEO Jay Sharman, psychologically fans need to be able to say to themselves, I want to go to the game because the experience is better than what I can get at home. Most teams know they're not clearing that bar right now - and that the bar is only going to continue to rise - which is why you're seeing a little bit of shiny rattle going on.[39]

ARTICLE 1.3
TECHNOLOGY IN SPORT: INSIDE THE STADIUM OF THE FUTURE

Mark Samuels

Tottenham Hotspur Football Club wants fans to think of its new state-of-the-art stadium as a destination first and a sports ground second.

Tottenham Hotspur Football Club – with a brand new, state-of-the-art stadium – hopes to use technology to re-think how football fans spend their Saturday afternoons or even longer.

"We want to take what is intrinsically Tottenham, to embrace it and to take it to the next level. We want to make Tottenham a destination because there are so many reasons to visit the stadium – we want to create Destination Tottenham," says Donna-Maria Cullen, executive director at Spurs.

....

The stadium includes HPE Aruba technology with 1,641 Wi-Fi Access Points that provide Wi-Fi coverage everywhere. The core wired network infrastructure, meanwhile, enables the operation of the stadium's critical services, such as CCTV, building management systems, audio visual technologies, and ticketing.

Finally, 700 HPE Bluetooth beacons work in conjunction with a newly created Spurs App to give fans location services, helping fans navigate bars, restaurants and retail stores. The aim is that this infrastructure provides the foundations for digitally enabled fan experiences, both now and into the future, says Lee.

"Technology is key to design-thinking for the stadium, whether that's for access systems, cashless technologies, Wi-Fi coverage, or incorporating the signal of all four of the major UK mobile providers," he says. "Ultimately it's about producing an infrastructure and a backbone that allows us to embrace new technologies as they come out. We want to be able to constantly incorporate those within the stadium."

Like Lee, Sanjeev Katwa, head of technology at Tottenham Hotspur, says digital infrastructure is the key to providing new types of customer experiences at the ground. The new stadium is fully cashless. All major contactless debit and credit cards are accepted, as well as mobile and wearable payment systems, including Apple Pay and Google Pay.

"If you look at that experience, we've got 100 percent cashless in retail, catering and even programme sales," says Katwa. "Most people nowadays in London don't have cash in their pockets. If you're having a good time and your team is winning, you're just going to keep on spending more. So, I believe technology has enabled those new revenue opportunities."

Fans are encouraged to arrive early at the new stadium to make the most of their day out. While fans arriving earlier helps boost profits, Katwa says it also helps Spurs manage the flow of customers to different areas and ensures high-quality experiences around the ground. Once again, technology plays a key enabling role.

"We do security checks at the bottom of the ramp to accessing the stadium and we use technology for that using PDAs," says Katwa. "If we didn't put the technology infrastructure in place, I don't believe we'd be able to meet that fan experience that our customers want. I think we're giving people different choices and different experiences – and I believe technology is enabling all of that."

Fans at this digitally enabled stadium have a huge amount of choice. Outside the ground, the Tottenham Experience houses the Spurs Shop, which at 23,000 square-feet is the largest retail space of any football club in Europe. The Experience is home to a range of other attractions, including stadium tours, and the Club Museum and Archive.

Inside the ground, the new stadium includes a host of bars and restaurants. The Market Place is a fan zone that includes food and drink outlets inspired by London's street-food market scene. At the rear of The Market Place in the 17,500-seater South Stand is the 65-metre Goal Line Bar, which is the longest bar in Europe.

Other facilities include a series of feature bars, a specially designed family area and top-price corporate facilities. These executive areas include suites, lodges serving Michelin-Star-calibre food, sky lounges, and The Tunnel Club, a glass-walled restaurant and bar that gives cash-rich supporters a behind-the-scenes view of the players' tunnel.

These pioneering facilities are a far cry from the traditional pie-and-pint served up to football fans. But while Michelin-starred food and craft beers might sound more enticing, getting football fans to accept the shift away from a short, sharp 90 minutes of raucous support to a full day of 'experiences' will be not be easy.

Match day traditions – many of which are passed from one generation to the next – matter to football fans. I'm an Aston Villa fan and my support is all about traditions; parking our car in the same place, buying sweets from the same shop, eating over-cooked burgers from the same van outside the ground, chatting with strangers about our shared passion for something beyond our control.

There's nothing intrinsically special about these experiences, but there's something warm, comfortable and perfect about these traditions. If the nature of football support is to change, then fans must willingly embrace that shift. It's a transformation of which Katwa is only too aware – and, while changing fan behaviours is a challenge, he believes Spurs fans will begin to relish the new experience.

"People have been coming to this area for many years, way before many of us were even born. The idea is to invite people to get here at least two hours earlier, to spend time with us and enjoy the choice. Ultimately, you give fans and customers choice, and I think that will also drive additional revenue," he says.

Sporting goods

Sporting goods represent tangible products that are manufactured, distributed, and marketed within the sports industry. Consumer retail purchases of sporting goods equipment, athletic footwear, and athletic apparel increased to $69.9 billion for the categories tracked by the National Sporting Goods Association (NSGA) in 2018, an increase of 1 percent versus 2017.[40]

The footwear category experienced the largest dollar gains in the walking shoes segment. The gym/fashion sneaker segment was second, followed by basketball and aerobic shoes. With respect to equipment, a decrease in hunting and firearms was offset by slight increases in a host of other categories, including golf, camping, bicycle equipment, and fishing tackle. The top dollar generator in the apparel category was golf, followed by swimming, which saw a slight decrease from 2017. Fitness categories increased across the board, led by yoga with a 3 percent increase; hiking equipment was up 4 percent and was a top performer for the second year in a row.[11]

Although sporting goods are usually thought of as sports equipment, apparel, and shoes, there are a number of other goods that exist for consumers of sport. Sporting goods also include licensed merchandise, collectibles, and memorabilia.

Licensed merchandise

Another type of sporting goods that is growing in sales is licensed merchandise. **Licensing** is a practice whereby a sports marketer contracts with other companies to use a brand name, logo, symbol, or characters. In this case, the brand name may be a professional sports franchise, college sports franchise, or a sporting event. Licensed sports products usually are some form of apparel such as team hats, jackets, or jerseys. Licensed sports apparel accounts for 60 percent of all sales of licensed sporting goods.[42] Other licensed sports products, such as novelties, sports memorabilia, trading cards, and even home goods, remain popular.

According to IBIS World,[43] licensed retail sales of sports-based merchandise declined 7.6 percent in 2020 due to COVID causing stores to temporarily shut down and demand waning. The $7 billion (US) industry has experienced some volatility in recent years as fan access and viewership across the majority of sports leagues has declined. While demand for products created in the

Table 1.2 Retail Sales of Licensed Merchandise Based on Sports Properties, by League, United States and Canada: 2018

League	Retail Sales
MLB	$3.88 billion
NFL	$3.72 billion
NBA	$2.87 billion
NHL	$1.1 billion
NASCAR	$0.86 billion
MLS	$0.8 billion
PGA Tour	$0.35 billion
Other	$2.55 billion

licensed sports industry is influenced by several variables, including consumer income, access, shifting demographics, and sports participation, it is hoped that as consumers regain confidence, spending on discretionary sports apparel is expected to increase.

Most of the major American sports leagues are cultivating licensed dollar growth in emerging, fast-growing markets like China (and to a lesser extent, Southeast Asia and South Korea), Mexico, Brazil, and other selected Latin American countries. In addition, growth is also occurring in Europe. France and Spain are surprisingly strong areas of growth, but the biggest gains are coming from Central and Eastern Europe. Middle Eastern countries, in particular the United Arab Emirates (UAE) and Saudi Arabia, are also especially popular targets for licensing. In the United States, the most notable investments are in licensing steaming rights for viewing games, and, to a lesser extent, virtual gambling and gaming licensing. E-commerce and innovative location-based merchandising, specifically, are driving most of the gains in licensed retail sales in the United States and Canada (see Table 1.2).[44]

Collectibles and memorabilia

According to David Yoken, the founder and CEO of Boston-based Collectable, the total value of the U.S. sports memorabilia market amounts to $5.4 billion annually, which includes the total gross merchandise volume (GMV) from eBay, independent auction houses, online retail venues, and other sources.[45]

Collectibles represent one of the earliest examples of sports marketing, tracing their roots to the 1880s when baseball cards were introduced. Consider life before the automobile and the television. For most baseball fans, the player's picture on the card may have been the only chance to see that player. Interestingly, the cards were featured as a promotion in cigarette packages rather than bubble gum. Can you imagine the ethical backlash that this practice would have produced today?

Photo 1.1
A sports collector's dream – the Baseball Hall of Fame's plaque gallery

Credit: Shutterstock, ID 247004004 by Nagel Photography

Although the sports trading card industry reached $1.2 billion in 1991, industrywide yearly sales plummeted to $700 million in 1995, and are now estimated to be about $200 million. There are signs, however, of an industry rebound, with modern players doing very well.[46]

What caused this collapse? One answer is too much competition. David Leibowitz, an industry analyst, commented that "With the channel of distribution backed up and with too much inventory, it was hard to sustain prices, let alone have them continue to rise." At the beginning of the 1980s there were only a few major card companies, such as Topps, Donruss, and Fleer, but by the early 1990s six different companies, more than ever before, were producing cards. The combination of a flooded sports card market and cartoon fad cards has hurt the sports trading card industry. Other problems include labor problems and scandals in sports, escalating card prices, and kids with competing interests (mainly related to too much time on their devices). However, this challenge of competing interests may perhaps turn into the biggest opportunity due to the selling and trading of cards through digital platforms.

Personal training for sports

Another growing category of sports is **personal training**. According to the U.S. BLS, employment opportunities for fitness workers are expected to increase more than 10 percent from 2016 to 2026, which is faster than the average of all occupations.[47] Much of this growth is attributed to increasing awareness of the health benefits of regular exercise. However, these products are produced to benefit participants in sports at all levels and include fitness centers, health services, sports camps, and instruction.

Fitness centers and health services

When the New York Athletic Club was opened in 1886, it became the first facility opened specifically for athletic training. From its humble beginnings in New York, the fitness industry has seen an incredible boom. "Pumping iron" was a common phrase in the 1970s and early 1980s. Moreover, the 1970s aerobics craze started by Dr. Ken Cooper added to the growth of health clubs across the United States.

It is no secret that a physically fit body is becoming more important to society. The growth of the fitness industry follows a national trend of people caring more about their health and certainly has been accelerated due to COVID health concerns. In 1993, there were 11,655 clubs in the United States billed as "health and fitness" centers. By 2018, this number had grown to a record high of 39,570 clubs, as well as a record high 71.5 million users.[48] Why are people joining health clubs in record numbers? Some of the reasons for the fitness boom, like streaming exercise classes, were highlighted earlier in the chapter.[49]

Sports camps and instruction

Sports camps are organized training sessions designed to provide instruction in a specific sport (e.g., basketball or soccer). Camps are usually associated with instructing children; however, the "fantasy sports camp" for aging athletes has received considerable attention in the past few years. Fantasy sports camps typically feature current or ex-professional athletes, and the focus is more on having fun than actual instruction. Nearly every sport at every level now offer camps, including MLB teams, Notre Dame football, LA Galaxy soccer, the PGA Tour Experience, and the Richard Petty Driving School.

Along with camps, another lucrative sports service is providing personal or group instruction in sports. The difference between instruction and camps is the ongoing nature of the instruction versus the finite period and intense experience of the camp. For example, taking golf or tennis lessons from a professional typically involves a series of half-hour lessons over the course of months or sometimes years. Contrast this with the camp that provides intense instruction over a week-long period.

Sports information

The final type of sports product that we discuss is sports information. **Sports information** products provide consumers with news, statistics, schedules, and stories about sports. In addition, sports information can provide participants with instructional materials. Sports-specific newspapers (e.g., *The Sporting News*), magazines (e.g., *Sports Illustrated*), web sites (e.g., www.skysports. com), television (e.g., The Golf Channel), and radio (e.g., WFAN) can all be considered sports information products. All these forms of media are experiencing growth both in terms of products and audience. Consider the following example of new sports information media.

Created in the vein of a radio show, podcasts are generally cheap to produce, and they provide a platform for individuals to broadcast their message to the public. Specifically, in the world of sports there are countless podcasts built around sports talk, sports media, pop culture, sports stories, and so on. If you want to hear a podcast about college football coaches, the NBA draft, and everything in between, chances are there's a specific podcast for you. Popular podcasts such as *Pardon My Take* have anywhere from 750,000 to 1.5 million listeners per episode.[50]

Although there a growing number of alternatives, the most popular source of sports information is still the World Wide Web, as accessed through computers, tablets, smartphones, and other mobile devices. The top sports websites are listed in Figure 1.5. Today, consumers are more connected than ever, with more access and deeper engagement, thanks to the proliferation of devices and platforms. The playing field for the distribution of sports content has never been deeper or wider. In fact, social media exchanges are now standard practice in our daily lives. Not only do consumers have more devices to choose from, but they own more devices than ever before. Connected devices such as smartphones and tablets have become constant companions to consumers on the go and in the home. The rapid adoption of second-screen alternatives has revolutionized shopping and viewing experiences. Publishers of sports-related content and advertisers seeking to reach sports enthusiasts have more options than ever to connect with fans as they consume all things sports. For instance, the 2018 Winter Olympic Games was the largest Olympics ever on social media platforms, with 300 million users, more than 1.6 billion video views, and 3 billion minutes viewed.[51]

Sports fans are the biggest consumers of media via cross-platform devices. A recent study revealed that, among all sports fans, 30 percent livestream sporting events to their mobile phone or tablet. Furthermore, 80 percent of respondents said they have juggled multiple screens while consuming sports, including messaging other fans or searching for player stats or live scores on their mobile devices or computers, while simultaneously watching the game on television.[52]

New alternatives such as augmented reality (AR) and virtual reality (VR) also are increasingly being used in the sports industry to create new experiences for audiences, allowing fans sitting at home to feel like they have a front row seat. Interactive games within a team's arena or stadium can even put the fan in the middle of the action as a participant, albeit a virtual one. For example, NBA AR Basketball enables users to designate an "AR Portal" and subsequently walk through it into a 3D video recorded from an earlier game. The MLB Ballparks app uses AR to allow fans to access live data while they watch a baseball game in a stadium, gaining the ability to interact with detailed stats and data visualizations. When it comes to VR, the Golden State Warriors are one of the first teams to jump into the "viewing vantage point" technology, placing VR cameras in a courtside seat to provide a premium experience to dedicated fans.[53]

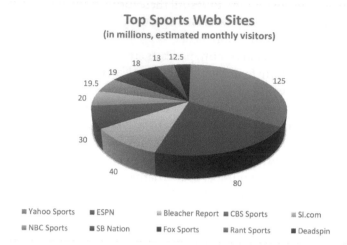

Top Sports Web Sites
(in millions, estimated monthly visitors)

- ■ Yahoo Sports   ■ ESPN   ■ Bleacher Report   ■ CBS Sports   ■ SI.com
- ■ NBC Sports   ■ SB Nation   ■ Fox Sports   ■ Rant Sports   ■ Deadspin

Figure 1.5
Top sports websites

Source: Adapted from: www.ebizmba.com/articles/sports-websites

Web Capture 1.2
Ski.com provides information for ski enthusiasts

Courtesy: Ski.com

Sport media giants like ESPN are constantly looking for new ways for consumers to access sports content. ESPN's multilayered web portal affords consumers access and tracks consumer behavior across the growing list of media and Web platforms. Considering the global nature of sport, looking across the multiplatform universe is essential. That is why ESPN has developed the following seven cross-media principles to further solidify and integrate multimedia and Web platform usage and analysis. ESPN's principles still ring true today.[54]

- New media create new strata of users: When a new technology is introduced, early adopters will gravitate to it, while others will not. As such, the new technology enters a complex matrix of media behavior;
- New metrics are not required in the analysis of cross-media research: It requires metrics that unite behavior across different platforms;
- The focus needs to be both on media users and their usage: It is important to evaluate how many people are using different combinations of media and for what length of time they engage with each platform;
- A heavy user of one medium is a heavy user of other media as well: A person who is a heavy Internet user will tend to watch more TV than average, listen to radio more than average, et. al. This finding was consistent across all studies and is applicable to sports fans specifically and media users as a whole;
- Cross-media usage is not a zero-sum game: Being part of one media behavior more often than not mean that a user is engaged in another one less, because the media pie is getting bigger overall. A generation or more ago, media use was constrained to specific locations and limited usage opportunities. With digital media, constraints are lifted – as users, in what the researchers labeled "new markets of time" – can consume media throughout the day, wherever they want to;
- Simultaneous usage is widespread but limited: People are using multiple media, but they're not often doing so at the same time. Simultaneous use is a widespread behavior – 56 percent of persons in Nielsen's Convergence Panel watched TV and used the Internet at the same time – but only did so for a few minutes each day; and
- People choose the best available screen for their location: For ESPN, this means that cross-media behavior isn't about convergence – it's about the opportunity to follow the sports consumer throughout the day, fulfilling specific needs and building various touchpoints.

The multidimensional nature of the sports product

As you can see from our previous discussion, there are a wide variety of sports products. Our earlier definition of the *sports product* incorporated the distinction between goods and services. Although this is a traditional approach to categorizing consumer products, the complexity of the sports product makes the goods–services classification inadequate. Consider the rich diversity of the sports products that we have just considered. Everything from a hockey puck to the NCAA championship game at the Final Four in basketball is included in our definition. Because of this diversity and complexity, we have added an additional dimension to the sports product known as the body-mind continuum. The body-mind continuum is based on the notion that some sports products benefit consumers' minds, whereas other products act on consumers' bodies. Figure 1.6 illustrates the multidimensional nature of sports products using two dimensions: goods-services and body-mind. These dimensions make up the **sports product map**.

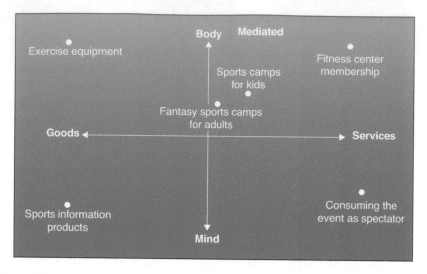

Figure 1.6
The multidimensional nature of sports products using two dimensions: goods–services and body–mind

As you can see, we have positioned some sports products on this map. Exercise equipment is shown as a good that works on the body of the consumer. At the other end of the map, attending or watching a sporting event is considered a service that acts on the mind of consumers. Perhaps we can best describe the differences based on the mind-body and goods-services dimension by exploring sports camps. Sports camps for children are primarily instructional in nature. The primary product being sold is the opportunity for kids to practice their physical skills. However, the fantasy camp targeting adults is a product that acts more on the mind than the body. The adults are purchasing the "fantasy" to interact with professional athletes rather than engaging in physical training.

Understanding where sports products fall on this map is critical for sports marketers. Marketers must understand how they want their sports product to be perceived by consumers so they can understand what benefits to stress. For example, the marketers of a sporting event may want to sell the intangible excitement or the tangible features of the arena. This strategic decision is based on a number of factors that will be considered in detail throughout this text.

Producers and intermediaries

Producers and intermediaries represent the manufacturers of sports products or the organizations that perform some function in the marketing of sports products. Organizations or individuals that perform the function of producer or intermediary include team owners, sanctioning bodies, agents, corporate sponsors, media, and sporting goods manufacturers. In the following paragraphs, we take a look at each of these producers and intermediaries as they relate to the various sports products.

Sports labor

Owners of professional sports franchises, partnerships that own sporting events, and universities that "own" their athletic teams all represent producers of sporting events. One of the unique aspects of the sports industry is that businesspeople often purchase a team because they always dreamed of becoming involved in sports. Typically, sports owners are entrepreneurs who have made their riches in other businesses before deciding to get involved in the business of sports. All too often these owners may be realizing a dream, but fail to realize a profit. Just think of the risks of owning your own team. Pro sports teams have seasonal revenue streams, few chances to expand, and frequent labor problems, and are dependent on the health of just a select few employees.

Many sports-related financial ownership deals – be it racehorses, minor league baseball teams, or box lacrosse franchises – score high on appeal and low on profits, unless the team spigot is affiliated with one of the premier teams or leagues. Historically, owners have a huge emotional investment, as well as a financial incentive to turn a profit. However, consider that even after a flood of new national television cash, 14 of the NBA's 30 teams lost money in the 2016-2017 season before collecting revenue-sharing payouts, and 9 finished in the red even after accounting for those payments, according to confidential NBA financial records obtained by ESPN.com.[55] On the opposite end of the spectrum are teams like the Dallas Cowboys, the world's most highly valued sport franchise worth $5 billion.[56]

Most professional sports teams are owned by individual investors who have invested their personal fortunes to buy their franchises, which they often operate as a public trust. The Washington Football Team (formerly Redskins), Wizards, and Capitals are owned by individuals and their investment teams. Corporate ownership of a major league sports team is rare, but exists. The New York Red Bulls are owned by Red Bull GmbH, and the Atlanta Braves are owned by Liberty Media. However, several recent corporate ownerships of professional sports teams have fizzled, including the Disney Company's ownership of the then-Anaheim Angels and the Mighty Ducks. The Los Angeles Dodgers were owned for several years by News Corp., before the company sold the team to an investor group from Boston, who in 2012 sold the team for $2.15 billion to Guggenheim Baseball Management, which includes former Los Angeles Laker Magic Johnson. Interestingly, the NFL forbids corporate ownership of franchises.

Sanctioning bodies

Sanctioning bodies are organizations that not only market sports products, but also, more important, delineate and enforce rules and regulations, determine the time and place of sporting events, and provide athletes with the structure necessary to compete. Examples of sanctioning bodies include the NCAA, NFL, NHL, IOC (International Olympic Committee), and MLB. Sanctioning bodies

Web Capture 1.3
NCAA: one of the most powerful sanctioning bodies

*Source:*www.ncaa.com

can be powerful forces in the sports industry by regulating the rules and organizing the structure of the leagues and sporting events.

The PGA (Professional Golf Association) of America is one of the largest sanctioning bodies in the world. The PGA's more than 29,000 members promote the game of golf to "everyone, everywhere." In addition to marketing the game of golf, the PGA organizes tournaments for amateurs and professional golfers, holds instructional clinics, and hosts trade shows.[57] Although the PGA has a long history of advancing golf, other sport-sanctioning bodies are surrounded by controversy. Look no further than the four sanctioning bodies of boxing (WBO, WBC, WBA, and IBF), the NCAA, the IOC, FIFA, or NASCAR, and you will find no shortage of scandal and corrupt officials.

Sponsors

Sponsors represent a sport intermediary. As noted earlier, corporations can serve as a consumer of sport. However, corporations also supply sporting events with products or money in exchange for association with the event. The relationship between the event, the audience, and the sponsor is referred to as the *event triangle*.[58]

The basis of the event triangle is that the event, the audience, and the sponsor are all interdependent and depend on each other to be successful. All three groups work in concert to maximize the sport's exposure. The events showcase talented athletes and attract the audience who watch the event in-person or through some medium. The audience, in turn, attracts the sponsor, who pays the event to provide them with access to the audience. In addition, the sponsor promotes the event to the audience, which helps the event reach its attendance goals. It is safe to say that sponsors represent an important intermediary between the event and the final consumers of sports – the audience.

Media

Earlier in this chapter, we commented on the growth and variety of media bringing sporting events to consumers. In fact, the media, which is considered an intermediary, may be the most powerful force in sports today, and is getting stronger. The primary revenue generator for these networks is selling prime advertising time. As the price of advertising time increases, so does the cost of securing broadcast rights; however, the networks are willing to pay.

Sports organizations cannot survive without the mass exposure of the media, and the media needs sports to satisfy the growing consumer demand for this type of entertainment. As the demand for sports programming increases, innovations in media will continue to emerge. Today's consumers want to be engaged, demanding up-to-the-minute platforms that provide exclusive content, statistics, and interactive forums based on live on-the-field action. Engagement not only extends brand support but also provides consumers with the opportunity to have real-time interaction, enabling the procurement of exclusive content and a sense of belonging. All the while, professional and collegiate leagues, teams, and sponsors struggle to stay abreast of these second- or third-screen alternatives. Even when consumers are at the event, they are using digital platforms to deepen their level of engagement and drive value for sponsors.

Agents

Another important intermediary in bringing the athlete to the consumer is the sports **agent**. From a sports marketing perspective, sports agents are intermediaries whose primary responsibility is leveraging athletes' worth or determining their bargaining power. The first "superagent" in sports was Mark McCormack (see box, "Sports marketing hall of fame"). Prior to his emergence, agents had never received the exposure and recognition that they enjoy today. Interestingly, it is not the agents themselves who have provoked their current rise to prominence, but rather the increased bargaining power of their clients.

The bargaining power of athletes can be traced to two factors. First, the formation of new leagues in the 1970s, such as the American Basketball Association (ABA) and the World Hockey Association (WHA), resulted in increased competition to sign the best athletes. This competition drove the salaries to higher levels than ever before and made agents more critical. Second, free agency and arbitration have given players a chance to shop their talents on the open market and question the final offer of owners. In addition, owners are now able to pay players higher salaries because of multibillion-dollar national television contracts and cable television revenues.

Although most people associate agents with contract negotiations, agents do much more. The following are some of the other responsibilities of agents:[59]

- Assess and sign new talent.
- Determine the value of the player's service and convince a club to pay the player his or her market value.

- Develop the compensation package to suit the player's needs.
- Protect the player's rights under contract (and within the guidelines set by the collective bargaining agreement).
- Counsel the player about postcareer security, both financial and occupational.
- Find a new club upon player free agency.
- Handle marketing and promotional activities.
- Advise an athlete on the effect their personal conduct has on their career.

ARTICLE 1.4
SPORTS MARKETING HALL OF FAME

Mark McCormack

Many people trace the beginnings of modern sports marketing to one man – Mark McCormack. In 1960, Mark McCormack, a Cleveland lawyer and one-time star amateur golfer, signed an agreement to represent Arnold Palmer. McCormack offered to take on Palmer's business contracts and fan mail. An early clothing endorsement deal was worth the grand sum of $4,000, and negotiations were fierce over additional $500 payments for extra exposure of the company's logo. With this star client in hand, McCormack began the International Management Group, better known as IMG. Today, IMG is a global leader in sports, events, media, and fashion, operating in more than 30 countries. The agency represents and manages some of the world's greatest sports figures and fashion icons; stages hundreds of live events and branded entertainment experiences annually; and is one of the largest independent producers and distributors of sports media. IMG also specializes in sports training; league development; and marketing, media, and licensing for brands, sports organizations, and collegiate institutions.

Before McCormack, many star athletes used friends and business associates to handle simple contract negotiation and endorsement deals. But the business discipline then, if it could be called that, was unrefined at best. Players like Yogi Berra and Mickey Mantle often were paid in vast quantities of the product they were pitching instead of cash. Fraud and embarrassing, buffoonish ads were commonplace. McCormack came in with a far different approach, accurately foreseeing the explosive growth of TV sports and the utility of sports for corporate America to reach male consumers. He used both as potent tools to strike ever-increasing salaries and endorsement deals and, in turn, helped change the economic landscape of pro sports. Over the subsequent four decades, McCormack landed just about every major name there was as a client, particularly in golf and tennis. Jack Nicklaus, Tiger Woods, Bjorn Borg, John McEnroe, the Williams sisters, Derek Jeter, John Madden, and Jeff Gordon all are represented by IMG.

In addition to his contribution to sports marketing in the United States, McCormack has globalized sports marketing. He opened an Asian office of IMG in Tokyo in 1969, led in the sponsorship of events in Europe, and continued to expand into Middle Eastern markets. One example of McCormack's enormous reach into international markets is IMG's Trans World International (TWI). TWI is the largest independent producer of sports programming in the world. One of its shows, *Trans World Sports*, is viewed in more than 325 million homes in over 76 countries. Additionally, IMG manages and creates sporting events such as the Skins Game, Superstars Competition, and CART races.

Unfortunately for the sports world, Mr. McCormack died in May 2003 at the age of 72. McCormick's work ethic and strict attention to conduct and detail, arguably helped to set the standards of ethics and professionalism in sport. In 2014, IMG was acquired by WME, a leading global entertainment agency, to form Endeavor.

Sources: Susan Vinella, "Sports Marketing Pioneer Dead at 72"; "IMG's McCormack Hailed as Visionary," *Plain Dealer*, May 17, 2003, a1; Eric Fisher, "IMG Founder McCormack Spiced Up Sports Industry," *The Washington Times*, May 18, 2003, c3

Sports equipment manufacturers

Sports equipment manufacturers are responsible for producing and sometimes marketing sports equipment used by consumers who are participating in sports at different levels of competition. Some sporting equipment manufacturers are associated with a single product line, whereas others carry a multitude of sports products. For example, Platypus Sporting Goods only manufactures cricket balls. In contrast, Wilson manufactures football, volleyball, basketball, golf, tennis, baseball, softball, racquetball or squash, and youth sports equipment.

Although it is obvious that equipment manufacturers are necessary to supply the equipment needed to produce the competition, they also play an important role in sports sponsorship. Sports equipment manufacturers become sponsors because of the natural relationship they have with sports. For instance, Rawlings, one of the best known baseball glove manufacturers, sponsors the American and National League Gold Glove Award, which is given to the best defensive players in their position. Molten sponsors the NCAA Men's Volleyball Championship by supplying the official game balls. In addition, Spalding is the official game ball of the WNBA.

Basic marketing principles and processes applied to sport

The sports marketing mix

Sports marketing is commonly associated with promotional activities such as advertising, sponsorships, public relations, and personal selling. However, sports marketers also are involved in product and service strategies, pricing decisions, and distribution issues. These activities are referred to as the **sports market-ing mix**, which is defined as the coordinated set of elements that sports orga-nizations use to meet their marketing objectives and satisfy consumers' needs.

The basic marketing mix elements are the sports product, price, promotion, and distribution. When coordinated and integrated, the combination of the basic marketing mix elements is known as the *marketing program.* The marketing mix or program elements are controllable factors because sports marketing man-agers have control over each element. In the following sections, we take a closer look at the four marketing mix elements as they apply to the sports industry.

Product strategies

One of the basic sports marketing activities is developing product strategies. In designing product strategies, decisions regarding licensing, merchandising, branding, and packaging are addressed. In addition, sports marketing managers are responsible for new product development, maintaining existing products, eliminating weak products, and identifying new markets.

For instance, the NBA is trying to expand its brand into Africa and could form a separate business unit to develop the game. In another branding exam-ple, SoFi will pay $600 million for the naming rights to the new LA stadium. The Chicago Fire rebranded their logo in advance of a move to Soldier Field for the 2020 season. The list goes on, and we will continue with more examples and explore product strategies throughout the text.

Because so much of sports marketing is based on services rather than goods, understanding the nature of services marketing is critical for the sports market-ing manager. Services planning entails pricing of services, managing demand for services, and evaluating service quality. For instance, sports marketing man-agers want to know fans' perceptions of ticket ushers, concessions, parking, and stadium comfort. These service issues are especially important in today's sports marketing environment because fans equate value with high levels of customer service.

Distribution strategies

Traditionally, the role of distribution is finding the most efficient and effective way to get the products into the hands of the consumers. Issues such as inven-tory management, transportation, warehousing, wholesaling, and retailing are all under the control of distribution managers. The advent of sporting goods superstores such as Dick's Sporting Goods and Recreational Equipment Inc. (REI), the availability of sports memorabilia on the Home Shopping Network (HSN), and the online marketing of sports products (e.g., Finish Line, https://finish-line.com) are examples of the traditional distribution function at work. Sports marketing managers are also concerned with how to deliver sports to specta-tors in the most effective and efficient way. Questions such as where to build a new stadium, where to locate a recreational softball complex, or how to distribute tickets most effectively are potential distribution issues facing sports marketers. Of course, the most effective media to use to deliver sport content is another distribution issue.

Pricing strategies

One of the most critical and sensitive issues facing sports marketing managers today is pricing. Pricing strategies include setting pricing objectives, choosing a pricing technique, and adjusting prices over time.

The price of tickets for sporting events; fees for personal seat licenses, pay-per-view, and television sports programming; and the rising costs of participating in recreational sports such as golf are all examples of how the pricing function affects sports marketing.

Promotion strategies

Just ask someone what comes to mind when they think of sports marketing, and the likely response is advertising. They may think of athletes such as Naomi Osaka or Peyton Manning (retired) endorsing a product or service. Although advertising is an element of promotion, it is by no means the only one. In addition to advertising, promotional elements include communicating with the various sports publics through sponsorships, public relations, personal selling, or sales promotions. Together these promotional elements are called the *promotion mix*. When designing promotional strategies, sports marketers must consider integrating their promotions and using all aspects of the promotion mix.

The exchange process

Understanding the exchange process is central to any successful marketing strategy. As generally defined, an **exchange** is a marketing transaction in which the buyer gives something of value to the seller in return for goods and services. For an exchange to occur, several conditions must be satisfied:

- There must be at least two parties.
- Each party must have something of value to offer the other.
- There must be a means for communication between the two or more parties.
- Each party must be free to accept or decline the offer.
- Each party must believe it is desirable to deal with the other(s).

Traditionally, a marketing exchange consists of a consumer giving money to receive a product or service that meets their needs. Other exchanges, not involving money, are also possible. For example, trading a Mike Trout rookie baseball card for a Mookie Betts card represents a marketing exchange between two collectors.

Examples of elements that make up other exchanges appear in Figure 1.7. The two parties in the exchange process are called *exchange players*. These two participants are consumers of sport (e.g., spectators, participants, or sponsors) or producers and intermediaries of sport. Sports spectators exchange their time, money, and personal energy with sports teams in exchange for the entertainment and enjoyment of watching the contest. Sports participants exchange their time, energy, and money for the joy of sport and the better quality of life that participating in sports brings. In sponsorships, organizations exchange money or products for the right to associate with a sporting event, player, team, or other sports entity.

Although these are rather elementary examples of the exchange process, one of the things that makes sports marketing so unique is the complex nature of the exchange process. Within one sporting event, multiple exchanges will occur. Consider a NASCAR event. There are exchanges between spectators and the track ownership (i.e., money for entertainment); spectators and product vendors who are licensed by NASCAR (i.e., money for goods associated with racing); track owner and NASCAR sanctioning body (i.e., money for organizing the event and providing other event services); media and NASCAR (i.e., event broadcast coverage for money); product sponsors and driving team owner (i.e., promotional benefits for money); and track owner and driving team owner (i.e., producer of the competition for money). As you might imagine, trying to sort out all these exchanges, much less determine the various marketing strategies involved in each exchange, is a complicated puzzle that can only be solved by having a full understanding of the industry within each sport. Although the nature of each sporting event and industry

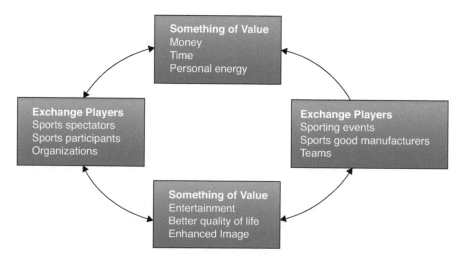

Figure 1.7
Model of the sports marketing exchange process

is slightly different, designing a marketing strategy incorporates some fundamental processes that span the sports industry.

The strategic sports marketing process

Sports marketers manage the complex and unique exchange processes in the sports industry by using the strategic sports marketing process. The **strategic sports marketing process** is the process of planning, implementing, and controlling marketing efforts to meet organizational goals and satisfy consumers' needs.

To meet these organizational goals and marketing objectives, sports marketers must first anticipate consumer demand. Sports marketers want to know what motivates consumers to purchase, how they perceive sports products or services, how they learn about a sports product, and how they choose certain products over others.

One way sports marketers anticipate demand is by conducting marketing research to gather information about the sports consumer. Another way that sports marketers anticipate demand is by monitoring the external environment. Sports analytics is a growing field that allows us to explore market competition (i.e., those other entertainment options vying for the same consumer dollar), demographic trends (i.e., what sports are most popular with Generation Z and how will they consume them), political/legal trends (i.e., pay for play in the NCAA or legalized sports betting), and economic trends (i.e., how will a downturn in the economy impact sponsorship spending or attendance at sporting events).[60]

[handwritten margin note: How consumers put demand on sports market.]

Next, sports marketers examine different groups of consumers, choose the group of consumers at which to direct the organization's marketing efforts, and then determine how to position the product or service to that group of consumers. These market-selection decisions are referred to as *segmentation, targeting,* and *position.* The final aspect of the planning phase is to offer products that are

ARTICLE 1.5
WHAT CAN BE DONE TO CLOSE THE MERCHANDISE GAP?

The perpetual disparity between the availability – and marketing – of men's and women's apparel is symbolic of how female fans are viewed.

by Shira Springer

Pink it and shrink it.

Not long ago, that's how leagues, teams, and sports apparel companies catered to female fans. The result: Pink hats and pink jerseys in ill-fitting women's sizes. And lots of dissatisfied customers. The bigger message to female fans: The sports world doesn't value you, at least not enough to figure out what you really want.

Now, female fans enjoy more options. Some good. Some questionably fashion forward. But while apparel makers have mostly moved on from pink-it-and-shrink-it, there's an undeniable residual effect from that approach. Female fans remain an underserved demographic.

Next time you're in a sports store or a pro shop, look around. Sports apparel sections for men dwarf sports apparel sections for women. Sometimes women's sections don't exist at all. Sometimes it takes a special order to get a particular jersey. Sometimes the children's section is the only place where women can find the style and fit they want.

Let's call it the Merchandise Gap

Maybe it doesn't prompt the same sense of outrage and call to action as the Gender Pay Gap. But the Merchandise Gap matters because it reflects the way female fans are viewed. Again, it goes to whether they're valued or not. It also speaks to inclusivity. Part of being a fan is wearing team gear. When it's hard to get team merchandise that looks authentic and fits well, it creates an invisible barrier, an impression that real fandom is for some and not others.

Teams, leagues, and apparel manufacturers are starting to recognize the incredible diversity of female fans

That's a lot to put on a piece of clothing. But consider the case of Boston Bruins fan Victoria Carter.

With the Bruins playing in the 2019 NHL Winter Classic, all Carter wanted was a jersey to celebrate the event, an authentic jersey in her size. She couldn't find one. She took to social media and asked, "Why do men and kids get authentic and replica Winter Classic jerseys, but not women?" She documented her search as it stretched from several days to several weeks.

"It made me question, 'Where do I rank in terms of fandom?'" Carter said. "You can talk to me and my friends who are female sports fans and we know what we're talking about. But when it comes to being able to represent that through the clothing that we're wearing, we have to do a lot more work. Hunt around a little more. It's almost like you have to jump through hoops to, in a bizarre sort of way, prove your fandom."

It shouldn't feel like that when, according to a recent Nielsen Sports study, nearly 50 percent of women surveyed across the Americas, Asia, and Europe consider themselves interested or very interested in sports. And when according to statistics, women drive 70 to 80 percent of consumer purchases. And when sports leagues and teams will be increasingly dependent on female fans for growth because they've likely maxed out male interest.

Apparel company Fanatics knows that from experience. Its women's business is its fastest-growing category.

In 2018, the company's sales of women's merchandise across all sports and leagues was up over 20 percent. That was the third consecutive year of over 20 percent growth. On the supply side, Fanatics says that it offers more than 125,000 women's-specific products. Beyond its official fan jerseys, the company takes particular pride in its partnerships with brands such as DKNY to produce a variety of products. Think sneaker dresses, cropped hoodies, and leggings with team logos.

The NBA offers a women's collection that ranges from replica jerseys to wedge boots with team logos. There's also NBA partnerships with Top Shop, Forever 21, and Levi's.

Say what you will about sandals dotted with team logos or Top Shop's cropped team sweatshirts. They're not for everyone. But they show how leagues and apparel companies are trying to satisfy female fans. They also illustrate how difficult that can be.

The idiocy of pink-it-and-shrink-it was that it treated female fans as a singular stereotype. In reality, they're incredibly diverse. As apparel makers dive into that diversity, it's OK if they produce logo-festooned purses and tie-ins with big-name brands. Inclusion comes in many styles.

But let's not get lost in the volume of the women's collections and forget about the Victoria Carters out there. At its core, the Merchandise Gap is about female fans not having the same apparel options as male fans and kids.

What can be done to close the Merchandise Gap? What can be done for women who simply want to walk into sports stores and buy team jerseys that fit well? Lisa Piken Koper, the NBA's senior vice president of merchandising partnerships, grew up a die-hard sports fan unhappy with pink and unisex options. Now, privy to how merchandising decisions get made, here's her advice: Let retailers and leagues know what you want. Create demand.

"I would love to hear from more female fans," said Piken Koper. "We love feedback. We'd love to hear more about what's missing from our assortment. Why can't you buy it and how can we help you?"

Piken Koper recalled how the league miscalculated with the Nike Therma Flex hoodie. Last year, female fans complained that the NBA didn't offer the hoodie for women. This year, the NBA and Nike made sure there was a women's version available. As for Carter, her social media campaign for a women's Winter Classic jersey got personal responses from Fanatics, the Bruins, and the NHL, including a 45-minute conference call with four league executives. They discussed how the NHL can do better by female fans.

Leagues, teams, and apparel companies would be smart to keep up the conversation and stock up for the future.

Source: Shira Springer. "What can be done to close the Merchandise Gap? The perpetual disparity between the availability – and marketing – of men's and women's apparel is symbolic of how female fans are viewed." *Sports Business Daily*, May 6, 2019. www.sportsbusinessdaily.com/Journal/Issues/2019/05/06/Opinion/Springer.aspx

promoted, priced, and distributed in ways that appeal to the targeted consumers. Article 1.5 illustrates how many of the professional sports leagues have attempted to target women and design products that will appeal to the female fan for years but still have a long way to go to satisfy this market.

Summary

The sports industry is experiencing tremendous growth, and sports marketing is playing an important role in this emerging industry. Chapter 1 provided a basic understanding of sports marketing and the sports industry. Sports marketing is "the specific application of marketing principles and processes to sport products and to the marketing of nonsports products through association with sport." The study and practice of sports marketing is complex and interesting because of the unique nature of the sports industry.

Today, sports organizations define their businesses as entertainment providers. In addition, sports organizations know that to be successful in the competitive environment of sports they must practice a marketing orientation. An organization with a marketing orientation concentrates on understanding consumers and providing sports products that satisfy consumers' needs.

Sports marketing will continue to grow in importance as sports become more pervasive in the U.S. culture and around the globe. This phenomenal growth of the sports industry can be seen and measured in a number of ways. We can identify growth by looking at the increasing numbers of sport spectators, the growth of media coverage, the increase in sports participation, rising employment opportunities, and the growth in sports internationally. To better understand this growing and complex industry, a simplified model of the consumer–supplier relationship was presented.

The simplified model of the consumer–supplier relationship in the sports industry consists of three major elements: consumers of sport, sports products, and producers and intermediaries. Three distinct types of sports consumers are identified in the model. These consumers of sport include spectators who observe sporting events, participants who take part in sporting events, and sponsors who exchange money or product for the right to be associated with a sporting event. The spectators, participants, and sponsors use sports products.

A sports product is a good, service, or any combination of the two that is designed to provide benefits to a sports consumer. The primary sports product consumed by sponsors and spectators is the sporting event. Products related to the event are athletes such as Kei Nishikori and arenas such as the Staples Center, which both provide their own unique benefits. Other categories of sports products common to the sports industry include sporting goods (e.g., equipment, apparel and shoes, licensed merchandise, collectibles, and memorabilia), personal training services for sports (e.g., fitness centers and sports camps), and sports information (e.g., news and magazines). Because there are a variety of sports products, it is useful to categorize these products using the sports product map.

Producers and intermediaries represent the third element of the simplified model of the consumer–supplier relationship in the sports industry. Producers include those organizations or individuals that help "manufacture" the sporting event, such as owners, sanctioning bodies, and sports equipment manufacturers. Intermediaries are also critical to the sports industry because they bring the sport to the end user of the sports product. Sponsors, the media, and agents are the three intermediaries presented in this chapter.

Although sports marketers must have a thorough understanding of the sports industry to be successful, the tool of their trade is the sports marketing mix. The sports marketing mix is defined as the coordinated set of elements that sports organizations use to meet their marketing mix objectives and satisfy consumers' needs. The elements of the marketing mix are sports products, distribution or place, pricing, and promotion.

In addition to the marketing mix, another central element of marketing is the exchange process. The exchange process is defined as a marketing transaction in which the buyer gives something of value to the seller in return for goods and services. One of the things that makes the sports industry so unique is the complex nature of the exchange process and the many exchanges that take place within a single sporting event.

To manage the complexities of the sports industry and achieve organizational objectives, sports marketers use the strategic sports marketing process. The strategic sports marketing process consists of three major parts: planning, implementation, and control. The planning process begins by understanding consumers' needs, selecting a group of consumers with similar needs, and positioning the sports product within this group of consumers. The final step of the planning phase is to develop a marketing mix that will appeal to the targeted group of consumers and carry out the desired positioning. The second major part of the strategic sports marketing process is putting the plans into action or implementation. Finally, the plans are evaluated to determine whether organizational objectives and marketing goals are being met. This third, and final, part of the strategic sports marketing process is called control.

Planning
Implementation
Control

Key terms

- agent
- amateur sporting event
- benefits
- exchange
- goods
- licensing
- marketing myopia
- marketing orientation
- organized sporting events
- participants
- personal training
- producers and intermediaries
- professional sports
- sanctioning body
- services
- simplified model of the consumer-supplier relationship
- spectators
- sport
- sporting event
- sporting goods
- sports equipment manufacturers
- sports information
- sports marketing
- sports marketing mix
- sports product
- sports product map
- sports sponsorship
- strategic sports marketing process
- unorganized sports

Review questions

1 Define *sports marketing*, and discuss how sports are related to entertainment.
2 What is a marketing orientation, and how do sports organizations practice a marketing orientation?
3 Discuss some of the ways that the sports marketing industry is growing.
4 Outline the simplified model of the consumer–supplier relationship in the sports industry.
5 What are the three distinct types of sports consumers? What are the different types of spectators? How are sports participants categorized?
6 Define *sports products*. What are the different types of sports products discussed in the simplified model of the consumer–supplier relationship in the sports industry?

7   Describe the different producers and intermediaries in the simplified model of the consumer-supplier relationship in the sports industry.

8   What are the basic elements of the sports marketing mix?

9   What is the marketing exchange process, and why is the exchange process critical for sports marketers?

10 Define the *strategic sports marketing process*, and discuss the various elements in the process.

Exercises

1   Provide five recent examples of sports marketing that have been in the news and describe how each relates to our definition of sports marketing.

2   How does sport differ from other forms of entertainment?

3   Provide an example of a sports organization that suffers from marketing myopia and another that defines its business as entertainment. Justify your choices.

4   Attend a high school, college, and professional sporting event and comment on the marketing orientation of the event at each level of competition.

5   Provide three examples of how you would measure growth in the sports marketing industry. What evidence do you have that the number of people participating in sports is growing?

6   Discuss the disadvantages and advantages of attending sporting events versus consuming a sporting event through the media (e.g., television or radio).

7   Develop a list of all the sports products produced by your college or university. Which are goods and which are services? Identify ways in which the marketing of the goods differs from the services.

8   Choose any professional sports team and describe how it puts the basic sports marketing functions into practice.

Internet exercises

1   Using web sites, support the growth of the sporting goods industry.

2   Compare and contrast the web sites of three professional sports teams. Which site has the strongest marketing orientation? Why?

Notes

1   American Marketing Association. Available from: http://www.marketingpower.com/AboutAMA/Pages/DefinitionofMarketing.aspx, accessed May 10, 2014.

2   Kristi Lee Covington-Baker, *A History of Sports Marketing and the Media* (UMI Microform 1450380, Proquest Information and Learning Company, 2007).

3   Ibid.

4   David Biderman, "The Stadium-Naming Game," *The Wall Street Journal* (February 3, 2010).

5   Kristie McCook, Douglas Turco, and Roger Riley, "A Look at the Corporate Sponsorship Decision Making Process," *Cyber-Journal of Sport Marketing* [Online], vol. 1, no. 2 (1997).

6   Colby Weikel, *Sports Marketing: A Take on the History and the Future* (manuscript, UNC, 1998). Available from: www.unc.edu/~andrewsr/mts092/weikel.html.

7   David Arthur, Garry Dolan, and Michael Cole, "The Benefits of Sponsoring Success: An Analysis of the Relationship between Television Exposure and the Position of the Motorcycle Rider," *Cyber-Journal of Sport Marketing* [Online], vol. 2, no. 2 (1998). Available from: http://fulltext.ausport.gov.au/fulltext/1998/cjsm/v2n2/arthur22.htm.

8   PwC Sports Outlook, "At the Gate and Beyond." Available from: www.pwc.com/us/en/industry/entertainment-media/assets/2018-sports-outlook.pdf.

9   Nigel Pope, "Overview of Current Sponsorship Thought," *Cyber-Journal of Sport Marketing* [Online], vol. 2 (1998). Available from: www.cjsm.com/vol2/pope21.htm.

10 Kristi Lee Covington-Baker, *A History of Sports Marketing and the Media* (UMI Microform 1450380, Proquest Information and Learning Company, 2007).

11 Merriam-Webster, "Sport." Available from: www.merriam-webster.com/dictionary/sport.

12 John Mossman, "Denver to Host 2005 NBA All-Star Game," *The Associated Press* [Online], (June 17, 2003).

13 John Pollock, "WWE Announces Record Revenue for 2018, Breakdown of the Year" (February 7, 2019). Available from: www.postwrestling.com/2019/02/07/wwe-announces-record-revenue-for-2018-breakdown-of-the-year/.

14 Ajay K. Kohli and Bernard Jaworski, "Marketing Orientation: The Construct, Research Propositions, and Managerial Implications," *Journal of Marketing*, vol. 54, no. 2 (1990), 1-18.

15 "Sports – $614 Billion Global Market Opportunities & Strategies to 2022," *Research AndMarkets.com.* Available from: www.businesswire.com/news/home/20190514005472/en/Sports-614-Billion-Global-Market-Opportunities.

16 "Superfans: The Tribalism of Sports | Annals of Obsession | The New Yorker" (February 1, 2018). Available from: www.youtube.com/watch?v=aY6GTSDYDRo.

17 Maury Brown, "How The NFL Gained Back Viewers, But Lost Attendance." Available from: https://www.forbes.com/sites/sportsmoney/people/bizballmaury/#4ce06f7b207d.

18 Dennis Dodd, "College Football Can Look to KISS to Win Fans Back After Lowest Average Attendance in 22 Years" (March 25, 2019). Available from: www.cbssports.com/college-football/news/college-football-can-look-to-kiss-to-win-fans-back-after-lowest-average-attendance-in-22-years/.

19 "National Hockey League: Average Attendance at Regular Season Games 2008/09 to 2018/19." Available from: https://www.statista.com/statistics/243066/average-regular-season-attendance-in-the-nhl/.

20 Jessica Golden, "NBA Has Baller Season: Attendance, Ratings, Merchandise All See Huge Uptick" (April 13, 2018). Available from: https://www.cnbc.com/2018/04/12/nba-has-baller-season-attendance-ratings-merchandise-see-huge-uptick.html.

21 Russell Scibetti, "Looking at MLS Attendance Over the Years" (March 26, 2019). Available from: https://blog.koresoftware.com/blog/looking-at-mls-attendance-over-the-years.

22   Lucy Handley, "Super Bowl Draws Lowest TV Audience in More than a Decade, Early Data Show" (February 5, 2019). Available from: https://www.cnbc.com/2019/02/05/super-bowl-draws-lowest-tv-audience-in-more-than-a-decade-nielsen.html.

23   Joe Otterson, "2018 Winter Olympics Close Out as Least-Watched on Record, Down 7% From Sochi Games" (February 26, 2018). Available from: https://variety.com/2018/tv/news/2018-winter-olympics-ratings-2-1202710137/.

24   Clay Travis, "Cable vs. Streaming: How Does ESPN Navigate the Future?" (2019). Available from: https://www.outkickthecoverage.com/cable-vs-streaming-how-does-espn-navigate-the-future/.

25   Cynthia Littelton, "ESPN Loses 2 Million Subscribers in Fiscal 2018" (November 21, 2018). Available from: https://variety.com/2018/biz/news/espn-disney-channel-subscriber-losses-2018-1203035003/www.techdirt.com/articles/20181126/09313541105/espn-has-lost-14-million-viewers-7-years-thanks-to-cord-cutting.shtml.

26   Sports Business Media, "United States Market Report" (February 7, 2019). Available from: https://media.sportbusiness.com/2019/02/the-us-media-rights-market-2018-global-media-report-extract/.

27   Alexandra Licata, "42 States Have or Are Moving towards Legalizing Sports Betting – Here Are the States Where Sports Betting Is Legal" (August 2, 2019). Available from: https://www.businessinsider.com/states-where-sports-betting-legal-usa-2019-7.

28   PRRI, "Despite NFL's Woes, Football Remains America's Most Dominant Sport" (January 25, 2018). Available from: https://www.prri.org/press-release/despite-nfls-woes-football-remains-americas-dominant-sport/.

29   ESPN, "Sudden Vanishing of Sports Due to Coronavirus Will Cost At Least $12 Billion, Analysis Says" (May 1, 2020). Available from: https://www.espn.com/espn/otl/story/_/id/29110487/sudden-vanishing-sports-due-coronavirus-cost-least-12-billion-analysis-says; "UK Sports Industry Worth £23.8 Billion and Holds Nearly 1 Million Jobs." Available from: https://www.careerbuilder.co.uk/uk/share/aboutus/pressreleasesdetail.aspx?sd=5%2F2%2F2013&id=pr52&ed=12%2F31%2F2013.

30   Kevin Gallagher, "Media Rights Will Continue to Propel Sports Revenue" (November 28, 2018). Available from: https://www.businessinsider.com/media-rights-propel-sports-revenue-2018-11.

31   Nigel Pope, "Overview of Current Sponsorship Thought" [Online]. *Cyber-Journal of Sport Marketing*, vol. 2, no. 1 (1998). Available from: http://fulltext.ausport.gove.au/fulltext/1998/cjsm/v2n1/pope21.htm.

32   "Global Sports Sponsorship Spend to Reach $65 Billion in 2019." Available from: https://ministryofsport.com.au/global-sports-sponsorship-spend-to-reach-65-billion-in-2019/.

33   Barry Janoff, "Sponsorship Spend in '18 to Top Record $24B in North America, $65.8B Worldwide" (January 9, 2018). Available from: http://nysportsjournalism.squarespace.com/na-sponsor-spend-to-top-24b-19/?SSScrollPosition=1.

34   Geoffrey Smith, "Sports: Walk, Don't Schuss," *Businessweek* (December 7, 1997).

35   Raja Dutta, "A Combined Global Audience of 1.12 Billion Watched the FIFA World Cup Final between France and Croatia" (December 26, 2018). Available from: https://sportsbeatsindia.com/a-combined-global-audience-of-1-12-billion-watched-the-fifa-world-cup-final-between-france-and-croatia/.

36   Pete Evans, "Scotiabank Pays Big for Arena Naming Rights, But Did It Break the Bank?" *CBC News* (September 4, 2017). Available from: https://www.cbc.ca/news/business/scotiabank-arena-naming-rights-1.4271688.

37   "College Athletes in America May Be Allowed to Profit from their Talent." Available from: https://www.economist.com/united-states/2019/09/28/college-athletes-in-america-may-be-allowed-to-profit-from-their-talent.

38   Merrit Kennedy, "Tiger Woods Rises Again – And Sponsors Are Celebrating His Resilience" (April 15, 2019). Available from: https://www.npr.org/people/466454757/merrit-kennedy.

39   "In-Stadium Technology Just 'an Expensive Dot Along a Continuum'" (March 26, 2019). Available from: https://johnwallstreet.com/in-stadium-technology-scoreboards/.

40   NSGA, "NSGA's Sporting Goods Market Report Shows Retail Sales Reach $69.9 Billion" (May 14, 2019). Available from: https://www.nsga.org/news/news-releases/association-news-archives/nsga-releases-2019-sporting-goods-market-report/.

41   "NSGA's Sporting Goods Market Report Shows Retail Sales Reach $69.9 Billion" (May 15, 2019). Available from: https://www.bicycleretailer.com/announcements/2019/05/15/nsgas-sporting-goods-market-report-shows-retail-sales-reach-699-billion#.XZJFUC2ZNQY.

42   "NSGA's Sporting Goods Market Report Shows Retail Sales Reach $69.9 Billion" (May 15, 2019). Available from: https://www.bicycleretailer.com/announcements/2019/05/15/nsgas-sporting-goods-market-report-shows-retail-sales-reach-699-billion#.XZJFUC2ZNQY.

43   "IBIS World, Licensed Sports Apparel Stores Industry in the US – Market Research Report" (November 30, 2020). Available from: https://www.ibisworld.com/united-states/market-research-reports/licensed-sports-apparel-stores-industry/.

44   "Sports-Based Licensing Stumbles with 1.4% Growth in the U.S. & Canada" (August 27, 2019). Available from: https://www.thelicensingletter.com/sports-based-licensing-stumbles-with-1-4-growth-in-the-u-s-canada/.

45   David Seideman, "Tech Entrepreneur Determines First True Estimate of U.S. Sports Memorabilia Market: $5.4 Billion" (September 19, 2018). Available from: https://www.forbes.com/sites/davidseideman/2018/09/19/tech-entrepreneur-determines-first-true-estimate-of-sports-memorabilia-market-5-4-billion/#2fdbf76652e8.

46   Charles White, "Feature: The Sports Trading Card Industry Is Fueled by the Digital Age" (May 12, 2019). Available from: https://www.wruf.com/headlines/2019/05/12/feature-the-sports-trading-card-industry-is-fueled-by-the-digital-age/.

47   Tyler Spraul, "What Is the Job Market Like for a Personal Trainer?" (August 25, 2020). Available from: https://www.exercise.com/learn/what-is-the-job-market-like-for-a-personal-trainer/.

48   Wellness Creative Co., "Gym Market Research and Industry Stats" (January 15, 2021). Available from: https://www.wellnesscreatives.com/gym-market-statistics/#market; Melissa Rodriguez, "Latest IHRSA Data: Over 6 Billion Visits to 39,570 Gyms in 2018" (March 28, 2019). Available from: https://www.ihrsa.org/about/media-center/press-releases/latest-ihrsa-data-over-6b-visits-to-39-570-gyms-in-2018/.

49   Ben Midgley, "The Six Reasons the Fitness Industry Is Booming" (September 26, 2018). Available from: https://www.forbes.com/sites/benmidgley/2018/09/26/the-six-reasons-the-fitness-industry-is-booming/#5b16952506db.

50   Salvador Lorenz, "Culture" (2018). Available from: https://vocal.media/unbalanced/best-sports-podcasts-of-2018.

51   Olympic Winter Games PyeongChang, "Global Broadcast and Audience Report" (2018). Available from: https://stillmed.olympic.org/media/Document%20Library/OlympicOrg/Games/Winter-Games/Games-PyeongChang-2018-Winter-Olympic-Games/IOC-Marketing/Olympic-Winter-Games-PyeongChang-2018-Broadcast-Report.pdf.

52   Jen Booten, "30 Percent of Fans Now Stream Sports to Their Phones, Tablets" (February 12, 2018). Available from: https://www.sporttechie.com/30-percent-fans-now-stream-sports-phones-tablets/.

53   Russell Karp, "How Technology Is Changing the Sports Fan Experience" (April 6, 2019). Available from: https://medium.com/swlh/how-technology-is-changing-the-sports-fan-experience-6f32a5bf921d.

54   Mike Reynolds, "ESPN Espouses 'Seven Principles of Cross-Media Research'" (July 28, 2009). Available from: https://www.multichannel.com/news/espn-espouses-seven-principles-cross-media-research-258647.

55   Brian Windhorst and Zach Lowe, "Confidential Report Shows Nearly Half of the NBA Lost Money Last Season. Now What?" (September 19, 2017). Available from: https://www.espn.com/nba/story/_/id/20747413/a-confidential-report-shows-nearly-half-nba-lost-money-last-season-now-what.

56   Kurt Badenhausen, "The World's 50 Most Valuable Sports Teams 2019" (July 22, 2019). Available from: https://www.forbes.com/sites/kurtbadenhausen/2019/07/22/the-worlds-50-most-valuable-sports-teams-2019/#641dd15a283d.

57   "The PGA of America." Available from: https://www.pga.com/pga-of-america/about.

58   Phil Schaaf, *Sports Marketing: It's Not Just a Game Anymore* (Amherst, MA: Prometheus Books, 1995).

59   Betterteam (2021). Available from: https://www.betterteam.com/sports-agent-job-description.

60   Matt McLaughlin, "Sports Data Analytics: How Teams Use Data to Gain Edge" (December 13, 2108). Available from: https://biztechmagazine.com/article/2018/12/how-data-analytics-revolutionizing-sports.

Contingency framework for strategic sports marketing

After completing this chapter, you should be able to:

- Understand the contingency framework for strategic sports marketing.
- Describe the strategic sports marketing process.
- Describe the major internal contingencies and explain how they affect the strategic sports marketing process.
- Describe external contingencies and explain how they affect the strategic sports marketing process.
- Discuss the importance of monitoring external contingencies and environmental scanning.
- Explain and conduct a SWOT analysis.
- Define the internal and external contingencies and relate them to the strategic sports marketing process.

The foundation of any effective sports organization is a sound, yet flexible, strategic framework. The process should be systematic and well organized, but must be readily adaptable to changes in the environment, as the following article illustrates. Each strategic marketing process may have unique characteristics, but the fundamentals are all the same. To help make sense of the complex and rapidly changing sports industry, we use a contingency framework to guide the strategic sports marketing process. For the remainder of this chapter, let us look at an overview of this process.

DOI: 10.4324/9780429030673-3

ARTICLE 2.1
FUTURE OF MARKETING – A SNEAK PEEK INTO 2020 AND BEYOND

Years roll on, technology keeps advancing, customers evolve, and brands are left with no choice but to keep adapting. Customer is definitely the king and their thirst for convenience has now reached an all-time high. To stay competitive and in the race, brands need to ensure that their marketing initiatives keep up to the evolving technologies and meet the needs of the ever-convenient customer. A rich customer experience being the focus of all marketing endeavors is merely an understatement today. Let's look at a few things that brands should do to ensure that they are in a position of strength in 2020 and beyond.

Voice technology – An "echo"-ing opportunity for brands to redefine customer engagement

Voice technology is making all the right sounds and is expected to be one of the most disruptive technologies in the years to come. A lot of experts around the world believe voice to be the next big thing for advertisers, mainly because of its ability to connect to people in a humane, and natural way. It's like we are talking to another human. Here lies the opportunity for brands to make a mark. Since the scope for personalization here is immense, the content for voice needs to be curated in a particular tone and feel that appeals to people.

When it comes to voice, establishing a genuine connection with the people is the key for brands. Voice has the ability to evoke emotional reactions out of people, which makes the setting of tone doubly important. The other important part is the response, which needs to be precise, relevant, and timely. The rate at which Artificial Intelligence and data analytics is advancing, it won't be long before voice technology achieves a near perfect response ratio.

To cut a long story short, brands have a massive opportunity to further their prospects by enhancing customer engagement like never before. Voice technology in marketing is certainly one for the future. These numbers do tell a story.

Fact file

- Findings by comScore suggest that 50% of all searches by 2020 will be voice searches.
- 55% of adults in the USA will have a smart speaker by 2022, as per a report by OC & C Strategy Consultants.

  - Tech giant Capgemini suggests that 24% of people prefer to use a voice assistant over visiting a website. Findings also reveal that out of the 71% of consumers who are satisfied with voice technology, 52% of them cite convenience, 48% love the hands-free scenario, and 41% prefer the automated shopping bit.

Augmented/virtual reality – the chance to bring the world to the customers' feet

If AR and VR already make your jaw drop, wait till it gains full traction and becomes more accessible. It's no secret the amount of money that social media giants like Facebook, Instagram, and Snapchat are spending on these technologies. For instance, Facebook shelled out around US $2 billion to acquire Oculus VR. Through AR and VR, brands can promote, advertise, and showcase their products and services to consumers in the most surreal and immersive of ways.

For consumers, it's convenience at its highest level. Imagine taking a trip to the Caribbean islands, trying out the dress you saw at the store the other day, checking out exactly how the $2,000 couch would look like at your living room, visiting house after house before zeroing in on which one to buy – all from the comfort of your house by either putting on a VR wearable or checking out multidimensional videos on your preferred internet-enabled device. Yes, that's how immersive, engaging, and convenient it will soon get for consumers across the globe. After all, there is a reason why these social media giants are spending so much on AR/VR.

For brands to be in a position of strength, they must resort to AR/VR storytelling from now itself. A year or so down the line, the technology will only evolve and competition will only stiffen. The following stats do paint a picture:

Fact file

- Recent studies show that the global AR Ad Revenue is expected to go beyond US $2 billion by 2022.
- The installed base of VR headsets is forecast for a surge up to 37 million by 2020.
- The market size for AR/VR is expected to be worth 192.7 billion US dollars by 2022.

Influencer marketing – the need for a wise and judicious brand advocacy

Influencer marketing is not new to brands. If anything, some might even feel that it should be considered as an ongoing trend, or one of the near past. But it's far from true. Influencer marketing of the near future will be a tad different to what it is now. Presently, it's more or less all about targeting people with over 100,000+ followers and asking them to advocate the brand messaging. But influencer marketing will soon evolve to be much more than that. Customers are getting smarter and brands too are getting wiser.

Soon, apart from individual influencers, there will be a rise in demand for influencer groups comprising of people closely connected to one another. This will give brands a better chance to create an impression as their outreach channel will not be focused on any one particular influential channel. The other thing that consumers will demand for is increased transparency and authenticity.

It has to be understood that the primary reason why people have moved on from traditional advertising to social influencer listening is because they lost faith in those ads. Now, the cost of influencer marketing is skyrocketing. Consumers know this fact. The last thing brands would want is for consumers to perceive the influencers as commissioned brand validators or co-branders. The future would require brands to do some digging before targeting influencers as consumers will hunt for signs of sincerity and authenticity.

Early days are over. Influencer marketing is evolving.

Fact file

- The net-worth of influencer marketing industry is expected to be around $10 billion by 2020.
- As per 94% marketers, transparency and authenticity are key to the success of influencer marketing.

Video marketing – freedom of speech and expression to brands

Video marketing is already big today and nothing is scheduled for a change in the years to come. Video is an easy to the eye, interactive, and fun way for brands to communicate with its consumers. Sometimes they can communicate more through a 30 second video as opposed to a 1500 word blog article. This trend is one for the future as well because the popularity of on-demand video is all set to keep increasing. Then there is social media videos which is perhaps the biggest sensation going around in the world right now.

Social Giants like Facebook, Instagram, and Snapchat have laid the perfect foundation for brands to make the most of their marketing and advertising endeavors through the 'Live Video feature.' The biggest benefactors have been e-commerce brands as they can promote product descriptions, and demo tutorials in a mighty effective way. Looking at the future, advertising and promotion will soon reach a whole new level once AR integrated video starts surfacing in a more streamlined manner. As mentioned earlier, AR videos are definitely the next big thing for brands and marketers to focus on.

While brands will be busy leveraging the might of video marketing in the time to come, they might want to focus a little on the SEO perspective as well. After all, the competition is going to be cutthroat and brands would definitely want their inch of visibility. Video optimization of strategically targeted keywords therefore will be the key behind effective ranking on YouTube or any other popular video-centric forum. Refer to the points below and you will know why video marketing will make a lot of noise in the years to come.

Fact file

- By 2022, over 82% of all consumer internet traffic will be online videos.
- By 2021, Facebook might be an all-video platform with no place for text as per prediction by one of its executives.
- There will be close to 1 million minutes of video surfacing the internet on a per second basis by 2020.

Source: Aditya Kathotia. (April 10, 2019). "Future of marketing – A sneak peek into 2020 and beyond".

What is the contingency framework?

Sports marketing managers must be prepared to face a continually changing environment. As Burton and Howard pointed out, "marketers considering careers or already employed in sports marketing must be prepared for unexpected, often negative actions that jeopardize a sports organization's brand equity."[1] Think about what can happen over the course of an event or a season. The team that was supposed to win the championship cannot seem to win a game or the likely cellar dwellers end up contending for championships. Take, for example, the St. Louis Cardinals who were off to what many Cardinal fans would identify as an abysmal start in 2018. Ownership and fans alike thought change was needed to reawaken the team. They ousted manager Mike Matheny midstream and hired Mike Shildt as his replacement. The result of this change afforded the team an opportunity to contend for the playoffs. Whether it be mid-season or season-long struggles e.g., these unpredictable outcomes require contingency planning. Historically dramatic positive turnarounds experienced by teams such as the Detroit Tigers, who lost 406 games from 2002 through 2005 and had not seen a winning season since 1993, and then who then go on to win the American League Championship and go to the World Series in 2006 and 2012, are easier to manage than the negative outcomes. The New Orleans Saints are a great example of a team that faced tremendous odds after suffering displacement from Hurricane Katrina and then went on to unexpectedly make the 2006 NFL playoffs and win the Super Bowl in 2010. In fact, Hurricane Katrina and its impact on the city of New Orleans and the Saints ranks as one of the most compelling examples of the changing environment that marketers cannot plan for.

Other unexpected events are commonplace in the sports marketing landscape. The star player gets traded or injured halfway through the season. Attendance at the sporting event is affected by poor weather conditions. Leagues are shut down by lockouts. Team owners threaten to move the franchise, build new stadiums, and change personnel. Or in the worst case scenario, a pandemic strikes and the entire sport is shut down. All this affects the sports marketing process.

At the collegiate level, a different set of situations may alter the strategic marketing process. For example, players may be declared ineligible because of grades, star players may leave school early to join the professional ranks, programs may be suspended for violation of NCAA regulations, or conferences may be realigned.

Sports marketers need to be prepared for either positive or negative changes in the environment. These factors are out of the sports marketer's control, but they must be acknowledged and managed. Sports marketers must be prepared to cope with these rapid changes. One model that provides a system for understanding and managing the complexities of the sports marketing environment is called the **contingency framework for strategic sports marketing**.

Contingency approaches

Contingency models were originally developed for managers who wanted to be responsive to the complexities of their organization and the changing environments in which they operate.[2] Several elements of the contingency framework make it especially useful for sports marketers. First, sports marketers operate in unpredictable and rapidly changing environments. They can neither predict team or player success nor control scheduling or trades. A quote by former New York Mets Marketing Vice President Michael Aronin, who spent 13 years with Clairol, captures the essence of this idea: "Before, I had control of the product, I could design it the way I wanted it to be. Here the product changes every day and you've got to adapt quickly to these changes."[3]

Second, the contingency approach suggests that no one marketing strategy is more effective than another. However, one particular strategy may be more appropriate than another for a specific sports organization in a particular environment. For example, sports marketers for the Boston Red Sox have years of tradition on their side that influence their strategic planning. This marketing strategy, however, will not necessarily meet the needs of the relatively new teams such as FC Cincinnati of MLS. Likewise, strategies for an NCAA Division I program are not always appropriate for a Division II program. The contingency framework can provide the means for developing an effective marketing strategy in all these situations.

Third, a contingency model uses a systems perspective, one that assumes an organization does not operate in isolation but interacts with other systems. In other words, although an organization is dependent on its environment to exist and be successful, it can also play a role in shaping events outside the firm. Think about the Chicago Blackhawks and all the resources required from the environment to produce the core product - entertainment. These resources include professional athletes, owners, management and support personnel, and minor league franchises to supply talent, facilities, other competitors, and fans. The different environments that the Chicago Blackhawks actively interact with and influence include the community, the NHL, sponsors, employees and their families, and the sport itself. Understanding the relationship between the organization and its many environments is fundamental to grasping the nature of the contingency approach. In fact, the complex relationship that sports organizations have with their many publics (e.g., fans, government, businesses, and other teams) is one of the things that makes sports marketing so complicated and so unique.

One way of thinking about the environments that affect sports organizations is to separate them on the basis of internal versus external contingencies. The external contingencies are factors outside the organization's control; the internal are considered controllable from the organization's perspective. It is important to realize that both the internal and external factors are perceived to be beyond the control, though not the influence, of the sports marketer.

The essence of contingency approaches is trying to predict and strategically align the strategic marketing process with the internal and external contingencies. This alignment is typically referred to as strategic fit or just "fit." Let us look at the contingency approach shown in Figure 2.1 in greater detail.

The focus of the contingency framework for sports marketing, and the emphasis of this book, is the strategic sports marketing process. The three primary components of this process are planning, implementation, and control. The planning phase begins with understanding the consumers of sports. As previously discussed, these consumers may be participants, spectators, or perhaps both. Once information regarding the potential consumers is gathered and analyzed, **market selection decisions** can be made. These decisions are used to segment markets, choose the targeted consumers, and position the sports product against the competition. The final step of the planning phase is to develop the sports marketing mix that will most efficiently and effectively reach the target market.

Effective planning is merely the first step in a successful strategic sports marketing program. The best-laid plans are useless without a method for carrying them out and monitoring them. The process of executing the marketing program, or mix, is referred to as implementation. The evaluation of these plans is known as the control phase of the strategic marketing plan. These two phases, implementation and control, are the second and third steps of the strategic sports marketing process.

Figure 2.1
Contingency framework for strategic sports marketing

As you can see from the model, a contingency framework calls for alignment, or fit, between the strategic marketing process (e.g., planning, implementation, and control) and external and internal contingencies. Fit is based on determining the internal strengths and weaknesses of the sports organizations, as well as examining the external opportunities and threats that exist. **External contingencies** are defined as all influences outside the organization that can affect the organization's strategic marketing process. These external contingencies include factors such as competition, regulatory and political issues, demographic trends, technology, culture and values, and the physical environment. **Internal contingencies** are all the influences within the organization that can affect the strategic marketing process. These internal contingencies usually include the vision and mission of the organization, organizational goals and strategies for reaching those goals, and the organizational structure and systems.

The **strategic sports marketing process** was defined in Chapter 1 as the process of planning, implementing, and controlling marketing efforts to meet organizational goals and satisfy consumers' needs (see also Figure 2.2) and is the heart of the contingency framework. The **planning phase**, which is the most critical, begins with understanding the consumers of sport through marketing research and identifying consumer wants and needs. Next, market

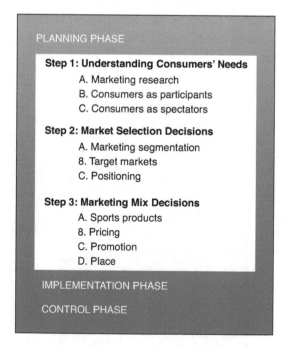

Figure 2.2
Strategic sports marketing process

selection decisions are made, keeping the external and internal contingencies in mind. Finally, the **marketing mix**, also known as the *four Ps*, is developed and *integrated* to meet the identified sports consumer needs.

Once the planning phase is completed, plans are executed in the **implementation phase**. In this second phase of the strategic sports marketing process, decisions such as who will carry out the plans, when the plans will be executed, and how the plans will be executed are addressed. After implementing the plans, the third phase is to evaluate the response to the plans to determine their effectiveness. This is called the **control phase**. The strategic sports marketing process and its three phases will be described in detail in the remainder of the book. Let's turn to a discussion of the internal and external contingencies for the rest of this chapter.

Internal and external contingencies

A complex relationship exists between internal contingencies and the strategic marketing process. Sports marketers must ensure that the marketing strategies are aligned with the broader organizational purpose. Factors controlled by the organization such as its vision and mission, organizational objectives, and organizational culture must be considered carefully. Additionally, this organizational strategy is often based on changes that occur in the environment. It is at this point that external and internal contingencies must complement one another. Let's take a further look at the various factors that make up the internal and external contingencies and gain an appreciation for just how much they can influence the strategic marketing process.

Internal contingencies

Internal contingencies are all influences within and under the control of the sports organization that can affect the strategic sports marketing process. Typically, the internal or controllable factors, such as designing the vision and mission, are the function of top management. In other words, these organizational decisions are usually made by top management rather than sports marketing managers. The more marketing oriented the organization, the more the marketing function becomes involved in the initial development and refinement of decisions regarding the internal contingencies. Irrespective of their involvement, sports marketers should have an understanding of internal contingencies and how they influence the strategic marketing process. Let us describe some of the internal contingencies that sports marketers must consider within the contingency framework.

Vision and mission

One of the first steps in developing a strategic direction for an organization is shaping a vision. The **vision** has been described as a long-term road map of where the organization is headed. It creates organizational purpose and identity. A well-written vision should be a prerequisite for effective strategic leadership in an organization. The vision should address the following:

- Where does the organization plan to go from here?
- What business do we want to be in?
- What customer needs do we want to satisfy?
- What capabilities are required for the future?

As you can see, the organizational questions addressed in the vision are all oriented toward the future. The mission, however, is a written statement about the organization's present situation. The purpose of a written mission statement is to inform various stakeholders (e.g., consumers, employees, general public, and suppliers) about the direction of the organization. It is particularly useful for motivating employees internally and for communicating with consumers outside the organization. Here are examples of mission statements constructed by Under Armour[4] and the Kent State University Athletic Department.[5]

Mission of Under Armour

To make all athletes better through passion, science and the relentless pursuit of innovation.

Mission and objectives of Kent State University Athletic Department

Mission: The mission of Kent State Athletics is to graduate student-athletes and win championships. #FlashesForever

Vision: We are nationally recognized for the exemplary character, achievements, and contributions of our student-athletes to better our society.

Core Values:
- Student-athlete well-being: We are committed to the health, safety, academic, athletic and personal growth of each student.
- Integrity: We do the right thing and hold each other accountable.
- Respect: We respect all people, their culture, beliefs, identity and thought.
- Stewardship: We are responsible guardians of the University's resources, relationships and reputation.
- Family: We are a collaborative team supporting one another.

These mission statements address several key questions:

- What business are we currently in?
- Who are our current customers?

- What is the scope of our market?
- How do we currently meet the needs of our customers?

In addition to addressing these four key questions, mission statements often have accompanying core values that further articulate the strategic framework of an organization. In fact, these core values are fundamental to carrying out the vision and mission of the organization and, as Web Capture 2.1 demonstrates, guiding principles may often serve as a supplement to the strategic roadmap, further defining and articulating organizational strategy.

How do the mission and vision influence the strategic sports marketing process? Both the vision and mission define the consumers of sport in broad terms. For example, Under Armour sees its customers from a global perspective. Also, the vision and mission define the products and services that are being marketed to consumers. The vision and mission also help to identify the needs of consumers, and ultimately guide the marketing process in meeting these needs.

Nike provides an excellent illustration of the dependent relationship among vision, mission, and the strategic marketing process. Originally, the product was aimed toward the serious track athlete who wanted a low-priced, high-quality performance shoe for competition. By 1969, Nike had begun to build a strong brand reputation as the shoe for competitive athletes. Over time, however, Nike redefined and broadened its vision and mission. In 1978, footwear represented 97 percent of Nike's total sales. Today, this percentage has decreased to roughly 66 percent as Nike produces footwear, equipment, and apparel to meet the needs of almost every consumer in global markets.[6] Nike's strategic decision to sell more than just high-performance footwear aimed only at serious athletes has

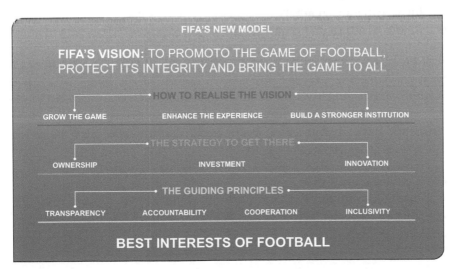

Web Capture 2.1
FIFA's new model accentuating its vision

Source: FIFA.com; https://publications.fifa.com/en/annual-report-2020/the-global-game/the-vision-2020-2023/

changed the entire marketing mix. Now, more Nike products are being sold at more places than ever before. In fact, Nike's mission is,

> to do everything possible to expand human potential. We do that by creating groundbreaking sport innovations, by making our products more sustainably, by building a creative and diverse global team and by making a positive impact in communities where we live and work.[7]

Organizational objectives and marketing goals

Organizational objectives

The **objectives** of the organization stem from its vision and mission. They convert the vision and mission into performance targets to be achieved within a specified timeframe. Objectives can be thought of as signposts along the road that help an organization focus on its purpose as stated in the mission statement. More specifically, an objective is a long-range purpose that is not quantified or limited to a time period.

Organizational objectives are needed to define both financial and strategic direction. Organizational leaders typically develop two types of objectives: financial and strategic. Financial objectives specify the performance that an organization wants to achieve in terms of revenues and profits. Achieving these financial performance objectives is critical to the long-term survival of the organization. Some examples of financial objectives include the following:

- Growth in revenues
- Increase in profit margins
- Improved return on investment (ROI)

Strategic objectives are related to the performance and direction of the organization. Achieving strategic objectives is critical to the long-term market position and competitiveness of an organization. Whereas strategic objectives may not have a direct link to the bottom line of an organization, they ultimately have an impact on its financial performance. Here are a few examples of general strategic objectives:

- Increased market share
- Enhanced community relations efforts
- Superior customer service

For example,

> the objectives of FIFA are: (a) to improve the game of football constantly and promote it globally in the light of its unifying, educational, cultural and humanitarian values, particularly through youth and development programmes; (b) to organise its own international competitions;

(c) to draw up regulations and provisions governing the game of football and related matters and to ensure their enforcement; (d) to control every type of association football by taking appropriate steps to prevent infringements of the Statutes, regulations or decisions of FIFA or of the Laws of the Game; (e) to use its efforts to ensure that the game of football is available to and resourced for all who wish to participate, regardless of gender or age; (f) to promote the development of women's football and the full participation of women at all levels of football governance; and (g) to promote integrity, ethics and fair play with a view to preventing all methods or practices, such as corruption, doping or match manipulation, which might jeopardise the integrity of matches, competitions, players, officials and member associations or give rise to abuse of association football.[8]

Marketing goals

Marketing goals guide the strategic marketing process and are based on organizational objectives. A **goal** is a short-term purpose that is measurable and challenging, yet attainable and time specific. The mnemonic SMARTER, which stands for specific, measurable, acceptable/attainable, realistic/reachable, timely, extending, and rewarding, is often used to help define the framework of marketing goals. As https://managementhelp.org/planning/index.htm#anchor1384873 articulates, goals and strategies should be SMARTER. A SMARTER goal or objective is:

Specific - For example, it is difficult to know what someone should be doing if they are to pursue the goal to "work harder." It is easier to recognize "implement marketing strategies."

Measurable - It is difficult to know what the scope of "implement marketing strategies" really is. It is easier to appreciate that effort if the goal is "implement 12 in-game marketing strategies."

Acceptable - If I'm to take responsibility for pursuit of a goal, the goal should be acceptable to me. For example, I'm not likely to follow the directions of someone telling me to implement 12 in-game strategies if I also have other duties such scanning tickets or facility supervision. However, if you involve me in setting the goal so I can change my other commitments or modify the goal, I'm much more likely to accept pursuit of the goal as well.

Realistic - Even if I do accept responsibility to pursue a goal that is specific and measurable, the goal won't be useful to me or others if, for example, the goal is to "implement 12 in-game marketing strategies in the next 5 minutes."

Timeframe - It may mean more to others if I commit to a realistic goal to "implement 12 in-game marketing strategies during the course of the home opener." However, it will mean more to others (particularly if they are planning to help me or guide me to reach the goal) if I specify that I will implement one marketing strategy at each television timeout during the course of the game, rather than including the possibility that I will implement all at halftime.

Extending – The goal should stretch the performer's capabilities. For example, I might be more interested in implementing a strategy that I know will have an impact on engagement or the way that I implement it will extend my capabilities.

Rewarding – I'm more inclined to implement a market strategy if it will contribute to enhancing fan engagement in such a way that it may have a positive impact upon the game atmosphere/environment.[9]

 Here is a sampling of common marketing goals:

- Increase ticket sales by 5 percent over the next year.
- Introduce a new product or service each year.
- Generate 500 new season ticketholders prior to the next season.
- Over the next 6 months, increase awareness levels from 10 to 25 percent for women between the ages of 18 and 34 regarding a new sports product.

Although multiple goals are acceptable, goals in some areas (e.g., marketing and finance) may conflict, and care must be taken to reduce any potential conflict. After developing marketing goals, the organization may want to examine them based on the following criteria:

- ***Suitability*** – The marketing goals must follow the direction of the organization and support the organization's business vision and mission.
- ***Measurability*** – The marketing goals must be evaluated over a specific timeframe (such as the examples just discussed).
- ***Feasibility*** – The marketing goals should be within the scope of what the organization can accomplish, given its resources.
- ***Acceptability*** – The marketing goals must be agreed upon by all levels within the organization. Top management must feel that the goals are moving the organization in the desired direction; middle managers and first-line supervisors must feel the goals are achievable within the specified timeframe.
- ***Flexibility*** – The marketing goals must not be too rigid, given uncontrollable or temporary situational factors. This is especially true when adopting the contingency framework.
- ***Motivating*** – The marketing goals must be reachable but challenging. If the goals are too easy or too hard, then they will not direct behavior toward their fulfillment.
- ***Understandability*** – The marketing goals should be stated in terms that are clear and simple. If any ambiguities arise, people may inadvertently work against the goals.

- *Commitment* - Employees within the sports marketing organization should feel that it is their responsibility to ensure goals are achieved. As such, managers must empower employees so everyone in the organization is committed and will act to achieve goals.
- *People participation* - As with commitment, all employees in the organization should be allowed to participate in the development of marketing goals. Greater employee involvement in setting goals will foster greater commitment to goal attainment.
- *Linkage* - As discussed earlier, marketing goals must be developed with an eye toward achieving the broader organizational objectives. Marketing goals incongruent with organizational direction are ineffective.

Organizational strategies

Organizational strategies are the means by which the organization achieves its organizational objectives and marketing goals. Whereas the organizational vision, mission, objectives, and goals are the "what," the organizational strategy is the "how." It is, in essence, the game plan for the sports organization. Often labeled as marketing objectives and action plans, these are the specific activities that each major function (e.g., department, etc.) must undertake to ensure that it is effectively implementing each strategy. Organization strategies should be clearly worded to the extent that people can assess if the standards have been met or not. They should be definable and articulate the specific, measurable results produced while implementing strategies. Just as football teams adopt different game plans for different competitors, sports organizations must be able to readily adapt to changing environmental conditions. Remember, flexibility and responsiveness are the cornerstones of the contingency framework.

In general, there are four levels of strategy development within organizations: corporate strategy, business strategy, functional strategy, and operational strategy. The relationship among these strategy levels is shown in Figure 2.3. Notice that there must be a good fit among the levels, vertically and horizontally, for the firm to succeed.

Corporate-level strategies represent the overall game plan for organizations that compete in more than one industry. Business-level strategies define how a business unit gains advantage over competitors within the relevant industry. Functional-level strategies are those developed by each functional area within a business unit. For example, the strategic sports marketing process is the functional-level strategy developed by sports marketing managers, just as financial strategy is the purview of their finance manager counterparts. The operational-level strategies are narrower in scope. Their primary goal is to support the functional-level strategies. Let us take a look at the relationship among the four levels of strategy at the Maloof Companies to see how a good fit among strategies can lead to

Figure 2.3
Relationships between levels of strategy

enhanced organizational effectiveness, while noted conflict and disparity can adversely impact an organization's strategy and effectiveness.

The Maloof Companies[10] are a diversified group of business ventures including entertainment, sports, hotels, casinos, banking, food and beverage, and transportation headquartered in Albuquerque, New Mexico, and operated in New Mexico, Colorado, and Nevada. The Maloof family owns the Palms, a $285 million hotel casino just off the Las Vegas Strip with a 42-story tower and 447 guestrooms. In addition to their gaming business, the Maloofs have exclusive proprietorship rights to the distribution of Coors beer throughout New Mexico. The Maloof Companies also are the largest single shareholder in Wells Fargo Bank, which operates banks and branches in 23 states throughout the United States with over $200 billion in assets and 15 million customers.

The Maloofs are in the process of expanding their business into the entertainment industry with the development of Maloof Productions and Maloof Music. Maloof Productions is committed to developing and producing quality television and motion picture entertainment. Also of interest is that the Maloof Companies are best known for being the previous owners of the Sacramento Kings of the National Basketball Association (NBA) and the Sacramento Monarchs of the Women's National Basketball Association (WNBA) as well as most recently adding to their portfolio a 15 percent minority share (Bill Foley retains the majority share, 85 percent) of the newly launched NHL franchise the Vegas Golden Knights.

They acquired a minority interest in the Kings in 1998 and took majority control the following year, with Joe and Gavin operating the franchise. As part of the purchase of the Kings, they also acquired the team's sister franchise in the WNBA, the Sacramento Monarchs. The Maloofs operated the Monarchs until 2009, when the WNBA was unable to find a new owner and the team folded. In 2013, the Maloofs sold the majority share of the Sacramento Kings (65 percent) and Sleep Train Arena to a group led by TIBCO Software chairman Vivek Ranadivé at a valuation of more than $534 million.

Prior to the sale of the majority interest, the Maloofs, the once favored entity of Sacramento sports consumers, fell out of favor with the fans. Dissonance occurred, as ticket sales continued to decline and rumors of moving the franchise followed. Their topsy-turvy reign as majority owners of the team created strategic implications that hurtled the organization downward. However, in contrast to their NBA franchise ownership, the strategic initiatives deployed to procure minority ownership in the NHL franchise flourished and helped capture the hearts of Las Vegas with a stunning inaugural season in 2017-2018. Traditionally, the corporate strategy for the Maloof Companies has been based on competing in all of these industries. The corporate strategy has allowed the Maloof Companies to obtain the broader organizational goals and pursue its vision and mission.

At the business level, Maloof management specified strategies for each business unit within each of the industry segments. For example, the Golden Knights, Kings, and the Monarchs would each have a unique business-level strategy, even though they are in the same industry sector - sports. These strategies were aimed at gaining competitive advantage within each relevant industry. However, each business-level strategy must support the corporate-level strategy, goals, vision, and mission.

At Maloof Companies, there are numerous functional areas within the organization. For example, the Kings' functional areas included finance and administration, general management and operations, business affairs, civic affairs, sales, and marketing. Leadership within each of these functional areas would be responsible for designing their own strategies to meet their respective business-level strategies.

Finally, within the functional areas such as sales and marketing, operational-level strategies were developed. Promotion, ticket sales, product, and pricing strategies must all be designed and coordinated to attain the sales and marketing objectives set forth in the functional-level strategy. As you can see, sports marketing managers responsible for each operational unit must be concerned with satisfying not only their own goals, but also the objectives of the broader organization.

Corporate level

Most professional sports franchises are owned by individuals or corporations that have many business interests. Sometimes these businesses are related, and sometimes the professional sports franchise is nothing more than a hobby of a wealthy owner. Today, the latter is becoming far less common as corporations include sports franchises in their portfolio. Even more rare is the sports franchise owned and operated as the primary, if not sole, source of owner income (e.g., the Mike Brown family and the Cincinnati Bengals).

There are typically two types of diversified companies - those that pursue related diversification and those that pursue unrelated diversification. In related diversification, the corporation will choose to pursue markets in which it can achieve synergy in marketing, operations, or management. In other words, the corporation looks for markets that are similar to its existing products and markets. The underlying principle in related diversification is that a company that is successful in existing markets is more likely to achieve success in similar markets. Unrelated diversification, however, refers to competing in markets that are dissimilar to existing markets. The primary criteria for choosing markets are based on spreading financial risk over different markets.

Professional sports franchises can be owned privately by one or more individuals, publicly owned corporations, or some combination of both. Corporate ownership of a major league sports team is becoming rarer. Most teams are owned by individual investors who have staked their personal fortunes to buy their franchises, which they often operate as a public trust. The Washington Football Team, Wizards, and Capitals are owned by individuals and their investment teams.

On the corporate side, the Chicago Cubs are owned by the Tribune Company and the Atlanta Braves are owned by Time Warner. However, several recent corporate ownerships of professional sports teams have fizzled, including the Disney Company's ownership of the then-Anaheim Angels and the Mighty Ducks. The Los Angeles Dodgers were owned for several years by News Corp., before the company sold the team to an investor group from Boston, who in 2012 sold the team to the Guggenheim Baseball Management, which includes former Los Angeles Laker Magic Johnson.

DEVELOPING CORPORATE-LEVEL STRATEGY

Corporate-level strategies must make three types of decisions. First, top managers must determine in which markets they want to compete. Sports organizations have a core product and service, plus they also compete in ancillary markets. The core product has been defined as the game itself and the entertainment provided to consumers, whereas secondary markets include sale of licensed merchandise, fantasy sports camps, sports magazines, sports art, and so on. The leaders of a sports organization must also attempt to identify ways of capitalizing on the similarities in markets. For instance, fans for the core product often represent a natural target market for additional products and services. Companies such as Comcast, (Philadelphia 76ers, Flyers, Wells Fargo Arena, Universal Pictures, NBC, and most recently SKI) can realize the benefits of this type of vertical integration. As Scott Rosner noted in 2010:

> by owning the team, playing facility and local media distribution channel, the company captures the lion's share of revenue generated by the team. It dominates the local marketplace, where fans are most passionate about the local team and can be most effectively monetized. Corporate owners with a local or regional focus are more successful than those with a national or global focus.[11]

On the international front, an example may include the Singapore Sports Council's "Vision 2030." Under the Vision 2030 initiative, the Ministry of

Community Development, Youth and Sports (MCYS) and the Singapore Sports Council (SSC) will work with the public, private, and people sectors to jointly develop proposals on how sport can best serve Singapore's future needs. Sports will be used as a strategy for individual development, community bonding, and nation building in the next two decades.[12]

The second type of decision deals with enhancing the performance within each of the chosen markets. Top managers constantly need to monitor the mix of markets in which the organization competes. This evaluation might lead to decisions that involve pursuing growth in some markets or leaving others. These decisions are based on the performance of the market and the ability of the organization to compete successfully within each market.

The third type of decision involves establishing investment priorities and placing organizational resources into the most attractive markets. For a sports organization, this could involve decisions regarding stadium renovation, player contracts, or investing more heavily in merchandising. Corporate decisions within a sports organization must constantly recognize that the core product, the competition itself, is necessary to compete in related markets.

Business-level strategy

The next level of strategic decision making is referred to as business-level, or competitive, strategies. Business level strategies are based on managing one business interest within the larger corporation. The ultimate goal of business-level strategy decisions is to gain advantage over competitors. In the sports industry, these competitors may be other sports organizations in the area or simply defined as entertainment, in general.

One strategic model for competing at the business level features four approaches to gaining the competitive advantage. These approaches include low-cost leadership, differentiation, market niche based on lower cost, and market niche based on differentiation. The choice of which of the four strategies to pursue is based on two issues: strategic market target and strategic advantage.

Strategic market targets can include a broader market segment or a narrow, more specialized market niche. Strategic advantage can be gained through becoming a low-cost provider or creating a real or perceived differential advantage.

The focus of low-cost leadership is to serve a broad customer base at the lowest cost to any provider in the industry. Although there may be a number of competitors pursuing this strategy, there will be only one low-cost leader. Many minor league teams compete as low-cost leaders due to the lower operating costs relative to their major league counterparts. Differentiation strategies attempt to compete on the basis of their ability to offer a unique position to a variety of consumers. Typically, companies differentiate themselves through

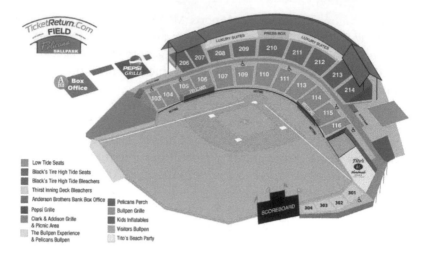

Web Capture 2.2

The Myrtle Beach Pelicans use a low-cost market niche strategy

Source: TicketReturn.com Field: www.milb.com/myrtle-beach/tickets/ticket-information

products, services, or promotions. With differentiation strategies, companies can charge a premium for the perceived value of the sports product. Professional sports franchises attempt to differentiate themselves from competitors by providing a high-quality product on and off the field. This is done through a unique blend of sports promotion, community relations, stadium atmosphere, and a winning team.

Although low-cost leadership and differentiation strategies have mass-market appeal, the market niche strategies are concerned with capturing a smaller market segment. These market segments may be based on consumer demographics, geographic location, lifestyle, or a number of other consumer characteristics. Within the market niche chosen, sports organizations can gain strategic advantage through a focus on low cost or differentiation. Leagues, conferences, and television networks often develop niche strategies targeting audiences that appeal to specific groups with a common set of interests (e.g., NFL Network, Big Ten Network, Golf Channel). Another example of the low-cost market niche strategy is the Pro Rodeo Cowboys Association (PRCA), whose events are priced inexpensively between $10 and $15.

Functional-level strategy

Each functional area of the organization (e.g., marketing, personnel, and operations) must also develop a game plan that supports the business-level and corporate-level initiatives. Again, the contingency framework calls for "fit" between each level of strategy within the organization. It is also important to coordinate among each functional area. For example, the marketing strategies should dovetail with personnel and operations strategies. The strategic marketing process discussed earlier provides the functional-level strategy for the organization's marketing efforts.

Operational-level strategy

Each strategy at the operational level must fit the broader strategic marketing process. This often requires integration across marketing functions and often, within the strategic sports marketing process, several narrower strategies must be considered. Plans must be designed, implemented, and evaluated in areas such as promotion, new product and service development, pricing, sponsorship, and ticket distribution. For example, the Los Angeles Dodgers unveiled an operational-level promotion strategy to increase attendance by offering fans an "all you can eat" ticket. The right-field pavilion at Dodger Stadium was converted into the special section, giving some 3,000 fans as many hot dogs, peanuts, popcorn, nachos, and sodas as they wanted. Season ticket savings versus buying advance purchase single-game tickets are approximately 20 percent, $24 versus $30.[13] Numerous other major league teams are taking note and testing this idea as well.

Organizational culture

Culture is described as the shared values, beliefs, language, symbols, and tradition that is passed on from generation to generation by members of a society. Culture can affect the importance placed on sports by a region or nation, whether we participate in sports, and even the types of sports we enjoy playing or watching. A similar concept applied to organizations is called organizational culture. **Organizational culture** is the shared values and assumptions of organizational members that shape an identity and establish preferred behaviors in an organization.

As one of the internal contingencies, organizational culture influences the sports marketer in a number of ways. First, the organizational culture of a sports organization dictates the value placed on marketing. For instance, just look at the numbers of people employed and the titles of front office personnel at a variety of sports organizations. These are just two important indicators of the marketing orientation of the organization and the importance of the marketing function.

Second, organizational culture is important because it is linked with organizational effectiveness. That is, a positive culture is associated with an effective organization. A positive culture rewards employees for their performance, has open communication, has strong leadership, encourages risk taking, and is adaptive. The ability to adapt to change is one of the most important dimensions from the contingency framework perspective.

Third, the organizational culture of professional sports organizations and college athletic programs not only has an impact on the effectiveness of the organization, but also can influence consumers' perceptions of the organization. For example, the NFL's Raiders, under former owner Al Davis, had an organizational culture that valued risk taking and doing anything necessary to get the job done. This organizational culture translated to the team's successful and ruthless performance on the field. Subsequently, the fans began to adopt this outlaw image. Ultimately, the black and silver bad boys of football have attracted a fan following that has come to expect this rebel image.

University athletic departments and their programs are also defined by the organizational culture. Athletic programs are known to either value education or attempt to win at all costs and be marred in scandal. Recent scandals such as those at the University of Maryland (Jordan McNair and D. J. Durkin), The Ohio State University (Urban Meyer), Baylor University (Art Briles), the University of Miami (Nevin Shapiro), and Penn State University (Jerry Sandusky) have tainted the reputation of these universities known for their high-quality academics and tarnished the image of their elite athletic programs. In each of these cases, actions of the athletic program have influenced consumers' perceptions of the university at large, and may ultimately influence the broader university culture.

External contingencies

External contingencies are all influences outside the organization that might affect the strategic sports marketing process. External contingencies include competition; technology; cultural and social trends; physical environment; the political, legal, and regulatory environment; demographics; and the economy. Let us take a brief look at each of these factors and how they might affect sports marketing strategy.

Competition

Assessing the competitive forces in the **marketing environment** is one of the most critical components in the strategic sports marketing process. **Competition** is the attempt all organizations make to serve similar customers. Sellers realize that to successfully reach their objectives they must know who the competition is – both today and tomorrow. In addition, sellers must understand the strengths and weaknesses of their competitors and how competitors' strategies will affect their own planning.

Access to sports content is at 15-year high across television, with content creators producing more than 134,000 hours of sports news, event, anthology, and commentary. Eighty-six of the top 100 telecasts viewed live or on the same day were sport related. Furthermore, viewership figures and advertising revenue suggests there's more to come. Much of the growth of live programming has been due to the dramatically expanded coverage of college sports on channels such as ESPN and the Big Ten Network. The Big Ten currently receives an average of $433 million a year from Fox and ESPN for between 51 and 54 football games. Audiences have ranged from 500,000 viewers to more than 12.9 million viewers for an Ohio State vs. Wisconsin matchup. The PAC-12 solidified a deal for $250 million a year from Fox and ESPN for 44 games. Meanwhile, the SEC package on CBS remains a "bit" undervalued, averaging approximately 4.9 million viewers in 2017, at a bargain price of $55 million per year. The scramble for lucrative TV deals have shaken up decades-old conference alignments and threaten the very structure of college sports.[14]

Technology is changing so fast and media companies are morphing at such a rate that it will be difficult to predict exactly what the landscape will look like in the future.[15] Over-the-top (OTT) streaming platforms are infiltrating the industry. These media services are offered directly to consumer (e.g., Netflix, Amazon Prime, Peacock) and are ultimately changing the way live sport is consumed. Furthermore, the sport industry is ripe for disruption. Across the global sports media landscape an already fragmented environment is becoming more pixelated.[16] There is no doubt that consumer behavior has been transformed by technology, and as part of that enhancement OTT delivery is becoming the new norm. Disney, along with domestic rivals FOX, NBC, Universal, CBS, and Turner Broadcasting System are all plotting to partner or launch new or enhanced sports streaming apps and services, and new players such as Amazon, YouTube, and Facebook continue to look to expand their presence in the sports marketplace. Table 2.1 illustrates the relative market share (subscribers) of the primary players in sport.

The nature of competition

Sports marketers most often categorize their competition as product related. There are three types of product-related competition. The first of these is termed **direct competition**, the competition between sellers producing similar products and services. High school football games on a Friday night in a large metropolitan area pose direct competition in that the "product" being offered is very similar. One interesting example of direct competition is found in the game schedule of the NBA Indiana Pacers. High school basketball is so popular in Indiana that the Pacers rarely play a home game on Friday or Saturday night because of the competition posed by high school games.

Another type of product competition is between marketers of substitute products and services that are seen as similar alternatives. For example, when several professional sports teams have scheduled games that overlap, a consumer may have to choose to attend the Philadelphia 76ers (NBA), the Philadelphia Phillies (MLB), or the Philadelphia Eagles (NFL). Another example of substitute products is when spectators choose to watch a sporting event on television or listen to a radio or web broadcast rather than attend the event.

The third type of product-related competition, called **indirect competition**, is more general in nature and may be the most critical of all for

Table 2.1 College sports TV: the main players

Network	Subscribers (millions)
BEIN Sport	21,977
Big Ten Network	58,240
ESPN	86,263
ESPN2	86,154
ESPN News	63,027
ESPNU	63,799
Fox Sports 1	83,491
Fox Sports 2	57,613
Golf Channel	70,831
MLB Network	59,106
NBA-TV	45,945
NBC Sports Network	83,683
NFL Network	68,398
Outdoor Channel	35,372
Sportsman Channel	26,437
TBS Network	90,916
The Tennis Channel	55,011
Turner Network Television	89,929

Source: www.broadcastingcable.com

sports marketers. Marketers of sporting events at any level realize their true competition is other forms of entertainment. Professional, collegiate, and high school sporting events compete with restaurants, concerts, plays, movies, and all other forms of entertainment for the consumer dollar. In fact, a study was conducted to examine how closely other forms of entertainment are related to sports.[17] Preliminary findings suggest that respondents' most preferred entertainment activities are going out to dinner, attending parties, playing sports, watching movies, attending sporting events, attending live music or theater, watching TV, shopping for pleasure, watching sports on TV, dancing, and gambling. In addition, video games seem to be competing in the same "entertainment space" as watching sports on TV. Obviously, the video game industry has capitalized on this notion by creating a multitude of sports-related video games. Some people fear that today's interactive, virtual reality video games may replace watching "real games" on TV. Similarly, playing sports and gambling are perceived to be in the same perceptual space. Sport marketers may want to better understand the excitement and risks associated with gambling and add these attributes when marketing sports participation.

Indirect competition is present when even the popular USC and UCLA football games fail to sell out their respective home stadiums (the L.A. Memorial Coliseum and the Rose Bowl). There is simply too much entertainment competition in Southern California compared with Ann Arbor, Michigan (University of Michigan) or South Bend, Indiana (Notre Dame).

Technology

Technology represents the most rapidly changing environmental influence. New technologies affect the field of sports marketing daily. Some advances in technology have a direct impact on how sports marketers perform their basic marketing functions, whereas others aid in the development of new sports products. For example, new technologies are emerging in advertising, stadium signage, and distributing the sports product. The development of mobile apps and web sites remains one of the fastest growing technologies to affect sports marketing (see Appendix B for examples of web sites of interest to sports marketers). Web sites have been developed to provide information on sports (e.g., www.espn.com), sites of sporting events (e.g., www.daytona500.com), teams (e.g., www.clevelandbrowns.com), and individuals (e.g., www.lebronjames.com). The likes of Hulu, Sony PlayStation Vue, Dish Network's Sling TV, A&T's Direct TV Now, and Fubo.tv have collectively shaken up the sports media landscape. Numerous bundle packages have been developed to enable consumers á la carte programming. The value propositions, which include myriad options and no fixed-term contracts, have been extremely attractive to Millennials and Generation Zers who have never had cable subscriptions.[11] While these OTT services remain a work in progress, sports broadcasters and rights holders alike must realize that consumer viewing habits are changing

Web Capture 2.3
SportingNews.com providing sports information via the Internet

Source: SportingNews.com

and OTT and catch-up content are increasingly favored over traditional linear TV. Traditionally sports rights holders have positioned themselves as business-to-business (B2B) businesses, linking lucrative contracts to particular networks. However, to stay atop of the scoreboard these players may be required to alter their tactics and adopt new strategies that can meet the expectations and demands of today's viewers. As Colin Smith, managing director of NASCAR Digital Media noted, more people are turning to mobile devices and second screen platforms to consume NASCAR content and if this continues . . . this means personalization, intelligent recommendations, and fresh approaches to content discovery offerings.[19] ESPN.com is still the king of sports information on the Internet and part of sports fans' daily routines securing 118.6 million unique visitors each month in 2017.[20]

In addition, the Internet has emerged as another popular way to broadcast live events to fans. Beginning in 1995 AudioNet, Inc. (www.audionet.com) was one of the pioneers of live game broadcasts via the Internet and video streaming. Today, each of the major leagues offers its fans opportunities to follow games online. MLB's premium app offers a number of valuable features to baseball fans including access to in-game highlights, expanded data for every player on all 30 MLB rosters, and breaking news for every team all for less than $20 annually.[21]

The University of Nebraska game against San Jose State on September 2, 2000, was the first ever intercollegiate football game to be video webcast. The webcast resulted in more than 200,000 video streams around the world. Nebraska Athletic Director Bill Byrne summed it up nicely by stating that "we believe the Internet brings us one step closer to our fans, particularly those who are miles from home and have limited access to our normal radio and TV broadcasts."[22] Today, people not only are recording shows to be viewed later, but they can also call up their shows from on-demand channels or watch them on their laptops, phones, or tablets.[23] Back in 2007, the NCAA Men's Basketball Championship was an example of how far things had come in a few years. March Madness on Demand allowed fans to watch live game broadcasts of CBS Sports television coverage of the NCAA Championship on their computer for free. Today, events like the Super Bowl and March Madness are communal. They afford even geographically restricted consumers the opportunity to watch events simultaneously, engaging in the interactive and immediate nature of the mediums, further optimizing and extending the mobile-specific experiences of their audiences.

In addition to providing information and game coverage to consumers, the Internet has emerged as a popular alternative to purchasing tickets at a box office. For example, MLB Advanced Media, LP (MLBAM), the interactive media and Internet company of MLB, serves as the Internet provider of tickets for MLB, while StubHub, owned by eBay, serves as the official MLB reseller. StubHub currently is the official ticketing partner of Major League Baseball. StubHub has in excess of 200 partners globally, and their North American business partners include more than 130 properties across the major leagues and venues including MLB, NBA, NHL, MLS, and the NCAA.[24]

The following article presents an excellent look at globalization trends that have, or will, dramatically altered the way spectators consume sport.

ARTICLE 2.2
ON THE INDUSTRY'S RADAR

The rise of streaming is bringing major sporting events to a global audience and pushing up media rights revenues and will drive media sport rights revenues up 75% in the period 2018–2025 from $48.6 billion to $85.1 billion according to a study from Rethink TV.

In the Globalization Lifts TV Sports Rights Past $85 Billion Future, Sports Rights Forecast to 2025 report, the analyst observed that football will increase its already dominant share of that pie from 25.1% ($12.8 billion) in 2018 to 37.4% ($31.9 billion), primarily through increased viewership of Europe's top leagues in other regions, especially Asia Pacific, including China, and North America. The report added that other sports will also benefit from the fan base expansion generated by globalisation and greater streaming distribution, notably basketball.

Rethink added that a strong subtext of the report is that direct-to-consumer services are creeping up on the sports rights industry, with what it called "stealthily with deadly intent" for broadcasters. It noted the likes of Amazon disrupting the traditional field and warned that sporting rights holders will themselves have to adapt to the growing reality of DTC if they are to have a future as major players in sports video distribution.

Another key finding is that the analyst believes that the maturation of streaming is now bringing another major gear shift, both by intensifying competition for rights and changing the viewing experience, with greater levels of personalization and interactivity, as well as innovations in presentation with proliferation of ancillary content.

Rethink also sees the availability of audience data linked to advanced analytics as having created the potential for making changes in the sports themselves, considering fans behavior during viewing, as has occurred in the case of basketball in the USA. It also cited a growing appreciation that sports rights are part of a bigger picture that includes fan participation and the other sources of sports monetization for the leagues or ultimate rights owners. The partnership between Discovery and PGA Golf is an example of connecting premium rights with fan participation.

However, the report also highlighted a persistent problem in the industry: piracy. It said that streaming has also stimulated piracy to the extent that content protection has become a factor in the rights auctions alongside quality of viewing experience, so that contracts no longer go automatically to the highest bidder.

Source: Joseph O'Halloran, "Globalization to take TV sports rights past $85BN by 2024." Rapidtvnews. com (September 2019). Available from: www.rapidtvnews.com/2019092957428/globalisation-to-take-tv-sports-rights-past-85bn-by-2024.html#ixzz61hZuWeXx

Today, every major professional sports team either has an analytics department or an analytics expert on staff. Items that utilize statistical algorithms and integrate digital technologies (e.g., real-time motion tracking) are becoming more prevalent. In fact, the popularity of data-driven decision making in sports has trickled down to the fans, requiring sports leagues to employ at least one full-time "number cruncher" to perform statistical analysis for the league, teams, players, and fans.[25] Teams and leagues have also formed partnerships with high-tech companies, such as that between the NBA and Synergy Sports, an organization whose vision is "for global sports at every level to have the content and technologies to raise their game and create a more immersive experience."[26] The leagues and teams recognize the value these technology-based partnerships provide, and they have become part of the sport business culture.

Interestingly, many owners have emerged from high-tech companies who are using their technology experience and financial strength to benefit their sports franchises. Examples of high-tech owners include, but are not limited to, Vivek Ranadivé, co-owner and chairman of the NBA Sacramento Kings; Steve Ballmer, owner of the NBA Los Angeles Clippers; the late Paul Allen, former owner of the Seattle Seahawks, Portland Trail Blazers, and Seattle Sounders and cofounder of Microsoft; Robert J. Pera, owner of the Memphis Grizzlies, who was a hardware engineer for Microsoft before founding Ubiquiti Networks; Everett R. Dobson, owner of the Oklahoma City Thunder and CEO of Dobson Technologies; Ted Leonsis, owner of the Washington Capitals, Washington Wizards, and former America Online executive; web marketer Daniel Snyder, owner of the Washington Football Team; Ken Kendrick, owner of the Arizona Diamondbacks and Datatel; the late Hiroshi Yamauchi, former Nintendo president and owner of the Seattle Mariners, who in fact sold the team to Nintendo in 2004; and Mark Cuban of the Dallas Mavericks and founder of broadcast.com. More recent collaborations include TIBCO's chief Vivek Ranadivé utilizing the company's Spotfire technology with the Golden State Warriors and more recently the Sacramento Kings and former Microsoft CEO Steve Ballmer, who recently bid $2 billion to acquire the Los Angeles Clippers.

So far, our discussion of technology has been based more on how technology influences spectators and the distribution of sport. But how do technologically advanced products affect sports participants and their performance? Although most sporting goods have experienced major technological improvements since the early 1990s, two sports that live and die by technology are golf and tennis. In the golf industry, one company that positions itself based on cutting-edge technology is E21. E21 differentiates itself by having the exclusive ability to manufacture golf products using E21 scandium metal alloys. These products include both shafts and driver heads. The huge advantage this offers the advanced player is lighter weight and better feel and consistency – something every player wants in a club. This newer competitor to titanium will help E21 capture more market share in the nearly $5.5 billion golf equipment market that has grown with increased play during COVID.[27]

Technology is even becoming a unique way to differentiate in the highly competitive sports apparel market. For example, Ralph Lauren's $295.00 Polo Tech Shirt contains sensors that send heart rate, stress level, and energy output to a paired app. Apparel companies realize that it is all about making the experience personal and unique, and while many battle over athletes and weekend warriors, most understand the urgency to embrace digital transformation. Textronics, Inc., a pioneer in the field of electronic textiles, has produced NuMetrex, a brand of clothes that monitor the body. In 2005, they developed a bra that featured electronic sensing technology that was integrated right into the knit of the fabric for women wishing to monitor their heart rate while they exercise.[28] FastCompany chose the most innovative companies in sports for 2021 during the pandemic, and they included the NBA for its novel ways to return to play and support fans, Zwift for holding the first Virtual Tour de France, and Cyclon, the world's first subscription-based shoe service to bring recyclable sportswear to runners.[29]

Global brands such as Nike and Apple are continuously improving upon product developments that link technology and sport. In 2016, the new Apple Watch Nike+ was released. The watch, which can be integrated with various fitness apps not only from other sports apparel companies but also the likes of key competitors such as Fitbit and Garmin, demonstrates a marketer's nirvana and how they thrive on inertia.[30] The better a brand knows its customers, the more it can tailor its products and communication to enhance brand loyalty. Few doubt that the applications for data will continue to increase and many believe that when brands figure how to make technology seamless, there will be a huge potential audience.

Although some marketers have a hard time grasping the special language of technology, they still agree that a whole new culture of technology has

Web Capture 2.4
STX showing its latest advances in lacrosse technology

Source: STX, LLC (www.stx.com/womens-lacrosse)

emerged. Owner Mark Cuban of the Dallas Mavericks states that the Mavericks constantly strive to push the tech envelope to make the exchange more valuable to their fans and customers.[31] Dan Helfrich, CEO and Chair of Deloitte Consulting, shares,

> What's exciting about technology is that it never stops evolving – and therefore its application in sport will continue to grow. All aspects of a sports experience – for the athlete, the coach, the general manager, the owner, the fan in stadium, the fan at home – can be enhanced by smartly incorporating technology. Those that embrace tech will win both more games and more loyal customers.[32]

Venues such as Mercedes-Benz Stadium are also bringing a multitude of new technologies to the sporting world. Partnerships with official systems integrator IBM favor integration, where no one piece of equipment can work in a vacuum. The idea is to create a smarter stadium that features a Passive Optical Network (PON) to ensure fast, reliable Wi-Fi; video displays; and digital signage while consuming less power. The PON is the first of its kind to ever be used in an NFL stadium. The goal of the integration is to allow fans to enjoy all of the technology that it has to offer without worrying about what goes on behind the scenes.[33] Daktronics, an industry leader in creating scoreboard systems and displays, has created a 360-degree, 63,000-square-foot HD Halo video board. Collectively the video board along with the 2,000-plus video displays throughout the venue will ensure that every fan has a perfect view of the action.

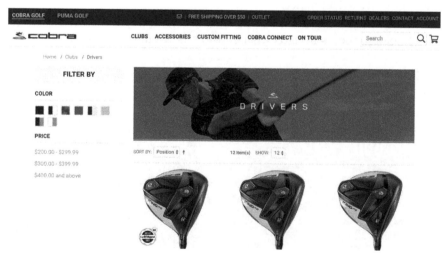

Ad 2.1

Cobra stresses improved performance based on its technological product improvements

Source: Cobra Golf

Cisco Connected Stadium underscores the commitment to creating a new standard for sports venues. As the official technology partner for multiple professional sports organizations, Cisco Connected Stadium encompasses state-of-the-art technology, featuring a platform that integrates access, communication, entertainment, and operations, helping to take the fans' experience and stadium operations to the next level. For example, digital signs ensure "smart" traffic flow; fans can purchase merchandise or concessions while in their seat by ordering from a mobile device; onsite ticket kiosks enable fans to upgrade seats in real-time. Luxury suites have the opportunity to include multimedia amenities for premium video content, and Cisco TelePresence technology may even enable new forms of player-to-fan communications.[34]

Rapid changes in technology make it difficult for many teams and stadiums to keep up. A few years back *Popular Mechanics* looked at 30 NFL stadiums and identified five technologies that at the time led the league in innovation; however, today many of these innovations are expected features. Topping the list was the Dallas Cowboys Stadium. Who would have expected Cowboys owner Jerry Jones to ignore the cliché that everything is bigger in Texas? The Lone Star State's venue has a seating capacity of over 100,000, a $1.2 billion price tag, and houses a pair of 2,100-inch HDTVs. The $40-million screens span 60 yards and are five times the size of the screens at Atlanta's Turner Field. The second item on the list was innovation at the State Farm Stadium, home of the Arizona Cardinals, and the introduction of a retractable *field*. The notion to install the departing lawn began with the owner's desire to play games on natural grass. Third on the list was the architectural framework of Lumen Field, home to the Seattle Seahawks. Decibels were an important part of the equation for then-Seahawks owner and Microsoft cofounder Paul Allen. The design resulted in 135 decibels, nearly as loud as a jet plane, creating one of the loudest stadiums in professional football. Fourth on the list was the giant sunroof of Reliant Stadium in Houston, Texas. The facility was an answer to fans' cry to view football outdoors. The fifth recognized advancement was associated with the development of the MetLife Stadium, home to the New York Giants and the New York Jets, and its efforts to make the stadium "sustainable." The venue creates less pollution, conserves water and energy, and reduces the environmental impact of its operation.[35]

In other stadium technology advancements, numerous sports, including football, baseball, and golf events, accept Apple Pay, which enables consumers to make secure purchases in stadiums, stores, apps, and on the web, or MasterCard PayPass, a "contactless" payment option giving fans the chance to pay for their purchases under $25 with a simple tap of their PayPass-enabled card or device on specially equipped merchant terminals. With these pay options sports fans spend less time standing in line or fumbling for cash at concession stands and more time catching the on-field action.[36] With the recent advancement in blockchain and cryptocurrency technology, look for these concepts to continue to expand. Most will likely become a mainstay for sporting organizations, especially since enhancements as well as the future of use of these products and the potential incorruptible digital ledgers are not only inviting to consumers but to sport organizations as well.

Computer-driven video sport (eSports) is another area of technological impact. Douglas Lowenstein, president of Entertainment Software Association (ESA), believes,

> The video game industry is entering a new era, an era where technology and creativity will fuse to produce some of the most stunning entertainment of the 21st century. Decades from now, cultural historians will look back at this time and say it is when the definition of entertainment changed forever.[37]

Video sports games, a subset of the video gaming industry, are called simulations because of their lifelike approximation of real sporting events. In fact, the danger for franchises lies in fans caring more about these games and simulations than they do the "real" sports. Newzoo predicts that by 2021 eSport revenues could reach $1.65 billion. Sponsorships, advertising, media rights, game publisher fees, and tickets and merchandise accounted for nearly $905 million in revenue generated in 2018. Prize money in eSports exceeds that of traditional sports (NBA, $13 million; The Masters, $11 million; Confederations Cup, $20 million), with a total prize pool of $24.7 million. The global eSports audience was expected to reach 474 million in 2021, which includes 234 million dedicated eSports fans and 215 million occasional viewers who tune in to YouTube's gaming channel or Twitch, a dedicated gaming channel on the web. The most popular game is Dota 2, followed by League of Legends and Counter Strike.[38]

The sport video games today are much more interactive than the "pong" environments of the past. Conceptually, today's games include multiplayer online platforms that provide free-to-play interactive experiences with state-of-the-art motion controls. The leading interactive sports software brand in the world is Electronic Arts (EA) Sports (www.easports.com), with games including *FIFA Soccer, Madden NFL, NFL Blitz, NHL Hockey, Fight Night Champion, NBA Live, Tiger Woods PGA Tour*, and *NCAA Football*. In fact, versions of games such as *Madden NFL* and *FIFA Soccer* have had sales of approximately $93 million and $90 million, respectively, since their inception. EA has been a dominant player in the market; however, as Table 2.2 demonstrates, it has not been without competition. The late Paul Allen, cofounder of Microsoft and former owner of the Portland Trail Blazers, believed that "the only thing holding back sports simulation products is the level of reality that can be achieved."

Video sports participation is not just limited to the couch potato or kids in the living room. Pro gaming leagues are now becoming the rage and viable sports entities of their own. CPL, or the Cyberathlete Professional

Table 2.2 Top 10 sports video games worldwide

Title	Release Year	Publisher
1. *NBA 2K20*	2019	2K Sports
2. *Madden NFL 20*	2019	EA Sports
3. *FIFA 19*	2018	EA Sports
4. *Rocket League*	2015	Psyonix
5. *FIFA 21*	2020	EA Sports
6. *MLB The Show 20*	2020	SIE/Sony
7. *NBA 2K18*	2017	2K Sports
8. *NBA 2K21*	2020	2K Sports
9. *FIFA 20*	2019	EA Sports
10. *NHL 20*	2019	EA Sports

Source: Ranker Games. (2021, June 25). "The most popular sports video games right now." www.ranker.com/list/most-popular-sports-video-games-today/ranker-games

League, has been around since 1997, and the NBA 2K League, a joint venture between the NBA and Take-Two Interactive, is the first official sports league operated by a U.S. professional sports league. For instance, Major League Gaming has a contract with the USA Network, and ESPN has a show called *Madden Nation*, which shows gamers playing Madden NFL. There is even the World Cyber Games, which is the largest global electronic sports tournament that includes multiple divisions and represents a variety of nations.

Cultural and social trends

Perhaps the most important aspects of any culture are the shared and learned values. **Cultural values** are widely held beliefs that affirm what is desirable by members of a society. Several of the core values of interest to sports marketers include individualism, youthfulness, achievement and success, and family.

Sports are symbolic of many core values. In fact in reference to America, what could be more American than baseball, our national pastime? ESPN used this rich tradition in a series of television advertisements promoting its MLB coverage. These advertisements claim "It's baseball – you're American – watch it."

All these core values are directly or indirectly relevant to sports marketing. For instance, certain sports or sporting events stress individualism. Individualism is based on nonconformance or the need to be unique. Nothing could be more directly linked to individualism than the X-treme Games, featuring sports such as skateboarding and street luge. The central or underlying values inherent in all sports are achievement and success. Virtually every sports marketing theme is either directly or indirectly linked to the achievement and success of an individual athlete or a team.

Youthfulness is another core value that is continually stressed by sports marketers. People participate in sports and watch sports to feel young and have fun. Those in the mature market are making strides at staying in shape; they are also watching their own age cohorts still participating in sports at a professional level via any number of senior tours (men's and women's golf, tennis, and bowling). In addition, products like Just for Men are endorsed by sports legends Emmitt Smith, Keith Hernandez, and Michael Waltrip, who all use the product to "stay looking great."

Another core value is family and the need to feel a sense of belonging. Engagement in culture and sport can take many forms. According to the SFIA, for years, rates of inactivity could be directly linked to the state of household incomes. The lower the income, the more likely people were to be inactive. The good news is that in 2019 the income gap became smaller. Inactivity dropped for four of the five household income brackets. The largest decline in inactivity was in the $25,000 to $49,000 household income group, dropping 8.6 percent, followed by those with household incomes between $50,000 and $75,000 dropping 7.9 percent. The largest household income bracket, $100,000 and higher, had the only increase, at 1.9 percent.[39]

According to the SFIA, team sports, which foster a sense of "group identity," continue to play an important role in the lives of American children, teaching

Photo 2.1

The mature market: staying young and having fun in record numbers

Credit: Shutterstock, ID# 696624586 by Ruslan Huzau
URL: www.shutterstock.com/image-photo/couple-playing-tennis-696624586

young people to socialize, solve problems, resolve disputes, experience the benefits of hard work, understand different personalities, and gain self-confidence and direction.[40] They are a significant part of the fabric of American culture. Participation in team sports increased in 2019 for the first time since 2016. This can be attributed, in part, to significant levels of participation in sports such as basketball (the most played team sport), baseball, and indoor/outdoor soccer. Specifically, according to the SFIA, as of 2019 team sports had 29 million youth participants, the main driver of the team sport market.[41] Basketball led the pack for team participation, with 24,917,000 participants, a 1.6 percent increase from 2014. Baseball came in second with 15,804,000 participants. Outdoor soccer was third with 11,913,000 participants, and saw the highest yearly increase (4.5 percent). Indoor soccer added an additional 5,536,000 participants. Ultimate Frisbee (–15.5 percent) and rugby (–10.8 percent) with roughly 1,392,000 participants, had the single largest yearly decline. Ultimate Frisbee, softball, roller hockey, touch football, ice hockey, and paintball all saw decreases over a 5-year period.[42]

Physical environment

The **physical environment** refers to natural resources and other characteristics of the natural world that have a tremendous impact on sports marketing. For instance, the climate of a region dictates the types of sports that are watched and played in that area. In fact, various sports were developed because of the physical characteristics of a region. Skiing and hockey in the northern United States and surfing on the coasts are obvious examples. Sports marketers attempt to control the physical environment for both spectators and sports participants. For example, NRG Stadium has a 50/80 rule. The 50/80 rule is a guideline to help fans prepare for game day. The organization makes the roof decisions on a case-by-case basis each game by considering numerous factors, including environment and weather. The organization will consider opening the roof when game time temperature is projected to be between 50 and 80 degrees, therefore providing an optimal viewing and playing environment. The goal of the 50/80 rule is to provide the most comfortable environment possible for spectators to enjoy a Houston Texans game.[43]

Artificial turf replaced natural grass surfaces in stadiums in the late 1960s. In the new millennium, all new stadiums being built have switched back to natural grass. Grass not only seems to be easier on the athletes in terms of avoiding potential injuries, but fans also seem to appreciate the "natural" look of grass. Likewise, domed stadiums seem to have run their (un)natural course, with Minneapolis being a rare exception.

The newer stadiums are all open-air venues, which have greater appeal for spectators. An interesting example of state-of-the-art stadium technology designed to control the physical environment is the new Cardinals Stadium in Arizona with the first rollout playing surface. At the touch of a button, the grass field slides in and out of the stadium along 13 steel rails. The purpose of the sliding field is threefold: it eliminates indoor watering and related humidity problems; allows the field to soak up direct sunlight; and leaves behind 152,000 square feet of unobstructed floor space for things such as concerts, conventions, and expos.[44]

In addition to the climate, the physical environment of sports marketing is concerned with conservation and preserving natural resources. This trend toward conservation is most often referred to as "green marketing." Marketing ecologically responsible products and being conscious about the effects of sports on the physical environment is one of the concerns of green marketing. For instance, many golf course management groups have come under attack from environmentalists concerned about the effect of phosphate-based chemicals used in keeping golf courses green. Other groups have criticized the sport of fishing as cruel and unusual punishment for the fish.

Political, legal, and regulatory environment

Sports marketers are continually faced with **political, legal, and regulatory environments** that affect their strategic decisions. Politics have always played a major role in sports and are becoming an increasingly important part of the sports landscape. In professional sports, politicians are involved in promoting or discouraging passage of stadium tax issues. Since 1953, most stadiums have been owned by city governments. The question is, "How far does one go in sacrificing taxpayers' wealth to promote civic pride?" Additional evidence of the relationship between government and sports marketing is the growing number of sports commissions. Since 1980, the number of sports commissions, designed to attract sporting events to cities, states, or regions has increased; in fact, the National Association of Sports Commissions has more than 750 member organizations and 2,400 sport tourism professionals.[45]

The legal environment of sports has certainly taken on a life of its own in the new millennium. Sports officials (i.e., league commissioners, judges, sports arbitrators, coaches, and athletic directors) are continually confronted with legal challenges that arise on and off the playing field. These officials must be adept at interpreting the language of collective bargaining, recruiting student-athletes, understanding Title IX, avoiding antitrust issues, licensing team logos, and handling other sports law issues.

One of the most famous pieces of legislation, passed in 1972 under President Richard Nixon, was Title IX. Simply, Title IX states that "no person in the United States shall, on the basis of sex, be excluded from participation in, be denied the benefits of, or be subjected to discrimination under any education program or activity receiving Federal financial assistance." Interestingly, the law that has had the most dramatic impact on the growth of women's sports participation does not even mention the word "sports." Perhaps the most famous Title IX decision was a 1997 ruling by the U.S. Supreme Court in the *Brown University v. Cohen* case. The courts ruled that Brown University did not meet any part of the three-step Title IX compliance.

This three-part test includes the following:

1   Are opportunities for female and male athletes proportionate to their enrollment?
2   Does the school have a history of expanding athletic opportunities for the underrepresented sex?
3   Has the school demonstrated success in meeting the needs of those students?

Unfortunately, Title IX implementation has led to reduction in men's sports programs. Rather than adding women's sports programs, universities have chosen to cut men's sports such as baseball and wrestling to address the problem of proportionality.

As mentioned earlier, sports legal issues involve much more than Title IX and antitrust issues. Recent examples of sports legal issues in the news include cases of breach of contract, player-on-player/coach/fan violence, and trademark infringement. NBA commissioner Adam Silver handed down a total of $6,899,999 million in fines to 978 players in the 2020–2021 season.[46] The NBA has been a strict enforcer of policies and fines since the Pacers–Pistons brawl in 2004. Arguably the most violent fight in NBA history, with less than 1 minute left in the game, the Indiana Pacers scuffled with the Detroit Pistons players and ultimately rushed the stands, involving some drunken Detroit Pistons fans.

Due to the billions of dollars of sports-licensed merchandise sold each year, a more common legal issue in sport is trademark violation. In one example, American Media, Inc. (parent company of the *National Enquirer* and *Globe*) was sued by the U.S. Olympic Committee (USOC) for using images of Olympic athletes without their consent and using the word "Olympics" in a publication entitled *Olympics USA*.[47] Similarly, the IOC has filed a lawsuit against 1,800 web sites abusing the Olympic name.[48] In yet another example, nearly 10,000 counterfeit clubs, including Titleist, Ping, and Callaway, were confiscated in China.

A regulatory body or agency is responsible for enacting laws or setting guidelines for sports and sports marketers. Regulatory agencies can be controlled by either governmental or nongovernmental agencies. One example of a nongovernmental regulatory body that has tremendous control over sports and sports marketing practices is the Fédération Internationale de Football Association (FIFA). FIFA is the international federation for the world's most popular sport, soccer. FIFA, which was formed in 1904, promotes soccer through development programs for youth and supervises international competition to ensure the rules and regulations of the game are being followed. In addition, FIFA is responsible for maintaining the unified set of rules for soccer called the *Laws of the Game.*

Although FIFA is concerned with regulating the game itself, it also controls many facets outside the game that have an impact on sports marketing. For example, FIFA is committed to improving stadiums for the fans and protecting them against the rising costs of attendance. Another example of FIFA's control over sports marketing is that virtual advertising - superimposing marketing messages on the field during televised broadcasts - is forbidden.

In addition, FIFA works with ISL Marketing to secure sponsors for major soccer events, such as the World Cup. As a regulatory agency, FIFA attempts to make sure that the sponsors do not intrude in any way on the integrity of the game. FIFA does not attempt to influence how companies do their own business; however, they do their best to ensure that sponsors do not influence the game itself.

FIFA's focus is to make a difference in people's lives while creating balance and understanding of who they serve. Their mission - develop the game, touch the world, build a better future - articulates both a challenge and an opportunity. Their promise to strive for the game, for the world, reflects FIFA's emphasis and responsibility to not only promote its core product, soccer, but to reach out to its world stakeholders by extending the core, using football as a symbol of hope and integration. FIFA President Joseph Blatter describes the delicate but beneficial relationship between FIFA, its consumers, and sponsors as follows: "We see it as our duty to take on the social responsibility that comes hand in hand with our position at the helm of the world's most loved sport. Join us in uniting forces to develop the game, touch the world and build a better future!"[49]

As sport continues to grow so do the regulatory and marketing concerns that affect its strategic framework. Commercial exploitation and the perceived inequalities that accompany its presence are prevalent in today's sport environment. Hence, so are the lawsuits that contest its framework. Governing agencies struggle to stay abreast of reform challenges. For example, in a landmark decision handed down on August 8, 2014, a federal judge ruled in favor of the plaintiff in the *Ed O'Bannon v. NCAA* antitrust case, knocking down the restrictions against college athletes profiting off their name, image and likeness. The injunction will not preclude the NCAA from implementing rules capping the amount of compensation, but the NCAA will not be permitted to set this cap below the cost of attendance. The landmark decision will have a significant impact upon the future regulatory environment and as the accompanying article illustrates, sanctioning bodies can often struggle to retain control.

ARTICLE 2.3
SPORTS AND POLITICS: WORLD OF UNCERTAINTY

The NBA's China crisis is not a foreign situation for American sports – and it promises to come up again.

As the controversy unfolded, workers in Shanghai took down a sign promoting the Oct. 10 game between the Los Angeles Lakers and the Brooklyn Nets.

Photo: GETTY IMAGES

Six years ago, Scott Blackmun, then-CEO of the U.S. Olympic Committee, said U.S. athletes should "comply" with Russia's anti-LGBT propaganda law as Team USA prepared for the 2014 Winter Games in Sochi.

Russia Today heavily promoted his comments. But condemnation was intense back home, where the law was seen as both an affront to gay rights and to the fundamental American expectation of free expression. The USOC had to issue clarifications, emphasizing that the body found the law inconsistent with Olympic values and that the compliance remark was for athletes' safety.

Last week, the NBA's own foreign political controversy in China threatened the very foundation of the league's rapid growth, dominating business, sports and political news for a week. But it was hardly the first time a sports property has found itself caught between domestic politics and foreign affairs as it seeks a global stage, and it surely won't be the last.

As in the USOC's case, NBA Commissioner Adam Silver eventually found a middle ground: He expressed regret for the offense caused by Rockets general manager Daryl Morey's tweet in support of Hong Kong protestors that ignited the firestorm, but he did not apologize and pledged that the league would "protect our employees' freedom of speech."

Though aware of the sensitive issues at stake, NBA Commissioner Adam Silver made clear the league will "protect our employees' freedom of speech."

The explosive nature of the fight between Silver and the totalitarian Chinese government may not be matched any time soon. But the problem of balancing American values against the political and cultural norms of other nations is sure to rise again. Western sports properties are increasingly pursuing China's tantalizing growth prospects at a time when their own customers, athletes and employees expect them to speak out on social causes. Individual athletes are now celebrated for becoming engaged in politics, and marketing experts say major sponsors also crave to be seen as "standing for something."

But one country's brand-safe social cause is another country's third rail. In just 27 months, the Winter Olympics head to Beijing, where controversies like the one the NBA is embroiled in could well reappear for any number of nations or brands. It has led to an open question about where the line should be between offering domestic political opinions and commenting on foreign affairs.

"We're American citizens, I think we have a social civic responsibility to be active in causes we believe in," Jacksonville Jaguars owner Shahid Khan, who was born in Pakistan, said from the stage at the Yahoo Finance All Markets Summit in New York. "Do we have that same responsibility to really opine on sovereign matters in other countries? I think that's the critical issue."

The International Olympic Committee, national Olympic committees and their sponsors have struggled with this balance for decades. Those who've experienced it have seen how the result has allowed those properties to maintain an altruistic brand in the West while still being welcome in China, North Korea and other totalitarian states.

"It's a fragile alignment, it's hard to keep together," said Terrence Burns, executive vice president of global sports for Engine Shop. "By necessity, they have to be extraordinarily adroit, diplomatically, and frankly respectful of every culture, in every nation, that they choose to work with."

Expect the China issue to come roaring back after the 2020 Summer Olympics in Tokyo, when final preparations for the 2022 Winter Games in Beijing kick off. When Beijing hosted the 2008 Summer Games, human rights advocates hammered Coca-Cola, Visa and others for supporting China through the Games. Visa even scrapped an early Olympics campaign tag line, "Go Humans!" in favor of "Go World!" amid concerns that the former would draw extra attention to China's human rights record.

USA Basketball managing director Jerry Colangelo got a first-hand look at China's passion for the sport during the FIBA Basketball World Cup this summer.

To a certain extent, criticism is unavoidable for multinationals, and often critics will seek to amplify cross-border differences for their own gain. The Chinese government is known for using these situations to rally nationalist sentiment, and President Donald Trump eagerly framed two of his leading critics from the sports world, Warriors coach Steve Kerr and Spurs coach Gregg Popovich, as hypocrites last week for their non-engagement on Hong Kong questions.

But problems can be mitigated by ensuring that companies and employees know the facts before speaking out, said Michael Payne, a former marketing chief of the IOC and a longtime consultant to Olympic brands, including Alibaba.

"When you're going to start commenting about geopolitics, or national interests and politics, you really need to make sure you're fully up to speed on it, and you know your history and background, otherwise you're going to slip up on a banana skin," Payne said.

The IOC has not totally disengaged from countries' internal politics, Payne said. In the Middle East, the Olympic movement has "very carefully" navigated the issue of women's equality, through "slow cajoling and coaching" to put women on equal sports footing. "Frankly, with more progress than most politicians are seeing," Payne said.

As American leagues globalize, they'd be wise to seek out more international staffers and train themselves on other perspectives – and to generally be more risk-averse when it comes to global communications, experts said.

"When we work with our global partners in the Olympic space, it's so innate that you look at things through so many more lenses than the gut reaction from the American seat," said Ann Wool, president of Ketchum Sports & Entertainment, which has advised Olympic sponsors such as Chinese computing giant Lenovo and Procter & Gamble.

Jerry Colangelo, managing director of USA Basketball, spent several weeks this summer in China for the FIBA Basketball World Cup. He said the Chinese people love the NBA and there's lots of common ground, but the Hong Kong situation requires sensitivity

"It is inevitable that because of where we are in today's world that there were going to be some roadblocks," said Colangelo. "And well, here we are."

Additional reporting by John Lombardo.

Source: Ben Fischer, "The NBA's China crisis is not a foreign situation for American sports – and it promises to come up again." *Streets and Smith's Sport Business Daily* (October 14, 2019), accessed September 24, 2020. www.sportsbusinessdaily.com/Journal/Issues/2019/10/14/Sports-and-Society/NBA-China.aspx

Demographics

Assessing the **demographic environment** entails observing and monitoring population trends. These trends are observable aspects of the population such as the total number of consumers and their composition (i.e., age or ethnic background) or the geographic dispersion of consumers. Let us look at several aspects of the demographic profiles, including size of the population, age of the population, shifts in ethnic groups, and population shifts among geographic regions.

Size of the population

Currently, the world population is approximately 7.79 billion and growing. The U.S. population stands at 332 million, which is the world's third largest behind China and India, both of which are growing at a rapid pace. It is estimated that there is a net gain of one person every 8 seconds in the United States and almost a net gain of approximately 2.5 per second worldwide.[50] This is of special interest to marketers of sports entities who are considering expansion into international markets.

Age

Age is one of the most common variables used in segmenting and targeting groups of consumers. As such, sports marketers must continually monitor demographic shifts in the age of U.S. consumers. The "graying of America" has and will continue to exert a huge influence. Many Americans are now living into their 70s, 80s, and beyond. In fact, in the United States the growth in the number and proportion of older adults is unprecedented. Two factors – Americans are living longer lives than in previous decades and aging baby boomers encompass a proportionally larger demographic segment – combine to impact this growth in the number of older adults. By 2060, the number of older adults is projected to double from more than 46 million to more than 98 million. This will be the first time in history that the number of older adults outnumbers children under the age of 5. In 2030, when the last baby boomer turns 65, the demographic landscape of our nation will have changed significantly, hence one of every five Americans – about 72 million people – will be an older adult.[51]

Another statistic from the 2020 census is that the U.S. population of 65 and older grew by more than a third (34%) over the last decade.[52] With new technological advances bringing about breakthroughs in medicine, a lower mortality rate, and preventive approaches to health, Americans are living longer.

Moreover, the 79-million-strong baby boom generation has already entered midlife and will soon age. In fact, if you add 65 years to January 1, 1946 you get January 1, 2011; therefore, the retirement age of the baby boomer has arrived. Four out of every 10 adults in the United States are baby boomers. In 2018, baby boomers ranged in age from 54 to 72 years. Also of significance is the baby bust generation (children of baby boomers) that follows in the wake of its parental tidal wave. In 2018, an estimated 6.4 percent of the U.S. population was younger than 5 years of age.[53]

Shifts in ethnic groups

The United States has been called a melting pot because of its diversity and multiethnic population, providing promise that all immigrants can be transformed into Americans, forging a new alloy built upon freedom, civic responsibility, and the crucible of democracy. Today, the number of white

Americans is diminishing. Immigrants today come not from Europe but overwhelmingly from Asia and Latin America and account for 60 percent of the nation's population growth in the last decade. A sizeable and growing number of young people come from families with one white and one minority parent, as more adults form families across racial and ethnic lines. By far the largest group among this sector have Hispanic and white European ancestry. In 2015, the Census Bureau tested a unified question that treated Hispanic origin like race, which in fact may be how most Americans think; the result was that almost 30 percent of Hispanics indicated a second ethno-racial origin. Today, roughly 45 percent of American children under the age of 5 belong to minority groups. By 2050, non-Hispanic whites will account for only 54 percent of the U.S. population. In terms of sheer size, just over 121 million people represent either the African American, Asian, or Hispanic ethnic groups. All three of these ethnic groups have rising income levels, which translate into more purchasing power.[54] Although all minority groups are growing, the fastest-growing segment has been Hispanics. Hispanic buying power is estimated to be $1.7 trillion.[55] This number is sure to rise in the years to come.

These ethnic groups are important subcultures that share a portion of the larger (white) American culture, but also have unique consumption characteristics. There are a number of benefits in developing a marketing mix that appeals to specific ethnic groups. The accompanying article describes how the National Basketball Association has recognized the value of ethnic diversity.

ARTICLE 2.4
REPORT: NBA STILL LEADS MEN'S PRO SPORTS IN DIVERSITY HIRING

The NBA continues to lead the way in men's professional sports in racial and gender hiring practices, according to a diversity report released Tuesday.

The league earned an A+ for racial hiring practices and a B for gender hiring practices for an overall grade of an A. That keeps the NBA "significantly above" other professional sports, according to the report's author Richard Lapchick, the director of The Institute for Diversity and Ethics in Sport.

"The NBA remains the industry leader among men's sports for racial and gender hiring practices even with the increased grading scales introduced last season," Lapchick said.

The report states that the NBA league office has the best record for people of color in men's professional sports at a 36.4 percent employment rate.

The league, which was first to have three team owners who are people of color, now has seven women who served as team presidents/CEOs during the 2017–2018 season – the highest among men's professional sports.

The report states there are also more NBA general managers and head coaches of color than in the past.

The general managers who are people of color doubled from last season from 10 percent to 20 percent overall, which puts the NBA well ahead of other men's sports leagues.

That's a big positive, Lapchick said.

As for head coaches, there were 30 percent of all NBA head coaches were people of color last season. But following the coaching changes at the end of this past season one-third of all NBA head coach are now people of color.

The same trend has trickled down to the assistant coach level, where the percentage of people of color increased from 45.4 percent in the 2016–2017 to 45.7 percent this past season.

Likewise, there was an increase in the percentage of people of color as vice presidents at the team level too, increasing to 25.4 percent this past season, up nearly six percent from the previous season.

Lapchick also said that in two of the other categories that were reclassified – team management and team professional staff – the percentage of people of color increased significantly from 23.4 percent to 31.2 percent and from 32.6 percent to 39.5 percent, respectively.

Lapchick had some concerns when it comes to gender hiring at the team level, a category which dropped for the third straight year.

The percentage of women decreased for team vice presidents and team professional staff. Women who held team vice president positions made up 23.5 percent, a slight decrease from last year's study. The percentage of women in team professional staff positions decreased by 2.9 percentage points from 40.1 in to 37.2 percent.

"It's something we are keeping an eye on," Lapchick said. "In men's sports in general gender hiring is a major concern."

However, Lapchick said the NBA still outpaces other leagues in gender hiring.

Despite those slight drop-offs in gender hiring, Lapchick called Commissioner Adam Silver and the NBA the "industry leaders" among all men's professional sports leagues in overall racial and gender hiring practices.

Source: NBC Sports.com, 2018. Report: NBA still leads men's pro sports in diversity hiring. Associated Press, June 26, accessed September 24, 2020. https://nba.nbcsports.com/2018/06/26/report-nba-still-leads-mens-pro-sports-in-diversity-hiring/

Population shifts

The latest count of the U.S. population highlighted that the demographic center of gravity continued to shift away from the Northeast and Midwest, with shifts in individual states becoming even more significant. As with the last decade, the 2020 census revealed that the greatest population shift continues to be in the South and West.[56]

With respect to the movement of the population in the United States, the South grew fastest at 10.2 percent, the West was second fastest at 9.2 percent, followed by the Northeast at 4.1 percent.

Utah was the fastest growing state at a rate of 18.4 percent since the 2010 census. West Virginia was the fastest shrinking state with a rate of 3.2 percent.[57]

There is no definitive explanation for this shift, although some believe it is due to the previously discussed aging of America or the growth of employment opportunities in these areas. It's interesting to note that until 1957 when the Brooklyn Dodgers moved to Los Angeles, there were no MLB teams west of St. Louis.

Along with exploring population shifts by state, sports marketers must assess the dispersion of people within an area. Are people moving back to urban areas, or is the "flight to the suburbs" still occurring? The 2020 censuses showed the greatest growth to be in suburban areas and out of metropolitan areas, especially given COVID.[58] There are still fewer people living in or moving back to the central city. These measures of population dispersion are having an impact on where new professional teams are locating and where new stadiums are being built (e.g., the Atlanta Braves Stadium, Truist Park).

The economy

The economic environment is another important but uncontrollable factor for sports marketers to consider. Economic factors that affect sports organizations can be described as either macroeconomic or microeconomic elements. A brief explanation of each follows.

Macroeconomic elements

Economic activity is the flow of goods and services between producers and consumers. The size of this flow and the principal measure of all economic activity is called the gross national product (GNP). The business cycle, which closely follows the GNP, is one of the broadest macroeconomic elements. The four stages of the business cycle are as follows:

- *Prosperity* - The phase in which the economy is operating at or near full employment, and both consumer spending and business output are high.
- *Recession* - The downward phase, in which consumer spending, business output, and employment are decreasing.
- *Depression* - The low phase of the business cycle, in which unemployment is highest, consumer spending is low, and business output has declined drastically.
- *Recovery* - The upward phase when employment, consumer spending, and business output are rising.

Each cyclical phase influences economic variables, such as unemployment, inflation, and consumers' willingness to spend. Decisions about the strategic sports marketing process are affected by these fluctuations in the economy. Ticket sales may boom during times of economic growth. In addition, the growth period may have an even greater impact on corporate demand for luxury boxes and season tickets. If the country is in either a recession or a depression, consumers may be reluctant to purchase nonessential goods and services such as sporting goods or tickets to sporting events. Mistakenly, the sports industry sometimes seems to operate under the "ignorance is bliss" philosophy when it comes to the economy. As Steve Wilstein points out, "salaries for athletes kept rising, TV deals soared, and ticket prices spiraled ever upward as if the leagues were living in their own fantasyland, immune to economic cycles."[59] Although Wilstein believes the sports that are hardest hit by the economy are those already on the periphery (e.g., the Women's Professional Bowling Tour), even the major sports are hit hard by a poor economy.

Although the relationship between the purchase of sporting goods and tickets to sporting events is likely to be associated with good economic times, this may not always be the case. During a recession or depression, sports may serve as a rallying point for people. Consumers can still feel good about their teams, even in times of economic hardship. This is one of the important, but sometimes neglected, societal roles of sport.

Microeconomic elements

Whereas **macroeconomic elements** examine the big picture, or the national income, **microeconomic elements** are those smaller elements that make up the big picture. One of the microelements of concern to sports marketers is consumer income level. As economist Paul Samuelson points out, "Mere billions of dollars would be meaningless if they did not correspond to the thousand and one useful goods and services that people really need and want."[60] Likewise, having sports products would be meaningless if consumers could not afford to purchase them. A primary determinant of a consumer's ability to purchase is income level.

Consumer income levels are specified in terms of gross income, disposable income, or discretionary income. Of these types of income, discretionary is of greatest interest to sports marketers. This is the portion of income that the consumer retains after paying taxes and purchasing necessities. Sports purchases are considered a non-necessity, and therefore are related to a consumer's or family's discretionary income. According to an analysis by The Conference Board, slightly more than half (51 percent) of American households have some discretionary income they can spend on non-necessities.[61] In addition, the number of families with discretionary income is expected to rise slightly over the next decade.

Sports advocates argue that new stadia and consumer spending on sports support local economic growth. The local economic benefits from a major professional sports team are typically derived from four major sources of spending: (1) attendance (tickets and parking) at the games; (2) concession items sold at the games such as food and merchandise; (3) spending before and after the events for other consumption items such as meals; and (4) taxes paid to local government on spending for the previous three categories. Others argue that spending on sport has little impact and that professional sport is an economic drain. The following quote summarizes this notion.

> People have a limited amount of discretionary income. They may use it on attendance at professional sporting events. In the absence of pro sports, they will spend the money elsewhere – lower-level sporting events, the movies, etc. The same is true for large corporations. If they don't buy sky boxes, they will entertain their clients elsewhere (i.e., restaurants). Sports facilities generate very few jobs. For a local economy, player management (and that may come from outside) and low-level game day employment (vendors, etc. . . .). A modest factory or a small research facility has far more impact.[62]

Monitoring the external contingencies

As discussed, external contingencies are dynamic, and sports marketers must keep abreast of these continually changing influences. A systematic analysis of these external factors is the first step taken by sports marketers using the contingency framework. In addition, as the sports industry becomes more competitive, one of the keys to success will be identifying new market opportunities and direction through assessing the external contingencies. The method used to monitor the external contingencies is known as environmental scanning.

Environmental scanning

An outward-looking, environmental focus has long been viewed as a central component of strategic planning. In fact, it has been argued that the primary focus of strategic planning is "to look continuously outward," to have foreseeability, and to keep the organization in step with the anticipated changes in the external environment. This process of monitoring external contingencies is called environmental scanning. More formally, **environmental scanning** is a firm's attempt to continually acquire information on events occurring outside the organization so it can identify and interpret potential trends.[63]

A sports organization can do several things to enhance its environmental scanning efforts. First, the organization can identify who will be responsible for environmental scanning. The only way to move beyond the pressures of daily business activities is to include environmental scanning responsibilities in the job description of key members of the organization.

Second, the organization can provide individuals conducting the environmental scan with plenty of information on the three Cs: customers, competition, and company. An organization's scanners cannot correctly monitor the environment without having a solid base of information about the following: customer expectations and needs; the strengths, weaknesses, distinctive competencies, and relative market positioning of the competition; and the strengths, weaknesses, distinctive competencies, and relative market positioning of your own company - as well as the major developmental opportunities that await exploitation.

Third, the organization can ensure integration of scanned information through structured interactions and communication. All too often, information needed to recognize new market opportunities is identified but never gets disseminated among the various functional areas. That is, marketing, finance, and operations may all have some information, or pieces to the puzzle, but unless these individuals share the information, it becomes meaningless. Organizations with the most effective environmental scanning systems schedule frequent interactions among their designated scanners.

Fourth, the organization can conduct a thorough analysis of ongoing efforts to improve the effectiveness of environmental scanning activities. This systematic study consists of evaluating the types of scanning data that are relevant and available to managers. This focus on previous environmental scanning efforts can often lead to the identification of new market opportunities.

Fifth, the organization can create a culture that values a "spirit of inquiry." When an organization develops such a spirit, it is understood that the environmental scanning process is necessary for success. In addition, it is understood that environmental scanning is an ongoing activity that is valued by the organization.

Environmental scanning is an essential task for recognizing the external contingencies and understanding how they might affect marketing efforts. However, there are two reasons why environmental scanning practices may fail to identify market opportunities or threats. First, the primary difficulty in effectively scanning the environment lies in the nature of the task itself. As scanning implies, sports marketers must look into the future and predict what will likely take place. To make matters even more difficult, these predictions are based on the interaction of the complex variables previously mentioned, such as the economy, demographics, technology, and so on. Second, predictions about the environment are based on data. Sports marketers are exposed to enormous amounts of data and only with experience can individuals selectively choose and correctly interpret the "right data" from the overwhelming mass of information available to them.

Assessing the internal and external contingencies: SWOT analysis

To this point, we have looked at both the external and internal contingencies. To guide the strategic sports marketing process, an organization conducts a SWOT analysis. SWOT is an acronym for strengths, weaknesses, opportunities, and threats. The strengths and weaknesses are controllable factors within the organization. In other words, a firm must evaluate its strengths and weaknesses based on the internal contingencies. The opportunities and threats are assessed as a result of the external contingencies found in the marketing environment. These elements may be beyond the control of the sports organization.

The strategic sports marketing process must first examine its own internal contingencies. These internal strengths and weaknesses include human resources, financial resources, and whether organizational objectives and marketing goals are being met with the current marketing mix. Products and services, promotional efforts, pricing structure, and methods of distribution are also characterized as either strengths or weaknesses.

After assessing the organizational strengths and weaknesses, the firm identifies external opportunities and threats found in the marketing environment. As discussed earlier in the chapter, sports marketing managers must monitor the competition; demographic shifts; the economy; political, legal, and regulatory issues; and technological advances. Each of these external factors may affect the direction of the strategic marketing process.

The intent of conducting a SWOT analysis is to help sports marketers recognize or develop areas of strength capable of exploiting environmental opportunities. When sports marketers observe opportunities that match a particular strength, a strategic window is opened. More formally, **strategic windows** are limited periods of time during which the characteristics of a market and

Web Capture 2.5
NCAA capitalizes on the new opportunities based on the growth in women's sports

Source: NCAA © National Collegiate Athletic Association, 2020

Table 2.3 Assessing external contingencies

1. **Social** – What major social and lifestyle trends will have an impact on the sports participants or spectators? What action has the firm been taking in response to these trends?

2. **Demographics** – What impact will forecast trends in size, age, profile, and distribution of population have on the firm? How will the changing nature of the family, the increase in the proportion of women in the workforce, and changes in ethnic composition of the population affect the firm? What action has the firm taken in response to these developments and trends? Has the firm reevaluated its traditional sports products and expanded the range of specialized offerings to respond to these changes?

3. **Economic** – What major trends in taxation and in income sources will have an impact on the firm? What action has the firm taken in response to these trends?

4. **Political, legal, and regulatory** – What laws are now being proposed at federal, state, and local levels that could affect the strategic marketing process? What recent changes in regulations and court decisions have affected the sports industry? What action has the firm taken in response to these legal and political changes?

5. **Competition** – Which organizations are competing with us directly by offering a similar product? Which organizations are competing with us indirectly by securing our customers' time, money, energy, or commitment? What new competitive trends seem likely to emerge? How effective is the competition? What benefits do our competitors offer that we do not?

6. **Technological** – What major technological changes are occurring that affect the sports organization and sports industry?

the distinctive competencies of a firm fit together well and reduce the risks of seizing a particular market opportunity. For example, IMG, a leading sports and entertainment marketing company, has created "IMG X Sports" to capitalize on the growing popularity in extreme and lifestyle sports and IMG College to capitalize on the growing popularity of college sports. In addition to capitalizing on strengths, sports marketers develop strategies that eliminate or minimize organizational weaknesses.

At this stage, you should have a broad understanding of how each of the external contingencies may affect your marketing plan. Table 2.3 provides a common list of questions to consider when developing the opportunities and threats (OT) portion of your SWOT analysis.

Summary

Chapter 2 provides an overview of the contingency framework for the strategic sports marketing process. Although there are many ways to think about constructing a sports marketing plan, it is best to lay a foundation that is prepared for the unexpected. The contingency framework is especially useful for sports marketers because of the complex and uncertain conditions in which the sports organization operates. The unexpected changes that occur over the course of a season or event may be positive or negative. The changes that occur may be either controllable or uncontrollable events that affect the sports organization. The contingency framework includes three major components: the internal contingencies, the external contingencies, and the strategic sports marketing process. Uncontrollable occurrences are typically in the marketing environment and are referred to as external contingencies, whereas internal contingencies are within the control of the organization (sometimes beyond the scope of the marketing function). The heart of the contingency framework is the strategic sports marketing process, which is defined as the process of planning, implementing, and controlling marketing efforts to meet organizational goals and satisfy consumers' needs.

Internal contingencies, thought of as managerial, controllable issues, include the vision and mission of the sports organization, organizational objectives and marketing goals, organizational strategies, and organizational culture. The vision and mission of the sports organization guide the strategic sports marketing process by addressing questions such as: What business are we in? Who are our current customers? What is the scope of our market? How do we currently meet the needs of our customers? The organizational objectives and marketing goals stem from the vision and mission of the sports organization. The objectives of the organization are long term and sometimes unquantifiable. Alternatively, marketing goals are short term, measurable, and time specific. It is extremely important to remember that the marketing goals are directly linked to decisions made in the strategic sports marketing process. Another internal contingency that influences the strategic sports marketing process is organizational strategy. The organizational strategy is how the sports organization plans on carrying out its vision, mission, objectives, and goals. There are four different levels of strategy development within the organization: corporate-level strategies, business-level strategies, functional-level strategies, and operational-level strategies. Marketing is described as a functional-level strategy. The operational-level strategies such as pricing and promotion must fit the broader strategic sports marketing process. A final internal contingency is the organizational culture or the shared values and assumptions of organizational members that shape an identity and establish preferred behaviors in an organization.

The external contingencies that affect the strategic sports marketing process include competition; technology; cultural and social trends; physical environment; political, legal, and regulatory environment; demographic trends; and the economy. As with any industry, understanding competitive threats that exist is critical to the success of all sports organizations. Competition for sporting events and sports organizations comes in many forms. Typically, we think of competition as being any other sporting event. However, other forms of entertainment are also considered competitive threats for sports organizations. Technological forces represent another external contingency. Advances in technology are changing the way that consumers watch sports, play sports, and receive their sports information. Cultural and social trends must also be carefully monitored. Core values, such as individualism, youthfulness, and the need for belonging, can have an impact on the target markets chosen and how sports products are positioned to spectators and participants. The physical environment, such as the climate and weather conditions, is another external contingency that can have a tremendous influence on the success or failure of sporting events. Another of the uncontrollable factors is the political, legal, and regulatory environment. Proposed legislation, such as the banning of all tobacco advertising and sponsorship at sporting events, could have a tremendous impact on the motor sports industry. Demographic trends are another critical external contingency that must be monitored by sports marketers. For instance, the graying of America will bring about changes in the levels of participation in sports and the types of sports in which the "mature market" will participate. Finally, economic conditions should be considered by sports marketers. Sports marketers must monitor the macroeconomic elements, such as the national economy, as well as microeconomic issues, such as the discretionary income of consumers in the target market.

Because the marketing environment is so complex and dynamic, sports marketers use a method for monitoring external contingencies called environmental scanning. Environmental scanning is the sports organization's attempt to acquire information continually on events occurring outside the organization and to identify and interpret potential trends. Sports marketers must continually monitor the environment to look for opportunities and threats that may affect the organization.

External and internal contingencies are systematically considered prior to the development of the strategic marketing process. The process that many organizations use to analyze internal and external contingencies is called a SWOT analysis. SWOT is an acronym for strengths, weaknesses, opportunities, and threats. The strengths and weakness are internal, controllable factors within the organization that may influence the direction of the strategic sports marketing process. For example, human resources within the organization may represent strengths or weaknesses. However, the opportunities and threats are uncontrollable aspects of the marketing environment (e.g., competition and the economy). The purpose of conducting a SWOT analysis is to help sports marketers recognize how the strengths of their organization can be paired with opportunities that exist in the marketing environment. Conversely, the organization may conduct a SWOT analysis to identify weaknesses in relation to competitors.

Key terms

- competition
- contingency framework for strategic sports marketing

- control phase
- cultural values
- culture
- demographic environment
- direct competition
- economic activity
- environmental scanning
- external contingencies
- goal
- implementation phase
- indirect competition
- internal contingencies
- macroeconomic elements
- market selection decisions
- marketing environment
- marketing mix
- microeconomic elements
- objectives
- organizational culture
- organizational strategies
- physical environment
- planning phase
- political, legal, and regulatory environment
- strategic sports marketing process
- strategic windows
- technology
- vision

Review questions

1 Describe the contingency framework for strategic sports marketing. Why is the contingency approach especially useful to sports marketers?
2 Outline the strategic marketing process, and comment on how it is related to the external and internal contingencies.
3 Define *marketing environment*. Are all the elements of the marketing environment considered uncontrollable? Why or why not?
4 What is environmental scanning? Why is environmental scanning so important? Who conducts the environmental scan, and how is one conducted?
5 Define *competition*. What are the different types of competition?
6 How has technology influenced the sports marketing industry? Discuss how "out-of-market" technology benefits sports spectators.
7 Identify several cultural and social trends in our society, and describe their impact on sport and sports marketing.
8 What are the core American values, and why are they important to sports marketers?

9 How does the physical environment play a role in sports marketing? How can sports marketers manipulate or change the physical environment?

10 Define the political and regulatory environment. Cite several examples of how this can influence or dictate sports marketing practices.

11 Describe the different demographic trends of interest to sports marketers. How will these demographic trends influence the strategic marketing process?

12 Differentiate between macro- and microeconomic elements. Which (macro or micro elements) do you feel plays an important role in sports marketing? Why?

13 How can sports marketers assess the external environment? What are some sources of secondary data that may assist in understanding the current and future external environment?

Exercises

1 Interview the marketing manager of a local college or professional sports organization and develop a list of the uncontrollable factors that were unexpected throughout the last season.

2 Interview the marketing manager of a sporting goods retailer or sports organization about the company's strategic sports marketing process. Ask how the external and internal contingencies affect planning.

3 Find two sports organizations that, in your opinion, have effective mission and vision statements. How do they promote these statements and how are they reflected in the organization?

4 Describe all the ways the changing marketing environment will have an impact on NASCAR racing. How should NASCAR prepare for the future?

5 Your university's athletic program has a number of competitors. List all potential competitors and categorize what type of competition each represents.

6 Find examples of how technology has influenced the sporting goods industry, a professional sports franchise, and the way spectators watch a sporting event. For each example indicate the technology that was used prior to the new technology.

7 Develop advertisements for athletic shoes that reflect each of the core American values discussed in this chapter.

8 Interview five international students and discuss the core values used by sports marketers in their culture. Do these values differ from the core American values? For example, do the British value individualism more or less than Americans? What evidence do the students have to support their claims?

9 How does the physical environment of your geographic area or location play a role in sports marketing?

10 Describe how changing demographic trends have led to the development of new sports leagues, the shifting of professional sports franchises, and new sports products. Provide three specific examples of each.

Internet exercises

1 Experience a portion of any sporting event via web broadcast. What did you enjoy the most about this experience, and what could be done to improve this technology?

2 Find three sports products on the Internet that stress technological innovation. Do the companies communicate their technological advantages differently?

3 Search the Internet for articles or sites that discuss the pros and cons of the banning of tobacco advertisements at sporting events.

4 Go to the Internet and find census data to support what sports fans in 2030 might look like from a demographic perspective.

Notes

1 Rick Burton and Dennis Howard, "Recovery Strategies for Sports Marketers: The Marketing of Sports Involves Unscripted Moments Delivered by Unpredictable Individuals and Uncontrollable Events," *Marketing Management*, vol. 9, no. 1 (Spring 2000), 43.

2 W. Richard Scott, *Organizations: Rational, Natural, and Open Systems* (Upper Saddle River, NJ: Prentice Hall, 1987), 87–89.

3 Bernard J. Mullin, Stephan Hardy, and William Sutton, *Sport Marketing* (Champaign, IL: Human Kinetics Publishers, 1993), 16.

4 Under Armour, "Under Armour Mission." Available from: https://www.uabiz.com/company/mission.cfm, accessed July 6, 2010.

5 Kent State University, "Kent State Intercollegiate Athletics Mission Statement and Objectives." Available from: https://www.kentstatesports.com/athleticDepartment/missionStatement, accessed 2012.

6 D. Tighe, "Statista, Revenue Share of Nike Worldwide in 2021 by Product Category" (August 3, 2021). Available from: https://www.statista.com/statistics/412760/nike-global-revenue-share-by-product/.

7 Nike Mission Statement. Available from: https://about.nike.com/

8 "FIFA Statutes" (June 2019 edition). Available from: https://digitalhub.fifa.com/m/784c701b2b848d2b/original/ggyamhxxv8jrdfbekrrm-pdf.pdf.

9 "Strategic Planning Facilitator Guide Government of Newfoundland and Labrador, Department of Innovation," *ManagemenHelp.org* (2020). Carter McNamara, "How to Do to Planning." Available from: https://managementhelp.org/planning/index.htm#anchor1384873.

10 Maloof Family Information. Available from: https://www.arcoarena.com/default. asp?lnopt=4&pnopt=0.

11 Scott Rosner, "Team Ownership Could Fade with Comcast – NBC Universal Deal," *Sports Business Journal* (March 2010).

12 Sport Singapore, "Sport as Strategy, Opportunity for All" (February 13, 2012). Available from: https://www.sportsingapore.gov.sg/newsroom/media-releases/2012/2/sport-as-strategy-opportunities-for-all.

13 "Food for Thought: Dodgers Offer All-You-Can-Eat Seats," *The Associated Press State & Local Wire* (January 12, 2007).

14 Sam Mamudi, "Study Shows Sports TV Success," *SportsWatch* (January 24, 2012).

15 Andy Staples, "Why WWE's Network Deal Could Signal a Way Forward for College Football," *Sports Illustrated* (May 24, 2018).

16 Michael Long, "Live and Direct: A Look across the OTT Landscape," *Sports Pro* (October 18, 2017). Available from: https://www.sportsmedia.com/from-the-magazine/live-and-direct-a-look-across-the-ott-lanscape.

17 M.D. Shank and K. Verderber, "Understanding the Nature of Sports Competition," *International Conference on Sport & Society*, Marquette, MI (June 1999).

18 Michael Long, "Live and Direct: A Look across the OTT Landscape," *Sports Pro* (October 18, 2017). Available from: https://www.sportsmedia.com/from-the-magazine/live-and-direct-a-look-across-the-ott-lanscape.

19 NASCAR.com, "NASCAR Digital Media Records Historic Day." Available from: https://www.nascar.com/en_us/news-media/articles/2014/2/24/nascar-digital-media-records-historic-day.html, released February 24, 2014, accessed February 28, 2014.

20 ESPN, 2018. Available from: https://espnmediazone.com.

21 Major League Baseball. Available from: https://www.mlb.com/apps/mlb-app.

22 Ken Kerschbaumer, "Cornhusker Fans Surf for Tackles," *Broadcasting and Cable* (August 28, 2000).

23 Rich Heldenfels, "Watching TV is Different Experience Today," *Akron Beacon Journal* (February 2012).

24 Stubhub, "Partners." Available from: https://www.stubhub.com/about-us.

25 Eric Fisher, "Numbers Game," *Sports Business Journal* (September 27, 2010).

26 "Synergy Sports." Available from: https://synergysports.com/.

27 "Golf Company Featured on the Golf Channel," *Market Wire* (November 21, 2006), E21.

28 "Textronics Expands into UK with NuMetrex Clothes that Monitor the Body," *Business Wire* (September 12, 2006).

29 FastCompany, "The 10 Most Innovative Companies in Sports" (March 9, 2021). Available from: https://www.fastcompany.com/90600328/sports-most-innovative-companies-2021.

30 Tom Wasserman, "Why Sports Apparel Brands are Becoming Tech Companies," *Forbes* (January 3, 2017). Available from: https://www.forbes.ocm/sites/rackspace/2017/01/03/why-sports-apparel-brands-are-becoming-rech-companies/#14a93bde63e2.

31 Blog Maverick, "The Mark Cuban WebLog." Available from: http://blog-maverick.com/, accessed February 25, 2014.

32 Dan Helfrich, Personal interview with CEO and Chair, Deloitte Consulting.

33 Donny Dicaprio, "Exploring the Innovative Tech Plans for the Falcons' New Stadium," *Sports Illustrated* (August 17, 2016). Available from: https://www.si.com/tech-media/2016/08/17/atlanta-falcons-mercedes-benz-stadium-technology.

34 "Cisco Connected Stadium Solution." Available from: https://www.cisco.com/c/dam/en_us/solutions/industries/docs/sports/Connected_Stadium_Datasheet.pdf.

35 Jeremy Repanich, "Top 5 Technologies in NFL Stadiums," *Popular Mechanics* (2011).

36 "Twelve Baseball Parks to Use MasterCard PayPass Technology this Season" (September 27, 2006). Available from: http://www.finextra.com/fullpr.asp?id=11531.

37 "Essential Facts about the Computer and Video Game Industry," *Entertainment Software Association* (2006). Available from: https://www.theesa.com/archives/files/Essential%20Facts%202006.pdf.

38   Alex Gray, "The Explosive Growth of Esport, World Economic Forum" (July 3, 2018). Available from: https://www.weforum.org/agenda/2018/07/the-explosive-growth-of-esports/.

39   SFIA 2020 Sports, "Fitness, and Leisure Activities Topline Participation Report."

40   Sport and Fitness Industry Association, *SFIA US Trends in Team Sports Report*, Silver Spring, MD (2013).

41   SFIA 2020 Sports, "Fitness, and Leisure Activities Topline Participation Report."

42   Ibid.

43   Eric Berger, "The Houston Texans Think Their Fans Are Weather Wimps. Are You? Chron" (August 11, 2013). Available from: https://blog.chron.com/weather/2013/08/the-houston-texans-think-their-fans-are-weather-wimps-are-you/.

44   Scott Wong, "New-Age Stadium is on a High-Tech Roll," *The Arizona Republic* (August 10, 2006).

45   National Association of Sports Commissions, "NASC Playbook" (December 2013). Available from: http://issuu.com/nasc92/docs/playbook_dec13_final_hires, accessed June 17, 2014.

46   "NBA Fines and Suspensions, Spotrac." Available from: https://www.spotrac.com/nba/fines-suspensions/2020/.

47   David Dusek, "Busted: Nearly 10,000 Counterfeit Golf Clubs Seized in China" (August 16, 2021). Available from: https://golfweek.usatoday.com/2021/08/16/busted-nearly-10000-counterfeit-golf-clubs-seized-china/.

48   "Olympic Committee Sues Tabloid Owner" (September 12, 2000). *Denver Business Journal*. Available from: https://www.bizjournals.

49   FIFA, "For the Good of the Game" (1996). Available from: https://www.fifa.com/aboutfifa/federation/mission.html.

50   U.S. Census Bureau, "U.S. and World Population Clock." Available from: https://www.census.gov/popclock/.

51   Sandra Colby and Jennifer Ortman, "The Baby Boom Cohort in the United States: 2012 to 2060" (May, 2012). Available from: https://www.census.gov/prod/2014pubs/p25-1141.pdf.

52   US Census 2020, "65 and Older Population Grows Rapidly as Baby Boomers Age" (June 25, 2021). Available from: https://www.census.gov/newsroom/press-releases/2020/65-older-population-grows.html.

53   U.S. Census Bureau, "State and Country Quick Facts" (2013). Available from: http://quickfacts.census.gov/qfd/states/00000.html, accessed June 17, 2014.

54   "Minorities Getting Closer to the Majority," *CNN* (May 11, 2006). Available from: https://www.cnn.com/2006/US/05/10/hispanics/index.html.

55   Parker Morse, "Six Facts about the Hispanic Market that May Surprise You," *Forbes* (January 9, 2018). Available from: https://www.forbes.com/sites/forbesagencycouncil/2018/01/09/six-facts-about-the-hispanic-market-that-may-surprise-you/#6686e01c5f30.

56   BBC News, "U.S. Census: Five Key Takeaways on Population Trends" (April 26, 2021). Available from: https://www.bbc.com/news/world-us-canada-56896154.

57   Harry Stevens and Nick Kirkpatrick, "How America's 'Places to Be' Have Shifted Over the Past 100 Years," *The Washington Post* (May 12, 2021). Available from: https://www.washingtonpost.com/nation/interactive/2021/census-population-changes/.

58   Yan Wu and Luis Melgar, "Americans Up and Moved During the Pandemic. Here's Where They Went," *Wall Street Journal* (May 11, 2021). Available from:

https://www.wsj.com/articles/americans-up-and-moved-during-the-pandemic-heres-where-they-went-11620734566.

59 Steve Wilstein, "Think the NBA Can't Go Belly Up? Think Again," *Associated Press* (September 26, 2003). Available from: http://news.mysanantonio.com.

60 Paul A. Samuelson, *Economics*, 10th ed. (New York: McGraw Hill, 1976).

61 Lynn Franco, *The Marketers Guide to Discretionary Income* (New York: The Conference Board Inc., November, 2007).

62 Brian Reich, "Baseball and the American City" (April 30, 2001). Available from: https://www.stadiummouse.com/stadium/economic.html.

63 Matthew D. Shank and Robert A. Snyder, "Temporary Solutions: Uncovering New Market Opportunities in the Temporary Employment Industry," *Journal of Professional Services Marketing,* vol. 12, no. 1 (1995), 5–17.

PART II
Planning for market selection decisions

Research tools for understanding sports consumers

After completing this chapter, you should be able to:

- Discuss the importance of marketing research to sports marketers.
- Explain the fundamental process for conducting sports marketing research.
- Identify the various research design types.
- Describe the process for questionnaire development.
- Understand how to prepare an effective research report.

As the following study on the Railcats illustrates marketing research is a fundamental tool for understanding and ultimately satisfying customers' needs. As described in Chapter 1, one way of demonstrating a marketing orientation is to gather information used for decision making. Another way of establishing a marketing orientation is to disseminate information and share the marketing information with those responsible for making decisions. Marketing research is viewed as an essential element in marketing-oriented organizations.

The information gathered through marketing research can be as basic as where consumers live, how much money they make, and how old they are. Research also provides information for decision makers in identifying marketing opportunities and threats, segmenting markets, choosing and understanding the characteristics of target markets, evaluating the current market positioning, and making marketing mix decisions.

More specifically, marketing research may provide answers to questions such as the following:

- What new products or services would be of interest to consumers of sport?
- What do present and potential consumers think about our new advertising campaign?
- How does the advertising and promotion mix affect purchase decisions?
- What are the latest changes or trends in the sport marketplace?

DOI: 10.4324/9780429030673-5

- How are consumers receiving sports information and programming?
- What are sports fans spending, and what are they buying?
- Who are the biggest sponsors of professional sports leagues or college sports?
- How interested are fans in my team, my players, and in the sport itself?
- How do consumers perceive my team, league, or event relative to competitors?
- What is the best way to promote my sports product or service?
- Who participates in sports, and in what sports are they participating? Also, where are they participating, and how often?
- Are current consumers satisfied with my sports products and services? What are the major determinants of customer satisfaction?
- What price are consumers willing to pay for my sports product or service?
- What image does the team, player, or event hold with current consumers and potential consumers?

MARKETING RESEARCH IN ACTION: THE GARY SOUTHSHORE RAILCATS

Since their inception, the Gary Southshore RailCats have utilized market research to enhance the strategic planning and business success of the organization. The Southshore RailCats, currently a member of the modern American Association of Independent Professional Baseball, conducted a detailed study prior to their first official game to gather information that would guide the planning phase of their strategic marketing process. At the time under the ownership of Victory Sports Group LLC, Southshore RailCats CEO Mike Tatoian and former General Manager Roger Wexelberg were able to successfully combine the power of sports and grassroots marketing to provide an exciting and memorable experience while adding to the quality of life in Northwest Indiana. The RailCats' mission is to provide Northwest Indiana with an exceptional level of fun, affordable family entertainment in a safe and enjoyable atmosphere. To ensure that fans received this opportunity, the organization sought to identify and determine if marketing services and investment opportunities were of an investment scale to which a capable private operator under a contractual agreement could achieve economic success. The goal of the RailCats organization was to offer marketing/sponsorship of such services and facilities at a reasonable cost to the consumer public, therefore validating rights fee expenditures. A self-administered survey of area consumers ($N = 1,034$) served as the primary data collection instrument to examine the identified research objectives. The survey was segmented into seven categories: interest levels, awareness, attendance/purchase characteristics, media/entertainment choices, level of importance, fan characteristics, and demographics. The intention of the research was to assist the Southshore RailCats to make informed decisions consistent with common organizational goals. In addition, the study was designed to look at how survey responses differed according to fan demographics. For instance, were males more likely than females to attend a RailCats game in the future?

Some of the contents of the survey included information specific to:

- I am planning to attend a RailCats game this coming season.
- I am more likely to a attend a game on a weekend than weekday.
- I prefer to attend games that have promotional giveaways.
- The quality of play will influence my attendance to a RailCats game.
- The RailCats organization is actively involved in the community.
- Which of the following best describes with whom you may attend a RailCats game?
- If available, would you purchase a mini season ticket plan for the upcoming season?
- Please identify the number of games you would prefer to purchase.
- Please rank from most likely to least likely the following items that may influence your attendance at a RailCats game (day of game, fireworks, opponent, premium giveaways, theme nights).
- Please rank preference of media sources for information of local sports teams.
- What is your zip code?
- What is your gender?
- What year were you born?

Source: Center for Sport Recreation and Tourism Development, KSU/Gary Southshore RailCats Feasibility Study

These are just a few of the questions that may be addressed through marketing research. As the following article illustrates, making false assumptions in today's world can have dire consequences.

ARTICLE 3.1
WE ARE WRONG ABOUT MILLENNIALS; THEY ARE SPORTS FANS

Many sports executives fear that the root cause of declining TV viewership and aging audiences is the disengagement of millennials from live sports. But the belief that millennials are to blame is misplaced.

We aren't losing fans, we are fighting short attention spans.

From Nielsen data, in the 2016–2017 regular season, NFL ratings among millennials declined to 9 percent. However, the number of millennials watching the NFL actually increased from the prior season by 2 percent. The ratings decline was caused by an 8-percent drop in the number of games watched and a 6-percent decline in the minutes watched per game. The same was true for MLB, NBA, and NHL. With so many sports options across so many screens, fans of all ages are clicking away from low stakes or lopsided games.

Millennials versus Gen X: the wrong way to segment sports fans

As sports executives seek to build new direct-to-consumer channels, McKinsey's proprietary research suggests that age is an ineffective way to target digital sports fans.

Millennials are sports fans too. Although more Gen Xers follow sports closely than millennials (45 percent versus 38 percent), the gap disappears for NBA, UFC, MLS, EPL, and college sports.

Most millennials have cable. As of November 2016, 78 percent of millennials had cable, satellite, or telco TV service at home. That's pretty close to the 84 percent of Gen Xers with pay TV.

It's not about getting older; it's about having kids. It's true that on average, millennials watched 28 percent fewer hours per week of TV in 2016 than people their age did in 2010, whereas Gen X viewing slipped by only 8 percent over the same period.

However, when Nielsen segments millennials into those living with parents, those living on their own, and those starting their own families (at age 27, all three segments are about equal in size), big differences emerge. Millennials with kids watch 3 hours and 16 minutes of live TV a day, fully 55 percent more than millennials living on their own and just 14 percent less than Gen Xers under 49. Millennials living on their own spend 15 percent more time out of their homes and are 31 percent more likely to own a multimedia device than millennials with kids.

Millennials still watch live games. Millennial sports fans watch just 6 percent fewer live games per week than Gen X.

Everyone's digital. Virtually everyone in Gen X owns a smartphone, as do millennials. The two groups own multimedia devices (36 percent versus 40 percent) and use online subscription video on demand (68 percent versus 75 percent) at nearly the same rates. And they both spend over 5 hours a day on smartphones and PCs.

A difference of degree: streaming and social media

For all the similarities in technology adoption and viewing behaviors, millennials differ from their parents' generation in two ways that matter to sports rights holders.

Millennials stream sports more often. They stream almost twice as much as Gen X (56 percent versus 29 percent). They are also more likely to admit to using unauthorized sports streaming sites (20 percent versus 3 percent).

Millennials are social fans. While millennials and Gen X use sports sites and apps equally, significantly more millennials follow sports on social media. For example, 60 percent of millennial sports fans check scores and sports news on social media versus only 40 percent for Gen X. Twice as many millennials use Twitter, and five times as many use Snapchat or Instagram for that purpose. YouTube dominates sports highlights for millennials.

However, the gap is closing: Gen X is growing social media usage 38 percent faster than millennials.

Implications: targeting digital sports fans

Given the similar trends in sports viewing among millennials and Gen X, how should sports marketers target digital fans?

- Target mobile viewers of live streams. In predicting the number of live sports events watched per week, we found that generation (i.e., millennial versus Gen X) was not statistically significant. Those who watch live sports on mobile, however, watch 20 percent more live sports events than those who do not.
- Convert the pirates. Fans who admit to watching unauthorized streams watch 22 percent more games (across all platforms) than those who do not.
- Target moms. Male sports fans with children watch 14 percent fewer live games than those without, but women with children watch 24 percent more sports events than those with no kids.
- Promote tickets on social media. Teams know to target fans making more than $100,000 a year (51 percent of whom attend live games versus 40 percent of those earning less than $100,000), but they may not know that 56 percent of fans who follow athletes or teams on social media attend games (versus only 30 percent of fans who do not).
- Highlights are the gateway to subscription video. Fans who consume more than 30 minutes a day of sports highlights are three times as likely to subscribe to sports OTT services as fans who do not.

Implications: innovating the digital sports experience

The problem of declining attention spans will not be solved merely by replatforming TV video for PCs and mobile devices. As sports marketers develop new digital products – including services for livestreamed events, highlights, fan commentary, news, analysis, etc. – they should design for new, digital behaviors that cut across generations:

- Shorter viewing sessions (e.g., with whip-around viewing and quick navigation to other games).
- One-click tune-ins from social media or search, prompted by alerts on high-stakes game situations.
- Convenient access, for example, the ability to watch any game for my favorite team or player or fantasy player, regardless of the TV network on which they are broadcast.
- Rapid, simple sign-on and payment (ideally using fingerprints or other biometrics).
- Quick navigation between fantasy sports rosters and live streams, especially for avid DFS players (and sports bettors).

Gen X wanted its MTV. Millennials have fear of missing out. Both generations are consuming digital sports voraciously, at the expense of traditional TV viewing. Sports marketers who target the right digital behaviors, rather than traditional viewer segments, and develop digital products to take advantage of them will build stronger fan bases than ever before.

Source: Singer, Dan, 2017. https://www.sportsbusinessjournal.com/Journal/Issues/2017/09/18/Opinion/ Singer.aspx?hl=millennial+singer&sc=0

Marketing research, as defined by the American Marketing Association (2004/2014), is: the process or set of processes that links the consumers, customers, and end users to the market through information - information used to identify and define marketing opportunities and problems; generate, refine, and evaluate marketing actions; monitor marketing performance; and improve understanding of marketing as a process. Marketing research specifies the information required to address these issues, designs the method for collecting information, manages and implements the data collection process, analyzes the results, and communicates the findings and their implications. More specifically, **sports marketing research** is the systematic process of collecting, analyzing, and reporting information to enhance decision making throughout the strategic sports marketing process.

Three key issues emerge from this definition. First, marketing research must be systematic in its approach. Systematic research is both well organized and unbiased. The well-organized nature of good research depends on adherence to the marketing research process, which is discussed later in this chapter. Researchers must also be careful not to make up their minds about the results of a study prior to conducting it; therefore, researchers must conduct the study in an unbiased manner.

Second, the marketing research process involves much more than collecting data and then reporting them back to decision makers. The challenge of research lies in taking the data collected, analyzing them, and then making sense of the data. Marketing researchers who can collect data, dump them in the computer, and spit out reports are a dime a dozen. The most valuable marketing researcher is the person who has the ability to examine the data and then make recommendations about how the information should be used (or not used) in the strategic marketing process.

Third, the importance of marketing research is found in its ability to allow managers to make informed decisions. Without the information gathered in research, management decision making would be based on guessing and luck. As General Robert Neyland, University of Tennessee's legendary football coach, once said about the forward pass, "Three things can happen and two of them are bad!"[1]

Finally, the definition states that marketing research is useful throughout the entire strategic sports marketing process. Traditionally, the focus of marketing research has been on how the information can be used in better understanding consumers during the planning phase of the strategic sports marketing process. It is also important to realize that marketing research is relevant at the implementation and control phases of the strategic marketing process. For example, research is used in the control phase to determine whether marketing goals are being met.

The marketing research process

As previously mentioned, marketing research is conducted using a systematic process, or the series of interrelated steps shown in Figure 3.1. Before we discuss each step in the research process in greater detail, two points should be kept in

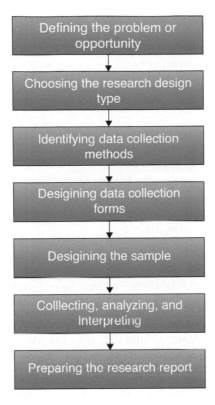

Figure 3.1
Marketing research process

mind. First, the basic framework or process for conducting marketing research does not change, although every marketing research problem will be different. For example, the Detroit Red Wings may engage in research to understand fan satisfaction or the effectiveness of a between-period promotion. Each of these research questions is different. However, the basic marketing research process used to address each question is the same.

Second, you should understand that the steps of the research process are interdependent. In other words, defining the problem in a certain way will affect the choice of research design. Likewise, selecting a certain type of research design will influence the selection of data collection tools. Let us now examine each of the steps in the research process.

Defining the problem or opportunity

The first and most important step of the marketing research process for sports marketers is to define the problem or opportunity. **Problem definition** requires the researcher to specify what information is needed to assist in either solving problems or identifying opportunities by developing a **research problem statement**. If the research addresses the correct problem or opportunity

Table 3.1 Issues addressed at initial research meeting
• A brief background or history of the organization or individual(s) requesting the research
• A brief background of the types of research the organization has done in the past, if any
• The information the organization wants and why (i.e., what they plan to do with the information once it is obtained)
• The targeted population of interest for this research
• The expectations in terms of the timeframe for the research and costs of conducting the study

and seeks to properly define the problem or opportunity, then the project could be successful. However, the data collected may be useless if they are not the information needed by the sports marketing manager.

How does the researcher identify problems or opportunities that confront the sports organization? Initially, information is gathered at a meeting between the researcher and his or her client. In this meeting, the researcher should attempt to collect as much information as possible to better understand the need for research. Table 3.1 shows a list of the typical questions or issues addressed at the first information-gathering meeting. Keep in mind that the ultimate goal of these meetings is to ensure that there is a clear understanding between the researcher and the decision makers as to the nature and role of the research and how it relates back to the need for information in the decision-making process.

Research objectives

Based on this initial meeting, the researcher should have collected the proper information to develop a set of research objectives: guidelines that establish an agenda of research activities necessary to implement the research process. **Research objectives** describe the various types of information needed to address the problem or opportunity. Each specific objective will provide direction or focus for the rest of the study.

Here is an example of the research objectives developed for the NASCAR Sponsorship Study conducted by Sponsorship Research and Strategy (SRS).[2] The purpose of the study was to provide information that would assist NASCAR sponsors in planning, evaluating, and justifying their NASCAR sponsorships. More specifically, the research objectives were as follows:

- Identify the benefits associated with NASCAR sponsorships.
- Record fan preferences for sales promotions.

- Identify lucrative market segments among NASCAR fans.
- Develop an extensive profile of NASCAR fans.
- Examine fan attitudes toward NASCAR and NASCAR sponsors.
- Analyze sponsorship effectiveness for different types of NASCAR sponsorships (e.g., car vs. league).
- Provide a comparative basis for sponsorship performance among NASCAR drivers.
- Provide a comparative basis for sponsorship performance among official NASCAR sponsors in selected product categories.

How would NASCAR or any sports entity go about measuring whether these objectives have been reached? The accompanying article describes this growing concern as it relates to sponsorship ROI. As the International Events Group (IEG) narrative illustrates, not defining evaluation tools in accordance with objective measures and/or failing to analyze research outcomes completely can be more dangerous than not measuring at all.

ARTICLE 3.2
CASE STUDY: A SPONSORSHIP MEASUREMENT SOLUTION

Complex challenges require new tools

Sponsorship impact is not one-dimensional. A partnership's ability to meet its goals depends on a series of interconnected variables.

Marketers long ago recognized that the sponsorship equation is not a simple one. They responded by reinventing the way they activate and execute partnership programs, developing big new ideas and using the latest technology to make sponsorships more relevant and engaging.

But when it comes to measurement, evaluation tools have not kept up with the pace of change. As the case study on the following pages shows, well-intentioned attempts that don't ask the right questions, or fail to analyze research outputs completely, can be more dangerous than not measuring at all, as they lead to false deductions and wrong decisions.

It also reveals that the solution does not need to be invented, merely applied.

First, brands must incorporate deep knowledge of how sponsorship works in shaping perceptions and driving changes in attitude and behavior into each step, ensuring the right partnership is targeted to the right group and activated in the right ways.

Second, marketing science – which already determines results for traditional media campaigns – must be applied to close the loop and determine ROI. The metrics, models and analyses used by brands to determine the effectiveness of their advertising can be adapted and scaled for partnerships of all types, including sports, entertainment, events and causes.

Figure 3.2

Making the right decisions

IEG Consulting engaged with a premium whiskey brand that was in the middle of a multi-year auto racing sponsorship to determine how the investment was performing against multiple objectives and whether it was delivering ROI. Chief among the brand's goals: acquiring one million new consumers.

In the process of gathering the necessary data to model the brand's return, the full picture of the program emerged, revealing that if true accountability and smart analytics had been incorporated from the start, the brand's objectives, execution and results would have been dramatically different.

Audience

The brand made its initial decision to sponsor motorsports based on research that showed a high percentage of whiskey drinkers among fans of the sport.

A deeper dive into the purchasing habits and lifestyles of racing fans revealed that they were much more likely to purchase non-premium brands and drank whiskey only on special occasions. In direct opposition to the sponsor brand's positioning, they were more likely to drink whiskey as a shot or mixed with soft drinks.

If the brand had the right data at the start, it could have targeted its racing efforts to build loyalty among the niche audience of its consumers. It could have transitioned its focus to suites and skyboxes at race tracks instead of trying to convert the fans in the grandstands.

Media value

Broadcast reports showed that the brand received significant exposure during telecasts of races. Translating impressions into advertising equivalencies showed a 2:1 return vs. the sponsorship fee.

However, analysis of survey research determined that little to no awareness was generated for the responsible drinking campaign that was a focal point of the brand's messaging through signage and on-car exposure and a key goal of the sponsorship. The broadcasting of an already well-known brand name was not a primary objective.

Survey research

Sixteen waves of pre- and post-race research were conducted in key markets. On the surface, a number of outputs indicated positive movement as a result of exposure to the sponsorship,

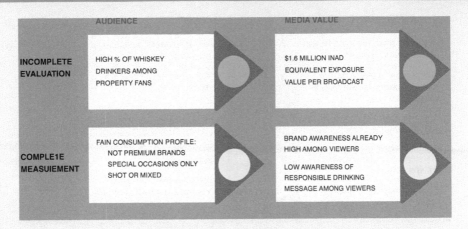

Figure 3.3

including higher awareness of retail and on-premise activity and increased likelihood of associating the brand with key image attributes and benefits.

Applying historical insights from sponsorship research that indicate a greater impact with current consumers vs. non-consumers, IEG's analysis determined that this pattern repeated itself here: There was virtually no increase in awareness of promotions or positive brand associations among consumers of competitive brands. Additionally, research into activity among two other whiskey brands that also were racing sponsors indicated better results for the competitors.

ROI

Finally, survey results showed an increase in intent to purchase the brand. Additionally, the brand's overall sales increased during the term of the sponsorship.

But when modeling was applied to the drivers of business, it was clearly determined that the sponsorship was not among them. These sophisticated analytics were able to show the client that it had acquired only 10,000 new customers – not one million – as a result of its racing program.

Linking sponsorship investments with business results

Marketing science applications such as the ROI modeling used in the spirits brand case study are typically thought of in the context of traditional media campaigns. But leading brands are putting these analytics to work for partnerships ranging from six-figure single-market deals to nine-figure global platforms.

More marketers will follow suit as the accountability bar continues to rise. Nearly two-thirds of CMOs say that ROI – the direct impact of expenditures on business results – will be a primary measure of marketing effectiveness.*

Sponsorship – because it delivers true engagement – is poised to claim a better seat at the marketing table, but only if it can demonstrate its contributions to the enterprise. But

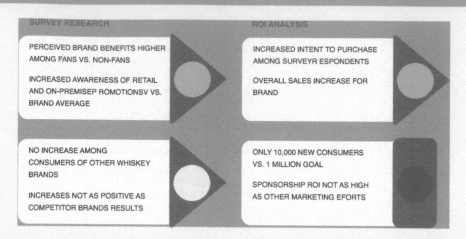

SURVEY RESEARCH	ROI ANALYSIS
PERCEIVED BRAND BENEFITS HIGHER AMONG FANS VS. NON-FANS	INCREASED INTENT TO PURCHASE AMONG SURVEYR ESPONDENTS
INCREASED AWARENESS OF RETAIL AND ON-PREMISEP ROMOTIONSV VS. BRAND AVERAGE	OVERALL SALES INCREASE FOR BRAND
NO INCREASE AMONG CONSUMERS OF OTHER WHISKEY BRANDS	ONLY 10,000 NEW CONSUMERS VS. 1 MILLION GOAL
INCREASES NOT AS POSITIVE AS COMPETITOR BRANDS RESULTS	SPONSORSHIP ROI NOT AS HIGH AS OTHER MARKETING EFORTS

Figure 3.4

measuring multifaceted engagement rather than one-dimensional reach and evaluating the complex ecosystem of sponsorship – with its ability to impact multiple audiences – requires at least the same level of data, rigor and analysis that is used to assess the other tools in the marketing arsenal.

This is not as daunting as it may sound. The techniques and analytic approaches of marketing science have become much more accessible and are flexible to the amount of data available. Much of the data needed to develop meaningful models and analyses is routinely captured by companies in the course of business.

Brands that have already taken this step know how their sponsorship investments are performing and how to make them work better.

In addition, their partnerships have gained a place in the strategic planning process, alongside other elements of the marketing mix rather than isolated and an afterthought. And, these brands are fostering better partnerships with rightsholders through a shared, fact-based understanding of the value exchange and what is needed for both to succeed.

Brands that don't take this step will see sponsorship budgets reduced in favor of marketing communications that can prove their value.

*IBM Global CMO Study, October, 2011

Source: From "A Sponsorship Measurement Solution," IEG October, 2011. Ukman, L. and Krasts, M.; www. sponsorship.com/ieg/files/07/07903e35–98d1–4f1c-b318–7524b3104222.pdf. Credit: IEG

Writing a marketing research proposal

To ensure agreement between the researcher and the client on the direction of the research, a research proposal is developed. A **research proposal** is a written blueprint that describes all the information necessary to conduct and control the study. The elements of the research proposal include background for

Table 3.2 Marketing research proposal outline

Background and History

Defining the Problem or Opportunity

Research Objectives

Research Methodology

   a. Sample

   b. Procedures

   c. Topical areas

Time Estimate

   a. Design of instrument

   b. Data collection

   c. Data entry

   d. Data analysis

   e. Final report preparation

Cost Estimate

the study and research objectives based on the need for the research, research methodology, timeframe, and cost estimates. An outline for developing a research proposal is shown in Table 3.2.

Choosing the research design type

Once the researcher is certain that the problem is correctly defined, the research design type is considered. The **research design** is the framework for a study that collects and analyzes data. Although every study is unique and requires a slightly different plan to reach the desired goals and objectives, three research design types have emerged: exploratory, descriptive, and causal designs. The type and nature of the design are highly dependent upon desired outcomes. Whatever research design or designs are ultimately chosen, it is important to remember the crucial principle in research is that the design of the research should stem from the problem.[3]

Exploratory designs

Exploratory designs are useful when research problems are not well defined. For instance, the general manager for the RailCats may say that ticket sales are down, but he is unsure why. In this case, an exploratory research design would be appropriate because there is no clear-cut direction for the research. The research is conducted to generate insight into the problem or to gain a better understanding of the problem at hand. For example, the researcher may recommend examining minor league baseball attendance trends or conducting one-on-one interviews with team management to determine their ideas about the lack of attendance. Because exploratory research design types address vague problems, a number of data collection techniques are possible. These data collection techniques will be addressed during the next phase of the research process.

Descriptive designs

If the research problem is more clearly defined, then a descriptive design is used. A descriptive design type describes the characteristics of a targeted group by answering questions such as who, what, where, when, and how often. The targeted group or population of interest to the decision maker might be current season ticket holders, people in the geographic region who have not attended any games, or a random group of people in the United States.

The RailCats study used a descriptive research design. The targeted group in this case was fans who may potentially attend RailCats home games. Characteristics of the group of interest in the study included where the fans were coming from (geographic area), how often they attended games, when they were most likely to attend games (weekends, weekdays, day, or evening), and demographics (age, race, and gender).

In addition to describing the characteristics of a targeted group, descriptive designs show the extent to which two variables differ or correlate. For example, a researcher may want to examine the relationship between game attendance and merchandising sales. Using the RailCats example, researchers wanted to understand the relationship between age of the fans and likelihood of attending games in the future. A descriptive research design type would allow us to examine the relationship or correlation between these two variables (age and future attendance).

If a positive relationship were found between age and likelihood of attending games in the future, then the older you get, the more likely you would be to attend future RailCats games. That is, as the age of the fan increases, the likelihood of going to future games also increases (see Figure 3.5a). However, a negative relationship means that as age increases, the likelihood of going to games decreases (see Figure 3.5b). Knowing the shape of this relationship will help the RailCats marketers make decisions on whom to target and how to develop the appropriate marketing mix for this group. What do you think the relationship between age and attendance would look like?

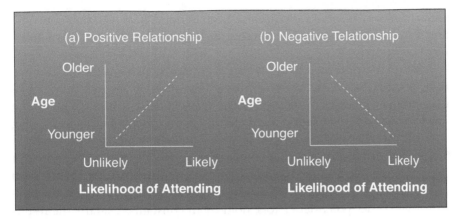

Figure 3.5
Descriptive research designs

Causal designs

Using a descriptive design, we can explore the relationship between two variables, such as age and likelihood of attending games in the future. However, what this does not tell us is that age causes the likelihood of attending to either increase or decrease. This can only be determined through a causal design.

Causal designs are useful when problems are very clearly defined. More specifically, causal designs examine whether changing the level of one variable causes the level of another variable to change. This is more commonly called a cause-and-effect relationship.

In an example of a causal design, the Southshore RailCats could conduct a study to determine whether varying the level of advertising on a local radio station has any effect on attendance. In this case, level of advertising is the independent variable and attendance is the dependent variable. The **dependent variable** is the variable to be explained, predicted, or measured (i.e., attendance). The **independent variable** is the variable that can be manipulated or altered in some way (i.e., level of advertising or perhaps whether to advertise at all).

To show cause-and-effect relationships, three criteria must be satisfied. The first criterion for causality is that the occurrence of the causal event must precede or be simultaneous to the effect it is producing. Using our example, advertising must precede or occur at the same time as the increase in attendance to demonstrate a cause-and-effect relationship.

The second criterion for causality involves the extent to which the cause and the effect vary together. This is called **concomitant variation**. If advertising expenditures are increased, then season ticket sales should also increase at the same rate. Likewise, when advertising spending is decreased, season ticket sales should also decline. Keep in mind, however, that concomitant variation does not prove a cause-and-effect relationship, but it is a necessary condition for it.

A third criterion used to show causal relationships requires the elimination of other causal factors. This means that another variable or variables may produce changes in the dependent variable. This possibility is called a spurious association or spurious correlation. In the dynamic sports marketing environment, it could be difficult to isolate and eliminate all possible causal factors. For instance, an increase in attendance may be due to the success of the team, ticket prices, and addition of other promotions (e.g., bobblehead night) rather than increased advertising. A researcher must attempt to eliminate these other potential factors, hold them constant, or adjust the results to remove the effects of any other factors.

Identifying data collection techniques

As with the previous steps in the research process, decisions regarding data collection techniques are very much a function of problem definition and research design type. If the research problem is loosely defined and requires an exploratory research design, then there are more alternatives for collecting that information. However, for well-specified problems using a causal design, the choice of data collection techniques decreases dramatically.

Data collection techniques can be broadly categorized as secondary or primary.

Secondary data refer to data that were collected earlier but are still related to the research question. These data may come from within the sports organization or from outside the organization. For example, useful internal secondary data might include a history of team merchandise sales figures, event attendance figures, or fan satisfaction studies that were conducted previously. External secondary data, or data from outside the organization, may come from any number of the sources presented later in this chapter.

Although a researcher should always try to use existing data before conducting his or her own inquiries, it is sometimes impossible to find data relevant to the problem at hand. In that case, research must turn to the other data collection alternative, primary data. **Primary data** are information gathered for the specific research question at hand.

Before turning our discussion to the various types of primary and secondary data, it is important to note that both types of data are useful in understanding consumers. For example, sports marketers from the Chicago Bears may want to look at trends in merchandising sales for each NFL team before undertaking a study to determine why their sales have decreased. In this case, secondary data are a useful supplement to the primary data they would also need to collect.

Secondary data

As just mentioned, secondary data may be found within the sports marketing organization (internal secondary data) or from outside sources (external secondary data). External secondary data can be further divided into the following categories:[4]

- Government reports and documents
- Standardized sports marketing information studies
- Trade and industry associations
- Books, journals, and periodicals

Government reports and documents

As we discussed in Chapter 2, environmental scanning is an essential task for monitoring external contingencies. Government reports and documents are excellent sources of data for sports marketers exploring the marketing environment. Government sources of data can provide demographic, economic, social, and political information at the national, state, and local levels. This information is generally abundant and can be obtained at no cost. There are thousands of government sources that are useful for environmental scanning. In fact, many are now published on the Internet. Let us look at a few of the most useful sources of government data.

Bureau of the Census of the U.S. Department of Commerce (www.census.gov)

The Bureau of the Census is one of the most comprehensive sources of secondary data that are readily available via the Internet. Here are some of the census documents that may be of interest: Census of Population, Census of Retail Trade, Census of Service Industries, and Census of Manufacturing Industries.

Chambers of Commerce

Usually, Chambers of Commerce have multiple sources of demographic information about a specific geographic area, including education, income, and businesses (size and sales volume). This type of information can be helpful to sports marketers conducting research on teams or events within a metropolitan area.

Small Business Administration (www.sba.gov)

Small Business Administration (SBA)-sponsored studies can be a valuable source for the environmental scan. The sources include statistics, maps, national market analyses, national directories, library references, and site selection.

Photo 3.1
The growing number of women's sport participants is being monitored through secondary marketing research

Source: Elissa Unger

Standardized sports marketing information studies

Although government sources of secondary data are plentiful, they are generally more useful for looking at national or global trends in the marketing environment. Standardized sports marketing information studies, such as the ESPN Sports Poll or Sports Marketing Analytics (www.sportsmarketanalytics.com), focus more specifically on sports consumers and markets. In fact, these sources of secondary data can provide extremely specialized information on consumers of a specific sport (e.g., golf) at a specific level of competition or interest (avid golfers). Table 3.3 shows the table of contents for a standardized study available for better understanding the golf market in North America.

These studies are called standardized because the procedures used to collect the information and the types of data collected are uniform. Once the

Table 3.3 North American Golf Report table of contents

Executive Summary

Golf Supply

2022 Golf Supply

- Golf supply by country
- Population per holes

Golf Development

- Development by country
- Golf course openings
- Recent golf course openings
- New openings by state

Golf Participation

- Participation by country
- Participation by state
- Number of golfers by state

Regional Breakdown of Supply, Growth, and Participation in Golf-Related Goods

- Imports and Exports by Country

Source:www.golf-research-group.com/reports/report/22/content.html

information is collected, it is then sold to organizations that may find the data useful. Although the data collected are more specific than other sources of secondary data, the data may still not directly address the research question. Table 3.4 shows a sampling of the standardized sources of secondary data that may be useful to sports marketers.

Trade and industry associations

There are hundreds of associations that can be helpful in the quest for information. Sports associations range from the very broad in focus (e.g., NCAA) to the more specific (e.g., National Skating Suppliers Association). For example, the Women's Sports Foundation (www.womenssportsfoundation.org), established in 1974 by Billie Jean King, works to improve public understanding of the benefits of sports and fitness for females of all ages. To support this educational objective, the foundation has a number of publications and research reports that serve as excellent sources of secondary data. In fact, the Women's Sports Foundation now has a cyberlibrary that contains years of information gathered on topics and issues such as business, coaching, ethics, gender equity,

Table 3.4 Standardized sports marketing information studies

Team Marketing Report

The Sports & Fitness Industry Association (SFIA), whose information was based on approximately 40,000 interviews encompassing youth and adult sports participation

The National Sporting Goods Association (NSGA), which publishes an annual report examining trends and patterns in 51 sports and activities

IEG's Sponsorship Report

PwC Sport Survey

Nielsen Sports Reports

Physical Activity Council's (PAC) Sports, Fitness and Leisure Activities Topline Participation Report

Kantar Media Reports

American Sports Data's American Sport Analysis Reports

National Golf Foundation's Golf Business Publications

Gallup Poll's Sports Participation Trends

MRI-Simmons Sports Fan Study

ESPN Harris, Sports & Sports Nation Poll

Snow Sports Industries America (SIA)

Bleacher Report

history, homophobia, leadership and employment, media, medical, participation, sexual harassment, special needs, and training and fitness. Here is just a small sampling of trade and sport associations:

American Marketing Association
European Association for Sport Management
Institute of Sport and Recreation Management
National Association Collegiate Directors of Athletics
National Association of Sports Commissions
National Collegiate Athletic Association
National Sporting Goods Association
North American Society for Sport Management
Sport Management Association of Australia and New Zealand
Sport Marketing Association
Sports & Fitness Industry Association (formerly SGMA)

Books and journals

A comprehensive list of journals related to sport follows the books listed here.

Books

Contemporary Sport Marketing (Zang & Pitts)

IEG's Complete Guide to Sponsorship

Introduction to Sport Marketing (Stewart & Smith)

Sport Marketing (Mullins, Hardy, & Sutton)

Sport Marketing: A Strategic Perspective (Shank & Lyberger)

Sport Marketing (Pitts and Stotlar)

Sport Marketing (Fullerton)

Sport Marketing: Canadian (O'Reilly)

Sport & Entertainment Marketing (Kaser)

Team Marketing Report's Newsletter

Cases in Sport Marketing (Donovan)

Cases in Sport Marketing (McDonald and Milne)

Case Studies in Sport Marketing (Pitts)

Developing Successful Sports Marketing Plans (Stotlar)

Sports Marketing: Global Marketing Perspectives (Schlossberg)

Sports Marketing: It's Not Just a Game Anymore (Schaaf)

Sports Marketing: Famous People Sell Famous Products (Pemberton)

Sports Marketing: The Money Side of Sports (Pemberton)

Sports Marketing/Team Concept (Leonardi)

The Elusive Fan: Reinventing Sports in a Crowded Marketplace (Rein, Kotler, and Shields)

Marketing of Sport (Chadwick and Beech)

Team Sports Marketing (Wakefield)

Keeping Score: An Inside Look at Sports Marketing (Carter)

Ultimate Guide to Sport Marketing (Graham, Neirotti, and Goldblatt)

Sports Marketing: Managing the Exchange Process (Milne and McDonald)

Academic journals of interest to sports marketers

European Sport Management Quarterly

International Journal of Sport Management, Recreation and Tourism

International Journal of Sports Marketing and Sponsorship

Journal of Advertising

Journal of Services Marketing

Journal of Sport & Tourism

Journal of Sport and Social Issues

Journal of Sport Behavior

Journal of Sport Management

Journal of Sport Tourism

Sports Business Journal

Sport Management Review

Sport Marketing Quarterly

The Journal of Intercollegiate Athletics

The Journal of Sport

Primary data

Data collected specifically to answer your research questions are called primary data. There are a wide variety of primary data collection techniques. Again, remember that your method of collecting primary data depends on your earlier choice of research design. Let us look briefly at some of the primary data collection methods and their pros and cons.

Depth interviews

Depth interviews are a popular data collection technique for exploratory research. Sometimes called "one-on-ones," depth interviews are usually conducted as highly unstructured conversations that last about an hour. *Unstructured* means that the researcher has a list of topics that need to be addressed during the interview, but the conversation can take its natural course. As the respondent begins to respond, new questions may then emerge that require further discussion.

The primary advantage of depth interviews is that they gather detailed information on the research question. Researchers may also prefer depth interviews to other primary methods when it is difficult to coordinate any interface with the target population. Just think of the difficulty in trying to organize research using professional athletes as the target population. For instance, a sports marketing researcher may want to determine what characteristics a successful athlete-endorser requires. To address this research question, depth interviews may be conducted with professional athletes who have been successful endorsers, athletes who have never endorsed a product, brand managers of products being

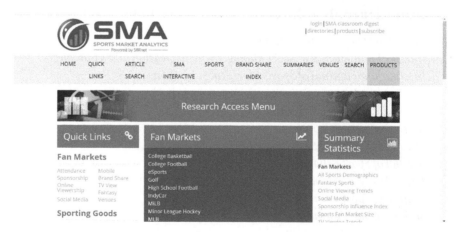

Web Capture 3.1
Sport Market Analytics is an excellent source of primary and secondary data

*Source:*www.sportsmarketanalytics.com

endorsed, or any other individuals who may provide insight into the research question. The responses given in these interviews then would be used to determine the characteristics of a successful endorser.

Depth interviews may also be appropriate when studying complex decision making. For example, researchers may want to find out how others influence your decision to attend a sporting event. The information gathered in the depth interviews at the initial phase of this research may then be used in the development of a survey or some other type of primary research. In yet another example, depth interviews were used in a study to understand the decision-making process used by corporate sponsors.[5]

Focus groups

Another popular exploratory research tool is the focus group. A **focus group** is a moderately structured discussion session held with 8 to 10 people. The discussion focuses on a series of predetermined topics and is led by an objective, unbiased moderator. Much like depth interviews, focus groups are a qualitative research tool used to gain a better understanding of the research problem at hand. For instance, focus groups may be useful in establishing a team name or logo design, deciding what food to offer for sale in the concession areas,

Photo 3.2a
Focus group room with adjoining observation room enhances implementation

Source: Kent State University

Photo 3.2b
Continued

determining how best to reposition an existing sporting goods retailer, or learning what kinds of things would attract children to a collegiate sporting event. Let us look a few examples of sports organizations that have used focus groups.

In 2018, Major League Soccer solicited FC Cincinnati season ticket holders to participate in focus groups to determine local soccer fans' perception of the sport, the club, and other local professional sports teams prior to MLS awarding the expansion team. The focus groups were part of MLS due diligence efforts to investigate market potential and support prior to awarding the expansion franchise. They sought to solicit opinions, ideas, and experiences to better serve fans in the future. A project to determine if public funding was supported by taxpayers for the new Minnesota Vikings stadium was commissioned by the Metropolitan Sports Facilities Commission, the agency that owned and operated the 28-year-old Metrodome. The commission utilized five focus groups conducted in various cities; each group had between 9 and 11 participants who were identified as potential November voters, not big sports fans, and not following the Vikings stadium debate. Results show that participants would approve a variety of funding mechanisms, including openness to a statewide sales tax.[6] Another example, as part of their off-season efforts to improve their team and their public image, the Mets have cut single-game ticket prices by an average of 14 percent, an attempt to increase revenues and coax spectators back to Citi Field. The team's season-ticket, ticket-plan, and group-ticket holders will receive an additional 10 percent discount. David Howard, the Mets' executive vice president of business operations, said after conducting in-season market research and holding focus groups with fans, the Mets decided to make these price adjustments. "Largely what we're doing here is a result from the feedback we've received from our customers," he said. "We feel we are the people's team."[7]

Conducting focus groups, like those in Cincinnati, Minnesota, and New York, requires careful planning. Table 3.5 provides questions and answers that must be considered when planning and implementing focus groups.

Table 3.5 Planning and implementing focus groups

Q. How many people should be in the focus group?

A. Traditionally, focus groups are composed of 8 to 10 people. However, there is a current trend toward having minigroups of 5 to 6 people. Minigroups are easier to recruit and allow for better and more interaction among focus group participants.

Q. How many people should I recruit if I want 8 people in my group?

A. The general rule of thumb is to recruit 25 percent more people than the number needed. For example, if you are planning on holding minigroups with 6 people, you should recruit 8. Unfortunately, some respondents will not show up for the group, even if there is an incentive for participation.

Q. What is a good incentive for participants?

A. Naturally, a good incentive depends largely on the type of individual you want to attract to your group. For example, if your group wants to target runners who might be participating in a local 10K race, $30 to $50 may be the norm, including dinner or light snacks. However, if your group requires lawyers to discuss the impact of Title IX on the NCAA, an incentive of $75 to $100 may be more appropriate. In addition to or instead of cash, noncash incentives could also serve. For example, free tickets or merchandise may work better than cash for some groups.

Q. Where should the focus group be conducted?

A. The best place to conduct focus groups is at a marketing research company that has up-to-date focus group facilities. The facility is usually equipped with a one-way mirror, videotape, microphones connected to an audio system, and an observation room for clients. In addition, more modern facilities have viewing rooms that allow the client to interact with the moderator via transmitter while the group is being conducted.

Q. How should I choose a moderator?

A. There is no rule of thumb, but research has identified a set of characteristics that seem to be consistent among good moderators. These characteristics

continued

Table 3.5 *continued*

include the following: quick learner, friendly leader, knowledgeable but not all-knowing, excellent memory, good listener, a facilitator – not a performer, flexible, empathic, a "big-picture" thinker, and a good writer. In addition, a good moderator should have a high degree of sports industry knowledge or product knowledge.

Q. How many groups should be conducted?

A. The number of groups interviewed depends on the number of different characteristics that are being examined in the research. For example, Notre Dame may want to determine whether regional preferences exist for different types of merchandise. If so, two groups may be conducted in the North, two groups in the South, and so on. Using the previous example, if lawyers were the participants in a focus group, two or three total groups may suffice. Any more than this and the information would become redundant and the groups would become inefficient.

Q. What about the composition of the group?

A. A general rule of thumb is that focus group participants should be homogenous. In other words, people within the group should be as similar as possible. We would not want satisfied, loyal fans in the same group as dissatisfied fans. Similarly, we would not want a group to be composed of both upper-level managers and the employees who report to them. In the latter case, lower-level employees may be reluctant to voice their true feelings.

Projective techniques

Another source of data collection is through the use of projective techniques. **Projective techniques** refer to any of a variety of methods that allow respondents to project their feelings, beliefs, or motivations onto a relatively neutral stimulus. Projective techniques were developed by psychologists to uncover motivations or to understand personality.[8] The most famous projective technique is the Rorschach test, which asks respondents to assign meaning to a neutral inkblot. Although the Rorschach may not have value for sports marketing researchers, other projective techniques are useful. For instance, sentence completion, word association, picture association, and cartoon tests could be employed as data collection techniques. Figure 3.6 demonstrates the use of sentence completion to gain insight into consumer attitudes toward Nike. The responses to these sentences could be analyzed to determine consumer perceptions of the target market for Nike (question 1), the brand image of Nike (question 2), and product usage (question 3).

Surveys

Data collection techniques are more narrowly defined for descriptive research design types. As stated earlier, a descriptive study describes who, where, how

---

Sentence Completion Test

1. People who wear Nike footwear are _____ .
2. When I think of Nike, I _____ .
3. I would be most likely to buy Nike shoes for _____ .

Figure 3.6
Sentence completion test

much, how often, and why people are engaging in certain consumption behaviors. To capture this information, the researcher would choose to conduct a survey. Surveys allow sports marketing researchers to collect primary data such as awareness, attitudes, behaviors, demographics, lifestyle, and other variables of interest. For example, the Cleveland Guardians handed out roughly 30,000 surveys over 14 games to understand fans' perceptions of the team's on-the-field winning prospects, the team's logo, the quality of the team's management and commitment to winning, and pricing issues.[9]

An additional illustration of survey research can be found in a study of global rugby fans. The survey claims to be the largest survey ever conducted to assess sport market trends, with over 88 distinct markets contacted. World Rugby survey results suggest enormous rises in the number of rugby followers and fans, with nearly 800 million followers globally. In fact, the research claims that one in every nine people on the planet considers themselves a rugby follower.[10]

Surveys that are considered "snapshots" and describe the characteristics of a sample at one point in time are called **cross-sectional studies**. For example, if a high school athletics program wanted to measure fan satisfaction with its half-time promotions at a basketball game, a cross-sectional design would be used. However, if a researcher wanted to investigate an issue and examine responses over a longer period of time, a **longitudinal study** would be used. In this case, fan satisfaction would be measured, improvements would be made to the half-time promotions based on survey responses, and then fan satisfaction would be measured again at a later time. Although longitudinal studies are generally considered more effective, they are not widely used due to time and cost constraints.

Experiments

For well-defined problems, causal research is appropriate. As stated earlier, cause-and-effect relationships are difficult to confirm. **Experimentation** is research in which one or more variables are manipulated while others are held constant; the results are then measured. The variables being manipulated are called independent variables, whereas those being measured are called dependent variables.

An experiment is designed to assess causality and can be conducted in either a laboratory or a field setting. A laboratory, or artificial, setting offers the researcher greater degrees of control in the study. For example, Major League Baseball may want to test the design of a new logo for licensing purposes. Targeted groups could be asked to evaluate the overall appeal of the logo while viewing it on a computer. The researchers could then easily manipulate the color and size of the logo (independent variables) while measuring the appeal to fans (dependent variable). All other variation in the design would be eliminated, which offers a high degree of control.

Unfortunately, a trade-off must be made between experimental control and the researchers' ability to apply the results to a "real purchase situation." In other words, what we find in the lab might not be what we find in the store. Field studies are conducted to maximize the generalizability of the findings to real shopping experiences. For example, MLB could test the different colors and sizes of logos by offering them in three different cities of similar demographic composition. Then, MLB could evaluate the consumer response to variations in the product by measuring sales. This common approach to experimentation used by sports marketers is called test marketing.

Test marketing is traditionally defined as introducing a new product or service in one or more limited geographic areas. Through test marketing, sports marketers can collect many valuable pieces of information related to sales, competitive reaction, and market share. Information regarding the characteristics of those purchasing the new products or services could also be obtained. For years, the IMG Academy has served as a test market for brands like Gatorade, Under Armour, Motus, and Airweave. It is a win–win deal. For the Academy, it affords the opportunity to provide attendees with equipment. For the brands, it serves as a test marketing hotbed, affording test marketing on athletes and the opportunity to expand business offerings. For example, Gatorade's focus is beyond sport drinks, and it conducts research on items such as nutrition bars and breakfast foods. The access helps to foster relationships and serves as an innovation pipeline. Another test market occurred in Columbus, Ohio, for the National Lacrosse League (NLL). Columbus, known as a good test market city because of its demographic composition, featured a star-studded demonstration match. If the game drew more than 5,000 spectators, the league was likely to consider Columbus as a strong possibility for a new franchise.[11] Columbus did not enter the league, but the NLL is now 12 teams strong (www.nll.com).

Although test marketer information is invaluable to a sports marketer wanting to roll out a new product, it is not without its disadvantages. One of the primary disadvantages of test marketing is cost and time. Products must be produced, promotions or ads developed, and distribution channels secured – all of which cost money. In addition, the results of the test market must be monitored and evaluated at an additional cost. Another problem related to test marketing is associated with competitive activity. Often, competitors will offer consumers unusually high discounts on their products or services to skew the results of a test market. In addition, competitors may be able to quickly produce a "me-too" imitation product or service by the time the test market is ready for a national rollout.

The problems of cost, time, and competitive reaction may be alleviated by means of a more nontraditional test market approach called a **simulated test market**. Typically, respondents in a simulated test market participate in a series of activities, such as (1) receiving exposure to a new product or service concept, (2) having the opportunity to purchase the product or service in a laboratory environment, (3) assessing attitudes toward the new product or service after trial, and (4) assessing repeat purchase behavior.

Analytics

Sophisticated data storage and data mining software programs, often labeled business intelligence, have been around for years. Traditionally, it was labeled decision support. Today, companies have made a tremendous investment to make sure that their information is consistent, accurate, and well-integrated. That information provides the basis of business analytics.

The term **analytics** first surfaced not in business magazines but in the sports pages. Many attribute the coming of this analytical craze to the likes of *Moneyball*. In 2003, author Michael Lewis published details of practices deployed by Oakland A's general manager Billy Beane. The best-selling author noted the team's use of statistical techniques to drive organizational decisions specific to on-field practices and player valuation. The impetus was a limited budget requiring the procurement of "good valuation bargains." Historically, sports like baseball and football have provided a laboratory for statistical analysis.[12] Historians suggest that the integration dates back to the 1940s, when Branch Rickey commissioned statistical analysis as the general manager of the Brooklyn Dodgers, but today it is commonplace to have an entire data analytics group employed by a team or even by individual athletes to maximize optimal decision making.[13]

Nonetheless, writers of newspapers and magazines began discovering the way baseball and football owners were using the vast mountains of data to select the best players and figure out how to use them. Today, franchises continue to explore a variety of analytical data techniques to drive organizational decision making. Companies use analytics to create a competitive advantage, and in many cases, create hope and businesses. According to Davenport and Herrin, the success is attracting a great deal of attention and inquiries, and often executives question how their companies can get in the game.[14]

Historically, analytics and business intelligence were used in a very narrow functional area, often limiting use and outcomes. Today, we're seeing a broad enterprise-wide, more strategic approach to using analytics for competitive differentiation. In order for it to really be valuable to the organization, users need to make an incremental investment in business intelligence and analytical capabilities.[15] It's a question of going that last mile and integrating and optimizing the information for decision making, not just for processing transactions.[16] Today teams from all leagues, such as the Oakland A's, New England Patriots, Orlando Magic, Tampa Bay Lightning, and FC Cincinnati, use techniques to enhance their decision making.

Davenport and Harris classify analytics into three distinct categories: descriptive, predictive, or prescriptive.[17] Descriptive analytics incorporates the procurement, organizing, and detailing of specific qualities of the data. While this analysis has merit, descriptive analytics provides no information about why something happened or what may occur in the future.[18] Predictive analytics, utilizing procured data sources, integrates data to assist with forecasting future trends. Predictive analytics are useful for predicting trends; however, as Mondello and Kamke note, one cannot assume any explicit cause/effect relationship. Prescriptive analytics do precisely what the term delineates: they incorporate methods such as optimization and experimental design to provide an additional layer of analysis, offering suggestions for implementing solutions to problems.[19]

Davenport and Kim identify three major stages of analytical thinking: framing the problem, solving the problem, and communicating and acting.

Stage One: Framing the Problem:	1	Problem recognition
	2	Review of previous findings
Stage Two: Solving the Problem	1	Modeling
	2	Data collection
	3	Data analysis
Stage Three: Results	1	Orientation of presentation
	2	Course of action[20]

Although each stage is deemed important, it is critical for the problem to be identified correctly. An incorrect definition of the problem significantly affects the entire framework and outcome analysis. Once the problem is framed, researchers should explore and identify variables, methods, and analysis techniques. Finally, communication of outcomes to the respective audience should be detail oriented, often including infographics, to enhance message delivery. As Modello and Kamke noted, leaders in sport business and sales are becoming increasingly savvy with analytics, and these data-driven techniques have become a competitive advantage in driving business strategies, further challenging the industry to invest resources or risk the possibility of falling behind the competition.[21]

Designing data collection instruments

Once the data collection method is chosen, the next step in the marketing research process is designing the data collection instrument. Data collection instruments are required for nearly all types of data collection methods. Guides

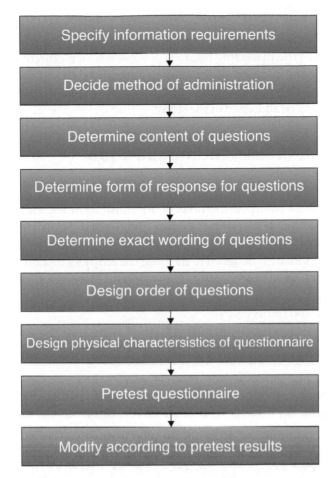

Figure 3.7
Designing a questionnaire

Source: Churchill. IM/TM – Basic Marketing Research, 3/E, 3E. © 1996 South-Western, a part of Cengage Learning, Inc.

are necessary for depth interviews and focus groups. Data collection forms are needed for projective techniques. Even experiments require data collection instruments.

One of the most widely used data collection instruments in sports marketing is the questionnaire or survey. All forms of survey research require the construction of a questionnaire. The process of designing a questionnaire is shown in Figure 3.7.

Specify information requirements

As the first step of **questionnaire design**, the information requirements must be specified. In other words, the researcher asks what information needs to be gathered via the questionnaire. This should be addressed in the initial step of the research process if the problem is carefully defined. Remember, in the first step of the marketing research process, research objectives are developed based on the specified information requirements. The research objectives are a useful starting point in questionnaire design because they indicate what broad topic will be addressed in the study.

Decide method of administration

The method of administration is the next consideration in questionnaire design. The most common methods of administration are via mail, phone, e-mail, web sites, or personal interview. Each method has its own unique advantages and disadvantages that must be considered (see Table 3.6). For example, if a short questionnaire is designed to measure fan attitudes toward the new promotion, then a phone survey may be appropriate. However, if the research is being conducted to determine preference for a new logo, then mail or personal interviews would be necessary.

Determine content of questions

The content of individual questions is largely governed by the method of administration. However, several other factors must be kept in mind. First,

Table 3.6 Comparison of methods of administration

Issues	Methods of administration			
	Mail	Telephone	Stadium and event interviews	Web-based
Costs	Inexpensive	Moderately expensive	Most expensive because of time	Inexpensive
Ability to use complex survey	Little, because self administered	Same	Greatest, because interviewer is present	Little, because self administered
Opportunity for interviewer bias	None	Same	Greatest, because interviewer is present	None
Response rate	Lowest	Low	High	Low
Speed of data collection	Slowest	High	Medium to high	High

What is your New Year's Resolution?

---

    a.   Lose Weight

    b.   Spend More Time with Family & Friends

    c.   Ouit Smoking

    d.   Get Out of Debt

    e.   Other

VOTE

Figure 3.8
New Year's resolution survey

does the question address at least one research objective? Second, are several questions necessary to answer an objective? Contrary to popular belief, more is not always better. Third, does the respondent have the information necessary to answer the question? For example, respondents may not be able to answer questions regarding personal seat licenses (PSLs) if they do not have a full understanding or description of what is meant by a PSL. Finally, will the respondent answer the question?

Sometimes respondents possess the necessary information, but they elect not to respond. For instance, questionnaires may sometimes ask sensitive questions (e.g., about income levels) that respondents will not answer.

Determine form of response

After deciding on the content of the questions, the form of response should be considered. The form of the response is dependent on the degree of structure in the question. Unstructured questionnaires use a high number of open-ended questions. These types of questions allow respondents to provide their own responses rather than having to choose from a set of response categories provided by the researcher. The following are examples of open-ended questions:

- How do you feel about personal seat licenses?
- How many years have you been a season ticket holder?
- How will the personal seat license affect your attitude toward the team?

Determine exact wording of questions

One of the most rigorous aspects of questionnaire design is deciding on the exact wording of questions. When constructing questions, the following pitfalls should be avoided:

- **_Questions should not be too lengthy_** - Lengthy, run-on questions are difficult to interpret and have a higher likelihood of being skipped by the respondent.
- **_Questions should not be ambiguous_** - Clarity is the key to good survey design. For instance, "Do you like sports?" may be interpreted in two very different ways. One respondent may answer based on participation, whereas another may answer from a spectator's viewpoint. In addition, there may be ambiguity in how the respondent defines sports. Some respondents would call billiards a sport, whereas others may define it as a game.
- **_Questions should not be double barreled or contain two questions in one_** - For example, "Do you enjoy collecting and selling baseball cards?" represents a double-barreled question. This should be divided into two separate questions: "Do you enjoy collecting baseball cards?" and "Do you enjoy selling baseball cards?"
- **_Questions should not lack specificity_** - In other words, clearly define the questions. "Do you watch sports on a regular basis?" is a poorly written question in that the respondent does not know the researcher's definition of _regular_. Does the researcher mean once per week or once per day?
- **_Questions should not be technical in nature_** - Avoid asking respondents a question that will be difficult for them to answer. For instance, "What type of swing weight do you prefer in your driver?" may be too technical for the average golfer to answer in a meaningful fashion.

Determine question sequence

Now that the question wording has been determined, the researcher must determine the proper sequence of the questions. First, a good questionnaire starts with broad, interesting questions that hook the respondents and capture their attention. Similarly, questions that are more narrow in focus, such as demographic information, should appear at the end of the questionnaire. Second, questions that focus on similar topical areas should be grouped together. For example, a fan satisfaction questionnaire may include sections on satisfaction with concessions, stadium personnel, or game promotions.

Finally, proper question sequencing must consider branching questions and skip patterns. Branching questions direct respondents to questions based on answers to previous questions. For example, the first question on a questionnaire may be, "Have you ever been to a RailCats game?" If the respondents answer "yes," they might continue with a series of questions concerning customer satisfaction. If the respondents answer "no," then they might be asked to skip forward to a series of questions regarding media preferences. Platforms such as SurveyMonkey and Qualtrics make the use of these techniques much easier; however, it is important to keep in mind that in some formats, branching questions and skip patterns are sometimes confusing to respondents.

Design physical characteristics of questionnaire

One of the final steps in the questionnaire development process is to carefully consider the physical appearance of the questionnaire. If the questionnaire is cluttered and looks unprofessional, respondents will be less likely to cooperate and complete the instrument. Other questionnaire design issues include the following:

- Questionnaire should look simple and easy to fill out.
- Questionnaire should have subheadings for the various sections.
- Questionnaire should provide simple and easy-to-understand instructions.
- Questionnaire should leave sufficient room to answer open-ended questions.

Pretest

After the questionnaire has been finalized and approved by the client, the next step in the questionnaire design process is to pretest the instrument. A **pretest** can be thought of as a "trial run" for the questionnaire to determine if there are any problems in interpreting the questions. In addition to detecting problems in interpreting questions, the pretest may uncover problems with the way the questions are sequenced.

An initial pretest should be conducted with both the researcher and respondent present. By conducting the pretest through a personal interview, the researcher can discuss any design flaws or points of confusion with the respondent. Next, the pretest should be conducted using the planned method of administration. In other words, if the survey is being conducted over the phone, the pretest should be conducted over the phone.

The number and nature of the respondents should also be considered when conducting a pretest. The sample for the pretest should mirror the target population for the study, although it may be useful to have other experienced researchers examine the questionnaire before full-scale data collection takes place. The number of people to pretest depends on time and cost considerations. Although pretests slow down the research process, they are invaluable in discovering problems that would otherwise make the data collected meaningless.

Designing the sample

After the data collection instrument has been designed, the research process turns to selecting an appropriate sample. A **sample** is a subset of the population of interest from which data are gathered that will estimate some characteristic of the population. Securing a quality sample for sports marketing research is critical. Researchers rarely have the time or money to communicate with everyone in the population of interest. As such, developing a sample that is representative of this larger group of consumers is required.

To design an effective and efficient sample, a variety of sampling techniques are available. Sampling techniques are commonly divided into two categories: **nonprobability sampling** and **probability sampling**. The primary characteristic of nonprobability sampling techniques is that the sample units are chosen subjectively by the researcher. As such, there is no way of ensuring whether the sample is representative of the population of interest. Probability sampling techniques are objective procedures in which sample units have a known and nonzero chance of being selected for the study. Generally, probability sampling techniques are considered stronger because the accuracy of the sample results can be estimated with respect to the population.

Nonprobability sampling

The three nonprobability sampling techniques commonly used are convenience, judgment, and quota sampling. **Convenience sampling techniques** are also called accidental sampling because the sample units are chosen based on the "convenience" of the researcher. For example, a research project could be conducted to assess fans' attitudes toward high school soccer in a large metropolitan area. Questionnaires could be handed out to fans attending Friday night games at three different high schools. These individuals are easy to reach but may not be representative of the population of interest (i.e., high school fans in the area).

Other researchers may approach the same problem with a different data collection method. For example, three focus groups might be conducted to gain a better understanding of the fans' attitudes toward high school soccer. Using this scenario, long-time, loyal soccer fans might be chosen as participants in the three focus groups. These participants represent a **judgment sample** because they are chosen subjectively and, based on the judgment of the researcher, they best serve the purpose of the study.

A quota sampling technique may also be used to address the research problem. In **quota sampling**, units are chosen on the basis of some control characteristic or characteristics of interest to the researcher. For instance, control characteristics such as gender and year in school may be appropriate for the soccer study. In this case, the researcher may believe there may be important distinctions between male and female fans and between freshmen and seniors. The sample would then be chosen to capture the desired number of consumers based on these characteristics. Often, the numbers are chosen so that the percentage of each sample subgroup (e.g., females and juniors) reflects the population percentages.

Probability sampling

As stated earlier, the stronger sampling techniques are known as probability sampling. In probability sampling, the sample is chosen from a list of elements called a sampling frame. For example, if students at a high school define the population of interest, the sampling frame might be the student directory. The sample would then be chosen objectively from this list of elements.

Although there are many types, a simple random sample is the most widely used probability sampling technique. Using this technique, every unit in the sampling frame has a known and equal chance of being chosen for the sample. For example, Harris Interactive (www.harrisinteractive.com/) e-mails a random and representative sample of the U.S. population drawn from a database of more than 6.5 million respondents who have agreed to cooperate. Respondents who agree to participate are directed to the appropriate URL for each survey. The Internet-based methodology allows Harris to randomly sample a minimum of 10,000 people each month on various topics of interest to decision makers in the sports and entertainment industry. A probability sampling technique, such as simple random sampling, allows the researcher to calculate the degree of sampling error, so the researcher knows how precisely the sample reflects the true population.

Sample size

Another question that must be addressed when choosing a sample is the number of units to include in it, or the sample size. Practically speaking, sample sizes are determined largely on the basis of time and money. The more precise and confident the researchers want to be in their findings, the greater the necessary sample size.

Another important determinant in sample size is the homogeneity of the population of interest. In other words, how different or similar are the respondents? To illustrate the effect of homogeneity on sample size, suppose the

RailCats are interested in determining the average income of their season ticket holders. If the population of interest includes all the season ticket holders and each person has an income of $50,000, then how many people would we need to have a representative sample? The answer, because of this totally homogeneous population, is one. Any one person that would be in our sample would give us the true income of RailCats' season ticket holders.

As you can see from this brief discussion, sample size determination is a complex process based on confidence, precision, and the nature of the population of interest, time, and money. Larger samples tend to be more accurate than smaller ones, but researchers must treat every research project as a unique case that has an optimal sample size based on the purpose of the study.

Data analysis

After the data are collected from the population of interest, data analysis takes place. Before any analytical work occurs, the data must be carefully scrutinized to ensure their quality. Researchers call this the editing process. During this process, the data are examined for impossible responses, missing responses, or any other abnormalities that would render the data useless.

Once the quality of the data is ensured, coding begins. Coding refers to assigning numerical values or codes to represent a specific response to a specific question. Consider the following question:

How likely are you to attend a RailCats' game in 2022?

1. Extremely unlikely
2. Unlikely
3. Neither unlikely nor likely
4. Likely
5. Extremely likely

The response of *extremely unlikely* is assigned a code of 1, *unlikely* a code of 2, and so on. Each question in the survey must be coded to facilitate data analysis.

After editing and coding are completed, you are ready to begin analyzing the data. Although there are many sophisticated statistical techniques (and software programs) to choose from to analyze the data, researchers usually like to start by "looking at the big picture." In other words, researchers want to describe and summarize the data before they begin to look for more complex relationships between questions.

Often, the first step in data analysis is to examine two of the most basic informational components of the data - central tendency and dispersion. Measures of central tendency (also known as the mean, median, and mode) tell us about the typical response, whereas measures of dispersion (range, variance, and standard deviation) refer to the similarity of responses to any given question.

To give us a good feel for the typical responses and variation in responses, frequency distributions are often constructed. A frequency distribution, such as the one shown in Table 3.7, provides the distribution of data pertaining to categories of a single variable. In other words, frequency distributions or one-way tables show us the number (or frequency) of cases from the entire sample that fall into each response category. Normally, these frequencies or counts are also converted into percentages.

After one-way tables or frequency distributions are constructed, the next step in data analysis involves examining relationships between two variables. A cross-tabulation allows us to look at the responses to one question in relation to the responses to another question. Two-way tables provide a preliminary look at the association between two questions. For example, the two-way table shown in Table 3.8 explores the relationship between the likelihood of going to RailCats' games and gender. Upon examination, the two-way table clearly shows that females are less likely to attend RailCats' games in the future than males. Implications of this finding may include the need to conduct future research to better understand why females are less likely to attend RailCats' games than males and the design of a marketing mix that appeals to females.

Preparing a final report

The last step in the marketing research process is preparing a final report. Typically, the report is intended for top management of the sports organization, who can either put the research findings into action or shelve the project. Unfortunately,

Table 3.7 Frequency distribution or one-way table		
How likely are you to attend a RailCats' game in 2022?		
	Respondents	
	Number	Percent
1. Extremely unlikely	88	9.1
2. Unlikely	60	6.2
3. Neither unlikely or likely	336	34.6
4. Likely	201	20.7
5. Extremely likely	169	17.4
NA	118	12.0
Total	972	100.00

Table 3.8 Two-way table of cross-tabulation

How likely are you to attend a RailCats' game in 2022?

	Gender	
	Male	Female
1. Extremely unlikely	35	53
2. Unlikely	28	32
3. Neither unlikely or likely	178	158
4. Likely	111	90
5. Extremely likely	101	68
NA	56	62
Total	509	463

the greatest research project in the world will be viewed as a failure if the results are not clearly communicated to the target audience.

How can you prepare a final report that will assist in making decisions throughout the strategic marketing process? Here are some simple guidelines for preparing an actionable report:

- **Know your audience** - Before preparing the oral or written report, determine your audience. Typically, the users of research will be upper management, who do not possess a great deal of statistical knowledge or marketing research expertise. Therefore, it is important to construct the report so it is easily understood by the audience who will use the report, not by other researchers. One of the greatest challenges in preparing a research report is presenting technical information in a way that is easily understood by all users.
- **Be thorough, not overwhelming** - By the time they are completed, some written research reports resemble volumes of the *Encyclopedia Britannica*. Likewise, oral presentations can drag on for so long that any meaningful information is lost. Researchers should be sensitive to the amount of information they convey in an oral research report. Oral presentations should show only the most critical findings, rather than every small detail. Generally, written reports should include a brief description of the background and objectives of the study, how the study was conducted (**methodology**), key findings, and marketing recommendations. Voluminous tables should be located in an appendix.
- **Carefully interpret the findings** - The results of the study and how it was conducted are important, but nothing is as critical as drawing conclusions from the data. Managers who use the research findings often

have limited time and no inclination to carefully analyze and interpret the findings. In addition, managers are not only interested in the findings alone; they also want to know what marketing actions can be taken based on the findings. Be sure you do not neglect the implications of the research when preparing both oral and written reports. The following articles represents the importance of using research to address and tackle important issues in sport.

ARTICLE 3.3
STRUCTURAL REPRESENTATION IN AMERICAN SPORT: FACTORS OF RACE AND SOCIOECONOMIC STATUS IN FOOTBALL

The purpose of this study was to find out whether or not black NFL players attend higher quality schools than black students in general regarding financial status, and the same for white NFL players. The other rather important purpose of this paper was to analyze whether or not there were any significant differences in socioeconomic backgrounds and race between the players and their owners, general managers, and coaches through the demographics of their respective high schools. In sum, the study sought to discuss opportunity within our economy. Specifically, it focused on how that opportunity relates to socioeconomic status, race, and football in our society.

The research questions were as follows: Do black NFL players attend schools with higher or lower socioeconomic statuses than other black students? Do white NFL players attend schools with higher or lower socioeconomic statuses than other white students? Lastly, were there any socioeconomic background/racial differences between the NFL players and the owners, general managers, and coaches?

In sociology of sport, questions about football productivity were not all that new. In 1969, John Rooney was searching for the 'football fever' and used the hometowns of players in the NCAA to find a marked variation in the capacity of regions to produce college football players. Yetman and Eitzen (1973) extended this research by examining player productivity in the United States and used demographic variables such socioeconomic status, occupational structure, degree of urbanization, and racial composition. Forty-five years ago, Yetman and Eitzen got identical results. More recent studies (Allison et al., 2017; White et al., 2017) showed that football players come from areas that are more black and more poor. The question becomes, who is benefiting from this consistency? There has only been a dearth of research that analyzed the long-term beneficiaries such as the owners, general managers, and coaches.

To interrogate this further, this study matched the perceived race with the individual players, of the 2016 NFL season, to find out if black NFL players attend higher quality schools than black students in general as well as completing the same procedure for white NFL players and every other race. In addition, this study also found data on the high school demographics of the NFL owners, general managers, and head coaches using variables of race and socioeconomic status such as: the racial composition of the school and the percent of poverty in the district. All data was collected from 2016 National Center for Education Statistics (NCES), 2016 Common Core of Data (CCD) for public schools, 2016 Private School Universe Survey (PSS) for private schools, and pro-football-reference.com.

An assessment of the 1893 NFL players' race and socioeconomic information revealed 67.7% of the NFL players were black. 26.3% of the players were white, 0.58% of them were Hispanic with the other races making up the rest of the population.

On average NFL players go to schools that have a higher percentage of black students than students in general (28.3% compared to 15.4%). NFL players also go to schools that have less white students than students in general (45.8% compared to 53.0%). NFL players go to schools that have a higher percentage of their school district in poverty than students in general (21% compared to 19.4%) but that is due to the fact that the racial composition of the NFL is mostly black. White NFL players go to schools much more financially advantaged than black NFL players and all students in general. Black NFL players go to high schools that are slightly more financially advantaged than black students in general. However, both NFL players and black students in general still go to high schools that are way more financially disadvantaged than white NFL players and white students in general.

Of the 98 owners, general managers, and head coaches, 85.7% of them were white (84 out of 98). There were 11 black administrators which made up 11.2% of the population and 1 Hispanic head coach which made up 1.0% (1 out of 98).

NFL owners on average went to high schools that were 60.5% white, 12.7% black, 11.6% Hispanic, and 23.5% of the school districts were identified to be in poverty. NFL general managers on average went to high schools that were made up of 63.4% white students, 16.0% black students, 11.6% Hispanic, and 19.2% of the school district was in poverty. NFL head coaches on average went to high schools that were 56.8% white, 14.0% black, 20.2% Hispanic, and 17.3% of the school district was in poverty.

NFL owners, general managers, and head coaches do go to schools that are more white and financially advantaged than the NFL players (19.3% compared to 21%). NFL owners, general managers, and head coaches also go to schools that are more white and financially advantaged than students in general.

In conclusion, although brain injury and paralysis are a risk when playing football, nearly 70% of the NFL is black when only 13.3% of the United States is reported to be black. The overrepresentation of poorer black people as NFL players and underrepresentation in decision-making positions suggests structural forces at play which encourage this development. It seems that from an early age these athletes have grown into this football identity that was maintained by American hegemonic ideology and systematic discrimination keeping them out of positions of power. In terms of social identity, it could be said that this lack of social representation of black youths in poverty making it in higher positions within the NFL works to constrain the future they believe is possible for themselves. As the study points out, race plays a role in determining the financial background of the players, students in general, and even the long-term beneficiaries.

Source: White, Kris 2020

References

Allison, R., Davis, A. & Barranco, R. (2016). A comparison of hometown socioeconomics and demographics for Black and White elite football players in the U.S. International Review for the Sociology of Sport, 15(1), 1–15.

Rooney, J. (1969). Up from the mines and out from the prairies: Some geographical implications of football in the United States. Geographical Review, 59(4), 471–492.

White, K., Wilson, K., Yim, B., Donnelly, M., Mulrooney, A., Lyberger, M., & Walton-Fisette, T. (2017, November). Blind side: High school economics and becoming an NFL player. Paper presented at North American Society for the Sociology of Sport, Windsor, Canada.

Yetman, N., & Eitzen, D. (1973). Some social and demographic correlates of football productivity. Geographical Review, 63(4), 553–557. doi:10.2307/213921 (2016).

Summary

Chapter 3 focuses on the tools used to gather information to make intelligent decisions throughout the strategic sports marketing process. More specifically, the chapter describes the marketing research process in detail. Marketing research is defined as the systematic process of collecting, analyzing, and reporting information to enhance decision making throughout the strategic sports marketing process.

The marketing research process consists of seven interrelated steps. These steps are defining the problem; choosing the research design type; identifying data collection methods; designing data collection forms; designing the sample; collecting, analyzing, and interpreting data; and preparing the research report. The first step is defining the problem and determining what information will be needed to make strategic marketing decisions. The tangible outcome of problem definition is to develop a set of research objectives that will serve as a guide for the rest of the research process.

The next step in the marketing research process is to determine the appropriate research design type(s). The research design is the plan that directs data collection and analysis. The three common research design types are exploratory, descriptive, and causal. The choice of one (or more) of these design types for any study is based on the clarity of the problem. Exploratory designs are more appropriate for ill-defined problems, whereas causal designs are employed for well-defined research problems.

After the research design type is chosen, the data collection method(s) is selected. Once again, decisions regarding data collection are contingent upon the choice of research design. Data collection consists of two types – secondary and primary. Secondary data refers to data that were collected earlier, either within or outside the sports organization, but still provide useful information to the researcher. Typically, sources of secondary data include government reports and documents; trade and industry associations; standardized sports marketing information studies; and books, journals, and periodicals. Primary data are information that is collected specifically for the research question at hand. Common types of primary data collection techniques include, but are not limited to, in-depth interviews, focus groups, surveys, and experiments.

The fourth step in the research process is to design the data collection instrument. Regardless of whether you are collecting data by in-depth interviews, focus groups, or surveys, data collection instruments are necessary. The most widely used data collection technique in sports marketing research is the questionnaire. As such, it is important that sports marketing researchers understand how to construct a questionnaire properly. The steps for questionnaire design include specifying information requirements, deciding the method of administration (i.e., mail, phone, and stadium interview), determining the content of questions, determining the form of response for questions, deciding on the exact wording of the questions, designing the order of the questions, designing the physical characteristics of the questionnaire, pretesting the questionnaire, and modifying it according to pretest results.

Once the data collection forms are constructed, the next step in the research process is choosing a sampling strategy. Rarely, if ever, can we take a census where we communicate with or observe everyone of interest to us in a research study. As such, a subset of those individuals is chosen to represent the larger group of interest. Sampling strategy identifies how we will choose these individuals and how many people we will choose to participate in our study.

Data analysis is the next step in the marketing research process. Before the data can be analyzed, however, they must be edited and coded. The editing process ensures the data being used for analysis are of high quality. In other words, it makes sure that there are no problems, such as large amounts of missing data or errors in data entry. Next, coding takes place. Coding refers to assigning numerical values to represent specific responses to specific questions. Once the data are edited and coded, data analysis is conducted. The method of data analysis depends on a variety of factors, such as how to address the research objectives. The last step in the marketing research process is to prepare a final report. Oral and written reports typically discuss the objectives of the study, how the study was conducted, and the findings and recommendation for decision makers.

Key terms

- concomitant variation
- convenience sampling techniques
- cross-sectional studies

- data collection techniques
- dependent variable
- experimentation
- focus group
- independent variable
- judgment sample
- longitudinal study
- marketing research
- methodology
- nonprobability sampling
- pretest
- primary data
- probability sampling
- problem definition
- projective techniques
- questionnaire design
- quota sampling
- research design
- research objectives
- research problem statement
- research proposal
- sample
- secondary data
- simulated test market
- sports marketing research
- test marketing

Review questions

1 Define sports marketing research. Describe the relationship between sports marketing research and the strategic marketing process.
2 What are the various steps in the marketing research process?
3 Define problem and opportunity definition and explain why this step of the research process is considered the most critical.
4 What are some of the basic issues that should be addressed at a research request meeting?
5 Outline the steps in developing a research proposal.
6 Define a research design. What are the three types of research designs that can be used in research? How does the choice of research design stem from the problem definition? Can a researcher choose multiple designs within a single study?
7 Describe some of the common data collection techniques used in sports marketing research. How does the choice of data collection technique stem from the research design type?

8   What are some of the central issues that must be considered when conducting focus groups?
9   What are the pros and cons of laboratory studies versus field studies?
10 Outline the nine steps in questionnaire design. What are some of the most common errors in the wording of questions?
11 Define nonprobability sampling and probability sampling techniques. What are three types of nonprobability sampling?
12 What is a sampling frame? How do researchers decide on the appropriate sample size for a study?
13 What are some of the guidelines for preparing oral and written research reports?

Exercises

You are interested in purchasing a new minor league baseball franchise. The franchise will be located in your area. To reduce the risk in your decision making, you have requested that a sports marketing firm submit a detailed research proposal. The following questions pertain to this issue:

1   What is the broad problem/opportunity facing you in this decision? Write the research objectives based on the problem formulation.
2   What type of research design type do you recommend?
3   The sports marketing firm has submitted the following preliminary questionnaire. Please provide a detailed critique of their work.

> Age: _____ Gender: _____
> Are you likely to go to a baseball game at the new stadium?
> Yes _____ No _____
> How many minor league games did you go to last year?
> 0-3 _____ 4-6 _____ 6-9 _____ 10+ _____
> What types of promos would you like to see?
> Beer Night_____ Straight-A Night_____ Polka Night_____

4   Now that you have looked at their survey, create a questionnaire of your own. Would any other data collection techniques be appropriate, given the research problem?
5   What sampling technique(s) do you recommend? How is the correct sample size determined, given your choice of sampling technique?

Internet exercises

1   Using secondary data sources on the Internet, find the following and indicate the appropriate URL (Internet address):

    a   Number of women who participated in high school basketball last year
    b   Attendance at NFL games last year
    c   Sponsors for the New York City Marathon
    d   Universities that offer graduate programs in sports marketing

2   Using the Internet, find at least five articles that relate to the marketing of NASCAR.

3   Using the Internet, locate three companies that conduct sports marketing research. What types of products and services do the companies offer?

Notes

1   https://www.espn.com/classic/s/beano_tenmia.html.

2   Beano Cook, "The Third Saturday in October" (October 17, 2001). Available from: https://www.espn.com/classic/s/beano_tenmia.html; NASCAR Sponsorship Study, "Sponsorship Research and Strategies." Available from: http://sponsorstrategy.com/_wsn/page9.html.

3   Gilbert Churchill, *Basic Marketing Research*, 3rd ed. (Ft. Worth, TX: Dryden Press, 1996).

4   Ibid.

5   Kristie McCook, Douglas Turco, and Roger Riley, "A Look at the Corporate Sponsorship Decision Making Process," *Cyber-Journal of Sport Marketing*, vol. 1, no. 2 (1997). Available from: http://fulltext.ausport.gov.au/fulltext/1997/cjsm/v1n2/mcook.htm.

6   Jay Weiner, "New Focus Group Report, Showing Surprising Openness to Sales Tax, Could Be Key to Vikings Stadium Effort" (May 4, 2010). Available from: www.minnpost.com/politics-policy/2010/05/new-focus-group-report-showing-surprising-openness-sales-tax-could-be-key-vi.

7   Mike Sielski, "After Losing Season, Mets Slash Ticket Prices" (November 4, 2010). Available from: http://online.wsj.com/news/articles/SB1000142405274 87035069045755 92780665674228.

8   Gilbert Churchill, *Basic Marketing Research*, 3rd ed. (Fort Worth, TX: Dryden Press, 1996).

9   "Cleveland Indians Look to Long-Term Viability through Market Research," *Akron Beacon Journal* (April 16, 1999).

10   Colin Brooke, "World Rugby Make Remarkable Claim about the Number of Global Rugby Fans" (August 6, 2019). Available from: www.rugbypass.com/news/world-rugby-make-remarkable-claim-number-global-rugby-fans/, accessed September 24, 2020; Craig Mertz, "Pro Lacrosse League to Test Local Support," *The Columbus Dispatch* (July 7, 2000), 5D.

11   "ESPN 3D to Show Soccer, Football, More." Available from: www.ESPN.com (January 5, 2010).

12   M. Modello and C. Kamke, "The Introduction and Application of Sports Analytics in Professional Sport Organizations: A Case Study of the Tampa Bay Lightning," *The Journal of Applied Sport Management*, vol. 6, no. 2 (2014).

13   P. Dizikes, "How Numbers Can Reveal Hidden Truths about Sports" (2013). Available from: https://news.mit.edu/2013/how-numbers-can-reveals-hidden-truths-about-sports-0301.

14   T. Davenport and J. Herrin, "Competing on Analytics. Interview Conducted by Paul Michelman," *Harvard Business Review* (March 15, 2007). Available from: https://hbr.org/ideacast/2007/03/harvard-business-ideacast-34-c.html.

15   Ibid.

16   Ibid.

17 T. Davenport and J. Harris, *Competing on Analytics* (Boston, MA: Harvard Business School Press, 2007).

18 M. Modello and C. Kamke, "The Introduction and Application of Sports Analytics in Professional Sport Organizations: A Case Study of the Tampa Bay Lightning," *The Journal of Applied Sport Management*, vol. 6, no. 2 (2014).

19 Ibid.

20 Ibid., and T. Davenport and J. Kim, *Keeping Up with the Quants* (Boston, MA: Harvard Business School Press, 2013).

21 T. Davenport and J. Kim, *Keeping Up with the Quants* (Boston, MA: Harvard Business School Press, 2013).

Understanding participants as consumers

After completing this chapter, you should be able to:

- Define participant consumption behavior.
- Explain the simplified model of participant consumption behavior.
- Describe the psychological factors that affect participant decision making.
- Identify the various external factors influencing participant decision making.
- Describe the participant decision-making process.
- Understand the different types of consumer decision making.
- Discuss the situational factors that influence participant decision making.

Think about the sports and recreational activities in which you participated during the past month. Maybe you played golf or tennis, lifted weights, or even went hiking. According to data from the Physical Activity Council Participation Report (see Figure 4.1), while age clearly affects how someone participates, what they do can also be age dependent.

At this point, you may be asking yourself, "Why are sports marketers concerned with consumers who participate in sports, their age, and their gender?" Recall from our discussion of sports marketing in Chapter 1 that one of the basic sports marketing activities was encouraging participation in sports. Sports marketers are responsible for organizing events such as the Boston Marathon, the Iron Man Triathlon, or the Gus Macker 3-on-3 Basketball Tournament in which thousands of consumers participate in sports. Moreover, sports marketers are involved in marketing the equipment and apparel necessary for participation in sports. As you might imagine, sports participants constitute a large and growing market both in the United States and internationally.

To successfully compete in the expanding sports participant market, sports organizations must develop a thorough understanding of participant

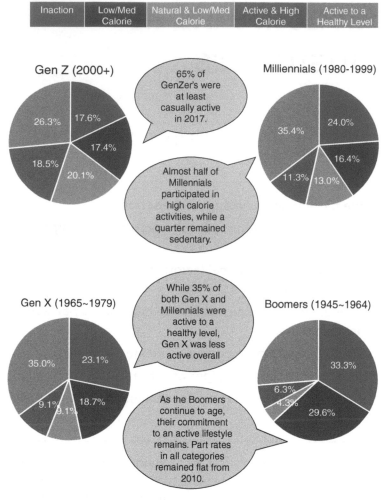

Figure 4.1

Participation rates segmented by generations, U.S. population, age 6+

Source: 2018 Physical Activity Council Participation Report

consumption behavior and what affects it. **Participant consumption behavior** is defined as actions performed when searching for, participating in, and evaluating the sports activities that consumers believe will satisfy their needs. You may have noticed this definition relates to the previous discussion of marketing concepts and consumer satisfaction. Sports marketers must understand why consumers choose to participate in certain sports and what the benefits of participation are for consumers. For instance, do we play indoor soccer for exercise, for social contact, to feel like part of a team, or to enhance our image? Also, the study of participant consumer behavior attempts to understand when,

Photo 4.1
Father and son fishing together: the benefits of sports participation

Source: Shutterstock.com, BlueOrange Studio

where, and how often consumers participate in sports. By understanding consumers of sports, marketers will be in a better position to satisfy their needs.

The definition of participant consumption behavior also incorporates the elements of the participant decision-making process. The **decision-making process** is the foundation of our model of participant consumption. It is a five-step process that consumers use when deciding to participate in a specific sport or activity. Before turning to our model of participant consumption behavior, it must be stressed that the primary reason for understanding the participant decision-making process is to guide the rest of the strategic sports marketing process. Without a better understanding of sports participants, marketers would simply be guessing about how to satisfy their needs.

Model of participant consumption behavior

To help organize all this complex information about sports participants, we have developed a model of participant consumption behavior that will serve as a framework for the rest of our discussion (see Figure 4.2). At the center of our model is the participant decision-making process, which is influenced by three components: (1) internal or psychological processes such as motivation, perception, learning and memory, and attitudes; (2) external or sociocultural factors, such as culture, reference groups, and family; and (3) situational factors that act on the participant decision-making process.

Participant decision-making process

Every time you lace up your running shoes, grab your tennis racquet, or dive into a pool, you have made a decision about participating in sports. Sometimes these decisions are nearly automatic because, for example, you might jog nearly every day. Other decisions, such as playing in a golf league, require more careful consideration because of the time and cost involved. The foundation of our **model of participant consumption behavior** is trying to understand how consumers arrive at their decisions.

Participant decision making is a complex cognitive process that brings together memory, thinking, information processing, and making evaluative judgments. The five steps that make up the process used to explain participant decision making are shown in Figure 4.2. It is important to remember that every individual consumer arrives at decisions in a slightly different manner because of his or her own psychological makeup and environment. However, the five-step participant decision-making process, moving from problem recognition through post-participation evaluation, is relatively consistent among consumers and must be understood by sports marketers to develop strategies that fit with consumers' needs.

As we progress through the participant decision-making process, let us consider the case of Jack, a 33-year-old male who just moved from Los Angeles to Cincinnati. Jack has always been active in sports and would like to participate in an organized sports league. Because of work and family commitments, Jack only has the time to participate in one league. He is unsure about what sport to

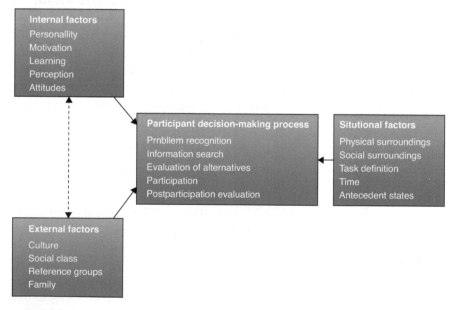

Figure 4.2
Model of participant consumption behavior

participate in, although he does have a few requirements. Because he is a new-comer to the city, Jack would like to participate in a team sport to meet new people. Also, he wants the league to be moderately competitive so as to keep his competitive juices flowing. Finally, he would like to remain injury free, so the sport needs to be non- or limited contact. Let us see how Jack arrives at this important decision by using the participant decision-making process.

Problem recognition

The first step in the participant decision-making process is problem recognition. During problem recognition, consumers realize they have a need that is not presently being met. **Problem recognition** is the result of a discrepancy between a desired state and an actual state large enough and important enough to activate the entire decision-making process.[1] Stated simply, the desired state reflects the "ideal" of the participant. In other words, what is the absolute best sport for Jack to participate in, given his unique needs? If there is a difference between ideal and actual levels of participation, then the decision-making process begins.

The desire to resolve a problem and to reach goals, once recognized by consumers, is dependent on two factors: (1) the magnitude or size of the discrepancy and (2) the relative importance of the problem. Let us look at how these two factors would affect problem recognition. Jack currently jogs on a daily basis and wants to participate in a competitive, organized, and aggressive team sport. Is the discrepancy between actual state (individual, recreational, and nonaggressive) and desired state (team play, competitive, and aggressive) large enough to activate the decision-making process? Let's assume that it is and consider the second condition of problem recognition, the importance of the problem.

The second condition that must be met for problem recognition to occur is that the goal must be important enough to Jack. Some consumers may recognize the difference between participating in recreational sports versus an organized league. Would the benefits of participating in the new organized league (hopefully making some friends and being more competitive) outweigh the time, expense, and energy required to play? If the problem is important enough to Jack, then he moves on to the next stage of the decision-making process – information search.

What strategic implication does problem recognition hold for sports marketers? Generally, we would first identify the actual and desired states of sports participants or potential participants. Once these states have been determined, sports marketers can offer activities and events that will fill these needs and eliminate "problems." In addition, sports marketers can attempt to alter the perceived ideal state of consumers. For example, it is common for health clubs to show the "ideal" body that can be achieved by purchasing a membership and working out. Media is continually an avenue in which the ideal and actual

Photo 4.2
Many consumers see a discrepancy between the "ideal" and "actual" body

Source: Shutterstock.com, Diego Cervo

body are forever challenged, as seen in the following video: www.common-sensemedia.org/blog/research-what-parents-need-to-know-about-kids-media-and-body-image video.

Information search

After problem recognition occurs, the next step in the participant decision-making process is information search. **Information search** occurs when a participant seeks relevant information that will help resolve the problem. The sources of information sought by consumers can be broken down into two types: internal and external sources.

   Internal sources of information are recalled from our own memories and are based on previous exposure to sports and activities. The internal information activated from memory can provide us with a wealth of data that may affect the decision-making process. Jack has spent most of his life participating in sports and recreational activities, so information based on past experience is readily available. For instance, because Jack has played in an organized league in the past, he would use internal information to recall his experiences. Did he enjoy the competition of organized sport? Why did he stop participating in the sport? **External sources** of information are environmentally based and can occur in three different ways. First, Jack might ask **personal sources**, such as friends or family, to provide him with information about possible organized team sports in which to participate.

EPIC PASSES

Web Capture 4.1
Explore the Vail Resort, online information source

Source: Vail Resorts; www.vail.com/

Friends and family are important information sources that can have a great deal of influence on our participation choices. Second, **marketing sources**, such as advertisements, sales personnel, brochures, and web sites on the Internet are all important information sources. In fact, sports marketers have direct control over this source of information, so it is perhaps the most critical from the perspective of the sports organization. The third type of external information source is called an **experiential source**. Jack may watch games in several different sports leagues to gather information. His decision is influenced by watching the level of competition.

Some participants may require a great deal of information before making a decision, whereas others require little to no information. The amount of information and the number of sources used is a function of several factors, such as the amount of time available, the importance of the decision, the amount of past experience, and the demographics and psychographics of the participants.

The extent of the information search also depends on the **perceived risk** of the decision. Perceived risk stems from the uncertainty associated with decision making and is concerned with the potential threats inherent in making the wrong decision. For individual sports participants, perceived risk surfaces in many different forms. Perceived risk may be the embarrassment of not having the skill necessary to participate in a competitive league (social risks) or being concerned about the money needed to participate (economic risks). Also, an important perceived risk for many adult participants is health and safety (safety risks).

At this stage of the participant decision-making process, sports marketers must understand as much as they can about the information sources used by consumers. For instance, marketers for the Cincinnati Recreational Commission want to know the information sources for teams, the most effective way to provide teams with information, how much information is desired, and to whom they should provide this information. Moreover, sports marketers want to understand the perceived risks for potential participants such as Jack. This information is essential for developing an effective promotional strategy that targets both teams and individual participants.

Evaluation of alternatives

Now that the information search has yielded all the available participation alternatives that have some of the basic characteristics that appeal to Jack, he must begin to evaluate the alternatives. Jack thinks about all the organized team sports in which he might participate and chooses a subset to which he will give further consideration. The few sports given the greatest consideration are called the **evoked set** of alternatives. Jack's evoked set might consist of four sports: softball, basketball, bowling, and indoor soccer.

After consumers develop their evoked set, which is composed of acceptable alternatives, they must evaluate each sport based on the important features and characteristics. These features and characteristics that potential consumers are looking for in a sport are called **evaluative criteria**. The evaluative criteria used by Jack include team sport, organized or league play, moderate level of competition, and moderately aggressive sport. It is important to realize that each of the four evaluative criteria carries a different weight in Jack's overall decision-making process. To continue with our example, let us say that Jack attaches the greatest importance to participating in a team sport. Next, Jack is concerned with participating in a league or organized sport. The level of aggression is the next most important criterion to Jack. Finally, the least important factor in choosing from among the four sports is the level of competition.

In complex decision making, Jack would evaluate each of the sports against each of the evaluative criteria. He would base his final decision regarding participation on which sport measures best against the various factors he deems important. The two most important criteria - team sport and league play - are satisfied for each of the four sports in the evoked set. In other words, all the sports that Jack is evaluating are team sports, and all have league play. Therefore, Jack moves on to his next criteria, level of aggression. Ideally, Jack wants to remain injury free, so he eliminates indoor soccer and basketball from further consideration. Bowling seems to be a clear winner in satisfying these criteria, and Jack is aware of several competitive bowling leagues in the area. Therefore, Jack decides to participate in a bowling league.

The **evaluation of alternatives** has two important implications for sports marketers. First, sports marketers must ensure their sports are included in the evoked set of potential consumers. To accomplish this objective, consumers must first become aware of the alternative. Second, sports marketers must understand what evaluative criteria are used by potential consumers and then develop strategies to meet consumers' needs based on these criteria. For example, marketers of bowling have determined that there are two different participant bowling markets: league or organized and recreational bowlers.

Recreational bowlers are growing in numbers and care most about the facilities at which they bowl and the related services provided. The evaluative criteria used by recreational bowlers might include the type of food served, other entertainment offered (e.g., arcade games and billiards), and the atmosphere of the bowling alley. League bowlers, however, constitute a diminishing market. This segment of bowlers cares most about the location of the bowling center and the condition of the lanes.[2]

Participation

The evaluation of alternatives has led us to what marketers consider the most important outcome of the decision-making process – the participation decision. The participation stage of the decision-making process might seem to be the most straightforward, but many things need to be considered other than actually deciding what sport to play. For instance, the consumer's needs may shift to the equipment and apparel needed to participate. Jack may decide that he needs a new bowling ball, shoes, and equipment bag to look the part of bowler for his new team. Thus, marketers working for equipment manufacturers are interested in Jack's participant consumption behavior. In addition, Jack may have to decide which bowling alley offers the best alternative for his needs. He may choose a location close to home, one that offers the best price, or the alley that has the best atmosphere. Again, these criteria must be carefully considered by sports marketers, because participants make choices regarding not only what sports they want to participate in but also where they want to participate.

Other things might occur that alter the intended decision to participate in a given sport. At the last minute, Jack's coworkers may talk him out of playing in a competitive men's league in lieu of a co-rec, work league. There might be a problem finding an opening on a roster, which would also change Jack's decision-making process at the last moment. Perhaps the bowling team that Jack wanted to join is scheduled to play during a trip that he had planned. All these "unexpected pleasures" may occur at the participation stage of the decision-making process.

Post-participation evaluation

You might think that the decision-making process comes to an abrupt halt after the participation decision, but there is one more very important step – **post-participation evaluation**. The first activity that may occur after consumers have made an important participation decision is **cognitive dissonance**. This dissonance occurs because consumers experience doubts or anxiety about the wisdom of their decision. In other words, people question their own judgment. Let us suppose Jack begins participating in a competitive bowling league, and the first time he bowls, he is embarrassed. His poor level of play is far worse than that of everyone else on the team. Immediately, he begins to question his decision to participate. Whether dissonance occurs is a function of the importance of the decision, the difficulty of the choice, the degree of commitment to the decision, and the individual's tendency to experience anxiety.[3] Jack does not know his teammates well and only paid $50 to join the league, so he may decide to quit the team. However, he does not want to let his team down and ruin his chance of making new friends, so high levels of dissonance may cause him to continue with the team. In either case, the level of dissonance that Jack feels is largely based on his own personality and tendency to experience anxiety.

Another important activity that occurs after participation begins is evaluation.

First, the participant develops expectations about what it will be like to play in this competitive bowling league. Jack's expectations may range from thinking about how much physical pain the sport will cause to thinking about how many new friends he will make as a result of participating. Next, Jack evaluates his actual experience after several games. If expectations are met or exceeded, then satisfaction occurs. However, if the experience or performance is poorer than expected, then dissatisfaction results. The level of satisfaction Jack experiences will obviously have a tremendous impact on his future participation and word-of-mouth communication about the sport.

Types of consumer decisions

We have just completed our discussion of Jack's decision-making process and have failed to mention one very important thing: Not all decisions are alike. Some are extremely important and, therefore, take a great deal of time and thought. Because we are creatures of habit, some decisions require little or no effort. We simply do what we have always done in the past. The variety of decisions that we make about participation in sport can be categorized into three different types of participation decision processes. The decision processes, also known as levels of problem solving, are habitual problem solving, limited problem solving, and extensive problem solving.

Habitual problem solving

One type of decision process that is used is called **habitual problem solving** (or **routinized problem solving**). In habitual problem solving, problem recognition occurs, followed by limited internal information search. As we just learned, internal search comes from experiences with sports stored in memory.

Therefore, when Jack is looking for information on sports next year, he simply remembers his previous experience and satisfaction with bowling. The evaluation of alternatives is eliminated for habitual decisions because no alternatives are considered. Jack participates in bowling again, but this time there is no dissonance and limited evaluation occurs. In a sense, Jack's decision to participate in bowling becomes a habit or routine each year.

2. Limited problem solving

The next type of consumer decision process is called **limited problem solving**. Limited problem solving begins with problem recognition and includes internal search and sometimes limited external search. A small number of alternatives are evaluated using a few evaluative criteria. In fact, in limited problem solving, the alternatives being evaluated are often other forms of entertainment (e.g., movies or concerts). After purchase, dissonance is rare and a limited evaluation of the product occurs. Participation in special sporting events, such as a neighborhood 10K run or charity golf outing, are examples of sporting events that lend themselves to limited problem solving.

3. Extensive problem solving

The last type of decision process is called **extensive problem solving** (or **extended problem solving**) because of the exhaustive nature of the decision. As with any type of decision, problem recognition must occur for the decision-making process to be initiated. Heavy information search (both internal and external) is followed by the evaluation of many alternatives on many attributes. Postpurchase dissonance and postpurchase evaluation are at their highest levels with extensive decisions. Jack's initial decision to participate in the bowling league was an extensive decision due to his high levels of information search, the many sports alternatives he considered, and the comprehensive nature of his evaluation of bowling.

For many people who are highly involved in sports, participation decisions are more extensive in nature, especially in the initial stages of participating in and evaluating various sports. Over time, what was once an extensive decision becomes routine. Participants choose sports that meet their needs, and the decision to participate becomes automatic. It is important for marketers to understand the type of problem solving used by participants so the most effective marketing strategy can be formulated and implemented.

Psychological or internal factors

Now that we have looked at the participant decision-making process, let us turn our focus to the internal, or psychological, factors. Personality, motivation, learning, and perception are some of the basic **psychological** or **internal factors** that will be unique to each individual and guide sports participation decisions.

Personality

One of the psychological factors that may have a tremendous impact on whether we participate in sports, the sports in which we participate, and the amount of participation is personality. Psychologists have defined **personality** as a set of consistent responses an individual makes to the environment.

Although there are different ways to describe personality, one common method used by marketers is based on specific, identifiable personality traits. For example, individuals can be thought of as aggressive, orderly, dominant, or nurturing.[4] Consider the potential association between an individual's personality profile and the likelihood of participating in a particular sport. The self-assured, outgoing, assertive individual may be more likely than the apprehensive, reserved, and humble person to participate in any sport. Moreover, the self-sufficient individual may participate in more individual sports (e.g., figure skating, golf, or tennis) than the group-dependent individual.

Much has been said about Millennials, Generation X, and Baby Boomers, but what about Generation Z? Generation Z, also known as the post-Millennial generation, includes those born from 1997 to 2015.[5] The "Z" Generation grew up with the Internet, mobile phones, and social media. Sport interest and engagement

Photo 4.3

A growing number of consumers participate in high-risk sports

Source: Shutterstock.com, Vitalii Nesterchuk

show that this group is more interested in basketball and soccer than other generations. They are less interested in football, baseball, and golf than their predecessors. Generation Z is more likely to participate in team sports like basketball and soccer, but running, swimming, and bicycling are this generation's most popular sport activities. Therefore, the sports industry may have to up the ante and enhance its level of efficiency in communicating to this up-and-coming generation. Another study found Generation Xers to be more interested in fast-paced, high-risk activities, such as rock climbing and mountain biking.[6] As such, action sports may be a good choice for the happy-go-lucky, venturesome personality type of the Generation Xers. Action or extreme sports are defined as the pantheon of aggressive, non-team sports, including snowboarding, inline skating, super modified shovel racing, wakeboarding, ice and rock climbing, mountain biking, and snow mountain biking.[7] The relationship between sports participation and personality traits can be seen in Table 4.1. As illustrated, golfers most often described themselves as responsible, family oriented, self-confident, and intelligent. The poorest descriptors for golfers were *bitter, sick a lot, extravagant*, and *risk-averse*. Interestingly, golfers described themselves as team players, although they participate in this highly individual sport.

Although personality and participation may be linked, take care not to assume a causal relationship between personality and sports participation. Some researchers believe sports participation might shape various personality traits (i.e., sport is a character builder). Other researchers believe we participate in sports because of our particular personality type. To date, little research supports the causal direction of the relationship between personality and participation in sport.

Table 4.1 Golfers' self-reported traits and personality characteristics

Poorest descriptors	Percentage	Best descriptors	Percentage
Born again	16	Practical	60
Attractive	15	Competent	61
Non-mainstream	14	Ambitious	61
Lonely	8	Sensitive	62
Fun-loving	8	Team player	63
Virgin	6	Fun-loving	64
Risk-averse	6	Intelligent	66
Extravagant	6	Confident	70
Always sick	3	Family-oriented	75
Bitter	3	Responsible	80

Source: Yankelovich Partners, "How Golfers Are Likely to Describe Themselves"

Not only does personality dictate whether someone participates in sports, but it may also be linked with participation in particular types of sports. The violent, aggressive personality type may be drawn to sports such as mixed martial arts, football, boxing, or hockey. The shy, introverted personality type may be more likely to participate in individual sports, such as tennis and running. Knowing the relationship between participation and personality profiles can help sports marketers set up the strategic sports marketing process so it will appeal to the appropriate personality segment. In addition, sports marketers of large participant sporting events use personality profiles to attract potential corporate sponsors who may want to appeal to the same personality segment.

Motivation

Why do people participate in sports? What benefits are people looking for from participating in sport, and what needs does participating in sport satisfy? McDonald, Milne, and Hong,[8] drawing on Maslow's human needs hierarchy, present evidence illustrating that consumers possess multiple and unique motivations – including achievement, competition, social facilitation, physical fitness, skill mastery, physical risk, affiliation, aesthetics, aggression, value development, self-esteem, self-actualization, and stress release – for participating in particular sport activities. Steve Jennison highlighted that

> sport has the ability to enhance people's lives, improve health status, and increase participation rates to support development of a physically active city. It can also unite communities and nations through success in international competition and major events through pride, passion, and participation.[9]
>
> (Hull City)

Additional studies suggest there are three basic reasons for participation in sport (see Table 4.2). Finally, studies have looked at understanding the motives for participation in a specific sport. For example, Rohm, Milne, and McDonald[10] recently explored the motives of runners (see Table 4.3 for segmentation of runners by motives).

The study of human motivation helps to better understand the underlying need to participate in sports. **Motivation** is an internal force that directs behavior toward the fulfillment of needs. In our earlier discussion of the participant decision-making process, problem recognition resulted from having needs that are not currently being met. As the definition indicates, motivation is discussed in terms of fulfilling unmet needs. Although there is no argument that all humans have needs, there is disagreement about the number of needs and the nature of them.

One popular theory of human motivation based on classification of needs is called **Maslow's hierarchy of needs** (see Figure 4.3). Maslow's hierarchy of needs consists of five levels. For a video interpretation of Maslow's hierarchy of needs, see: www.youtube.com/watch?v=O-4ithG_07Q. According to Maslow, the most basic, primitive needs must be fulfilled before the individual can progress to the next level of need. Once this higher level of need is satisfied, the

Table 4.2 Why people participate in sports

Personal improvement

Release of tension or relaxation, sense of accomplishment, skill mastery, improved health and fitness other people's respect for one's athletic skill, release of aggression, enjoyment of risk taking, personal growth, development of positive values, and sense of personal pride

Sport appreciation

Enjoyment of the game, sport competition, and thrill of victory

Social facilitation

Time spent with close friends or family and sense of being part of a group

Why people play sport	Why people don't play sport
Improve fitness/skill level	No time/too busy
Make new friends	Family/home/work commitments
Sense of belonging/peer pressure	Too competitive
Fun and enjoyment	Lack motivation or confidence
Fame or money	Cost too expensive
Achievement of goals	Physically unable

Source: George Milne, William Sutton, and Mark McDonald, "Niche Analysis: A Strategic Measurement Tool for Managers," *Sport Marketing Quarterly*, vol. 5, no. 3 (1996), 17–21

Table 4.3 Segmentation of runners by motives

"I find running to be both relaxing and is the primary way along with a good diet that I keep up my plan for good health and fitness." – Female 50+ years old, 18 miles/week, 4 days/week

"Running is very important because I use running to relieve stress and to think about what is bothering me. I use running to clear my head. Running is important to maintain fitness and to counteract my poor diet of late." – Male, <25 years old, no mileage reported

continued

Table 4.3a & b *continued*

Social competitors

"Running is one of the greatest joys of life. Keeps the body, mind, and spirit soaring. Running with friends is special. Competition pushes me to new levels. Can travel to races and see new places. I can share stories with runners from all over the world." – Female, 25–39 years old, runs 40 miles/week, 5 days/week

"I just recently started running 3 yrs. ago. I used to weigh 317 lbs. I'm now down to 245. Before I leave work I change and go directly to a 1/2-mile track located on the way home. My running is very important: it relieves a lot of stress and is something that is within my control. I have made many acquaintances at the track. We all motivate each other. If someone misses one day everybody is aware and concerned. That alone motivates you to keep going. Besides I am trying to get down to 199lbs." – Male, 40–49, runs 24 miles/week, 6 days/week

Actualized athletes

"I love to run. I've always been athletic and enjoyed team sports. But running is different. It's a solitary sport. It pits me against me. I'm 42 yrs. old and I know I've yet to reach my potential as a runner. My best yrs. are behind me and I know I'll never be world class but I still have room to improve and I'll keep trying, training, testing. It makes me fit. It makes me happy. I love to run." – Male, 40–49 years old, runs 35 miles/week, 5 days/week

Devotees

"It is a big part of my life. It's like brushing your teeth – it's a gift I give myself every day or almost everyday. It is who I am and I never want not to run. It's the most wonderful total feeling in life. It has made me grow in so many ways and also appreciate life so much more. You can do it anywhere at any time – no expense." – Male, 50+ years old, runs 38 miles/week, 6 days/week

"It's part of who I am. Running is the most important free time activity I have besides spending time with my kids. I'm a happier person when I get my running." – Female, 25–39, runs 20 miles/week, 4 days/week

Source: Andrew J. Rohm, George R. Milne, and Mark McDonald, "A Mixed-Method Approach for Developing Market Segmentation Typologies in the Sports Industry," *Sport Marketing Quarterly*, 2006, 15, 29–39, © 2006 West Virginia University

individual is then motivated to fulfill the next higher level of need. Let us look at the hierarchy of needs as it relates to participation in sports.

The first and most basic level of needs in Maslow's hierarchy are called **physiological needs**. These are the biological needs that people have - to eat, drink, and meet other physiological needs. For some individuals, there may be a physiological need to exercise and have some level of activity. Once this lower-order need is met, safety needs are addressed. **Safety needs** are concerned with physical safety, as well as the need to remain healthy. Sports equipment manufacturers address the need participants have for physical safety.

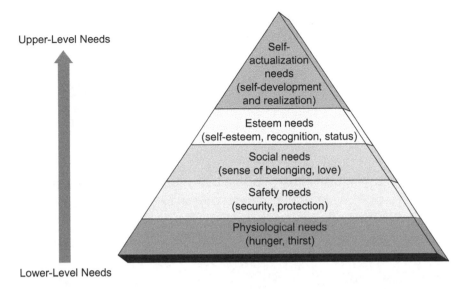

Upper-Level Needs

Lower-Level Needs

Figure 4.3

Maslow's hierarchy of needs

Source: A. H. Maslow, *Motivation and Personality*, 2nd ed. (New York: Harper and Row, 1970). Reprinted with permission of Pearson Education, Inc., Upper Saddle River, NJ

With respect to the need for health, many participants cite that the primary reason for joining health clubs is to maintain or improve their health.

The next need level is based on **love and belonging**. Many people choose to participate in sport because of the social aspects involved. One of the early need theories of motivation includes "play" as a primary social need.[11] For some individuals, sports participation is their only outlet for being part of a group and interacting with others. The need to be part of a team and to be respected by teammates has been demonstrated in a number of studies.

As these social needs are satisfied, **esteem** needs of recognition and status must be addressed. Certainly, sport plays a major role in enhancing self-esteem, and the impact of sport participation on enhanced self-esteem has been well documented. For instance, research has been conducted at Queensland University of Technology in Australia exploring what motivates participants in extreme sports. Professor Robert Scheitzer explains,

> far from the traditional risk-focused assumptions, extreme sports participation facilitates more positive psychological experiences and express human values such as humility, harmony, creativity, spirituality, and a vital sense of self that enriches everyday life.[12]

Finally, the highest-order need, **self-actualization**, should be met. This refers to the individual's need to "be all that you can be" and is usually fulfilled through participation in mountain climbing, triathlons, or any sport that pushes an individual to the utmost of his or her physical and mental capacities. For example, ultramarathons in which runners compete in 100K road races

Photo 4.4
Sports participants fulfilling the need for self-actualization

Source: Shutterstock.com, Dudarev Mikhail

certainly test the will of all participants. Another example of self-actualization can be found in the amateur athlete who trains his or her whole life for the Olympic Games.

As a sports marketer, you may be able to enhance strategies for increasing participation if you identify and understand the needs of consumers. In some instances, participation might fill more than one need level. Consumers may satisfy physiological needs, safety needs, social needs, esteem needs, or possibly self-actualization needs. For instance, marketing a health club membership might appeal to consumers wanting to fulfill any of the need levels in the hierarchy. The members' physiological needs are being met through exercise. Safety needs might be met by explaining that the club has state-of-the-art exercise equipment that is designed to be safe for all ages and fitness levels. Social needs are addressed by describing the club as a "home away from home" for many members. The need for esteem for health club members might be easily satisfied by depicting how good they will look and feel after working out. Finally, self-actualization needs may be fulfilled by working out to achieve the ideal body.

The needs that have just been presented can be described in two ways: motive direction and motive strength. Motive direction is the way that a consumer attempts to reduce tension by either moving toward a positive goal or moving away from a negative outcome. In the case of sports participation, an individual wants to get in good physical condition and may move toward this goal by running, biking, lifting weights, and so on. Likewise, this same individual may want to move away from eating fatty foods and drinking alcohol.

Of particular interest to sports marketers is the strength of the sports participation motive. Motivational strength is the degree to which an individual chooses to actively pursue one goal over another. In sports marketing, the strength of a motive is characterized in terms of **sports involvement**. Sports involvement is the perceived interest in and personal importance of sports to an individual participating in a sport.[13]

Triathletes are an excellent example of an extreme level of sports involvement because of the importance placed on training for events. In their study, Hill and Robinson demonstrated that extreme involvement in a sport affects many aspects of the athletes' lives.[14] Participation could have positive effects, such as increased self-esteem, improved moods, and a better sense of overall wellness. Conversely, high involvement in a sport (e.g., triathlon) may produce neglected responsibilities of work, home, or family and feelings of guilt, stress,

Photo 4.5
The high-involvement cyclist

Source: Shutterstock.com, Ljupco Smokovski

and anxiety. Said simply, extremely involved individuals frequently have a difficult time balancing their lives.

Sports marketers are interested in involvement because it has been shown to be a relatively good predictor of sports-related behaviors. For example, a study found that level of involvement was positively related to the number of hours people participate in sports, the likelihood of planning their day around a sporting event, and the use of sports-related media (e.g., television, newspaper, or magazines).[15] Knowledge of sports involvement can help sports marketers develop strategies for both low- and high-involvement groups of potential participants.

Perception

Think for a moment about the image you have of the following sports: soccer, hockey, and tennis. You might think of soccer as a sport that requires a great deal of stamina and skill, hockey as a violent and aggressive sport, and tennis as a sport for people who belong to country clubs. Ask two friends about their images of these same sports, and you are likely to get two different responses. That is because each of us has our own views of the world based on past experience, needs, wants, and expectations.

Your image of sport results from being exposed to a lifetime of information. You talk to friends and family about sports, you watch sports on television, and you listen to sports on the radio. In addition, you may have participated in a variety of sports over the course of your life. We selectively filter sports information based on our own view of the world. Consumers process this information and use it in making decisions about participation.

The process by which consumers gather information and then interpret that information based on their own past experience is described as perception. **Perception** is defined as the complex process of selecting, organizing, and interpreting stimuli such as sports.[16] Ultimately, our perception of the world around us influences participant consumer behavior. The images that we hold of various sports and of ourselves dictate, to some extent, what sports we participate in. One of the primary goals of sports marketing is to shape your image of sports and sports products.

Before sports marketers can influence your perceptions, they must get your attention. **Selective attention** describes a consumer's focus on a specific marketing stimulus based on personal needs and attitudes. For example, you are much more likely to pay attention to advertisements for new golf clubs if you are thinking about purchasing a set.

Sports marketers fight with other sports and nonsports marketing stimuli for the limited capacity that consumers have for processing information. One job of the sports marketer is to capture the attention of the potential participant. But how is this done? Typically, sports marketers capture our attention through the use of novel promotions, using large and colorful promotional materials, and developing unique ways of communicating with consumers.

While sports marketers attempt to influence our perceptions, each participant brings a unique set of experiences, attitudes, and needs that affect the perceptual process. Generally speaking, consumers perceive things in ways that are consistent with their existing attitudes and values. This process is known as **selective interpretation**. For example, those who have played hockey all their life may not see it as a dangerous and violent sport, whereas others hold a different interpretation.

Finally, **selective retention**, or the tendency to remember only certain information, is another of the influences on the perceptual process. Selective retention is remembering just the things we want to remember. The hockey player does not remember the injuries, the training, or the fights – only the victories.

Although sports marketers cannot control consumers' perceptions, they can and do influence our perceptions of sports through their marketing efforts. For example, a sports marketer trying to increase volleyball participation in boys ages 8 to 12 must first attempt to understand their perception of volleyball. Then the sports marketer tries to find ways of capturing the attention of this group of consumers, who have many competing sports and entertainment alternatives. Once they have the attention of this group of potential participants, a marketing mix is designed to either reinforce their perception of volleyball or change the existing image.

In addition to understanding these consumers' images of volleyball, sports marketers are also interested in other aspects of perception. For instance, how do potential participants perceive advertisements and promotional materials about the sport? What are the parents' perceptions of volleyball? Do the parents

Ad 4.1
Titleist highlighting the latest technology in their driver lines

*Source:*www.titleist.com/golf-clubs/golf-drivers

perceive volleyball to be costly? The answer to all these questions depends on our own unique view of the world, which sports marketers attempt to understand and shape.

Learning

Another psychological factor that affects our participation decisions is learning. **Learning** is a relatively permanent change in response tendency due to the effects of experience. These response tendencies can be either changes in behavior (participation) or in how we perceive a particular sport. Consumers learn about and gather information regarding participation in various sports in any number of ways. **Behavioral learning** is concerned with how various stimuli (information about sports) elicit certain responses (feelings or behaviors) within an individual. **Cognitive learning**, however, is based on our ability to solve problems and use observation as a form of learning. Finally, **social learning** is based on watching others and learning from their actions. Let us look briefly at these three theories of learning as they apply to sports participation.

Behavioral learning

One behavioral learning theory of importance to sports marketers is operant conditioning. Conditioning teaches people to associate certain behaviors with certain consequences of those behaviors. A simplified model of operant conditioning is illustrated in Figure 4.4.

Let us illustrate the model of operant conditioning using participation in snowboarding. We may decide to try snowboarding (specific behavior) as a new sport. Next and unfortunately, our behavior is punished as we continually fall down, suffer social embarrassment, and feel uncomfortably wet and cold. Finally, the likelihood of our engaging in this behavior in the future is decreased because of the negative consequences of our earlier attempts at snowboarding. However, if we are rewarded through the enjoyment of the sport and being with others, then we will continue to snowboard more and more.

Figure 4.4
Model of operant conditioning

Figure 4.5
Model of cognitive learning

The theory of operant conditioning lies at the heart of loyalty to a sport. In other words, if the sports we participate in meet our needs and reinforce them, then we will continue to participate in those sports. The objective of the sports marketer is to try to heighten the rewards associated with participating in any given sport and diminish any negative consequences.

Cognitive learning

Although much of what we learn is based on our past experience, learning also takes place through reasoning and thought processes. This approach to learning is known as cognitive learning. Cognitive learning is best known as learning through problem solving or insight, as shown in Figure 4.5.

Consider a goal that concerns some of us – weight loss. Once this goal is established, consumers search for activities that allow them to achieve the goal. The activities necessary to achieve weight loss might include dieting, participating in aerobics, weight training, playing basketball, or jogging. When consumers finally realize what specific activities they feel are necessary to achieve the desired goal, insight occurs. Finally, and hopefully, the goal of weight loss is achieved.

By using the concept of cognitive learning, the first focus of sports marketers is to understand the goals of potential consumers or participants. In addition, marketers must make potential participants aware of how the sport or sports product will help participants achieve their goals.

Social learning

Much of our learning takes place by watching how others are rewarded or punished for their actions. This way of learning is called social learning. As children, we watched our friends, family members, and our heroes participate in various sports. To a large extent, this early observation and learning dictate the sports in which we choose to participate later in life. In social learning, we not only see someone benefiting from sport, but we also learn how to participate in the sport ourselves.

Those individuals we choose to observe and the process of observation are called models and modeling, respectively. The job of the sports marketer is to present positive models and present sports in a positive light, so others will perceive the benefits of sports participation. For example, Serena Williams may be seen as a role model for young African American athletes thinking about participating in tennis and Tiger Woods in golf, while Tom Brady may be a model for young men interested in football.

Attitudes

Because of the learning and perceptual processes, consumers develop attitudes toward participating in sports. **Attitudes** are learned thoughts, feelings, and behaviors toward some given object. What is your attitude toward participation in bowling? One positive aspect of bowling is the chance to interact socially with other participants. However, bowling does not burn a lot of calories and may be seen as expensive. Your overall attitude toward bowling is made up of these positive and negative aspects of the sport.

Attitudes represent one of the most important components of the overall model of sports participation because they ultimately guide the decision-making process. Our attitudes are formed on the basis of an interaction between past experience and the environment in which we live. A simple model of attitude formation or how attitudes are developed is shown in Figure 4.6.

As the model of attitude formation suggests, an attitude is based on our thinking, feeling, and actions toward a sport. These three components interact to form an overall attitude. Let us look briefly at its three components: cognitive, affective, and behavioral.

The **cognitive component** of attitude holds the beliefs that people have toward the object. Beliefs can be either a statement of knowledge regarding bowling or thoughts someone has toward bowling. They are neither right nor wrong and vary from individual to individual. For example, here are some beliefs about participation in bowling that consumers might hold:

- Bowling is expensive.
- Bowling is time consuming.
- Very few women bowl.
- Bowling is for old people. (*Note:* The largest participant group for bowling is 18- to 34-year-olds.)

The **affective component** of attitude is based on feelings or emotional reactions to the initial stimulus. Most beliefs, such as the ones shown for cognitive attitude, have a related affective evaluation. More recently, affects, or feelings, have taken a more central role in explaining attitudes than beliefs or behaviors. In other words, some people equate attitudes with feelings that are held toward an object.[17] Here are some potential affective statements:

- I hate bowling.
- Bowling is a boring sport.

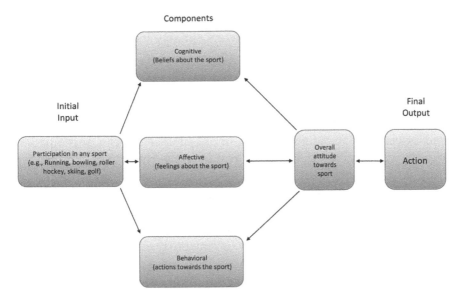

Figure 4.6
Model of attitude formation

Source: Adapted from Del Hawkins, Roger Best, and Kenneth Coney. *Consumer Behavior: Building Marketing Strategy*, 7th ed. (© 1998 The McGraw-Hill Companies, Inc., New York)

The final component is called the **behavioral component** and is based on participants' actions. In other words, does the individual participate in bowling? How often does the individual bowl? What are the individual's behavioral intentions, or how likely will he or she be to bowl in the future?

Generally, sports marketers must understand consumer attitudes to maintain or increase participation in any given sport. Only after attitudes are assessed can sports marketing strategies be formulated to improve upon or change existing attitudes. In our previous example, bowling equipment manufacturers and bowling alley management companies would need to change the beliefs that potential participants have about bowling. Additional strategies may attempt to change potential participants' feelings about bowling by repositioning the sport's current image. Finally, marketers may get potential participants to try bowling, which could lead to possible changes in their beliefs and feelings about the sport.

Sociological or external factors

Now that we have looked at the major internal or psychological factors that influence participation decisions, let us turn our attention to the sociological factors. The **sociological or external factors** are those influences outside the individual participant that affect the decision-making process. The external factors are also referred to as sociological because they include all aspects of society and interacting with others. The external factors discussed in this chapter include culture, social class, reference groups, and family.

Culture

Participating in sports and games is one of the most long-standing traditions of civilization. Since the time of the ancient Greeks, participation in sports was expected and highly valued.[18] In the United States, sports are criticized for playing too important a role in our society. Many detractors frown at public monies being spent to finance private stadiums for professional athletics or institutions of higher education spending more on a new coach than on a new president for the university. Coaches and managers are always under the intense scrutiny of athletic directors, club owners, and the media. In fact, in today's sporting world, managing has become one of the most volatile jobs. Although wages are not always in the limelight like the wages of star players, top managers do earn a handsome amount. Some of these wages even match the wages of top players. For example, Arsenal's Arsene Wenger, who signed a contract extension in 2017, is the longest-standing manger in the Premier League, making £8.9 million per year. Jose Mourinho of Manchester United makes £15 million and Pep Guardiola £15.3 million per year at Manchester City, while their counterpart Fabio Capello in the Chinese league earns £8.98 million per year, and Marcello Lippi earns £18 million per year with the Chinese national team. Are these salaries a testimony to the intense work they do? Or is it the lopsided sociological identity and emphasis that is transparent throughout the industry? As the accompanying article (4.1) illustrates, sports are part of the global arena that ties together entertainment, lifestyle, occupation, and business. However, as other cultures try to emulate sports participation patterns in the United States, the question is not how to do it but, is that the most appropriate model to emulate?

Culture is the set of learned values, beliefs, language, traditions, and symbols shared by a people and passed down from generation to generation. One of the most important aspects of this definition of culture includes the learning component. **Socialization** occurs when we learn about the skills, knowledge, and attitudes necessary for participating in sports. Sports marketers are interested in better understanding how the **consumer socialization** process takes place and how they might influence this process.

A model of sports socialization is presented in Figure 4.7, which provides a framework for understanding how children learn about sports. Although the sports socialization process begins at increasingly younger ages, it extends throughout the life of the individual. Sports marketers are interested in learning how the socialization process differs on the basis of gender, income, family lifestyle, and the number of children in the family.

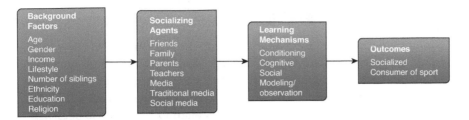

Figure 4.7
Model of consumer socialization

Source: Adapted from Mowen, John, 1993. *Consumer Behavior*, 3rd ed. (New York: Macmillan, 1993)

Socializing agents also have a tremendous impact on the process. These factors represent direct and indirect influences on children. Sports marketers are also interested in understanding the relative impact of each socializing agent on a child's interest in participating in sports. For instance, is watching parents or professional athletes a better predictor of sports participation among children? One study has shown that children look to parents first, but if they are unacceptable or unwilling role models, children turn to other people.[19]

The learning mechanisms of observation and reinforcement are just two ways to facilitate the socialization process. As discussed earlier, observation refers to looking to others as models for sports participation. For example, older siblings may serve as models for sports participation at earlier ages, whereas friends may become a more important learning mechanism as children age. Reinforcement may occur as children receive praise for participation in sport from parents, coaches, and friends.

The final element in the socialization model is the emergence of a socialized sports participant. Here, the child becomes actively engaged in sports participation. From the sports marketer's perspective, when children participate in sports at an early age, they may have better potential to become lifelong participants. Certainly, sporting goods manufacturers are interested in having children associate their brands with the enjoyment of sport at the earliest possible age.

ARTICLE 4.1
MARKETING AND PROMOTION OF THE OLYMPIC GAMES

Introduction
Sport plays one of the most significant roles in everyday life of people around the world, whether those who actively participate in it or just spectators and supporters. In most western countries, this part of social life is widely reported on and reflected by the mass media.

Today, sport has not only become great entertainment, occupation and lifestyle, but solid business as well. In the world of sports, marketing, promotion and advertisement are fundamental tools for generating great profits. Each year, entrepreneurs and executives involved in the sport industry face serious issues, whether ones of defining ways to persuade advertisers to buy commercial time during the sport event or alluring customers to purchase some particular equipment for sports.

Particularly huge profits are associated with marketing and advertising of Olympic Games. Nowadays, Olympic Games have become one of the most large-scale and profitable global media events. Though, the situation was not always like that. Starting as ancient Greek religious festival, where athletes competed in honor of Zeus and being revived in late nineteenth century as completely athletic games, Olympics ended up with becoming one of the most celebrated and profitable media events in the world.

The current article will explore the issue of marketing-mediated sport events on the example of Olympic games and will touch upon the issues of promotion of properly the Games, advertising athletes and participants, sources of profit for conducting the Games, technologies used in Olympic marketing, new trends in marketing of Olympics and emerging threats to sports marketing. The issue will be discussed both in theoretical and practical network and is aimed at tracing the compliance of theoretical findings on advertisement, promotion and sponsorship strategies, with the practical implementation thereof on the example of one of the most profitable events in the sense of advertising, the Olympic Games. Thus, the work will focus on the issue of current developments of Olympic marketing and steps to be done in both theoretical and practical way to ensure further effectiveness and attractiveness of Olympic marketing programs.

Distinctive features of Olympics marketing

The Olympic games is the global arena for the best athletes in the world and a venue for unity and cooperation of people around the globe. Together with that, since the beginning of the last century, the games have acquired powerful advertising function. In 20s and 30s, this function was primary political and aimed at ideological propaganda of certain regime, most often dictatorship, like communism or nazism, while by late twentieth century it acquired purely economic dimension, becoming one of the most suitable places for advertising, marketing and generating considerable sums of money.

Today's Olympics is one of the most popular and most watched events in the world. For that reason, each 4-year period states compete for the right to host the games and show their country and attractions to thousands of Olympic enthusiasts who are going to come at the venue to watch the Games and millions of others watching them on TV. Broadcasting companies, in their turn, pay considerable sums of money to buy the rights for transmission of the Games. For instance, NBC, an national American broadcasting company, paid the sum of $3.5 billion to receive the right to transmit five Olympic games for the period of 2000–2008.

Nevertheless, this deal is considered a very successful one, since NBC has already return those $3.5 billion and received even more by selling advertising during the broadcast of the Games. The officials of the Company prefer not to disclosure the actual price of their advertising spots, but some sources of the industry assert that prime-time spots 30 seconds long may cost about $600,000. Of course, this sum doesn't go in line with $2 million cost of commercials 30 seconds long during Super Bowl of 2002. Notwithstanding the price, the demand for advertising spots is very high. Already in November 2001, NBC has sold 90% of its advertising spots to be broadcast during Olympic Games.

The advertisement strategy in Olympics significantly differs from other events. In Olympic Games, there are limited ways of attaining revenues from advertisement – either athletic endorsement in Olympics, or purchasing broadcasting rights and in such way promotion the TV Company, or sponsorship. Thus, in Olympics, there are no merely advertisers, there are sponsors. Sponsorship involves not only financial support of the revenue, but providing products and services, technologies, expertise and personnel to help in the organization of the Games. Revenue on sponsorship makes up about 32% of the total Olympic marketing revenues. The Olympic Games provide incomparable returns for the sponsors. They benefit from the marketing platform based on the ideals and values and increased opportunities from the company's showcasing, sales, community outreach programs and internal rewards.

"Without the support of the business community, without its technology, expertise, people, services, products, telecommunications, its financing – the Olympic Games could not and cannot happen. Without this support, the athletes cannot compete and achieve their very best in the world's best sporting event," stated Dr Jacques Rogge, the President of International Olympic Committee (International Olympic Committee Official Website).

The example of great benefits derived from the sponsorship can be the Coca-Cola Company, which used Olympic Games to advertise and sell its products for quite long period of time. In Athens, it has purchased the right to be the "official soft drink" of the Games and paid solid sums for numerous advertising spots. At 1984 Olympic Games in Los Angeles, Coca Cola was the second leading advertiser having spent $30,875,000 on promotion of its drinks. At 1996 Olympics in Atlanta, Coca Cola spent $73,645,900 on promotion (Eastman, 2000), becoming the leading advertiser of the Games and making Olympics its biggest and most important event in promotional company.

Promotion of sportsmen

In summer 2001, the Olympic Committee of the United States announced a new promotional campaign aimed at developing interrelation of United States Olympic Team and public. This was to be attained with three commercials picturing in humorous way three sportsmen trying to get into the Olympic Team. Each commercial ended with a slogan "The U.S. Olympic team. They're not just out there every four years, they're out there every day."(Dedyukhina, 2004). Chairman of NBC Sports and Olympics Dick Ebersol said that his company conducts the policy of raising awareness of U.S. Olympic team with the aim of making athletes more familiar to viewers, particularly the young ones for them to follow the sportsmen of the team throughout Olympics.

Athletic endorsement in Olympics

During the Olympic Games, virtually all the athletes carry a huge number of advertisements on their clothes. Numerous outfit companies such as Nike, Adidas or Oakley provide sportsmen with new equipment and clothes designed to facilitate movement and improve performance and at the same time advertise their new products to millions of viewers. Athletes can have various kinds of deals, while some are paid for appearance in a definite outfit, others just get them at no cost. Generally, skis, snowboards, skates and other equipment needed for Olympic games is considerably expensive, and the only opportunity for many athletes is to get sponsored by a sports-outfit company to cover the cost of their equipment. The companies greatly benefit from such deals since by this way their equipment is advertised by the world's most famous sportsmen. Often the companies modify the models of their outfit used by sportsmen to decrease their price and adapt them to the condition of consumers.

Olympic licensing and merchandise

Olympic licensing programs are targeted to market officially licensed products and merchandise from the Organizing Committee, National Committees and IOC. Olympic souvenirs and other merchandise bring a huge amount of money to the organizers. Consumers at the venue of the Games are certain to purchase some little things which would remind them of Olympics, such as official golden or silver coins of Olympic Games, wallets with Olympic symbols and a number of other souvenirs with Olympic logos.

Thus, today Olympics have become a mixture of ancient ideals of sportive perfection and today's reality associated first of all with commerce. Marketing and advertising are essential things in the organization of the Games since they are targeted to cover great expenses of such global event. Though, despite overwhelming dominance of commercial element, the Games still try to preserve the level and ideals of the Ancient Greece. Thus, there are strict tools aimed at maintaining the purity of the competition and the athletes who win the games become people of national pride.

Use of technology in Olympic marketing strategies

From the perspective of mass-media, the Olympics become undoubtedly a testing field for the new technologies. As the essential part of the Olympic ideal of the universalism, (Verdier, 1996, p. 59) the International Olympic Committee tries to make every possible effort to ensure everyone around the globe the access to Olympic information irrespective of location. Although the goal started as idealistic, today the infrastructure and technological developments are able to achieve this task. The information age offers the developments in the communication technologies which reorients the mode the consumers experience the Olympics in a broad range of traditional, developing and yet untested mass-media. This in particular concerns the vast potential of the Internet. Though, in Olympics, this medium is has somewhat limited action range due to the actions of the IOC Press Commission and

Radio and Television Commission (Verdier, 1996, p. 62) as a reply to request of other forms of media rights holders. Technologies available for use in the Internet, such as streaming video footage of Olympics on the web, were prohibited. Thus, the limits were placed on the possibility of reorientation of media usage for watching the Games. As to the finding out about the Games, internet, as a assessable and far-reaching information tool has large potential for reorientation of the media forms for the informative exposure of the Games.

Historically, radio was the second media or one supplement to television in exposure of the Games. Recent developments in the availability of mobile connection and satellite communication channels have afforded radio networks with relevant infrastructure to provide improved live coverage of the Games (Verdier, 1996, p. 61).

Of course, the main coverage media of the Olympics is television. Television broadcasting rights traditionally constitute 50% of the Olympic marketing revenue. The estimated number of Olympics viewers is 3.7 billion people in 220 countries and territories (Information from International Olympic Committee Official website). Thus, television is the engine that has pushed the growth of the entire Olympic movement. Over the past two decades, increases in the broadcast revenues have provided the Games with unusually large financial base. Though, this revenue is drawn for the broadcasting rights solely, not on the money derived from the viewers. Olympic committee adheres to the principles of free TV coverage and declines offers for broadcast on a pay per view platform since such practice contradicts the Olympic Broadcast Policy, targeted at making the Games viewed by as much number of people as possible. The fundamental Olympic principle, set forth in the Olympic Charter, provides the maximum presentation of the event by broadcasters all around the globe for everybody having access to the television. Therefore, broadcasting rights are sold only to those companies, who guarantee the broadcasting of the Games on their territory free of charge.

Methods of signal transmission of radio, television or Internet, have greatly developed by the advancements in transmission technologies, including satellites, microwave or fiber optic technology. Therefore it should be noticed that developments in communication technologies, both complimentary and peripheral to the Internet advancements, reorient the mode of informing the audience of the Olympic Games and exposing the main events. This is mainly based not only on huge increase in the number of media tools and facilities, but the capability and quality of new technologies.

Theoretical findings on sports marketing

There are very few studies that focus on particular issue of sports promotion, but instead there is a considerable number of mediated sports research which touch upon different aspects of the marketing connected to sports. Moreover, the issue of promotion is generally included in the broader sphere of marketing, which enhances not only the audiences of the program, but economic and social issues of sponsorship, globalization, political manipulation and commercialization. Therefore, sport marketing covers a broad range of issues such as selling sports events to television distributors and advertisers, and a few studies have covered the question of ongoing and increasing commercialization of sport events (Wenner, 1998).

Despite prevailing usage of televised marketing practices of professional sports that occupied the networks and mass media around the world to the great extent by the early 1990s, a very limited number of researches has been made in regards of the effects of televised sports marketing.

Farrell (1989) called marketing of the sports transmitted by television the creation of modern spectacles, McAllister (1997, 1998) perceived televised sports as a tool for the sponsorship of the products, but there are very few studies which explored the link between sport marketing and televised program promotion. Since the prices for acquiring right to broadcast sport events of paramount importance keep growing at enormous rate (Goldstein, 1996), considerable number of research on marketing has naturally focused on the issue of how the networks pay for these excessively expensive broadcasts.

For example, NBC paid more than $3.5 billion for the right to transmit Olympic games from 2000 to 2008. Moreover, cities hosting the Games pay more than a billion dollars each to attract the games and host the visitors (Fortune, 1996). Marketing is the only tool with which NBC and Olympic host cities can turn their debts into profits. For example, in 1976 in Montreal, due to sponsorship, a billion dollar loss was converted into $215 million profit for the city. According to the estimations of the Fortune magazine in 1996, the Atlanta city spent more than 2 billion dollars to host the games in 1996 but due to sponsorship they were returned with surplus. Although the television companies have a number of other income sources, none of them is larger and more profitable than sponsorship. To the contrast with spot advertising, sponsorship is defined by McAllister (1998) as "the funding of an entire event, group, broadcast, or place by one commercial interest in exchange for large amounts and special types of promotion connected with the sponsored activity" (p. 357). This resulted in such deviations as the Sunkist Orange Bowl, Winston Cup racing series, the Virginia Slims tennis tournaments, and presenting Visa as the main official credit card of the 1998 Winter Olympic Games. One of the very appropriate definition of sponsorship is the one defining it as a paid effort of the advertiser to tie its name to event or venue which strengthens its brand in a positive, yet in not obviously commercial way. Therefore, sponsorship, particularly one of Olympic Games, is different from merely advertising, since it involves not only financial support of the event, but provision of technology, equipment, services and products, expertise and relevant staff to assist the organization of the venue.

It is understood that marketing of sports is a big business and it requires elevated attention of researchers. Work by O'Neal, Finch, Hamilton, and Hammonds (1987) on the topic of features of sports that make it particularly attractive to the corporate sponsors, pay special attention to the finding that the sport rises excitement of viewers and thus lowers their anti-commercial self-protection mechanisms, making them more sensitive to advertising. According to the studies of Eastman (2000), if this phenomenon works between the content of program and commercials, it should also work between the sport program and promotions of other programs. This study confirms that advertisement of other programs during major sport events, in particularly Olympics, has great impact on the popularity of the promoted programs. But the excitement effect works in two directions: as the sports environment makes the promotion of other programs more effective, exciting commercials of other programs render sport events even more exciting. These conclusions are made on the basis of two theories, theory of expectance and theory of excitation transfer. Expectancy theory states that expectations about programs, sport programs in particular, might either enhance or diminish the effect of promos for other programs. Excitation-transfer theory stands for the fact that promotions that are able to excite viewers may transfer these emotions to the sport programs. In that way, promotions of televised sport event help create excitement about upcoming sport events and potentially increase their ratings, while promos for other programs, such as movies or prime-time series generally gain elevated effectiveness just by the fact of being placed within sport environment. Studies of Izod (1996) concluded that broadcasters have the real levels of power to present the myths to the audience as a real-life fact and shape the view of audience on the Olympic Games. Developing this issue, Puijk (1997) explored the effect of the 1994 Lillehammer Olympics on creating the image of the host country, and Stevenson (1997), on the basis of the analysis of 2000 Olympics staging, presumed that mythology connected with the games will have dramatic impact on world vision of Sydney as a city and a culture. These studies have provided comprehensive arguments that mega sporting events gave the ability and power to create and shape identities, cultures, attitudes, adding to the research of the marketing mediated sports particular social and economic significance.

New trends in Olympics marketing

It was shortly mentioned above that there is a growing trend towards changing the format of Olympic Games advertising which provides the ground to assert that millions of dollars spent by the corporate sponsors for advertising in the framework of Olympic Games do not guarantee a considerable profit from their investments. To succeed in the actual environment, more elaborate strategies are needed.

Today, a growing number of big companies which traditionally spent substantial amounts to associate their brands with the image and idea of Olympic Games ask the question if the Games are worth it. The most recent example is provided by Xerox Company which decided to cease its 40-year Olympic games sponsoring history. Olympics 2004 in Athens, which took 42 million euros of the Company's investments are the last games funded by Xerox (Dedyukhina, 2004). Instead, the company plans to direct its resources into other initiatives aimed at drawing customers' attention and loyalty.

Numerous data provided on Olympic sponsorship indicate that large-scale funding of Olympics is becoming less efficient for promotion of the companies that it had been earlier. The results of the poll carried out by American Dynamic Logic Company (Dedyukhina, 2004) show that only 25% of American viewers and only 12% of Europeans pay considerable attention to the commercials connected to the Olympic Games. Specialists insist with increasing faith that major companies have to review their traditional strategies of sponsorship. To make the financial assistance to the Games bring a solid commercial return, these companies need to elaborate more targeted marketing steps that take into consideration not only geographic differences between Europeans and Americans, for instance, but also the differences in interests of various consumer groups.

Over the last few decades, many major global companies have made huge investments targeted on associating their brand with the Olympic Games. For instance, Coca-Cola spent $145 million on advertising and sponsorship programs in 2004 Olympics in Athens (International Olympic Committee Official Website). Other official sponsors of the Games, such as McDonalds, Kodak, Samsung, Panasonic, Adidas and Visa in total spent $1.3 billion during the same games. The games enjoy such popularity with big corporations because these corporations encounter growing difficulties in introducing themselves to the mass audience and get feedback on their advertisement. Some estimates show that average Americans are subject to about 3000 commercials per day. This information overload causes growing resistance to perceiving marketing and advertising information. Therefore, Olympic Games are viewed as a perfect tool for delivering advertisement to millions of viewers worldwide. This argument is supported by enormous audience and great number of replays of the Games over the limited timeline. However, with increased commercial exploitation of the Olympic Games, it becomes evident hat not each sponsor is successful in benefiting from its Olympics-related promotion. For example, Samsung's promotional campaign in Sydney turned out to be surprisingly ineffective. Their $40 million of advertising investments returned in only 1 billion dollars of income. Very often other firms are even less lucky. For example, during the winter 1994 Olympics in Lillehammer, 43% of interviewed people failed in correctly name the Olympic sponsors. They mixed up Pepsi with Coke and American Express with Visa.

There emerges another aspect of the problem. It becomes evident that being official Olympic sponsor is not necessary to gain benefits from the Games' image. An entire parasite movement, or ambush marketing, has emerged, when major companies put their advertisement in major places near the venue of the Games or during the Games without paying sponsorship fees. As it was mentioned, this phenomenon is called parasite, or ambush, marketing. As sponsorship of the Games becomes increasingly lucrative, increasing number of companies create association with their company's products and the Games. The term of ambush marketing is used in marketing industry to denote the strategy of a company, which is not an official sponsor of the event, but, because of the fact that its promotional company is focused on the Games or any other event, creates an illusion of being one of the official sponsors. For instance, in 1996 Olympics in Atlanta, Nike Company located its slogans outside but very close to sporting arenas of the Games, which hampered the efficiency of Adidas, an official sponsor's, promotional campaign.

The scale of such abuses has so greatly grown up that the organizers of the Games had to take to extraordinary measures. For instance, during Olympics in Sydney, Pepsi cans were taken from the viewers by the organizers, since Coca-Cola was an official sponsor of the event. Athens organizers took unprecedented steps and protected rights of their sponsors by removing 10,000 billboards from the city, averting in such way potential ambush marketers and leaving space only for their official sponsors. This action cost Olympics organizers 750,000 euros.

Conclusions

One of the main reasons of inefficiency of Olympic Games is that companies have not decided definitely on their expectations from sponsoring Olympics. Sponsorship can prove effective only in case when the company hits its potential targeted audience that relates itself to the Olympics and associates itself with them. Sponsors' attempts to attract consumers around the world are useless as long as their image and activity is conceived differently in various parts of the world. For instance, there is no point in trying to influence American and European people in the same way with Olympic advertisement. According to the same Dynamic Logic poll data (Dedyukhina, 2004), only 58% of Americans and 39% of Europeans understand that it is predominantly due to sponsors that Olympic games take place and can be broadcasted on TV. Another example is the result of the same poll where 66% of American people and only 51% of Europeans attach particular importance to advertisement with the Olympic logos.

This fact can be accounted to cultural and lifestyle differences between Europe and America. First of all, in general terms Americans tend to be more susceptible to promotion and advertising techniques. Secondly, Americans practice a healthy lifestyle cult, which results in elevated interest in sporting events and more involvement in them. The third factor contributing to the popularity of the Olympic games in USA is strong belief in victory of American team. The games are of bigger interest to Americans because their team is more likely to win more medals. Thus, they are more positive toward Olympics and everything connected with them, commercials in particular.

Moreover, it is calculated that private investments in Olympics always turn out to be more effective than the public ones. For instance, Olympic Games in Los Angeles, the most successful games in terms of commerce, gained $335 million mostly due to private investments. Other examples are 1996 Atlanta, 1992 Barcelona and 2000 Sydney Games that were most efficient in the financial return and funded primarily by private capital. To the contrast, in 2004 Athens games, where ratio of public and private capital was 3:1, were not paid off and Greece still has the problems with its foreign debt. Future 2008 Games in Beijing will cost about $28–30 million, which will be absolute record in cost for all Olympic history. It is very unlikely that the organizers of the Games will manage to cover such expenses with revenues from the Olympics.

Therefore it is evident that the myth of high effectiveness of Olympic Games doesn't correspond to today's realities. To benefit from Olympic advertisement, development of more sophisticated strategies is necessary. Mere putting advertisement on billboards and transmitting commercials with Olympic symbols on TV is not longer enough. It is indicative that some companies like Samsung gave launched a special Wireless Olympic Works program. Within this program, more than 14,000 mobile phones are distributed at no cost to the members of Olympic committee, mass media and politicians for them to be able to receive the information on the Games online. In this way the company acquires loyalty of different consumer groups.

These improved strategies are likely to strengthen the factor of sponsorship in the business field. Sponsorship and merchandising will become the major factor of growth on American sports market along with a global one. It is calculated that sponsorship spending is to increase by 8% a year, while broadcasting right will enter the period of recession due to already high inflation on TV broadcast rights.

The conclusion drawn from the information above is ambiguous one. From the one hand, the economic impact of the Olympic Games is enormous and can transcend the very event itself. Thus, according to Lawrence Davidson, professor of business economics and public policy in IU's Kelley School of Business, having done several studies on economic impacts of other important sporting events, such as The Brickyard 400, Pan American Games, the Indianapolis 500 and the Final Four of the NCAA Basketball Tournament, came to conclusion that most people are aware of huge economic influence of the Olympic Games due to global audience, but also, there are serious long-term impacts which are often overlooked until the Games are finished. "The Olympics make people aware of your country and what's there. It's a way to make a statement to the world that your community is a destination," he said (Stevenson, 1997).

From the other hand, new trends, discussed above, illustrate some inefficiency of traditional advertising methods in the Olympic Games are obvious. Therefore, there is a need to fill the gap in theoretical studies on the issue of Olympic promotion strategies with the finding of a new promotion, advertising and sponsorship methods and approaches. Taking into account urgent need for a brand-new vision of marketing, due to advancement of new technologies and complication of marketing instruments, such necessity is more than obvious.

References

1. Dedyukhina A. (August 30, 2004) Focusing the Olympic Flame. Expert, #31 (431)
2. Eastman S.T. (2000) Research in Media Promotion. Lawrence Erlbaum Associates. Place of Publication: Mahwah, NJ. 231.
3. Farrell T. B. (1989). "Media rhetoric as social drama: The Winter Olympics of 1984". Critical Studies in Mass Communication, 6, 158–182.
4. Fortune. (1996, July 22). Fortune's Olympic fact sheet, 58–59.
5. Goldstein M. (1996, July 1). "Analysis and commentary". Business Week, 33.
6. Izod J. (1996). Television sport and the sacrificial hero. Journal of Sport & Social Issues, 22, 173–193.
7. McAllister M. P. (1997). "Sponsorship, globalization, and the Summer Olympics". In K. T. Frith (Ed.), Undressing the ad: Reading culture in advertising (pp. 35–63). New York: Peter Lang.

8. McAllister M. P. (1998, April 2). Super Bowl advertising as commercial celebration. Paper presented at the annual meeting of the Broadcast Education Association, Las Vegas, NV.

9. O'Neal M., Finch P., Hamilton J., & Hammonds K. (1987). Nothing sells like sports. Business Week, 48–53.

10. Puijk R. (1997). Global spotlights on Lillehammer. Belfordshire, England: John Libby.

11. Stevenson D. (1997). Olympic arts: Sydney 2000 and the cultural Olympiad. International Review for the Sociology of Sport, 32(2), 227–238.

12. Verdier, M., and the ITU, (June/July, 1996.) The Olympic Games and the Media. Olympic Review Vol xxv-9

13. Wenner L. A. (Ed.). (1998). MediaSport. New York: Routledge.

14. International Olympic Committee Official Website www.olympic.org/uk/organisation/facts/introduction/index_uk.asp

Source: Lee, Johnny, K., 2005. "Marketing and Promotion of the Olympic Games." *The Sport Journal*, Volume 21, U.S. Sport Academy. ISSN 1543–9518

Aside from the learning that takes place during the socialization process, values represent another important aspect of any culture. **Values** are widely held beliefs that affirm what is desirable in a culture. Whereas freedom is often an American priority, countries like Sweden are often more attuned to openness. America's main belief is rights for all through freedom, while Sweden's main concern is with all being accepted and resolving issues through other means such as working together to come to a solution.[20] Swedish citizens want to be able to have security and trust in their country. Several of the core values that reflect U.S. culture are shown in Table 4.4, and most have remained consistent as well as prominent over time. Can you think of some that may have changed over time?

Some of the core American values listed in Table 4.4 have intimate ties to sports participation in the United States. Obviously, the last value mentioned, fitness and health, relates directly to our preoccupation with participating in sports. The activity value has a direct impact on the way Americans spend their leisure time, including sports participation. Likewise, achievement and success is a theme that is continually underscored as consumers participate in sports.

Although they are not directly related, other core U.S. values may tangentially affect sports participation. For example, the value of individualism and being oneself may manifest itself in the types of sports or activities in which we choose to participate. Many sports, such as surfing, hang-gliding, climbing, and hiking, allow a consumer to express his or her own

Table 4.4 Core American values	
Core American value	Descriptor
Achievement and success	Sense of accomplishment
Activity	Being active or involved
Efficiency and practicality	Saves time and effort; solves problems
Progress	Continuous improvement
Material comfort	Money; status
Individualism	Being themselves
Freedom	Democratic beliefs
External conformity	Adaptation to society
Humanitarianism	Overcoming adversity: supporting
Charity	Giving to others
Youthfulness	Looking and acting young
Fitness and health	Exercise and diet

Source: Leon Shiffman and Leslie Kanuk, *Consumer Behavior*, 5th ed. (Upper Saddle River, NJ: Prentice Hall, 1994)

personality. Youthfulness is also expressed through participation in sport as consumers keep "young at heart" by staying active. Consumers may also participate in sporting events to help raise money for charities. One of the most visible charitable influences in sport today is developing breast cancer awareness. Athletes in professional, collegiate, and even youth levels will often be seen wearing pink gear to show their support for those fighting the disease.

Social class

Throughout history, people within various cultural systems have been grouped together based on social class. Whether it is the "haves" versus the "have nots" or the "upper class" versus the "lower class," social class distinctions have always been present. **Social class** is defined as the homogeneous division of people in a society sharing similar values, lifestyles, and behaviors that can be hierarchically categorized.

Important to this definition is the idea that individuals are divided into homogeneous classes, or strata. Typically, social strata are described in terms of a hierarchy ranging from lower to upper class. Consumers are grouped into the

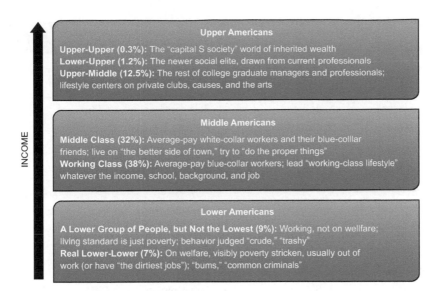

Figure 4.8
The structure of social class

Source: Richard P. Coleman, "The Continuing Significance of Social Class to Marketing," *Journal of Consumer Research*, vol. 10 (December 1983), 265–280

various social classes based on the interaction of a number of factors. Occupation, income, and education are usually considered the three primary determinants of social class. In addition, possessions (e.g., home and car) and affiliations (e.g., club membership, professional organizations, and community organizations) are also believed to be important factors.

Although researchers agree that there are distinct social strata, there is little agreement on how many categories there are in the hierarchy. For instance, some researchers believe a seven-tiered structure (as illustrated in Figure 4.8) explains social class in the United States. Others, however, believe in a simple two-tiered system (i.e., upper and lower).

Regardless of the class structure, sports marketers are interested in social class as a predictor of whether consumers will participate in sports and, if they do participate, the types of sports in which they might participate. Table 4.5 shows the relationship between average household income and participation in 22 selected sports activities.

Other research has shown that more than one in four Americans would like to have more time for leisure activities such as bowling and softball. A disproportionate number of those people who want more leisure time are lower-income, blue-collar workers.[21] In addition, the Rand Corporation conducted a study finding that sport participation gaps among youth exist between lower-income

Activity	Household income (in thousands)	Activity	Household income (in thousands)
Basketball	$58	Roller hockey	$73
Bowling	$60	Running/jogging	$63
BMX bicycling	$49	Sailing	$82
Day hiking	$66	Saltwater fishing	$64
Downhill skiing	$83	Snorkeling	$83
Fitness bicycling	$71	Snowboarding	$63
Fitness swimming	$69	Soccer	$59
Fitness walking	$66	Surfing	$74
Football (tackle)	$54	Tennis	$68
Golf	$80	Tent camping	$58
Horseback riding	$65	Yoga/t'ai chi	$68

Table 4.5 Household incomes for select sports and activities

Source: Sports & Fitness Industry Association, www.sfia.org

family and those in the middle and upper class. More specifically, only 52 percent of lower-income families indicated their children (between 6th and 12th grade) participate in sports compared with 66 percent of middle- and upper-class families.[22]

Reference groups

Classic advertising slogans like "Be Like Mike" (Michael Jordan) and "Witness" (LeBron James) illustrate the power of reference group influence. More formally, **reference groups** are individuals who influence the information, attitudes, and behaviors of other group members. Sports participation is heavily influenced through the various reference groups to which an individual may belong. In these classic advertising campaigns, hordes of children have identified with and created an association between athletes, representing a wide array of sports, and their respective sport products.

These types of reference groups, which have an impact on our participation in sports as well as on our purchase of sports products, are called aspirational groups. Although many famous athletes recognize the influence they can have on children, others refuse to accept the responsibility that reference groups can influence consumer demands (e.g., the now-retired Charles Barkley of the NBA stating, "I am not a role model"; entertainer Rihanna stating "I can't really say I'm a role model").

ARTICLE 4.2
SPORTS MARKETING HALL OF FAME

The Babe: Babe Didrikson Zaharias

Mildred "Babe" Didrikson Zaharias was known by sports fans all over as the "best at everything." Her early success as an all-around athlete began as she played on basketball, softball, and track and field teams, named the Golden Cyclones, sponsored by the Employers Casualty Insurance Company. Babe represented the Golden Cyclones by herself in the 1932 Olympic track and field qualifying trials and entered eight of the 10 events. She ended up winning six of the events, and her legend was born. As an amateur, Babe won two gold medals and one silver in track and field events at the 1932 Olympics. She began a professional career that included stints in basketball, baseball, boxing, football, and hockey. Didrikson's most impressive sport of all, however, was golf. Returning to amateur status in golf, Babe ran up an unprecedented 17 straight wins, including a victory in the 1947 British Women's Amateur – never before won by an American. In 1949, she was one of the founding members of the LPGA.

In addition to her impressive athletic achievements, Babe was the consummate sports promoter and marketer. For example, she participated in publicity stunts such as harness racing and pitched against New York Yankee Joe DiMaggio. She published a book of golfing tips, had her own line of golf clubs through Spalding Sporting Goods, and appeared in movies such as the classic *Pat and Mike*. Through her example and performance, Babe Didrikson Zaharias legitimized women's sports. Her excellence in so many sports made her a marketer's dream. Just imagine her today.

Source: Elizabeth Lynn, *Babe Didrikson Zaharias: Champion Athlete* (New York, Chelsea House, 1989)

Celebrity athletes are not the only individuals who have an impact on sports participation. Friends and coworkers are also considered a **primary reference group** because of the frequent contact we have with these individuals and the power they have to influence our decisions. Many of us participate in sports because friends and coworkers urged us to join their team, play a set of tennis, or hit the links. Primary reference groups may exert a powerful influence among high-school athletes as participation continues to grow at this level.

Family

Another primary reference group that has one of the greatest influences on sports participation is the family. As you might guess, family plays a considerable role because sports marketers target families as spectators. But how does **family influence** affect participation in sport? Consider families of friends or your own family. It is common for family members to exert a great deal of influence on one another with respect to decisions about sports participation

Photo 4.6
Girls' sport participation is eroding traditional gender roles

Source: Shutterstock.com, Lipik Stock Media

and activities. For example, children may either directly or indirectly get parents involved in a sport (e.g., inline skating, soccer, or biking) so the entire family can participate together. Conversely, parents may urge their kids to get off the couch and get involved in sports.

Traditionally, fathers have had the greatest impact on their children's (mostly their sons) sports participation. Dad might have encouraged junior to play organized football because he did or go fishing because his father took him fishing. Of course, these scenarios are vanishing, as is the traditional family structure.

Long gone are the days of the mom, dad, two kids, and a dog. Long gone is the *Leave It to Beaver* mentality where fathers are breadwinners and mothers are homemakers. Today's modern family structure typically includes dual-income families with no kids, divorced parents, single parents, or parents who are dually employed with kids.

Each of these modern family structures may influence participation in sports for both adults and children. For instance, dual-income families with no kids may have the time and the money to participate in a variety of "country club" sports. However, single or divorced parents may face time and financial constraints. Sports products such as the "10-minute workout" and 30-minute aerobic classes are targeted to working moms on the move. In addition, the tremendous increase in sales of home exercise equipment may be traced back to the constraints of the modern family structure.

ARTICLE 4.3

HIGH SCHOOL SPORTS PARTICIPATION INCREASES FOR 28TH STRAIGHT YEAR, NEARS 8 MILLION MARK

by NFHS on September 06, 2017

Led by the largest one-year increase in girls participation in 16 years, the overall number of participants in high school sports increased for the 28th consecutive year in 2016–17, according to the annual High School Athletics Participation Survey conducted by the National Federation of State High School Associations (NFHS).

Based on figures from the 51 NFHS member state high school associations, which includes the District of Columbia, the number of participants in high school sports reached an all-time high of 7,963,535. The increase of 94,635 participants from 2015–16 is the largest one-year jump in overall participation since the 2008–09 school year.

Thanks to increases in all of the top 10 participatory sports, the number of girls participants reached an all-time high of 3,400,297. The increase of 75,971 from the previous year is the largest one-year jump since the 2000–01 sports participation report.

Competitive spirit registered the largest increase among girls sports with an additional 18,712 participants, followed by outdoor track and field (8,508), volleyball (8,470), soccer (6,810) and lacrosse (5,423).

"As we celebrate the 45th anniversary of Title IX this year, this report on girls participation numbers underscores the significance of that important decision in 1972," said Bob Gardner, NFHS executive director. "It is great to see an ever-increasing number of girls taking advantage of that opportunity to compete in high school sports."

Seven of the top 10 boys sports registered increases from the previous year, led by soccer (9,912), outdoor track and field (9,003), and cross country (8,580). Overall participation for boys in 2016–17 was 4,563,238, an increase of 18,664 from the previous year.

Participation in 11-player football was down 25,901 from the previous year, although the numbers in 6- and 8-player football were up from the 2015–16 season. The overall number of participants in football (6, 8, 9 and 11 player) in 2016–17 was 1,086,748, down 25,503 from the 1,112,251 in the 2015–16 season.

While the number of participants in high school football declined, the number of schools offering the sport increased by 52 schools in 11-player – from 14,047 to 14,099 – and by nine schools in 6-, 8- and 9-player – from 1,349 to 1,358.

With 14,099 high schools offering 11-player football, the decrease of 25,901 participants amounts to fewer than two individuals (1.8) per school, and an overall decrease of 2.5 percent.

Football remains the No. 1 participatory sport for boys at the high school level by a large margin. Track and field is second with 600,136 participants, followed by basketball (550,305), baseball (491,790) and soccer (450,234).

"While we are concerned when any sport experiences a decline in participation, the numbers do not substantiate that schools are dropping the sport of football," Gardner said. "The NFHS and its member state high school associations have worked hard to reduce the risk of injury in high school football, and we are pleased at the continued strength of the sport across the country."

Amazingly, this year's survey indicated that more than 60 different sports were offered by high schools nationwide, from judo and kayaking, to fencing and rugby, to snowboarding and rodeo. Some of the more popular non-traditional high school sports were badminton (17,184), archery (9,767), crew (5,179) and fencing (4,100).

The top 10 states by participants remained the same; however, Florida moved ahead of Michigan to seventh position this year. Texas and California topped the list again with 834,558 and 800,364 participants, respectively, followed by New York (367,849), Illinois (341,387), Ohio (340,146), Pennsylvania (319,153), Florida (310,567), Michigan (295,647), New Jersey (283,655) and Minnesota (239,289).

The participation survey has been compiled since 1971 by the NFHS through numbers it receives from its member associations. The top 10 sports for boys and girls and the year-by-year participation totals are listed below in Figure 4.9. The complete 2016–17 High School Athletics Participation Survey is available at www.nfhs.org/ParticipationStatistics/ParticipationStatistics/

Children's ability to participate in organized sport may also be hampered by the single-parent family, although women are increasingly taking on the traditional male sex role of coach, sports participant, and sports enthusiast. Also, fathers are increasingly encouraging daughters to participate in sport, another sign of changing sex roles.

Situational factors

Now that we have looked at how psychological and sociological factors influence the participant decision-making process, let us turn to situational factors.

TEN MOST POPULAR BOYS PROGRAMS

	Schools			Participants	
1.	Basketball	18,214	1.	Football – 11-Player	1,057,407
2.	Track and Field – Outdoor	16,299	2.	Track and Field – Outdoor	600,136
3.	Baseball	15,979	3.	Basketball	550,305
4.	Cross Country	15,087	4.	Baseball	491,790
5.	Football – 11-Player	15,099	5.	Soccer	450,234
6.	Golf	13,223	6.	Cross Country	266,271
7.	Soccer	12,188	7.	Wrestling	244,804
8.	Wrestling	10,629	8.	Tennis	158,171
9.	Tennis	9,725	9.	Golf	141,466
10.	Swimming & Diving	7,342	10.	Swimming & Diving	138,364

TEN MOST POPULAR GIRLS PROGRAMS

	Schools			Participants	
1.	Basketball	17,934	1.	Track and Field – Outdoor	494,477
2.	Track and Field – Outdoor	16,658	2.	Vollyball	444,779
3.	Vollyball	15,992	3.	Basketball	430,368
4.	Softball – fast Pitch	15,440	4.	Soccer	388,339
5.	Cross Country	14,880	5.	Softball – fast Pitch	367,405
6.	Soccer	11,823	6.	Cross Country	226,039
7.	Tennis	10,121	7.	Swimming & Diving	170,797
8.	Golf	10,076	8.	Tennis	158,171
9.	Swimming & Diving	7,721	9.	Competitive Spirit Squads	144,243
10.	Competitive Spirit Squads	6,541	10.	Lacrosse	93,473

Figure 4.9

www.nfhs.org/articles/high-school-sports-participation-increases-for-28th-straight-year-nears-8-million-mark/

Unlike psychological and sociological factors, which are relatively permanent in nature, situational factors are temporary aspects that affect participation. For instance, the culture in which we make our participation decision is considered a long-term environmental factor. Likewise, personality is a set of consistent responses that we make to our environment. However, **situational factors** are those temporary factors within a particular time or place that influence the participation decision-making process.[23]

Consider the following examples of situational influences on **participant behavior**. Your best friend is in town, and, although you do not normally enjoy golfing, you do so anyway to spend time with your friend. You typically run five miles per day, but an unexpected ice storm puts a halt to your daily exercise routine. You have to study for final exams, so you settle for a 30-minute workout versus your normal 75 minutes. Each of these examples represents a different type of situational influence on participant decision making.

Consumer researchers have identified five situational influences that affect decision making. The five primary types of situational influences include physical surroundings; social surroundings; time; reason for participation, or task definition; and antecedent states. Let us briefly look at each in the context of participant decision making.

Physical surroundings

The location, weather, and physical aspects of the participation environment make up the **physical surroundings**. In sports participation, the physical surroundings play an extremely important role in decision making. When the weather outside is good, people who might not participate in sports normally do so. Likewise, the weather can have a situational influence on where we choose to participate. The runner described in the earlier example may decide to jog indoors rather than skip the workout. In addition to the weather, location might influence our decision to participate. For example, nonskiers may be tempted to try skiing if they are attending a sales conference in Vail or Aspen. Other aspects of the physical environment, such as a perfectly groomed championship golf course or scenic biking trail, can also influence our participation decisions in a positive manner. From the perspective of the sports marketer, any attempt to increase participation must carefully consider the physical surroundings. Even the worst athletes in the world enjoy playing in nice facilities.

Social surroundings

The effect of other people on a participant during participation in a sport is another situational influence, called **social surroundings**. In other words, who we are with may have a positive or negative impact on participation decisions. The earlier golf example presented a case where the presence of a friend caused the person to participate. Likewise, golfing in the presence of unfamiliar coworkers at a corporate outing can be an unpleasant and intimidating experience. In this case, participation might be avoided altogether.

Crowds represent another social situation that is usually avoided. For example, if the tennis courts or golf courses are full, you might decide to participate in another sport that day. Biking and hiking represent two other activities where crowds are usually perceived to have a negative impact on participation. In other words, people generally do not like to bike or hike in large crowds. However, some people may take pleasure when participating among large crowds. Consider, for example, runners who feel motivated when participating in events with thousands of other runners.

Time

The effect of the presence or absence of **time** is the third type of situational influence. In today's society, there are increasing time pressures on all of us. Changes in family structure, giving rise to dual-income families and single parents, have made time for participation in sports even scarcer. Slightly more than half of all U.S. residents under the age of 50 complain of a lack

Photo 4.7
Time needed for marathon training may limit participation

Source: Shutterstock.com, Suzanne Tucker

of leisure time, and this percentage is even higher for dual-income families. How many times have you heard someone say, "I don't have the time to work out today"?

Because of time constraints, sports marketers are concentrating on ways to make our participation activities more enjoyable and more time effective. For example, few of us can afford to take five hours out of our day to enjoy 18 holes of golf. As such, golfing associations are always communicating ways to speed up play. Similarly, few of us feel that we have the time to drive to the gym each day. The marketers' response to this was the development of the shorter, higher-intensity workout benefitting the enormous home health equipment industry.

ARTICLE 4.4
SITUATIONAL FACTORS SHAPE OUR NEW YEAR'S RESOLUTIONS

The most popular 2019 New Year's resolution in every U.S. state

The start of a new calendar year is a time for reflection and new beginnings. It prompts us to rethink how we make choices and spend our time, and helps us re-prioritize what matters most to us in the near future.

Even if you're a proponent of living every month with intention whether it's the start of another year or not, New Year's is still a great reminder to do so.

Life gets busy, so each year it's helpful to reflect on where you're headed and where you'd like to go. If those two destinations differ, then it may be a great opportunity for you to select a New Year's resolution and set your new course – you and your health deserve it.

At Vitagene, we're focused on helping every individual live a healthy life by providing information about their unique genetic makeup.

There is so much that goes into one's well-being and physical needs, including their DNA and lifestyle. With that in mind, we wanted to learn more about Americans' plans for health and happiness in 2019.

Methodology

To find this out, we conducted a survey of over 1,450 Americans across every state and D.C. We asked them which New Year's resolution they plan to set for 2019, as well as which types of resolutions are easiest and most difficult to keep.

We also asked how long they've typically been able to keep resolutions. After analyzing our data, we were able to determined the most popular New Year's resolution in each state and get an overall picture of Americans' 2019 plans.

The most popular 2019 New Year's resolution in every state

When looking at the results by state, we found that there is significant variation across the country.

The resolutions that appear as the top choice in at least one state are 'exercise to get in shape' (18 states), 'diet to lose weight' (16), 'save money' (9), 'eat healthier in general' (5), 'learn a new skill' (1), 'get a (new) job' (1), and 'something for self care' (1).

Interestingly, it is more common for states in the South or Northeast to want to save money compared to those in the West or Midwest, which are more focused on exercise or dieting.

The states that are most unlike any other are Wyoming, Minnesota, and South Carolina, which were the only ones to select 'learn a new skill,' 'something for self care,' and 'get a (new) job,' respectively.

All other states share their most popular New Year's resolution with other states in the nation.

Which states are best and worst at keeping resolutions?

We also wanted to see how long Americans are able to keep their resolutions and if there's any variation based on location – our data shows that there definitely is.

Based on how many locals reported that they could keep them for a year or more, South Dakota (37.5%), Alaska (35.3%), Minnesota (31.0%), Maryland (31.0%) and Iowa (28.6%) proved to be the best at holding onto their New Year's goals.

THE MOST POPULAR 2019
New Year's Resolutions

AL save money	KY diet to lose weight	ND exercise to get in shape
AK exercise to get in shape	LA save money	OH diet to lose weight
AZ exercise to get in shape	ME save money	OK exercise to get in shape
AR exercise to get in shape	MD save money	OR exercise to get in shape
CA diet to lose weight	MA eat healthier in general	PA diet to lose weight
CO exercise to get in shape	MI exercise to get in shape	RI exercise to get in shape
CT diet to lose weight	MN something for self care	SC get a job, or get a new job
DE save money	MS save money	SD diet to lose weight
DC diet to lose weight	MO exercise to get in shape	TN diet to lose weight
FL diet to lose weight	MT eat healthier in general	TX exercise to get in shape
GA eat healthier in general	NE diet to lose weight	UT exercise to get in shape
HI exercise to get in shape	NV diet to lose weight	VT exercise to get in shape
ID exercise to get in shape	NH exercise to get in shape	VA eat healthier in general
IL diet to lose weight	NJ diet to lose weight	WA save money
IN save money	NM diet to lose weight	WV diet to lose weight
IA diet to lose weight	NY eat healthier in general	WI exercise to get in shape
KS exercise to get in shape	NC save money	WY learn a new skill

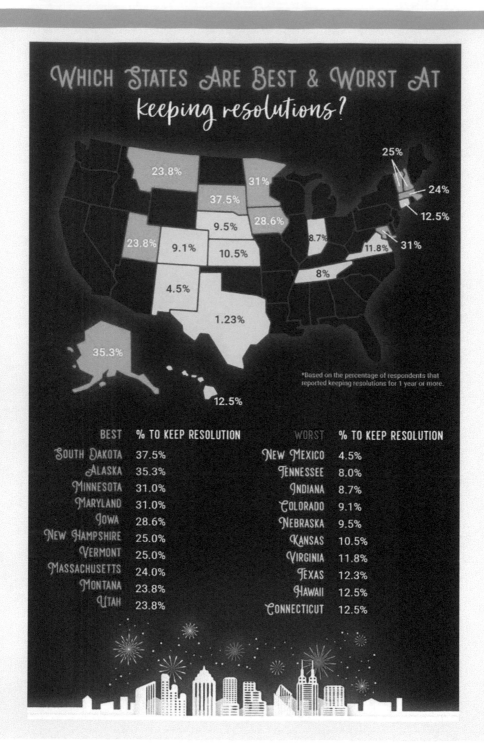

WHICH STATES ARE BEST & WORST AT keeping resolutions?

23.8%
31%
37.5%
9.5%
28.6%
23.8% 9.1% 10.5%
8.7%
11.8% 31%
8%
4.5%
1.23%
35.3%
12.5%

25%
24%
12.5%

*Based on the percentage of respondents that reported keeping resolutions for 1 year or more.

BEST	% TO KEEP RESOLUTION	WORST	% TO KEEP RESOLUTION
SOUTH DAKOTA	37.5%	NEW MEXICO	4.5%
ALASKA	35.3%	TENNESSEE	8.0%
MINNESOTA	31.0%	INDIANA	8.7%
MARYLAND	31.0%	COLORADO	9.1%
IOWA	28.6%	NEBRASKA	9.5%
NEW HAMPSHIRE	25.0%	KANSAS	10.5%
VERMONT	25.0%	VIRGINIA	11.8%
MASSACHUSETTS	24.0%	TEXAS	12.3%
MONTANA	23.8%	HAWAII	12.5%
UTAH	23.8%	CONNECTICUT	12.5%

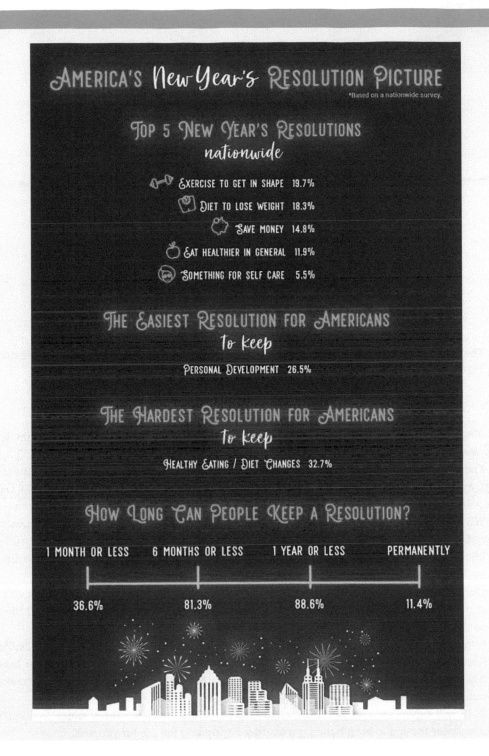

America's *New Year's* Resolution Picture
*Based on a nationwide survey.

Top 5 New Year's Resolutions
nationwide

- Exercise to get in shape 19.7%
- Diet to lose weight 18.3%
- Save money 14.8%
- Eat healthier in general 11.9%
- Something for self care 5.5%

The Easiest Resolution for Americans
to keep

Personal Development 26.5%

The Hardest Resolution for Americans
to keep

Healthy Eating / Diet Changes 32.7%

How Long Can People Keep a Resolution?

1 MONTH OR LESS	6 MONTHS OR LESS	1 YEAR OR LESS	PERMANENTLY
36.6%	81.3%	88.6%	11.4%

The five states that have the toughest time doing so are New Mexico (4.5%), Tennessee (8.0%), Indiana (8.7%), Colorado (9.1%), and Nebraska (9.5%).

America's New Year's resolution picture

Finally, we decided to zoom out and look at our survey results nationwide. We found that the top resolutions by state align with the national picture very closely.

The five most popular New Year's resolutions are 'exercise to get in shape' (19.7%), 'diet to lose weight' (18.3%), 'save money' (14.8%), 'eat healthier in general' (11.9%), and 'something for self care' (5.5%).

We also asked respondents what they found to be the easiest and most difficult types of resolutions to keep.

26.5% said that personal development resolutions, such as learning a hobby or reading more, have been the easiest to keep going.

On the flip side, 32.7% said that healthy eating or diet changes were the most difficult to hold onto. This is a good reminder of how important it is for everyone to understand their genetic background and find the diet that is right for their body.

In general, our data shows how difficult it can be in general to keep a resolution. 36.6% of Americans report that they generally are only able to keep theirs for one month or less. 81.3% are able to keep them for six months or less, and only 11.4% say they're able to make permanent changes.

2019 will be an exciting year for many reasons – the most important of which is that it's another year for you to keep building a healthy, happy, and full life for yourself.

New Year's resolutions are a great way to jumpstart that process, and we hope our survey results helped you to decide on yours, or at least got the wheels turning for you.

*Source:*https://vitagene.com/blog/most-popular-2019-new-years-resolution/, December 19, 2019, accessed September 24, 2020

Reason for participation, or task definition

Another situational influence, **task definition**, refers to the reasons that occasion the need for consumers to participate in a sport. In other words, the reason the consumer participates affects the decision-making process. Some participants may use Jet-Skis or scuba dive once a year while they are on vacation. Other consumers may participate in a fantasy baseball camp once in a lifetime.

These examples represent special occasions or situational reasons for participating. Moreover, the participation occasion may dictate the sports apparel and equipment we choose. For example, a consumer participating in a competitive softball league might wear cleats, long softball pants, and batting gloves. However, the recreational participant playing softball at the company picnic would only bring a glove.

Antecedent states

Temporary physiological and mood states that a consumer brings to the participant situation are **antecedent states**. In certain situations, people may feel worn out and lack energy. This physiological state may motivate some people to work out and become reenergized at the end of a long day of work. However, feeling tired can elicit another response in others, such as "I'm too tired to do anything today." Promotion to combat these negative antecedent states can be seen in the following link, which was the Union of European Football Association's "Get Active Campaign": www.youtube.com/watch?v=uZX14W4rVCU.

Certainly, other situational mood states, such as being "stressed out," can activate the need to participate in sports or exercise. Yet feeling tired or hungry can cause us to decide against participation. At the very least, our mood can influence our decision to ride or walk 18 holes of golf.

It is important to remember that antecedent means "prior to" or "before." Therefore, the mood or physiological condition influences our decision making. For example, people who are experiencing bad moods may turn to sports to lift their spirits. Contrast this with those who feel great because they have just participated in a sporting event.

Summary

The focus of Chapter 4 is on understanding the sports participant as a consumer of sports. Sports marketers are not only concerned with consumers who watch sporting events but also with the millions of consumers who participate in a variety of sports. To successfully market to sports participants, sports marketers must understand everything they can about these consumers and their consumption behaviors. Participant consumption behavior is defined as the actions performed when searching for, participating in, and evaluating the sports activities that consumers believe will satisfy their needs.

To simplify the complex nature of participant consumption behavior, a model was developed. The model of participant consumption behavior consists of four major components: the participant decision-making process, internal or psychological factors, external or sociological factors, and situational variables. The participant decision-making process is the central focus of the model of participant consumption behavior. It explains how consumers make decisions about whether to participate in sports and in which sports to participate. The decision-making process is slightly different for each of us and is influenced by a host of factors. However, the basis of the decision-making process is a five-step procedure that consumers progress through as they make decisions. These five steps are problem recognition, information search, evaluation of alternatives, participation, and post-participation evaluation. The complexity of this process is highly dependent on how important the decision is to participants and how much experience consumers have had making similar decisions.

Internal or psychological factors are those things that influence our decision-making process. These psychological factors include personality, motivation, perception, learning, and attitudes. Personality is a set of consistent responses we make to our environment. Our personality can play a role in which sports we choose to participate in or whether we participate in any sports. For example, an aggressive personality type may be most likely to participate in boxing or hockey. Motivation is the reason we participate in sports. Some of the more common reasons we participate in sports are for personal improvement, appreciation of sport, or social facilitation. The strength of our motives to participate in sports is referred to as sport involvement. Another important psychological factor that influences our participation decisions is perception. Perception influences our image of the various sports and their participants as well as shaping our attitudes toward sports participation. Learning also affects our participant behavior. We learn whether to participate in sports because we are rewarded or punished by our participation (behavioral theories), because we perceive sports as a way to achieve our goals (cognitive theories), and because we watch others participating (social theories). A final internal or psychological factor that directly influences our sports participation decisions is attitudes. Attitudes are defined as learned thoughts, feelings, and behaviors toward some given object (in this case, sports participation). Our feelings (affective component of attitude) and beliefs (cognitive component) about sports participation certainly play a major role in determining our participation (behavioral component).

External or sociological factors also influence the participant decision-making process. These factors include culture, social class, reference groups, and family. Culture is defined as the learned values, beliefs, language, traditions, and symbols shared by people and passed down from generation to generation. The values held by people within a society are a most important determinant of culture. Some of the core American values that influence participation in sports include achievement and success, activity, individualism, youthfulness, and fitness and health. Social class is another important determinant of participant decision making. Most people erroneously associate social class only with income. Our social class is also determined by occupation, education, and affiliations. Another important sociological factor is the influence of reference groups. Reference groups are individuals who influence the information, attitudes, and behaviors of other group members. For example, our friends may affect our decision to participate in a variety of recreational sports and activities. One reference group that has a great deal of influence over our attitudes and participation behavior is our family.

The final component of the model of participant behavior is situational factors. Every decision that we make to participate in a given activity has a situational component. In other words, we are always making a decision in the context of some unique situation. Five major situational influences that affect participant decision making include physical surroundings (physical environment), social surroundings (interaction with others), time (presence or absence of time), task definition (reason or occasion for participation), and antecedent states (physiological condition or mood prior to participation).

Key terms

- affective component
- antecedent states
- attitudes
- behavioral component
- behavioral learning
- cognitive component
- cognitive dissonance
- cognitive learning
- consumer socialization
- culture
- decision-making process
- esteem
- evaluation of alternatives
- evaluative criteria

- evoked set
- experiential source
- extensive problem solving (or extended problem solving)
- external sources
- family influence
- habitual problem solving (or routinized problem solving)
- information search
- internal sources
- learning
- limited problem solving
- love and belonging
- marketing sources
- Maslow's hierarchy of needs
- model of participant consumption behavior
- motivation
- participant behavior
- participant consumption behavior
- perceived risk
- perception
- personality
- personal sources
- physical surroundings
- physiological needs
- post participation evaluation
- primary reference group
- problem recognition
- psychological or internal factors
- reference groups
- safety needs
- selective attention
- selective interpretation
- selective retention
- self-actualization
- situational factors
- social class
- socialization
- social learning
- socializing agents
- social surroundings
- sociological or external factors
- sports involvement
- task definition
- time
- values

Review questions

1 Define participant consumption behavior. What questions does this address with respect to consumers of sport? From a marketing strategy perspective, why is it critical to understand consumer behavior?

2 Outline the components of the simplified model of participant consumer behavior.

3 Outline the steps in the decision-making process for sports participation. What are the three types/levels of consumer decision making? How do the steps in the decision-making process differ for routine decisions versus extensive decisions?

4 Define personality. Why is it considered one of the internal factors of consumption behavior? Do you think personality is related to the decision to participate in sports? Do you think personality is linked to the specific sports we choose to play?

5 Describe Maslow's hierarchy of needs. How is Maslow's theory linked to sports marketing?

6 What is meant by the term *sports involvement* from the perspective of sports participants? How is sports involvement measured and used in the development of the strategic marketing process?

7 Define perception and provide three examples of how the perceptual processes apply to sports marketing.

8 Describe the three major learning theories. Which learning theory do you believe best explains the sports in which we choose to participate? Why is learning theory important to sports marketers?

9 Describe the three components of attitude. How do these components work together? Why must attitudes be measured to increase sports participation?

10 Define culture and explain the process of sports socialization. Describe the core American values.

11 Define social class and explain the characteristics of individuals at each level of the seven-tiered structure.

12 Explain how reference groups play a role in sports participation.

13 Discuss the traditional family structure and then the nontraditional family structure. How do today's nontraditional families influence sports participation? Is this for the better or the worse?

14 Explain each of the five situational factors that influence the participant decision-making process.

Exercises

1 Trace the simplified model of participant behavior for a consumer thinking about joining a health club. Briefly comment on each element of the model.

2 Ask three males and three females about the benefits they seek when participating in sports. What conclusions can you draw regarding motivation? Are there large gender differences in the benefits sought?

3   Interview five adult sports participants and ask them to describe the sports socialization process as it relates to their personal experience. Attempt to interview people with different sports interests to determine whether the socialization process differs according to the specific sports.

4   Watch three advertisements for any sporting goods on television. Briefly describe the advertisement and then suggest which core American value(s) are reflected in the theme of the advertisement.

5   Develop a survey instrument to measure attitudes toward jogging. Have 10 people complete the survey and then report your findings. How could these findings be used by your local running club to increase membership (suggest specific strategies)? Are attitudes and behaviors related?

6   Interview five children (between the ages of 8 and 12) to determine what role the family and other reference group influences have had on their decision to participate in sports. Suggest promotions for children based on your findings.

7   Prepare a report that describes how time pressures are influencing sports participation in the United States. How are sports marketers responding to increasing time pressures?

Internet exercises

1   Using the World Wide Web, prepare a report that examines sport participation in Australia. What are the similarities and differences in the sports culture of Australia versus that of the United States?

2   Find and describe two sports web sites that specifically appeal to children. How does this information relate to the process of consumer socialization?

3   Find and describe a web site for a health club. How does the information relate to the consumer decision-making process to join the club?

Notes

1   Del Hawkins, Roger Best, and Kenneth Coney, *Consumer Behavior: Building Marketing Strategy*, 7th ed. (New York: McGraw-Hill, 1998).

2   Ian P. Murphy, "Bowling Industry Rolls Out Unified Marketing Plan," *Marketing News* (January 20, 1997), 2.

3   Del Hawkins, Roger Best, and Kenneth Coney, *Consumer Behavior: Building Marketing Strategy*, 7th ed. (New York: McGraw-Hill, 1998).

4   Raymond B. Cattell, Herbert W. Eber, and Maurice M. Tasuoka, *Handbook for the Sixteen Personality Factors Questionnaire* (Champaign, IL: Institute for Personality and Ability Testing, 1970).

5   Nielsen, "How Celebs and Brands Can Get in the Game With Gen Z" (July 11, 2017). Available from: www.nielsen.com/us/en/insights/news/2017/how-celebs-and-brands-can-get-in-the-game-with-gen-z.html.

6   Douglas M. Turco, "The X Factor: Marketing Sport to Generation X," *Sport Marketing Quarterly*, vol. 5, no. 1 (1996), 21–23.

7   Terry Lefton and Bernhard Warner, "Alt Sportspeak: A Flatliner's Guide," *Brandweek* (January 27, 1997), 25-27.

8   Mark A. McDonald, George R. Milne, and JinBae Hong, "Motivational Factors for Evaluating Sport Spectator and Participant Markets," *Sport Marketing Quarterly*, vol. 11 (2002), 100-113.

9   Steve Jennison, "Pride, Passion, and Participation: A Strategy for Sport and Active Recreation in Hull 2008-2013," Sport England, The Humber Sports Partnership, and Hull City Council, Hull (2008).

10   Andrew J. Rohm, George R. Milne, and Mark A. McDonald, "A Mixed-Method Approach for Developing Market Segmentation Typologies in the Sports Industry," *Sport Marketing Quarterly*, vol. 15 (2006), 29-39.

11   Henry Murray, *Exploration in Personality: A Clinical and Experimental Study of Fifty Men of College Age* (New York: Oxford University Press, 1938).

12   Janice Wood, "What Motivates People to Do Extreme Sports?" *PsychCentral* (May 11, 2017). Available from: https://psychcentral.com/news/2017/05/11/what-motivates-people-to-participate-in-extreme-sports#1.

13   Fred M. Beasley and Matthew D. Shank, "Fan or Fanatic: Refining a Measure of Sports Involvement," *Journal of Sport Behavior*, vol. 21, no. 4 (1998), 435-443.

14   Ronald Paul Hill and Harold Robinson, "Fanatic Consumer Behavior: Athletics as a Consumption Experience," *Psychology & Marketing*, vol. 8, no. 2, (1991), 79-99.

15   Fred M. Beasley and Matthew D. Shank, "Fan or Fanatic: Refining a Measure of Sports Involvement," *Journal of Sport Behavior*, vol. 21, no. 4, (1998), 435-443.

16   Robert Sekuler and Randolph Blake, *Perception*, 2nd ed. (New York: McGraw-Hill, 1990).

17   John Kim, Jeen Su Lim, and Mukesh Bhargava, "The Role of Affect in Attitude Formation: A Classical Conditioning Approach," *Journal of the Academy of Marketing Science*, vol. 26, no. 2 (1998), 143-152.

18   Harry Edwards, *The Sociology of Sport* (Homewood, IL: Dorsey Press, 1973)

19   Elizabeth Moore Shay and Britto Berchmans, "The Role of the Family Environment in the Development of Shared Consumption Values: An Intergenerational Study," in Kim Corfman and John G. Lunch, Jr. (Eds.), *Advances in Consumer Research*, vol. 23 (Provo, UT: Association for Consumer Research, 1996), 484-490.

20   Kristy Meyer, "Core American Values Incorporated into Everyday Life," *Content.com* (March 30, 2009).

21   "Something to Wish for: Time to Relax," *US News and World Report* (November 11, 1996), 17.

22   Anamarie A. Whitaker, Garrett Baker, Luke J. Matthews, Jennifer Sloan McCombs, and Mark Barrett, "Who Plays, Who Pays? Funding For and Access to Youth Sports," Rand Corporation (2019). Available from: https://www.rand.org/pubs/research_reports/RR2581.html.

23   Russell Belk, "Situational Variables and Consumer Behavior," *Journal of Consumer Research*, vol. 2, no. 3 (1975), 157-163.

Understanding spectators as consumers

After completing this chapter, you should be able to:

- Understand the similarities and differences between spectator and participant markets.
- Describe the eight basic fan motivation factors.
- Explain how game attractiveness, economic factors, and competitive factors relate to game attendance.
- Describe the demographic profile of spectators and explain the changing role of women as spectators.
- Understand the relationship between stadium factors and game attendance.
- Discuss the components of the sportscape model.
- Describe the multiple values of sport to the community.
- Explain sport involvement from a spectator's perspective.
- Discuss the model of fan identification.

In Chapter 4, we examined participants as consumers. This chapter examines another group of consumers of great importance to sports marketers - spectators. Before we turn to our discussion of spectator consumption, two key points need to be addressed. First, the model of participant consumption behavior discussed in Chapter 4 can also be applied to spectator consumption. Think for a moment about your decision to attend sporting events. Certainly, there are sociological factors that influence your decision. For instance, reference groups such as friends and family may play a major role in influencing your decision to attend sporting events. Psychological factors, such as personality, perception, and attitudes, also affect your decision to attend sporting events or which sporting events to attend. For example, the more ambitious and aspiring you are, the more likely you may be to attend sporting events. In addition,

DOI: 10.4324/9780429030673-7

situational factors can affect your decision to attend sporting events. Maybe you were given tickets to the game as a birthday gift (e.g., task definition).

As you can see, the factors that influence participant decision making are also applicable to spectator decisions. However, the focus of this chapter is to understand why people attend sporting events and to examine what additional factors relate to game attendance. Rather than using the framework for participant consumption behavior, however, we concentrate on the wants and needs of spectators. Understanding the consumer's needs and wants, in turn, is important when developing an effective marketing mix for spectators.

The second key point addresses the basis for considering spectators and participants two separate markets. Many people who watch and attend sporting events also participate in sports, and vice versa. For example, you may watch March Madness and also play basketball on a recreational basis. Research has shown, however, that two different consumer segments exist.[1] In fact, marketing to "either participants or spectators would miss a large proportion of the other group." Let us look at Figure 5.1 to illustrate the differences between spectators and participants.

Each diagram in Figure 5.1 depicts the potential relationship between spectator and consumer markets for golf, basketball, NASCAR, and running. Golf (see Figure 5.1a) represents a sport in which there is a large crossover between participants and spectators. A study conducted by Milne, Sutton, and McDonald supports this notion, finding that 84 percent of the golf participant market

Photo 5.1
Happy Brazilian soccer fans commemorating victory, with the flag of Brazil swinging in the air

Source: Shutterstock.com

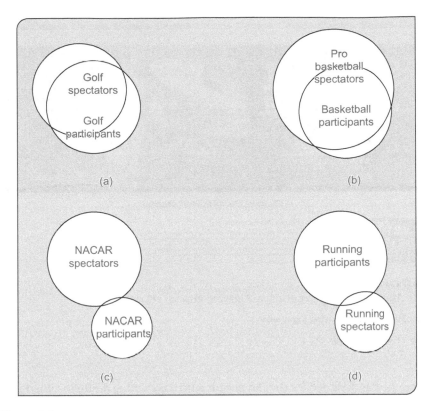

Figure 5.1
Relationship between spectator and participant markets

overlaps the golf spectator market.[2] In another study, it was found that 87.3 percent of the spectators in attendance at an LPGA event also participated in golf.[3]

A similar pattern is shown for basketball (see Figure 5.1b). The results of the study indicated an 81 percent overlap between basketball participation and watching pro basketball. Surprisingly, this same relationship did not exist for college basketball spectators. In that case, the overlap in the participation market and the college basketball spectator market was only 43 percent. The study also found that there was only a 36 percent overlap between spectators of professional basketball and spectators of college basketball – evidence that there are not only differences in spectators and participants but also among spectators at different levels of the same sport.[4]

The other two sports shown in Figure 5.1, NASCAR racing and running, demonstrate more extreme differences in the spectator and participant markets. There is virtually no overlap between the spectators and participants of NASCAR (see Figure 5.1c). Obviously, the NASCAR participant market is virtually nonexistent. However, new "fantasy camps" are springing up across the United States for spectators who want to try racing and include the likes of Mario Andretti (Indy Car) or Richard Petty (NASCAR). For example, participants can enroll in classes at the Richard Petty Driving Experience. The "Rookie

YES! We are OPEN and Booking Experiences.

BEST. EXPERIENCE. EVER.

MARIO ANDRETTI RACING EXPERIENCE, "WORLD'S FASTEST" DRIVING EXPERIENCE" You can DRIVE a full size, open wheel, Indy-style race car. By Yourself! Following drivers meeting with crew chief, training and instruction you get behind the wheel and drive an Indy-style race car for timed racing sessions on the Nation's Premier Race Tracks. There's no limit as to follow no instructor rides with you; you get one-on-one instruction from a spotter over your 2-Way In-Car Radio. You can pass the slower cars as you catch them. YES, passing is allowed in this once-in-a-lifetime, Indy-style racing experience.

Ride Alongs on SALE starting at $29.00

SALE ends TODAY!
0 8 3 9 5 8

Book Now or Buy a Gift Certificate

Web Capture 5.1

Mario Andretti Driving Experience: Allowing fans to feel racing thrills

Credit: Mario Andretti Driving Experience

URL: www.andrettiracing.com/

Experience" is designed for the "layperson who has a strong desire to experience the thrill of driving a Monster Energy NASCAR Cup race car." For prices starting at $599, racing enthusiasts can begin to experience driving around the track at speeds up to 145 mph. Top speeds vary according to driver ability, track location, and program. The company, attempting to cater to a number of audiences, offers a number of experiences ranging from a heart-pounding ride around one of the tracks with a professional instructor, $149.00, to the ultimate package, the Richard Petty Fantasy Experience, at a cost of $5,000.[5] The vast array of offerings help fulfill the needs, wants, and demands of the consumer audience.

Figure 5.1d depicts the potential participant and spectator markets for running. As opposed to the previous examples, the participant running market is much larger than the spectator running market. In addition to the size of the markets, there are also differences in motivations for spectators and participants. Participants, for instance, may be motivated to run for reasons of personal improvement. However, spectators are likely to watch to provide support to a family member or friend.

In addition to looking at the overlap (or lack thereof) between participants and spectators on a sport-by-sport basis, other research has explored the differences between these two groups for sports in general. Table 5.1 summarizes the findings of a study conducted by Burnett, Menon, and Smart,[6] which examined spectator and participant socioeconomic characteristics and media habits. Based on the results of this and other studies, sports participants and sports spectators seem to represent two distinct markets that should be examined separately by sports marketers.

Before we explore spectators in greater detail, it is important to note that this market can be differentiated into two groups on the basis of consumer behavior. The first group consists of spectators who attend the sporting event. The second group of spectators consumes the sporting event through some medium (e.g., television, radio, or OTT). This chapter is primarily concerned with understanding why consumers attend sporting events and what factors influence attendance and viewership. Let us begin by looking at some of the major factors that influence the decision to attend sporting events rather than watching them from the comfort of home.

Photo 5.2
The sport of bullfighting depicts a "lack of overlap" between sports participants and sports spectators, for very few have the courage and/or the skills to master the ring

Source: Shutterstock.com, Matej Kastelic

> ## Table 5.1 Differences between spectators and participants
>
> - Spectator and participant markets differ from each other with respect to socioeconomic characteristic and media habits.
> - Consumers categorized as heavy participants were more likely to be male, better-educated, white-collar workers, minorities, and young, compared with the heavy spectator group.
> - Consumers categorized as heavy participants also differ from heavy spectators with respect to media usage. Heavy participants are more likely to use business news-reporting media. In addition, heavy participants are more likely to watch intellectually appealing programming.
> - Compared with male participants, male spectators exhibit an interest in a wider variety of media especially television.
> - Heavy participants and heavy spectators are different with respect to how they can be reached by advertising and how they perceive advertising.
>
> *Source:* Adapted from John Burnett, Anil Menon, and Denise T. Smart, 1993, "Sports Marketing: A New Ball Game with New Rules," *Journal of Advertising Research* (September–October 1993) 21–33

Factors influencing attendance

It is opening day in New York, and the hometown Yankees are set to take on their rival, the Boston Red Sox. Fred has gone to the traditional opening day parade and then attended the ball game for the past five years. The game promises to be a great one because the Yankees are returning from last year's winning season and playing the rival Red Sox. Fred will be joined at the game by his eight-year-old son and a potential business client.

As this hypothetical scenario illustrates, there are a variety of factors influencing Fred's decision to attend the season opener. He wants to experience the new season, have the experience at the stadium, and watch the team that he has identified with since his childhood. As a businessman, Fred views the game as an opportunity to build a relationship with a potential client. As a father, Fred views the game as a way to bond with his son. In addition to these factors, Fred is prone to gambling and has placed a $50 bet on the home team. Finally, Fred thinks of opening day as an entertaining event that brings the whole community together, and, as a lifelong resident, he wants to feel that sense of belonging.

Certainly, the interaction of the factors mentioned affected Fred's decision to attend the game. Sports marketers must attempt to understand all the influences on game attendance to market effectively to Fred and other fans like him.

A variety of studies have examined some of the major issues related to game attendance. A study conducted by Ferreira and Armstrong[7] found that eight distinct factors influence game attendance. Factor 1 had eight significant loadings: crowd density, crowd noise, popularity of sport, opportunity to watch game on TV, player's popularity, amount of advertising, rivalry, and pace. All variables loading on Factor 1 included items related to the overall popularity of sport and were collectively labeled *popularity of sport*. Factor 2 outlined items related to overall *game attractiveness*, including opposing team quality, home team quality, strategy displayed, athleticism, and skill displayed. The third factor was based on *free offerings and promotions*, such as offerings of free T-shirts, prizes, free tickets, and promotions on concessions (e.g., dime-a-dog). Factor 4 denoted *pregame and in-game entertainment* items such as band, music, and pregame activities. Factor 5, labeled *physical contact*, conveyed the degree of physical contact displayed. Factor 6 included items that related to *convenience and accessibility*, such as seating arrangement, seat location/sightlines, location convenience, and parking. Factor 7, *facility*, signified items of facility newness and niceness. Finally, Factor 8 was labeled *cost* and referenced items related to ticket prices.

Other research has shown that that weather, parking and security,[8] ticket cost,[9] promotional events,[10] team success,[11] attributions for team success,[12] and the presence of star players[13] all play a role in sport consumption decisions.

Let's delve deeper into some of these critical drivers of game attendance, such as fan motivation factors, game attractiveness, economic factors, competitive factors, demographic factors, stadium factors, value of sport to the community, sports involvement, and fan identification.

Fan motivation factors

The foundation of any strategic sports marketing process is understanding why spectators attend sporting events, or **fan motivation factors**. Based on an extensive literature review, Trail et al.[14] proposed that nine different motives explain why individuals consume sport or are sport fans. Most of these motives are based on social and psychological needs: vicarious achievement, acquisition of knowledge, aesthetics, social interaction, drama/excitement, escape (relation), family, physical attractiveness of participants, and quality of physical skill of the participants. Trail and his colleagues also suggested that spectators attend games due to one or a combination of these motives.

Additional research by Wann has found eight basic motives for watching sport. The motives are categorized as self-esteem enhancement, diversion from everyday life, entertainment value, eustress, economic value, aesthetic value, need for affiliation, and family ties. It is important to note that these fundamental motives represent the most basic needs of fans. Because of this, the eight motives are often related to other factors, such as sports involvement and fan identification, which are discussed later in the chapter. Let us now examine the eight underlying motives of fans identified in a study conducted by Wann.[15]

- **Self-esteem enhancement** - Fans are rewarded with feelings of accomplishment when their favorite players or teams are winning. These fans more commonly are called "fair weather fans"; their association with the team is likely to increase when the team is winning and decrease when the team is doing poorly.

The phenomenon of enhancing or maintaining self-esteem through associating with winning teams has been called BIRGing, or basking in reflected glory.[16] When BIRGing, spectators are motivated by a desire to associate with a winner and thus present themselves in a positive light and enhance their self-esteem. Madrigal developed a model to explain why BIRGing might occur. He found that the three antecedent conditions that are related to BIRGing are expectancy disconfirmation, team identification, and quality of the opponent. In other words, BIRGing increases when the team does much better than expected, when the fan has high levels of association with the team, and when the team upsets stronger opponents.[17]

Spectators who dissociate themselves from losing teams because that negatively affects self-esteem accomplish this through CORFing, or cutting off reflected failure. The BIRGing and CORFing behaviors even have a high-tech influence on fans. A recent study found that fans are more likely to visit their team's website after a victory and less likely to visit the site after a defeat.[18]

A new construct has been posited to explain why some fans, although it may sound crazy, don't want to associate themselves with a winner. In this instance, although a team might have a winning record, fans may actually dissociate themselves from the team.

Reasons for such behavior, known as CORSing (cutting off reflected success), may include rebelliousness, jealousy, loyalty (to an earlier era, a previous style of play, prior coaching/management, etc.), a need for individuality (informally seen as a need to stand apart from the crowd), and possibly a fear of success (e.g., to ascend to new heights implies a chance for a greater fall). The CORSing fans do not want to be associated with the new era of winning; rather, they prefer to stay linked to the past. By CORSing, the fans are managing their self-image through an expression of individualism.[19]

- **_Diversion from everyday life_** - Watching sports is seen as a means of getting away from it all. Most people think of sports as a novel diversion from the normal routines of everyday life. In a recent article, University of Nebraska Cornhusker fans were cited as having intense emotional ties to the team, and it was stated that football served as a diversion from everyday life in Nebraska. "For several hours on a Saturday afternoon the struggling farmers of rural Nebraska - the inspiration for the school's nickname - can put aside their own problems and focus on someone else's."[20]

In a more horrific example, there was great debate about whether and when Oklahoma State, undefeated at the time, should play their football game scheduled against Iowa State after a tragic plane crash took the life of members of Oklahoma State's coaching fraternity, the head and assistant woman's basketball coach, in 2011. The game was played, for many thought that it would serve as a positive diversion; however, the game resulted in an overtime upset win in favor of Iowa State. In another more national example, Major League Baseball and other sports dealt with uncertainty of when they would resume their schedules after the events of September 11, 2001 or when and how play would resume during the pandemic. Ultimately, it was decided that play should go on to serve as a diversion and to ensure that the American way of life was not disrupted.

- ***Entertainment value-*** Entertainment is closely related to the previous motives for attendance. Sports serve as a form of entertainment to millions of people. As discussed in previous chapters, sports marketers are keenly aware of the heightened entertainment value of sports. In fact, one of the unique aspects of attending a sporting event is the uncertainty associated with the outcome. The drama associated with this uncertainty adds to the entertainment value of sports. Among spectators, the entertainment value of sports is believed to be the most highly motivating of all factors. In fact, Harris Interactive Company states that

contrary to popular belief, lowering ticket prices is not the best way - or even the most profitable way - to get people into seats. Creating an entertainment experience with flexible season tickets, VIP perks, etc., is a far better alternative. In short, people want to have fun, and for an increasing number of sports attendees this may have very little to do with the actual competition.[21]

A number of sports are attempting to find interesting and innovative ways to increase their entertainment value for the fans on the field of play by changing the rules of the game. As the accompanying article illustrates, college and professional officials alike continue to implement strategies that further enhance fan engagement and entertainment.[22]

ARTICLE 5.1
MLB EYES REDUCING PACE OF PLAY WITH NEW RULE CHANGES

MLB officially has announced the adoption of "several new rules" for this season, including the "somewhat controversial requirement that relief pitchers must face at least three batters or finish the inning before being taken out of the game," according to Steve Gardner of USA TODAY. MLB Commissioner Rob Manfred "pushed for the three-batter minimum as a way to cut down on the number of pitching changes during a game and speed up the pace of play."

Among other new rules: Each team will "add one player to its game-day roster, increasing the number of active players from 25 to 26." Then, starting Sept. 1 through the end of the regular season, active rosters of all teams will "increase to 28 players." Meanwhile, managers now will have 20 seconds to "decide whether to challenge an umpire's call," after previously having 30 seconds (USA TODAY, 2/13). In DC, Dave Sheinin notes most of the new rules were "long expected and many of them designed to speed up the pace of play – a longtime pet cause" of Manfred. The commissioner had "attempted to improve pace of game with some of his earlier rule changes, including the limit on mound visits and the introduction of the automatic intentional walk, but with little success." After some "modest improvement" in '18, the average game last season took 3 hours 10 minutes, an all-time high, while the average nine-inning game took 3:05, also an all-time high (WASHINGTON POST, 2/13).

TESTING THE FUTURE: In St. Louis, Rick Hummel cited a source as saying that nine Spring Training facilities, which also serve as venues for Florida State League games, "will be using" ABS (Automated Balls and Strikes) technology this spring. But Hummel noted it will be "in test mode only for the major-league games." Data will be "assembled from the spring games and then the system is set to be full bore" when the FSL uses it during the regular season (ST. LOUIS POST-DISPATCH, 2/12).

Source: Street and Smith's Sport Business Daily, February 13, 2020. Accessed July 24, 2020, www.sports businessdaily.com/Daily/Issues/2020/02/13/Leagues-and-Governing-Bodies/MLB.aspx?hl=pace+ of+play&sc=2

- *Eustress* - Sports provide fans with positive levels of arousal. In other words, sports are enjoyable because they stimulate fans and are exciting to the senses. For example, imagine the excitement felt by Indy fans when the announcer says, "Gentlemen, start your engines," or the anticipation surrounding the opening kickoff for fans at the Super Bowl.
- *Economic value* - According to Sport England, in terms of economic impact and broader economic value, it is evident that sports and sports-related activities make a substantial contribution to the economy and to the welfare of individuals and the society.[23] Often debated, this total economic value is accounted for through measures of participation, consumption (i.e. watching sport, gambling, and consumption of sportswear and equipment for recreational use), and employment. Items such as educational attainment, health, happiness, well-being, national pride, and other feel-good factors are often associated with value considerations, the net impact of which can contribute to community regeneration and development, enhanced environmental exchanges, reduced crime, volunteering, and engagement.[24] Not all of the wider benefits can be easily measured and are often debated, for in some instances, issues of potential conflict exist. For example, a subset of sports fans are motivated by the potential economic gains associated with gambling on sporting events. Their enjoyment stems

from having a vested interest in the games as they watch. Because this motive is only present for a small group of spectators, the economic factor is the least motivating of all factors. However, the number of spectators who gamble on sports continues to rise, especially among college students. Keith Whyte, executive director for the National Council on Problem Gambling, says, "college campuses bring together a lot of Internet access, a propensity for sports wagering, and most students have credit cards. We are seeing signs that it is becoming a problem." As states continue to adopt laws to legalize gambling, this will become an even greater problem in the future.

As Giuseppe Partucci noted, sport gambling has remained a popular pastime of sports fans everywhere. People turn to sports betting for a variety of reasons; some of them do it to escape their problems and relax.[25] He added that others bet on sports for a significant part of their income, so a slowdown in the economy will not affect the amount they wager. In fact, according to Partucci, legal sports books in Nevada report that the volume of wagers did not decline during the recent recession.[26] In addition, increasing efforts to legalize various types of e-sports, both in the United States and internationally, is expected to boost market growth in coming years.

In 2018, the U.S. Supreme Court overturned the federal ban known as the Professional and Amateur Sports Protection Act (PASPA). This decision, coupled with rising mobile betting trends, is likely to stimulate the growth of sports wagering in states across the United States. Additionally, Asia Pacific is projected to witness substantial growth in the years to come due to improving economic conditions. Macau and Hong Kong are the prominent sports betting revenue-generating regions.[27]

ARTICLE 5.2
DECLINING ATTENDANCE: HOW WORRIED SHOULD MLB BE?

MLB's 2019 season was the year of the home run, as 6,770 long balls were hit, more than 600 than the previous high, with 15 teams setting new individual records.

But while more baseballs made it to the stands, less fans were there to catch them.

Roughly 68.5 million fans attended MLB games during the 2019 regular season – down 1.7% from 69.7 million in 2018.

The 2019 campaign continued the concerning trend of declining MLB attendance figures: It represents a 14% decline from a high of 79.5 million in 2007. MLB total attendance has declined in six of the last seven seasons. It also means that total attendance has fallen below 70 million for a second consecutive season – and set the lowest mark for the league since 2003.

Despite its less-than-favorable attendance trend, Noah Garden points to baseball's overall popularity as signs that it is thriving in these uncertain times. As MLB's executive vice president of business and sales, he noted that over *41 million people attended Minor League Baseball games this season* – a 2.6% rise year-over-year. In total, nearly 110 million people visited both MLB and MiLB games in 2019 – hardly an indicator, he thinks, of a dying sport.

"If you think about it, it's over a hundred million people that have gone to see baseball," Garden said. "That's a number that we're proud of – and it's a big number. I think when you start to look at the game as a whole, you have to look at it sort of three-dimensionally."

When analyzing the different ways that MLB fans consume games, Garden says that three areas are carefully dissected: local ratings, national ratings, and digital properties. By each of these metrics, the league is witnessing growth, he added.

A *press release* from MLB on Sept. 30 shows that games on regional sports networks were rated number one in primetime on cable in 24 of the 25 United States markets where all 30 teams played. National TV also saw viewership spikes in 2019 across partners MLB on FOX (+8%), ESPN Sunday Night Baseball (+2%), and MLB on TBS (+10%).

Garden says that especially this year, MLB invested more into digital platforms like the MLB At Bat mobile application and Ballpark Pass. Downloads for the MLB At Bat app increased 18% year-over-year and reached over 2 billion users. Its Ballpark Pass – which allows fans to subscribe and purchase monthly ticket options on the MLB BallPark app – saw a 49% increase in purchases.

Although all these positive traits point to a healthy MLB, Garden says that the league's focused on the changes seen with season ticket holders. While he estimates that single-game ticket sales are up double-digits compared to 2018, season tickets have generally been on the decline. How to address this trend is something MLB is intent on, and one that he believes can help the league's future.

"I think the one step that we have taken on the subscription products has helped address that in a small way [and] is growing exponentially," Garden said. "I think we need to still figure out ways to combat that drop in season tickets generally. It's challenging, but we will solve that as well. And if all the numbers from a consumption standpoint continue to grow like they are today, this is a sport that's going to be around for a lot longer in the future than it has been in the past."

Arguably no team in MLB had a better 2018 offseason than the Philadelphia Phillies, and that led to off-the-field success in 2019. Celebrating its first season with free-agent signee Bryce Harper, the Phillies drew a combined 2.72 million fans to Citizens Bank Park, powered by an MLB-leading increase of 569,297 year-over-year. It also averaged 33,672 fans per home contest – a 26% increase year-over-year.

While Harper's impact can't be understated, Phillies' Senior Vice President of Ticket Operations John Weber says the team's other under-the-radar roster moves helped fuel this booming interest. Around the 13-year, $330-million Harper deal, Philly also brought on players such as Jean Segura, Andrew McCutchen, and J.T. Realmuto, building considerable buzz around the team.

By the time the team announced the *Harper signing on March 1*, as many as 100,000 fans already bought tickets for the upcoming season. Even though Weber knows the team underwhelmed with an 81–81 record, the hype from the last offseason stuck with fans – who he believes will continue to come to watch Harper and the Phils for years to come.

"I think we're excited about the future and I know our fans are excited for the future as well," Weber said. "The biggest takeaway is the fan support we received this year and knowing that it's there and knowing that it will continue as we move forward with a superstar like Bryce Harper."

While MLB attendance has seen recent struggles, a number of teams saw boosts in fan interest in 2019. The Los Angeles Dodgers followed up last season's World Series run by setting a franchise record by going 59–22 at Dodger Stadium. It averaged a league-leading 49,066 fans for a seventh consecutive season – a 4.3% increase year-over-year – while also setting a new single-season franchise attendance record.

Although Los Angeles' on-field success has lured in prospective fans, the experience around the ballpark is just as vital, said Erik Braverman, the Dodgers' senior vice president of marketing, broadcasting, and communications. Some of its most successful promotions ranged between historical and progressive.

Two notable nights the were Cody Bellinger Bobblehead Night and Fernando Valenzuela's Legends of Dodger Baseball Night – but neither was the biggest. One diversity-driven initiative that made news was its Mexican Heritage Night on May 8. Included with a jersey giveaway, the Dodgers sold over 20,000 packages as the biggest ticket pack in sports history, said Braverman. Its annual LGBT night took place on May 31 and attracted 54,307 fans – the biggest Dodger Stadium crowd since it finished stadium renovations in 2013.

"In 2018, we set a Dodger Stadium attendance record," Braverman said. "We followed it up with another record in 2019. Needless to say, we have our work cut out for ourselves for 2020, and couldn't be more excited about the challenge."

Another NL team that saw attendance rise in 2019 was the Milwaukee Brewers. Milwaukee finished the season with the eighth-highest average home attendance per game at 36,090 fans – a 2.5% bump compared to 2018's average of 35,195.

Despite being home to MLB's smallest market, Milwaukee fans have a great relationship with management, said Tyler Barnes, the Brewers' senior vice president of communications and affiliate operations. After coming off a 68-win season in 2015, team executives were honest in their desire to rebuild the team. Even though its 73–89 record in 2016 showed marginal growth, ticket sales reached 2.6 million – proof that fans would stick with the team, Barnes said.

Fast forward to 2019, and the Brewers' wish to remain loyal with its core audience is paying off. With an 89–73 record this season and a "less-is-more" approach on social media – focusing on quality content as opposed to frequent posts – Milwaukee drew in over 2.9 million visitors to Miller Park, eighth best in MLB. Even though their season ended in the NL Wild Card Game against the Washington Nationals, Barnes is happy that the fans from the team's rebuilding years have been able to see the tide change in recent years.

"We have always said that Brewers fans overdeliver in their support of the team," Barnes said. "The fans like the idea that we can compete with the biggest markets in sports. When we deliver on our promise to offer an entertaining experience for them, the support is unmatched."

On the other end of MLB's attendance spectrums are teams such as the Arizona Diamondbacks and Miami Marlins.

After finishing in second place in the NL West with an 85–77 record, the Diamondbacks attracted an average of 26,364 fans to Chase Field in 2019. Although this was good for the 17th-best in MLB this season, it was a 4.7% drop from the team's 2018 average of 27,687.

John Fisher, the Diamondbacks' senior vice president of ticket sales and marketing, isn't fazed by this season's below-average attendance numbers. Since 2014, the team has endured two 90+ loss seasons. Even given its inconsistency, he says that total home attendance always fluctuated between 2 and 2.3 million – peaking at 2.24 million in 2018.

"If the team is playing great, awesome, let's capitalize on it," Fisher said. "If the team is .500, if the team is having a tough season, there are things that we can do to program games in a way that gives people reasons to come out to the ballpark other than how the team's playing. We've seen that a lot over the years, but we're seeing some of that this year too."

In the two seasons since Adam Jones joined the Marlins as its chief revenue officer, the team has finished last in MLB in both total and average home attendance. It also was the only MLB team to attract fewer than one million total fans in both 2018 and 2019.

Despite the disappointment surrounding the Marlins' crowd, Jones says that some initiatives this season did perform well. The team released its new Marlins Membership package, which is a 365-day membership with added benefits and incentives. This new opportunity contributed to a higher customer retention rate in 2019 and a finish in the top 10 across MLB in terms of new full season equivalents, which refers to the sum of all the various ticket packages sold converted to one measurable number.

Jones also says that the team has tried to make the ballpark experience at Marlins Park more affordable. Its 305 Menu priced eight different stadium food and beverage items at either $3 or $5.

With a slight increase in average home attendance from 10,013 in 2018 to 10,016 in 2019, he believes that this is a better indicator of the direction the team's interest is going. If fans can continue to give the Marlins a chance, he's convinced that they will be rightly rewarded with a memorable experience.

"In terms of how we're going to continue to build is continuing to invest with [the fans]," Jones said. "Making sure that your dollars are not a reason why an individual or a business will choose not to attend the Marlins game. We understand time is a more valuable consideration to many consumers. That's where we need to continue to build value into our experience to be able to earn that investment of time."

While there are many ways that MLB and its teams are addressing attendance, Sam Yardley, Two Circles' senior vice president of consulting, thinks that the one real remedy to this is better competition. He noted that outside of the NL Central, the playoff teams were pretty much set in stone.

In a recent *FiveThirtyEight.com article*, eight teams had already clinched playoff berths or had 90% or greater odds of clinching by Sept. 13. Only the AL Wild Card race and NL Central race were still being decided. While the St. Louis Cardinals ultimately won the NL Central, the Brewers' runner-up position still guaranteed them a wild card spot.

Heading into the 2019 playoffs, four teams – the Dodgers, Rays, Twins, and Yankees – reached the 100-win mark. Conversely, four others – the Marlins, Orioles, Royals, and Tigers – exceeded 100 losses for the first time since 2002. With the talent gap between baseball teams seemingly widening, Yardley believes that this has hurt the sport – and it shows in this year's latest attendance numbers.

"The competitive balance of the league is not where it once was," Yardley said. "I think that has harmed ticket sales because the product put on the field is less and less interesting for fans of teams that are already 30 games back by mid-July."

Source: Moran, Eddie, 2019. Another Year Of Declining Attendance: How Worried Should MLB Be? Fan Experience. October 7, accessed September 24, 2020. https://frntofficesport.com/mlb-attendance-2019-2/

- *Aesthetic value* - Sports are seen by many as a pure art form. Basketball games have been compared with ballets, and many fans derive great pleasure from the beauty of athletic performances (e.g., gymnastics, figure skating, beach volleyball, and body building).
- *Need for affiliation* - The need for belonging is satisfied by being a fan. Research has shown that reference groups, such as friends, family, and the community, influence game attendance. The more an individual's reference group favors going to a game, the more likely the person will attend games in the future. Additionally, individuals who become fans of a team later in life (adolescence and adulthood) are more likely to be influenced by friends in forming an attachment with a particular team.[28]

  In addition to influencing game attendance, one study found that reference groups can also affect other game-related experiences, such as perceived quality of the stadium, perceived quality of the food service, overall satisfaction with the stadium, and perceived ticket value.[29] For instance, individuals who perceive their reference group as opposing going to games will also have less satisfaction with the stadium environment.
- *Family ties* - Some sports spectators believe attending sporting events is a means for fostering family togetherness. The entire family can spend time together, and lines of communication may be opened through sports. Interestingly, women are more motivated than men to attend sporting events to promote family togetherness.[30] Research has also shown that "fathers" are the persons who have the greatest influence in becoming a

fan of a specific team. This is especially true for individuals who became fans early in life (preteen years). In fact, brand identification in sport often occurs at an early age and is significantly linked to family influences. In the majority of these instances, sport consumers become exclusive consumers, often consumers for life. These allegiances last a lifetime, and these findings have important implications for sports marketers in creating opportunities for fathers to interact with children in team-related activities.[31]

ARTICLE 5.3
SPORTS MARKETING HALL OF FAME

David Stern

David Stern served as the commissioner of the NBA for over three decades from 1984 to 2014. Stern shepherded the NBA from a struggling sport to a global entertainment superpower. He is considered one of the best commissioners in sport history and the best in NBA history. Prior to Stern, the NBA had a shaky network reputation, plummeting attendance figures, and no television contract.

During his tenure as commissioner, Stern took a floundering NBA and turned it "into an entity that is the envy of professional sports – an innovative, multifaceted, billion-dollar global marketing and entertainment company whose future literally knows no bounds." Stern redefined the NBA and focused his marketing efforts on licensing, special events, and home entertainment. The league went from the arena business to radio, television, concessions, licensing, real estate, and home video – all under Stern's leadership. When the NBA was experiencing a public relations nightmare because of the number of players believed to be on drugs, it was again Stern who cleaned up the mess.

The All-Star Weekend, the made-for-television NBA lottery, making basketball the most popular sport in America with kids, and marketing the NBA across the world were all part of the sports marketing legacy that is David Stern. In addition, Stern helped the NBA develop an international presence in countries such as China and India, making it one of the fastest internationally growing sport franchises.

David Stern left an enduring legacy. He turned the NBA into a professional organization that is innovative, multifaceted, and a billion-dollar empire though marketing and entertainment. League revenues saw more than a 30-fold increase. Stern helped launch the WNBA, the draft lottery, the G League and helped to create the Dream Team. Under his watch the league expanded to 30 teams. Television revenues expand from $20 million in 1984 to more than $24 billion (9 years) in 2014, and now the NBAs finals are broadcast in more than 215 countries. NFL Commissioner Roger Goodell noted that he was a driving force in sports for decades. While NHL Commissioner Gary Bettman noted that he was a man of great vision and energy who taught him how to be a commissioner and, more importantly, how to try to be a good person. Stern is also known for his contribution and commitment to social responsibility by launching the NBA Cares program. The league's players and teams donate millions of dollars and hours of community service to the youth. Stern passed away at the age 77 as a result of complications arising from a brain hemorrhage on January 1, 2020.

Sources: Adapted from: E. M. Swift, 1991, "Corned Beef to Caviar," *Sports Illustrated,* June 3, 74–87. Credit line: Time, Inc.

Front Office Sports. Front Office Sports info@frntofficesport.com, January 2, 2020

ARTICLE 5.4
GLOBAL SPORTS BETTING MARKET EXPECTED TO REACH NEARLY $155.49 B BY 2024

The sports betting market revenue is projected to expand past USD 134.5 Billion by 2027, according to data provided by Transparency Market Research. It is boosted by the stronger presence of online betting.

FinancialBuzz analyzed the sports betting market based on several research reports showing future growth of the sector, with sports betting currently holding about 70% of the global gambling revenue. The web portal also highlighted recent significant deals involving FansUnite and Askott; GAN and Cordish; Boyd Gaming and FanDuel, IGT in Colorado casinos; and Scientific Games with Vaix.ai.

FinancialBuzz.com, a financial news informational web portal, has analyzed the sports betting market, noting that it continues to gain popularity among people of all generations as online betting is gradually becoming more mainstream.

The portal cites data provided by a Zion Market Research report that indicates sports betting holds about 70% of the global gambling revenue, which is more than any other sectors, including those of lotteries, casinos, and poker, among other forms of gambling. As for which sports are the most popular, European football attracts the greatest betting revenue, and is then closely followed by baseball.

FinancialBuzz also notes that numerous technological developments have helped propel the market to new highs. The stronger presence of online betting has completely transformed the process of sports betting, making it easier, faster and more convenient to place bets. On the other hand, the strict regulations by various governments are still an obstacle for the online market. Nevertheless, according to the report, the global sports betting market was valued at around USD 104.31 Billion in 2017 and is expected to reach approximately USD 155.49 Billion by 2024 while growing at a healthy CAGR (compound annual growth rate) of 8.83% between 2018 to 2024.

Despite legal restrictions, regionally and country wise, in 2018 the market had already produced more than USD 48.9 Billion in worldwide revenue and is projected to expand past USD 134.5 Billion by 2027, according to data provided by Transparency Market Research.

FinancialBuzz also delved into recent news involving FansUnite Entertainment, GAN, Boyd Gaming Corporation, International Game Technology (IGT), and Scientific Games Corporation.

FansUnite Entertainment and Askott Entertainment just announced breaking news that the two companies, have entered into a definitive amalgamation agreement to create one of Canada's leading online gaming companies, focused on sports betting, esports wagering and casino games.

The combined FansUnite and Askott will have four live business-to-consumer (B2C) platforms that have generated over CDN$350 million in wagers since inception and will have over 300,000 registered members.

FansUnite and Askott will have four executed business-to-business (B2B) contracts, two of which are currently live and generating revenue with leading esports companies. Two esports themed casino games will be released on multiple casino games aggregators platforms this year with more games currently in development. Also, applications have been completed for gaming licenses for B2C and B2B;

According to a recent report by Grandview Research, the global online gambling market size was valued at USD 53.7 billion in 2019 and is expected to grow at a compound annual growth rate (CAGR) of 11.5% from 2020 to 2027.

GAN is a business-to-business supplier of online gambling software-as-a-service solutions to the U.S. land-based casino industry. The company has developed a proprietary internet gambling enterprise software system, GameSTACK, which it licenses principally to land-based U.S. casino operators as a turnkey technology solution for regulated real-money internet gambling, encompassing internet gaming, internet sports gaming and virtual Simulated Gaming. Recently GAN had announced that Cordish Gaming Group, the global gaming division of The Cordish Companies, has engaged GAN as their enterprise software Platform provider to power their new "PlayLive!" branded Internet gambling business in the State of Pennsylvania, complementing the development of two new Live!-branded gaming facilities in Philadelphia and Pittsburgh.

Boyd Gaming Corporation and FanDuel Group recently announced the debut of FanDuel Sportsbooks at four Boyd Gaming properties: Blue Chip Casino Hotel and Spa in Michigan City, Indiana; Diamond Jo Casino in Dubuque, Iowa; Diamond Jo Casino in Northwood, Iowa; and Belterra Casino Resort in Florence, Indiana.

IGT announced earlier this month that its PlaySports platform will power retail and mobile sports betting at Wild Card Saloon and Sasquatch Casino in Black Hawk, Colorado. Owned and operated by privately held gaming company, Ed & Shirley's Inc., both casinos will leverage IGT PlaySports kiosks, platform and mobile technologies to give their patrons choice and convenience for how, when and where they place sports bets. "Offering omni-channel sports betting via the IGT PlaySports solution will introduce an exciting new dimension of gaming to Wild Card Saloon and Sasquatch Casino that sports fans throughout Colorado are ready to embrace," said Ed Smith, Ed & Shirley's Inc. President. "We've leveraged IGT's expertise and trusted technology to create a sports betting program that gives players choice and convenience for wagering on their favorite teams."

Scientific Games Corporation announced earlier in March that it had partnered with Vaix. ai to offer sports bettors personalized recommendations and tailored betting choices through the OpenMarket branch of the OpenSports product suite. Vaix.ai will offer an Artificial Intelligence (AI) model through OpenSports that enhances the sports betting experience. By providing sports, league, team, event, and market recommendations to bettors in real-time, the companies aim to further personalize sports betting through Scientific Games' OpenMarket solution. OpenMarket is the industry's first one-stop content marketplace, giving Scientific Games' partners access to top-tier sports betting intelligence, data feeds and tools without the need for complex integrations and financial agreements.

Source: www.yogonet.com/international/noticias/2020/06/24/53713-global-sports-betting-market-expected-to-reach-nearly-15549-b-by-2024

Game attractiveness

Another factor related to game attendance is the perceived attractiveness of each game. **Game attractiveness** is a situational factor that varies from game to game and week to week. The perceived quality of a single game or event is based on the skill level of the individuals participating in the contest (i.e., the presence of any star athletes), team records, and league standings. In addition to these game-attraction variables, if the game is a special event (opening day, bowl game, or all-star game), game attractiveness is heightened. The more attractive the game, the more likely attendance will increase.

Economic factors

Both controllable and uncontrollable **economic factors** can affect game attendance. Controllable economic factors include aspects of the sports marketing environment that can be altered by sports marketers, such as the price of tickets and the perceived value of the sports product. Uncontrollable economic factors are things such as the average income of the population and the economic health of the country.

Generally, the greater the perceived value of the game and the greater the income of the population, the greater the game attendance. Surprisingly, one study found that attendance has no relationship to increased ticket prices.[32] In other words, raising ticket prices does not negatively affect game attendance. Other researchers, however, have found just the opposite.[33]

Competitive factors

As discussed in Chapter 2, competition for sporting event attendance can be thought of as either direct (other sports) or indirect (other forms of entertainment). Ordinarily, the less competition for spectators' time and money, the more likely they will be to attend your sporting event.

One form of direct competition of interest to sports marketers is the televised game. Television continues to be used by almost all fans to follow sports. However, according to Kantar's 2013 Global Sports Media Consumption Report, well over half (59 percent) of sports fans state that their sports consumption has changed in some way in the last two years.[34] Whether it be consumption via high definition, consumption online (which now surpasses print alternatives), or the use of digital access in the use of social networking platforms, the trends of use of traditional media consumption are changing. Some of the underlying trends can only be good news to the industry. In fact, fans in the United States spend an average of 8 hours a week watching sport content, and fans in most markets are spending more time consuming sports than ever before. The era of digital and second-screen usage garners opportunity, and according to Kantar's editor Frank Dunne, whoever said the pie doesn't get any bigger was wrong.[35] In fact, more and more fans are consuming sport on Internet-connected devices without - crucially - taking away viewers from television. Dunne noted that digital has added new layers to the experience, offering more ways of viewing and discovering the alchemy that turns digital into dollars is the holy grail for sports rightsholders and brands. We are in an era where primary and second-screen choices, as well as digital choices, continue to develop; however, many in the industry are still trying to map out a strategy and are not alive to its true potential. Sports marketers need to understand spectators' media habits and motivations to appeal to these growing segments. In addition, sports marketers want to learn whether to treat the viewing audience as a separate segment or whether it overlaps with spectators who attend games.

Some of these issues were addressed in a series of studies conducted to understand consumers' motivations for watching televised sports. Overall, the excitement, enthusiasm, and entertainment value associated with the telecasts are the primary motivating factors.[36] Interestingly, the need for watching televised sports differed by gender. Women indicated they were more motivated to watch sports for the social value and the fact that friends and family were already doing so. Men, however, were motivated to watch sports on television because they enjoy the telecasts and find them entertaining.

With respect to their viewing behavior, men are more interested in watching sports on television, want more sports coverage, watch more sports coverage, and follow it up by watching news reports of the action more frequently than do their female counterparts. In short, men appear more highly involved in televised sports.

How does consuming the game via some alternative media such as radio, webcast, or television affect game attendance? One study examined the influence of television and radio broadcasting on the attendance at NBA games. The results indicated that television broadcasts of home games would have a negative impact on attendance, with more than 60 percent of the fans indicating they would watch the game on television rather than attending. However, watching televised sports can also have a positive impact on home game attendance. For instance, the more one watches away games on television, the more one attends home games. In addition, the more one listens to the radio (for both home and away games), the greater the likelihood of attending home games.[37]

Demographic factors

Demographic factors or variables, such as population, age, gender, education, occupation, and ethnic background, are also found to be related to game attendance. Although the number of women attending sporting events is greater than ever before, males are still more likely to be in attendance. The sports that possess male fan bases include the NFL, college football, and Major League Baseball. The most avid female fans flock to figure skating, the NFL, and Major League Baseball.

In addition, male sport fans tend to be younger and more educated and have higher incomes than that of the general population. With the exception of baseball, the majority of ticket holders at sporting events now have annual income levels of $80,000 or more. According to the most recent census data, only 15 percent of American households reach this level of income, a relatively small market segment.[38] Interestingly, the National Hockey League, PGA Tour, and ATP (tennis) have the greatest percentage of fans with household incomes over $50,000.[39]

As you might imagine, it is very difficult to come up with the profile of the typical sports fan because of the varying nature of sport. However, it is important not to generalize and run the risk of neglecting a potentially huge market.[40] Figure 5.2 presents the demographic profile of Americans who consider themselves sports fans.

Stadium factors

New stadiums are being built across the United States. Moreover, team owners who cannot justify or afford new stadiums are moving to cities that will build a new facility or attempt to renovate the existing stadium. Obviously, these stadium improvements are believed to affect the bottom line for team owners or for university presidents.

Stadium factors refer to variables such as the newness of the stadium, stadium access, aesthetics or beauty of the stadium, seat comfort, and cleanliness of the stadium. One study found that all these factors are positively related

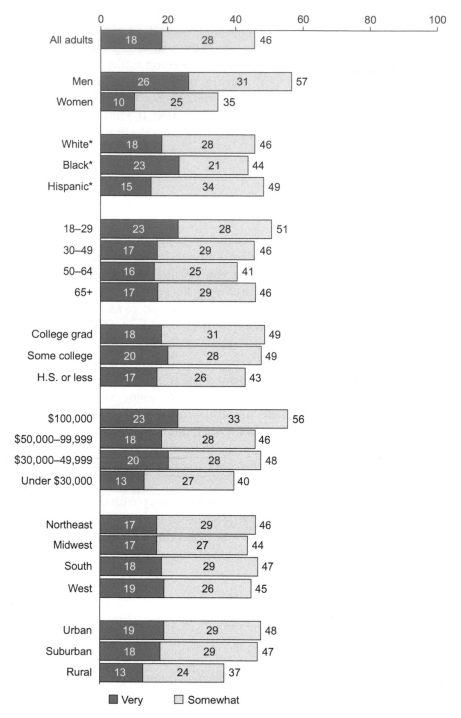

Figure 5.2
Who's a sports fan?

Source: Americans to Rest of World: Soccer Not Really Our Thing, page 8. Pew Research Center, http://www.pewsocialtrends.org/2006/06/14/americans-to-rest-of-world-soccer-not-really-our-thing/

to game attendance. That is, the more favorable the fans' attitude toward the stadium, the higher the attendance.[41]

Similar results were found in a study conducted for *Money* magazine by IRC Survey Research Group.[42] This study looked at what 1,000 sports fans value when attending professional sporting events. The major findings, in order of importance, are:

- Parking that costs less than $8 and tickets under $25 each
- Adequate parking or convenient public transportation
- A safe, comfortable seat that you can buy just a week before the game
- Reasonably priced snack foods, such as a hot dog for $2 or less
- Home team with a winning record
- A close score
- A hometown star who is generally regarded as being among the sport's 10 best players
- Reasonably priced souvenirs
- A game that ends in less than three hours
- A wide variety of snack foods

Interestingly, the four most important things identified in the study were unrelated to the game itself. If you make people pay too much or work too hard, they would rather stay home. Apparently, only after you are seated in your comfortable chair with your inexpensive food do you begin to worry about rooting for the home team.

In addition, spectators were concerned about having a clean, comfortable stadium with a good atmosphere. Part of the positive atmosphere is having strict controls placed on rowdy fans and having the option of sitting in a non-alcohol section of the stadium. An emerging area of some importance to new stadium design, as well as to stadium rehabilitation, is the need to provide more and larger restrooms. Because stadium atmosphere seems to be so important to fans, let us examine it in greater detail.

Sportscape

As you might have noticed, stadium atmosphere appears to be a critical issue in game attendance. Recently, studies have been conducted in the area of stadium environment or "sportscape."[43] **Sportscape** refers to the physical surroundings of the stadium that affect the spectator's desire to stay at the stadium and ultimately return to the stadium. Figure 5.3 shows the relationship between these sportscape factors and spectator behavior.

As shown in Figure 5.3, sportscape factors include stadium access, facility aesthetics, scoreboard quality, seating comfort, and layout accessibility. Each sportscape factor serves as input to the spectator's affective response or judgment of pleasure or displeasure with the stadium. The affective response, as

Photo 5.3
New sports facilities such as the AT&T Stadium in Dallas influence attendance

Source: dallascowboys.com

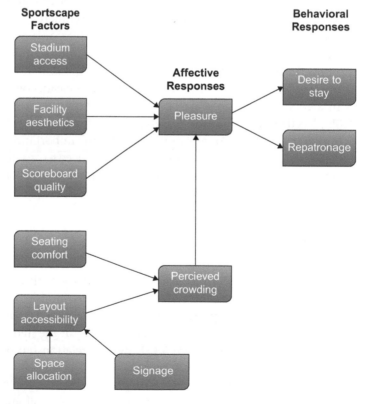

Figure 5.3
Model of sportscape

Source: K. L. Wakefield, J. G. Blodgett, and H. J. Sloan, 1996, "Measurement and Management of the Sportscape," *Journal of Sport Management,* 10(1): 16, Human Kinetics

we learned in Chapter 4, is the "feeling" component of attitudes. Similarly, the affective response with the sportscape is the feeling of perceived pleasure or displeasure the spectator has with the stadium. The perceptions of the stadium sportscape are linked to behavioral responses or actions of the spectator. In this case, the two behavioral responses are the desire to stay in the stadium and repatronage, or returning to the stadium for future events. Let us further examine the sportscape factors and their impact on spectators' pleasure.

Stadium accessibility

Many of us have left sporting events early to avoid traffic hassles or walked long distances to get to a game because of limited parking. For example, I recently attended a game at Wrigley Field in Chicago and, because of limited parking spaces, had to walk over 3 miles to get to the game. By the time I reached my seat, it was the third inning! This experience certainly resulted in displeasure with the entire game experience.

Stadium access includes issues such as availability of parking, the ease of entering and exiting the parking areas, and the location of the parking relative to the stadium. From the spectator's perspective, anything that can make it easier to get in and out of the stadium quicker will positively affect a return for future games.

Facility aesthetics

Facility aesthetics refers to the exterior and interior appearance of the stadium. The exterior appearance includes stadium architecture and age of the stadium. New stadiums, with unique architectural designs, are springing up across the United States. For example, the Dallas Cowboys' AT&T Stadium seats 80,000, making it the fourth-largest stadium in the NFL by seating capacity. However, the seating capacity is expandable. The maximum capacity of the stadium, including standing room, is 110,000. The Party Pass sections are behind seats in each end zone and on a series of six elevated platforms connected by stairways. At the time of its development, it was the largest domed stadium in the world and had the world's largest column-free interior and the largest high-definition video screen, which hangs from 20 yard line to 20 yard line. Additionally, new innovative stadia are being built around the world. Construction began in 2021 at the Bramley-Moore Dock for the Everton Football Club. In a very market-orientated approach, both fans and non-fans were consulted on the design, which promises to provide a billion pound boost to the local Liverpool economy.[44] With the environment in sharp focus, the designers of the SoFi Stadium, home to the NFL Rams and Chargers, have created an artificial lake around the facility. This will not only create a beautiful landscape feature, but with 100% recycled water, can be used to irrigate the greenery around the stadium.[45] The creativity seen in this example and with all new stadium designs is becoming the norm as prices skyrocket into the billions of dollars for construction costs.

Although the external beauty adds to the stadium aesthetics, the interior can also play a major role in fan satisfaction and attendance. The interior of the stadium includes factors such as color of the stadium walls, facades, and seats; the presence of sponsors' signage; and the presence of symbols from the team's past. For example, The Metrodome, the domed home of University of Minnesota football, was rated the poorest stadium in the Big Ten Conference because of its sterile game day atmosphere, hence its recent destruction. It was so bad that the university decided to build a standalone stadium on campus that opened in September 2009. TCF Bank Stadium, sometimes referred to as either "The Bank" or "The Gopher Hole," is the football stadium for the Minnesota Golden Gophers college football team at the University of Minnesota in Minneapolis, Minnesota. The 50,805-seat on-campus "horseshoe"-style stadium is designed to support future expansion to seat close to 80,000 people. TCF Bank Stadium, which cost $288.5 million, features 39 suites, 59 loge boxes, 1,000 outdoor club seats, 300 indoor club seats, a club lounge, a 20,000-square-foot facility for the marching band, and several locker rooms. The stadium's field is laid out in an east–west configuration, with the open end of the stadium facing campus. This layout, similar to that of Memorial Stadium, provides a view of downtown Minneapolis. Compare these design features with Fenway Park in Boston, one of the oldest and most unusual stadiums in the United States, and you can see how aesthetics can vary from one facility to the next. As former pitcher Bill Lee stated, "Fenway Park is a religious shrine. People go there to worship." Obviously, professional sports franchises are not the only ones who care about facility aesthetics. University marketers and athletic departments are equally concerned with their venues. In a recent article, the top 10 college football venues were ranked based on atmosphere and aesthetics, tradition, and how well the team plays at home. The number-one stadium in college sport was Ohio Stadium - The Ohio State University. The rest of the best in college facilities are the following: (2) Beaver Stadium - Penn State University, (3) Tiger Stadium - Louisana State University, (4) Michigan Stadium - University of Michigan, (5) Ben Hill Griffin Stadium, also known as the "Swamp," at the University of Florida, (6) The Rose Bowl - UCLA, (7) Autzen Stadium - University of Oregon, (8) (9) Darrell K. Royal Texas Memorial Stadium - University of Texas, and (10) Notre Dame Stadium - Notre Dame University.[46]

Scoreboard quality

One of the specific interior design considerations that represents a separate dimension of sportscape is **scoreboard quality**. In fact, the scoreboard in some stadiums is seen as the focal point of the interior. Throughout the game, fans continually monitor the stadium scoreboard for updates on scoring, player statistics, and other forms of entertainment, such as trivia contests, cartoon animation, and music videos. Examples of scoreboard quality range from the traditional scoreboard at Fenway Park, which is manually operated, to the NFL's biggest scoreboard, at Dallas Cowboys Stadium.

Cowboys Stadium is home to the world's largest outdoor digital display. The scoreboard at Cowboys Stadium is approximately 60 yards long. The 2,100-inch display weighs in at approximately 600 tons, spans 25,670 square feet, features back-to-back high-definition LED screens, and has two small screens at each end to accommodate the stadium end zone fans. Stadium scoreboards such as those at Cowboys Stadium, Heinz Field in Pittsburgh, and AT&T Park in San Francisco are designed to create pure entertainment. Most of the entertainment will be produced like a TV show and feature in-stand giveaways, trivia contests, features on players, and facts and figures about the field. Rick Fairbend, the executive producer/broadcast manager for the Steelers, said that "[the fans] will be amazed at the whole entertainment package from now on."

Even smaller colleges like Coastal Carolina University are enjoying the benefits of custom scoreboards. Underscoring the importance of the scoreboard is Warren Koegel, former athletic director at Coastal Carolina University, who believes that fans are used to high-definition TV and large-screen displays, so they made the decision to invest in top-of-the-line equipment.

Perceived crowding

As shown in Figure 5.3, seating comfort and layout accessibility are the two factors that were found to be determinants of spectators' perceptions of crowding. Perceived crowding, in turn, is believed to have a negative influence on the spectator's pleasure. In other words, spectator pleasure decreases as perceived crowding increases.

Perceived crowding not only has an impact on pleasure but also on spectator safety. For example, English football grounds are moving away from terraces (standing areas renowned for hooliganism and violence) and toward a requirement of all-seated facilities. There has been a great deal of debate about reintroducing terracing. However, based on a report that identified all-seating as the factor that contributes the most to spectator safety, the British government has no plans to bring back terraces at English football grounds.[47]

Seating comfort

Seating comfort refers to the perceived comfort of the seating and the spacing of seats relative to each other. Anyone who has been forced to sit among the more than 110,000 fans at a University of Michigan football game can understand the influence of seating on the game experience. Likewise, those who have been fortunate enough to view a game from a luxury box or club seat also know the impact of seating on enjoyment of the game. Luxury boxes often offer top-of-the-line amenities, while the club seats provide the customer with the padded seat luxuries of a private box without the privacy. Club-level seats commonly include climate-controlled lounges, multiple TV sets, buffets, parking benefits, concierge service, and more space between rows of seats.

Chris Bigelow, president of a facility management company, contends that more seating capacity in our stadiums will not guarantee financial success in the future. Less capacity with a higher level of comfort may be a much more profitable route to attracting fans. The trend should not be for more seats in a venue but for better seating. Bigelow states, "Our culture is willing to pay for comfort."[48]

Layout accessibility

Layout accessibility refers to whether spectators can move freely about the stadium. More specifically, does the layout of the stadium make it easy for spectators to get in and out of their seats and reach the concession areas, restrooms, and so on? To facilitate access to these destinations, there must be proper **signage** to direct spectators, and there must be adequate **space allocation**. Inadequate space and signage cause spectators to feel confused and crowded, leading to negative feelings about the game experience.

As stated previously, all the sportscape factors affect spectators' feelings about the game experience. These positive or negative feelings experienced by spectators ultimately affect their desire to stay in the stadium and return for other games. Although all the sportscape factors are important, research has shown that perceived crowding is the most significant predictor of spectators having a pleasurable game experience. In addition, the aesthetic quality of the stadium was found to have a major impact on spectators' pleasure with the game.[49] The findings of sportscape research present several implications for sports marketers and stadium or facilities managers. First, stadium management should consider reallocating or redesigning space to improve perceived crowding. This might include enlarging the seating areas, walkways, and the space in and around concession waiting areas. Second, before spending the money to do major renovations or even building a new stadium to improve aesthetic quality, focus on more inexpensive alternatives. For instance, painting and cleaning alone might significantly improve the aesthetic value of an aging stadium.

UCLA has moved the Pauley Pavilion renovation process forward and has expanded and improved the building that has been a campus landmark for more than 40 years and the home court of 38 NCAA championship teams. The goal was to dedicate the restored Pauley Pavilion on October 14, 2010, to honor Coach John Wooden on his 100th birthday; unfortunately, the great Coach John Wooden's long life fell a little more than four months short of his 100th birthday.

Among the many enhancements being considered were a new retractable seating system to bring spectators closer to the court and new concession areas, restrooms, and modern arena technology to enhance fan experience; new and expanded locker rooms, medical treatment and media rooms and dedicated practice facilities; and a main lobby that would serve as a central entrance and celebrate UCLA's illustrious athletic tradition. These types of changes have provided the Bruin faithful with a first-class facility that spectators feel good about, at a cost much lower than that for new construction.[50]

Based on the studies conducted by Wakefield and his colleagues, there seems to be no doubt that the stadium atmosphere, or sportscape, plays a pivotal role in spectator satisfaction and attendance. Moreover, the pleasure derived from the sportscape causes people to stay in the stadium for longer periods of time. Certainly, having spectators stay in the stadium is a plus for the team, who will profit from increased concession and merchandise sales. In describing the importance of the sportscape, Wakefield states, "Effective facility management may enable team owners to effectively compete for consumers' entertainment dollars even when they may be unable to compete on the field."[51]

Value of sport to the community

Values, as you will recall, are widely held beliefs that affirm what is desirable. In this case, values refer to the beliefs about the impact of sport on the community. Based on the results of a recent study, spectators' perceptions of the impact of professional sport on a community can be grouped into eight value dimensions (see Table 5.2 for a brief description of values).

As you might expect, each value is related to spectators' game attendance and intentions to attend future games. For instance, spectators who believe sports enhance community solidarity are more likely to attend sporting events. Sport marketers should carefully consider these values and promote positive values when developing marketing strategy.

Table 5.2 Eight value dimensions of sport to the community

- Community solidarity – Sport enhances the image of the community, enhances community harmony, generates a sense of belonging, and helps people to feel proud

- Public behavior – Sport encourages sportsmanship, reinforces positive citizenship, encourages obedience to authority, and nurtures positive morality

- Pastime enjoyment – Sport provides entertainment and brings excitement

- Excellence pursuit – Sport encourages achievement and success, hard work, and risk taking

- Social equity – Sport increases racial and class equality and promotes gender equity

- Health awareness – Sport reduces drug abuse, encourages exercise, and promotes an active lifestyle

- Individual quality – Sport promotes character building and encourages competitive traits

- Business opportunity – Sport increases community commercial activities, attracts tourists, and helps community economic development

Source: James J. Zhang, Dale G. Pease, and Sai C. Hui, 1996, "Value Dimensions of Professional Sport as Viewed by Spectators," *Sports and Social Issues* February 21: 78–94, Sage Publications

ARTICLE 5.5
CAREER SPOTLIGHT

Marc Reeves, International Commercial Director, NFL

Career questions

1. What are your roles and responsibilities? What's on your agenda?

It is essentially to grow the fan base of the NFL around the world and to increase and maximize sponsorship opportunities. We have to not only export the brand and the game that is being played here in the States, but also create new assets around the world that are locally relevant and then tie them back and grow interest in the NFL.

To understand the markets that are most ripe for growth and to work out ways to link to who our fans are. . . . In markets where the NFL is known, we need to raise awareness. In other markets, it's to get the fans to understand that the NFL is more than just the Super Bowl and cheerleaders.

2. What could the NFL do better on the global scale? What is the NFL's international vision?

We have to package the game.

Make it palatable for audiences who don't understand it. We have to do a better job educating people about the game because very few people know the rules.

There are five local offices (in New York, China, Japan, Mexico, and the U.K.) and we had to figure out local sponsorships. For instance, the international game every year is being held in England right now. We have to figure out how to build local sponsorships around that and also maximize value for the existing partners of the NFL.

So a lot of it will be how do we work with sponsorships and local business and then also make them a marketing function so that they are helping to grow interest in the sport.

3. What are the plans for the next five years? Is there a chance for another NFL Europa?

To grow the avid fan base of the league. We have done a lot of research that shows that there are people aware of the NFL, but there are few avid fans depending on the countries.

No. I think we realized that fans around the world want the best product. We know based on the fact that each of the last three England NFL games sold out in 90 minutes or less.

4. What career advice do you have for people wanting to go into the sports industry?

To specifically focus on the value that you can add to any organization. And the second part is also to look beyond the obvious, like the agencies and the leagues and teams. There are a lot of great opportunities at some of the brands, tourist boards, and other areas that are involved in sports and there is a lot less competition for those jobs.

Sports involvement

In Chapter 4, involvement was examined in the context of sports participation. Measures of sports involvement have also been used to understand spectator behavior. From the spectator's perspective, **sports involvement** is the perceived interest in and personal importance of sports to an individual attending sporting events or consuming sport through some other medium. What sports are people most interested in? Just 4 percent of adults in this country rate soccer as their favorite sport to watch, compared with 34 percent who say this about football, 14 percent about basketball, and 13 percent about baseball, according to a Pew Research Center study.[52] Fan interest and involvement in the remaining sports can be seen in Table 5.3.

Detailed studies have looked at the involvement levels of golf spectators, baseball spectators, Division I women's basketball spectators, and sports

Table 5.3 What's your favorite sport? Favorite sports to watch by interest in sports news			
	Follow sports		
	All adults %	Very/Somewhat closely %	Not very/Not at all closely %
Football	34	45	26
Basketball	14	18	11
Baseball	13	14	12
Soccer	4	6	2
Auto racing	4	4	4
Ice skating	3	1	5
Ice hockey	3	3	3
Golf	2	2	3
Tennis	2	2	2
Boxing	2	1	2
Wrestling	1	1	1
Other	5	2	8
None	12	1	20
Don't know	1	*	1
	100	100	100
Number of respondents	2,250	1,029	1,216

Source: Americans to Rest of World: Soccer Not Really Our Thing, page 9. Pew Research Center, https://news.gallup.com/poll/4735/sports.aspx

spectators in general.[53] In addition, a study has examined the cross-cultural differences in sport involvement (see Spotlight on International Sports Marketing). Generally, these studies have shown that higher levels of spectator involvement are related to the number of games attended; the likelihood of attending games in the future; and the likelihood of consuming sport through media, such as newspapers, television, and magazines. Also of importance, high-involvement spectators were more likely to correctly identify the sponsors of sporting events.

ARTICLE 5.6
SPOTLIGHT ON INTERNATIONAL SPORTS MARKETING

A comparative analysis of spectator involvement:
United States vs. United Kingdom

As the field of sports marketing expands into international markets, the success of U.S. sports entities will depend on understanding the core consumer abroad – the international sports fan. Recently, a study was conducted to better understand the domestic and U.K. sports fan by measuring sports involvement and by exploring the relationship between sports involvement and sports-related behaviors.

The findings indicated that there are two dimensions of sports involvement that are consistent across the U.S. and U.K. sample. The cognitive dimension refers to the way that consumers think about sports, and the affective dimension is the way that consumers feel about sports. Both the cognitive and affective factors were positively related to viewing sports on television, reading about sports in magazines and newspapers, attending sporting events, and participating in sports. That is, higher levels of involvement are related to more viewing, reading about, and attending sporting events.

There were some differences in the responses of people from the United States and the United Kingdom. People from the United Kingdom spent less time each week watching sports on television; however, they were more likely to read the sports section of the newspaper on a daily basis. Compared with the U.S. sample, people from the United Kingdom were less interested in local sports teams as opposed to national teams. Finally, the British respondents were more likely than their American counterparts to perceive sports as necessary, relevant, and important.

There were no significant differences in the responses of people from the two countries concerning (1) the likelihood of planning your day around watching a sporting event, (2) hours spent reading sports-related magazines, and (3) participation in sports-related activities.

Source: Adapted from Matthew D. Shank and Fred Beasley, 1998, "A Comparative Analysis of Sports Involvement: U.S. vs. U.K.," Advertising and Consumer Psychology Conference, Portland, OR, May

Fan identification

Sports involvement was previously defined as the level of interest in and importance of sport to consumers. A concept that extends this idea to a sports organization is fan identification. Two contrasting examples of fan identification were seen with the movement of NFL franchises. When the Cleveland Browns moved to Baltimore, Browns fans became irate, holding protests and filing lawsuits to try to stop the team's move.[54] However, when the Houston Oilers moved to Nashville relatively little fan resistance was observed, indicating low levels of fan identification.

Sports marketers are interested in building and maintaining high levels of fan identification for organizations and their players. If high levels of identification are developed, a number of benefits can be realized by the sports organization. Before examining the benefits of fan identification, let us take a closer look at what it is. **Fan identification** is defined as the personal commitment and emotional involvement customers have with a sports organization.[55] A conceptual framework was developed by Sutton, McDonald, Milne, and Cimperman for understanding the antecedents and outcomes of fan identification.[56] The model is shown in Figure 5.4.

Managerial correlates are those things such as team characteristics, organizational characteristics, affiliation characteristics, and activity characteristics that directly contribute to the level of fan involvement. Team characteristics include, most notably, the success of the team. Typically, the more successful the team, the higher the level of fan identification – because people want to associate themselves with a winner (BIRGing). However, some fans see loyalty to the team as more important than team success. For instance, the Chicago Cubs continued to have high levels of fan identification even when they did not win the World Series for over a century.

Organizational characteristics also lead to varying levels of fan identification. In contrast to team characteristics, which pertain to athletic performance,

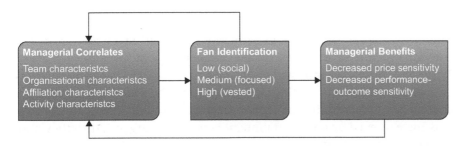

Figure 5.4
Model for fan identification

Source: William A. Sutton, Sport Marketing Quarterly

organizational characteristics relate to "off-the-field" successes and failures. Is the team trying to build a winning franchise or just reduce the payroll? Is the team involved in the community and community relations? Is the team owner threatening to move to another city if a new stadium is not built with taxpayers' monies? An example of the impact of team and organizational characteristics on fan identification was provided by the Florida Marlins. As soon as the team won the 1997 World Series (team characteristic that should foster high fan identification), the owner talked about selling the team, and the organization traded several of its star players (organizational characteristic that will diminish fan identification).

Affiliation characteristics refer to the sense of community that a fan builds as a result of a team. According to Sutton and colleagues, "The community affiliation component is . . . defined as kinship, bond, or connection the fan has to a team. Community affiliation is derived from common symbols, shared goals, history, and a fan's need to belong."[57] As discussed in a study on the impact of sports on the community, the sports team provides fans with a way to feel connected to the community and fulfill the need for affiliation. In addition, the more a fan's reference group (friends and family) favors going to games, the more the individual identifies with the team.[58]

Activity characteristics represent another antecedent to fan identification. In this case, activity refers to attending sporting events or being exposed to events via the media. As technology continues to advance, sports fans are afforded more opportunities to watch their favorite team via cable or pay-per-view, listen to games via radio, or link to broadcasts from anywhere via the Internet. With increased exposure, fan identification should be enhanced.

The interaction of the four preceding factors will influence the level of fan identification. An individual's level of identification with a team or player can range from no identification to extremely high identification. However, for simplicity, Sutton et al. describe three distinct categories of fan identification.[59]

Low identification

Fans who attend sporting events primarily for social interaction or for the entertainment benefit of the event characterize low-level identification. These "social fans" are attracted by the atmosphere of the game, promotions or events occurring during the competition, and the feelings of camaraderie that the game creates. Although this is the lowest level of fan identification, if fans are reinforced by the entertainment benefits of the game, then they may become more involved.

Medium identification

The next higher classification of fan involvement is called medium identification, or focused fans. The major distinguishing characteristic of these fans is that they identify with the team or player but only for the short term. In other words, they may associate with the team, or player, if it is having an especially good year. However, when the team starts to slump or the player is traded, "focused" identification will fade. As with low-level identification, a fan that experiences medium levels of identification may move to higher levels.

High identification

The highest classification of fan involvement is based on a long-term commitment to the sport, team, or player. These vested fans often recruit other fans, follow the team loyally, and view the team as a vital part of the community. Fans classified as high involvement exhibit a number of concrete behavioral characteristics. Most important, high-identification fans are the most likely to return to sporting events. Moreover, high-involvement fans are more likely to attend home and away games, have been fans for a greater number of years, and invest more financially in being a fan.

Managerial benefits

The final portion of the fan identification model put forth by Sutton et al. describes the outcomes of creating and fostering vested fans. One outcome is that high-identification fans have decreased price sensitivity. Price sensitivity refers to the notion that small increases in ticket prices may produce great fluctuations in demand for tickets. Fans that stick with the team for the long run are more likely to be season ticket holders or purchase personal seat licenses to get the right to purchase permanent seats. Fans that exhibit low levels of identification may decide not to purchase tickets, even for small increases in ticket prices.

Another outcome of high levels of fan identification is decreased performance-outcome sensitivity. Stated simply, fans who are vested will be more tolerant of poor seasons or in-season slumps. Fans will be more likely to stick with the team and not give up prime ticket locations that may have taken generations to acquire.

Summary

In this chapter, we explored the spectator as a consumer of sport. Although there are many people who both participate in and observe sports, research suggests that there are two distinct segments of consumers.

There are a variety of factors that influence our decision to attend sporting events. These factors include fan motivation, game attractiveness, economic factors, competitive factors, demographic factors, stadium factors, value of sport to the community, sports involvement, and fan identification. Fan motivation factors are those underlying reasons or needs that are met by attending a sporting event. Researchers believe that some of the primary reasons fans attend sporting events are enhancement of self-esteem, diversion from everyday life, entertainment value, eustress (feelings of excitement), economic value (gambling on events), aesthetic value, need for affiliation, and time with family members.

Another factor that influences our decision to attend sporting events is game attractiveness. Game attractiveness refers to the perceived value and importance of the individual game based on which teams or athletes are playing (e.g., is it the crosstown rival, or is Kevin De Bruyne in town?), the significance of the event to the league standings, whether the event is postseason versus regular season competition, or whether the event is perceived to be of championship caliber (e.g., the four majors in golf or the NCAA Final Four). In general, the greater the perceived attractiveness of the game, the more likely it is we will want to attend.

Economic factors also play a role in our decision to attend sporting events. As we discussed briefly in Chapter 2, the economic factors that may affect game attendance can be at the microeconomic level (e.g., personal income) or macroeconomic level (e.g., state of the nation's economy). Although these are uncontrollable factors, the sports organization can attempt to control the rising cost of ticket prices to make it easier for fans to attend sporting events.

Competition is another important factor that influences our decision to attend sporting events or observe them through another medium. Today, sports marketers must define the competition in broad terms – as other entertainment choices such as movies, plays, and theater compete with sporting events. Interestingly, sports organizations sometimes compete with themselves for fans. For example, one study found that televising home basketball games had a negative impact on game attendance.

Demographic factors such as age, ethnic background, and income are also related to spectator behavior. There is no such thing as a profile of the typical spectator. However, spectators are more likely to be male, young, more educated, and have higher incomes than that of the general population.

Perhaps the most important factor that influences attendance is the consumer's perception of the stadium. Stadium atmosphere appears to be a critical issue in attracting fans. The stadium atmosphere, or environment, has been referred to as the sportscape. The sportscape is the physical surroundings of the stadium that affect spectators' desire to stay at the stadium and ultimately return to the stadium. The multiple dimensions of sportscape include stadium access, facility aesthetics, scoreboard quality, seating comfort, and layout accessibility.

Another factor influencing game attendance and the likelihood of attending sporting events in the future is the perceived value of sport to the community. A study found that the more value attributed to sport, the more likely people were to attend. The value dimensions of sport to the community include community solidarity (bringing the community together), public behavior, pastime enjoyment (entertainment), pursuit of excellence, social equity, health awareness, individual quality (builds character), and business opportunities.

As discussed in Chapter 4, sports involvement refers to the consumer's perceived interest in and the importance of participating in sport. Sports involvement has a related definition for those observing sporting events. High-involvement spectators are more likely to attend sporting events, read sports magazines, and plan their entire day around attending a sporting event.

A final factor related to spectator behavior is fan identification. Fan identification is the personal commitment and emotional involvement customers have with the sports organization. The characteristics of the team, the characteristics of the organization, the affiliation characteristics (sense of community), and the activity characteristics (exposures to the team) all interact to influence the level of fan identification. The higher the level of fan identification, the more likely fans are to attend events.

Key terms

- aesthetic value
- demographic factors
- diversion from everyday life
- economic factors
- economic value
- entertainment value
- eustress
- facility aesthetics
- family ties
- fan identification
- fan motivation factors
- game attractiveness
- layout accessibility
- need for affiliation
- scoreboard quality
- seating comfort
- self-esteem enhancement
- signage
- space allocation
- sport involvement
- sportscape
- stadium access
- stadium factors

Review questions

1 Describe the differences and similarities between spectators and participants of sport.
2 Discuss the spectators' eight basic motives for attending sporting events. Which of these are similar to the motives for participating in sports?
3 Provide two examples of how game attractiveness influences attendance.

4   What are the economic factors that influence game attendance? Differentiate between the controllable and uncontrollable economic factors.

5   Describe the typical profile of spectators of women's sporting events. How would a sports marketer use this information in the strategic sports marketing process?

6   Discuss, in detail, the sportscape model and how the sportscape factors affect game attendance.

7   What are the value dimensions of professional sport to the community? How would sports marketers use these values in planning the strategic sports marketing process?

8   Define sports involvement from the spectator perspective. Why is it important to understand the levels of involvement among spectators?

9   Discuss, in detail, the model of fan identification and its implications for sports marketers.

10 Explain the relationship among the eight basic fan motivation factors and the other factors that influence game attendance (i.e., game attractiveness, economic factors, competitive factors, demographic factors, stadium factors, value to the community, sports involvement, and fan identification).

Exercises

1   Go to a high school sporting event, college sporting event, and professional sporting event. At each event, interview five spectators and ask them why they are attending the events and what benefits they are looking for from the event. Compare the different levels of competition. Do the motives for attending differ by level (i.e., high school, college, and professional)? Are there gender differences or age differences among respondents?

2   Go to a sports bar and interview five people watching a televised sporting event. Determine their primary motivation for watching the sporting event. Describe other situations in which motives for watching sporting events vary.

3   Attend a women's sporting event and record the demographic profile of the spectators. What are your observations? Use these observations and suggest how you might segment, target, and position (market selection decisions) if you were to market the sport.

4   Attend a collegiate or professional sporting event. Record and describe all the elements of sportscape. How do these affect your experience as a spectator?

5   Ask 10 consumers about the value they believe a professional sports team would (or does) bring to the community. Then ask the same people about the value of college athletics to the community. Comment on how these values differ by level of competition.

6   How will marketing play a role in revitalizing the following sports: baseball, tennis, and cricket? How has marketing played a role in the increased popularity in the following sports: golf, basketball, and soccer?

Internet exercises

1. Find examples via the Internet of how sports marketers have attempted to make it easier for fans to attend sporting events.
2. Locate two web sites for the same sport - one for women and one for men (e.g., women's basketball and men's basketball). Comment on differences, if any, in how these sites market to spectators of the sport.
3. Locate two web sites for the same sport - one American and one international (e.g., Major League Soccer and Premier League). Comment on differences, if any, in how these sites market to spectators of the sport.

Notes

1. John Burnett, Anil Menon, and Denise T. Smart, "Sports Marketing: A New Ball Game with New Rules," *Journal of Advertising Research* (September–October 1993), 21-33.
2. George R. Milne, William A. Sutton, and Mark A. McDonald, "Niche Analysis: A Strategic Measurement Tool for Managers," *Sport Marketing Quarterly*, vol. 5, no. 3 (1996), 17-22.
3. Ibid.
4. Ibid.
5. *Richard Petty Driving Experience*. Available from: http://www.nascarracingexperience.com/.
6. John Burnett, Anil Menon, and Denise T. Smart, "Sport Marketing: A New Game with New Rules," *Journal of Advertising Research*, 33 (October 1993), 21-33.
7. Mauricio Ferreira and Ketra L. Armstrong, "An Exploratory Examination of Attributes Influencing Students' Decisions to Attend College Sport Events," *Sport Marketing Quarterly*, vol. 13 (2004), 194-208.
8. R. D. Hay and C. P. Rao, "Factors Affecting Attendance at Football Games," in M. Etzel and J. Gaski (Eds.), *Applying Marketing Technology to Spectator Sports* (South Bend, IN: University of Notre Dame Press, 1982), 65-76; Roger G. Noll, "Attendance and Price Setting," in Roger G. Noll (Ed.), *Government and the Sports Business* (Washington, DC: The Brookings Institute, 1974), 115-157; Dominic H. Rivers and Timothy D. DeSchiver, "Star Players, Payroll Distribution, and Major League Baseball Attendance," *Sport Marketing Quarterly*, vol. 1 (2002), 164-173.
9. Hal Hansen and Roger Gauthier, "Factors Affecting Attendance at Professional Sport Events," *Journal of Sport Management*, vol. 3 (1989), 15-32; James J. Zhang, Dael G. Pease, Stanley C. Hui, and Thomas J. Michaud, "Variables Affecting the Spectator Decision to Attend NBA Games," *Sport Marketing Quarterly*, vol. 4, no. 4 (1995), 29-39.
10. James R. Hill, Jeff Madura, and Richard A. Zuber, "The Short Run Demand for Major League Baseball," *Atlantic Economic Journal*, vol. 10 (1982), 31-35; Mark McDonald and Daniel Rascher, "Does Bat Day Make Cents? The Effect of Promotions on the Demand for Major League Baseball," *Journal of Sport Management*, vol. 14 (2000), 8-27.

11   Robert A. Baade and Laura J. Tiehen, "An Analysis of Major League Baseball Attendance, 1969-1987," *Journal of Sport & Social Issues*, vol. 14, no. 1 (1990), 14-32; J. A. Schofield, "Performance and Attendance at Professional Team Sports," *Journal of Sport Behavior*, vol. 6 (1983), 196-206.

12   S. E. Iso-Ahola, "Attributional Determinants of Decisions to Attend Football Games," *Scandinavian Journal of Sports Sciences*, vol. 2 (1980), 39-46; Daniel L. Wann, Angie Roberts, and Johnnie Tindall, "The Role of Team Performance, Team Identification, and Self-Esteem in Sport Spectators' Game Preferences," *Perceptual & Motor Skills*, vol. 89 (1999), 945-950.

13   Roger G. Noll, "Attendance and Price Setting," in R. G. Noll (Ed.), *Government and the Sports Business* (Washington, DC: The Brookings Institute, 1974), 115-157; J. Michael Schwartz, "Causes and Effects of Spectator Sports," *International Review of Sport Sociology*, vol. 8 (1973), 25-45.

14   Galen Trail, Dean F. Anderson, and Janet Fink, "A Theoretical Model of Sport Spectator Consumption Behavior," *International Journal of Sport Management*, vol. 1 (2000), 154-180.

15   Daniel L. Wann, "Preliminary Validation of the Sport Fan Motivation Scale," *Journal of Sport & Social Issues* (November 1995), 337-396.

16   Robert B. Cialdini, Richard J. Borden, Avril Thorne, Marcus R. Walker, Stephen Freeman, and Lloyd R. Sloan, "Basking in Reflected Glory: Three (Football) Field Studies," *Journal of Personality and Social Psychology*, vol. 34 (1976), 366-375.

17   Robert Madrigal, "Cognitive and Affective Determinants of Fan Satisfaction with Sporting Events," *Journal of Leisure Research*, vol. 27 (Summer 1995), 205-228.

18   Filip Boen, Norbert Vanbeselaere, and Jos Feys, "Behavioral Consequences of Fluctuating Group Success: An Internet Study of Soccer-Team Fans," *The Journal of Social Psychology*, vol. 142 (2002), 769-782.

19   Richard M. Campbell, Jr., Damon Aiken, and Aubrey Ken, "Beyond BIRGing and CORFing: Continuing the Exploration of Fan Behavior," *Sport Marketing Quarterly*, vol. 13 (2004), 151-157, © 2004 West Virginia University.

20   Malcolm Moran, "For Nebraska, Football Is Personal," *USA Today* (October 27, 2000).

21   "Get Them Out to the Ballpark - and Off of the Couch," Harris Interactive, *Sporttainment News*, vol. 1, no. 3 (June 12, 2001).

22   "Rule Changes in College Football." Available from: www.phoenixsports.com/list_articles.php?cappers_article_id123=459&show=articles.

23   Sport England, "Economic Value of Sport in England" (2013). Available from: www.sportengland.org/media/3174/economic-value-of-sport-summary.pdf.

24   Ibid.

25   "The True Statistics of Sports Gambling," *online sportsbetting picks* (July 25, 2011). Available from: Online-sportsbetting-picks.com/the-true-statistics-of-sports-gambling, accessed December 9, 2013.

26   Ibid.

27   Hexa Research, "Sports Betting Market Estimated to Expand at a Robust CAGR by 2025." Available from: www.digitaljournal.com/pr/4153823#ixzz5fKkGUGB4.

28   Richard Kolbe and Jeffrey James, "An Identification and Examination of Influences That Shape the Creation of Professional Team Fan," *International Journal of Sports Marketing and Sponsorship*, vol. 2 (2000), 23-38.

29 Daniel C. Funk, Lynn L. Ridinger, and Anita M. Moorman, "Exploring Origins of Involvement: Understanding the Relationship Between Consumer Motives and Involvement with Professional Sport Teams," *Leisure Science*, vol. 26 (2004), 35–61.

30 Daniel L. Wann, "Preliminary Validation of the Sport Fan Motivation Scale," *Journal of Sport & Social Issues* (November 1995), 337–396.

31 Richard Kolbe and Jeffrey James, "An Identification and Examination of Influences That Shape the Creation of Professional Team Fan," *International Journal of Sports Marketing and Sponsorship*, vol. 2 (2000), 23–38.

32 Robert A. Baade and Laura J. Tiechen, "An Analysis of Major League Baseball Attendance, 1969–1987," *Journal of Sport & Social Issues*, vol. 14 (1990), 14–32.

33 Brad Edmondson, "When Athletes Turn Traitor," *American Demographics* (September 1997).

34 Kantar Media Sports, "Global Sports Media Consumption Report 2013, PERFORM" (May 2013).

35 Ibid.

36 Walter Gantz, "An Exploration of Viewing Motives and Behaviors Associated with Televised Sports," *Journal of Broadcasting*, vol. 25, no. 3 (1981), 263–275.

37 James Zhang and Dennis Smith, "Impact of Broadcasting on the Attendance of Professional Basketball Games," *Sport Marketing Quarterly*, vol. 6, no. 1 (1997), 23–32.

38 Noel Paul, "High Cost of Pro-Sports Fandom May Ease Attendance at Most Major Events Drop – And Ticket Prices Are Expected to Follow," *Christian Science Monitor* (November 19, 2001), 16.

39 "2003 ESPN Sports Fan Poll Is Now Available," *Sporting Goods Manufacturers Association*

40 Donna Lopiano, "Marketing Trends in Women's Sports and Fitness," *Women's Sports Foundation*.

41 Kirk L. Wakefield and Hugh J. Sloan, "The Effects of Team Loyalty and Selected Stadium Factors on Spectator Attendance," *Journal of Sport Management*, vol. 9, no. 2 (1995), 153–172.

42 Jillian Kasky, "The Best Ticket Buys for Sports Fans Today," *Money*, vol. 24, no. 10 (October 1995), 146.

43 Kirk L. Wakefield, Jeffrey G. Blodgett, and Hugh J. Sloan, "Measurement and Management of the Sportscape," *Journal of Sport Management*, vol. 10, no. 1 (1996), 15–31.

44 Tom Mallows, "Sport Business Nation, Everton Breaks Ground on New Staidum at Bramley Moore Dock" (August 10, 2021). Available from: https://royalbluemersey.sbnation.com/2021/8/10/22618060/everton-new-stadium-latest-breaks-ground-bramley-moore-dock-bill-kenwright-farhad-moshiri.

45 Sam Lubell, "How SoFi Stadium Makes a Revolutionary Design Promise: A Place for All to Play," *LA Times* (September 2, 2020). Available from: https://www.latimes.com/entertainment-arts/story/2020-09-02/sofi-stadium-architecture-park.

46 Matt Fitzgerald, "Best College Football Stadiums: Ranking the NCAA Gridiron's Premier Venues" (July 17, 2021). Available from: https://sportsnaut.com/best-college-football-stadiums/.

47 "British Sports Minister Says 'The Terraces Are History'" (October 1997). Available from: www.nando.net/newsroom/sport.../feat/archive/102297/ssoc45127.html.

48 Chris Bigelow, "IAVM News, International Association of Assembly Managers, Coppell, TX, formerly" (2005). Available from: www.iaam.org/facility_manager/pages/2005_Aug_Sep/STADIUMS.HTM.

49 Kirk L. Wakefield, Jeffrey G. Blodgett, and Hugh J. Sloan, "Measurement and Management of the Sportscape," *Journal of Sport Management*, vol. 10, no. 1 (1996), 15–31.

50 Andy Hemmer, "Gardens Gets Skyboxes in Makeover," *Cincinnati Business Courier Inc.*, vol. 11, no. 48 (April 10, 1995), 1.

51 Kirk L. Wakefield, Jeffrey G. Blodgett, and Hugh J. Sloan, "Measurement and Management of the Sportscape," *Journal of Sport Management*, vol. 10, no. 1 (1996), 15–31.

52 Pew Research Study, "Americans to the Rest of the World: Soccer Not Really Our Thing" (June 14, 2006).

53 Deborah L. Kerstetter and Georgia M. Kovich, "An Involvement Profile of Division I Women's Basketball Spectators," *Journal of Sport Management*, vol. 11 (1997), 234–249; Dana-Nicoleta Lascu, Thomas D. Giese, Cathy Toolan, Brian Guehring, and James Mercer, "Sport Involvement: A Relevant Individual Difference Factor in Spectator Sports," *Sport Marketing Quarterly*, vol. 4, no. 4 (1995), 41–46.

54 Geoff Hobson, "Just Another Sunday," *The Cincinnati Enquirer* (December 7, 1996).

55 William A. Sutton, Mark A. McDonald, George R. Milne, and John Cimperman, "Creating and Fostering Fan Identification in Professional Sports," *Sport Marketing Quarterly*, vol. 6, no. 1 (1997), 15–22.

56 Ibid.

57 Ibid.

58 Ibid.

59 Ibid.

6 Segmentation, targeting, and positioning

After completing this chapter, you should be able to:

- Discuss the importance of market selection decisions.
- Compare the various bases for marketing segmentation.
- Understand target marketing and the requirements of successful target marketing.
- Describe positioning and its importance in market selection decisions.
- Construct a perceptual map to depict any sports entity's position in the marketplace.

Market selection decisions are the most critical elements of the strategic sports marketing process. In this portion of the planning phase, decisions are made that will dictate the direction of the marketing mix. These decisions include how to group consumers together based on common needs, whom to direct your marketing efforts toward, and how you want your sports product to be perceived in the marketplace. These important market selection decisions are referred to as segmenting, targeting, and positioning (STP). In this chapter, we examine these concepts that are the heart of our strategic sports marketing process. Let us begin by exploring market segmentation, the first of the market selection decisions.

Segmentation

Not all sports fans are alike. You would not market the X Games to members of the American Association of Retired People (AARP). Likewise, you would not market the PGA's Champions Tour to Generation Zers. The notion of mass marketing and treating all consumers the same has given way to understanding the unique needs of groups of consumers. This

DOI: 10.4324/9780429030673-8

concept, which is the first market selection decision, is referred to as market segmentation. More specifically, **market segmentation** is defined as identifying groups of consumers based on their common needs.

Market segmentation is recognized as a more efficient and effective way to market than mass marketing, which treats all consumers the same. By carefully exploring and understanding different segments through marketing research, sports marketers determine which groups of consumers offer the greatest return on investment for the organization.

If the first market selection decision is segmentation, then how do sports marketers group consumers based on common needs? Traditionally, there are six common bases for market segmentation. These are demographics, socioeconomic group, psychographic profile, geographic region, behavioral style, and benefits. Let us take a closer look at how sports marketers use and choose from among these six bases for segmentation.

Bases for segmentation

The bases for segmentation refer to the ways that consumers with common needs can be grouped together. Six bases for segmenting consumer markets are shown in Table 6.1.

Table 6.1 Common bases for segmentation of consumer markets

Demographic	Geographic
• Age	• World region
• Gender	• Country
• Ethnic background	• Country region
• Family lifecycle	• City
Socioeconomic	• Physical climate
• Income	**Behavioral**
• Education	• Frequency of purchase
• Occupation	• Size of purchase(s)
Psychographic	• Loyalty of consumers
• Lifestyle	**Benefits**
• Personality	• Consumer needs
• Activities	• Sport product features desired
• Interests	
• Opinions	

Demographic segmentation

One of the most widely used techniques for segmenting consumer markets is **demographic segmentation**. Demographics include such variables as age, gender, ethnic background, and family life cycle.

Segmenting markets based on demographics is widespread for three reasons. First, these characteristics are easy for sports marketers to identify and measure. Second, information about the demographic characteristics of a market is readily available from a variety of sources, such as the government census data (census.gov) described in Chapter 3. Third, demographic variables are closely related to attitudes and sport behaviors, such as attending games, buying sports merchandise, or watching sports on our mobile devices.

ARTICLE 6.1
TECHNICAL REPORT – SPORT ENGLAND MARKET SEGMENTATION

The Sport England market segmentation is built primarily from the 'Taking Part' and 'Active People' surveys[1], and helps explain individual's motivations, attitudes, behaviour and barriers towards sport and active recreation. It is underpinned by key socio-demographic variables, thereby ensuring that the segments can be geographically quantified and appended to both customer records and the Electoral Roll. Therefore, every adult in England can have a Sport England segment appended to them, whilst a market segment profile can be counted at any geographic level within England down to postcode.

It was this key requirement to be able to geographically quantify and append the classification to customer records which drove the methodology adopted for this project. Key socio-demographic variables were used as the link between the sport and active recreation details in the two sport surveys. It was also this common set of indicators that enabled us to link our sport data to other datasets. This enabled us to apply the classification outside the restricted set of individuals who responded to Active People and Taking Part.

Using the 'Taking Part' survey a series of propensity models were built to predict the likelihood an individual would have to take part in an activity or have a particular motivation or attitude towards sport and active recreation. The 'Taking Part' survey was used as it contained attitude and motivation questions and therefore provided the most comprehensive insight, whilst 'Active People' insight was used to enhance our understanding of each segment. Propensity modelling is a statistical technique that assigns the probability of displaying a particular behaviour/ attitude to each demographic category. The differences in these probabilities are measured for significance by comparing across the sample population as a whole. Those models which show the most significance are subsequently extrapolated across the whole England adult population.

Source: Technical Report – Sport England Market Segmentation (2010)

http://segments.sportengland.org/querySegments.aspx

Age

Age is <u>one of the most simplistic yet effective demographic variables used to segment markets</u>. Not only is age easy to measure, but it is also usually related to consumer needs. In addition, age of the consumer is highly correlated with other demographic characteristics, such as income, education, and stage of the family life cycle. A number of broad age segments exist, such as the children's market, the teen market, and the mature market. Care must be taken, however, not to stereotype consumers when using age segmentation. How many 13-year-olds do you know who think they are 20, and how many 75-year-olds think they are 45?

Children

There has always been a natural association between children and sports. However, sports marketers are no longer taking this huge children's market for granted – and with good reason. Children have tremendous influence on purchasing decisions within the family and are increasingly purchasing more and more on their own.[1]

Children, up to age 11, wield $1.2 trillion in annual purchasing power in direct and indirect purchasing, and their opinions today influence consumer trends far into the future, as 25 percent of brand preferences persist to adulthood, creating a large loyal consumer base.[2] Table 6.2 describes what sports are

Web Capture 6.1
A wide array of youth football programs exist that target participation in youth football and cheerleading

Source: Reprinted with permission of Cleveland Browns Inc. (2020)

Table 6.2 Core participation in select sports

Percentage of kids ages 6 to 12 who participated on a regular basis

	2008	2013	2017	2018	2017–18 change	# kids in 2018
Baseball	16.5%	14.2%	13.1%	13.6%	+3.3%	4,100,000
Basketball	16.6%	16.0%	14.1%	14.1%	–0.3%	4,200,000
Bicycling	27.7%	19.8%	16.0%	15.7%	–2.2%	4,700,000
Cheerleading	n/a	1.8%	2.2%	2.6%	+18.2%	775,000
Field hockey	n/a	0.6%	0.4%	0.4%	–7.8%	110,000
Flag football	4.5%	2.8%	3.3%	3.3%	–0.3%	989,000
Tackle football	3.7%	3.5%	2.9%	2.8%	–4.0%	839,000
Golf	5.0%	4.9%	4.9%	4.9%	0.0%	1,400,000
Gymnastics	2.3%	2.9%	3.1%	3.4%	+8.5%	1,000,000
Ice hockey	0.5%	1.1%	1.2%	1.1%	–12.5%	324,000
Lacrosse	0.4%	0.8%	0.9%	1.0%	+4.7%	296,000
Soccer (outdoor)	10.4%	9.3%	7.7%	7.4%	–3.3%	2,200,000
Softball (fast-pitch)	1.0%	1.1%	1.1%	1.2%	+4.9%	359,000
Swimming (team)	n/a	1.6%	1.4%	1.4%	+1.6%	417,000
Tennis	n/a	4.1%	4.1%	4.3%	5.1%	1,300,000
Track and field	1.0%	1.1%	1.1%	1.0%	–10.0%	307,000
Volleyball (court)	2.9%	2.7%	2.7%	2.8%	+5.5%	846,000
Wrestling	1.1%	0.7%	0.6%	0.7%	–14.2%	218,000

Source:www.aspenprojectplay.org/youth-sports-facts/participation-rates

growing and declining in the 6–12-year-old market, an important set of data for the sports industry and marketers to monitor.

Teen and tween Gen Z kids, ages 10–17, account for $44 billion in discretionary spending each year. This generation of consumers is expected not to slow down in the near future and will be responsible for nearly $143 billion of direct spending soon.[3] Tweens, 8–12-year-olds, "heavily influence" spending by parents, and 80 percent of all global brands now deploy a "tween strategy."[4] As Dan Cook, at Rutgers University, noted, "kids not only want things, but parents seems to yield to that influence at an alarmingly high rate."[5]

Presently, 20 percent of U.S. families spend more than $12,000 a year, or $1,000 per month, on youth sports per child.[6] Children are participating in sports and are identifying with teams, players, and brands at younger ages each year. In fact, according to market research firm Packaged Facts, Gen Z teens and young adults have a buying power exceeding $500 billion, a disposable spending ability that is comparable to the GDP of many countries, including Belgium, Poland, Sweden, Thailand, and Venezuela.[7] As you can imagine, sports marketers have recognized and are capitalizing on the power of the kids' market. They realize children will become the sporting goods consumers, fans, and season ticket holders of the future. As such, they have segmented markets and targeted youth accordingly.

Target young kids

Examples of sports marketers reaching the kids' market are plentiful. For instance, Build-a-Bear Workshops has collaborated with Major League Baseball to find new customers, targeting the 12 and under market segment. Targeting this age group affords Build-a-Bear the opportunity for youth sports fans to build their own little team mascot web capture 6.2.

All major league sports have developed their own initiatives to reach the youth market. The NFL Foundation supports the game at the youth level and promotes positive player development. Through youth football grant programs and partnerships, hundreds of thousands of children have been given the opportunity to learn about the game of football, get physically fit, and interact positively with adult mentors, all in a safe and accessible environment.[8]

NFL PLAY 60 is the League's national youth health and wellness campaign to encourage kids to get physically active for at least 60 minutes a day. Since PLAY 60 launched in 2007, the NFL has committed more than $352 million to youth health and fitness through PLAY 60 programming, grants, and media time for public service announcements.

The NFL PLAY 60 has over 73,000 schools and 38 million children engaged and constructed more than 265 "youth fitness zones" nationwide. In one

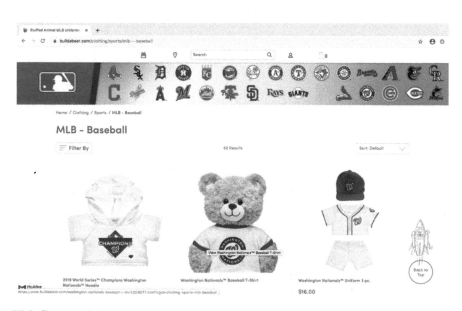

Web Capture 6.2
Build-a-Bear

Source: www.buildabear.com/collections/sports/mlb – baseball

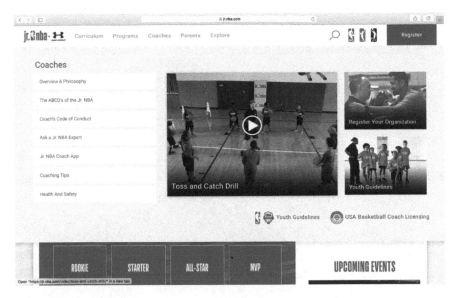

Web Capture 6.3

Demographic segmentation of NBA Jr., creating a new, loyal fan base

*Source:*https://jr.nba.com

study, conducted by the Cooper Institute through its NFL PLAY 60 Fitness-Gram Project, the program seems to be working. The research revealed annual improvements in aerobic capacity and body mass index for students participating in NFL PLAY 60 programming when compared to schools not utilizing NFL PLAY 60 programs.[9]

In 2015, the National Basketball Association launched Jr. NBA. It's a participation program designed to enhance the youth basketball experience for players ages 6-14, coaches, parents, teams, and organizations. There are programs and activities designed to grow the game and instructional tips and information designed to enhance coaching effectiveness and parental involvement in youth basketball.

Like the other leagues, the National Hockey League and the National Hockey League Players' Association have also identified the need to grow the game of hockey. Their "Learn to Play Initiative" (LTP), a joint (NHLPA/NHL) grassroots hockey initiative, was created to offer more families an opportunity to see what makes youth hockey great. For first-time participants to the sport, this program changes the way hockey is offered to inspire new families to join the hockey community and provide an age-appropriate program based on the latest child development research. With certified coaches, led by former NHL players, the on-ice program will teach the basic skills of ice hockey.[10]

Teens

Just as with the younger user segment, the total number of teens is also expected to rise. According to the U.S. Census Bureau, by 2050, the population between

Photo 6.1
Professional sports are realizing the importance of the kids' market to their long-term success

Source: Shutterstock.com, Christopher Penler

the ages of 10 and 19 will reach 44 million, although these ages will make up a smaller percentage of the total population than today.[11]

With this potential amount of purchasing power, it can be understood why sporting goods are one of the top advertising categories for teens. One key to reaching this teen market is to involve them in the marketing process and engage them in the brand. What brands (or leagues, in this case) are hot with teens? Figure 6.1 shows the pro sports of interest to the teen market, including differences between males and females.

Although teens represent a sizable and important market, sports marketers must do a better job of understanding this group, or it will be lost. For instance, American teens are not tuning in to sporting events in large numbers, at least not compared with the general population. As shown in Figure 6.2, only the NBA attracts a share of greater than 10 (which represents the percentage of viewers watching the sport at that point in time). Fortunately for soccer, the highest shares for teen viewers were Liga MX and MLS.[12]

While TV viewership may diminishing, there is an increasing use of media among young people. Teen's lives today are primarily a story of technology facilitating increased consumption. Today's multitasking teens (ages 13 to 18) used entertainment screen media (not at school or for homework) for an unbelievable average of seven hours and 22 minutes each day in 2019.[13]

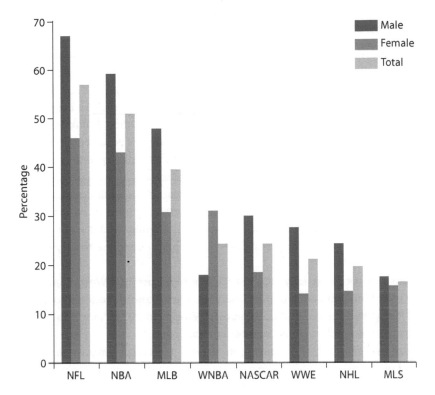

Figure 6.1

Prosports that appeal to teenagers: youth who say they are very or somewhat interested in the sport

Source: The Futures Company

What can sport marketers do to better reach teens and those slightly older in Generation Z (born between 1997 and 2012)? As the accompanying article illustrates, the sports industry is (re)thinking consumption patterns to grasp a further understanding of this demographic that will become increasingly important.

ARTICLE 6.2
HERE TO STAY: GENERATION Z'S IMPACT ON SPORTS CONTENT STRATEGY

Generation Z is already impacting modern culture and that's unlikely to change.

The generation, born after 1997, will make up 40 percent of consumers by 2020 and already has a direct spending impact of $143 billion dollars. A recent panel at South by Southwest discussed strategies to capture their attention, as well as how Gen Z will radically shift the way content is distributed. "They're going to be huge," said Kathleen Grace, CEO of the production studio New Form. "They're coming for us, and it's pretty cool. They consume differently than any other generation."

The under-22 demographic consumes more than 3.5 hours of video daily, a majority of which is on mobile devices, according to Dude Perfect Chief Business Officer Jeff Toney. Much of the video is consumed in short snippets and by brand influencers connecting with the audience, a strategy that cultivates a special trust as well as offering plenty of engagement for those content creators nimble enough to stay ahead of the curve.

"You can't become predictable," Toney said. "One unfortunate thing is the generation is a little ADD, 'Entertain me now if, I don't like it, I have 1,000 other options to be distracted with.' . . . The challenge is between continuing something that is popular and doubling down on what works, but, in parallel, introducing fresh, new concepts to continue to engage the audience."

The impact on sports is yet to be fully felt, but it's coming, said John West, founder of Whistle, a sports and entertainment media brand. "The young generation is redefining sports; less watching on TV, less attending live traditional sports," West said. "They're still followers, but on social and they're able to follow niche, non-traditional sports."

That surge in non-traditional sports activity is driven by direct involvement. The proliferation of digital media allows participatory sports to reach more people looking to try and improve instead of passively watching elite athletes. Activities such as CrossFit and rock climbing benefit from improved exposure, which in turn can help spur participation numbers. But West, who has three children in Generation Z, said he often sees them outside recreating videos they see on platforms like Dude Perfect, from there they film it, edit it and add music before sharing and challenging their peers.

"To us, sports has been defined by leagues," Toney said. "Traditionally, it's only a select few who can compete on the professional level. But people who don't have those inherent genes are competitive and like to compete with friends."

Advertising consumption habits are beginning to change with those content shifts.

A Nielsen study found the demographic has an 86 percent recall rate of products, suggesting massive potential for stickiness. But according to West, Generation Z is also more likely to find content when it's shared by a friend and allows them to engage directly. It's incumbent on platforms to provide the influencers and creators to establish genuine and authentic relationships with their key audience, which Generation Z users feel they can trust more.

"This generation views social influences and creators as their new celebrities," West said. "There's a relationship that can be developed that is tough to develop with LeBron James and Tom Brady."

To that end, Toney said it's important for creators to give users a view behind the curtain to get to know them better. For sports teams, in particular, that means showcasing its athletes away from competition. By and large, Generation Z cares far more about the name on the back of the jersey than the front. "When I was growing up, I'd follow the Detroit Tigers, doesn't matter who's on the team," Toney said. "Nowadays, you're not following a sport, you're following a player because they fall in love with the personalities."

West said that despite how much older generations want to believe the social influence won't stick, he doesn't expect this media model to go anywhere. "It's amazing to me in traditional media and sports, they're still skeptical the influencer is a fad," he said. "We don't see any data that when a 24-year-old turns 25, they un-wire. The habits they're forming now are generational shifts that grow up with them. "Embracing the power of social entertainers and the brands they've built organically is step one. "It's up to sports media to adapt accordingly.

Credit: Pat Evans

Rightsholder: Front Office Sports

URL: https://frntofficesport.com/generation-z-sports/. Accessed September 24, 2020

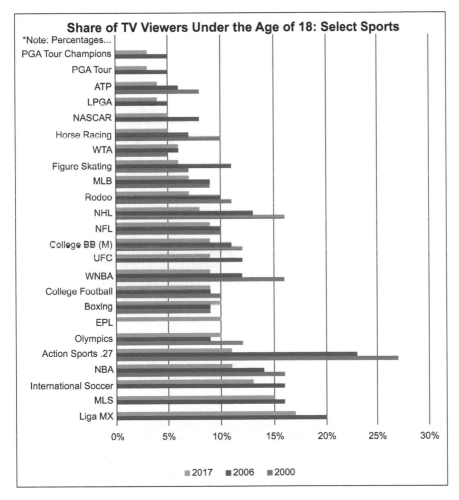

Figure 6.2
Share of TV viewers who are under 18 for selected sports in the United States

Source: Sport Business Journal: By John Lombardo and David Brought, June 5, 2017 www.sportsbusiness daily.com/Journal/Issues/2017/06/05/Research-and-Ratings/Viewership-trends.aspx

The mature market

Another market that is expected to increase at a staggering pace is the older age groups, otherwise known as the "mature market." The number of Americans age 65 and older is *projected to nearly double* from 52 million in 2018 to 95 million by 2060, and the 65-and-older age group's share of the total U.S. population will rise from 16 percent to 23 percent.[14]

In fact, every day, about 10,000 people in the United States turn 65, and by the year 2030, roughly one out of every five Americans will be aged 65 years and older.[15] Stereotypically, the elderly are perceived to be inactive and thrifty. Nothing could be further from the truth. The mature market is living longer for a variety of reasons and becoming more physically active. The mature market makes up nearly 25 percent of health club membership, and this number is expected to grow.[16]

The 50-plus age group controls over 80 percent of disposable income and holds over $8 trillion in spending power. Contrary to the widespread view of older populations as an economic burden, an AARP report "clearly shows that older adults are not a drain on society but a growing demographic that is transforming markets and is a key driver of economic growth, innovation and new value creation benefiting people of all ages," says Jean Accius, senior vice president for thought leadership and international affairs for AARP.[17] As a result, sports marketers are capitalizing on this growing market in a variety of ways.

Traditionally, senior citizen discounts have been promoted in Major League Baseball and their affiliates. For example, the former New York Yankees minor

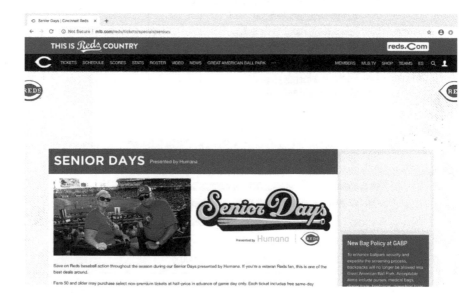

Web Capture 6.4
Cincinnati Reds targeting the mature market through Senior Days

*Source:*www.mlb.com/reds/tickets/specials/seniors

league affiliate, the Trenton Thunder, created the 55+ fan club called the Senior Diamond Club, providing tickets, discounts on merchandise, and other special promotional offers to seniors. Promotions such as Baseball Bingo and half-priced wine were designed to strengthen the relationship between the Thunder and the teams' senior fans.[18]

Other examples of sports markets being segmented by age can be seen in the growing number of "senior" sporting tours and events. The Champions Tour of the PGA has nearly the following of the regular tour events. Although not as successful as the golf tour, other professional senior tours include tennis (ATP Champions Tour) and bowling (PBA50 Tour).

Seniors are also becoming more active as sports participants. The fastest-growing participation sports for seniors, classified as age 55 and older, include bicycling, fishing, and bird/wildlife viewing. Table 6.3 shows some of the sports of interest for the maturing baby boomer market (ages 55+).

On a more organized front, National Senior Games is the largest multi-sport competition in the world open to those 50 and older. The National Senior Games started in 1987 with 2,500 athletes participating in 15 sports. By 2019, these numbers grew to nearly 14,000 athletes competing in 20 sports, illustrating the rising numbers of seniors who are remaining active.[19] In yet another example, the International Tennis Federation offers a seniors global tour with more than 26,000 participants in 450 tournaments spanning 70 nations. The ITF Championships include a senior division (50-60+) and supersenior division (65-85+).

These examples of senior athletes are representative of the mature market worldwide and demonstrate what a vibrant, independent, and viable segment this is for sport marketers.

Gender

A number of marketing executives in the sports industry have increasingly taken note that women have become crucial to their fan bases. Female fans have been so crucial that organizations such as FIFA, NFL, NASCAR, MLB, NBA, and NHL have focused promotional efforts on enhancing the female audiences, with much success. For example, some 30-40 percent of women count themselves baseball fans, 35 percent of basketball fans are women, 47 percent of football fans are female, and an estimated 43 percent of MLS fans are female.[20]

The NFL has long realized the importance of women fans and has developed evolving strategic plans to attract them and keep them interested in a traditionally male-oriented sport. Based on research conducted by the NFL, women fans do not want to be treated differently from men. NFL Commissioner Roger Goodell stated, "(Women) fans want to be treated as real fans because they love the game, understand the game, and want to have the opportunity to experience the game just as anyone else does."[21]

Table 6.3 Top 25 sports/activities by participants in 2019, ages 60+

	Sport/activity	2019 participants (000s)	1-year change	3-year avg. change
1	Walking for fitness	111,439	0.4%	1.1%
2	Treadmill	56,823	5.7%	3.1%
3	Dumbbells/hand weights	51,450	0.3%	0.0%
4	Running/jogging	50,052	1.2%	1.9%
5	Hiking (day)	49,697	3.8%	5.7%
6	Bowling	45,372	–0.9%	–0.4%
7	Road/paved surface bicycling	39,388	0.9%	0.9%
8	Fishing (freshwater/other)	39,185	0.5%	0.9%
9	Stationary cycling (recumbent/upright)	37,085	1.1%	0.9%
10	Weight/resistance machines	36,181	–0.5%	0.4%
11	Elliptical motion/cross-trainer	33,056	–0.5%	0.9%
12	Yoga	30,456	6.0%	5.1%
13	Free weights (barbells)	28,379	2.0%	2.3%
14	Swimming for fitness	28,219	2.3%	2.0%
15	Camping	28,183	2.8%	2.1%
16	Basketball	24,917	2.9%	3.7%
17	Dance, step, and other choreographed exercise to music	23,957	7.0%	3.2%
18	Bodyweight exercise and bodyweight accessory–assisted training	23,504	–2.8%	–2.2%
19	High-impact/intensity training	22,044	2.0%	1.0%
20	Wildlife viewing more than 1/4 mile from home/vehicle	20,040	–2.5%	–1.1%
21	Tennis	17,684	–0.9%	–0.7%
22	Baseball	15,804	–0.5%	2.3%
23	Camping (RV)	15,426	–3.5%	–0.9%
24	Stair-climbing machine	15,359	2.2%	0.6%
25	Table tennis	14,908	–4.4%	–3.5%

*Source:*www.physicalactivitycouncil.com/pdfs/current.pdf

Despite the obvious male overtones of the increasingly popular mixed martial arts scene – as exhibited by the success of the Ultimate Fighting Championship (UFC) – fans of the female persuasion are also flocking to the popular sport. Some estimate as many as 44 percent of UFC fans are women.[22] In fact, for a sport that used to be known as little more than a glorified bar brawl, mixed martial arts fights have been branded and stamped with a marketable seal of approval by sponsors and UFC stakeholders alike.

Sports and non-sports brands have recognized the need for a strategic approach to targeting a growing female market (both participants and spectators), as the accompanying article indicates.

ARTICLE 6.3
WOMEN IN SPORTS: ARE BRANDS KEEPING UP?

Women in sports: was this year's FIFA Women's Cup the game changer?

Gender equality in advertising is the holy grail. Same for the sporting industries, where – perhaps apart from in tennis – female sports stars haven't achieved the same level of notoriety as their male counterparts. Or at least, that seemed to be the case until this year's FIFA Women's World Cup.

While 2019 may have been the year that the world cast an eye on women in sports, marketers and researchers have realized that this isn't a one-off trend.

For instance, a recent report from IBM – Change to win: achieving competitive advantage in the sports industry – reveals some 150 million people watched the UEFA Women's Euro 2017 and 51,211 people attended the finale of the Mexican 16-team Liga MX Femenil the same year, which marked a record for women's football.

When women's football just became football

Many marketers anticipate a growing level of intrigue in women's sport following the Women's World Cup (WWC). "What has changed is women," says BBD Perfect Storm's managing director New Macho, Fernando Desouches. "And brand communications are reflecting and reinforcing this change."

Campaigns such as Dove's 'Real Beauty' in 2005, followed by Always' 'Like a Girl' in 2014 and Sport England's 'This Girl Can' of 2015 have paved the way for female empowerment. "Women now feel more comfortable and attracted to sports that were previously more exclusively available to men, like football or rugby," adds Desouches. "This is definitely not a one-off. It's part of a social evolution, and it's very good for brands and society at large."

Nationwide's director of campaigns and public policy, Tanya Joseph – also the architect of 'This Girl Can' – agrees that the success of these campaigns has only served to increase public attention when it comes to championing women's sport. Looking back on the iconic campaign she worked on, Joseph has personally seen the impact that 'This Girl Can' had on the industry.

"It changed the way we sell sport to women, the way women are portrayed in sports advertising, and the way women think about sport," she says. It prompted subsequent campaigns to mimic the trailblazing approach. Just think of Bodyform's 'Blood' campaign, which pioneered the use of red blood on-screen, defying the tradition of using blue liquid to represent menstrual blood.

The WWC became a historical moment in advertising. "It helped to normalise [gender roles]," according to James Kirkham, chief business officer at Copa90. "It was when women's football just became football."

How brands are rethinking their approach

Rather than separate sports because of gender, the tournament brought women up to the same level playing field as their male counterparts. For Kirkham, it caused "a seismic shift in interest, spawning countless shows, new programming and media documentation, and exactly the right positive noise, too. The WWC wasn't the only element, but it has been an important cultural moment for changing attitudes around women's sport."

And brands are seeing women's sport as equally important as men's, according to Marzena Bogdanowicz, head of marketing and commercial at the FA's Women's Football division.

There's no doubt that gender stereotypes continue to exist in the advertising industry, despite efforts and regulations from organizations such as the Advertising Standards Authority, yet the sporting sector has been somewhat neglected.

"Beauty standards for women have been redefined and are now becoming more relaxed," says Desouches. "But other less visible stereotypes, like the narrow way brands define the notion of success for men, have not yet been addressed properly. Brands that solely address men are more at risk of becoming obsolete than those also targeting women because they've had to actively adjust their message."

Looking back on the WWC, Bogdanowicz remembers the work the FA put in, revealing just how much planning it took to get it right: "From the media, to the rights holders, to the brands that support, the FA has spent time with its commercial partners, media and broadcasters to align positioning and discuss how, as a collective, we can help change attitudes."

Which is why, she believes, the interest in women's sport and marketing women in sport won't waver, especially with the Lionesses' match against Germany in November followed by the 2021 UEFA Women's Euro.

There are many more opportunities for brands to take advantage of this new space – with brands like Nike having already created a dedicated women's kit, Lucozade creating a first-ever footballers (male or female) on-product, and Budweiser promoting women on their multi-packs – all actively embracing the challenge and participating in these social discussions.

But it requires a team effort. "Sports and brands need to work really hard together to entrench the change," says Joseph.

This boy can

"But using authentic images [of sports] is a massive challenge to lots of brands," she adds. "Playing sport and being active involves sweat, mud, blood and grimacing, things which most brands shy away from."

Showcasing the reality of women playing sports, rather than glamourising or glossing over it, has the power to push society into new terrain. It begins a discourse that is different from the way in which men are represented in sport, where often the conversation centres around hyper-competition – the reason why many male sports stars still don't reveal their sexualities for fear that it could have repercussions on their career progression. "Undoubtedly right now there's uncertainty about masculinity and how to present it," explains Kirkham. "People do not want to create the wrong types of communication in this climate."

But some marketers – like Bogdanowicz – believe that the shift in focus, moving the limelight away from male sports stars to females, has impacted the way the public view masculinity. "There've been some cases where the element of masculinity has softened, as a result, in its portrayal," she says. Although, of course, progress is slow and difficult to measure. For marketers like Joseph it's not the issue with stereotyping that's the problem, but the way in which brands are carelessly using these ideals. "Stereotyping is a helpful way of conveying messages swiftly, but I do have a problem with harmful gender stereotypes – ones that tell us 'real girls' don't play sports like rugby or that makeup and sport don't go together."

As public interest in women's sport continues, brands will increasingly recognize the traction they can gain from tapping into these audiences, not to mention possibly revolutionizing the way men are perceived in this field. Desouches expects businesses to invest further in brands that are targeting women through sports, not just sports brands – but suggests that rather than mimic male ads, they need to find a unique way in which to engage these newfound consumers. He predicts that "genderless communications in sports marketing" could be something to look out for.

As Joseph concludes: "There is potential for a really bright future for sports marketing. It just needs brands to want to build long-term relationships with individuals/teams/sports to understand their audiences and what they are looking for."

Credit: Atkins, Olivia, 2019. Women in sports: Are brands keeping up? The Drum. November 05

URL: www.thedrum.com/news/2019/11/05/women-sports-are-brands-keeping-up, accessed September 24, 2020

More women are participating in sports, and more women are watching sports. Stereotypes are quickly eroding as females are also choosing to participate in traditionally male-only sports. One such example of females participating in a historically male sport is football. Nationwide, 1,240 girls played on high school tackle football teams in the 2018 season, according to a survey by the National Federation of State High School Associations. That represents the most female participation in the history of the sport at the high school level.[23] Some 59 professional women's football teams in three main divisions exist across the Women's Football Alliance.[24] The league is even attracting some national sponsors like Secret (see Web Capture 6.5).

The other barrier that women are crossing is the sport industry job market. As Article 6.4 discusses, women are taking on more prominent roles in global sport business, like the Olympic Games.

Web Capture 6.5
Women's Football Alliance promoting equality and opportunity

Source: www.wfaprofootball.com

ARTICLE 6.4
WOMEN AT THE FOREFRONT OF THE U.S. OLYMPIC MOVEMENT

- Women at the forefront of U.S. Olympic Movement – The USOC's Sarah Hirshland and Susanne Lyons, along with IOC members Anita DeFrantz and Kikkan Randall, are part of the new, female-led U.S. Olympic movement.

  - www.sportsbusinessdaily.com/Journal/Issues/2019/01/07/Olympics/USOC-women.aspx?hl=women%27s+participation+in+sport&sc=0

You've heard of the glass ceiling keeping women out of the corner office. But over the past decade, researchers have identified another challenge facing female executives: the "glass cliff."

That's the term coined when academics discovered that women are far more likely to ascend into senior leadership when companies face crisis. Therefore, they face a tougher job from the start than their male counterparts – they start on a cliff and must pull the organization back from the brink, or get pushed off.

Which brings us to the U.S. Olympic Committee, still working to emerge from the vast USA Gymnastics sex abuse scandal. With a new all female CEO/board chair duo, its leadership ranks include women at a level never before seen in major sports.

Along with CEO Sarah Hirshland and Chair Susanne Lyons, America's two International Olympic Committee members are women – Anita DeFrantz and Kikkan Randall – as are eight of 15 members of Hirshland's executive cabinet. So is Kathy Carter, CEO of the USOC-Los Angeles 2028 commercial joint venture and the country's top Olympic sales executive.

To be clear, most of them pre-date the scandal – only Hirshland and Carter are entirely new to the Olympics; Lyons has served on the board since 2010 and became chair Jan. 1. But at a time when the USOC is under pressure from Congress, abuse victims and its own athletes to make profound changes quickly, it's women who will determine the organization's crucial next steps.

In recent interviews with Sports Business Journal, the female leaders spoke about the dual feelings of opportunity and moral imperative they face. As the former CMO of Visa, Lyons for most of her career strove to be simply a leader for all purposes, not a "woman leader" per se. Now, her gender is central to the task.

"We recognize that some of our sisters were not served well by our movement, and I think we feel a special obligation to them to make sure we are at our best and that we do the best work of our lifetime to make things better for them," she said.

That's the challenge facing Lyons, Hirshland and their teams: To restore stability and confidence in the USOC, while also recognize their unprecedented position and help other women thrive.

"I think it's a story that I hope we all look at in 20 years and say it shouldn't be a story any more," Hirshland said. "It's a story that should go away, but it's a story right now because it is unusual. And to the extent that telling it makes it more common, or more comfortable, or more normal, then it should be a story."

The Olympics are a natural environment for female executives and administrators to thrive. It's the only major sports property that over-indexes with female audiences, and the Games are the only time when women athletes are given equal billing with men, if not in some cases more.

Commercially and competitively, Team USA is growing ever-more dependent on women. In three of the last four Olympics, American women have won more medals then the men, and Title IX has put American women in a position to dominate their global competitors in many sports for years to come.

But at the same time, Olympic sports can be extremely traditional and hierarchical. Without the promise of fame and high salaries that major professional leagues can offer to ambitious young executives, Olympic sport federations tend to be led by former competitors and coaches, and reliant on volunteers who often spend decades around the sport, tying modern management to a culture from decades ago.

"We make the assumption that if we get more women into these leadership positions that it's going to lead to these massive institutional changes," said Cheryl Cooky, a Purdue professor and author of the book "No Slam Dunk: Gender, Sport and the Unevenness of Social Change." "But the institutions themselves are gendered. That's the important piece. We tend to forget about that."

Indeed, 48 of the 50 American national governing bodies that report to the USOC have male CEOs, though their volunteer boards are much more diverse. International sport federations are not much better, and the Olympic program still betrays traces of the paternalism of an earlier era. For example, women road cyclists will tackle a much less interesting course than men in Tokyo, and the Olympics have refused overwhelming demand by female bobsledders to add a four-person race in the Winter Games to match the men's program.

In talking to the USOC's new leaders, much of the conversation focused on how they can use their positions to bring more women into leadership positions, both inside the USOC and elsewhere in the sprawling movement.

Lyons specifically noted the poor track record of converting female athletes into sport administrators, and promised action on that front. Even though most sports generate roughly the same number of male and female Olympians, administrators and coaches are overwhelmingly men.

> We recognize that some of our sisters were not served well by our movement, and I think we feel a special obligation to them to make sure we are at our best and that we do the best work of our lifetime to make things better for them.
>
> Susanne Lyons
> Board Chair

"I think we have to take much more definitive action to begin to help women begin to, in the early stages of their career, develop those skills so they can be considered for those roles," Lyons said.

If they succeed, future executives wouldn't have to pursue hiring diversity at the expense of the relationships and specialized experience that drive the Olympic industry. Today, there's a tension between finding new blood and maximizing influence. Hirshland, for instance, was specifically chosen as CEO because she brought an outside perspective, Lyons said, but the board was aware of the steep learning curve.

"I think it's very possible to find a handful of women to jump into a handful of roles, but at the end of the day, you know that's not systemic change," Hirshland said. "[Systemic change] is creating a long-term pipeline where there is this constant pattern of development. Because in a perfect world, you're not bringing in people from outside the Olympic movement."

The USOC requires at least half of the candidates for every job be women or minorities. However, it does not mandate that for governing bodies – that level of control over day-to-day hiring would be politically difficult and unwieldy – leaving just USA Fencing (Kris Ekeren) and the U.S. Tennis Association (Katrina Adams) with female chief executives. Many of the NGBs have only a handful of staff, Hirshland noted, so they don't have sufficient turnover to drive quick change.

But the USOC is looking to play a stronger hand in overseeing the governing bodies after the Ropes & Gray report revealed that its hands-off approach was one reason Larry Nassar's abuse went undetected for so long. According to Nicole M. LaVoi, co-director of the Tucker Center for Research on Girls & Women in Sport at the University of Minnesota, change could happen swiftly if the USOC really wanted. Simply tie funding to minimum diversity goals in the executive or board ranks, LaVoi said.

She noted, however, that there's risk in potentially being seen as catering to women exclusively.

"If women leaders start making changes that look like they're benefiting women, people freak out," LaVoi said. "But if men come in and hire other men, nobody bats an eye because that's normal. There's lots of reasons women are reluctant to make those kinds of sweeping changes, because they get a lot of backlash."

In the post-Nassar world, female leaders could face less of the perception risk that LaVoi notes because empowering women is closely correlated with better serving athletes in general, of whom half are women.

As the USOC reels from the sex abuse cases, one of the new administration's top tasks is to become more "athlete-centric." In its report on the Nassar case, the law firm Ropes & Gray criticized the USOC for putting more effort into managing the bureaucracy than serving athletes.

Lyons, Hirshland and DeFrantz, the U.S.'s senior IOC representative who is one of four vice presidents of the global body, all said gender issues played a role in the USOC's inadequate response to Nassar.

"I think if there was something that we underestimated, it was really the impact of the power dynamics [between athletes and doctors, coaches and administrators]," Lyons said, "and as is true in most of society, often the person in power is male and the person who is not is female."

DeFrantz speculated that Nassar's victims didn't get taken seriously because he enjoyed presumed legitimacy as a male doctor. "[People] thought that just couldn't be happening," she said.

That power dynamic is perhaps still the defining issue for women in sports, said Cooky, the Purdue professor. Male athletes are almost never subordinate to a woman; female athletes are routinely subordinate to men.

Female Olympians simply have a different experience. The women on Team USA at the Pyeongchang Winter Games were more than a year younger than the men on average. In Rio, U.S. women were on average seven months younger. And female superstars tend to grasp fame at younger ages than men.

"There are some very unique things about being a female athlete," said Randall, who won an eight-year term on the IOC in an athletes-only vote in Pyeongchang. "In my case, I was still in the prime of my athletic performance and I wanted to start a family, and I had to wonder if sponsors and the team would still support me. Women tend to have to take on a lot of different things at once."

Randall, a cross-country skier, won Olympic gold in February – 22 months after her son, Breck, was born and two months before she was diagnosed with breast cancer. Then she joined the IOC Women's Commission.

She said visibility – simply being in key positions – is important to women and girls. "It's a very positive thing for the USOC to have so many strong women because I think that's going to plant the idea in more athletes' minds that maybe that's something they want to do," Randall said, "and we can start developing more women sport leaders."

Three-time bobsled medalist Elana Meyers Taylor, now president of the Women's Sports Foundation, said she's had just two female coaches in a 12-year career. "Without a doubt, my personal experience has been completely different from even that of my husband," Taylor said, referring to fellow bobsledder Nic Taylor.

"You're always fighting that good ol' boys club that kind of runs the system, and having women in leadership roles brings that unique perspective on how to navigate those types of political climates," Taylor said.

Internationally, the old boys' club has already taken notice. In Tokyo in November for the Association of National Olympic Committees meeting, Lyons and Hirshland sat together behind an American flag – an unprecedented show of female leadership in the organization. "There were a lot of people who were coming up and taking pictures of us," Hirshland recalls. "That was a big deal."

DeFrantz was the fifth female IOC member ever when she was first appointed in 1986. Today there are 32 current members. The IOC has set a goal of full gender equality in Olympic Games participation; however, the international federations are overwhelmingly led by men. "We used to have at least one woman on the executive board of every international federation on the Olympic [Summer] and Olympic Winter Games program," DeFrantz said. "There has been some backsliding of late, which needs to be corrected."

The U.S. has to be judicious in deciding when and how to exert its influence in the Olympic movement, but Hirshland promises action abroad. "I can tell you that the three of us are going to be really active internationally," Hirshland said. "That doesn't mean we won't be careful and it doesn't mean we won't be respectful. But we're going to be very active."

Internally, Hirshland has participated in a networking group of women from the USOC and the NGBs based in Colorado Springs that meets regularly, but she has a long-term goal of a talent development program that would specifically find and develop possible executives.

Like is often the case with female leaders who find themselves on the "glass cliff," the leaders of the USOC face extraordinary expectations. Society assumes women will bring a more team-oriented and empathic approach to leadership, and Cooky notes, sometimes believes those mere traits can push change faster than is practical.

But along with the high stakes is a sense of optimism about what can change. "I'm excited and happy," DeFrantz said. "A disaster brings us here in part, and that's horrible. But the future is going to be exciting."

A lot is riding on Hirshland and Lyons' success. Historically, the Olympics put women in the forefront of sports before anyone else, and today the Games are still sold to sponsors as a unique way of celebrating the country's full range of diversity. The stakes are high – for the USOC, the Olympics overall and women in sports in general.

"I'm really optimistic about putting these women in positions of leadership," LaVoi said. "And I really hope they succeed, because we so desperately need them to. There are a lot of people who care very deeply about this, and I hope they get the support they need to change the culture."

Credit: Fischer, Ben, 2019. Women at the forefront of U.S. Olympic Movement. Sports Business Journal, January 7

URL: www.sportsbusinessdaily.com/Journal/Issues/2019/01/07/Olympics/USOC-women.aspx?hl=women%27s+participation+in+sport&sc=0, accessed September 24, 2020

Ethnic background

Segmenting markets by **ethnic background** is based on grouping consumers of a common race, religion, and nationality. Ethnic groups, such as African Americans (13.4 percent of the U.S. population), Hispanic Americans (18.3 percent of the U.S. population), and Asian Americans (5.9 percent of the U.S. population)[25] are increasingly important to sports marketers as their numbers continue to grow. When segmenting based on ethnic background, marketers must be careful not to think of stereotypical profiles but to understand the unique consumption behaviors of each group through marketing research. We know that in the United States, these ethnic groups will continue to grow until the now-minority segment becomes the majority. These shifts will have a huge impact on sports marketing in the future.

What sport is currently best positioned to appeal to the growing ethnic markets? Most agree that soccer and the MLS have and will have the most numerous and most engaged fans, although the MLS will need to compete against other soccer leagues from around the world (e.g., the Premier League) for fans.

Ricardo Fort, Coke's Head of Global Sponsorships, reinforces this notion.

> As the profile of an American fan becomes more international, particularly Hispanic, soccer is likely to be the biggest winner. Thanks to the growth of the MLS, the increasing availability of international soccer content in open TV and, mostly, the incredible global success of the women's national team, new generations of fans will be as familiar with the Mbappes and Alex Morgans as their grandparents were with the Joe Montanas and their parents are with the Tom Bradys.[26]

An article by Mike Valdes-Fauli aptly points out that understanding the Hispanic subculture's love of sport goes well beyond soccer and has major implications for sports marketers. For example, Latino sports fans are more likely than non-Latinos (54 percent to 48 percent) to support organizations that support their sports entity. Hispanics follow a greater variety of sports, beyond just soccer, and also engage via mobile devices some 75 percent of the 90 hours they spend per month online. Simply put, this is a huge and growing market of importance and finding athletes and teams that resonate with Hispanic audiences will promise a huge return on investment.[27]

The NFL, NBA, and MLB have all been positioning themselves for the ethnic shifts by creating more international exposure through exhibition and regular season games, merchandising, and media coverage. For example, the NBA's Basketball Without Borders, an instructional camp organized by the NBA and FIBA, has had more than 2,300 participants from more than 120 countries. On the other hand, sports like NASCAR and the NHL that have historically appealed to a predominantly white fan base will continue to struggle and need to adapt or risk declines in fans.[28]

Sports media is also quickly moving to appeal to specific to ethnic groups. For example, NBC launched its Spanish sports network, then known as Deportes Telemundo, in 1987. *ESPN Deportes*, the premier Spanish-language sports daily, was introduced in 2001. The sports network includes some 2,500 hours of programming and more than 500 events annually across television, radio, streaming, and in print demonstrating their ongoing commitment to Hispanic sports fans in the United States.[29] Similarly, there are Spanish-language web sites corresponding to the main English site.

The Hispanic market is not the only ethnic segment of interest to sport marketers. In the United States, Asian Americans have the highest median household income of any ethnic group of $87,194, which is nearly $20,000 higher than that of non-Hispanic whites.[30] With over $1 trillion in purchasing power and spending 21 percent more than the average household in the United States, Asian Americans are the fastest-growing and most-educated segment and a highly reachable group in the country. Moreover, they have large population centers in major cities that are home to multiple pro sports franchises. When it comes to putting fans in the stands and merchandise in their homes and offices,

Asian Americans should be a sports marketer's dream[31] (www.marketingcharts. com/demographics-and-audiences/asian-american-108591). Whether it's the Hispanic market, Asian market, or any other ethnic market, sport organizations are realizing the critical nature of understanding and catering to these growing segments for all sports products and services.

Family life cycle

The family life cycle was a concept developed in the 1960s to describe how individuals progress through various "life stages," or phases of their life. A traditional life cycle begins with an individual starting in the young, single "life stage." Next, an individual would progress through stages such as young, married with no children; young, married with children; to, finally, older with no spouse. As you can see, the traditional stages of the family life cycle are based on demographic characteristics such as age, marital status, and the presence or absence of children.

Today, the traditional family life cycle is no longer relevant. In 2018, 3.2 per 1,000 people in the United States are divorced, a number that has actually declined over time. While this might be encouraging, the marriage rate is also declining, more people are cohabiting than ever before,[32] and changes in family structure such as these have led marketers to a more modern view of the family life cycle, shown in Figure 6.3.

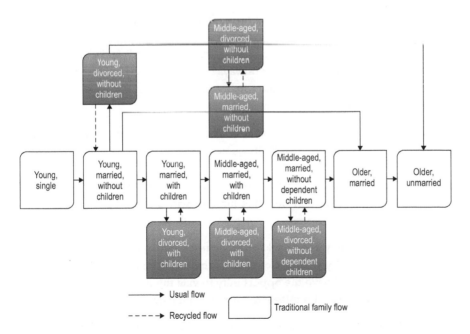

Figure 6.3
Modern family life cycle

Sports marketers segmenting on the basis of family life cycle have a number of options. Do they want to appeal to the young and single, the elderly couple with no kids living at home, or the family with young children? Sports that are growing in popularity, such as biking, segment markets based on a stage of the family life cycle. Just imagine the incompatible biking needs of a young, single person versus a young, married couple with children.

Professional sports have come under increased scrutiny in the past decade for their lack of family values, making it more difficult to market to the family unit. Rising ticket prices, drunken fans, and late games to accommodate televised scheduling have all been cited as examples of professional sports becoming "family unfriendly." Realizing this, sports marketers have tried to renew family interest in sports and make going to the game fun for the entire family.

There are numerous examples of sports marketers trying to become more family friendly. Take a look at the following example from the Indianapolis Colts.

ARTICLE 6.5
COLTS UNVEIL FAMILY-FRIENDLY ACTIVITIES, BENEFITS FOR 2019 GAME DAYS

Colts communications

Indianapolis – The Indianapolis Colts today announced several opportunities and benefits that will welcome and engage even more kids and families at Colts games at Lucas Oil Stadium this season.

"Our fans are our family, and each home Colts game is a family reunion," said Carlie Irsay-Gordon, Colts vice chair and owner. "That's why we're always focused on creating more activities and programming that will engage and entertain the whole family, including fans of all ages."

Some of the programming and benefits include:

- **Infants at homes games**. Beginning this season, children aged 24 months and younger will no longer need tickets to attend home Colts games when accompanied by a parent or guardian. Children 25 months and older will still need regularly-priced tickets.
- **Colts "Family Day."** The Colts will celebrate Family Day at the Colts–Cleveland Browns preseason game on Sun., August 17 and welcome families with special opportunities to enjoy time together on game day.

As such, the Colts will offer a "Family Four Pack" that includes four game tickets for $60. Family Four Packs can be purchased by visiting Colts.com/family. In addition, children 18 and under in attendance at that game will have the opportunity to visit the field post-game. More details on the post-game field visits will be released later this summer.

- **Youth Gameday Giveaway**. During each game of the 2019 season, a special Colts-branded arm sleeve will be available to all youth aged 15 and under. There is a limit of one item per child per game, and the child must be present to redeem the item. The items will be available at any Guest Services kiosk in the stadium.

- **Colts Kids' Club Meal.** Special Colts Kids' Club Meals – consisting of a hot dog, apple slices, string cheese and apple juice – are available on game days for $5. Kids' Meals can be purchased at Concession Stands 148, 331, 513 and 540, as well as the East & West Club Street Grill.
- **"First Colts Game" pins.** For those attending their first Colts game, "My First Colts Game" pins will be available at any Guest Services kiosk in the stadium. The team offers special birthday pins to fans celebrating a birthday at a home game.
- **Mamava lactation stations.** Last season, the Colts installed three lactation pods at the stadium, providing an option for nursing mothers who prefer a private location to breastfeed or pump at games or other stadium events. Created by Mamava, the suites are self-contained pods with comfortable seating, a fold-down table, interior lighting, an electrical outlet, a USB port and a door that can be locked for privacy. The three pods are located at:

  - Street Level, southwest corner near Section 132.
  - Street Level, northeast corner outside of Sections 108–110.
  - Terrace Level, southeast corner outside of Sections 518/619.

In addition to the pods, the Mother's Room is another private lactation area, located on the Loge Level next to the stadium administrative offices near Sections 307/407.

- **American Family Insurance Touchdown Town.** As in past years, the Colts will host fans at Touchdown Town, which is free and open to the public, before home Colts games. Located along South St. north of Lucas Oil Stadium on home game days, Touchdown Town features fun activities for kids and families, including the Colts Play 60 Zone, a 40-yard dash, face and hair painting, autographs and photo opportunities, live music and entertainment and much more.
- **Child Wristbands.** During game days and other events at Lucas Oil Stadium, guests may request a wristband for themselves and their child, which includes the guest's name, seat location and a preferred phone number to be contacted if the child is lost. Guests may pick up wristbands from Guest Services kiosks located at:

  - Street Level, southeast corner near Section 121
  - Street Level, southwest corner near Section 135
  - Club/Log Level, southwest corner adjacent to Section 330
  - Terrace Level, northwest corner by elevator lobby across from Section 519
  - Terrace Level, southeast corner by elevator lobby across from Section 545

Credit: Colts.com. June 24, 2019

URL: www.colts.com/news/colts-unveil-family-friendly-activities-benefits-for-2019-game-days, accessed September 24, 2020

Pygmy Boats is the original manufacturer of precision, pre-cut stitch and glue kayak kits in North America. In the last 32 years our designs have been awarded "Best Kayak Kit" and "Best Wooden Kayak" and are enjoyed by thousands around the world. Started in 1986 by boat designer and software engineer, John Lockwood, Pygmy Boats produced North America's first computer designed wooden sea kayaks. Whether a paddler is novice or advanced in technique, we have a boat kit to suit your needs. Kits are 1/3 the price and 30% lighter than fiberglass with equal durability.

Ad 6.1
Pygmy's segmentation on the basis of the family life cycle

Credit: Pygmy

URL: www.pygmyboats.com

The hope for family focus such as that of the Colts is to raise the standard of fan behavior on game days, making the environment more appropriate for families. Moreover, many sports organizations have instituted specific family nights, which include tickets, parking, promotional items, and food for a reduced price to encourage family attendance.

Socioeconomic segmentation

Thus far, we have discussed demographic variables such as age, gender, ethnic background, and family life cycle as potential ways to segment sports markets. Another way of segmenting markets that was found to be an excellent predictor of consumer behavior is through **socioeconomic segmentation**. As previously defined, **social class** is a division of members of a society into a hierarchy of distinct status classes, so that members of each class have relatively the same status and members of all other classes have either more or less status.

Although most people immediately equate social class with income, income alone can be a misleading predictor of social class. Other factors such as educational level and occupation also determine social standing. Usually, income, education, and occupation are highly correlated. In other words, individuals with higher levels of education typically have higher income and more prestigious occupations. Based on these factors (income, education, and occupation), members of a society are artificially said to belong to one of the social class categories. The traditional social class categories are upper-, middle-, and lower-class Americans. Participation in certain sports has been associated with the various social strata. For instance, golf and tennis have been called "country club" sports. Polo is a sport of the "rich and famous." Bowling is usually thought of as one of the "blue-collar" sports of the working class. NASCAR has also traditionally and stereotypically been tagged with "good ol' boys" and "blue-collar" values. However, NASCAR has turned into a multibillion-dollar-a-year industry and a marketing success story. During this tremendous growth, the sport is moving beyond its "good-ol'-boy" mentality and reaching new markets. Just consider the demographics of the NASCAR fan.[33]

The typical fan base breakdown of a NASCAR consumer shows that:

- 62 percent/38 percent male to female
- 33 percent have children
- Top markets include LA; NY; Atlanta; Dallas; Chicago
- Average household income of $80,500/yr
- 25 percent multicultural audience (up from 20 percent in 2011)

As with sex roles, the relationship between social class and sport is now shifting. Golf is now being enjoyed by people of all income levels, and sports like mixed martial arts continue to attract both blue- and white-collar populations. While there appears to be valid evidence to support the notion that sport participation is related to social class, studies of sport have found that the higher one's social class, the greater one's involvement in sports.[34] Many believe that sport and entertainment are perfectly suited to capitalize on the social qualities of a "New America." In an era where the web and social media are eliminating physical and cultural boundaries and creating a larger global community, sport

Photo 6.2
Polo is a sport that has typically appealed to the upper class

Credit: Shutterstock, ID# 63037606 by fritz16

URL: www.shutterstock.com/image-photo/ebreichsdorf-austria-september-10-polo-european-63037606

provides a platform to augment these "pastime" exchanges. Although these exchanges are often still tied to economic factors, that is, what one can afford, sport serves as an escalator that provides opportunity.

Attending a professional sporting event, once affordable for the whole family, is now a more costly endeavor; therefore, today's consumers tend to weigh the pros and cons of attending against the array of entertainment alternatives, that is, media and other forms of non-sport entertainment. Some choose to spend the money, others not, but the opportunity for exchange still exists. In addition, as the roles of social class continue to shift, so do value exchange components that affect their purchasing decisions. In many instances, season ticket options to these events, which used to be readily affordable, can only be enjoyed by wealthy corporate season ticket holders.

Psychographic segmentation

Psychographic segmentation is described as grouping consumers on the basis of a common lifestyle preference and personality. Because personality alone is very difficult to measure and has not been linked directly to sports behavior, few sports marketing practitioners find it useful alone. The results of one recent study suggest that individuals who are most likely to identify with a team are those who seek out and enjoy social exchanges. The researchers suggest that marketing plans should be designed to emphasize communal aspects of events and that individuals rated high on extraversion, agreeability, and materialism may be more responsive to such promotions. Psychographics, however, looks more toward lifestyle preferences and less toward specific personality measures or traits.

Psychographic segments are believed to be more comprehensive than other types of segmentation, such as demographic, behavioral, or geodemographic. As consumer behavior researcher Michael Solomon points out, "Demographics allow us to describe *who* buys, but psychographics allows us to understand *why* they do."[35] For this reason, many sports marketers have chosen to segment their markets on the basis of psychographics. To gain a better understanding of consumers' lifestyles, marketers assess consumers' **AIO dimensions**, or statements describing activities, interests, and opinions (AIO). The three AIO dimensions are shown in Table 6.4.

Typically marketers quantify AIOs by asking consumers to agree or disagree with a series of statements reflecting their lifestyle. These statements can range from measures of general interest in sports to measures focusing on a specific sport. As seen in Table 6.4, many of these AIO dimensions relate indirectly or directly to sports. For example, social events, recreation, and products may have a direct link to sports, whereas club memberships, fashion, community, and economics may be indirectly linked.

Psychographic segmentation is sometimes linked directly to or even thought of as synonymous with lifestyle sports. In an excellent chapter in the book

Table 6.4 AIO dimensions

Activities	Interests	Opinions
Work	Family	Themselves
Hobbies	Home	Social issues
Social events	Job	Politics
Vacation	Community	Business
Entertainment	Recreation	Economics
Club membership	Fashion	Education
Community	Food	Products
Shopping	Media	Future
Sports	Achievements	Culture

Source: Journal of Advertising Research

Sport and Society, Belinda Wheaton describes the essence of lifestyle sports such as skateboarding, surfing, climbing, and snowboarding, to name a few. Wheaton described the distinctive nature of this "category" of sport as a desire for consumers of the sport to live a certain "style of life." She goes on to describe some of the unique characteristics of lifestyle sports. For example, these sports are based on the consumption of new objects (boards, bikes, etc.) and often involve new technologies. Lifestyle sports participants emphasize the creative, aesthetic, and performative expressions of their activities. Some practitioners refer to their activities as art rather than sport. Most of the lifestyle sports are individual rather than team oriented and stress personal goals rather than traditional competition.[36] These "lifestyle" sports represent an excellent example of the in-depth nature of psychograph segments and are illustrated in Table 6.5.

Marketers can also segment and target consumers by combining their lifestyles, obtained through AIOs, with their values. This method is called VALS, which is an acronym for values and lifestyles.[37] Values are "desirable, trans-situational goals, varying in importance, that serve as guiding principles in people's lives." The VALS model places consumers into one of eight segments based on their values. These segments range from innovators at the top to survivors at the bottom. Consumers are further segmented based on their affinity for ideals, achievement, and self-expression. For example, a consumer categorized as an innovator who values achievement would be motivated to seek products and services that convey status and success to others. Knowing this, marketers are able to tailor strategies that reach these types of consumers and impact them accordingly. Some researchers consider the VALS method "more elegant and fundamental" than the AIO approach.

Table 6.5 Claritas PRIZM premier social groups

Source: Claritas

Credit: © Claritas LLC, 2018

Geographic segmentation

Geography is a simple, but powerful, segmentation basis. Certainly, this is critical for sports marketers and as long-standing as "rooting for the home team." All sports teams use **geographic segmentation**; however, it is not always as straightforward as it may initially seem. For instance, the Dallas Cowboys, Chicago Bulls, Atlanta Braves, and the Notre Dame Fighting Irish were all known as "America's Team" at one time or another.

Geographic segmentation can be useful in making broad distinctions among local, regional, national, and international market segments. International or multinational marketing is a topic of growing interest for sports marketers. For example, Major League Baseball has developed an MLB International web presence that focuses on increasing awareness of the sport across the globe and started to play a number of international series prior to COVID.[38] NBA games are televised in 215 countries in 50 languages.[39] The NFL has also expanded internationally and now broadcasts regular season games in more than 234 countries, and Super Bowl LIV was streamed to 170 countries.[40] As the article below indicates, the leagues are realizing that the key to growth is going global, but the politics are not always easy or pleasant.

ARTICLE 6.6
THE NBA'S CHINA CRISIS IS NOT A FOREIGN SITUATION FOR AMERICAN SPORTS – AND IT PROMISES TO COME UP AGAIN

Six years ago, Scott Blackmun, then-CEO of the U.S. Olympic Committee, said U.S. athletes should "comply" with Russia's anti-LGBT propaganda law as Team USA prepared for the 2014 Winter Games in Sochi.

Russia Today heavily promoted his comments. But condemnation was intense back home, where the law was seen as both an affront to gay rights and to the fundamental American expectation of free expression. The USOC had to issue clarifications, emphasizing that the body found the law inconsistent with Olympic values and that the compliance remark was for athletes' safety.

Last week, the NBA's own foreign political controversy in China threatened the very foundation of the league's rapid growth, dominating business, sports and political news for a week. But it was hardly the first time a sports property has found itself caught between domestic politics and foreign affairs as it seeks a global stage, and it surely won't be the last.

As in the USOC's case, NBA Commissioner Adam Silver eventually found a middle ground: He expressed regret for the offense caused by Rockets general manager Daryl Morey's tweet in support of Hong Kong protestors that ignited the firestorm, but he did not apologize and pledged that the league would "protect our employees' freedom of speech."

The explosive nature of the fight between Silver and the totalitarian Chinese government may not be matched any time soon. But the problem of balancing American values against the political and cultural norms of other nations is sure to rise again. Western sports properties are increasingly pursuing China's tantalizing growth prospects at a time when their own customers, athletes and employees expect them to speak out on social causes. Individual athletes are now celebrated for becoming engaged in politics, and marketing experts say major sponsors also crave to be seen as "standing for something."

But one country's brand-safe social cause is another country's third rail. In just 27 months, the Winter Olympics head to Beijing, where controversies like the one the NBA is embroiled in could well reappear for any number of nations or brands. It has led to an open question about where the line should be between offering domestic political opinions and commenting on foreign affairs.

"We're American citizens, I think we have a social civic responsibility to be active in causes we believe in," Jacksonville Jaguars owner Shahid Khan, who was born in Pakistan, said from the stage at the Yahoo Finance All Markets Summit in New York. "Do we have that same responsibility to really opine on sovereign matters in other countries? I think that's the critical issue."

The International Olympic Committee, national Olympic committees and their sponsors have struggled with this balance for decades. Those who've experienced it have seen how the result has allowed those properties to maintain an altruistic brand in the West while still being welcome in China, North Korea and other totalitarian states.

"It's a fragile alignment, it's hard to keep together," said Terrence Burns, executive vice president of global sports for Engine Shop. "By necessity, they have to be extraordinarily adroit, diplomatically, and frankly respectful of every culture, in every nation, that they choose to work with."

Expect the China issue to come roaring back after the 2020 Summer Olympics in Tokyo, when final preparations for the 2022 Winter Games in Beijing kick off. When Beijing hosted the 2008 Summer Games, human rights advocates hammered Coca-Cola, Visa and others for supporting China through the Games. Visa even scrapped an early Olympics campaign tag line, "Go Humans!" in favor of "Go World!" amid concerns that the former would draw extra attention to China's human rights record.

To a certain extent, criticism is unavoidable for multinationals, and often critics will seek to amplify cross-border differences for their own gain. The Chinese government is known for using these situations to rally nationalist sentiment, and President Donald Trump eagerly framed two of his leading critics from the sports world, Warriors coach Steve Kerr and Spurs coach Gregg Popovich, as hypocrites last week for their non-engagement on Hong Kong questions.

But problems can be mitigated by ensuring that companies and employees know the facts before speaking out, said Michael Payne, a former marketing chief of the IOC and a longtime consultant to Olympic brands, including Alibaba.

"When you're going to start commenting about geopolitics, or national interests and politics, you really need to make sure you're fully up to speed on it, and you know your history and background, otherwise you're going to slip up on a banana skin," Payne said.

The IOC has not totally disengaged from countries' internal politics, Payne said. In the Middle East, the Olympic movement has "very carefully" navigated the issue of women's equality, through "slow cajoling and coaching" to put women on equal sports footing. "Frankly, with more progress than most politicians are seeing," Payne said.

As American leagues globalize, they'd be wise to seek out more international staffers and train themselves on other perspectives – and to generally be more risk-averse when it comes to global communications, experts said.

"When we work with our global partners in the Olympic space, it's so innate that you look at things through so many more lenses than the gut reaction from the American seat," said Ann Wool, president of Ketchum Sports & Entertainment, which has advised Olympic sponsors such as Chinese computing giant Lenovo and Procter & Gamble.

Jerry Colangelo, managing director of USA Basketball, spent several weeks this summer in China for the FIBA Basketball World Cup. He said the Chinese people love the NBA and there's lots of common ground, but the Hong Kong situation requires sensitivity.

"It is inevitable that because of where we are in today's world that there were going to be some roadblocks," said Colangelo. "And well, here we are."

Credit: Ben Fischer. Sports and politics: World of uncertainty. Sports Business Journal, Oct. 14

URL: www.sportsbusinessdaily.com/Journal/Issues/2019/10/14/Sports-and-Society/NBA-China.aspx?hl=china+nba+&sc=0, accessed September 24, 2020

The physical climate also plays a role in segmenting markets geographically. Classic examples include greater demand for snow skiing equipment in Colorado and surfboards in Florida. However, Colorado ski resorts have the greatest number of sports tourists who come from Florida, hardly thought of as a snow ski mecca. Therefore, segments of sports consumers may exist in unlikely geographic markets. In this example, the psychographics of the sports consumer may be more important in predicting behavior than geographic location.

Although the climate plays an important role in sports, marketers have attempted to tame this uncontrollable factor. For instance, tons of sand was shipped to Atlanta, creating beach-like conditions, for the first ever Olympic beach volleyball competition in 1996. The creation of domed stadiums has also allowed sports marketers to tout the perfect conditions in which fans can watch football in the middle of a blizzard in Minnesota or during the middle of a thunderstorm in Houston, Texas. More recently, stadium design has taken its next step forward. Seven new state-of-the-art stadiums with advanced open-air cooling technology are being built from scratch for the 2022 World Cup event.[41]

Behavioral segmentation

For sports marketers engaged in the strategic sports marketing process, two common goals are attracting more fans and retaining them. Behavioral segmentation lies at the heart of these two objectives. **Behavioral segmentation** groups consumers based on how much they purchase, how often they purchase, and how loyal they are to a product or service.

Interestingly, in today's professional sports environment, loyalty is an increasingly important topic. Many professional sports teams have held their fans and cities hostage, and cities are doing everything they can to keep their beloved teams. One estimate is that nearly $11 billion of taxpayer money has been spent on 54 ballparks, arenas, and stadiums in North America since 2006 alone.[42] This new construction and renovation was done largely to keep team owners satisfied and curb any threat of moving. In the NFL alone, the cost of the last 10 stadiums constructed was nearly $13 billion,[43] all of this done to keep owners and loyal fans coming back.

Franchises and players within each team move so rapidly that fan loyalty becomes a difficult phenomenon to capture. The day of the lifelong fan is over. Because of this, fans may identify more with individual players or even coaches (e.g., Aaron Judge and the Yankees, LeBron James and the Lakers, or Nick Saban and University of Alabama football) than they do with teams. According to some sports marketing experts, next to wins, fans like to see famous faces on the field. This is true even in team-dominated sports, such as football.

Fans may be more concerned with the individual performance of Raheem Sterling than they are with Manchester City. Certainly, sports marketers have to monitor this trend of diminishing loyalty to a team. However, some sports fans show extreme loyalty by purchasing personal seat licenses. PSLs require fans to pay a leasing fee for their seats. This fee would guarantee the consumer his or her seat for several years. The PSL, of course, demonstrates the extreme devotion of a group of fans. For example, NFL fans in Dallas had to pay PSLs of up to $150,000 just for the right to purchase season tickets at the Dallas Cowboys AT&T Stadium.

Sports marketers have recently taken a lesson in loyalty marketing from other industries and are creating loyalty marketing programs. A study by Pritchard and Negro[44] found that these programs are effective when they build on the genuine affinity fans have for their teams rather than rewarding attendance alone. Increasing fan interaction with players, coaches, and the entire organization through direct access or personal communication was shown to be much more important to the success of loyalty programs than rewarding attendance. Roughly two-thirds of MLB teams have loyalty programs, and the nature and number of these programs are in growth mode. Much of the growth in loyalty programs is spurred by the increasing amount of fan data collected to better understand preferences. The following article provides some of the best practices in fan loyalty programs.

ARTICLE 6.7
FAN LOYALTY PROGRAMS: SEVEN BEST PRACTICES

The ins and outs of team loyalty programs

Airlines, hotels and retailers have long found success using loyalty programs to retain their very best customers.

Below, marketing executives and fan engagement specialists with the Boston Red Sox, Minnesota Wild, New York Jets and San Francisco 49ers share tips, tactics and best practices on getting the most out of fan loyalty programs.

#1) Make it frictionless

Reward programs should reward fans for what they already do – buying season tickets, coming to games, interacting on social media, etc.

"You want to limit friction – keep it as close as possible to their current behavior. Don't make them jump over hoops," said Tim Zue, Boston Red Sox executive vice president and chief financial officer.

#2) Keep redemption items fresh

Teams need to update redemptions items on a regular basis to maintain fan interest and participation.

Just ask the New York Jets. The team learned that items that excited fans in the first two years of the Jets Rewards program were not so exciting in years three and four.

"We had to identify new and exciting redemption items. We didn't understand that would be a continual process," said Seth Rabinowitz, New York Jets senior vice president of marketing and fan engagement.

#3) Prioritize intangible rewards

Most season ticket holders already own jerseys and other team merchandise. As a result, properties should prioritize experiences – dinners with team executives, player experiences, etc. – as fan rewards.

"People want intangibles, things that are hard to find," said Marie Troje, Minnesota Wild vice president of customer service and retention.

Intangible rewards also help keep a lid on expenses, she added. "Using experiences instead of hard costs helps keep expenses low."

The San Francisco 49ers placed more focus on experiences after noticing that Faithful Rewards members were accruing points but not using them. The team infrequently offered game worn jerseys and autographed items as part of auctions or sweepstakes.

"People are gun shy of turning in points for a sweepstakes, because it's a lottery, and auctions, because there is only one winner," said Matt Crowell, San Francisco 49ers senior manager of member experience.

As a result, the team increased its investment in game day experiences. That includes participation in pre-game ceremonies, access to the player tunnel and post-game press conferences.

"Before we had small quantities of cool things and large quantities of lackluster things. We raised the bar and made it more experiential."

While experiences are in demand, they can be difficult to access. To get around that challenge, teams need to drive home the importance of rewards programs – and unique experiences – to departments that can offer them up. That includes team personnel, game day operations and building operations staff.

The Minnesota Wild, for example, works with Xcel Energy Center operations staff to access concert tickets for the Wild Rewards program.

"If they understand what we're doing, we can all benefit," said Troje.

#4) Reward behavior, not dollars spent

Teams have three options in how fans can earn points: the amount of money they spend, the actions they take, or a combination of the two.

A growing number of teams are prioritizing behaviors over dollars spent.

The New York Jets made a conscious decision to let season ticket holders earn points on their actions, not the amount of money they spend.

"A bigger disposable income does not make a bigger fan. Everyone is equal in their fandom. You earn the same points because you're contributing to the home field advantage," said Rabinowitz.

#5) Hire a dedicated staffer

Teams should have a dedicated staffer to ensure success from rewards programs.

The Minnesota Wild have a full-time staffer who is responsible for managing redemptions and making sure Wild Rewards members are happy. The employee works out of the team's office during the day and staffs a kiosk at home games.

"(Rewards) programs sometimes fall on someone's plate, and they don't get the attention they need. We have someone focus on it day in and day out."

#6) Don't limit programs to season ticket holders

While most teams use loyalty programs to reward season ticket holders, a growing number are expanding the programs to reach a larger audience.

The New York Jets this year rolled out Jets Rewards to single-game ticket purchasers, while the Boston Red Sox are piloting Red Sox Rewards with Red Sox Nation, the team's official fan club.

#7) Go slow on commercialization

Loyalty programs should be used to reward loyal customers, not to bombard them with corporate logos and commercial messages. Properties need to look for sponsors that add value to loyalty programs, not distract from them.

Source: Sponsorship.com, 2017. Fan Loyalty Programs: Seven Best Practices. IEG, October 10, accessed September 24, 2020. www.sponsorship.com/Report/2017/10/10/The-Ins-and-Outs-Of-Team-Loyalty-Programs/Fan-Loyalty-Programs – Seven-Best-Practices.aspx

Along with behavioral segmentation based on loyalty to a team or sports product, consumers are frequently grouped on the basis of other attendance or purchasing behaviors. For instance, lifelong season ticket holders represent one end of the usage continuum, whereas those who have never attended sporting events represent the other end. A unique marketing mix must be designed to appeal to each of these two groups of consumers.

Benefits segmentation

The focus of **benefits segmentation** is the appeal of a product or service to a group of consumers. Stated differently, benefits segments describe why consumers purchase a product or service or what problem the product solves for the consumer. In a sense, benefits segmentation is the common denominator in all types of marketing segmentation in that every purchase is made to satisfy a need. Benefits segmentation is also consistent with the marketing concept (discussed in Chapter 1) that states that organizations strive to meet customers' needs.

Major shoe manufacturers, such as Nike, focus on *benefits sought* to segment markets. In fact, Nike's vision is to bring inspiration and innovation to every athlete in the world. This includes both the elite athletes and professional performers as well as the casual participant. Some consumers desire a high-performance cross-training shoe, whereas others want a shoe that is more of a fashion statement. Nike is a fashion brand, and consumers who wear Nike products do not always buy them to participate in sport. Nike produces sportswear products from manufacturing waste, thereby enhancing the development opportunities that satisfy a consumer market, that is, sunglasses and jewelry. Nike focuses on personal benefit associated with the use of its products and the values satisfied by this product use.[45]

Golf ball manufacturers also try to design products that will appeal to the specific benefits sought by different groups of golfers. Pro V1x has enhanced aerodynamics and promotes the following benefits: low long game spin, high trajectory, drop and stop short game control, and soft feel. DT SoLo gives the ultimate combination of distance with soft feel and trusted quality and consistency. Tour Soft delivers responsive soft feel and commanding distance. The Titleist Velocity is designed to maximize distance for golfers seeking that benefit at a lower price. Sports marketers really hit a home run when they design one product that satisfies multiple needs (i.e., distance, feel, accuracy, durability, price) of consumers.

Choosing more than one segment

Although each of the previously mentioned bases for segmentation identifies groups of consumers with similar needs, it is common practice to combine segmentation variables. An example of combining segmentation approaches is found in a study of the soccer fan.[46] The resulting profile produced six distinct market segments that combine some of the various bases for segmentation discussed earlier in the chapter. These six segments are shown in Table 6.6.

Table 6.6 Six defined market segments for soccer fans

The Event Seeker

Defined as:

A soccer consumer who is primarily interested in the sport during major event moments like the Men's and Women's FIFA World Cup.

Traits/Characteristics:

- Equal ratio of male and female
- Primarily influenced by friends and peer groups
- Likely to have become a fan of the sport later life (age 25 onward)
- Significantly more interested in National Team soccer than Club Team fandom

The Agnostic

Defined as:

A soccer consumer who is a "fan of the sport" with interest in several domestic and international leagues and teams

Traits:

- 59% actively support more than 5 Club Teams
- Heavily influenced by an interest in star players

continued

Table 6.6 *continued*

- Most likely segment to wear their soccer jersey while watching a match
- Watch 4+ games a week on average

The Europhile

Defined as:

A soccer consumer who follows the sport domestically, but their primary fan interest lies in European soccer. An elite contingent of Europhiles (sometimes referred to as Euro snobs) are exclusively interested in European soccer.

Traits:

- Tend to skew male (64%) more than other fan personas
- The most hard core of all soccer personas, they are deeply vested in the sport
- Overwhelmingly interested in the Premier League
- 44% have attended a pro game outside the U.S.

Fanaticos

Defined as:

A soccer consumer who is mainly interested in futbol from Mexico or other Central and South American countries.

Traits:

- 68% female head of household
- Have grown up in a soccer culture with parents who loved the game
- 35% became a soccer fan before the age of 10

The Domestic:

Defined as:

A soccer consumer who follows the sport internationally, but their primary interest lies at home through interest in Major League Soccer and/or the U.S. National Teams.

Traits:

- Soccer persona with the highest interest in MLS
- Highly active on social media and heavily influenced by peer and friend group opinion
- Christian Pulisic is more revered than Lionel Messi

The Observer:

Defined as:

A soccer consumer who is primarily connected to the sport because of a family member's participation more than their own personal fandom.

continued

Table 6.6 *continued*

Traits:

- 61% female
- The lowest fan passion index of all soccer personas, but emotionally and financially connected to the game via other passions
- Pro soccer interest lies most closely aligns with US Men's and Women's National Teams
- 91% have not attended a game outside the United States

Source: Gilt Soccer, www.giltedgesoccer.com/wp-content/uploads/2018/09/GESM-Soccer-Fan-Personas_2018.pdf

Geodemographic segmentation

One of the most widely used multiple-segment approaches in sports is **geodemographic segmentation**. Although geographic segmentation and demographic segmentation are useful tools for sports marketers, combining geographic and demographic characteristics seems to be even more effective in certain situations. For instance, many direct marketing campaigns apply the principles of geodemographic segmentation.

The basis for geodemographic segmentation is that people living in close proximity are also likely to share the same lifestyle and demographic composition. Because lifestyle of the consumer is included in this type of segmentation, it is also known as geo-lifestyle. Geodemographics allows marketers to describe the characteristics of broad segments such as standard metropolitan statistical areas (SMSAs) all the way down to census blocks (consisting of roughly 340 houses).

The most common unit of segmentation for geodemography is the zip code. Claritas, Inc., a marketing firm leading the charge in geodemographics, established the PRIZM system in the 1970s. PRIZM is used to identify potential markets for products. PRIZM affords marketers the benefits of household-level precision in applications such as direct mail while at the same time maintaining the broad market linkages, usability, and cost-effectiveness of geodemographics for applications such as market sizing and site selection.[47] Each unit of geography was originally classified as 1 of 62 PRIZM clusters. However, PRIZM Premier, released in 2010, replaced the original PRIZM system and classifies every U.S. household into 68 segments, which have been given names that best characterize those populations. Some examples of the PRIZM Premier cluster categories were shown in Table 6.5.

Target markets

After segmenting the market based on one or a combination of the variables discussed in the previous section, target markets are chosen. **Target marketing** is choosing the segment(s) that will allow an organization to most efficiently and effectively attain its marketing goals.

Sports marketers must make a systematic decision when choosing groups of consumers they want to target. To make these decisions, each potential target market is evaluated on the basis of whether it is sizable, reachable, and measurable and whether it exhibits behavioral variation. Let us look at how to judge the worth of potential target markets in greater detail.

Evaluation of target markets: sizable

One of the first factors to consider when evaluating and choosing a potential target market is the size of the market. In addition to the current size of the market, sports marketers must also analyze the estimated growth of the market. The market growth would be predicted, in part, through environmental scanning, already discussed in Chapter 2.

Sports marketers must be careful to choose a target market that has neither too many nor too few consumers. If the target market becomes too large, then it essentially becomes a mass, or undifferentiated, market. For example, we would not want to choose all basketball fans as a target market because of the huge variations in social class, lifestyles, and consumption behaviors.

However, sports marketers must guard against a target market that is too small and narrowly defined. We would not choose a target market that consisted of all left-handed female basketball fans between the ages of 30 and 33 who live in San Antonio and have income levels between $40,000 and $50,000. This market is too narrowly defined and would not prove a good return on our marketing investment.

One common trap that marketers fall into with respect to the size of the potential market is known as the majority fallacy. The **majority fallacy** assumes that the largest group of consumers should always be selected as the target market. Although in some instances the biggest market may be the best choice, usually the competition is the fiercest for this group of consumers; therefore, smaller and more differentiated targets should be chosen.

These smaller, distinct groups of core customers that an organization focuses on are sometimes referred to as a market niche. **Niche marketing** is the process of carving out a relatively tiny part of a market that has a very special need not currently being filled. By definition, a **market niche** is initially much smaller than a segment and consists of a very homogeneous group of consumers, as reflected by their unique need. The differences between market segments and niches are highlighted in Table 6.7. Hutchins provides support for the use of niche marketing in the sports industry, emphasizing that niche sport properties should be aware of their influence on several different communities.[48]

Properties need to be aware of their image and be cognizant of the image potential and how their image may be attractive to potential sport properties. Focusing on the image intricacies, niche marketing may enable sport properties

Table 6.7 Market segments vs. market niches	
Segment	Niche
Small mass market	Very small market
Less specialized	Very specific needs
Top down (go from large market into smaller pieces)	Bottom up (cater to the smaller pieces of the market)

Source: Sports Marketing Quarterly

to enhance the linkage between the wants and needs of the consumer with sponsors and their athletic platforms. For these reasons, niche sport properties need to know how to best reach and connect with the different communities. Niche sport marketers should have a thorough grasp on each of these communities and what each of those communities looks like from a demographic and psychographic perspective. Organizations and sports such as professional bull riding, paintball leagues, hunting, and even professional gamblers and eaters have always been present but have increased in status and popularity with fans as well as sponsors over recent years.

These niche leagues and sports have the ability to reach a small target audience and have been seen to be more aggressive in collaborating with marketers. By providing alternative platforms to marketers, they have multiplied the sponsorship opportunities.

One specific example of a niche market is individuals (as opposed to corporations) who have financially invested in the sports franchise through the purchase of season tickets for many seasons. In addition to their financial investment, these loyal fans have a high emotional investment in the team. As previously discussed, to retain these valuable consumers, sports marketers must develop a specialized marketing mix to reinforce and reward the loyalty that these fans have shown to the organization. In addition to niche target markets, there are also niche sport products such as professional bass fishing, world's strongest man and woman competitions, or drag racing that all have their own unique, niche cultures and followers.

Reachable

In addition to exploring the size of the potential target market, its ability to be reached should also be evaluated. Reach refers to the accessibility of the target market. Does the sports marketer have a means of communicating with the desired target market? If the answer to this question is no, then the potential target market should not be pursued.

Traditional means of reaching the sports fan include mass media, such as magazines, newspapers, and television. In today's marketing environment,

Web Capture 6.6
Reaching women's sports fans on the Web

Source: https://washingtonspirit.com/

it is possible to reach a specific target market with the many forms of social media, virtual reality, augmented reality, and streaming. According to Sports Fan Graph, professional sports have recently been utilizing this avenue to promote leagues, teams, and athletes through Facebook. The NBA has over 38 million fan "likes" on Facebook and MLB 7.3 million "likes," while the NFL has over 17.6 million fan "likes." In fact when looking at the NFL, and including all 32 teams, almost 1 in 10 Americans have declared their support for an NFL team on Facebook.[49] In addition to web, cable, and satellite technology products, streaming services such as CBS All Access allow sports fans across the United States access to their favorite teams, leagues, and sports. This, of course, opens new geographic segments for sports marketers to consider.

Measurable

The ability to measure the size, accessibility, and purchasing power of the potential target market(s) is another factor that needs to be considered. For a market segment to represent a good target market, sport marketers must be able to identify and then measure the number of people in that segment. If a sport marketer has no measurable criteria to identify the size or scope of that market segment, a marketer may want to reconsider basing a marketing campaign on that segment. Segments may be composed of multiple criteria; however, for segments to be measurable, they should be evaluated against the following criteria:

- **Identifiable** - Differentiation among attribute measures must occur so they can be identified.
- **Accessible** - Market segments must be reachable through communication and distribution channels.
- **Sustainable** - Market segments should be sufficiently large to justify the resources required to target them.

- ***Unique needs*** - Clarify considerations and offerings as they relate to the needs of the consumer.
- ***Durable*** - Segments should be measured to identify stability and to minimize cost and the frequency of change.

One of the reasons demographic segmentation is so widespread is the ease with which characteristics such as age, gender, income level, and occupation can be assessed or measured. Psychographic segments are perhaps the most difficult to measure because of the complex interaction of personality and lifestyle.

Behavioral variation

Finally, if the target market is sizable, reachable, and measurable, sports marketers must examine behavioral variation. We want consumers within the target market to exhibit similar behaviors, attitudes, lifestyles, and so on. In addition, marketers want these characteristics to be unique within a target market. This component is the underlying factor in choosing any target market.

An example of behavioral variation among market segments is the corporate season ticket holder versus the individual season ticket holder. Although both corporate season ticket holders and individual season ticket holders may be fans at some level, their motivation for attending games and attitudes toward the team may be quite different. These variations would prompt different approaches to marketing to each segment.

How many target markets?

Now that we have evaluated potential target markets, do we have to choose just one or should we consider multiple markets? The answer depends largely on the organization's marketing objectives and its resources. If the firm has the financial and other resources to pursue more than one target market, it does so by prioritizing all potential target markets.

The market distinguished as the most critical to attaining the firm's objectives is deemed the primary target market. Other, less critical markets of interest are called secondary, tertiary, and so on. Again, a unique marketing mix may need to be developed for each target market, so the costs associated with choosing multiple targets are sometimes prohibitive.

Positioning

Segmentation has been considered and specific target markets have been chosen. Next, sport marketers must decide on the positioning of their sporting events, athletes, teams, and so on. **Positioning** is defined as fixing your sports entity in the minds of consumers in the target market.

Before discussing positioning, three important points should be stressed. First, positioning is dependent on the target market(s) identified in the previous phase of the market selection decisions. In fact, the *same* sport may be positioned differently to distinct target markets. As the spotlight demonstrated earlier in the chapter, the positioning of the NBA and other professional sports is changing with the opening of a new target market – women.

Second, positioning is based solely on the perceptions of the target market and how its members think and feel about the sports entity. Sometimes positioning is mistakenly linked with where the product appears on the retailer's shelf or where the product is placed in an advertisement. Nothing could be further from the truth. Position is all about how the consumer perceives your sports product relative to competitive offerings.

Third, the definition of positioning reflects its importance to all sports products. It should also be noted that sports leagues (XFL versus NFL), sports teams (e.g., Dallas Cowboys as "America's Team"), and individual sports (e.g., women participating in hunting has increased, while the number of male hunters has decreased), or the NFL's perennial bad boy Myles Garrett, must all be positioned by sports marketers.

How does the sports marketer attempt to fix the sports entity in the minds of consumers? The first step rests in understanding the target market's perception of the relevant attributes of the sports entity. The relevant attributes are those features and characteristics desired in the sports entity by the target market. These attributes may be intangible, such as a fun atmosphere at the stadium, or tangible, such as having cushioned seating. Golf manufacturers such as Slazenger have positioned their equipment as the "standard of excellence" and having "impeccable quality."

In another example, consider the possible product attributes for skateboards. Pricing status of the brand name, durability, quality of the wheels, and weight of the skate may all be considered product attributes. If serious, competitive skaters are chosen as the primary target market, then the skateboards may be positioned on the basis of quality of the wheels and materials used. However, if first-time, recreational skateboarders are considered the primary target market, then relevant product attributes may be price and durability. Marketers attempt to understand all the potential attributes and then which ones are most important to their target markets through marketing research.

Perceptual maps

Perceptual mapping is one of the few marketing research techniques that provides direct input into the strategic marketing planning process. It allows marketing planners to assess the strengths and weaknesses and to view the customer and the competitor simultaneously in the same realm. Perceptual mapping and preference mapping techniques have been a basic tool of the applied marketing research profession for years. It is one of the few advanced multivariate techniques that has not suffered very much from alternating waves of popularity and disfavor.[50]

Perceptual maps provide marketers with three types of information. First, perceptual maps indicate the dimensions or attributes that consumers use when thinking about a sports product or service. Second, perceptual maps tell sports marketers where different sports products or services are located on those dimensions. The third type of information provided by perceptual maps is how your product is perceived relative to the competition.

Perceptual maps can be constructed in any number of dimensions, based on the number of product attributes being considered. Figure 6.4 demonstrates a one-dimensional perceptual map, which explores the positioning of various spectator sports based on the level of perceived aggression or violence associated with the sports. This hypothetical example can be interpreted as follows:

Ad 6.2
Crucial Catch positions itself as the official licensee of the National Football League

*Source:*www.lids.com

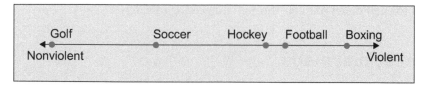

Figure 6.4
One-dimensional perceptual map of sports

Boxing is seen as the most violent or aggressive sport, followed by football, hockey, and soccer. However, golf is the least aggressive sport. These results would vary, of course, based on who participated in the research, how aggression or violence is defined by the researchers, and what level of competition is being considered (i.e., professional, high school, or youth leagues).

Although it is easy to conceptualize one-dimensional perceptual maps, the number of dimensions is contingent upon the number of attributes relevant to consumers. For example, Converse positions its shoes for multiple uses like action sports, basketball, cheerleading, cross-training, or fashion. New Balance, however, positions its shoes solely on the basis of running.

A study using perceptual mapping techniques found that consumers identify six dimensions of sport (shown in Table 6.8). Although it is possible to create a six-dimensional perceptual map, it is nearly impossible to interpret. Therefore, two-dimensional perceptual maps were constructed that compared 10 sports on the six dimensions identified by consumers.

Figure 6.5 shows a two-dimensional perceptual map using Dimension 4 (skill developed primarily with others versus skill developed alone) and Dimension 5 (younger athletes versus broad age ranges of participants). Interpreting this perceptual map, we see that football is considered a sport whose participants are younger athletes and skill is developed primarily with others. Compared with football, golf is seen as a sport for a broader range of participants with skills developed more on your own. Using these results, sports marketers can better understand the image of their sport from the perspective of various target markets and decide whether this image needs to be changed or maintained.

Table 6.8 Six dimensions or attributes of sports

Dimension 1	Strength, speed, and endurance vs. methodical and precise movements
Dimension 2	Athletes only as participants vs. athletes plus recreational participants
Dimension 3	Skill emphasis on impact with object vs. skill emphasis on body movement
Dimension 4	Skill development and practice primarily alone vs. primarily with others
Dimension 5	A younger participant in the sport vs. participant ages from young to older
Dimension 6	Less masculine vs. more masculine

Source: James H. Martin, "Using a Perceptual Map of the Consumer's Sport Schema to Help Make Sponsorship Decisions," *Sport Marketing Quarterly*, vol. 3, no. 3 (1994), 27–33

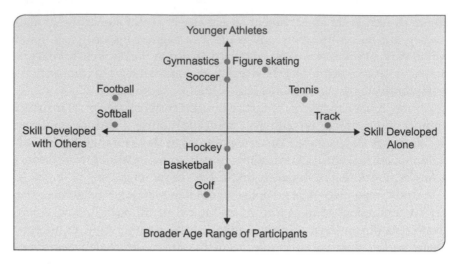

Figure 6.5
Two-dimensional perceptual map of sports

Repositioning

As suggested, sport marketers may use the results of positioning studies to change the image of their sport. For instance, the NCAA has repeatedly come under fire for a series of scandals off the courts and playing fields. The most notable NCAA crisis is massive and involved Division I men's basketball coaches, sportswear companies, agents, and amateur basketball clubs. It was a complex scheme that led to FBI investigations and the arrests of 10 men, including assistant coaches at Oklahoma State University, the University of Arizona, the University of Southern California, and Auburn University. The bribery scheme and fraud had been under investigation since 2015 and worked as follows: The coaches accepted cash bribes from sports agents and financial advisers in exchange for the coaches' influence to direct selected players and their families to retain the services of the agents, who provided the bribes once the players entered the NBA. In another scheme, adidas funneled six-figure payments to amateur players, through the coaches, for players to commit to schools with which the clothing company already had a business partnership. Obviously, these are not only crimes, but receiving benefits or payments from prospective agents or sponsors is considered a violation of the NCAA's rules.[51]

Obviously this is not the image the NCAA and the coaches wish to project. Thus, the NCAA and sport of men's basketball have been trying to **reposition** themselves or change the image or perception of the sports entity in the minds of consumers in the target market.

In response to this scandal, and in hopes of cleaning up the reputation of the sport, the NCAA created a task force to review issues and make recommended changes. Time will tell whether these recommendations will be implemented and what impact they will have on repositioning college basketball.[52] The NCAA is not the only sports entity attempting to reposition itself. Let's not forget the Houston Astros cheating scandal, giving baseball a black eye. Individual athletes can produce image problems for themselves or a city, as well as a sponsor. LeBron James and "The Decision" left himself, Cleveland, and Nike to re-establish an image and reposition within the sports industry. Even entire countries have cause to reposition their images, should they wish. For example, in December 2019, the Russian Athletics Federation was fined $10 million for breaching anti-doping rules. In addition to the monetary fine, more importantly, Russia was given a four-year ban from competing in all major sporting events. However, even though Russia as a country was banned, 335 Russian athletes participated as neutrals under a Russian Olympic Committee flag.[53]

While athletes are always shaping and honing their reputation or image, the advent of social media has created new challenges for athletes attempting to craft their public persona, as discussed in the accompanying article.

ARTICLE 6.8
THE ONLINE REPUTATION OF ATHLETES

The development of the Internet and Social Media has meant that athletes from all disciplines are having to manage their online reputations as the entire world eavesdrops on their daily lives, day and night. Nothing escapes their fans and the media who can make or break an athlete's reputation, his or her career, and even family life. The following is an overview of the risk factors and solutions involved with the online reputation of athletes.

The candour of athletes

An **American survey**(1), asking 200 athletes about their views on social media, revealed that:

- 53.8% use social media when and however they want. 84.6% of athletes personally use their own Twitter accounts. 23.1% get **their agent or agency** to send out their messages. 69.2% use social media to promote their club. 61.6% post messages about their team or club.
- 84.7% think that the reputation of sports stars has an impact on the **reputation of their club**. 38.5% think that some stars use social media to damage the reputation of their club.
- 53.9% know they will face disciplinary measures if they post negative messages about their team. 37.7% are required to follow the strict 'Social Media' guidelines laid out by their club.

Generally speaking, this study shows that **athletes are not aware of the growing dangers of online reputation** and the consequences their social media activity may elicit. There are, however, more and more athletes who are **starting to take better care of their image and**

that of their club. This is why it has become essential for clubs and athletes alike to agree on a 'Social Media' policy to confront potential online reputation problems.

An unforgiving world

In this day and age, being an elite athlete is no longer just about winning events. It also involves being 'flawless' in life, particularly in family life. And that's not all: rumours, critiques, and bad press(2) are all part of everyday life in a society that revolves around the Social Media. Before even setting foot on the pitch, **athletes are judged**. Spectators, fans and journalists know all about the slightest little slip-up committed by an athlete (for proof, see below). Forums thrive with mudslinging, insults and photo-shopped images that aim to do harm. Add to that the hounding journalists who push athlete's buttons to see how far they'll go, to get an angry or hostile reaction. Online harassment can destroy careers, marriages and the ability to earn a living. Athletes are therefore obliged to set up an online reputation management system to get rid of all undesirable online content.

The online reputation of athletes: rocketing risks

Rumours, unrestrained tweets, mudslinging, photo-shopped images, false accusations, personal info (telephone number and email) shared by millions of people on the Internet. Everything and anything can create bad buzz today and be turned into something harmful to

Photo 6.3
Events that occurred some years before and their digital footprints are still present on the first Google page of Lance Armstrong

an athlete's image. The list of things that could go wrong is endless: loss of credibility, career destruction, divorce, loss of sports and publicity contracts, ostracism, collateral damage for the club – everything is at risk these days for **athletes**. How then do you fight the potentially damaging effects of media coverage and rumours that spread like wildfire on the Web?

The online reputation of athletes: sports organizations get involved

Like athletes, sports organizations are protecting themselves against collateral damages that tarnish their reputation. More and more, they are taking control of the reputations of their athletes (who delegate their image to their agent or club). For example, the Italian Football Federation just took draconian measures regarding its players by prohibiting all social network communication (from tweets to posts to likes) during the World Cup in Brazil. An anticipated solution that aims at avoiding the types of scandal that tarnished the image of football (not to mention France) during the previous World Cup in South Africa.

Athletes are people like you and me

Following in the footsteps of political figures and showbiz celebrities, athletes are arousing the interest of fans and the Media, and since the advent of Web 2.0, the Web has been playing a lead role in how their image is perceived. For sports agents, it has become crucial to keep an eye on their athletes' images. By taking advantage of the online reputation dashboard, and monitoring their online reputation for free, agents get a global view of an **athlete's digital presence** and, when faced with trouble, can call upon the Digital Fortress solution.

URL: www.reputationvip.com/blog/online-reputation-of-athletes

Summary

Chapter 6 focuses on critical market selection decisions, also referred to as segmentation, targeting, and positioning. Segmentation, the first market selection decision, is identifying consumers with common needs. Typically, the bases for segmentation of consumer markets include demographics, socioeconomics, psychographics, behaviors, and benefits. Marketers using demographic segmentation choose groups of consumers based on common ages, gender, ethnic background, and stage of the family life cycle. Geographic segmentation groups people who live in similar areas such as cities, states, regions of the country, or even countries (e.g., the United States versus international markets). Socioeconomic segmentation groups consumers on the basis of similar income levels, educational levels, and occupations. Psychographic segments are especially useful to sports marketers; they are based on consumers' lifestyles, activities, interests, and opinions. Behavioral segments are groups of consumers that are similar on the basis of consumer actions, such as how often they purchase sports products or how loyal they are when purchasing a sports product. Finally, benefits segments are groups of consumers attempting to satisfy similar needs by consuming the sports product together. Sports marketers may choose to segment their markets using one of the previously mentioned segmentation variables (e.g., demographics) or combine several of the bases for segmentation (e.g., geodemographic).

Once market segments have been chosen, the next market selection decision is picking a target market. Target marketing is choosing the segment or segments that will allow the organization to most effectively and efficiently achieve its marketing goals. When evaluating potential target markets, care should be taken to ensure the markets are the right size (neither too large nor too small), reachable (accessible), and measurable (i.e., size, purchasing power, and characteristics of the segments can be measured) and that they demonstrate behavioral variation (i.e., consumers share common characteristics within the target market).

The final market selection decision is positioning. After the target market has been chosen, sports marketers want to position their products or fix them in the minds of the target markets. Positioning is based on the perception or image that sports marketers want to develop or maintain for the sports product. For example, a minor league baseball team may want to position itself as an inexpensive, family entertainment alternative. To understand how a sports product is positioned relative to its competition, perceptual maps are developed through marketing research techniques. By looking at perceptual maps, sports marketers can identify whether they have achieved their desired image or whether they need to reposition their sports product in the minds of the target market.

Key terms

- AIO dimensions
- behavioral segmentation
- benefits segmentation
- demographic segmentation
- ethnic background
- family life cycle
- geodemographic segmentation
- geographic segmentation
- market niche
- majority fallacy
- market segmentation
- market selection decisions
- mature market
- niche marketing
- perceptual maps

- positioning
- psychographic segmentation
- reposition
- social class
- socioeconomic segmentation
- target marketing

Review questions

1 Describe the key components of market selection decisions and indicate how market selection decisions are incorporated into the larger strategic marketing process.

2 What is market segmentation? Provide some examples of how sports marketers segment the sports participant market (those who play) and the sports spectator market (those who watch).

3 Discuss the various ways to segment the sports market based on demographics. Which of the demographic bases are the most effective when segmenting the sports market and why?

4 Describe, in detail, the family life cycle and how it is used as a strategic tool when segmenting sports markets. What stage of the family life cycle are you currently in? How does this affect your sports participation and spectator behavior?

5 Provide examples of sports you believe would appeal to each of the six social class categories (upper-upper through lower-lower). What sports appeal to all social class segments?

6 What are AIOs? What are VALS? Describe the similarities and differences in obtaining each and evaluate which is more effective at segmenting consumers for sports marketers.

7 Why is developing and maintaining an international presence important for sports marketers? What further considerations, if any, need to be taken into account when attempting to segment an international market? Provide several examples of the growth of international sports marketing.

8 What is behavioral segmentation? What are some of the common behaviors that sports marketers would use for segmentation purposes?

9 Define benefits segmentation and discuss why benefits segmentation is considered to be at the core of all segmentation. What benefits do you look for when attending a sporting event? Does your answer vary from event to event?

10 Define a target market. What are the requirements for successful target markets (i.e., how should each target be evaluated)? Provide examples of sports products or services that target two or more distinct markets.

11 How many target markets should a sports marketer consider for a single product?

12 Describe positioning and discuss how perceptual mapping techniques are used by sports marketers. What is repositioning?

Exercises

1 Find two advertisements for sports products that compete directly with one another. For example, you may want to compare Nike running shoes with Reebok running shoes or King Cobra golf clubs with Taylormade golf clubs. How is each product segmented, targeted, and positioned? Are there more differences or similarities in these market selection decisions?

2 How is the health and fitness industry segmented in general? Describe the segmentation, targets, and positioning of health and fitness clubs in your area.

3 You are hired as the director of sports marketing for a new minor league hockey franchise in Chicago, a city that already has an NHL team. Describe how you would segment, target, and position your new franchise.

4 Describe the primary target market for the following: NASCAR, the Kentucky Derby, "The Rhino" bowling ball, and the WNBA. Next, define a potential secondary target market for each of these sports products.

5 Interview five consumers who have recently attended a high school sporting event, five consumers who have recently attended a college sporting event, and five who have recently attended any professional sporting event. Ask them to identify why they attended this event and what benefits they were looking for. Were their needs met?

6 Develop a list of all the possible product attributes that may be considered when purchasing the following sports products: a tennis racquet, a basketball, and a mountain bike. After you have developed the list of attributes, ask five people which attributes they consider the most important for each product. Do all consumers agree? Are there some attributes that you may have omitted? Why are these attributes important in positioning?

7 How do you think the following races are positioned: Boston Marathon, "Run Like Hell" 5K Halloween Race, and the Bowling Green 10K Classic? Draw a two-dimensional perceptual map to illustrate the positioning of each race.

8 Provide examples of individual athletes, teams, and sports (leagues) that have had to develop repositioning strategies.

9 Find the web sites for three professional sports franchises and go to their ticket section. How many special promotions do they offer? Which segment of the population is being targeted by each promotion? Are any segments excluded? If so, create a promotion targeting that segment and explain why it would be effective.

10 Choose a professional sports team that performs poorly in attendance. Locate its Facebook page on the Internet. (If you cannot find it, choose another team.) Examine the content of the page. Are any special events or promotions being planned? How many friends/fans does the team have? As far as you can tell, what kinds of people are these (college students, professionals, families, etc.)? Develop a segmentation strategy that revolves around Facebook. How would you appeal to each segment?

Internet exercises

1   Using the Internet, find the demographic profile for fans attending the LPGA (women's tour) versus the PGA (men's tour). Are there differences? Use this information to comment on the market selection decisions for the LPGA.

2   Find two web sites that target children interested in sports and two web sites that target the mature market. Note any similarities and differences between the sites.

3   Find two web sites for soccer. One site should focus on U.S. soccer, whereas the other focus should be international. Comment on the relative positioning of soccer in the United States versus abroad based on information found on the Internet.

Notes

1   James McNeal, "Tapping the Three Kids' Markets," *American Demographics* (1998); James McNeal, "Kids in 2010," *American Demographics* (1999).

2   Vicom, "Kidfluence: How Kids Influence Buying Behavior" (March 26, 2018). Available from: https://www.viacomcbs.com/news/audience-insights/kidfluence-kids-influence-buying-behavior.

3   Fona, "Consumer Insight: Purchase Power of Today's Teens" (February 7, 2019). Available from: https://www.fona.com/purchase-power-of-todays-teens/.

4   Ibid.

5   Dan Cook, "Lunchbox Hegemony: Kids & the Marketplace, Then & Now," *LiP Magazine* (August 20, 2001).

6   Adam Shell, "Why Families Stretch Their Budgets for High Priced Youth Sports" (September 5, 2017). Available from: https://www.usatoday.com/story/money/2017/09/05/why-families-stretch-their-budgets-high-priced-youth-sports/571945001/.

7   Press Release, Packaged Facts, "U.S. Gen Z Youth Have Already Developed the Buying Power of a Small Country" (August 2, 2018). Available from: https://www.packagedfacts.com/about/release.asp?id=4386.

8   National Football League Foundation. Available from: www.nflfoundation.org/youth-football.

9   NFL. Available from: www.nfl.com/play60.

10   "Let's Get Playing." Available from: https://www.learntoplay.nhl.com.

11   "Office of Population Affairs." Available from: www.hhs.gov/ash/oah/facts-and-stats/changing-face-of-americas-adolescents/index.html.

12   "Christina Gough," *Statista* (March 4, 2019). Available from: www.statista.com/statistics/480119/cable-or-broadcast-tv-networks-extreme-or-action-sports-watched-within-the-last-12-months-usa/#s.

13   "Teen Social Media Statistics 2021 (What Parents Need to Know)." Available from: https://smartsocial.com/social-media-statistics/.

14   "Fact Sheet: Aging in the United States." Available from: www.prb.org/aging-unitedstates-fact-sheet/#footnote-1.

15   "United States Census." Available from: www.census.gov/library/stories/2019/12/by-2030-all-baby-boomers-will-be-age-65-or-older.html.

16 "IHRS Staff, 2019 Fitness Industry Trends Shed Light on 2020 & Beyond." Available from: www.ihrsa.org/improve-your-club/industry-news/2019-fitness-industry-trends-shed-light-on-2020-beyond/.

17 Kenneth Terrell, "Americans 50 and Older Would Be World's Third-Largest Economy, AARP Study Finds" (December 19, 2019). Available from: https://www.aarp.org/politics-society/advocacy/info-2019/older-americans-economic-impact-growth.html.

18 "MiLB Thunder Tickets." Available from: www.milb.com/trenton/tickets/senior diamondclub.

19 "NSGA, History of the NSGA." Available from: https://nsga.com/history/.

20 "The Shelf, Marketing to Sports Fans: Viewership & Demographics." Available from: www.theshelf.com/the-blog/sports-viewership.

21 Scott Goldberg, "Why the NFL Struggles to Attract Female Fans," Digital Wire Media (December 5, 2006). Available from: http://www.dmwmedia.com/news/2006/12/05/why-the-nfl-struggles-to-attract-female-fans, accessed June 18, 2014.

22 "The Medium." Available from: https://medium.com/@bob_6051/inside-the-numbers-mma-and-boxing-fans-cfef9e96522a.

23 Kelsey McKinney, "More High School Girls Are Playing Tackle Football" (September 2019). Available from: https://deadspin.com/more-high-school-girls-are-playing-tackle-football-than-1837378141.

24 "WFA." Available from: https://wfaprofootball.com.

25 "United States Census Bureau." Available from: www.census.gov/quickfacts/fact/table/US/IPE120218.

26 Mollie Simon, "Coca-Cola Stays in the World Cup Game with Largest Ever Marketing Campaign" (June 25, 2018). Available from: https://www.bizjournals.com/atlanta/news/2018/06/25/coca-cola-stays-in-the-world-cup-game-with-largest.html.

27 Mike Valdes-Fauli, "Passion For Sports: How Hispanics Are Driving the Sports Marketing Landscape." Available from: https://www.forbes.com/sites/forbesagencycouncil/2020/07/31/passion-for-sports-how-hispanics-are-driving-the-sports-marketing-landscape/?sh=1780abb246ed.

28 Isaac Mizrahi, "The Minority-Majority Shift. Two Decades that Will Change America. For Sports Marketing, It's Game On." Available from: www.forbes.com/sites/isaacmizrahi/2020/01/16/the-minority-majority-shift-two-decades-that-will-change-america-for-sports-marketing-its-game-on/#1d1c797715b8.

29 "ESPN Press Room." Available from: https://espnpressroom.com/us/media-kits/espn-deportes/.

30 Statista, "Median Household Income in the United States in 2019, by Race or Ethnic Group." Available from: www.statista.com/statistics/233324/median-household-income-in-the-united-states-by-race-or-ethnic-group/.

31 Nielsen Homescan & Total Media Fusion, "Asian-Americans Have Strong Purchasing Power. How Can Marketers Reach Them?" Available from: www.marketingcharts.com/demographics-and-audiences/asian-american-108591.

32 Marisa Lascala, "The U.S. Divorce Rate Is Going Down, and We Have Millennials to Thank" (February 27, 2019). Available from: www.goodhousekeeping.com/life/relationships/a26551655/us-divorce-rate/Change.

33 Nielsen Scarborough, "Demographics: A Snapshot of NASCAR's Fan Base, 2020." Available from: http://thedrivetoconnect.com/demographics-a-snapshot-of-nascars-fan-base-2/.

34 Tom C. Wilson, "The Paradox of Social Class and Sport Involvement," *International Review for the Sociology of Sport*, vol. 37, no. 1 (2002), 5–16.

35   Michael Solomon, *Consumer Behavior*, 3rd ed. (Upper Saddle River, NJ: Prentice Hall, 1996).

36   Barrie Houlihan and Dominic Malcolm, "Sport and Society." Available from: https://uk.sagepub.com/en-gb/eur/sport-and-society/book241826.

37   VALS, "Strategic Business Insights." Available from: http://www.strategicbusiness insights.com/vals/.

38   MLB International. Available from: https://www.mlb.com/international.

39   Kamil Karamali, "NBA Finals Broadcast to More Than 200 Countries, Thanks to One to One 40-Foot Truck" (June 3, 2019). Available from: https://globalnews.ca/news/5345286/nba-finals-world-feed-truck/.

40   "Super Bowl Live 2020." Available from: https://www.nfl.com/super-bowl/ways-to-watch/.

41   Al Jazeera (December 18, 2020). Available from: https://www.aljazeera.com/news/2020/12/18/ethiopia-offers-reward-for-intel-on-fugitive-tigrayan-leaders.

42   Jason Notte, "Your Tax Dollars At Play: How Stadium Tax Scams Pick Fans Pockets." Available from: www.forbes.com/sites/jasonnotte/2018/08/17/your-tax-dollars-at-play-how-stadium-tax-scams-pick-fans-pockets/#32cbc0446fb9.

43   Mark Gaughan and Sandra Tan, "The 10 Newest Stadiums in the NFL – And What Buffalo Can Learn From Them" (March 31, 2019). Available from: https://buffalonews.com/2019/03/31/a-look-at-the-10-newest-stadiums-in-the-nfl-and-what-it-means-for-buffalo/.

44   Mark Pritchard and Christopher Negro, "Sport Loyalty Programs and Their Influence on Fan Relationships," *International Journal of Sports Marketing and Sponsorship*, vol. 3 (2001), 317–338.

45   "Nike Swot 2021/ SWOTA Analysis of Nike." Available from: https://bstrategy hub.com/swot-analysis-of-nike-nike-swot-analysis/.

46   American Soccer Fan Personas. Available from: www.giltedgesoccer.com/wp-content/uploads/2018/09/GESM-Soccer-Fan-Personas_2018.pdf.

47   "Claritas Prizm Premier Segment Narratives 2018." Available from: http://kantar media.srds.com/common/pdf/claritas3.

48   "Niche Sports: An Underutilized Market for an Otherwise Inundated Industry." Available from: https://medium.com/@shutchens257/niche-sports-an-under-utilized-market-for-an-otherwise-inundated-industry-resm5333-caf54031fa98.

49   "The Most Liked NFL Teams on Facebook." Available from: www.trackalytics.com/the-most-liked-nfl-teams-on-facebook/page/1/.

50   Iza Gigauri, "Perceptual Mapping as a Marketing Research Tool for Brand Positioning," *SSRG International Journal of Economics and Management Studies*, vol. 6, no. 4 (2019), 73–79.

51   Dylan Scott, "NCAA Basketball's Bribery Scandal and Its March Madness Conspiracy Theory, Explained" (March 13, 2018). Available from: www.vox.com/2018/3/13/17109874/ncaa-scandal-fbi-basketball-march-madness.

52   The Associated Press, "Committee on College Basketball Proposes Changes, Including One-and-Done and Punishing Cheats" (April 25, 2018). Available from: www.azcentral.com/story/sports/ncaab/2018/04/25/committee-college-bas-ketball-proposes-sweeping-changes-aimed-improving-sport/547714002/.

53   Megan McCluskey, "Here's What to Know About the ROC and Why Russia Can't Compete at the Tokyo Olympics" (July 26, 2021). Available from: https://time.com/6084195/what-is-roc-olympics/.

PART III
Planning the sports marketing mix

Sports product concepts

After completing this chapter, you should be able to:

- Define sports products and differentiate between goods and services.
- Explain how sports products and services are categorized.
- Define branding and discuss the guidelines for choosing an effective brand name.
- Discuss the branding process in detail.
- Examine the advantages and disadvantages of licensing from the perspective of the licensee and licensor.
- Identify the dimensions of service quality and goods quality.
- Define product design and explain how product design is related to product quality.

Think about attending a Major League Baseball game at Wrigley Field in Chicago. Inside the stadium, you find vendors selling game programs, scorecards, Major League Baseball-licensed merchandise, and plenty of food and drink. An usher kindly escorts you to your seat assignment and ensures that your seat is clean before you begin to enjoy the entertainment. How do you feel? During the game, you are exposed to more product choices.

Every game experience presents us with a number of opportunities to purchase and consume sports products. Some of the products, such as the scorecards, represent a pure good, whereas others, such as the game itself, represent a pure service. Each sports product represents a business challenge with incredible upside and downside potential. In this chapter, we explore the multidimensional nature of sports products.

DOI: 10.4324/9780429030673-10

Defining sports products

A **sports product** is a good, a service, or any combination of the two that is designed to provide benefits to a sports spectator, participant, or sponsor. Within this definition, the market concept discussed in Chapter 1 is reintroduced. As you recall, the marketing concept states that sports organizations are in the business of satisfying consumers' needs. To do this, products must be developed that anticipate and satisfy consumers' needs. Sports marketers sell products based on the benefits they offer consumers. These benefits are so critical to marketers that sometimes products are defined as "bundles of benefits." For example, the sport of lacrosse has emerged as one of the nation's fastest-growing sports. Lacrosse has been tagged as "the fastest game on two feet," and those "feet" are rapidly moving across the country.[1] Colleges and high schools are now adding lacrosse to their athletic repertoire as the sport gains attention in the areas that knew little if anything about the game in the past. Lacrosse originated from Native Americans who often played the game as a way to train for warfare. The game may not be played for the same reasons today, but the action and intensity that are displayed are still highly competitive and exciting, providing a "bundle of benefits" for the consumer.

What has caused the game to spread so quickly? There are five main factors. (1) Increased visibility in the national media, (2) Growing concern for high-impact sports, that is, concussions, (3) Development of a professional league, (4) Growth of new high school and college programs, (5) Growth of youth programs. Knowledge of the game is spreading, making it no longer appear to be in the dark to the general public. The game is also very appealing.

Photo 7.1
This baseball, glove, and bat represent pure goods
Source: Shutterstock, ID# 62893237 by David Lee

It is fast-paced, full of non-stop action, provides great exercise, and is less expensive to play than many traditional sports. It is a good mix between many popular American sports such as football, basketball, and hockey. The whole of America is starting to discover lacrosse, resulting in increased participation rates that are spreading just as fast as the game itself.

In addition to sports and sporting goods, athletes can also be thought of as sports products that possess multiple benefits. For example, NBA teams are currently seeking players who can perform multiple roles on the court rather than those who have more specialized skills. The player who can rebound, is great defensively, dribbles well, and can play the post is invaluable to the franchise. The classic example of the "hybrid" player with multiple skills was Magic Johnson, who played center and guard in the 1980 NBA Finals. Today's NBA stars, such as Kevin Durant, LeBron James, or James Harden, exemplify the versatile player who offers many benefits to the team.

A number of athletes offer a unique bundle of benefits both on and off the court. Consider former star center Shaquille O'Neal. Shaq has been a top performer, helping teams such as the Lakers earn a three-peat championship, and he was one of three players in NBA history to be selected to the NBA All-Star Game for 15 seasons. In addition to Shaq's 18 seasons as a player, he was the oldest active player in the NBA, has made and appeared in several movies, raps, has written his autobiography, owns his own sportswear company, starred in his own reality show titled *Shaq vs.*, and is currently an NBA analyst for TNT. The 7-foot-1-inch center has been aligned with numerous endorsement contracts, from Taco Bell to Buick to Carnival Cruises, and has helped a number of non-profit organizations, most notably the Boys and Girls Clubs of America. Most recently, Shaq has utilized the social network of Twitter as a way to communicate with fans and enhance his brand. All of these activities contribute to the "product" we know as Shaq.[2]

Goods and services as sports products

Our definition of products includes goods and services. It is important to understand the differences in these two types of products to plan and implement the strategic sports marketing process. Because services such as watching a game are being produced (by the players) and consumed (by the spectators) simultaneously, there is no formal channel of distribution. However, when you purchase a pure good, such as a pair of hockey skates, they must be produced by a manufacturer (e.g., Bauer), sent to a retailer (e.g., Sports Authority), and then sold to you. This formal channel of distribution requires careful planning and managing. Let us explore some of the other differences between goods and services.

Goods are defined as tangible, physical products that offer benefits to consumers. Obviously, sporting goods stores sell tangible products such as tennis balls and racquets, hockey equipment, exercise equipment, and so on. By contrast, **services**

ARTICLE 7.1
CAREER SPOTLIGHT

Rodger Collins, Former President: Direct Store Delivery, Keurig DR Pepper Inc

Question: From your perspective, what is most successful . . . new to the world products, new product category entries, product line extensions, product improvement, or repositioning?

Answer: At Dr. Pepper marketing is implemented in four so called buckets. The first bucket is the heavy or core user. The second bucket is the light user. The third bucket would be the line extension or innovation, such as launching Dr. Pepper Cherry and using Kiss as the spokesman. Finally a cultural approach, for example, Dr. Pepper is targeting the Hispanic community.

Question: In looking at the consumers' perspective, which of the following do you target, discontinuous innovations, dynamic continuous innovations, or continuing innovations?

Answer: We look internally, where the value of a product or service is with the correct investment. An example would be the Crush brand, which was idle until we utilized the brand exploiting the flavor line with a powerful trademark and marketed it across the country. As for the citrus beverage line Mountain Dew holds the market. We look to utilize Sun Drop which is popular in the southeast and to become a player in this product line.

Question: How does your company go about implementing the new product development process?

Answer: We have a committee that receives concepts from our marketing department on all new products. All new products are developed internally through our research and development laboratory. We have doctors in our labs developing all of our new products. As for market categories, we test and launch products depending on market segmentation and focus groups.

Question: How does your company go about dealing with problems in marketing?

Answer: All market research is considered to be on the high end. Therefore it is discounted and we approach this utilizing low end numbers. Formulas are in place in this company to actualize all numbers into useable material.

Question: Can you give me some examples of your company's products and the product life cycle?

Answer: A good example would be Snapple; a twenty year old product that started as a high end, healthy beverage. Between competitors and a lack of advertising Snapple went from a growth to a mature to a declining product. Two years ago we had a product restage with new packaging, ads, and a conversion to the use of real sugar in the beverage. This plan has completely paid off. We must be careful because this beverage line is quick to decline because of competition and copy cats. We have another beverage that is in the introduction stage. This is Mott's Medley, which competes with V8's Fusion. We are in the early stages. We have priced this beverage low, so as to create a larger customer base. The jury is out. Finally we have Dr. Pepper. A beverage that is 100 years old that we do not feel has reached the maturity stage. We feel we are still in the growth stage. We believe line extensions will allow us to continue to grow despite the cycling of the market. As for declining brands, we have been harvesting Royal Crown Cola. We have put no money into it because of the competition of Coke and Pepsi and are somewhat treading water with this beverage. We have not deleted any brands, only packaging on many different products.

Question: How much stock does your company put into fads, classics, and seasonal products?

Answer: We never look at products like fads. We look at them as innovations. If we have the ability to manufacture and the capacity to distribute with no capital upstart we will look to utilize the product. We have very limited seasonal products, but Iced Tea and Lemonade sells better in the summer.

Question: What techniques do you employ in the product diffusion process to speed the adoptions of your products?

Answer: With our new products we utilize target marketing, the internet, and social media, especially when dealing with the younger demographic. As for an older demographic we employ coupons, especially at checkouts in grocery stores with a coupon printed on the back of the receipt.

Source: Interview conducted by authors in 2014. Updated 2019. M. Shank and M. R. Lyberger. Interview with R. Collins.

are usually described as intangible, nonphysical products. For instance, the competitive aspect of any sporting event (i.e., the game itself) or an experience such as receiving an ice-skating lesson or an usher wiping your seat reflects pure services.

It is easy to see why soccer balls and exercise equipment are classified as pure goods and why the intangible nature of the game constitutes a pure service, but what about other sports products? For example, sporting events typically offer a variety of pure goods (such as food, beverages, and merchandise). However, even these goods have a customer service component. The responsiveness, courtesy, and friendliness of the service provider are intangible components of the service encounter.

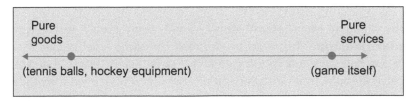

Figure 7.1
The goods–services continuum

Most sports products do not fall so neatly into two distinct categories but possess characteristics of both goods and services. Figure 7.1 shows the goods–services continuum. On one end, we have sporting goods. At the other end of the continuum, we have, almost exclusively, sports services. For example, a sports service that has received considerable attention in the past few years is the fantasy sports camp. Sports camps from a variety of team and individual sports have sprung up to appeal to the aging athlete. For instance, the Chicago Cubs Fantasy Camp offers lifelong memories and mementos for $3,995.00. During the week, campers receive the following tangible goods: a personalized uniform with name and number, engraved Louisville Slugger bat, baseball autographed by an instructor, baseball card with the camper's picture and camp stats, a DVD of the "Big Game" vs. the former major leaguers, a glossy 8″ × 10″ team photo, and an intangible opportunity to play with former and current Cubs players.

Thus far, the distinction between goods and services has been based on the tangible aspects of the sports product. In addition to the degree of tangibility, goods and services are differentiated on the basis of perishability, separability, and standardization. These distinctions are important because they form the foundation of product planning in the strategic sports marketing process. Because of their importance, let us take a look at each dimension.

Tangibility

Tangibility refers to the ability to see, feel, and touch the product. Interestingly, the strategy for pure goods often involves stressing the intangible benefits of the product. For example, advertisements for Nike's Dri-FIT performance apparel highlight not only the comfort of the product but also the way the clothing will make you "ready to take on the challenges of wild and wicked workouts." Similarly, Formula 1 racing is paired with TAG Heuer watches in a sponsorship agreement and product line that leverages the benefits of both brands by asking "What are you made of?" By pairing with Formula 1 racing, Tag Heuer hopes to capitalize on the intangible attributes of excitement, danger, excellence, and pushing yourself to be the best.

However, the strategy for intangible services is to "tangibilize them."[3]

Standardization and consistency

Another characteristic that distinguishes goods from services is the degree of **standardization**. This refers to receiving the same level of quality over repeat purchases. Because sporting goods are tangible, the physical design of a golf ball is manufactured with very little variability. This is even truer today, as many organizations focus on how to continuously improve their manufacturing processes and enhance their product quality.

Pure services, however, reflect the other end of the standardization and consistency continuum. For example, think about the consistency associated with different individual and team athletic performances. How many times have you heard an announcer state before a game, "Which team (or player) will show up today?" Meaning, will the team play well or poorly on that given day?

The Duke University men's basketball team, under the leadership of Mike Krzyzewski, has been one of the most consistent teams in college sports over the past 35 seasons. This, however, does not guarantee they will win the night you attend the game. In recent years, teams such as the high-performing Cowboys or Chargers have had successful regular seasons but have faced the embarrassing distinction of being eliminated in the first round of the NFL playoffs. Historically, the Buffalo Bills had the embarrassing distinction of being the only team ever to lose four consecutive Super Bowls.

Consider another example of the lack of consistency within a sporting event. You may attend a doubleheader and see your favorite team lose the first game 14 to 5 and win the second game of the day by a score of 1 to 0. One of the risks associated with using individual athletes or teams to endorse products is the high degree of variability associated with their performance from day to day and year to year. Because sports marketers have no control over the consistency of the sports product, they must focus on those things that can be controlled, such as promotions, stadium atmosphere, and, to some extent, pricing.

Perishability

Perishability refers to the ability to store or inventory "pure goods," whereby services are lost if not consumed. Goods may be inventoried or stored if they are not purchased immediately, although there are many costs associated with handling this inventory. The length of time a product may be inventoried, a product's **shelf life**, varies. Most sport and entertainment services have a limited shelf life and are perishable only during the life of the exhibition. Each exhibition has an exclusive time frame that encompasses a unique set of attributes; therefore, they cannot be renewed. Although future reproductions via video rebroadcast and match play may occur, the unique intangible characteristics cannot be renewed. For example, if one were planning to attend a 1:00 football game but had car trouble and ended up not arriving until 4:30, most likely, the exception being overtime or major delay, the shelf life of the exhibition would have expired. If a tennis professional is offering lessons, but no students enroll between the hours of 10:00 a.m. and noon, this time (and money) is lost. This "down time" in which the service provider is available but there is no demand is called **idle product capacity**. Idle product capacity results in decreased profitability. In the case of the tennis pro, there is a moderate inventory cost associated with the professional's salary.

Another example with much higher inventory costs is a professional hockey team that is not filling the stands. Consider the Ottawa Senators, one of the NHL teams with the poorest average attendance and lowest percentage of attendance in the last decade (31st in the 2019-20 season). The costs of producing one professional game include everything from the "astronomical" salaries of the players to the basic costs of lighting and heating the arena. If paying fans are not in the seats, the performance or service will perish, never to be recouped. As a general rule of thumb, the most perishable products in business are airline seats, hotel rooms, and athletic event tickets.

In an effort to reduce the problem of idle product capacity, sports marketers attempt to stimulate demand in off-peak periods by manipulating the other marketing mix variables. For example, if tennis lessons are not in demand from 10:00 a.m. to noon, the racquet club may offer reduced fees for enrolling during these times.

Separability

Another factor that distinguishes goods from services is **separability**. If a consumer is purchasing a new pair of running shoes at a major shoe store chain, such as the Foot Locker, the quality of the good (the Reebok shoes) can be separated from the quality of the service (delivered by the Foot Locker sales associate). Although it is possible to separate the good from the person providing the service, these often overlap. What this suggests is that manufacturers will selectively choose the retailers that will best represent their goods. In addition, manufacturers and retailers often provide detailed training to ensure salespeople are knowledgeable about the numerous brands that are inventoried.

As we move along the goods-services continuum from pure goods toward pure services, there is less separability. In other words, it becomes more difficult to separate the service received from the service provider. In the case of an athletic event, there is no separation between the athlete, the entertainment, and the fan. The competition is being produced and consumed simultaneously. As such, sport marketers can capitalize on a team or athlete when they are performing well. When things are going poorly, they may have to rely on other aspects of the game (food, fun, and promotions) to satisfy fans. The Green Bay Packers have sold the history and tradition of the team to the fans. Despite several losing seasons, the team has sold out every game since 1960, with the fans braving the elements in support of their team. These fans were rewarded with another Super Bowl victory in the 2010-2011 season.

Classifying sports products

In addition to categorizing products based on where they fall on the goods-services continuum, a number of other classification schemes exist. For sports organizations that have a variety of products, the concepts of product line and product mix become important strategic considerations. Let us look at these two concepts in the context of a goods-oriented sports organization and a services-oriented sports organization.

A **product line** is a group of products that are closely related because they satisfy a class of needs, are used together, are sold to the same customer groups, are distributed through the same type of outlets, or fall within a given price range. Wilson Sporting Goods sells many related product lines such as shoes, bats, gloves, softballs, golf clubs, and tennis racquets. The total assortment of product lines that a sports organization sells is the **product mix**. Table 7.1 illustrates the relationship between the product lines and product mix for Wilson Sporting Goods. The number of different product lines the organization offers is referred to as the breadth of the product mix. If these product lines are closely related in terms of the goods and services offered to consumers, then there is a high degree of product consistency.

Nike recently increased the breadth of its product mix by adding new brands and product lines. The company acquired Converse and its famous Chuck Taylor All-Star shoes, as well as Hurley International, a surf and skateboard apparel brand. Other new acquisitions include Cole Haan dress shoes and Umbro sports apparel. The strategic advantage of this related diversification is the use of Nike's established marketing muscle.[4] Synergy in distribution and promotion, as well as strong brand identification, has made Nike's launch into new markets a successful venture. Joycelyn Hayward, the manager of a sporting goods

Table 7.1 Wilson Sporting Goods product mix

Baseball	Basketball	Football	Golf	Racquetball	Soccer
Gloves	Accessories	Footballs	Irons	Racquets	Soccer balls
DeMarini bats	Basketballs	Tees/ accessories	Woods	Gloves	Protective gear
Baseballs	Uniforms		Wedges	Eyewear	
Protective gear		Youth	Putters	Racquetballs	Bags
Bags		Protective accessories uniforms NFL	Complete sets Balls	Footwear Bags	
Accessories					
Uniforms			Bags	String	
			Gloves	Accessories	
			Accessories retired models	Apparel	

continued

Table 7.1 *continued*

Volleyball	Softball Fastpitch	Softball Slowpitch	Squash	Tennis	Badminton
Outdoor balls	Gloves	Gloves	Racquets	Balls	Racquets
Indoor Balls	Bats	Bats	Bags	Footwear	Shuttlecocks
Uniforms	Balls	Balls	String	Legacy	String
Ball carts	Protective	Accessories	Grips	footwear	
Bags	gear			Accessories	
	Accessories			Platform	
				tennis	
				Court	
				equipment	
				Retired	
				models	
				Raquets	
				Bags	
				String	
				Grips	

Source: Wilson Sporting Goods, www.wilsonsports.com

store that carries Nike, summed it up best by saying, "Nike's ability to churn out innovative products and marketing plans has kept it ahead of rivals."[5]

Today, Nike is focusing on increasing their talent pool of athletes and expanding their growing product lines in new sports. For example, LeBron James joined the Phil Knight stable in 2003 for a $90-million, multiyear endorsement contract prior to playing a college or professional game. Nike certainly pinned its hopes on James to invigorate sales in the high-end market. This risk paid off, as 2005 was a record year for sales and profitability for Nike, who increased revenues by 12 percent from the previous fiscal year to $13.7 billion.[6] Nike, under the initial leadership of Knight, has moved into international markets, and these endeavors accounted for 61 percent of Nike's total of $37 billion of revenue in 2020.[7] Much of Nike's growth (21 percent in 2018) has been attributed to its most recent lineup of shoes and apparel products. Knight will always be remembered as the man who realized the true marketing power of sports celebrities.

The depth of the product lines describes the number of individual products that make up that line. The greater the number of variations in the product line, the deeper the line. For example, the Wilson basketball product line currently features 62 different basketballs, 6 of which are indoor and 56 of which are indoor/outdoor. Now, think about how the product concepts might relate to a more service-oriented sports organization, such as a professional sports franchise. All these organizations have gone beyond selling the core product, the game itself, and moved into other profitable areas, such as the sale of licensed

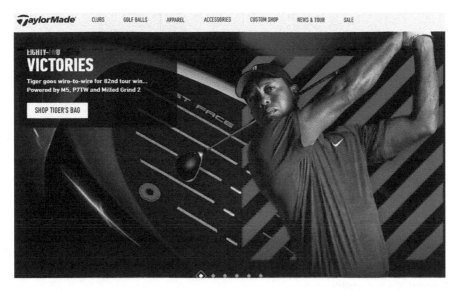

Web Capture 7.1
TaylorMade's split from Adidas Golf provided "freedom and independence" according to TaylorMade CEO David Abeles

Source: © 2019 TaylorMade Golf Company, Inc.

URL: www.taylormadegolf.com/

merchandise, memorabilia, and fantasy camps. In essence, sports organizations have expanded their product lines or broadened their product mix.

Understanding the depth, breadth, and consistency of the product offerings is important from a strategic perspective. Sports organizations might consider adding product lines and therefore, widen the product mix. For example, Nike is using this strategy and capitalizing on its strong brand name. Alternatively, the sports organization can eliminate weak product lines and focus on its established strengths. In addition, the product lines it adds may be related to existing lines (product line consistency) or may be unrelated to existing lines (product line diversification).

Another strategic decision may be to maintain the number of product lines but add new versions to make the line deeper. For instance, the MLS has 24 teams divided into Eastern and Western conferences, 21 in the United States and 3 in Canada. FC Cincinnati became the 24th team, and the league grew to 26 teams (Miami and Nashville) in 2020. All of these product planning strategies require examining the overarching marketing goals and the organizational objectives, as well as carefully considering consumers' needs.

Product characteristics

Products are sometimes described as "bundles of benefits" designed to satisfy consumers' needs.[8] These "bundles" consist of numerous important attributes

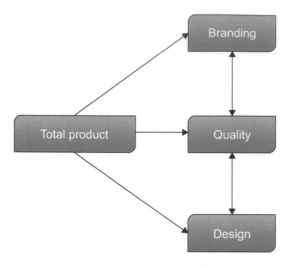

Figure 7.2
Product characteristics

ARTICLE 7.2
SPOTLIGHT ON INTERNATIONAL SPORTS MARKETING

The weirdest, wackiest, worst sports endorsements of all time

Endorsing products – either their own or someone else's – is a time-honored way for athletes to rake in the bucks. The first sports endorsements appeared as far back as the late nineteenth century, so there were bound to be a few mismatched collaborations and dubious products over the years, such as . . .

THE RAY LEWIS SNUGGIE: Yes, the one-piece-blanket-with-arms-that-you-wear. The official Ray Lewis Snuggie was bright purple, and part of his RL52 clothing line, which debuted in 2010.

SHAQUILLE O'NEAL'S SHAQ-FU VIDEO GAME: A pretty bad name and, according to gamers, a pretty bad game. And speaking of bad product names related to Shaquille O'Neal, there's also Shaq's Luv Shaq Vodka – a very punny brand of vodka that Shaq said he'd release in 2012, but that never hit the market. Hard to imagine why.

BEN ROETHLISBERGER'S BIG BEN'S BEEF JERKY: It was sold in Pittsburgh-area grocery stores. The name sounds a little, well, jerky, but the problem really came after he was accused of sexual assault in 2009 and 2010. Suddenly it didn't seem like a great idea to be talking about Big Ben's Beef anything. PLB Sports, the company that produced it, dropped both Ben and his beef.

RONALDINHO'S SEX-FREE CONDOMS: A very peculiar (if not completely contradictory) name for a product not usually endorsed by athletes.

MANNY RAMIREZ'S SUM POOSIE ENERGY DRINK: Speaking of strange names and, for that matter, sex. Not that it's supposed to be about sex exactly, even though there's a scantily clad, large-breasted woman on the pink bottle and the owner of Sum Poosie said he considered himself "the Larry Flynt of energy drinks."

CARSON PALMER'S AD FOR JOHN MORRELL SMOKED SAUSAGES: An extremely dubious print ad, exhorting you to "Go Longer" and showing then-hot-prospect Palmer shoving a long wiener into his mouth, which . . . well, you get it.

CHAD (JOHNSON) OCHOCINCO'S OCHOCINC-O'S, ROB GRONKOWSKI'S GRONK FLAKES, AND JUSTIN VERLANDER'S FASTBALL FLAKES: A group of cereal offenders. Ochocinc-O's were sold to benefit Feed the Children, but the phone number on the box was for a phone sex line instead of the charity. Gronk Flakes, meanwhile, are still carried in New England grocery stores, and Fastball Flakes sold like hotcakes (hotflakes?) in the Michigan market.

Source: Petras, Kathryn, Petras, Ross, 2017. The Stupidest Sports Book of All Time. Excerpts. https://blog.workman.com/the-weirdest-wackiest-worst-sports-endorsements-of-all-time

or characteristics that, when taken together, create the total product. These **product characteristics**, which include branding, quality, and design, are illustrated in Figure 7.2. It is important to note that each of the product characteristics interacts with the others to produce the total product. Branding is dependent on product quality, product quality is contingent on product design, and so on. Although these product features (i.e., branding, quality, and design) are interdependent, we examine each independently in the following sections.

Branding

What first comes to mind when you hear University of Notre Dame, Green Bay, or adidas? It is likely the Fighting Irish name, along with the Lucky Leprechaun ready to battle; the Packers and their synonymous relation with Green Bay, Wisconsin; and adidas's symbolic three stripes. All these characteristics are important elements of branding.

Branding is a name, design, symbol, or any combination that a sports organization (or individual athlete, as is the case with Cristiano Ronaldo) uses to help differentiate its products from the competition. Three important branding concepts are brand name, brand marks, and trademarks. A **brand name** refers to the element of the brand that can be vocalized, such as the Nike Air Jordan, the Pittsburgh Penguins, and the UNC Tar Heels. When selecting a brand name for sporting goods or a team name, considerable marketing effort is required to ensure the name symbolizes strength and confidence. Because choosing a name is such a critical decision, sports marketers sometimes use the following guidelines for selecting brand names:

- The name should be positive and distinctive, generate positive feelings and associations, and be easy to remember and to pronounce. For team names, the positive associations include those linked with a city or geographic area.
- The name should be translatable into a dynamite attitude-oriented logo. As an example of a successful logo choice, consider Kansas City's Major League Soccer team, who changed their name from the Wizards to Sporting Kansas City. CEO and managing partner Robb Heineman stated that the name change "continues the forward-thinking and innovation. This is all about our connection to the community and us trying to be innovative in what we're trying to do."[9]
- The name should imply the benefits the sports product delivers. For example, the name communicates the product attributes the target market desires.
- The name should be consistent with the image of the rest of the product lines, organization, and city. Again, this is especially important for cities naming their sports franchises. One example of this concept in action is MLS's Columbus Crew.[10] The Crew was chosen to represent the Columbus community in a positive manner. The name suggests the hard work, do-not-quit attitude that people in the Columbus community value.
- The name should be legally and ethically permissible. That is, the name cannot violate another organization's trademarks or be seen as offensive to any group of people. For example, a great many team names with reference to (and perceived negative connotations of) Native Americans have been changed or are under scrutiny (e.g., Miami University of Ohio Redskins to RedHawks, Washington Redskins to Washington Football Team and Atlanta Braves). The NCAA decided in 2005 to ban the use of American Indian mascots by sports teams during its postseason tournaments. Schools using American Indian mascots or nicknames would also be barred from hosting NCAA postseason tournaments.

While choosing a team/brand name is critical to marketing success, some teams and leagues haven't fared so well in the name game. For example, the National Lacrosse League has had a history of poor team names.[11] The name Colorado Mammoth conjures up images such as big, slow, and extinct – not exactly a good fit for a professional athletic team. In addition, some of the University of California institutions such as UC Santa Cruz and UC Irvine have struggled to develop a positive association with the brand names of Banana Slugs and Anteaters, respectively.

A **brand mark**, also known as the **logo** or **logotype**, is the element of a brand that cannot be spoken. One of the most recognizable logos in the world is the Nike Swoosh. Interestingly, Carolyn Davidson was paid just $35 in 1971 to create the logo that now adorns Nike products, as well as former CEO Phil Knight's ankle in the form of a tattoo. It's important for sports marketers to realize that

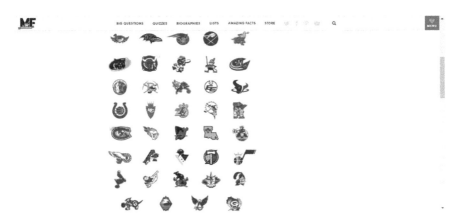

Web Capture 7.2
Sources on the Internet provide a definitive gallery of sports logos

Source: Fanning Creative (https://fanningcreative.carbonmade.com/), http://mentalfloss.com/article/53219/logo-mashups-all-teams-each-city

while the Nike logo was created for the paltry sum of $35, the cost of changing logos and nicknames can swell and eventually cost millions of dollars. Some of the incidental costs of changing your brand include surveys of constituent groups, designing the logo, retaining a marketing firm, developing a new ad campaign to create awareness, repainting facilities, buying new stationery, replacing signage, creating new uniforms, and even developing a new mascot costume.[12]

A **trademark** identifies that a sports organization has legally registered its brand name or brand mark and thus prevents others from using it. Unfortunately, product counterfeiting or the production of low-cost copies of trademarked popular brands is reaching new heights. Product counterfeiting and trademark infringement are especially problematic at major sporting events, such as the Super Bowl or Olympic Games. For example, Collegiate Licensing Co., a division of IMG Worldwide, which represents about 200 collegiate properties, found some 3,000 counterfeit items at football bowl games and the NCAA basketball tournament.

The branding process

The broad purpose of branding a product is to allow an organization to distinguish and differentiate itself from all others in the marketplace. Building the brand will then ultimately affect consumer behaviors, such as increasing attendance, merchandising sales, or participation in sports. However, before these behaviors are realized, several things must happen in the **branding process**, shown in Figure 7.3.

First, **brand awareness** must be established. Brand awareness refers to making consumers in the desired target market recognize and remember the brand name. Only after awareness levels reach their desired objectives can

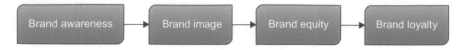

Figure 7.3
The branding process

brand image be addressed. After all, consumers must be aware of the product before they can understand the image the sports marketer is trying to project.

After brand awareness is established, marketing efforts turn to developing and managing a **brand image**. Brand image is described as the consumers' set of beliefs about brands, which, in turn, shape attitudes. Brand image can also be thought of as the "personality" of the brand. Organizations that sponsor sporting events are especially interested in strengthening or maintaining the image of their products through association with a sports entity (athlete, team, or league) that reflects the desired image. For instance, the marketers of Mercedes-Benz automobiles have established sponsorships with tennis events to reinforce a brand image of power, grace, and control.

Sports marketers attempt to manage beliefs that we have about a particular brand through a number of "image drivers," or factors that influence the brand image. The image drivers controlled by sports marketing efforts include product features or characteristics, product performance or quality, price, brand name, customer service, packaging, advertising, promotion, and distribution channels. Each of these image drivers contributes to creating the overall brand image. After shaping a positive brand image, sports marketers can then ultimately hope to create high levels of brand equity.

Another link in the branding process is developing high levels of brand equity. **Brand equity** is the value that the brand contributes to a product in the marketplace. In economic terms, it is the difference in value between a branded product and its generic equivalent. Consumers who believe a sport product has a high level of brand equity are more likely to be satisfied with the brand. The satisfied consumers will, in turn, become brand-loyal or repeat purchasers. Gladden, Milne, and Sutton have developed a unique model of assessing brand equity for the sports industry. The components of the model can be seen in Figure 7.4. The authors explain brand equity by extending the previous work of Aaker, who believes there are four major components of brand equity.[13] These are perceived quality, brand awareness, brand associations, and brand loyalty. Gladden, Milne, and Sutton describe the perceived quality of sport as the consumers' perceptions of a team's success. Obviously, this could be extended beyond the notion of a team to other sport products. Brand awareness is defined as the consumers' familiarity with a particular team or sport product. Brand associations refer to the intangible attributes of a brand or, in the case of sport, the experiential and symbolic attributes offered by an athletic team. The final component, brand loyalty, is defined

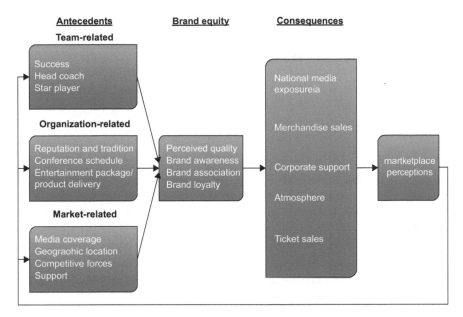

Figure 7.4
The conceptual model for assessing brand equity

as the ability to attract and retain consumers. As the authors point out, this is sometimes difficult because of the inconsistent and intangible nature of the sports product.[14]

When describing the full model of brand equity for sport, Gladden and his colleagues also discuss the antecedents and consequences of brand equity for a sports product. These antecedent conditions are particularly important for marketing managers to understand because they will have an impact on

ARTICLE 7.3
THESE PRO SPORTS TEAMS ARE RUNNING OUT OF FANS

Each year, tens of millions of Americans pour into arenas, parks, rinks and stadiums to see a professional sporting event in one of the four major American sports leagues – the NFL, NBA, NHL, and MLB.

But fans are now less inclined to go to games in person. Each league saw a decline in total attendance from 2008 to 2018. Fans are often unwilling to pay high ticket prices, and teams don't seem to care, as an increasing amount and share of their revenue comes from lucrative TV contracts as opposed to ticket sales. But not all teams are losing fans at an equal rate. Some have seen average attendance declines of more than a third over the last decade.

While it is tough to know exactly what is stopping fans from coming to games, losing is likely a top cause. Fans are simply not willing to pay top dollar to see a game that will probably end in disappointment for them. In fact, 10 of the 12 teams running out of fans played worse in 2018 than they had a decade earlier. Every team can have losing seasons, but franchises that always seem to come up short can lose the attention of their fans. Those squads are the hardest teams to root for.

Not all teams have attendance slumps for the same reason. Some teams, like the Philadelphia Phillies, usually have a packed stadium, but recent struggles seem to have impacted attendance. Other teams, like the Tampa Bay Rays, have never had strong attendance, and the one-time surge they experienced after their franchise-best season has long since dissipated. This is each MLB team's best season in franchise history.

To determine the teams losing the most fans, 24/7 Wall St. reviewed 10-year percentage changes in average attendance at regular season home games in the NHL, NBA, MLB, and NFL. Attendance figures are from ESPN and are as of the most recent completed season – the 2018–2019 season for the NHL and NBA, and the 2018 seasons for the NFL and MLB – and the season 10 years earlier. We considered only bottom three teams that saw at least a 10% decline in the average percentage of the stadium that was filled.

To avoid attendance declines based on a reduction in stadium capacity, franchises that built a new facility or moved to a new city in those years were excluded. The average percentage of capacity filled during home games in a season for the NHL, NBA, and NFL also came from ESPN and is as of the most recently completed regular season. In the case of the MLB, average capacity filled is based on the average home game attendance from ESPN and officially listed stadium capacities.

3. Philadelphia Phillies

- Avg. home attendance change 2008–2018: –35.3%
- 2008 avg. home game attendance (pct. capacity): 42,254 (97.1%)
- 2008 record: 92–70

Phillies fans were excited ahead of the 2008 MLB season as the team finally broke through and ended its 13-year playoff drought the year prior. In 2008, Philadelphia won what would be its second of five straight NL East titles on its way to a World Series championship. More than 97% of seats at Citizens Bank Park were occupied that season, accounting for over 42,000 fans per game – both figures ranked among the top five in baseball that year.

3. Philadelphia Phillies

- Avg. home attendance change 2008–2018: –35.3%
- 2018 avg. home game attendance (pct. capacity): 27,318 (63.4%)
- 2018 record: 80–82

This Phillies led the majors in total attendance from 2010 to 2012, but it can be tough to maintain enthusiasm for a team that has not made the playoffs since 2011. In 2018, an average of 27,318 fans per game came to Citizens Bank Park, near the middle of MLB attendance. Now that the team is playing better with the acquisition of superstar Bryce Harper, Philly fans are already returning to the ballpark in droves in 2019.

2. Tampa Bay Rays

- Avg. home attendance change 2008–2018: –35.9%
- 2008 avg. home game attendance (pct. capacity): 22,259 (52.8%)
- 2008 record: 97–65

Even when the Tampa Bay Rays are playing well, the team's stadium is rarely full. In 2008, the Rays won 97 games and made the postseason for the first time in team history, eventually losing in the World Series. Fans didn't seem to care, as the team's average home attendance was just over 22,000, or 52.8% of Tropicana Field's capacity.

2. Tampa Bay Rays

- Avg. home attendance change 2008–2018: –35.9%
- 2018 avg. home game attendance (pct. capacity): 14,258 (41.8%)
- 2018 record: 90–72

A decade after their first postseason run, the Rays are still a winning team, despite sharing a division with the high-powered Yankees and Red Sox, and the fans are still not showing up. Despite being 18 games over .500 in 2018, average attendance for Rays home games fell to 14,258 people per game, or just 41.8% of the Trop's capacity. Most teams are able to attract more than 2 million fans to their games over a season. The Rays haven't hit that mark since their inaugural season of 1998

1. Detroit Tigers

- Avg. home attendance change 2008–2018: –41.3%
- 2008 avg. home game attendance (pct. capacity): 39,538 (98.6%)
- 2008 record: 74–88

Following the team's 2006 World Series appearance, in which they lost to the St. Louis Cardinals, attendance at Detroit Tigers had been increasing. Though the team had a losing record, Comerica Park was typically close to full in 2008, with nearly 40,000 fans coming to each game.

1. Detroit Tigers

- Avg. home attendance change 2008–2018: –41.3%
- 2018 avg. home game attendance (pct. capacity): 23,212 (56.3%)
- 2018 record: 64–98

A four-season playoff drought may have, in part, spurred the exodus of Tigers fans. The team managed a string of postseason appearances in the early 2010s, but it has struggled since – and attendance suffered along with the team's performance. After peaking in 2013, attendance at Tigers games has consistently fallen, reaching 23,212 per game in 2018. This may also have something to do with the fact that Detroit is quickly losing residents, as once-available manufacturing jobs are gone. It may be difficult to convince some of the remaining fans to come to Tigers games if the team is unable to put together a winning season.

Credit: Grant Suneson

Rightsholder: 24/7 Wall Street

URL: https://247wallst.com/special-report/2019/07/09/sports-teams-running-out-of-fans-3/

the level of brand equity. The three broad categories of antecedents are team-related factors, organization-related factors, and market-related factors.

Team-related factors are further broken down into the success of the team, head coach, and star player(s). Previous research has shown that winning or success is still a critical factor in establishing a strong brand and in achieving the desired outcomes such as merchandise sales, media exposure, and so on. Although selling an inferior core product (i.e., losing team) is never easy, it is important to underscore the notion that sports marketers must do their best to enhance those aspects of the event experience that they can control. As the accompanying article illustrates, numerous teams still attract fans even after a series of losing seasons.

Although success is defined by wins and losses, it can also be thought of as the historical standard by which the team has been judged. Interestingly, the authors of the model also believe the head coach can be an important factor in establishing brand equity. The University of Minnesota received a tremendous boost when they hired basketball coach Tubby Smith, and The Ohio State University brand was bolstered with the hiring of former Florida head coach Urban Meyer. Similarly, a star player or players can boost brand equity, especially in the sports of baseball and basketball. For example, the LeBron phenomenon gave the struggling Cleveland Cavaliers a new image and chance to reposition their franchise with the drafting of James in 2003. This brand positioning strategy was changed when LeBron James and Chris Bosh signed matching 6-year $110.1 million contracts to join Dwayne Wade and the Miami Heat in 2010 and revised upon his return to Cleveland in 2014–2015. Now that LeBron has joined the LA Lakers, both teams will have a need to revise brand strategy.

The organization-related antecedents described in the model include reputation and tradition, conference and schedule, and entertainment package – product delivery. The reputation and tradition of the team off the field are believed to be factors in building brand equity. An excellent example of problems in the front office influencing fan perceptions and brand equity is that of the hapless Arizona Cardinals. Owner Bill Bidwell has been scrutinized and criticized by the fans and media for years because of bad choices made on and off the field.

The conference affiliation and schedule are also organizational factors influencing image. Gladden et al. believe college and professional teams who play in tougher conferences with long-standing rivals will create greater benefits for the team's equity in the long term. This must certainly hold some truth, as college teams and conferences are constantly realigning. Often this link is relative to attendance, market presence, and media exposure. From 2011 to 2014, there were wild rounds of realignment that helped to shape the collegiate landscape. Now all eyes are on 2023. Why 2023? That is when many of the power conferences' television contracts start expiring.

Finally, the entertainment aspect of sport created and managed by the organization will affect brand equity. As mentioned previously, this is one of the controllable elements of the largely uncontrollable sports industry.

Market-related antecedents are those things such as media coverage, geographic location, competitive forces, and support. Media coverage refers to the exposure the sport product receives in the media via multiple outlets such as radio, TV, newspaper, and the Internet. Obviously, the images portrayed in the media and amount of coverage can have a huge bearing on all aspects of brand equity. Geographic location is also related to equity in that certain areas of the United States are linked with certain types of sport. As described in Milne and McDonald,[15] "it may be easier to establish brand equity, and for a Division I men's basketball team in Indiana than it would be in Idaho." Competition must also be considered a market factor, and the authors of the model describe it as the most influential in creating equity. In some instances, competition can enhance the value of a brand, but more typically, competitive forces vying for similar consumers will weaken equity and its outcomes. Fan support is the final market force influencing equity. Quite simply, the greater the number of loyal fans or supporters, the greater the brand equity.

Although the preceding discussion has focused on the antecedents of brand equity to a sports product, the model also describes the related outcomes or consequences of establishing a strong brand. More specifically, the authors believe higher levels of brand equity will lead to more national media exposure, greater sales of team merchandise, more support from corporate sponsors, enhanced stadium atmospherics, and increased ticket sales.

How can marketers assess the equity of a brand such as the Yankees or Nike? One popular technique to measure brand equity evaluates a brand's performance across seven dimensions. Brand equity is then calculated by applying a multiple, determined by the brand's performance on the seven dimensions, to the net brand-related profits. These dimensions include leadership, or the ability of the brand to influence its market; stability, or the ability of the brand to survive; market, or the trading environment of the brand internationality or the ability of the brand to cross geographic and cultural borders; trend, or the ongoing direction of the brand's importance to the industry; support, or the effectiveness of the brand's communication; and protection of the owner's legal title.[16]

Although there are a number of ways to measure brand equity in consumer goods, there have been very few attempts to look at the equity of sports teams. One exception was a study that measured the brand equity of MLB franchises.[17] To measure brand equity, the researchers first calculated team revenues for each franchise. These revenues are based on gate receipts; media; licensing and merchandise; and stadium-oriented issues, such as concessions, advertising, and so on. The franchise value is then assigned a multiple based on growth projections for network television fees. Next, the total franchise value is subtracted from the value of a generic product to determine the brand equity. Because there is no such thing as a generic baseball team, the researchers used the $130 million fee paid by the two new expansion teams at the time of the study, Tampa Bay and Arizona. This $130 million fee, though low when compared with today's standards, represents the closest estimate to an unbranded team, because the new teams had yet to begin play.

Interestingly, only 7 of the 30 MLB teams show any brand equity. Based on the research, the following teams have positive brand equity (in rank order): New York Yankees, Toronto Blue Jays, New York Mets, Boston Red Sox, Los Angeles Dodgers, Chicago White Sox, and Texas Rangers. The teams with the lowest brand equity include the Pittsburgh Pirates and Seattle Mariners. Given the fact that many of these "brands" have been around for decades, the brand equity for MLB franchises is surprisingly low.

ARTICLE 7.4
SPORTS MARKETING HALL OF FAME

Phil Knight's biography

Nike co-founder, Philip Knight was born on February 24, 1938, in Portland, Oregon.

Knight was a middle-distance runner for the University of Oregon track team, where he encountered coach Bill Bowerman's obsession with improving running shoes. When Knight studied at the Graduate School of Business at Stanford, a professor, Frank Shallenberger instructed his students to write a paper on how they would create a new company. With his experience of Bowerman in his mind, Phil Knight's paper argued how profits could be generated by importing cheap but well-made running shoes from Japan. He put his theory into practice and Phil Knight and Bowerman each invested $500 in purchasing Tiger shoes from Japan. They founded Blue Ribbon Sports, Inc. in the early 1960s.

In their first year they cleared $364, but by 1969 sales had rocketed to a million dollars. The company was renamed Nike in 1972. They developed the "swoosh" logo and cultivated endorsers that included Michael Jordan, Tiger Woods and Pete Sampras.

In spite of receiving a lot of negative publicity because of their use of child labor in the Far East, by 2004 Nike was selling goods worth around $12bn annually and employing 24,000 staff worldwide. In November 2004 Phil Knight announced he was stepping down as chief executive, and also retired as chairman of the board of directors in 2016. On the Nike website, Phil Knight states his personal philosophy: "There is an immutable conflict at work in life and in business, a constant battle between peace and chaos. Neither can be mastered, but both can be influenced. How you go about that is the key to success." Forbes estimated Phil Knight's net worth at $37.6 billion.

*Source:*www.biogs.com/famous/knightphilip.html

Although the previous study used an economic basis for determining brand equity, other research has employed less precise, qualitative approaches. For example, a panel of sporting goods industry experts was asked to name the most powerful brands in sport. In this study of equity, sports brands were defined as those who directly manufacture sporting apparel, equipment, and shoes. Nike is in a league of its own when it comes to branding. Ever since the introduction of the Air Jordan basketball shoe, Nike has grown geometrically since the days when Phil Knight (the founder) sold shoes out of the trunk of his car.

Brand loyalty is one of the most important concepts to sports marketers, because it refers to a consistent preference or repeat purchase of one brand over all others in a product category. Marketers want their products to satisfy consumers, so decision making becomes a matter of habit rather than an extensive evaluation among competing brands.

In sports marketing, teams represent perhaps one of the most interesting examples of loyalty. It is common to hear us speak of people as being "loyal fans" or "fair-weather fans." The loyal fans endure all the team's successes and hardships. As the definition implies, they continue to prefer their team over others through thick and thin. Alternatively, the fair-weather fan will jump to and from the teams that are successful at the time. Sport and entertainment offers a unique platform to immerse the "brand-conscious." For example, youth often develop patterns of loyalty to athletic teams at a young age, some by the age of 36–42 months. Social exchanges and key influencers such as parents and families facilitate this brand identity. What are the determinants of fan loyalty to a team? Psychologist Robert Passikoff believes the interaction of four factors creates fan loyalty.[18] The first factor is the *entertainment value* of athletics. As we discussed in Chapter 5, entertainment value is one of the underlying factors of fan motivation. In addition, entertainment was discussed as one of the perceived values of sports to the community. The second component of fan loyalty is *authenticity*. Passikoff defines authenticity as the "acceptance of the game as real and meaningful." *Fan bonding* is the third component of fan loyalty. *Bonding* refers to the degree to which fans identify with players and the

Table 7.2 Psychological commitment to team scale

1. I might rethink my allegiance to my favorite team if this team consistently performs poorly.
2. I would watch a game featuring the [name of team] regardless of which team they are playing.
3. I would rethink my allegiance to the [name of team] if the best players left the team (i.e., transfer, graduate, etc.).
4. Being a fan of the [name of team] is important to me.
5. Nothing could change my allegiance to the [name of team].
6. I am a committed fan of the [name of team].
7. It would not affect my loyalty to the [name of team] if the athletic department hired a head coach that I disliked very much.
8. I could easily be persuaded to change my preference for the [name of team].
9. I have been a fan of the [name of team] since I began watching collegiate football.
10. I could never switch my loyalty from the [name of team] even if my close friends were fans of another team.
11. It would be unlikely for me to change my allegiance from the [name of team] to another team.
12. It would be difficult to change my beliefs about the [name of team].
13. You can tell a lot about a person by their willingness to stick with a team that is not performing well.
14. My commitment to the [name of team] would decrease if they were performing poorly and there appeared little chance their performance would change.

team. The bonding component is similar to the concept of fan identification discussed in Chapter 5. The fourth and final component of fan loyalty is the *history and tradition* of the team. For example, the Cincinnati Reds are baseball's oldest team and, although they may be lacking in other dimensions of loyalty such as attendance recently, they certainly have a long history and tradition with the fans in the greater Cincinnati area.

To measure fan loyalty, self-identified fans are asked to rate their hometown teams on each of the four dimensions. Interestingly, the fan loyalty measure does not specifically include a team performance component. Contrary to popular belief, Passikoff believes winning and loyalty do not always go hand in hand.

Another way to operationalize the loyalty construct has been developed by researchers Dan Mahony and his colleagues.[19] They believe that loyalty can be thought of as having two distinct components: attitudinal loyalty and behavioral loyalty. Attitudinal loyalty can be expressed as an individual's psychological commitment to the team (or PCT). To better understand how to measure PCT and what it means, Table 7.2 shows the scale developed by Mahony.

In our society, loyalty to sports teams at the high school, college, and professional levels is perhaps higher than it is for any other goods and services we consume. Unfortunately, team loyalty at the professional level is beginning to erode because of the constant threat of uprooting the franchise and moving it to a new town. This is perhaps one reason for the increased popularity of amateur athletics. Colleges will not threaten to move for a better stadium deal, and athletes do not change teams for better contracts (although they do leave their universities early for professional contracts). Historically, fan loyalty has been defined in four ways: pure entertainment – how well a team performs or how exciting the play; fan bonding – respect and admiration of players; history and tradition – if the game and the team are part of community beliefs and rituals; and authenticity – how well they play as a team or how well the stadium or managers/players present themselves in the community. To increase fan loyalty, many teams are establishing fan loyalty programs, pairing new technology with existing marketing principles. Technology facilitates engagement with fans during games through a variety of scoreboard and fan chatter platforms. These platforms could be expanded to all team branded touch points that a fan may encounter. These points include sports web sites, fantasy sports systems, and stores and bars in which sports fans purchase products.[20]

Lyberger, McCarthy, and Yim (2018) explored fan loyalty of professional sports teams. The study explored the presence, nature, engagement, and effectiveness of loyalty initiatives and assessed equity, amplification, and antecedent focus. Loyalty programs are typically driven by an app or card that is swiped at kiosks when fans enter a stadium or event. The fans benefit by earning points that can be redeemed for rewards such as free tickets, merchandise, and concessions. The teams benefit by collecting valuable information on their fan base that can later be used to direct strategic marketing decisions. Major League Baseball seems to have taken the lead in fan loyalty efforts; however, most, if not all professional, organizations have realized the corresponding benefits.[21]

Non-sport organizations also seek to develop customer loyalty through sport. In a Turnkey Intelligence survey conducted exclusively for *Sports Business Journal* and *Sports Business Daily*, respondents were screened and analyzed based on their general avidity levels.[22] Results revealed that overall, official brands got a good ride with NASCAR. For example, Subway, who was not even an official sponsor but a part-time sponsor on driver Carl Edwards's car, received the highest percentage of recognition among respondents in the quick-service restaurant category. In addition, according to NASCAR's Brian Moyer, managing director of market and media research, Nationwide did a good job of diversifying their partnership by tying in and integrating multiple drivers with multiple promotional efforts.[23] Gatorade also received high marks, specifically integrating the success of their partnership with Kroger for the Daytona 500, creating custom labels highlighting three flavors that integrated the race and driver.

Licensing

The importance of having a strong brand is demonstrated when an organization considers product licensing. Licensing is a contractual agreement whereby a company may use another company's trademark in exchange for a royalty or fee. A branding strategy through licensing allows the organization to authorize the use of brand, brand name, brand mark, trademark, or trade name in conjunction with a good, service, or promotion in return for royalties. According to author Steve Sleight, "Licensing is a booming area of the sports business with players, teams, event names, and logos appearing on a vastly expanding range of products."[24] The Annual Global Licensing Industry Survey released by LIMA revealed that retail and related revenue generated globally by the trademark licensing business rose 3.3 percent to US$271.6B. In addition, according to results, royalty revenue from sales of licensed merchandise and services rose 2.6 percent to $14.5 billion.[25] The report revealed Entertainment/Character licensing to be the largest industry category, accounting for $122.7 billion, or 43.8 percent of the total global licensing market. Corporate/Brand Trademarks generated US$58.8 billion in retail receipts for 21 percent of total revenues, followed by Fashion with $32.2 billion (11.5 percent) and Sports with $27.8 billion (9.9 percent).[26]

The global licensed sports merchandise industry is projected to grow at a significant rate in the near future. Many licensed sports merchandisers are acquiring a license to sell sports merchandise that incorporates copyrighted material similar to other licensing arrangements, a market in the past that was highly dominated by a few key players, for the agreement used in merchandise licensing is usually more complex.[27] Content-rich licensing properties that can perform well utilizing social media and identify directly with fans will continue to develop new licensed sales opportunities. The growing popularity of outdoor sports like football, cricket, and basketball is attracting teenagers to spend more on licensed sports merchandise. Increasing sports league activities across the globe are also creating new opportunities for key players to capture the market. For example, the La Liga and its franchisees are following the other global sporting events for building the brand value to increasing their revenue collections through merchandising.[28] The market is also driven by growing innovation and development activities to produce more attractive and stylish sports apparel and sports accessories. This, coupled with improved economic conditions across developing countries such as China and India, enables sports fans to spend more on licensed sports merchandise.

License Global's annual report brings together financial information from the world's most powerful brands. The study accounts for retail sales of licensed merchandise across all major sectors of business, from entertainment to sports, food and beverage, corporate brands, fashion, art and design, non-profits, and much more.[29] The report revealed that the Walt Disney Company, owner of ABC and ESPN, is the world's largest licensor. The Walt Disney Company had $54.7 billion in retail sales of licensed merchandise and led the pack by an astounding $28.2 billion. Sports organizations that

Photo 7.2
Future Redbirds in their St. Louis Cardinals licensed baby gear

Source: Matthew D. Shank

made the Top 150 include Major League Baseball $2.7B (27th), a drop from their previous $5.5B; National Football League $3.5 (16th); National Basketball Association $3.2B (20th); NFL Players Association $1.9B (36th); National Hockey League $1.3B (43rd); PGA Tour $1.42B (54th); WWE $1.0 B (52nd); NASCAR $1B (47th); Major League Soccer $420M (77th); Sports Afield $228M (100th); and Gold's Gym, owners of Dick's Sporting Goods, $147M (124th). Interestingly, The Ohio State University was the leader in collegiate licensing at 99th, with $232M in licensed merchandise sales. IMG, which includes IMG Collegiate Licensing and representation across a multitude of brands, was the top licensing agent, with $16B in licensed merchandise sales. Let's take a look at a few of the top sport properties and their plans for strategic growth.

1. Major League Baseball, $2.7 billion

The 30 clubs that make up Major League Baseball scored a number of profitable licensing deals. Originally, MLB recently announced a 10-year partnership that will launch in 2020 that will see Under Armour become the official uniform provider to MLB's 30 teams, and Fanatics gets the licensing rights to manage the manufacturing and distribution of all fan gear, including jerseys, name and number products, and post-season apparel, HOLD THE PRESSES - ROSTER CHANGE! According to Terry Lefton of Sports Business Daily, Under Armour is currently dealing with financial issues, and backing out of this deal would save them $50 million. As such, they're in no position to spend money, so the apparel company has decided to back out of the deal. Under Armour's loss has ended up being Nike's gain. Sports Business Daily is also reporting that with Under Armour backing out, Nike has swooped in themselves, and they will be the ones who will be taking on uniform and apparel duties for MLB once the 2020 season rolls around. The deal would leave Nike with licensing agreements with MLB, the NFL, and the NBA.[30] MLB is "licensing brands that are offering brasher statements and a more fashion-forward attitude" in its bid to "chase a younger audience," according to Janelle Nanos of the *Boston Globe*.[31] These deals helped MLB retain the top spot in sport licensing sales and further complement previous enactments. Previous enactments such as Topps, the first exclusive baseball card company of MLB in nearly 30 years, as well as others, including Ballpark Classics for ballpark-themed tabletop baseball games, ballpark-branded grass seed blends and fertilizers from the Scotts Miracle-Gro Company, and Tommy Bahama in a multi-year deal for a series of collector's edition Major League Baseball team shirts, are performing well, and others like Timex, Snapple, UTZ, Loot Crate, Carhart, and Kingsford have significant potential.

2. IMG College Licensing $16B

IMG College Licensing's partner institutions represent approximately 70 percent of the total retail sales in collegiate athletics, with the remaining sales coming from other collegiate institutions not represented by IMGCL. (Note: Collegiate Licensing Company clients include all major schools except The Ohio State University, Michigan State, University of Southern California, and Oregon.) Top-selling college brands included Michigan, Alabama, Texas A&M, Tennessee, Michigan State, Florida, Clemson, and LSU, as well as the NCAA and the College Football Playoff. Leading retailers of collegiate merchandise in the United States included Wal-Mart, Fanatics, Kohl's, Academy Sports & Outdoors, Dick's Sporting Goods, Sam's Club, Amazon, Follett, and Barnes & Noble. E-commerce and direct-to-consumer retail channels experienced the largest percentage growth. Some of the top product categories for growth included non-wool headwear, jerseys, women's fashion, footwear, and consumables. National marketing platforms developed by IMG Collegiate Licensing helped retailers put college front and center during key selling periods like back-to-school and holidays. Growth in college will come from data-driven brand strategies where collegiate institutions partner with best-in-class licensees that are invested in growing college brands at retail. With the largest female fan base of any sports league - more than 92 million - college brands are increasing their focus serving this consumer by developing more trendy products for lifestyle wear, as well as improving the merchandising of products to inspire purchases. Additionally, increased marketing to consumers through social selling will be a key way to grow college brands at retail. IMG represents a number of brands, including but not limited to AAA, Alfa Romeo, ABARTH, ArmorAll, Arnold Palmer, AS Roma, "Assassin's Creed," Aston Martin, Baby Gap, Banana Republic, BB King, Becks (Europe), Been Trill, Beyond Closet, Billboard, Brigitte Bardot, FC Barcelona, Budweiser (Europe), Bugatti, Bundesliga, Care Bears (Asia), Caesars Palace, Chris-Craft, Chevron, Chrysler, Collegiate Licensing Company, Corona (Europe), Cosmopolitan, Dee & Ricky, Delish, Dodge, Downton Abbey (Asia), Dolly Parton, Ducati, Dylan's Candy Bar, CrossFit, East India Company, Esquire, FC Internazionale, France Rugby Federation, Fiat 500, Fiat Professional, Football Greats Alliance (FGA), "Fortnite," Gap, Gene Simmons, Gola, George Best, Goodyear, Haribo, Harper's Bazaar, Janie and Jack, Jim Beam, John Wooden, Joyrich, Juventus FC, Kakao Friends, Kirsch, Lamborghini, Laura Ashley, 24 Hour Le Mans, Leffe, Li Na, Like Nastya, Marilyn Monroe (Asia), Michael Jackson, Millie Bobby Brown, Maserati, Maui & Sons, Miss Universe, MGM (Asia), National Lampoon, NFL (international), Norman Rockwell, Normal People, Pepsi, Pininfarina, Pink Panther, Professional Bull Riders, Queer Eye, RAM, Red Arrows, Real Madrid (Asia), Refinery29, Rocket League, Royal Ascot, Royal Air Force, Royal Marines, Royal Navy, Royal & Ancient, Rovio Angry Birds, Rugby World Cup 2023, Shinola, Stars On Ice, STP, Stella Artois, Sergio Tacchini, "Sesame Street" (Asia), Superdry, Tempur+Sealy, "Tetris" (Asia and Europe), Toes on the Nose, Tokidoki, Tom Clancy's "Rainbow Six," UEFA EURO 2020, UFC, Vail Resorts, Van Gogh Museum, Volkswagen, Wayne Gretzky, World Rugby, World Trade Center, World's Strongest Man, and Yamaha

3. National Football League, $3.5 billion/NFL Players Association $1.9B

The NFL has approximately 175 licensees selling more than 2,500 products such as apparel, sporting goods, football cards and collectibles, home furnishings, school supplies, home electronics, interactive games, home video, publishing, toys, games, gifts, and novelties.[32] Since the emergence of NFL Properties in 1963, licensing has become one of the most prevalent sports product strategies. The NFL, along with Nike, has inked a 10-year licensing deal that will make Fanatics the exclusive manufacturer and distributor of all Nike-branded NFL fan merchandise - except for kids' clothes - starting in 2020. That means that all adult NFL Nike gear - other than the jerseys and apparel worn by players and coaches on the field - will be produced by Fanatics. The goal, according to NFL Senior Vice President for Consumer Products Michelle Micone, is to be able to get gear into the hands of fans as fast as possible when new storylines spur demand - like when an unheralded rookie becomes a star player, or a team that was expected to perform poorly ends up having a breakout season. "We want to have the NFL Shop be the place where . . . anytime a fan wants to buy something, it's there," Micone said. "Just that instant gratification."[33]

NFLPA: Through its group licensing program, the NFLPA provides its licensees with rights to create player-identified products featuring more than 2,000 active NFL players that include more than 70 licenses across three categories: apparel, digital, and hard lines. Licensed products include mobile, digital, and console video games; trading cards; men's, women's, and youth jerseys and t-shirts; player murals; figurines; bobbleheads; drinkware; and memorabilia and collectibles, among others. Licensees leverage player rights to create products with local, national, and international appeal. The NFLPA is focused on several different player-centric licensing initiatives.

3. WWE $1.0 B

WWE consists of a portfolio of businesses that create and deliver original content 52 weeks a year to a global audience. It has aligned with a number of manufacturers who produce a range of consumer products in more than 85 countries. Collectively, WWE holds owns the rights for more than 200 licensees, including over 100 superstars, including The Rock, John Cena, Becky Lynch, and Undertaker, and legends like Stone Cold Steve Austin, Ultimate Warrior, and Ric Flair. They continue to have a strong presence in prominent retailers, that is, Wal-Mart, Amazon, and Target, and continue to expand and offer new innovative products. WWE partnerships include the likes of Foot Locker, Mattel, and Good Humor. They offer a diverse range of products across a wide range of demographics. WWE released "WWE 2K Battlegrounds" in 2020, which features a completely new gaming experience that incorporates arcade-style action and over-the-top design, and WWE will continue to offer new and exciting collaborations with key partners such as Mattel and Funko.

Web Capture 7.3
Licensed merchandise on the Web

Source: FansEdge, Incorporated

Advantages to the licensee

- The licensee benefits from the positive association with the sports entity. In other words, the positive attributes of the player, team, league, or event are transferred to the licensed product or service.
- The licensee benefits from greater levels of brand awareness.
- The licensee benefits by saving the time and money normally required to build high levels of brand equity.
- The licensee may receive initial distribution with retailers and potentially receive expanded and improved shelf space for their products.
- The licensee may be able to charge higher prices for the licensed product or service.

Disadvantages to the licensee

- The athlete, team, league, or sport may fall into disfavor. For example, using an athlete such as Terrell Owens is risky given his past behavior, off the field as well as on the field.
- In addition to the licensee, the licensor also experiences benefits and risks due to the nature of the licensing agreement.

Advantages to the licensor

- The licensor is able to expand into new markets and penetrate existing markets more than ever before.
- The licensor is able to generate heightened awareness of the sports entity and potentially increase its equity if it is paired with the appropriate products and services.

Disadvantages to the licensor

- The licensor may lose some control over the elements of the marketing mix. For instance, product quality may be inferior or price reductions may be offered frequently. This may lessen the perceived image of the licensor.

Based on all these considerations, care must be taken in choosing merchandising-licensing partnerships. Certainly, "the manufacturer of the licensed product should demonstrate an ability to meet and maintain quality control standards, possess financial stability, and offer an aggressive and well-planned marketing and promotional strategy."[34]

In addition to carefully choosing a partner, licensors and licensees must also be on the lookout for counterfeit merchandise. One estimate has it that billions worth of counterfeit sports products hit the streets each year. For instance, the NFL typically confiscates $15 million worth of fake goods during Super Bowl week. In an attempt to stop or reduce counterfeit merchandise, Olympic officials have previously used new DNA technology in which an official Olympic product has a special ink containing the DNA of an athlete. A handheld scanner determines whether the tag matches the DNA and whether the merchandise is legitimate.[35]

This problem has become so pervasive that the leagues now have their own logo cops who travel from city to city and event to event searching for violations. In addition to this form of enforcement, the Coalition to Advance the Protection of Sports Logos (CAPS; see www.capsinfo.com/) was formed in 1992 to investigate and control counterfeit products. Since 1993, CAPS has been involved in the seizure of more than 9 million pieces of counterfeit merchandise featuring the logos of various professional sports leagues and teams, colleges, and universities. How can consumers guard against fakes? CAPS offers the following suggestions to consumers who are purchasing sports products:[36]

- *Look for quality* - Poor lettering, colors that are slightly different from the true team colors, and background colors bleeding through the top color overlay are all signs of poor product quality.
- *Verification* - Counterfeiters may try to fake the official logo. Official items will typically have holograms on the product or stickers with moving figures, and embroidered logos should be tightly woven.
- *Check garment tags* - Poor-quality merchandise is often designated by split garment tags. Rarely, if ever, will official licensed products use factory rejects or seconds.

Quality

Thus far, we have looked at some of the branding issues related to sports products. Another important aspect of the product considered by sports marketers that will influence brand equity is quality. Let us look at two different types of quality: service quality and product quality.

Quality of services

As sports organizations develop a marketing orientation, the need to deliver a high level of service quality to consumers is becoming increasingly important. For instance, at NFL Properties (NFLP), service quality is taken to the highest levels. NFLP is highly committed to understanding the individualized needs of each of its sponsors. Every sponsor of the NFL receives the name of a primary contact at NFLP whom they can call at any time to discuss their marketing needs. They also recognize that each sponsor is in need of a unique sponsorship program, given their vastly different objectives and levels of financial commitment to the NFL.[37]

Although NFLP is an excellent example of an organization that values service quality, we have yet to define the concept. **Service quality** is a difficult concept to define, and as such, many definitions of service quality exist. Rather than define it, most researchers have resorted to explaining the dimensions or determinants of service quality. Unfortunately, there is also little agreement on what dimensions actually constitute service quality or how best to measure it.

Lehtinen and Lehtinen say service quality consists of physical, interactive, and corporate dimensions.[38] The physical quality component looks at the tangible aspect of the service. More specifically, physical quality refers to the appearance of the personnel or the physical facilities where the service is actually performed. For example, the physical appearance of the ushers at the game may affect the consumer's perceived level of service quality.

Interactive quality refers to the two-way flow of information disseminated from both the service provider and the service recipient at the time of the service encounter. The importance of the two-way flow of information is why many researchers choose to examine service quality from a dyadic perspective. This suggests gathering the perceptions of service quality from stadium employees, as well as fans.

The image attributed to the service provider by its current and potential users is referred to as corporate quality. As just discussed, product performance and quality are some of the drivers of brand image. Moreover, Lehtinen and Lehtinen also cited customer service as one of the image drivers. This suggests a strong relationship between corporate quality, or image of the team, and consumers' perceptions of service quality.

Groonos describes service quality dimensions in a different manner.[39] He believes service quality has both a technical and functional component. Technical quality is described as "what is delivered." Functional quality refers to "how the service is delivered." For instance, "what is delivered" might include the final outcome of the game, the hot dogs that were consumed, or the merchandise that was purchased. "How the service is delivered" might represent the effort put forth by the team and its players, the friendliness of the hot dog vendor, or the quick service provided by the merchandise vendor. This is especially important in sports marketing, as "the total game experience" is evaluated using both the "what" and "how" components of quality.

The most widely adopted description of service quality is based on a series of studies by Parasuraman, Zeithaml, and Berry.[40] They isolated five distinct dimensions of service quality. These **dimensions of service quality** constitute some of its fundamental areas and consist of reliability, assurance, empathy, responsiveness, and tangibles. Because of their importance in service quality literature, a brief description of each follows.

Reliability refers to the ability to perform promised service dependably and accurately. **Assurance** is the knowledge and courtesy of employees and their ability to convey trust and confidence. **Empathy** is defined as the caring, individualized attention the firm provides its customers. **Responsiveness** refers to the willingness to help customers and provide prompt service. **Tangibles** are the physical facilities, equipment, and appearance of the service personnel.

To assess consumers' perceptions of service quality across each dimension, a 22-item survey instrument was developed by Parasuraman, Zeithaml, and Berry. The instrument, known as SERVQUAL, requires that the 22 items be administered twice. First, the respondents are asked to rate their expectations of service quality. Next, the respondents are asked to rate perceptions of service quality within the organization. For example, "Your dealings with XYZ are very pleasant" is a perception (performance) item, whereas the corresponding expectation item would be "Customers' dealing with these firms should be very pleasant."

From a manager's perspective, measuring expectations and perceptions of performance allows action plans to be developed to improve service quality. Organizational resources should be allocated to improving those service quality areas where consumer expectations are high and perceptions of quality are low.

The original SERVQUAL instrument has been tested across a wide variety of industries, including banking, telecommunications, health care, consulting, education, and retailing. Most importantly, McDonald, Sutton, and Milne adapted SERVQUAL and used it to evaluate spectators' perceptions of service quality for an NBA team. The researchers fittingly called their adapted SERVQUAL instrument TEAMQUAL.[41]

In addition to finding that the NBA team exceeded service quality expectations on all five dimensions, the researchers looked at the relative importance of each dimension of service quality. More specifically, fans were asked to allocate 100 points among the five dimensions based on how important each factor is when evaluating the quality of service of a professional team sport franchise. As the results show in Table 7.3, tangibles and reliability are considered the most important dimensions of service quality. Tangibles, as you will recall from Chapter 5, form the foundation of the sportscape, or stadium environment.

Table 7.3 Importance weights allocated to the five TEAMQUAL dimensions

Dimensions	Allocation (%)
Reliability – ability to perform promised services dependably and accurately	23
Assurance – knowledge and courtesy of employees and their ability to convey trust and confidence	16
Empathy – the caring, individualized attention provided by the professional sports franchise for its customers	18
Responsiveness – willingness to help customers and provide prompt service	19
Tangibles – appearance of equipment, personnel, materials, and venue	24

Source: Mark A. McDonald, William A. Sutton, and George R. Milne, "TEAMQUAL: Measuring Service Quality in Professional Team Sports," Sport Marketing Quarterly, vol. 4, no. 2 (1995)

This study provides additional evidence that the tangible factors, such as seating comfort, stadium aesthetics, and scoreboard quality, play an important role in satisfying fans. Understanding fans' perceptions of TEAMQUAL is critical for sports marketers in establishing long-term relationships with existing fans and trying to attract new fans. As McDonald, Sutton, and Milne point out, "Consumers who are dissatisfied and feel that they are not receiving quality service will not renew their relationship with the professional sport franchise."

On the sports participation side, an excellent study was conducted to explore the determinants of service quality in the sport recreation industry or recreation center. The researchers, Ko and Pastore,[42] suggest that service quality is multidimensional and consists of four primary factors. Factor one is program quality, which refers to the range of programs, such as the variety of recreation and fitness programs offered, operating time or whether programs start and finish on time, and whether participants can get up-to-date information on programs. Factor two, interaction quality, is the level of customer-to-employee interaction and also customer-to-customer relationships. Outcome quality is the third factor and is based on physical change, or whether the participant realizes the health benefit he or she wished to obtain; valence, which refers to post-consumption or whether the overall experience was a good or bad one; and sociability, or social interaction, which motivates many participants to engage in physical activity. The final factor, environment quality, is the ambient condition, design, and equipment quality. All of these refer to the tangible, physical environment in which the consumption takes place.

Quality of goods

The quality of sporting goods that are manufactured and marketed has two distinct dimensions. The first **quality dimension of goods** is based on how well the product conforms to specifications that were designed in the manufacturing process. From this standpoint, the quality of goods is driven by the organization and its management and employees. The other dimension of quality is measured subjectively from the perspective of consumers or end users of the goods. In other words, does the product perform its desired function? The degree to which the goods meet and exceed consumers' needs is a function of the organization's marketing orientation.

From the sports marketing perspective, the consumer's perception of **product quality** is of primary importance. Garvin found eight separate quality dimensions: performance, features, reliability, conformance, durability, serviceability, aesthetics, and perceived quality (see Table 7.4).

Whether it is enhancing goods or service quality, most sports organizations are attempting to increase the quality of their product offerings. In doing so, they can better compete with other entertainment choices, more easily

Table 7.4 Quality dimensions of goods

Quality dimensions of goods	Description
Performance	How well does the good perform its core function? (Does the tennis racquet feel good when striking the ball?)
Features	Does the good offer additional benefits? (Are the golf club heads constructed with titanium?)
Conformity to specifications	What is the incidence of defects? (Does the baseball have the proper number of stitches, or is there some variation?)
Reliability	Does the product perform with consistency? (Do the gauges of the exercise bike work properly every time?)
Durability	What is the life of the product? (How long will the golf clubs last?)
Serviceability	Is the service system efficient, competent, and convenient? (If you experience problems with the grips or loft of the club, can the manufacturer quickly address your needs?)
Aesthetic design	Does the product's design look and feel like a high-quality product? (Does the look and feel of the running shoe inspire you to greater performance?)
Perceived quality	Is the product perceived to be long lasting? Does the product have a good reputation?

Source: Adapted from D. A. Garvin, "Competing on the Eight Dimensions of Quality," *Harvard Business Review* (November–December 1987), 101–109

increase the prices of their products, influence the consumer's loyalty, and reach new market segments willing to pay more for a higher-quality product.

Some sports franchises have been criticized for attempting to increase the quality of their overall products while driving up the price of tickets. Unfortunately, it is becoming more costly for the "average fan" to purchase tickets to any professional sporting event. Sports marketers have targeted a new segment (corporations) and overlooked the traditional segments.

Other criticisms have been directed at the NCAA and professional sports for making it too easy for athletes to leave school and turn professional. While the practice has been prevalent in both basketball and baseball for years, it is new to college football. This exodus of stars may have detrimental effects on "product quality" at the high school and college levels. While there is no minimum age for professional football players, the NFL mandates that you must be out of high school for at least three years before you are eligible to play. To be eligible for the draft, players must have been out of high school for at least three years and must have used up their college eligibility before the start of the next college football season. Underclassmen and players who have graduated before using all their college eligibility may request the league's approval to enter the draft early. Players are draft eligible only in the year after the end of their college eligibility. Before the draft, NFL Player Personnel staff members confirm the eligibility of draft prospects; that means researching the college backgrounds of approximately 3,000 college players each year. They work with NCAA compliance departments at schools across the country to verify the information for all prospects.[43] Even under the NFL's "Special Eligibility" route, requiring players to request special permission to enter the league, the players must still be three seasons removed from their high school graduation.[44] The reason for this rule is that it's believed that younger college players are not fully developed physically and are not ready for the physical demands of professional football.[45]

From a marketing standpoint, the fans are also suffering and may experience dissatisfaction when college players and high school players turn pro early. Teams no longer stay together long enough to capture the imagination of fans. Former Atlantic 10 Commissioner Linda Bruno stated, "It seems as soon as college basketball hooks on to a star, he's suddenly a part of the NBA. Athletes leaving early have definitely hurt the college game." Former University of Louisville head basketball coach Rick Pitino added the concern: "Quite frankly, I think college basketball is in serious trouble." Interestingly, the early departures that are making the college game less appealing are doing nothing to strengthen the quality of the NBA. The NBA is saturated with players whose games never had a chance to grow, or, as former Stanford coach Mike Montgomery put it, "will have to be nurtured through [their] immaturity."[46]

A final product feature related to perceptions of product quality is product warranties. **Product warranties** are important to consumers when purchasing expensive goods or hedonic purchases because they act to reduce the perceived risk and offset consumer sensitivity, that is, fear of replacement, associated with cognitive dissonance. Traditional warranties are statements indicating the liability of the manufacturer for problems with the product. For example, Spalding's line of Neverflat balls has a product redesign with a new membrane, a redesigned valve, and the addition of NitroFlate, a substance added to the ball during inflation that forms a barrier preventing seepage. Spalding has produced balls it says will not leak air for at least a year. It is backing that claim with a money-back guarantee.

Interestingly, warranties are also being developed by sports organizations. The New Jersey Nets offered their season ticket holders a money-back guarantee if they were dissatisfied with the Nets' performance. With the price of tickets skyrocketing for professional sporting events, perhaps these service guarantees will be the wave of the future. The Indiana Ice of the U.S. Hockey League offered their fans a similar deal. The Ice are so convinced local hockey fans will enjoy seeing the under-20 amateur team play next season, franchise officials are offering a money-back guarantee on season tickets.

Product design

Product design is one competitive advantage that is of special interest to sports marketers. It is heavily linked to product quality and the technological environment discussed in Chapter 2. In some cases, product design may even have an impact on the sporting event. For example, the latest technology in golf clubs does allow the average player to improve his or her performance on the course. The same could be said for the new generation of big-sweet spot, extra-long tennis racquets. In another example, the official baseball used in the major league games was believed to be "juiced up." In other words, the ball was livelier because of the product design. As a result of this "juiced up" ball, home run production increased, much to the delight of the fans. From a sports marketing perspective, anything that adds excitement and conjecture to a game with public relation problems is welcomed. In the end, what matters is not whether the ball is livelier but that the game is.

Baseballs are not the only products that are having an impact on the outcome of sporting events, and equipment changes aren't the only way to think about product design or redesign. Baseball is constantly looking for ways to make games shorter and thus more attractive to fans. In a recent rule change, the time a pitcher is allotted to deliver the ball with no runners on base has changed from 20 to 12 seconds. The price for each violation is a ball. It is hoped that this minor product redesign will have a major impact. Historic rule changes that have had a significant impact on the sport product include the designated hitter in baseball, the shot clock in basketball, or (in 1912) when hockey moved from seven to six players on the ice at one time.

Product design is important to sport marketers because it ultimately affects consumers' perceptions of product quality. Moreover, organizations need to monitor the technological environment to keep up with the latest trends that may affect product design. Let us look at this relationship in Figure 7.5.

As you would imagine, the technological environment has a tremendous impact on product design decisions. In almost every sporting good category, sports marketers communicate how their brands are technologically superior to the competition.

Figure 7.5
Relationship among product design, technology, and product quality

The golf equipment industry thrives on the latest technological advances in ball and club design. Bicycle manufacturers stress the technological edge that comes with the latest and greatest construction materials. Tennis racquets are continually moving into the next generation of frame design and racquet length. NordicTrack exercise equipment positions itself as technologically superior to other competing brands. Nike is continually developing new lines of high-tech sports gear in its state-of-the-art Sports Research Lab, which aided in the development of the NikeConnect experience platform. Tapping in to the new Nike NBA Jersey (via a special NFC chip located behind the Jock Tag) with the NikeConnect app unlocks personal, next-level access to athletes, exclusive offers, and the game on buyers' smartphones. In this case, the claim is that product design is actually influencing not only performance and function but tailoring the experience to the consumer.

The product design of sporting goods, in turn, influences consumer perceptions of product quality. By definition, **product design** includes the aesthetics, style, and function of the product. Two of the eight dimensions of the

Photo 7.3
Bike manufacturers must stress the importance of product design and technology

Source: Shutterstock, ID# 81690598 by Dudarev Mikhail

quality of goods are incorporated in this definition, providing one measure of the interdependency of these two concepts.

The way a good performs, the way it feels, and the beauty of the good are all important aspects of product design. Again, think of the numerous sporting goods that are purchased largely on the basis of these benefits. Consumers purchase golf clubs because of the way they look and feel. Tennis shoes are chosen because of the special functions they perform (cross-trainers, hiking, or basketball) and the way they look (colors and style).

Color has historically been an important factor in the design of almost all licensed merchandise. Recent trends show that in hats, jerseys, and jackets, anything that's black is "gold." The Las Vegas Raiders' silver and black are always near the top in NFL merchandise sales regardless of the team's record on the field. The Toronto Blue Jays adopted logo incorporates black and moves away from the reds and blues of the past. Although fans associate certain colors with their favorite teams (e.g., Dodger Blue or the Cincinnati Reds), MLB markets licensed products that deviate from the traditional colors. Baby blues, pinks, and camouflage are replacing the traditional team colors, and fans seem to be responding. Examples like these illustrate that color alone may be a motivating factor in the purchase of many sports products. Sports marketers, therefore, must consider color critical in product design.

Figure 7.5 also shows that product quality may influence product design to some extent. Sports organizations are continually seeking to improve the levels of product quality. In fact, having high-quality goods and services may be the primary objective of many firms. As such, products will be designed in the highest-quality manner with little concern about the costs that will be ultimately passed on to the consumers. Some major league sports organizations (e.g., New York Yankees and Detroit Red Wings) will design their teams to achieve the highest quality levels without cost consideration.

As new technologies continue to emerge, product design will become increasingly important. Organizations with a marketing orientation will incorporate consumer preferences to ensure their needs are being met with respect to product design for new and existing products. What will the future bring with respect to product design, technology, and the need to satisfy consumers? One hint comes to us via the athletic shoe industry. With advances in technology, customized shoes are now being produced for professional athletes. Gone are the days when recreational athletes could wear the same shoes as their professional counterparts. Today's professional athletes are demanding custom-fit and high-tech shoes, and weekend athletes will soon require the same. Companies such as Nike are now customizing certain features of their shoes to the mass market under the Nike ID (individualized design) name. A company such as Under Armour, who made headlines at the 2014 Olympics in Sochi for seemingly all the wrong reasons, that is, speed skating apparel deemed inferior, remained committed to its customers and ended up being vindicated, also cementing its place at the next two Olympics.

Another perspective on the future of product design is that the design of products will stem from demand and changes in the marketing environment. One such change is the emergence of a viable market for women's sports products. For instance, ski and snowboard companies are now turning their attention to women's products based on a growing number of women hitting the slopes. Historically, the only difference in men's and women's ski products was the color, but today there are product design changes that truly address women's needs. Skis for women are softer and lighter. Boots are more cushioned and designed to fit the foot and calf muscles of the female skier. All of these product changes try to capitalize on the marketing environment and satisfy the needs of a growing target market.[47]

Summary

Sports products are defined as goods, services, or any combination of the two that are designed to provide benefits to a sports spectator, participant, or sponsor. Within the field of sports marketing, products are sometimes thought of as bundles of benefits desired by consumers. As discussed in Chapter 1, sports products might include sporting events and their participants, sporting goods, and sports information. The definition of sports products also makes an important distinction between goods and services.

Goods are defined as tangible, physical products that offer benefits to consumers. Conversely, services are intangible, nonphysical products. Most sports products possess the characteristics of both goods and services. For example, a sporting event sells goods (e.g., concessions) and services (e.g., the competition itself). The classification of a sports product as either a good or a service is dependent on four product dimensions: tangibility, standardization and consistency, perishability, and separability. Tangibility refers to the ability to see, feel, and touch the product. In other words, tangibility is the physical dimension of the sports product. Standardization refers to the consistency of the product or the ability of the producer to manufacture a product with little variation over time. One of the unique and complex issues for sports marketers is dealing with the inconsistency of the sports product (i.e., the inability to control the performance of the team or athlete). Perishability is the ability to store or inventory product. Pure services are totally perishable (i.e., you cannot sell a seat after the game has been played), whereas goods are not perishable and can be stored or warehoused. Separability, the final product dimension, refers to the ability to separate the good from the person providing the service. In the case of an athletic event, there is little separation between the provider and the consumer. That is, the event is being produced and consumed simultaneously.

Along with classifying sports products by the four product dimensions, sports products are also categorized based on groupings within the sports organization. Product lines are groups of products that are closely related because they satisfy a class of needs. These products are used together, sold to the same customer groups, distributed through the same types of outlets, or fall within a given price range. The total assortment of product lines is called the product mix. The mix represents all the firm's products. Strategic decisions within the sports organization consider both the product lines and the entire product mix. For instance, an organization may want to add product lines, eliminate product lines, or develop new product lines that are unrelated to existing lines.

Products can also be described on the basis of three interrelated dimensions or characteristics: branding, quality, and design. Branding refers to the product's name, design, symbol, or any combination used by an organization to differentiate products from the competition. Brand names, or elements of the brand that can be spoken, are important considerations for sports products. When choosing a brand name, sports marketers should consider the following: the name should be positive and generate positive feelings, be translatable into an exciting logo, imply the benefits that the sports product delivers, be consistent with the image of the sports product, and be legally and ethically permissible.

The broad purpose of branding is to differentiate your product from the competition. Ultimately, the consumer will (hopefully) establish a pattern of repeat purchases for your brand (i.e., be loyal to your sports product). Before this can happen, sports marketers must guide consumers through a series of steps known as the branding process. The branding process begins by building brand awareness, in which consumers recognize and remember the brand name. Next, the brand image, or the consumers' set of beliefs about a brand, must be established. After the proper brand image is developed, the objective of the branding process is to develop brand equity. Brand equity is the value that the brand contributes to a product in the marketplace. Finally, once the brand exhibits high levels of equity, consumers are prone to become brand loyal, or purchase only your brand. Certainly, sports marketers are interested in establishing high levels of awareness, enhancing brand image, building equity, and developing loyal fans or customers.

One of the important sports product strategies that is contingent upon building a strong brand is licensing. Licensing is defined as a contractual agreement whereby a company may use another company's trademark in exchange for a royalty or fee. The licensing of sports products is experiencing tremendous growth around the world. Advantages to the licensee (the organization purchasing the license or use of the name or trademark) include positive association with the sports entity, enhancing brand awareness, building brand equity, improving distribution and retail relationships, and having the ability to charge higher prices. Disadvantages to the licensee are the possibility of the sports entity experiencing problems (e.g., athlete arrested or team performing poorly or moving). However, the licensor (the sports entity granting the permission) benefits by expanding into new markets, which creates heightened awareness. Yet the licensor may not have tight controls on the quality of the products being licensed under the name.

Quality is another of the important brand characteristics. The two different types of quality that affect brand image, brand equity, and, ultimately, loyalty, are the quality of services and the quality of goods. The quality of services, or service quality, is generally described on the basis of its dimensions. Parasuraman, Zeithaml, and Berry describe service quality as having five distinct dimensions: reliability, assurance, empathy, responsiveness, and tangibles. Reliability refers to the ability to perform a promised service dependably and accurately. Assurance is the knowledge and courtesy of employees and their ability to convey trust and confidence. Empathy is defined as the caring, individualized attention the firm provides its customers. Responsiveness refers to the willingness to help customers and provide prompt service. Tangibles are the physical facilities, equipment, and appearance of the service personnel. Using this framework, sports researchers have designed an instrument called TEAMQUAL to assess the service quality within sporting events.

The quality of goods is based on whether the good conforms to specifications determined during the manufacturing process and the degree to which the good meets or exceeds the consumer's needs. Garvin has conceptualized the quality of goods from the consumer's perspective. He found eight separate dimensions of goods quality: performance, features, conformity to specifications, reliability, durability, serviceability, aesthetic design, and perceived quality.

Product design is the final characteristic of the "total product." Product design is defined as the aesthetics, style, and function of the product. It is important to sports marketers in that it ultimately affects consumers' perceptions of product quality. For a sporting event, the product design might be thought of as the composition of the team. For sporting goods, product design has largely focused on the development of technologically superior products. In fact, the technological environment is believed to directly influence product design. Product design, in turn, enjoys a reciprocal relationship with product quality. In other words, product design affects perceptions of product quality and may influence product design.

Key terms

- assurance
- brand awareness
- brand equity
- brand image
- brand loyalty
- brand mark
- brand name
- branding
- branding process
- dimensions of service quality
- empathy

- goods
- idle product capacity
- licensing
- logo
- logotype
- perishability
- product design
- product characteristics
- product line
- product mix
- product quality
- product warranties
- quality dimensions of goods
- reliability
- responsiveness
- separability
- service quality
- services
- sports product
- standardization
- tangibility
- tangibles
- TEAMQUAL
- trademark

Review questions

1 Define sports products. Why are sports products sometimes called "bundles of benefits"?
2 Contrast pure goods with pure services using each of the dimensions of products.
3 Describe the nature of product mix, product lines, and product items. Illustrate these concepts for the following: Converse, Baltimore Orioles, and your local country club.
4 What are the characteristics of the "total product"?
5 Describe branding. What are the guidelines for developing an effective brand name? Why is brand loyalty such an important concept for sports marketers to understand?
6 Describe how an athlete's image has an impact upon brand development.
7 Define licensing. What are the advantages and disadvantages to the licensee and licensor?
8 Describe service quality and discuss the five dimensions of service quality. Which dimension is most important to you as a spectator of a sporting event? Does this vary by the type of sporting event?

9 Describe product quality and discuss the eight dimensions of product quality. Which dimension is most important to you as a consumer of sporting goods? Does this vary by the type of sporting good?

10 How are product design, product quality, and technology interrelated?

Exercises

1 Think of some sports products to which consumers demonstrate high degrees of brand loyalty. What are these products, and why do you think loyalty is so high? Give your suggestions for measuring brand loyalty.

2 Interview the individuals responsible for licensing and licensing decisions on your campus. Ask them to describe the licensing process and what they believe the advantages are to your school.

3 Construct a survey to measure consumers' perceptions of service quality at a sporting event on campus. Administer the survey to 10 people and summarize the findings. What recommendations might you make to the sports marketing department based on your findings?

4 Go to a sporting goods store and locate three sports products that you believe exhibit high levels of product quality. What are the commonalities among these three products? How do these products rate on the dimensions of product quality described in the chapter?

Internet exercises

1 Search the Internet for a sports product that stresses product design issues on its Web site. Then locate the Web site of a competitor's sports product. How are these two products positioned relative to each other on their web sites?

2 Search the Internet for three team nicknames (either college or professional) of which you were previously unaware. Do these team names seem to follow the suggested guidelines for effective brand names?

Notes

1 Kevin Burke, "Lacrosse: The Fastest Growing Sport in the Country" (2008). Available from: http://blog.dc.esri.com/2008/01/24/lacrosse-the-fastest-growing-sport-in-the-country/.

2 Shaquille O'Neal. Available from: http://cbs.sportsline.com/u/fans/celebrity/shaq; "Athletic Shoes by Shaquille O'Neal Now Available Only at Payless Shoe Source," *PR Newswire, Financial News* (January 14, 2004).

3 Christopher Lovelock, *Services Marketing* (Englewood Cliffs, NJ: Prentice Hall, 1984).

4 Boaz Herzog, "Rising with a Swoosh," *The Sunday Oregonian* (September 21, 2003), D1.

5 Joycelyn Hayward, Sporting Goods Store Manager. Personal Statement.

6   Nike Annual Report & Notice of Annual Meeting, Form 10-K, 2013, "Nike Annual Report & Notice of Annual Meeting, Form 10-K, 2013." Available from: www.fool.com/investing/2018/11/14/why-nike-is-up-21-in-2018.aspx.

7   "Nike Annual Report on Form 10-K, 2020. Nike Inc" (May), pp. 2, 25. Available from: https://s1.q4cdn.com/806093406/files/doc_downloads/2021/NKE-FY20-10K.pdf.

8   See, for example, Courtland Bovee and John Thill, *Marketing* (New York: McGraw-Hill, 1992), 252.

9   Terez Paylor, "Wizards Change Name to Sporting Kansas City," *Kansas City Star* (November 17, 2010). Available from: www.kansas. com/2010/11/17/1593465/wizards-change-name-to-sporting.html.

10 The Columbus Crew. Available from: www.thecrew.com.

11 Andrew Lupton, "The NLL Fails to Excel at the Team Name Game," *National Post* (f/k/a The Financial Post) (Canada), (January 8, 2007), S2.

12 Marcus Nelson, "Want a New Look? There's a Price," *The Palm Beach Post* (October 24, 2003).

13 David Aaker, *Managing Brand Equity* (New York: The Free Press, 1991).

14 James Gladden, George Milne, and William Sutton, "A Conceptual Framework for Assessing Brand Equity in Division I College Athletics," *Journal of Sports Management*, vol. 12, no. 1 (1998), 1–19.

15 George R. Milne and Mark A. McDonald, *Sport Marketing: Managing the Exchange Process* (Sudbury, MA: Jones & Bartlett, 1999).

16 Louis E. Boone, C. M. Kochunny, and Dianne Wilkins, "Applying the Brand Equity Concept to Major League Baseball," *Sport Marketing Quarterly*, vol. 4, no. 3 (1995), 33–42.

17 Ibid.

18 John Lombardo, "MLB Makes It 5 Firsts in a Row in Brand Keys Fan Loyalty Survey," *Street and Smith's Sports Business Journal*, vol. 8, no. 10 (August 25–31, 2003), 28.

19 Daniel F. Mahony, Robert Madrigal, and Dennis Howard, "Using the Psychological Commitment to Team (PCT) Scale to Segment Sport Consumers Based on Loyalty," *Sport Marketing Quarterly*, vol. 9 (2000), 15–25.

20 Michael Manoochehri, "Information Systems & Service Design" (2009). Available from: http://courses.ischool.berkeley.edu/i228/f10/files/A4_Michael_Manoochehri_0.pdf.

21 Jeff Summers, "Diamondbacks' Fan Loyalty Programs," *Bleacher Report* (April 21, 2010).

22 David Broughton, "Official Brands Get a Good Ride with NASCAR," *Sport Business Journal* (November 28–December 4, 2011).

23 Ibid.

24 Steve Sleight, *Sponsorship: What Is It and How to Use It* (London: McGraw-Hill, 1989).

25 www.licensing.org/news/global-revenue-from-licensed-goods-and-services-grows-to-us271-6-billion/.

26 The licensing industry continues to grow, according to License Global, 2019. "Licensing International's Annual Global Licensing Survey" (July 05, 2019. Available

from: https://www.licenseglobal.com/industry-news/licensing-biz-grows-nearly-9-billion.

27 www.prnewswire.com/news-releases/global-licensed-sports-merchandise-market-2018-2023-increasing-sports-league-activities-driving-the-licensed-sports-merchandise-market-growth-300708162.html.

28 www.prnewswire.com/news-releases/global-licensed-sports-merchandise-market-2018-2023-increasing-sports-league-activities-driving-the-licensed-sports-merchandise-market-growth-300708162.html.

29 www.licenseglobal.com/sites/default/files/Top150_2018_0.pdf.

30 www.forbes.com/sites/demetriusbell/2018/05/24/nike-2020-major-league-baseball-mlb-under-armour/#1daa2dd7ff00.

31 www.sportsbusinessdaily.com/Daily/Issues/2018/07/02/Marketing-and-Sponsorship/MLB-Licensing.aspx.

32 Scott Sillcox, "Licensed Sports Products and the Ebb and Flow of Time: What Can Change in 10 Short Years." Available from: licensedsports.blogspot.com, accessed March 3, 2014.

33 www.recode.net/2018/5/23/17380964/nfl-nike-fanatics-sports-gear.

34 Eddie Baghdikian, "Building the Sports Organization's Merchandise Licensing Program: The Appropriateness, Significance, and Considerations," *Sport Marketing Quarterly*, vol. 5, no. 1 (1996), 35–41.

35 Elliott Harris, "Spitting Image: Ink with DNA Could Put Counterfeiters on Spot at Olympics," *Chicago Sun Times* (June 8, 2000), 133.

36 Robert Thurow, 1996, "Busting Bogus Merchandise Peddlers with Logo Cops," *The Wall Street Journal* (October 24, 1997), B1, B14.

37 Rick Burton, "A Case Study on Sports Property Servicing Excellence: National Football League Properties," *Sport Marketing Quarterly*, vol. 5, no. 3 (1996), 23.

38 Jarmi R. Lehtinen and Uolevi Lehtinen, *Service Quality: A Study of Quality Dimensions* (Helsinki: Service Management Institute, 1982).

39 Christian Groonos, "A Service Quality Model and Its Marketing Implications," *European Journal of Marketing*, vol. 18 (1982), 36–44.

40 A. Parasuraman, Valarie Zeithaml, and Leonard Berry, "A Conceptual Model of Service Quality and Its Implications for Future Research," *Journal of Marketing*, vol. 49 (1985), 41–50.

41 Mark A. McDonald, William A, Sutton, and George R. Milne, "TEAMQUAL: Measuring Service Quality in Professional Team Sports," *Sport Marketing Quarterly*, vol. 4, no. 2 (1995), 9–15.

42 Yong Jae Ko and Donna L. Pastore, "Current Issues and Conceptualizations of Service Quality in the Recreation Sport Industry," *Sport Marketing Quarterly*, vol. 13, no. 3 (2004).

43 See National Football League Eligibility Rules, "NFL Regional Combines." Available from: www.nflregionalcombines.com/Docs/Eligibility%20rules.pdf, accessed June 20, 2014.

44 Ibid.

45 Chad Walters, "NBA and NFL Draft Eligibility Restrictions – Why?" *Lean Blitz* (February 15, 2013).

46   Jack McCallum, "Going, Going, Gone," *Sports Illustrated*, vol. 84, no. 20 (May 20, 1996), 52.

47   "Ski Industry Focusing on Women" (January 30, 2004). Available from: sports businessnews.com.

Managing sports products

After completing this chapter, you should be able to:

- Describe the characteristics of new products from an organizational and consumer perspective.
- Explain the various stages of the new product development process.
- Discuss the phases of the product life cycle and explain how the product life cycle influences marketing strategy.
- Determine the factors that will lead to new product success.
- Discuss the diffusion of innovations and the various types of adopters.

The article on innovation provides an interesting illustration of Nike's commitment to innovations that further athlete potential. The integration of digital and design with many of Nike's core products provide the everyday athlete as well as some of the world's top competitors access to many unique quality and design features. Obviously there is nothing new about fitness, fitness shoes, or even apparel, but when combined with digital and design innovation strategies, they create an exciting new realm of sport products that offer a competitive advantage in the marketplace. Nike continues to keep this in mind when executing a marketing strategy for their new and emerging sport products (see Article 8.1 below).

New sports products

Although it might seem as if new products are easy to describe and think about, "new" is a relative term. Think about purchasing season tickets to your favorite college basketball team for the first time. You might consider this a new product even though the tickets have been available for many years. In other instances, consumers may be exposed to a sport that utilizes a combination of

DOI: 10.4324/9780429030673-11

ARTICLE 8.1
NIKE NEWS

The defining innovations and products of 2018

December 20, 2018

At Nike, the opportunity to innovate is ripest when the challenge is re-imagining how fans and consumers interact with product, strengthening the emotional connection to sport and, of course, solving athlete problems to advance human potential. Here's what Nike did to accomplish that this year.

Breathing new life into retail

If the old model of brand retail was to sit as monolith – always telling, never listening – the future of commerce lies in creating dialogue. For Nike, this means Living Retail, a multi-faceted approach comprised of intersecting brick-and-mortar spaces and digital platforms predicated on fluid conversation and seamless adaptability. The idea is best expressed in Nike's new flagship program, House of Innovation, which debuted this year in Shanghai and New York. In both instances, all elements of the Living Retail approach are on full display from the Nike App at Retail to the data-informed product assortments of Nike Live.

House of Innovation 001 in Shanghai

- House of Innovation: Digitally enabled innovation, design and personalized service at Nike's two new flagship stores are unlike any other Nike retail experience. A Sneaker Lab on the fourth floor of NYC's House of Innovation 000 showcases the largest concentration of Nike footwear anywhere in the world; the Expert Studio features a paragon of one-on-one service that local Nike Members can book in-store and on the Nike App. Shanghai's House of Innovation 001 houses a digitally-enabled Center Court where shoppers can enjoy speaker sessions, workshops and digitally-led trialing sessions; and at Nike by You, NikePlus members can have one-on-one sessions with a designer to customize select shoes.
- Nike App at Retail: The interactive app was designed to intuitively bridge the worlds of tech and physical retail, all through the power of your smartphone (and at your nearest Nike store).
- Nike by Melrose: The first Nike Live concept store to open its doors houses a selection of product determined by Nike digital commerce data (things like buying patterns, app usage and engagement) to serve local NikePlus members exactly what they want.

Elevating the soul of sport

While Nike began with a simple remit, to make athletes better, it has matured to find a new, parallel truth: Solving discrete athlete problems requires a deft balance of the physical and the emotional. When this is met, new silhouettes are able to serve far beyond their initial intent. A sterling example: The Air Force 1 has transcended Nike's modern sport design since its arrival in 1982. Essential training apparel and new explorations of digital craft also serve as reminders of how the soul of sport regularly becomes the code of the street.

- Nigeria Football Federation kits: Imbued with the Naija spirit, the kits channel a healthy reserve of exuberance and represent the resoundingly cool culture of pure contemporary Nigeria.
- Earned Edition uniforms: Teams that make the NBA Playoffs will be rewarded with exclusive new uniforms – variations of each team's Statement or City Edition uniforms – that aim to supply fans with a tangible claim to both their team's heritage and current success streak.
- The 1 Reimagined: This 10-shoe collection – a result of 14 women spending two weeks in London to "make some cool shit" – gives a female perspective to the Air Force 1 and Air Jordan 1. The collection realizes a number of first-time efforts against the storied icons, ranging from increased stack heights to corset lacing.
- Nike City Ready: With the debut launch from Nike Women's Collections, an all-female design team delivered directional silhouettes that set a new benchmark for athleisure.
- Nike × A-COLD-WALL* Air Force 1: Award-winning London-based designer Samuel Ross pushed the storied Air Force 1 into a future state by employing Nike Flyleather, a super material that deftly balances the natural tactile qualities of leather with an important reduction in the planet's carbon footprint.
- Nike × MMW: Working with Nike's latest suite of digital tools (from atlas maps to computation algorithm), Matthew M Williams' unisex collection combined athlete data and human ingenuity to grant a purpose-led aesthetic to training.

Expanding breakthrough platforms

Innovation in cushioning platforms is at the forefront of Nike's consistent push for athlete advancement. In 2018, this was exhibited by a trio of rapidly scaling breakthrough platforms: Nike React, which is the softest, smoothest and most resilient foam Nike has ever created, provides consistent cushioning stride after stride; Nike ZoomX foam, which delivers 85 percent energy return – the greatest of any Nike foam – allows runners to go fast and far; and Nike Air, which, through expressive new designs, has redefined ride for all-day wear. All are predicated on progress, explicitly in building the broadest portfolio of choice. After all, personal preference is a critical component to performance.

Nike React Element 87

- Nike React Element 87: With wide grooves, the midsole of this new Nike Sportswear silhouette looks like an exaggerated version its performance running counterpart. The looser and wider pattern provides a softer ride for all-day comfort.
- Nike Zoom Pegasus Turbo: Inspired by the magic of the Nike Zoom Vaporfly 4%, this new running shoe houses the same highly responsive ZoomX foam in the midsole and takes

on the same aerodynamic shape of the heel. Because there's no carbon fiber plate, it provides a more comfortable kick runners crave during daily training runs.

- Air Max 270: The first 100-percent lifestyle Air unit, and its eponymous shoe, offers the biggest heel volume displacement for maximum Air cushion comfort.

Refining fit and ease of use is also critical to advancing performance. Continued growth of two technologies, the Nike FastFit tightening system that allows athletes to achieve 360-degree lockdown in a shoe with a single pull of a forefoot strap and the Nike Flyease closure system that connects a hook-and-loop strap to a wraparound zipper to allow a runner to put the shoe on or take it off in one fluid motion, enables athletes to easily dial in on preferred fit for ultimate performance. Both visible technologies are designed for function, but also open the door for striking new aesthetic treatments.

Air Jordan XXXIII

- Air Jordan XXXIII: Jordan's first laceless basketball shoe progresses the legacy of visible technology in the Jordan line by challenging a different aesthetic norm and proposes a new system for containment on court.
- Nike Air Zoom Pegasus 35 Flyease: It has the same performance elements as the Nike Air Zoom Pegasus 35 (a supportive Zoom Air and cushion foam midsole, an out-turned collar from the Achilles for comfort and a beveled heel), but with adaptive fit technology.

The promise of intelligent product

January 15, 2019

Michael Donaghu, Nike's VP of Innovation, explains how the future of fit lets Nike make real the decades-old dream: a custom shoe for everyone (yes, even you).

Michael Donaghu

There's an invention in human history that's older than you think. It's older than coins, paper and the alphabet. In fact, it dates back to 3500 BC, before Stonehenge or the Pyramids.

That ancient invention? The shoelace.

Think how many technologies have fallen away in the 5,000-plus years since shoelaces came on the scene. From VHS tapes to the horse-drawn carriage, they've come and gone – and yet the shoelace remains.

It remains, somehow, despite its imperfections. We've all had laces come undone on us, forcing a sudden time-out. And because the foot visibly swells throughout the day – even over the course of a single basketball game – we have to constantly tie and untie our shoes to get the fit just right.

Shoelaces: you had a good run. But we think we may have finally bettered you.

Inside the revolutionary Nike Adapt BB sits an intricate lace engine.

When we took on the challenge of finding the next lacing system for performance footwear, we knew the answer would be found in a personalized solution. That's because fit is a personal thing. Our mission is to solve problems for athletes, and delivering to their exact needs has always been the best path forward.

Earlier today, we debuted the Nike Adapt BB, a revolutionary basketball shoe with an intricate lace engine neatly closes around your entire foot. It remembers, via a paired app, how tight or loose you prefer your footwear – not just one setting, but in different situations like warm-ups, gameplay and while resting on the bench.

This, finally, is the precise performance fit our athletes have long demanded – exactly when they need it, with the push of a button or a tap on a phone.

And with your own personal fit, Nike has finally made countless dreams come true: a custom shoe for everyone.

> Our mission is to solve problems for athletes, and delivering to their exact needs has always been the best path forward.

As you could guess, I'm incredibly proud of the team that worked on Nike Adapt BB. Like the athletes we serve, I'll admit we are some pretty demanding perfectionists, and we have poured years into this project. It reminds me of one of the first projects of my Nike career: the Air Huarache, a shoe that fit, felt and definitely looked different. That instinct to challenge convention has never left me.

My starting point is always curiosity. I love probing and questioning what's out there, trying to get a feel of what's possible. I was a geography major in college, and the study of the intersection of human activity and the physical world around us has shaped my work more than I ever could've expected.

After all, what we're launching this week goes far beyond a shoe. Our long-term vision for innovation at Nike is a world in which intelligent products adapt at the speed of sport to improve an athlete's performance.

Shoes in our Nike Adapt platform – of which Nike Adapt BB is the first – can update and evolve after purchase, letting consumers opt in to provide you with new services and features through smartphone-like technology.

In other words, we've finally added firmware to footwear, letting us continuously improve the product you've already bought, responding as need be to changing preferences and environments.

> Our long-term vision for innovation at Nike is a world in which intelligent products adapt at the speed of sport to improve an athlete's performance.

What's more, you don't just connect with footwear through Nike Adapt. You connect with Nike.

What do I mean? Imagine a cycle, where opting in creates data about your activity to inform personalized guidance from Nike. And as your performance improves, we can connect you to new product and services for your new goals – and the cycle continues.

For most footwear out there, buying the shoe is the end of a transaction. But here, buying the shoe is just the beginning.

These conversations have the power to unlock benefits we've never seen before, bringing the latest sport science to all athletes everywhere, including real-time personalized training and guidance. It will also help us make products better, with feedback given in a first-of-its-kind true dialogue. It's a unique conversation between you, Nike and your shoes – one in which you decide what data you share with us, and when.

We started this journey in basketball because NBA athletes are some of the most demanding of their footwear. But we'll be expanding FitAdapt later this year across more performance and lifestyle categories and in even greater quantities.

Something tells me, in 5,000 years, shoes without a perfect fit may also be going the way of the horse-drawn carriage.

https://news.nike.com/news/defining-innovations-products-2018

techniques they are familiar with to create "new" and exciting alternatives, such as Bossaball.

Bossaball combines elements of different sports on a pitch of trampolines and bouncy inflatables. The popularity of Xtreme sports, soccer, and volleyball around the globe suggest the time could be right for this new product. There is obviously nothing new about volleyball, soccer, and jumping on a trampoline, but when combined, they create an exciting new sport. The founders of

Web Capture 8.1
The new sport of Bossaball combines volleyball, football, gymnastics, and capoeira and now draws large crowds

Source: www.Bossaballsports.com

Bossaball will have to keep this in mind when developing a marketing strategy for this emerging sports product. This sports product is new to spectators and participants alike.

Regardless of how you define "new products," they are critical to the health of any sports organization for two reasons. First, new products are necessary to keep up with changing consumer trends, lifestyles, and tastes. Second, as unsuccessful sports products are dropped from the product mix, new products must be introduced continually to maintain business and long-term growth.

One of the key considerations for any sports organization is to continually improve the products it offers to consumers. New products seek to satisfy the needs of a new market, enhance the quality of an existing product, or extend the number of product choices for current consumers. Before discussing the process for developing new products, let us look at the different types of **new sports products**.

ARTICLE 8.2
SPORTS MARKETING HALL OF FAME

Bill Rasmussen

It is nearly impossible to encounter a sports fan who does not perk up at the sound of "ESPN". Fans can usually tell you what ESPN is and what ESPN does, but they more than likely cannot tell you how the network came to fruition. A man named Bill Rasmussen is responsible for the ingenious plan that has helped make the sports world what it is today. Rasmussen, ESPN's founder, developed the 24-hour sports programming channel in the fall of 1979. At that time, he was simply looking for a way to broadcast the University of Connecticut basketball games but then stumbled upon satellite technology.

Rasmussen started his career in media. He first started working with a radio station in Amherst, Massachusetts then a career change landed him in Springfield where he spent eight years as a Sports Director and two years as a News Director and News Anchor. After Springfield, Rasmussen landed in New England to join the hockey team as their Director of Communications. Rasmussen only held this position for 3 years before he and the whole front office staff were abruptly fired. It was this moment that stirred Bill Rasmussen's dream of creating his own network, later to be known as ESPN.

As of today, ESPN reaches close to 100 million households and presents close to 25,000 live events and over 83,000 total live hours of studio and event programming. Some additional well-known ESPN entities include ESPN2, ESPN Classic, ESPNEWS, ESPN Deportes, and ESPNU. It is absolutely no question that Bill Rasmussen and his brilliant idea have truly left a significant mark on the sports world.

Along with being a businessman, a guest speaker, an author, and a number of additional roles, Bill Rasmussen still keeps his ties with ESPN very strong. Rasmussen says that he absolutely loves to turn on the TV and see what ESPN has become. He loves to see the new generation of personalities who are hosts and anchors. Rasmussen is avid supporter who continues to endorse and support enhancement efforts that continue to expand the wide range of coverage and offerings through the network. Thanks to Bill Rasmussen, the face of sports, the face of television, and the way we, quite literally, view both are forever changed!

Source: https://bill-rasmussen-speaker.com/bio/. Accessed May 18th, 2020

Types of new products

As noted previously, there is no universally accepted definition of new products. Instead, new products are sometimes described from the viewpoint of the sports organization versus the consumer's perspective. The organization's definition of a new product is based on whether it has ever produced or marketed this particular product in the past. This can be important for organizations trying to understand how the new sports product "fits" with their existing products.

However, newness from the consumer's perspective is described as any innovation the consumer perceives as meaningful. In other words, the new product could be a minor alteration of an existing product or a product that has never been sold or marketed by any organization. Looking at new products from the consumer's viewpoint helps sports organizations understand the most effective way to market the product. Let us examine the types of new products from the organizational and consumer perspectives in greater detail.

Newness from the organization's perspective

New-to-the-world products

Brand-new sports innovations, such as the first inline skates, the first sailboard, or the advent of arena football in 1987, all represent **new-to-the-world products**. These products were new to the organization selling the product as well as to the consumers purchasing or using the product.[1]

Another interesting, new-to-the-world sports product is the wireless ballpark. Raley Field, home of the AAA Sacramento River Cats baseball team, was one of the first to become one of professional sports' most technologically advanced venues. The River Cats were among the first teams to provide wireless access to customers in suites and the exclusive "Solon Club." The stadium is now wired for all fans who are able to operate laptop computers, PDAs, and other wireless devices from their seats for access to up-to-the-minute stats and replays. Additionally, fans can order food or tickets for future games right from their seat.[2] Today these innovations are inclusive in almost all stadium development projects. New state-of-the-art facilities such as Atlanta's Mercedes Benz Stadium accentuate the innovation and delivery options.

New product category entries

Sports products that are new to the organization, but not to the world, are referred to as **new product category entries**. For example, IMG, a sports, entertainment, and media company, acquired Host Communications in November of 2007. Several months earlier, IMG acquired the Collegiate Licensing Company, and collectively these two companies formed the foundation for IMG College, a division of IMG Worldwide, which provides unparalleled expertise and resources to the collegiate market through the use of licensing and multimedia rights services. IMG further expanded this platform with the acquisition of ISP Sports on July 28, 2010. In late 2018, IMG College and Learfield jointly announced a merger that created Learfield IMG College. The organization will support collegiate institutions, conferences, and arenas across the country with enhanced services, more consistent promotions, technological innovation, and greater economic opportunities. Learfield IMG College specializes in fully integrated solutions, including branding, licensing, and multimedia rights management; access to professional concessions, ticket sales, and fan engagement systems and support; publishing, radio, digital, and social expertise; and campus-wide business and sponsorship development.

> Completing this merger is an important step toward our mission to best support our partners – including universities, collegiate athletic departments and brands – with tailored services and capabilities that drive results that ultimately help fund the student-athlete experience. Our respective companies bring so much to the table, and by building on our collective resources, relationships and experiences, we will deliver new and enhanced opportunities for all our partners, said Learfield IMG College President and CEO Greg Brown.[3]

This acquisition further enhanced Learfield IMG College as the leading representative of colleges and universities in their efforts to maximize their revenue through media and marketing rights deals.

New Balance, known only for its footwear, acquired Brine, Inc., a recognized industry leader in soccer, lacrosse, field hockey, and volleyball. "Brine's history of manufacturing high-performance team sports products will enable us to broaden our offerings at the global level," said Jim Davis, chairman and founder of New Balance. "Brine's motto, 'Find Your Game,' speaks directly to their long-standing support of game improvement products and programs, and fits in well with New Balance's philosophy of promoting personal athletic achievements."[4]

In another example, Rawlings, a century-old company that has produced the official ball and helmet of Major League Baseball, was sold to Seidler Equity Partners and MLB. The $395-million deal that adds the professional league as a key investor gives MLB a chance to provide input and direction on the production. Rawlings, which is credited with introducing the first football shoulder pads, traces its roots to a small store in St. Louis opened by brothers George and Alfred Rawlings. Its gloves have been worn by baseball greats like Roberto Clemente and Mickey Mantle, and its baseballs have been the official, and exclusive, game balls of MLB since 1977. The company will remain based in St. Louis.[5] Additionally, a historic example specific to the athletic footwear landscape occurred when German-based manufacturer adidas announced it would be acquiring all outstanding shares of Reebok. Under the terms of the deal, adidas bought Reebok for $3.8 billion in 2006. For adidas, the merger strengthens its presence in global athletic footwear, apparel, and hardware markets – allowing for a more competitive vantage point, a more defined brand identity, a wider product offering, and a stronger presence in professional athletics. These products are not new to the sports consumers, but they are new acquisitions for the organizations.

Product line extensions

Product line extensions refer to new products being added to an existing product line. For instance, the addition of expansion teams in Major League Baseball or Daiwa's new Dendoh Marine Power Assist fishing reels, precision engineered with Daiwa's unique Power Lever for instant control of winding speed and power, are product line extensions. The NBA G-League is also a product line extension of the original National Basketball Association. The league is currently fielding 27 teams across the United States and was formerly known as the National Basketball Development League (NBDL), which started with 8 teams in the fall of 2001.

In another example of a product line extension, change is good, right? New Balance footwear thought so when they gave the New Balance 998 a brand-new look and tongue patch. The 998 comes dressed in shades of gray, green, and brown constructed out of leather, mesh, and suede materials. The versatile look of the shoe is then topped off with a new patch sewn on the tongue housing the "New Balance 998 Made in USA" branding. Last, the shoe also comes with an Abzorb sole unit to match the comfort with the aesthetics of the shoe.

Product improvements

Product improvements refer to current products that have been modified and improved, such as the new shoe addition to the long line of the Jordan Brand. Every year, the new game shoe sets the tone for the future of Jordan Brand. Authentic to futuristic, distinct features demonstrate Nike and acknowledge the fact that present-day athletes crave not only comfort and responsiveness but also style and innovation. Each shoe is built and constructed with that greatness in mind. Inspired by gravity-defying athletes and space travel, the new Air Jordan XXXIII was made to change the game of basketball. The new FastFit tightening system provides optimal lockdown and follows the Air Jordan tradition of boldly bringing the shoe's innovation to the exterior of the shoe.

Another example of a product improvement is the Wilson Pro Staff. As 20-time Grand Slam champion Roger Federer puts it, "the tuxedo finally got its shirt." The Swiss star worked closely with Wilson to help develop this racquet. The Pro Staff RF 97 model weighs in at a manageable 315 g, but there are other lighter models with bigger head sizes as well. The racquet has a noticeable weight to groundstrokes and is the perfect platform for those who like to dictate the baseline.[6]

Any sports team or individual that improves during the off-season can be considered a product improvement. Sometimes this improvement takes place because of trades or purchasing new players, and other times an enhanced product is the result of a new coach or players who are maturing and finally performing to their potential. In either case, product improvements represent an opportunity for sports marketers to promote the improvements (either real or perceived) in product quality.

A final example of a product improvement comes from the Chicago Cubs and their rearranging of a few group areas at Wrigley Field to free up room in the historic ballpark to allow more room for fans to mingle. The organization's proposed ballpark renovations included a 57,000-square-foot Jumbotron; larger home clubhouse equipped with a new weight room, medical area, players' lounge, batting cages, and media center; wider concourse; new restaurant club; improved concessions; more restrooms; enlarged and renovated skyboxes; new plaza area for pre- and post-game festivities; new office building to

---

ARTICLE 8.3
SPOTLIGHT ON SPORTS MARKETING ETHICS

Why American Universities Sponsor Commercial Sports

by Allen Sanderson and John Siegfried

Some 130 American universities field big-time commercialized football teams, each offering 85 grants-in-aid (aka athletic scholarships). Meanwhile, over 300 colleges sponsor men's basketball teams with 13 scholarship players each, all competing for slots in the National College Athletic Association's annual "March Madness" basketball tournament.

These two sports businesses collectively generate over $10 billion in revenue annually that flows to institutions whose primary purpose is to educate students and advance knowledge – not to entertain the public. Indeed, the charters of none of these universities even mention sports as part of their mission.

How did this come about, and why does it persist in an organizational structure that severely tests the integrity of players, coaches and administrators? For that matter, why does it persist at all in light of the evidence that the greatest revenue producer – football – poses serious health risks to players?

The sports connection seems especially baffling in light of the reality that fewer than two dozen programs earn revenues sufficient to cover their operating costs, let alone the costs of massive physical facilities and other indirect costs such as security. Indeed, once full-cost accounting is applied, the vast majority of universities must redirect funds to cover sports deficits – funds that might otherwise support academic programs.

Here, we offer some perspective on how commercialized college sports got started, what spawned their massive growth and why it is so difficult to reform or discontinue these activities in spite of repeated scandals.

In the beginning

The sports connection dates to the second half of the 19th century, when large state "land grant" universities were spawned by the Morrill Act of 1862, which funded them through gifts of federally owned lands. (Kansas State University was the first.) Over the next 40 years, many of these institutions found themselves with excess capacity as the supply of low-cost higher education outstripped demand. They responded with sports programs that raised their visibility and made them more attractive to sports-crazed young men.

Simultaneously – mostly at elite private colleges and universities – teenage boys sought camaraderie and recognition by organizing competitions in America's emerging team sports: football, baseball and basketball. Football rivalries began in 1869 with a game resembling rugby played between Princeton and Rutgers.

Over the next 35 years, rules changes morphed the sport into what looked a lot like modern football. The most important modifications occurred in 1905 after President Theodore Roosevelt demanded action to reduce the injuries resulting from what amounted to semi-organized mayhem. Indeed, in 1906, the forerunner organization to the National College Athletic Association took Roosevelt's threat to ban football seriously. One of its first actions was to require seven of the 11 players on each team be on the line of scrimmage when the ball was snapped (a rule still in effect today), thus eliminating the common tactic of offensive players linking arms and gaining a running head start toward the defensive line.

The University of Chicago was the first to pay its head football coach, Amos Alonzo Stagg, who was lured from his volunteer coaching position at Springfield College in 1892. Harvard built the first large permanent football stadium, with a seating capacity of 31,000, in 1903. With investments in staff and facilities, universities now needed to ensure sufficient revenues to pay their mortgages and coaches; thus began the focus on sports finances.

In those early years, intercollegiate competitions were usually organized by students, rendering universities potentially liable for injuries and the occasional death. With time, the universities managed to gain greater control over their teams, specifying who could play and under what rules. Closing ranks on the governance of intercollegiate athletics also enabled universities to improve their ability to use sports to recruit students to fill empty classroom seats.

Student recruitment remains one of the ostensible rationales for hosting commercialized intercollegiate sports, although there is little evidence that the boost to enrollment for schools with winning teams is either substantial or enduring. Moreover, most of the (limited) effect is simply to rearrange students among institutions rather than stimulate overall college attendance. In any event, one has to wonder whether students (or the institutions) are well served by marketing that conflates the quality of education offered with the win-loss records of their sports teams.

From the turn of the 20th century through the end of World War II, commercialized intercollegiate athletics remained on a reliably upward trajectory, supported by rising enrollment in higher ed. Meanwhile, enthusiasm for teams was bolstered by growing ranks of alumni, most of whom lived within driving distance of their alma maters.

Before 1950, costs remained largely under control because revenues were sufficiently modest that competition to buy better coaching staff and players was simply out of the question. Professional players were prohibited from participating in intercollegiate athletics controlled by the NCAA. Compensation to players in the form of tuition remission and reimbursement for room and board was an off-again, on-again affair – but did not absorb big bucks even when it was on-again because university residence halls were spare and food was basic.

A new era

Dramatic technological and demographic changes disrupted the college sports business in the decade immediately following World War II. The first of these changes was the market diffusion of television. The University of Pennsylvania got a jump on competitors, televising its home football games in 1940 for the then very thin ranks of television owners. A decade later, Penn was earning $150,000 (real money in 1950) for its annual football broadcasting rights. And that was just the beginning. In 1950, only 9 percent of U.S. households owned TVs; in 1960, market penetration had reached 90 percent. Sports, it should be noted, provided popular broadcasting content at low marginal cost because the games were already scheduled to be played even if the cameras weren't around. Payments for TV rights was lagniappe.

For a variety of reasons, live spectator demand for college and university sports events also increased sharply after the war. First, the G.I. Bill increased college and university enrollment, adding to the ranks of loyal alumni as veterans graduated. Second, the post-war baby boom increased interest in college and university sports as the population of teenage boys and young men spiked in the late 1950s and early 1960s.

Football

In 1951, the NCAA decided to prohibit televised college football because it thought the opportunity to watch games on TV would cut into live gate attendance and receipts. Penn, however, refused to stop televising its games, precipitating the threat of a boycott by other NCAA teams.

Penn backed off. But in 1952, tempted by the prospect of a large and growing payoff, the NCAA concocted its own "Television Plan," which endured for decades. The scheme was anchored by an agreement among NCAA members to broadcast only a single Saturday afternoon football game (or a single game in each region) and to limit the number of appearances by any team in order to spread the wealth sufficiently to build and sustain support for the overall scheme.

All told, revenue from college sports broadcasting rights has increased by 1,500 percent since the Supreme Court decision liquidating the NCAA football broadcasting cartel.

The rights to broadcast the weekly game were auctioned off to the three major television networks, creating competition that led to rapid fee escalation. But the Television Plan's division of the revenues plainly favored less popular teams. In a challenge in 1984 by the University of Oklahoma, the Supreme Court decided that the agreement violated the Sherman Antitrust Act, thus ending the plan after 32 years. In the meantime, broadcast rights fees for college football had grown significantly, rivaling ticket sales as the largest source of college football revenue.

Basketball

The commercialization of men's college basketball developed more slowly. The first intercollegiate championship was the 1938 National Invitation Tournament, sponsored by the Metropolitan Basketball Writers Association and held in New York City – then ground-zero for interest in the sport. The NCAA started a competing tournament in 1939, and the two tournaments co-existed uneasily until 1970, when the NCAA flexed its muscles by prohibiting any team invited to its tournament from participating in the NIT. That precipitated a prolonged antitrust challenge by the NIT – one only settled in 2005, when the NCAA purchased the NIT. Since then, the NIT has been run as a consolation prize tournament for teams that don't make the cut for the main show.

The NCAA's three-week men's basketball tournament was first called "March Madness" by a television broadcaster in 1982. But the tournament organizers weren't the sort to leave a dime on the table. They trademarked March Madness soon thereafter and have been aggressively enforcing their exclusive right to it since 1995. All told, the tournament brings in over $1 billion annually, enough to cover virtually all of the NCAA's formidable organizational costs.

The pot of gold

Surprisingly, in light of the 1984 Supreme Court decision dismantling the cartel on college football broadcasting, TV rights revenues have subsequently soared.

The immediate impact was, as to be expected, negative. Advertising rates fell by two-thirds immediately after the court swept aside the NCAA's Television Plan. But soon thereafter, regional conferences, first collectively and later individually, began to market their member teams' broadcast rights. They soon discovered that football fans were drawn to regional rivalries, and the rise of the cable sports networks – notably ESPN and Fox Sports – gave them almost as much market power for broadcast rights tailored to each conference's geographic presence as the NCAA had possessed with its national cartel.

The burgeoning pot of gold might have been competed away in bidding wars for star athletes. But the NCAA recognized the importance of using its cartel power to control these outlays at about the same time that revenues began to mushroom.

In the immediate aftermath of World War II, the NCAA adopted what it called a "sanity code" (on the grounds that paying players was "insane") that forbade any compensation to the athletes, including tuition remission or the cost of room and board. This code lasted only a few years, however. And in 1951, just as the NCAA was asserting control of college sports broadcast rights via the Television Plan, athletic scholarships (called grants-in-aid, which include tuition, room, board, health insurance, books and some incidentals) came back to stay. Compensation exceeding grants-in-aid, however, has been forbidden ever since.

Player costs were not really brought under control until 1973, though, when the NCAA capped the number of grants-in-aid that could be offered by a team as well as the size of the grants. Football was initially restricted to 105 scholarships, which was lowered to 95 in 1978 and 85 in 1992. As a further cost-containment measure, freshmen were declared eligible to play on varsity teams, thus reducing the number of scholarship players needed to field competitive teams.

Tightening the monopsony

One might have expected the most talented young players to bypass college – with its snug cap on compensation – and head for the pros, where money talks. Some basketball players, including superstars Kevin Garnett and LeBron James, did just that, going directly to the National Basketball Association from high school. But in 2007, the NBA extended a helping hand to the NCAA, requiring players to wait at least one year after their high school classes had graduated before they could be employed. The NFL raised the ante in this regard, requiring three years to pass after high school.

This has been rationalized in any number of ways – most notably, as a way to ensure that players have adequate training and time to mature before facing the less forgiving environment of the pros. Maybe. But it's worth noting that 18-year-olds are still welcome to fight the Taliban. Or, for that matter, to play big-league hockey or baseball, join the rodeo circuit or drive 200-plus miles an hour in NASCAR races.

One need not be excessively cynical to assume that universities like the rule because it guarantees them a steady supply of talent at a low, capped price. The NBA and NFL have less to gain. But they do benefit because the value of players who have been trained and tested in big-time college sports is easier to assess. It probably doesn't hurt either that funneling players through colleges generates goodwill among college-sports-mad legislators who, if they wished, could turn a gimlet eye on the market power exercised by the professional leagues.

The commercial value of virtually all sports programming got an added boost with the arrival of the cheap digital video recorder, which allowed viewers to record programs to view later while fast-forwarding through the ads. This reduced revenue from most programming – but not, ironically, from sports, where the audience seems to be hooked on live action. As a consequence, the cost of ad time on sports programming is as much as triple that of popular prime-time entertainment. All told, revenue from college sports broadcasting rights has increased by 1,500 percent since the Supreme Court decision liquidating the NCAA football broadcasting cartel.

> Funneling players through colleges generates goodwill among college sports-mad legislators who, if they wished, could turn a gimlet eye on the market power exercised by the professional leagues.

Following the money

At first blush, then, it's hard to understand why colleges lose money on football and men's basketball while their professional counterparts (the NFL and NBA) are immensely profitable, as evidenced by the ever increasing market value of their franchises. Granted, the professional sports cartels have the decided advantage of being able to threaten to leave town unless local taxpayers cough up a new stadium – something Ohio State can't do to Columbus. Moreover, the NFL and NBA only have to keep about 30 owners each in line, rather than several hundred heterogeneous institutions.

On the other hand, the professional leagues have to contend with players who have free-agency rights after an initial probationary contract period, and must bargain collectively with the players' labor union – as opposed to simply stipulating uniform, grant-in-aid compensation. On balance, these financial pluses and minuses seem to favor the universities and the NCAA. So what's wrong with this picture?

A partial explanation for most colleges' grim bottom lines is that, while player costs may be limited by the cartel, there are still ways to compete away the surpluses ensured by the combination of fat broadcast rights and caps on player costs. For one thing, training facilities and stadiums must be kept in a whole lot better shape than classrooms. For another, the market for high-profile coaches is very competitive. Indeed for over 24 assistant coaches make $1 million or more per plus year, while at minimum, 25 head coaches make $4.15 million or more per year. Dabo Swinney of Clemson ($9,315,600) and Alabama's Nick Saban ($8,857,000) top the ranks at the collegiate level.[8]

Assuming that university administrators understand all this as well as we do, why do these institutions continue to field so many money-draining operations?

First, consider Title IX of the 1972 Higher Education Amendments, which addresses gender equity at colleges and universities. Title IX requires these institutions to provide approximately equal opportunities and funding for male and female athletes. Thus athletic departments of universities that play men's basketball or football are required to field a wider array of resource-draining teams – something the NFL avoids. (So does the NBA, except for its subsidiary, the Women's National Basketball Association, which has only recently begun to make a profit.)

A second possibility is that, while the costs of maintaining these athletic programs are tangible and measurable, university administrators are aware that much of the benefits that go to myriad university stakeholders are not. Students get the vicarious pleasure provided by the commercialized sports teams, along with the opportunity to participate in non-revenue sports as indirectly mandated by Title IX. Alumni, who follow football or basketball as a way to stay connected to their alma maters, often return the favor with contributions. Likewise, nearby towns get to identify with the fortunes of the teams – and their merchants may get a boost from gameday sales or the true bonanza associated with hosting a bowl game or basketball tournament. Coaches and other athletic staff earn far more than they would in jobs outside commercial sports. And then there's the need to stay on the good side of state legislators who control public universities' purse-strings – there's nothing like a winning team to keep lawmakers sweet.

Athletic departments of universities that play men's basketball or football are required to field a wider array of resource-draining teams – something the NFL avoids.

Using a little imagination, this list of stakeholders can be expanded until the cows come home. The NCAA supports a large bureaucracy that is paid from what amounts to taxes on member teams. As mentioned above, the NBA and NFL capture some of the value of the training provided by university commercial sports programs. And while broadcasters pay a lot of money for television rights, unless the networks miscalculate, some of the value (what economists call "producers' surplus") accrues to their bottom lines. Ditto for apparel makers, who presumably earn more on sports-branded clothes than they pay for the rights to the logos. And while none of these indirect beneficiaries is in a position to persuade university administrators to invest heavily in commercial sports, they do support a popular culture in which life without the rituals of big-time college football and basketball seem unimaginable.

The beginning of the end?

While big-time college sports are part of the American landscape, it's still worth examining whether the current iteration of this accidental industry represents a stable equilibrium. To put it another way, what could possibly go wrong?

First, while legislatures are inclined to turn a blind eye to the market power of the NCAA, the courts may not. Legal challenges to the NCAA's rigid cap on the amount "studentathletes" may be paid are winding their way through the courts. If the cartel rules were declared illegal, one would expect a bidding war for the best high school athletes, raising the cost of fielding commercialized college teams and, arguably, paring down the number of universities willing to make the investment. By the same token, the courts could rule that the NFL and NBA rules delaying access to athletes who skip college could further erode the supply of players willing to risk careerending injuries in return for scholarships and all the steak dinners they can eat.

Next, changing technologies could erode the value of the broadcast rights fueling both college and professional sports. The challenge to cable television from streaming apps has driven the cable companies to bid for the sort of exclusive programming that constitutes must-see TV. Sports has fit the bill perfectly. But as the trend toward cable-cutting accelerates (as is widely predicted), the cable companies won't be willing to pay as much for broadcast rights to keep patrons on the hook.

Finally, it's worth remembering that the NCAA is a cartel and, as with most cartels, there are powerful incentives for dominant members to seek other means of organization that give them a bigger share of the gravy. Specifically, the NCAA cartel could devolve into a few professional-like groupings – most likely, the five large power conferences that exist under the NCAA umbrella today – with more compensation for athletes and looser affiliations with the campuses. The sports programs of the remaining universities would find it harder to generate break-even revenue, at the very least forcing them to cut back on staffing salaries, gold-plated training facilities and the number of student-athletes on the payroll. At some point, university administrators may have to weigh the benefits accruing to big-time intercollegiate athletics against the costs of scrimping on the academic side of their mission.

It's not that breaking the link between commercial sports and higher education would be unprecedented. The NCAA dropped boxing in 1960 after a slew of injuries – and without much consequence for the institutions that had previously embraced it. For that matter, some of the most prestigious (and well-funded) universities today – Boston University, New York University, George Washington University, Caltech and three of the University of California campuses (Santa Barbara, Irvine and Riverside) – manage to excel without the cash or goodwill generated by football. Others choose to play it at the less-demanding, nonscholarship level (MIT, Chicago, Washington University, Emory, Carnegie Mellon, Johns Hopkins).

The marriage of commercial sports and higher education was not inevitable. Nor is it inevitable that the forces binding them together will – or should – hold indefinitely.

Source: Milken Institute Review

www.milkenreview.org/articles/why-american-universities-sponsor-commercial-sports

house team, stadium, and concession personnel; and, last, a seven-story hotel with a connected walkway.[7]

Repositioning

As defined in Chapter 6, repositioning is changing the image or perception of the sports entity in the minds of consumers in the target market. Sports products such as bowling and billiards are trying to reposition themselves as "yuppie sports activities" by creating trendy and upscale environments in sports facilities that are stereotypically grungy and old fashioned.[9]

Another repositioning example comes from the city of Moscow, the largest city in Europe with no modern arena to serve the sports and entertainment community. The city of Moscow, partnering with VTB Bank and AEG, built a massive $1.5-billion sport and entertainment complex to serve Europe's largest market. The arena/stadium project includes the VTB Bank stadium, with 6,750 club seats, 98 suites, and an expandable seating capacity that serves populations from 33,000–45,000. The VTB Bank Arena houses 1,632 club seats and 82 suites and has a seating capacity of 12,000, expandable to 15,000. These sports venues are targeted to attract mega-events such as FIFA World Cup competition.[10]

The most common examples of new products are repositioning and product improvements because of the limited risk involved from the organization's perspective. The rearrangement of existing sports products also has its advantages. For example, this type of new product can be developed more quickly than new-to-the-world or new product category entrants, and it already has an established track record with consumers.

However, new-to-the-world products must undergo enhanced research and development because they are new to the organization and to consumers. Moreover, more money must be invested because heavy levels of promotion are necessary to make potential consumers aware of the product. In addition, consumers must learn about the benefits of the new product and how it can help satisfy their needs.

Newness from the consumer's perspective

Another way to describe new products is from the perspective of consumers. New products are categorized as discontinuous innovations, dynamically continuous innovations, or continuous innovations.[11] New products are categorized on the basis of the degree of behavioral change required by consumers. Behavioral changes refer to differences in the way we use a new product, the way we think about a new product, or the degree of learning required to use a new product. For instance, a new extra-long tennis racquet does not require us to change the way we play tennis or to relearn the sport. However, extensive learning took place for many Americans exposed to soccer for the first time in the 1994 World Cup match, and the learning process continues. Similarly, learning will have to occur for the many Americans who will watch cricket or experience the growing sport of lacrosse for the first time. Let us look at the three categories of new products from the consumer's perspective in greater detail.

Discontinuous innovations are somewhat similar to new-to-the-world products in that they represent the most innovative products. In fact, discontinuous innovations are so new and original that they require major learning from the consumer's viewpoint and new consumption and usage patterns. Some of the "extreme sports," such as sky surfing, bungee jumping, and ice climbing, represented discontinuous innovations but are now becoming more mainstream. New "extremes" such as free diving, hang gliding, cave diving, base jumping, wakeskiing, and kite-surfing are also becoming popular.

Many Southerners who have had limited access to ice hockey may view this sport as a discontinuous innovation. Interestingly, a study found that spectator knowledge of hockey was found to be a significant predictor of game attendance and intention to attend hockey games in the future. An equally important finding in the study was that knowledge of hockey may vary based on sociodemographic variables. In other words, the fan's age, gender, educational level, income, and marital status influence the degree of hockey knowledge.[12]

Even distribution patterns for sport have required new consumption and usage patterns and therefore represent discontinuous innovation. For example, *Sports Business Journal* noted that programs such as Twitter and Instagram via smartphones could serve sports properties and brands and offer a real-time perspective of how people react to a game, a deal, or a critical decision. These instantaneous feed mechanisms provide information and even gratification for consumers searching for and desiring up-to-date news.

Dynamically continuous innovations are new products that represent changes and improvements but do not strikingly change buying and usage patterns. For instance, the titanium head and bubble shaft on a golf club or the liquid metal technology aluminum bat are innovations that do not change our swing but do represent significant improvements in equipment (and hopefully our game). When the shot-clock and three-point field goal were added to basketball, changes took place in how the game was played. Coaches, players, and fans were forced to understand and adopt new strategies for basketball. Most basketball enthusiasts believe these dynamically continuous innovations improved the sport.

The latest dynamically continuous innovations from the golf industry, which thrives on new product development, are the mainstream acceptance of the hybrid club and new surface geometrics of the golf ball. Many low- and high-handicap golfers are replacing their long irons with hybrids – a half-iron, half-wood alternative to the difficult-to-hit long irons. The innovative designs of the golf ball, which include the use of swirls or grooves rather than circular dimples, allow balls to fly like rockets in breezy conditions.

Software giant SAP has entered the next phase of its sponsorship strategy. They are now using sponsorship and a new strategy of consumerism to put a personal touch on their brand by using new information technology. This technology is adopted by consumers and then spreads to business and government applications. SAP paired up with three professional sports properties: the NBA; the NFL's San Francisco 49ers; and, more recently, MetLife Stadium, home of the NFL New York Giants and New York Jets. SAP plans to use this technology in order to enhance the fan experience. Examples of this include offering real-time statistics through NBA.com. This information was not available to the public until now. This is one way SAP is using sponsorship to introduce its brand to new customers.

EA Sports utilizes dynamically continuous innovations to enhance its critically acclaimed portfolio of brands such as The Sims, Madden NFL, EA Sports FIFA, Battlefield, Need for Speed, Dragon Age, and Plants vs. Zombies. EA constantly strives to deepen their focus on user experience, remain authentic, and continue to enhance the in-game likeness of many of their platforms. Development plays a vital role in EA's future. They continue to push forward to offer access to more games and content through industry-leading subscription services. By creating a gaming culture and using creativity, they continue to be at the forefront of creating dynamically continuous innovations in the gaming market. EA Sports added online scouting, online team play, and online attribute boost for co-op play to enhance functionality. Previous dynamically continuous innovations include customizable playbooks, diagrams, and testing sequences to better prepare athletes for specific opponents. Additionally, the software includes built-in teaching and reporting tools so coaches can analyze and track the tactical-skill development of their athletes. Instead of simply playing a video game for enjoyment, an athlete can play a game to test and train for upcoming on-field action. For example, a quarterback using the new tool can practice reading a defense, picking up blitzes, and making quick decisions on where to throw the ball, all based on the tendencies of the team he is going to play the upcoming weekend.

A final example of a dynamically continuous innovation comes from the world of trading cards. To remain competitive in a rapidly changing collective marketplace, Upper Deck developed the Shadow Box slot cards. These interchangeable acetate cards allowed collectors the opportunity to customize their own unique trading cards. This change represented a new buying behavior for a product (trading cards) that has been on the market for decades.

Continuous innovations represent an ongoing, commonplace change such as the minor alteration of a product or the introduction of an imitation product. A continuous innovation has the least disruptive influence on patterns of usage and consumer behavior. In other words, consumers use the product in the same manner that they have always used the product. Examples of continuous innovations include the addition of expansion teams for leagues such as NBA G-League, MLB, the WNBA, MLS, or even expanding the number of games in the season. Another example of a continuous innovation comes to us from the previous EA example and the world of sports video game technology. Absent a dynamically continuous innovation, very little may change from year-to-year in video games, such as Madden 2020 vs. Madden 2021. However, manufacturers often still deploy continuous innovation strategies. These strategies are inclusive of minor improvements, that is, color, graphics, packaging, or number of teams, and are often made to satisfy consumer demand or to further enhance sales of products lines. In fact, since many of these games are played much the same way that games were played in editions released decades before the need for continuous innovation, it may be more evident to further have an impact on sales.

We often could debate which new product category best represents a team that has built a new arena and changed its venue or any new sports product, but few new products fall neatly into the three categories. Rather, there is a continuum ranging from minor innovation to major innovation, based on how consumers perceive the new product. Knowing how consumers think and feel about a new product is critical information in developing the most effective marketing strategy. Before we talk more about the factors that make new products successful and spread through the marketplace, let us look at how new products are conceived.

The new product development process

Increased competition for sports and entertainment dollars, emergence of new technologies, and ever-changing consumer preferences are just a few of the reasons sports marketers are constantly developing new sports products. As Higgins and Martin point out in their research on managing sport innovations, "Clearly, the list of innovations in sports is extensive and appears to be increasing at a rapid rate. This would suggest that spectators are seeking new and better entertainment and participants are seeking new and better challenges."[13]

Many new sports products are conceived without much planning or happen as a result of chance. For instance, the modern sport of polo was created by British cavalry officers in India who wanted to show off their horsemanship in a more creative way than the parade ground allowed. Although polo represents a sport that was developed by chance, this is more the exception than the rule. More often than not, sports organizations develop new products by using a systematic approach called the **new product development process**. The phases in the new product development process include idea generation, idea screening, analysis of the concept, developing the sports product, test marketing, and commercialization. Let us briefly explore each phase in the new product development process.

Idea generation

The first phase of the new product development process is **idea generation**. At this initial phase, any and all ideas for new products are considered. Ideas for new products are generated from many different sources. Employees who work in product development teams, salespeople close to the consumers, consumers of sport, and competitive organizations are just a few of the potential sources of ideas for new sports products.

Naturally, a marketing-oriented sports organization will attempt to communicate with their consumers as much as possible to determine emerging needs. As we discussed in Chapter 3, marketing research plays a valuable role in anticipating the needs of consumers. Moreover, environmental scanning helps sports organizations keep in touch with changes in the marketing environment that might present opportunities for new product development. For instance, the entrepreneurs who established Ultimate Fighting understood that the environmental conditions would be conducive to success.

Idea screening

Once the ideas are generated, the next step of the product development process, **idea screening**, begins. During the idea screening phase, all the new

Table 8.1 New product screening checklist

Rate the new product concept using a 10-point scale. Score a "1" if the concept fails the question and a "10" if it meets the criterion perfectly.

Relative advantage
Does the new product offer a cost advantage compared with substitutes?
Does the new product have a value-added feature?
Is the new product directed at neglected segments of the marketplace?

Compatibility
Is the product compatible with corporate practices, culture, and value systems (i.e., the internal contingencies)?
Is the new product compatible with the market's environment (i.e., the external contingencies)?
Is the new product compatible with current products and services being offered (i.e., product mix)?

Perceived risk
Note: On the following questions, absence of risk should receive a higher score.
Does the consumer perceive an economic risk if they try the new product?
Does the consumer perceive a physical risk in adopting the new product?
Does the consumer fear the new technology will not perform properly?
Does the product offer a social risk to consumers?

A bottom-line score of 100 (10 points for each question) suggests a new product winner.
For most companies, a score of 70 or better signals a "go" decision on the new product concept. A risk-oriented company would probably consider anything that scores 50 or higher. A score of 30 or less signifies a concept that faces many consumer obstacles.

product ideas are evaluated and the poor ones are weeded out. An important consideration in the idea screening process is to examine the "fit" of the product with the organization's goals and consumer demand. The concept of new product fit is consistent with the contingency framework, which states that product decisions should consider the external contingencies, the internal contingencies, and the strategic sports marketing process. One formal idea screening tool for analyzing the "fit" of potential products is the new product screening checklist (see Table 8.1).

Sports marketers using some variant of this new product screening checklist would rate potential new product ideas on each item. As Table 8.1 indicates, a score of less than 30 would eliminate the new product from further consideration, whereas a score of 70 or more means the product would be further developed. Obviously, each sports organization must design its own new product screening checklist to meet the demands of its unique marketing environment and organization.

Analysis of the sports product concept or potential

By the third phase of the new product development process, poor ideas have been eliminated. Now the process continues as the firm begins to analyze potential new products in terms of how they fit with existing products and how consumers respond to these new products. As new product ideas begin to take shape, marketing research is necessary to understand consumers' perceptions of the new product concepts. One type of marketing research that is commonly conducted during the new product development process is referred to as concept testing.

During concept testing, consumers representative of the target market evaluate written, verbal, and pictorial descriptions of potential products. The objectives of concept testing are to understand the target market's reaction to the proposed product, determine how interested the target market is in the product, and explore the strengths and weaknesses of the proposed product. In some cases, consumers are asked to evaluate slightly different versions of the product so that sports organizations can design the product to meet the needs of consumers.

The most important reason for conducting a concept test is to estimate the sales potential of the new product. Often, this is done by measuring "intent

---

Table 8.2 Concept test for the Beach Soccer World Wide Tour

The sport of beach soccer is played on a 30-by-40-yard soft sand surface with five players on each team, including the goalie. There are three periods of 12 minutes, each with unlimited player substitutions (as in hockey). In the event of a tie, the game goes into a three-minute overtime period, followed by sudden-death penalty kicks. Beach Soccer World Wide (BSWW) would feature nation against nation (e.g., United States vs. Italy).

What is your general reaction to beach soccer?

How likely would you be to attend an event if the tour stopped in your city?

Would definitely attend

Probably would attend

Might or might not attend

Probably would not attend

Would definitely not attend

What do you like most about this concept of BSWW?

What could be done to improve the concept of BSWW?

Photo 8.1
Concept testing is used to understand consumer reactions to sports such as whitewater rafting

Source: Shutterstock, ID# 102918779 by Ammit Jack

to buy" responses from tested consumers. Using the results of concept testing, along with secondary data such as demographic trends, sports marketers can decide whether to proceed to the next step of the new product development process, drop the idea, or revise the product concept and reevaluate. Table 8.2 shows a hypothetical concept test for the Beach Soccer World Wide Tour, a new sports product that has been growing around the globe.

Developing the sports product

Based on the results of the concept test, design of the product begins in order to conduct further testing. Ideally, if the sports organization is employing a marketing orientation, then the product design and development stem from the consumer's perspective. For instance, Nike began its product design efforts for a new baseball glove by asking 200 college and minor league baseball players what they disliked about their current gloves. Eighteen months and $500,000 later, researchers designed a prototype glove that is lightweight, held together with plastic clips and wire straps, and resembles a white foam rubber clamshell. Nike was hoping this space-age design would not be perceived by baseball purists as too far afield from traditional models.[14] However, consumers didn't respond favorably, and Nike was forced to discontinue the glove line.

In the case of a sporting good, a prototype is usually developed so consumers can get an even better idea of how the product will function and look. Today's superior engineering technology allows manufacturers to develop more realistic prototypes in a shorter period of time. It is common for prototypes to then be sent to select individuals for further testing and refinement. For instance, new golf, tennis, and ski products are routinely sent to club professionals for testing.

Another consideration in **developing the sports product** is making preliminary decisions with respect to the planning phase of the strategic sports marketing process. Potential market selection decisions (segmentation, target markets, and positioning) are considered. Furthermore, packaging, pricing, and distribution decisions are also deliberated. These basic marketing decisions are necessary to begin the next phase of new product development – test marketing.

Test marketing

In the concept stage of new product development, consumers indicate they would be likely to purchase the new product or service. Now that the product has been designed and developed, it can be offered to consumers on a limited basis to determine actual sales. Test marketing is the final gauge of the new product's success or failure.

Test marketing allows the sports organization to determine consumer response to the product and also provides information that may direct the entire marketing strategy. For instance, test markets can provide valuable information on the most effective packaging, pricing, and other forms of promotion.

The three types of test markets that may be conducted include standardized test markets, controlled test markets, and simulated test markets.[15] In standardized test markets, the product is sold through normal channels of distribution. A controlled test market, also known as a forced-distribution test market, uses an outside agency to secure distribution. As such, the manufacturer of a new product does not have to worry about the acceptance and level of market support from retailers or those carrying the product because the outside agency pays the retailer for the test. A simulated test market uses a tightly controlled simulated retailing environment or purchasing laboratory to determine consumer preferences for new sports products. This type of test market may be especially important in the future as more and more sporting goods and services are being marketed through the Internet.

Whatever type of test market is chosen, it is important to keep several things in mind. First, test marketing delays the introduction of a new sports product and may allow time for the competition to produce a "me-too" or imitation product, thereby negating the test marketer's investment in research and development. Second, costs of test marketing must be considered, and these costs can be excessive. Third, the results of test marketing may be misleading. Consumers may be anxious to try new sports products, and competition may try to influence the sales figures of the tested product by offering heavy discounting and promotion of their own product. Finally, test marketing presents a special challenge for sports marketers because of the intangible nature of many sports services.

Commercialization

The final stage of new product development is **commercialization**, or introduction. The decision has been made at this point to launch full-scale production (for goods) and distribution. If care has been taken at the previous stages of new product development, the new product will successfully meet its objectives. However, even if a systematic approach to new product development is followed, more often than not, sports products fail. Just what is it that makes a small portion of new sports products successful, while the large majority fail? Let us look at some of the factors that increase the chances of new product success.

New product success factors

The success of any new sports product, such as the NFL sports theme parks or NASCAR SpeedParks, depends on a variety of **new product success factors**. First and foremost, successful products must be high quality, create and maintain a positive and distinct brand image, and be designed to consumer specifications. In addition to the characteristics of the product itself, the other marketing mix elements (pricing, distribution, and promotion) play a major role in the success of a new product. Finally, the marketing environment also contributes to the success of a new product. A brief description of these critical success factors is presented in Table 8.3. Let us evaluate how well the new NFL Super Bowl sports theme parks perform on each of the critical success factors.

Based on the critical success factors in Table 8.3, would you predict that the NFL Super Bowl sports theme parks will be profitable? The NFL Super Bowl sports theme parks would seem to perform well on each of the product characteristics. Families can immerse in an interactive experience with limited perceived risk. The NFL Super Bowl sports theme parks are safe and offer a variety of interactive experiences for all ages., Product complexity is low, further enhancing the sense of community, safety, and fun entertainment for the entire family. With the NFL branding, the sophisticated simulations, and the authenticity, the parks provide a truly unique and valuable opportunity to connect to consumers. The

Table 8.3 Critical success factors for new products

Product considerations

- Trialability – Can consumers try the product before they make a purchase to reduce the risk?

- Observability – Can consumers see the benefits of the product or watch others use the product prior to the purchase?

- Perceived complexity – Does the new product appear to be difficult to understand or use?

- Relative advantage – Does the new product seem better than existing alternatives?

- Compatibility – Is the new product consistent with consumers' values and beliefs?

Other marketing mix considerations

- Pricing – Do consumers perceive the price to be consistent with the quality of the new product?

- Promotion – Are consumers in the target market aware of the product, and do they understand the benefits of the product?

- Distribution – Is the product being sold in the "right" places and in enough places?

Marketing environment considerations

- Competition – Are there a large number of competitors in the market?

- Consumer tastes – Does the new product reflect a trend in society?

- Demographics – Is the new product being marketed to a segment of the population that is growing?

Source: Courtland L. Bovee and John Thill, *Marketing* (New York: McGraw-Hill, 1992), 307–309

activation, sponsored by Hyundai Motor Co., allows fans to get their head into the game through simulations of what it is like to train like an NFL player - from the three cone drill to the 40-yard dash, the parks are consistent with core values, and offer behind-the-scenes action with access to NFL Network, players, and celebrity interactions.

In addition to the product considerations, other marketing mix considerations have also been well thought out for the Super Bowl sports theme parks. The park is bound to generate some excitement prior to the game and further affords a vast array of opportunities for cross-promotion. The marketing environment also appears to be ready for the growth of the theme parks. The NFL Super Bowl is still one of the premier mega-events in the world. The NFL still has a huge and loyal following. Moreover, there are other interactive fan experiences but none with the backing of the NFL, so competition is limited. In summary, the NFL Super Bowl theme parks should perform well. The critical success factors are aligned well with objective measures, but only time will tell whether this new sports product will result in a victory.

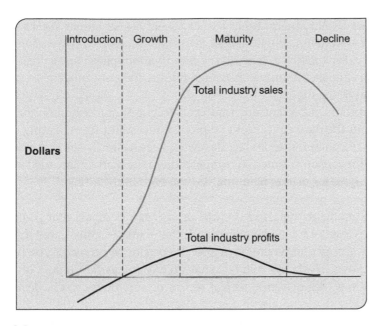

Figure 8.1
Product life cycle

Product life cycle

From the time a sports product begins the new product development process to the time it is taken off the market, it passes through a series of stages known as the **product life cycle** (PLC). The product life cycle was first introduced by Theodore Levitt in 1965 in a *Harvard Business Review* article titled "Exploit the Product Life Cycle."[16] The four distinct stages of the PLC are introduction, growth, maturity, and decline. As shown in Figure 8.1, the traditional PLC was originally developed by marketers to illustrate how the sales and profits of goods vary over time. However, other sports products, such as athletes, teams, leagues, and events, pass through four distinct phases over time. The sport product life cycle often differs from the traditional cycle because it affords sport organizations the opportunity for off-season enhancement. Companies like Dell Computer do not have an off season to further enhance or develop their product. This unique time lapse provides sport marketers the opportunity to modify strategies to enhance the life cycle of the product. Regardless of the nature of the sports product, the PLC is a useful tool for developing marketing strategy and then revising this strategy as a product moves through its own unique life cycle. Authors Rick Burton and Dennis Howard used the product life cycle as a tool to assess the current state of big league sports. Their conclusion was that all four big league sports (baseball, hockey, basketball, and football) have reached either late maturity or decline. The authors speculate that part of the reason for this decline is that professional sports leagues have experienced a variety of conflicting encounters including:

player strikes (MLB, August 1994; NHL, October 1994, September 2004 and 2012), player lockouts (NBA, July 1994, 1998, 2011; NFL, March 2011), player free agency and salary demands (all leagues, all the time), various player arrests, rising ticket prices (an annual custom), stadium referendums, franchise movement, and constant legal wrangling.[17]

The authors also point out that each league should examine its current position in the marketplace and be prepared to adjust its marketing strategy based on the phase of the product life cycle. These issues as well as the increased demand for consumer time and competition in the marketplace further accentuate the need for market planning. As expressed in the article,

> despite all the hype and rhetoric, a case can be made that professional sports leagues are marketable brands that require sophisticated marketing plans and an understanding of how the product is perceived, received, and purchased. If a brand is in late maturity or the earliest phases of decline, then new uses, new product features, or new markets must be developed.

The water bike is an excellent example of a sports product whose life cycle mirrors the shape of the conventional PLC. The water bike, or personal watercraft, had its first commercially successful introduction in the early 1970s. It had tremendous growth in the early 1990s. Sales of water bikes reached their peak in 1995 with 200,000 units sold. However, since then, unit sales have been steadily decreasing. It was not until 2012 that personal watercraft sales had a significant year-over-year increase, with growth of 10 percent. This was after

Photo 8.2
Extending the product life cycle of the water bike
Source: Shutterstock, ID# 158192810 by EpicStockMedia

plateauing at a 10 percent year-over-year decline in the 2011 season.[18] Industry insiders want to believe the water bike is in the maturity phase of the PLC and sales have merely reached their plateau. Others, however, contend the industry has developed an image problem because of the safety and pollution issues associated with the activity. In this case, water bike brands such as Jet Ski and Sea-Doo may need to find ways to extend the life of their products. Makers of personal watercraft have long been committed to changing the product to be more environmentally friendly, quieter, and safer.

Before we explore the four phases of the PLC, keep several important factors in mind. First, the PLC was originally developed to describe product categories, such as water bikes or baseball gloves, rather than specific brands, such as Sea-Doo or Mizuno. Second, the product life cycle was designed to monitor the industry sales and profitability of goods rather than services. Third, the traditional shape and length of the product life cycle are generalized. In other words, they are assumed to look the same for all products. In reality, the length of the PLC varies for each sports product. Some products die quickly, some seem to last forever, and others die and are then reborn. Collectively, these items as well as the opportunity for off-season enhancement require sport marketers to carefully consider the unique PLC of each of their products on the market. Let us now explore how the PLC can be used for decision making in the strategic sports marketing process.

Introduction

When a new sports product first enters the marketplace, the introduction phase of the PLC is initiated. Products such as the Mirror.co, which turns less than two feet of wall space into a personal fitness studio, or new leagues such as the Alliance of American Football (AAF), XFL, and Women's Professional Lacrosse League are excellent examples of sports products being introduced. Another sport product in the introductory phase is Heading Trainer by Soccer Innovations.[19] What makes the Heading Trainer so special? The ball is about half the weight of an ordinary ball and was made to teach kids the proper heading technique without the fear of impact from a regulation ball. Since concussions in all sport are a growing concern, the innovation provides an alternative that is safe and less impactful. If you've ever headed or been hit in the head by a normal soccer ball, you know it's not always the most pleasant feeling. This leads young players to shy away during heading drills, which means often they don't use the proper technique.[20]

The broad marketing goal of the first phase of the PLC for any sport product is to generate awareness and stimulate trial among those consumers who are willing to try new products. Typically, profits are low because of the high start-up costs associated with getting the product ready to market.

During the introduction phase, pricing of the sports product is determined largely by the type of image that has been determined in the positioning strategy. Generally, one of two broad pricing alternatives is usually chosen during the **introduction** of the product. If the product strategy is to gain widespread consumer trial and market share, a lower price is set. This low pricing strategy is termed penetration pricing. However, a higher-priced skimming strategy is sometimes preferred. The advantages of skimming include recouping the early marketing investment and production costs, as well as reinforcing the superior quality usually associated with higher prices.

Distribution of the new product is also highly dependent on the nature of the product. Usually, however, distribution is limited to fewer outlets. That is, there are a small number of places to purchase the product. Incentives are necessary to push the product from the manufacturer to the consumer. Promotion activity is high during the product's introduction to encourage consumers to try the new product. In addition, promotions are designed to provide consumers with information about the new product and to provide a purchase incentive.

Growth

Sales are usually slow as the new product is introduced. With the onset of the **growth** stage, sales of the product increase. In fact, a rapid increase in sales is the primary characteristic of the growth stage of the PLC. Because industry sales are growing, the broad marketing goal is to build consumer preference for the product and continue to extend the product line. Although competition is usually nonexistent or very weak at introduction, more competitors emerge during the growth phase. Promotion must stress the benefits of this brand over competitive brands.

For example, the sport of lacrosse is currently in the growth stage in the U.S. market. Years ago, lacrosse was played only in select East Coast cities and considered a sport for prep schools. For the last decade, according to the SFIA and the U.S. Lacrosse Participation Survey, lacrosse has been one of the fastest-growing team sports in the country. U.S. Lacrosse chapters have been established in 42 states, and nearly 826,000 people played on organized teams in 2017 compared to just over 250,000 in 2001. Overall, lacrosse achieved a total 7.1 percent year-over-year (YOY) increase and a 12.4 percent YOY increase in casual participation. Youth lacrosse is the fastest-growing segment of the sport, and total participation has increased 226 percent since 2001.[21]

Another example of a sport product in the growth phase, where more and more competitors are starting to enter the market, is Ultimate Fighting Championships. A recent UFC Fight Night event served as a driver for ESPN'S direct-to-consumer video service, procuring 568,000 subscriptions over the course of Friday and Saturday evening. This sum made the UFC event the largest event and subscription driver for the direct-to-consumer video service.[22]

When dealing with products in the growth phase, whether it be watching a UFC event on ESPN+, watching a sporting event at the local micro-brewery, engaging in an event through virtual reality, or streaming over the Internet, the product or the innovation becomes accepted in the market, and as a result, sales and revenues start to increase. Markets become more competitive, and businesses need to invest wisely in any marketing they undertake. They also

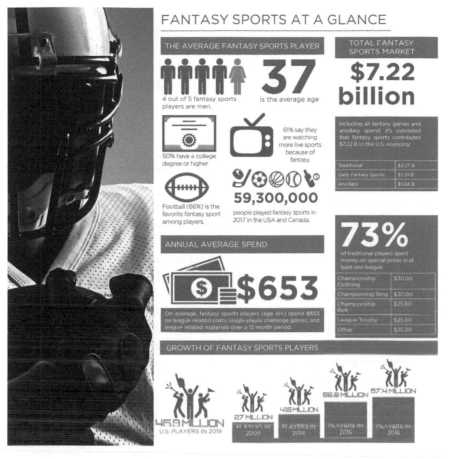

FANTASY SPORTS AT A GLANCE

THE AVERAGE FANTASY SPORTS PLAYER

37 is the average age

4 out of 5 fantasy sports players are men.

50% have a college degree or higher

61% say they are watching more live sports because of fantasy.

Football (66%) is the favorite fantasy sport among players.

59,300,000 people played fantasy sports in 2017 in the USA and Canada.

TOTAL FANTASY SPORTS MARKET

$7.22 billion

Including all fantasy games and ancillary spend, it's estimated that fantasy sports contributes $7.22 B to the U.S. economy:

Traditional	$3.27 B
Daily Fantasy Sports	$2.91 B
Ancillary	$1.04 B

ANNUAL AVERAGE SPEND

$653

On average, fantasy sports players (age 18+) spend $653 on league related costs, single-player challenge games, and league related materials over a 12 month period.

73% of traditional players spent money on special prizes in at least one league.

Championship Clothing	$30.00
Championship Ring	$30.00
Championship Belt	$25.60
League Trophy	$25.00
Other	$25.00

GROWTH OF FANTASY SPORTS PLAYERS

45.9 MILLION U.S. PLAYERS IN 2019

27 MILLION PLAYERS IN 2009

41.5 MILLION PLAYERS IN 2014

56.8 MILLION PLAYERS IN 2015

57.4 MILLION PLAYERS IN 2016

Infographic 8.1
Fantasy sports becoming big business as popularity continues to rise

Source: Fantasy Sports & Gaming Association

URL: https://thefsga.org/wp-content/uploads/2020/06/2020-Press-Kit.pdf

need to consider continuous innovations that include product modifications or improvements to the production process. The goal of marketing efforts at this stage is to differentiate a firm's offerings from other competitors within the industry. Thus, the growth stage requires funds to launch a newly focused marketing campaign as well as funds for continued investment in property, plant, and equipment to facilitate the growth required by the market demands. Normally, the industry is experiencing more product saturation at this stage, which may encourage economies of scale and facilitate development of a line-flow layout for production efficiency. Creating competitive advantages can offset the saturation in the marketplace and prohibit diminishing losses of return on investment.

During the growth stage, product differentiation occurs by making minor changes or modifications in the product or service. A premium is placed on gaining more widespread distribution of the product. Manufacturers must

409

secure outlets and distributors at this early phase of the PLC so the product is readily available. Finally, the prices during the growth phase are sometimes reduced in response to a growing number of competitors or held artificially high to enhance perceived quality. Let us look at some of the strategic decisions discussed thus far in the context of the growth of the fantasy sports industry.

Maturity

Eventually, industry sales begin to stabilize as fewer new consumers enter the saturated market. As such, the level of competition increases as a greater number of organizations compete for a limited or stable number of consumers. The primary marketing objective at **maturity** is to maintain whatever advantages were captured in growth and offer a greater number of promotions to encourage repeat purchases. Brand strategy shifts from "try me" to "buy one more than you used to." Unfortunately, profitability is also lessened because of the need to reduce prices and offer incentives. If attempts to maintain sales and market share are unsuccessful in the maturity stage, an organization may try several alternative strategies to extend the PLC before the product begins to decline and eventually die.

One household sport product in the maturity to decline phase of the product life cycle is the WNBA. These women are some of the most talented and skilled professional athletes in the world, yet, outside of WNBA circles, they remain largely unknown. Many claim the need for marketing to match their product. The trouble is defining that product and quite possibly the market. Is it a basketball, professionalism, competitiveness, or viewership market strategy? As the NBA/WNBA continues to try to figure out a winning formula, executives note that ultimately it is a business issue. Factors such as attendance and seasonal play continue to impact the league; WNBA games averaged 7,716 fans per game in 2017, the highest in six years but far from a significant improvement. WNBA games haven't averaged 8,000 fans per game since 2009, and the 2017 figure was down 28.9 percent from the league's all-time high attendance in 1998, which was the WNBA's second season.[23] Moving the season would be

---

Table 8.4 Extending the product life cycle

- Develop new uses for products.
- Develop new product features and refinements (line extensions).
- Increase the existing market.
- Develop new markets.
- Change marketing mix (e.g., new or more promotion, new or more distribution, and increase or decrease price).
- Link product to a trend.

Source: Joel Evans and Barry Berman, *Marketing*, 6th ed. (New York: Macmillan, 1992), 439

ARTICLE 8.4
UNDER ARMOUR FEELS THE PRESSURE OF THE US SPORTS RETAIL SECTOR

Author: Andria Cheng, emarketer

The slumping sporting goods retail sector is taking a toll on brands. Feeling the pinch is Under Armour, which posted a quarterly sales decline of 5% on Tuesday, its first ever quarterly drop.

Under Armour's direct-to-consumer sales surged 15%, but results were dragged down by a 13% slide in wholesale sales to specialty sports and other retailers.

In a conference call on Tuesday, Chief Executive Kevin Plank noted the challenges faced by the retail sector, describing it as "pinned in a multi-year struggle to evolve past its legacy architecture."

And he was not optimistic about change in the near future. "As we look to close out 2017, we do not expect these conditions to improve," he said.

Under Armour isn't alone. Larger rival Nike recently also reported declining North America fiscal Q1 wholesale revenue that led to flat companywide revenue growth. Meanwhile, in other sectors, toymakers Mattel and Hasbro have also been hurt by the bankruptcy filing of Toys "R" Us.

While bankruptcy filings of retailers from the Sports Authority to Gander Mountain have translated to promotional closeout sales that hurt demand at other retailers and forced other chains to cut their prices, the specialty retail sector is also grappling with the bigger issue of declining store traffic and increased online competition. Dick's Sporting Goods, for instance, is beefing up its own ecommerce site and vows to be more price competitive. To diversify and put more control into their own hands, brands like Under Armour and Nike also are expanding their own online sales or striking new deals with retailers like Kohl's for Under Armour and Amazon for Nike.

However, it's not just struggling retail traffic and increased online competition that's been hurting both Under Armour and Nike. The so-called athleisure trend has led retailers and fashion labels across the board to unveil their own style-oriented athletic collections, which appear to have crimped demand for performance-focused products.

Under Armour's Plank noted the shift to "lifestyle" from performance products, which he said represent some 90% of Under Armour's business. He said the company is seeking to shorten its product cycle time to be more responsive to what consumers want. "We're really focused on having product that's trend-right, style-right, fit-right, color-right and being there in the right place at the right time and at the right price."

But sports brands are dealing with some significant challenges. The basketball sneaker sector, primarily dominated by such shoes as Nike's $150–$200 Air Jordan line, is about "halfway through its five-year downward cycle," said NPD Group's sports industry analyst Matt Powell.

"The category will continue to be a drag on the industry," he said. "With a lack of compelling new technology to drive the performance business, we can expect performance shoes to remain soft for the balance of the year."

Not all major sneaker players are experiencing the same downturn. Adidas, which also owns Reebok, said in its most recent quarterly announcement that its global sales excluding currency impact jumped 19%. The combined sales growth of Adidas and Reebok in North America was 26%.

"Adidas repositioned itself in the U.S. market as a fresh brand with unique product to offer," Powell said. "Adidas will remain in this position for holiday, but, as no other major brands have stepped up, the athletic footwear industry as a whole will be impacted and we can expect overall sales to be soft closing out the year."

https://retail.emarketer.com/article/under-armour-feels-pressure-of-struggling-us-sports-retail-sector/59f8f1a4ebd4000aa48d8eb6

risky, but does holding its season in the summer months create advantages or disadvantages for the league? As NBA Commissioner Adam Silver noted, as the league continues to struggle to engage certain demographics, "we still have a marketing problem, and we gotta figure it out. We gotta figure out how we can do a better job connecting to young people and how they could become interested in women's basketball."[24]

Another illustration of a sport that observed its declining movement, decided to take corrective action, and developed and implemented new marketing strategies is NASCAR, specifically as it relates to sponsorship. Table 8.4 provides additional suggestions for sports marketers who want to extend the PLC.

Decline

The marketing goals for the **decline** stage of the PLC are difficult to pinpoint because decisions must be made regarding what to do with a failing product. These decisions are based largely on the competition and how the sports organization chooses to react to the competition.

The distinctive characteristic of the decline phase of the PLC is that sales are steadily diminishing. Several alternative strategies might be considered during the decline phase. One alternative is referred to as deletion. As the name implies, the product is dropped from the organization's product mix. A second alternative, **harvesting (or milking)**, is when the organization retains the sports product but offers little or no marketing support. A final alternative is simply maintaining the product at its current level of marketing support in the hope that competitors will withdraw from a market that is already in decline.

Other life cycle considerations

The PLC, although an excellent tool for strategic decision making, is not without limitations. These limitations include generalizing the length of the PLC,

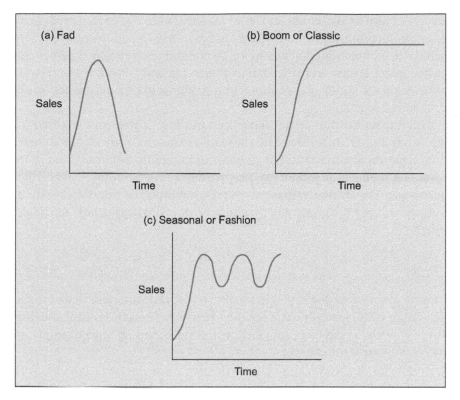

Figure 8.2
Selected product life cycle patterns

applying the PLC to broad product categories only, and using the PLC to ana-lyze "pure" sporting goods only. Each of these potential weaknesses of the PLC model is discussed in the following.

Length and shape of the PLC

Figure 8.1 depicted the traditional length and shape of the PLC. However, each product life cycle has its own unique shape and length, depending on the product under consideration and the nature of the marketing environment. Several variants of the typical PLC length, including the fad PLC, the classic PLC, and the seasonal PLC, are shown in Figure 8.2.

Fad

The **fad** PLC (Figure 8.2a) is characterized by accelerated sales and acceptance of the product followed by the decline stage. Often, sports marketers realize their products will be novelty items that get into the market, make a profit, and then quickly exit. These one-time, short-term offerings follow the volatile fad cycle. The ABA red, white, and blue basketball followed the fad cycle, as do many products in the golf equipment industry. Other examples of a fad cycle include the bobblehead doll as a sports promotion and retro-look jerseys and sports apparel. Fitness and fads seem to go hand in hand. While some exercise routines and machines have endured the test of time to become classics, others come and go in a flash.

High-impact aerobics might have been the first of the more modern fitness fads in the 1970s, followed by the cardio-fitness movement of the 1980s. Then came the incorporation of strength training into workouts, and more recent fads include the indoor cycling program called "spinning" and cardio-kickboxing. The latest and greatest exercise fad links the mind and body in routines such as P90X, yoga, and t'ai chi. Who knows what the next fad might bring?

Classic

Another variation of the PLC is characterized by a continuous stage of maturity (Figure 8.2b). Season tickets for the Green Bay Packers, Frisbees, baseball gloves and bats, tennis balls, and hockey sticks all represent other examples of the PLC known as the **classic**.

Seasonal

The **seasonal** life cycle is found in most sports where the sales of sports products rise and fall with the opening and closing day of the season. To combat the seasonal life cycle, some sports have adopted year-round scheduling. Most auto racing series are run on an 8- to 10-month schedule, giving sponsors almost year-round coverage. Professional tennis has also adopted a continual schedule, but this may not be the best thing for the sport.

When asked what he would do to cure the ills of tennis, former star and current TV analyst John McEnroe did not hesitate before responding,

> I would cut the amount of events. Now, there are too many tournaments, so people don't have any idea about what's really important. I would make a schedule that would be like the baseball or basketball season, so we wouldn't go 12 months a year.[25]

Somewhat surprisingly, the NBA used the "less-is-more" strategy more than 20 years ago, when the league was plummeting in popularity. David Stern, then a rookie commissioner, significantly cut the number of televised games to increase long-term interest in the sport. Numerous leagues have struggled and continue to struggle to balance seasonal life cycle offerings with consumer demand.

The fad, classic, and seasonal life cycles are three common variants of the traditional PLC. Other products, however, seem to defy all life cycle shapes and lengths. Consider skateboarding. Since its inception in the 1940s, skateboarding has been a fad in nearly every decade. As such, the culture of skateboarding has gradually made its way back into the mainstream. Now skateboarding seems to be here to stay. Skateboarding will make its debut at the Summer Olympic Games in Tokyo in 2021. As a result, the sport is likely to remain steady or continue to see growth. According to the National Sporting Goods Association, there were 5.5 million skateboarders in the United States in 2017. Skateboarding posted an unbelievable growth rate in participation for youth ages 7 to 17 from 1995 to 2010. Over that 15-year period, skateboarding has experienced 160 percent growth in total participation and a 213 percent increase in frequent participation and was second only to snowboarding in terms of percentage growth, which experienced 160 percent growth in total participation and a 257 percent increase in frequent participation.[26]

The level of product

Another consideration for developing marketing strategy based on the PLC is the level of the product. Historically, the PLC was based on total industry sales for an entire product category, such as basketball shoes, bowling balls, mountain bikes, or golf clubs. Although examining the PLC by category is useful, it is also necessary to understand the PLC by product form and product brand.

Product form refers to product variations within the category. For example, titanium woods, metal woods, and "wood" woods represent three variations in product form in the golf club product category. The potential marketing strategies for each of these product forms differ by the stage of the PLC. Titanium woods are in the growth stage, metal woods are in decline, and traditional woods are extinct.

In addition to looking at the product category and form, it is also beneficial to examine various brands. Within the titanium wood form, there are a variety of individual brands, such as Titleist, Ping, Taylormade, and Mizuno. Each of these brand's models may be in different stages of the PLC. Therefore, sports marketing managers must give full consideration to variations in the PLC based on the level of the product (category, form, and brand).

Type of product

The PLC was originally designed to guide strategies for goods. However, the notion of the PLC should be extended to other types of sports products. For instance, individual athletes can be thought of as sports products that move through a life cycle just as products do.

The phenomenal rise, success, and some fluctuations of stars like Tom Brady in the NFL, Tiger Woods of the PGA, and Shaun White from the U.S. Olympic Team demonstrate how numerous athletes may waver through the various phases of the product life cycle. The number of products that these stars endorsed has increased because everyone is aware of their star qualities. However, when these athletes become injured, retire, or encounter turmoil, there may be a significant change in their status within the product life cycle. The former Cleveland Cavaliers star LeBron James has gone through an entire life cycle in the Cleveland market. LeBron, even with his recent move to the LA Lakers, continues to retain market presence. At the same time, former New York Knicks and Houston Rockets star Carmelo Anthony, who had the best-selling jersey during the 2012–13 season, is in the decline phase of his PLC. Although trades are being explored, it is uncertain how the PLC will be affected by Anthony's future performance.

Interestingly, some individual athletes have a unique shape to their PLC. Think about former NBA MVP Shaquille O'Neal. He entered the decline phase of his playing career after being traded to the Cleveland Cavaliers in the 2009-10 season and then with the Boston Celtics in the 2010-11 season before retiring. Although Shaq was entering the decline phase of his playing career, numerous outside endeavors such as endorsements, albums, movie and TV appearances, and broadcasting have kept his career outside of basketball in the growth and maturity stages. A number of professional athletes have come out of retirement to reintroduce themselves. Mark Spitz attempted to come back to Olympic swimming 20 years after winning seven gold medals in Munich and was no longer able to compete. Jim Palmer, Bjorn Borg, Sugar Ray Leonard, Magic Johnson, and Muhammad Ali all tried to come back after years away from their respective sports and failed miserably. Arnold Palmer, with his incredible staying power, will undoubtedly stay in the maturity phase of his PLC and remain a classic even after his death. Many aging golfers, such as Tom Jenkins, who has won $10.5 million since 1998 on the senior circuit but won only once on the regular PGA Tour, are experiencing tremendous success on the senior circuit. Unfortunately, many athletes experience a life cycle that is best represented by the fad PLC. For instance, Brian Bosworth (Seattle Seahawks linebacker), Mark "The Bird" Fidrych (Detroit Tigers pitcher), and Buster Douglas (boxing) were all athletes who had short-term success, only to quickly fall into decline for a number of reasons.

Sports teams can also pass through the various phases of the PLC. For instance, the MLS awarded a franchise to Cincinnati, Ohio, in 2018, and it enters the introductory stage of its PLC in MLS, but many would consider this the continued growth stage as a franchise. In 2017, many considered the NFL Raiders to be in the decline phase as their stay in Oakland remained in limbo. When they enter the Las Vegas market, their PLC status will change. Likewise, the Sacramento Kings under previous majority owner the Maloof family were contemplating leaving Sacramento for a new, more appealing market after an

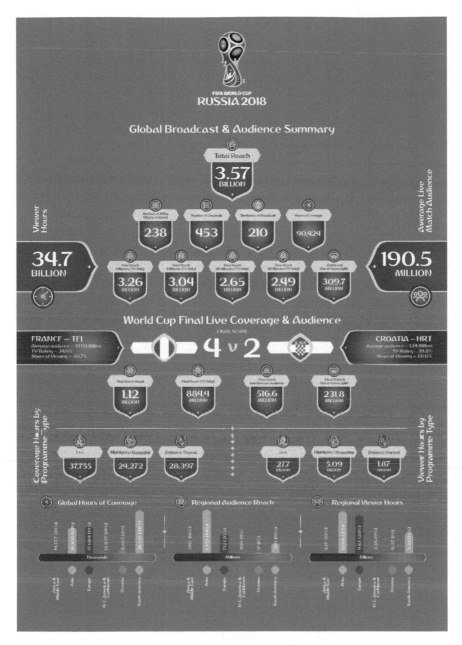

Infographic 8.2
Global broadcast and audience summary, FIFA World Cup Russia 2018

Source: FIFA

impasse in their new arena negotiations. However, the 2013 transaction created an exchange of ownership, offering the organization "an opportunity of adjustment" in the PLC, moving from decline to growth. Under new owner Vivek Ranadive, the Kings have developed new strategies to enhance their brand and its offerings to enhance the growth of the organization. Keep in mind that the revitalization of these product examples would each require completely different marketing strategies.

Professional and collegiate sports leagues also pass through the stages of the PLC. Many of the established leagues in the United States are going global and are currently in the introduction phase of their life cycles internationally. Therefore, the leagues have directed their marketing efforts toward making fans aware of them and generating interest. For example, international markets are attracting a lot of attention by major sports leagues/structures world-wide, as the accompanying infographic illustrates.

Each level of sports product must receive careful consideration by sports marketers because of the strategic implications. Sometimes the interaction of athlete, team, and league PLCs can make strategic decisions even more challenging. Take the case of Zion Williamson, forward for the New Orleans Pelicans in the NBA. The New Orleans Pelicans could be seen to be in the growth phase, and the NBA could be seen to be in the maturity phase of the PLC, while Williamson is at the introductory stage of his career with New Orleans. As complex as this seems, sports marketers must remember not to neglect any of these products. Decisions will be made about the perceived relevance of each of these types of products.

Diffusion of innovations

New sports and sports products, or **innovations**, are continually being introduced to consumers and pass through the various stages of the product life

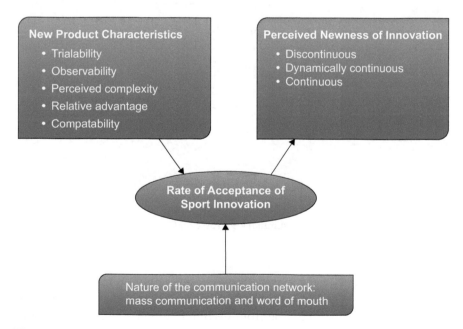

Figure 8.3
Model of the rate of diffusion

cycle, as described in the previous section. Initially, new sports and sports products are purchased or tried by a small number of individuals (roughly 2.5 percent of the marketplace). Then, more and more people begin to try the new product. Consider the "metal wood" in golf. When this innovation was first introduced in the late 1970s, only the boldest "pioneers" of golf were willing to adopt the new technology. Now, every golfer carries metal woods in their bag.[27]

The rate at which new sports products spread throughout the marketplace is referred to as the **diffusion of innovation**.[28] The rate of acceptance of a sport innovation is influenced by three factors, which are shown in Figure 8.3. The first factor affecting the rate of diffusion is the characteristics of the new product. These characteristics, such as trialability, observability, perceived complexity, relative advantage, and compatibility, were discussed earlier in the chapter in the context of new product factors. The interaction of these factors can accelerate or slow the rate of diffusion. Perceived newness, the second factor that influences the rate of diffusion, refers to the type of new product from the consumer's perspective (continuous, dynamically continuous, and discontinuous innovations). Typically, continuous innovations have a faster rate of acceptance because they require no behavioral change and little disruption for the adopter. The third factor is the nature of the communication network. The rate and way in which information is shared about a new sports product are critical to its success, as well as the speed of acceptance. Most marketers conceptualize the communications network for innovations as a two-step flow of information. In the first step, the initial consumers try a new product, or opinion leaders are influenced by mass communication such as advertising, sales promotions, and the Internet. Then, in the second step, opinion leaders use word-of-mouth communication to provide information about the new product to the rest of the target market. Martin and Higgins believe this two-step flow of information is especially important to sports innovations because, "unlike typical consumer purchase decisions, which involve only the individual, recent studies show that of the consumers who attend sporting events, less than 2 percent attend by themselves."[29]

The diffusion of innovations is an important concept for sports marketers to understand because of its strategic implications. Stated simply, the marketer must know the stage of the life cycle and the characteristics of the consumers likely to try the product at any given stage. Let us examine the characteristics of each group as a product spreads throughout the marketplace.

Types of adopters

There are several **types of adopters. Innovators** represent those consumers who are the first to adopt a new sports product as it enters the marketplace. Because they are the first to adopt, these consumers carry the highest risk associated with the new product. These risks may be social (what will others think of the product?), economic (costs are high and drive up the price), and performance (will the product perform as it was intended?). This younger and usually high-income group of consumers is also known for the high degree of interaction and communication they have with other innovators.

The next group of consumers to adopt a new sports product is the **early adopters**. As with the innovators, this group is also characterized by high social status. It is perhaps the most important group to sports marketers, however, because these consumers carry high degrees of opinion leadership and word-of-mouth influence. As just discussed, these individuals are the key players in communicating the value of new sports products to the majority of consumers.

Once the new sports product has spread past the early stages of the product life cycle, the **early majority** is ready for adoption. This group is above average in social status but more deliberate in their willingness to try new products. In addition, this group is heavily influenced by information provided by the innovators and early adopters.

The **late majority** adopt innovations in the late stages of maturity of the product life cycle. As their name implies, over half (roughly 60 percent) of the market has now purchased or tried the new product before the late majority decide to do so. These individuals are skeptical and have less exposure to mass media.

The final group of adopters is known as **laggards**. These individuals are oriented toward the past and tend to be very traditional in the sports products they choose. They begin to adopt products in the declining stage of the product life cycle. Clearly, prices must be reduced, and promotions encouraging trial and widespread distribution must all be in place for laggards to adopt new products.

Summary

Few sports products are critical to the success of any organization. Newness, however, can be thought of in any number of ways. The organizational perspective on newness depends on whether the firm has marketed the product in the past. From the organizational perspective, new products are categorized as follows: new-to-the-world products, new product category entries, product line extensions, product improvements, and repositioning.

Conversely, newness from the consumer's perspective is based on the consumer's perception of whether the product represents an innovation. From the consumer's perspective, new products are classified as discontinuous innovations, dynamically continuous innovations, or continuous innovations. Discontinuous innovations represent the most innovative new products, whereas continuous innovations are simply improvements and often have a faster rate of acceptance.

Regardless of how new products are classified, organizations are constantly searching for the next innovation that will help the firm achieve its financial objectives. Rather than leave this to chance, many organizations use a systematic approach called the new product development process. The new product development process consists of the following phases: idea generation, idea screening, analysis of the concept, developing the sports product, test marketing, and commercialization. Idea generation considers any and all ideas for new products from sources such as employees, competitors, and consumers. During the idea screening phase, these new product ideas are screened, and the poorer ones are eliminated. To perform this task, organizations sometimes use a new product screening checklist. In the third phase, analysis of the sports product concept, marketing research is used to assess consumer reaction to the proposed product. More specifically, concept tests are used to gauge the product's strengths and weaknesses, as well as consumer intent to use the new product. Next, a prototype of the new product is designed so that consumers can get an even better idea about the product. In addition, preliminary decisions regarding marketing strategy are established. In the sixth stage, the new product is test marketed. Depending on the product and the market conditions, sports marketers may use standardized, controlled, or simulated test markets. The final stage of the new product development process is commercialization, in which the new product is formally introduced in the marketplace. Whether the product succeeds is a function of a number of factors, such as product considerations (e.g., trialability and relative advantage), other marketing mix variables (e.g., pricing), and marketing environment considerations (e.g., competition).

As a new product reaches commercialization, it moves through a series of four stages known as the product life cycle. The PLC is an important marketing concept in that the stage of the life cycle dictates marketing strategy. The four stages of the PLC are introduction, growth, maturity, and decline. At introduction, the marketing goal is to generate awareness of the new sports product. The broad goal of the growth phase is to build consumer preference for the sports product and begin to expand the product line. During maturity, the number of promotions is increased, and marketers seek to maintain any competitive advantage they have obtained during growth. Finally, the product goes through decline, where decisions must be made regarding whether to delete the product or extend the life cycle.

Although each product has a life cycle, the length of that life and the speed at which a product progresses through the four stages are unique for each product. Some sports products grow and decline at a rapid pace. These are known as fads. Other products, which seem to last in maturity forever, are called classics. The most common life cycle for sports products is known as seasonal. Other life cycle considerations are the level and type of product. For example, sports marketers might analyze the life cycle of leagues, teams, and individual athletes, as well as other types of sports products.

The rate of diffusion is the speed at which new products spread throughout the marketplace. The rate of diffusion, or speed of acceptance, is based on three broad factors: new product characteristics (e.g., trialability and observability), perceived newness (e.g., discontinuous innovation), and the nature of the communications network. It is critical that sports marketers monitor the rate of diffusion and understand the characteristics of consumers who try new products as they spread throughout the marketplace.

Innovators are the first group of consumers to try a new product. They are generally younger, have higher incomes, and have a strong tolerance for risk. The next group of consumers to try a sports product is the early adopters. This is a larger group than the innovators, and, as such, they are key consumers to target. After the product has passed through the initial stages of the product life cycle, the early majority adopt the product. This group is above average in income but more deliberate in trying new things. The late majority adopts the product during the late stages of maturity, and, finally, the laggards may try new products. Strategically, sports marketers must adopt a different marketing mix when marketing to each new product adopter group.

Key terms

- classic
- commercialization
- continuous innovations
- decline
- developing the sports product
- diffusion of innovation
- discontinuous innovations
- dynamically continuous innovations
- early adopters
- early majority
- fad
- growth
- harvesting (or milking)
- idea generation
- idea screening
- innovations
- innovators
- introduction
- laggards
- late majority
- maturity
- new product category entries
- new product development process
- new product success factors
- new sports products

- new-to-the-world products
- product form
- product life cycle
- seasonal
- test marketing
- types of adopters

Review questions

1   What is meant by a "new sports product"? Describe a "new sports product" from the organization's perspective and from the consumer's perspective.
2   What is the difference between discontinuous, dynamically continuous, and continuous innovations? Provide examples of each to support your answer.
3   Describe, in detail, the new product development process.
4   Why is test marketing so important to sports marketers in the new product development process? What are the three types of test markets? Comment on the advantages and disadvantages of each type of test market.
5   What are the critical success factors for new sports products?
6   Describe the product life cycle concept. Why is the product life cycle so critical to sports marketers? What is it used for? How can the product life cycle be extended?
7   What are some of the variations in the shape of the traditional product life cycle?
8   Define the diffusion of innovations. What are different types of adopters for innovations? Describe the characteristics of each type of adopter.

Exercises

1   For each of the following sports products, indicate whether you believe they are discontinuous, dynamically continuous, or continuous innovations: WNBA, titanium golf clubs, and skysurfing.
2   Contact the marketing department of three sporting goods manufacturers or sports organizations and conduct a brief interview regarding the new product development process. Does each organization follow the same procedures? Does each organization follow the new product development process discussed in the chapter?
3   In what stage of the product life cycle is Major League Baseball? Support your answer with research.
4   Find an example of a "new sports product." Develop a survey using the critical success factors for new sports products and ask 10 consumers to complete the instrument. Summarize your findings and indicate whether you think the new product will be successful based on your research.
5   Some people think boxing may be in the decline phase of the product life cycle. Develop a strategy to extend the product life cycle of boxing.

Internet exercises

1   Search the Internet and find examples of three new sports products recently introduced in the marketplace.

2   Find three web sites of professional athletes in any sport. In what stage of the product life cycle are these athletes? Support with evidence found on the Internet.

3   Search the Internet for an example of a new sports product that could be classified as a fad. Describe the product and why you think the product is a fad.

Notes

1   William Zikmund and Michael d'Amico, *Marketing*, 4th ed. (St. Paul: West, 1993).

2   "Raley Field Pioneers the First Wireless Ballpark; Stadium Launches WiFi-Wireless Technology-Application Throughout Ballpark to Better Serve Fans," *Business Wire* (September 3, 2003).

3   www.learfield.com/2018/12/learfield-img-college-complete-merger/.

4   Donna Goodison, "New Balance Adds Brine to Beef Up Sports Shoes," *The Boston Herald* (August 9, 2006).

5   www.wsj.com/articles/newell-brands-to-sell-rawlings-brands-for-395-million-1528203488.

6   www.independent.co.uk/extras/indybest/outdoor-activity/tennis/best-tennis-rackets-for-beginners-control-under-100-intermediate-players-wilson-babolat-head-a7835226.html.

7   Matt Snyder, "Chicago Approves $500 Million in Renovations to Wrigley Field," *CBSSports.com* (July 24, 2013). Available from: https://www.cbssports.com/mlb/news/chicago-approves-500-million-in-renovations-to-wrigley-field/.

8   James Crabtree-Hannigan, "Dabo Swinney, Nick Saban and the 10 Highest-Paid College Football Coaches in 2019," *Sportingnews.com* (January 13, 2020). Available from: www.sportingnews.com/us/ncaa-football/news/highest-paid-college-football-coaches-2019-dabo-swinney-nick-saban/1tm0hym5dtina1ms02d-4davsfp.

9   Mark Glover, "Taking the Cue – New Billiard Parlors Cater to Family Crowds and Aren't Shy about Giving Hustlers the Heave," *The Sacramento Bee* (January 15, 1996).

10 Don Muret and John Lombardo, "AEG Involved in Massive Moscow Sports Complex," *Street & Smith's Sports Business Journal* (March 28–April 3, 2011). Available from: www.sportsbusinessdaily.com/Journal/Issues/2011/03/28/Facilities/AEG-Russia.aspx?hl=All%20Sport&sc=0, accessed June 19, 2014.

11 Del Hawkins, Roger Best, and Kenneth Coney, *Consumer Behavior: Building Marketing Strategy*, 7th ed. (New York: McGraw-Hill, 1998), 248–250.

12 James J. Zhang, Dennis W. Smith, Dale G. Pease, and Matthew T. Mahar, "Spectator Knowledge of Hockey as a Significant Predictor of Game Attendance," *Sport Marketing Quarterly*, vol. 5, no. 3 (1996), 41–48.

13 Susan Higgins and James Martin, "Managing Sport Innovations: A Diffusion Theory Perspective," *Sport Marketing Quarterly*, vol. 5, no. 1 (1996), 43–50.

14 Bill Richards, "Nike Plans to Swoosh into Sports Equipment but It's a Tough Game," *The Wall Street Journal* (January 6, 1998), A1.

15 Gilbert Churchill, *Basic Marketing Research*, 3rd ed. (Fort Worth: Dryden Press, 1996).

16 Theodore Levitt, "Exploit the Product Life Cycle," *Harvard Business Review* (November 1965).

17 Rick Burton and Dennis Howard, "Professional Sports Leagues: Marketing Mix Mayhem," *Marketing Management*, vol. 8, no. 1 (1999), 37.

18 "PWC Sales Improving in 2012," *PowerSportsBusiness* (September 25, 2012). Available from: http://www.powersportsbusiness. com/top-stories/2012/09/25/pwc-sales-improving-in-2012/.

19 www.sportsproductreview.com/.

20 Ibid.

21 SFIA, "SFIA 2013 Participation Topline Report" (2013). Available from: www.uslacrosse.org/sites/default/files/public/documents/about-us-lacrosse/participation-survey-2017.pdf.

22 Front Office Sports (January 21, 2019). Available from: https://frntofficesport.com/.

23 www.washingtonpost.com/news/early-lead/wp/2018/04/20/adam-silver-one-of-the-wnbas-problems-is-that-not-enough-young-women-pay-attention-to-it/?utm_term=.87ce730eefdf.

24 Ibid.

25 David Hidgon, "Trim the Season to Grow the Game," *Tennis* (November 1996), 22.

26 "The Action Sports Market," *Active Marketing Group* (2007).

27 James P. Sterba, "Your Golf Shots Fall Short? You Didn't Spend Enough," *The Wall Street Journal* (February 23, 1996), B7.

28 Everett Rogers, *Diffusion of Innovations*, 3rd ed. (New York: Free Press, 1983).

29 Bernard J. Mullin, Stephen Hardy, and William Sutton, *Sports Marketing* (Champaign, IL: Human Kinetics Publishers, 1993).

Promotion concepts

After completing this chapter, you should be able to:

- Identify the promotion mix tools.
- Describe the elements of the communication process.
- Understand the promotion planning model.
- Compare the advantages and disadvantages of the various promotional mix tools.
- Understand the importance of integrated marketing communication to sports marketers.

Just ask anyone the first thing that comes to mind when they think of sports marketing, and they are likely to say advertisements produced by corporations such as Nike, Gatorade, and Anheuser Busch or events such as the World Cup, Super Bowl, the Masters, Daytona 500, and March Madness. Many of these advertisers utilize star athletes to endorse their products. Sports and sports celebrities have become a major spectacle of today's media culture. Sports celebrities have been looked upon as role models for decades, and with the technological advances in broadcast and interactive media, it appears that the famous and not-so-famous athletes are everywhere.[1] Some of the most widely utilized advertising spokespersons include famous athletes such as Lionel Messi (adidas, Gatorade, Huawei, Mastercard, Pepsi), Michael Jordan (Nike, Hanes, Gatorade, Upper Deck), Tiger Woods (Nike), LeBron James (Nike, Gatorade), Peyton Manning (Nike, Papa Johns, Nationwide, DirecTV, Gatorade), and Serena Williams (Audemars Piguet, Beats Electronics, Wilson Sporting Goods, Bumble, JPMorgan Chase). While many of the wealthy athletes make most of their money from endorsements, Floyd Mayweather makes the majority of his money from salary or winnings. Mayweather blew away the competition in 2017 by earning $285 million, which was driven almost entirely by his boxing match against UFC star Conor McGregor. Mayweather did not compete professionally over the past year.[2] As we have discussed, sports marketing is much

DOI: 10.4324/9780429030673-12

more than advertisements using star athlete endorsers. It involves developing a sound product or service, pricing it correctly, and making sure it is available to consumers when and where they ask for it. However, the necessary element that links the other marketing mix variables together is promotion.

Typically, the terms *promotion* and *advertising* are used synonymously. **Promotion**, however, includes much more than traditional forms of advertising. It involves all forms of communication to consumers. For many organizations, sports are quickly becoming the most effective and efficient way to communicate with current and potential target markets. The combination of tools available to sports marketers to communicate with the public is known as the promotional mix and consists of the following **promotion mix elements**:

- *Advertising* - a form of one-way mass communication about a product, service, or idea, paid for by an identified sponsor.
- *Personal selling* - an interactive form of interpersonal communication designed to build customer relationships and produce sales or sports products, services, or ideas.
- *Sales promotion* - short-term incentives usually designed to stimulate immediate demand for sports products or services.
- *Public or community relations* - evaluation of public attitudes, identification of areas within the organization in which the sports population may be interested, and building of a good "image" in the community.
- *Sponsorship* - investing in a sports entity (athlete, league, team, event, and so on) to support overall organizational objectives, marketing goals, and more specific promotional objectives.

Within each of the promotion mix elements are more specialized tools to aid in reaching promotional objectives. For example, sales promotions can take the form of sweepstakes, rebates, coupons, or free samples. Advertising can take place on Twitter, Instagram, Facebook, or television; in print; or as stadium signage. Sponsors might communicate through an athlete, team, or league. Each of these promotional tools is a viable alternative when considering the most effective promotion mix for a sports organization. Regardless of which tool we choose, the common thread in each element of the promotion mix is communication. Because communication is such an integral part of promotion, let us take a more detailed look at the communications process.

Communications process

The communications process is an essential element for all aspects of sports marketing. **Communication** is the process of establishing a commonness of thought between the sender and the receiver. To establish this "oneness" between the sender and the receiver, the sports marketer's message must be transmitted via the complex communications process.

The interactive nature of the communications process allows messages to be transmitted from sports marketer (source) to consumer (receiver) and from consumer (source) to sports marketer (receiver). Traditionally, sports marketers' primary means of communication to consumers has been through the various promotion mix elements (e.g., advertisements, sponsorships, sales promotions, and salespeople). Sports marketers also communicate with consumers via other elements of the marketing mix.

ARTICLE 9.1
SPORTS MARKETING HALL OF FAME

Bill Veeck

Bill Veeck undoubtedly changed the landscape of sports marketing. Because of his efforts, Veeck is often known and referred to as the Promotion King of Baseball. While the teams and organizations that Bill Veeck was a part of changed, his ingenious marketing ideas stayed true. We all are very aware of a multitude of promotional events that take place throughout the course of a sporting event. We have Bill Veeck to thank for that.

The best part about Veeck's eccentric marketing ideas would be the fact that he always had the fans in mind. He was always thinking about new and exciting ways to get the fans involved. One way he quite literally got the fans involved would be when he hosted the "Grandstand Manager's Day." Zach Taylor, who was the then manager of the St. Louis Browns, was able to take the day off from his typical roles during a game thanks to Bill Veeck. The fans were given large cards that basically instructed the team on how to play the game. The cards could tell the team and the manager when to steal a base, when to bunt, or even when to change pitchers. It really gave the fans the experience of being "in the game."

One of Veeck's most memorable promotions took place on August 19, 1951, when a pinch-hitter was announced in the bottom half of the first inning in a game between the St. Louis Browns and the Detroit Tigers. Over the furious objections of the Detroit manager, Red Rolfe, the batter was declared a legitimate member of the Browns. Bill Veeck, then owner of the Browns, cautioned his pinch-hitter before he left the dugout that "I've got a man in the stands with a high-powered rifle, and if you swing he'll fire." What was the fuss? Veeck sent in a 3-foot-7-inch man named Eddie Gaedel to pinch-hit for the Browns. Gaedel was promptly walked on four straight pitches and removed from the game for a pinch-runner. Gaedel was quoted as saying, "For a minute, I felt like Babe Ruth."

Veeck is responsible for several of the events and various "promotional nights" that still exist today. Some of these include "Ladies Night" and "Straight-A Night." These two events have held a very positive existence in ballparks for several years. One night, however, that did not have quite the success was "Disco Demolition Night."

"Disco Demolition Night" was one of Bill Veeck's infamous marketing endeavors. The idea of this night was for the fans to bring their disco albums to the park to eventually be burned in a bonfire after the game. The plan could have been a good one, had it not been for the riot that broke out when the fans stormed the field. This caused the White Sox to be forced to forfeit the second game of the day's doubleheader.

Nonetheless, Bill Veeck helped fill the stands for a number of different organizations by providing various forms of entertainment to all types of fans. In fact, Bill even hosted a "Good Old Joe Earley Night" that helped honor the "average Joe" fan. It is no question that Bill's fan-oriented marketing ideas set the tone for today's promotional events.

Source: Adapted from Bill Veeck, *Veeck as in Wreck: Autobiography of Bill Veeck* (New York: Simon and Schuster, 1962)

For example, the high price of a NASCAR Cup Series ticket communicates that it is a higher-quality event than the more inexpensive Xfinity Series. In addition to sports marketers communicating with consumers, consumers communicate back to sports marketers through their behavior. Most notably, consumers communicate whether they are satisfied with the sports product by their purchase behavior. In other words, they attend sporting events and purchase sporting goods.

The communications process begins with the source or the sender of the message. The source encodes the message and sends it through one of many potential communications media. Next, the message is decoded by the receiver of the message, and finally, feedback is given to the original source of the message. In the ideal world, messages are sent and interpreted exactly as intended. This, however, rarely occurs because of noise and interference.

Figure 9.1 shows a simplified diagram of the communications process. Each box in the figure represents one of the **elements in the communications process**. These elements are the sender, encoding, message, medium, decoding, receiver, feedback, and noise. To maximize communication effectiveness, it is necessary to have a better understanding of each of these elements in the communications process.

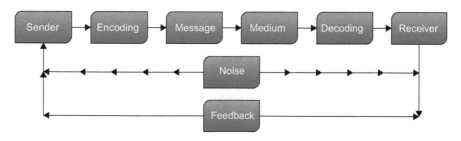

Figure 9.1
Communication process

Source: Solomon, Michael R., *Consumer Behavior*, 3rd Edition, © 1996, p. 194, Prentice-Hall

Source

The sender or **source** of the message is where the communication process always originates. In sports marketing, the source of messages is usually a star athlete. For example, you might think of Maria Sharapova shooting pictures with her Canon or Troy Polamalu washing his long hair with Head & Shoulders. Recently, Forbes published its rankings of the top 100 highest-paid athletes in 2019. The list collectively earned in excess of $4 billion over the last 12 months, of which 12.5 percent or $987 million was attributed to endorsement deals.[3] The list of elite athletes consists of players from 10 different sports and 25 different countries. A 2001 study conducted in California found that a photograph of the back of Michael Jordan's head was more recognizable to people than the faces of Bill Clinton, Newt Gingrich, and Jesus Christ.[4] Manata (2013) explained, while this may be hard to believe, it is the result of the widespread use of celebrity endorsements that causes people to see pictures or video of someone like Michael Jordan far more than some political, economic, or historical figures.[5]

Although these sources are all individual athletes, there are many other sources of sports marketing messages. The source of a message might also be a group of athletes, a team, or even the league or sports. Additional sources of sports marketing messages are company spokespeople such as John Solheim, the chairman of Ping Golf, or owners such as Mark Cuban of the Dallas Mavericks.

Sources do not always have to be well recognized and famous individuals to be effective. Sports marketers use actors playing the role of common, everyday sports participants to deliver their message from the perspective of the representative consumer of the sports product or service. Other effective sources are inanimate objects, such as the mascots affiliated with sport teams, leagues, and agencies. In addition, sports marketers rely on sales personnel to convey the intended message to consumers. Informal sources, such as friends, family, and coworkers, are also sources of marketing information and messages. As we learned in Chapters 4 and 5, reference groups play an important role in influencing purchase behavior and transmitting the marketing message.

Whatever the source, it is agreed by researchers that to be effective, the source must be credible. **Credibility** is the source's perceived expertise and trustworthiness. A very persuasive message can be created when a combination of these two factors (expertise and trustworthiness) is present in the source. For a source to be trustworthy, that person must be objective and unbiased. Certain athlete endorsers, such as former stars Peyton Manning, coach Mike Ditka, and Michael Jordan, are known for their perceived trustworthiness; however, others may seem more controversial. We sometimes look to friends and family as information sources because of their objectivity. In fact, word-of-mouth communication is believed to be extremely persuasive because the source of the message has nothing to gain from delivering the message. Additional unbiased sources are those "man-on-the-street" testimonies given by the common consumer. For example, many of us have seen infomercials that use "regular people" to describe how they lost weight or became physically fit by using the latest and greatest fitness equipment.

Source credibility is also enhanced when the sender of the message has perceived expertise. Naturally, an athlete such as LeBron James is believed to deliver expert messages when the product being promoted is related to athletics or, more specifically, basketball. At least, this is what Nike is counting on.

LeBron James, one of the NBA's most popular players, came directly out of high school and signed the richest shoe endorsement deal that any NBA rookie had ever signed. Nike signed James to a $90-million endorsement contract, narrowly beating out adidas, which was the sponsor of James's high school team. James signed endorsement deals with a range of other top companies. The NBA's top 10 earners made an estimated $540 million from salaries, endorsements, appearances, royalties, and media pacts, which is up more than $180 million for hoops' top earners from five years ago. James is the NBA's highest-paid player for the fifth straight year, earning $88.7 million, $53 million of which is off the court. Kobe Bryant was the last active basketball player to outearn King James,[6] and time will tell how his image will be used after his untimely death.

Other examples of athletes who endorse products related to their sport include current as well as former race car drivers such as Dale Earnhardt Jr. promoting Mountain Dew, Chevrolet, or Nationwide Insurance; Aaron Rodgers with State Farm; and tennis players such as Roger Federer promoting Nike tennis equipment. The general rule of thumb is that the message is more effective if there is a match-up, or congruence, between the qualities of the endorser and the product being endorsed. In fact, the **match-up hypothesis** states that the more congruent the image of the endorser with the image of the product being promoted, the more effective the message.

If the match-up hypothesis holds true, then why do companies pay millions of dollars to star athletes to promote their nonathletic products? For example, tennis star Maria Sharapova's style and beauty led to endorsement deals with fashion company Cole Haan and watch maker Tag Heuer, and golfer Phil Mickelson is an endorser for Rolex. First, consumers have an easier time identifying brands associated with celebrity athletes. Second, athletes are used to differentiate competing products that are similar in nature. For instance, most consumers know and associate Cristiano Ronaldo with Nike (with a deal reported at an estimated $1 billion over his lifetime). Ronaldo's association helps to create and maintain the desired image of Nike, which in turn differentiates it from other industry suppliers such as adidas.

Encoding

After the source is chosen, encoding takes place. **Encoding** is translating the sender's thoughts or ideas into a message. To ensure effective encoding, the source of the message must make difficult decisions about the message content. Will the receiver understand and comprehend the message as intended? Will the receiver identify with the message? In 1974, adidas launched its "Impossible Is Nothing" campaign. Originating from a quote taken from the great Muhammad Ali, the notation has been a powerful adidas slogan for many years, and many people will continue to remember the brand with the same philosophy for a long time to come. In 2011, adidas brought together sport, street, and style for the very first time, collectively highlighting that the company was willing to go "All in" for the consumer.[7] The campaign was the biggest marketing push in the brand's history. The premise behind the push was to create intimacy between their assets and the brand's fans and consumers. The goal was to help them create and enhance their own style while giving them the latest news on hot trends.[8] The plan was part of their strategic business plan – called Route 2015 – where the company set social and environmental targets that aimed to shape how they would grow and meet their business goals.[9] Today, sports-centric activities predominantly revolve around social media and community connect programs, which have helped adidas be one of the biggest players in sportswear. Adidas wants to close in on the market leader, that is, of course, a name familiar to many: Oregon-based Nike, who recently refined their "Just Do It" campaign. adidas, in response, launched "Creating the New" campaign. They believe that, through sport, they have the power to change lives. The company's "Creating the New" program is not only the attitude they hope will lead them into the future, it is also the name of their strategic business plan until the year 2020 to enhance their mission. They have introduced a number of strategic choices, such as speed, how they deliver; cities, where they deliver; and open source, how they create. In addition, they have introduced initiatives Portfolio, North America, Digital, and ONE adidas, that focus on enhancing corporate culture and marketing implementation strategies. At its core, adidas's "Creating the New" stands for an ambition to further drive top- and bottom-line growth by significantly increasing brand desirability. They are focusing on their brands as they connect and engage with consumers.[10]

Sources have a variety of tools that they use to encode messages. They can use pictures, logos, words, and other symbols. Symbols and pictures are often used in sports marketing to convey the emotional imagery that words cannot capture. The most effective encoding uses multiple media to get the message across (i.e., visually and verbally); presents information in a clear, organized fashion; and always keeps the receiver in mind.[11]

ARTICLE 9.2
SPOTLIGHT ON SPORTS MARKETING ETHICS

How brands should use celebrities for endorsements

It's not a new idea in marketing; celebrity endorsements sell products. And while not all brands subscribe to the celebrity endorsement theory, it's based in pretty simple logic.

433

People idolize celebrities, so when famous people are seen in advertisements promoting a new product, audiences are prompted to buy that product, either subliminally or directly.

There are methods to fine tune the effectiveness of endorsements, however, that lead to bigger impact. Here's a look at how brands can use celebrities to boost their sales:

The effects of endorsements on sales and loyalty

The potential positive effects on product sales cannot be understated. According to a Marketwatch claim in Social Media Week, just one endorsement can spell an increase in sales by 4%, almost immediately. That's why businesses, even small businesses would be foolish to resist the mere exploration of celebrity influencers to promote their brand. The effects would be substantial if the brand could find a prominent name who influences their audience.

When it comes to affecting brand loyalty one study entitled "Impact of celebrity endorsements on consumer brand loyalty: Does it really matter?" found that while the use of celebrity endorsers does not necessarily influence consumer brand loyalty celebrity, "endorsements are a powerful and useful tool that magnifies the effect of a campaign."

Celebrities inspire consumer confidence

The brand value added by celebrities is immediate and palpable. When a celebrity signs an endorsement deal with a product, an element of legitimacy is suddenly present in the company, simply because of the power of the name backing it up.

According to Ad Age, a brand that inks an endorsement contract with a celebrity or an athlete can see their stock rise up to .25 as soon as the news is made public. This represents an increase in perceived legitimacy from the celebrity's endorsement, even though the product has not changed at all.

The same article claims that on average, audiences are exposed to some 3,000 advertisements today across all media, leading to an element of marketing overexposure. Studies have shown that advertisements that use a celebrity, about whom many people already have positive feelings and impulses, grab an audience's attention more easily than a standard ad.

Endorsements have to be targeted accurately

It seems obvious, but in order for their impact to be shown, endorsements have to have a similar target audience that the "influencer" has to begin with. As Convince and Convert notes, using celebrities or athletes to promote something that their audience has little interest in will not produce a big marketing splash.

For example, you wouldn't see LeBron James promoting, say, makeup. He's one of the biggest stars on the planet, and yet without his celebrity being targeted accurately towards the potential users of products promoted by him, his effect will be relatively small. That's why athletes are typically used to promote products used in their fields, such as sports drinks or recovery products.

From the celebrity or athlete's perspective many times there has to be a cultural and values fit. "When it comes to endorsements, I work with brands that I feel align with my values," Hall of Fame Wide Receiver Jerry Rice told me a few years ago. "I accept ambassador roles with companies who have products I use or wear so that the relationship is authentic and not forced. You are agreeing to represent a certain company and you have a responsibility to represent them in the best possible way."

Celebrities carry a brand of their own

If the "influencer" has enough brand power of their own, they don't even need to explicitly endorse a product to see the effects of their influence on sales or to be used in promotional materials.

Take, for example, one major U.K. eyewear retail brand who decided to help its customers who have a penchant for British royalty. It's not that the Queen and her ilk have come right out and endorsed this particular brand, but they are smartly piggybacking on the strong brand of the royal family.

In this scenario, a retailer has keyed in on the influences that their customers find in everyday life, and offered a downloadable style guide to match their eyewear to one of the world's most prominent families.

Words of caution

It is important to remember to not forgo other marketing channels to focus on endorsements. As impactful as the presence of influencers is, it still needs to remain just a portion of a multi-channel approach in order to maximize its impact on the audience of a particular brand.

It is equally important to note that a celebrity endorsement alone does guarantee success. As the aforementioned "Impact of celebrity endorsements . . . " study astutely points out, "It is the combination of several factors especially the price and other elements that work together for the success of a brand and its acceptance in the minds of consumers as well as for its market offering."

And yes one of those "other elements" most assuredly means you better have a good product to start with else none of this matters.

Source: Steve Olenski Contributor, CMO Network. Published July 20, 2016

From Forbes. © 2016 Forbes. All rights reserved. Used under license

www.forbes.com/sites/steveolenski/2016/07/20/how-brands-should-use-celebrities-for-endor sements/#5f485ac25593

Message

The next element in the communications process is to develop the **message**, which refers to the exact content of the words and symbols to be transmitted to the receiver. Decisions regarding the characteristics of this message depend on the objective of the promotion, but sports marketers have a wide array of choices. These choices include one- versus two-sided messages, emotional versus rational messages, and comparative versus noncomparative messages.

The **sidedness** of a message is based on the nature of the information presented to the target audience. The messages can be constructed as either one- or two-sided. In a one-sided message, only the positive features of the sports product are described, whereas a two-sided message includes both the benefits and weaknesses of the product.

Another decision regarding the message in the promotion is whether to have an **emotional versus rational appeal**. A rational appeal provides consumers with information about the sports product so they may arrive at a careful, analytical decision, and an emotional appeal attempts to make consumers "feel" a certain way about the sports product. Emotional appeals might include fear, sex, humor, or feelings related to the hard work and competitive nature of sport.

A final message characteristic that may be considered by sports marketers is **comparative messages**. Comparative messages refer to either directly or indirectly comparing your sports product with one or more competitive products in a promotional message. For example, golf ball manufacturers often compare the advantages of their product with competitors' products.

Regardless of the **message characteristics**, the broad objective of promotion is to effectively communicate with consumers. What are some ways to make your sports marketing message more memorable and persuasive? Table 9.1 summarizes a few simple techniques to consider.

Table 9.1 Creating a more effective message

- Get the audience aroused.
- Give the audience a reason for listening.
- Use questions to generate involvement.
- Cast the message in terms familiar to your audience and build on points of interest.
- Use thematic organization – tie material together by a theme and present in a logical, irreversible sequence.
- Use subordinate category words – that is, more concrete, specific terms.
- Repeat key points.
- Use rhythm and rhyme.
- Use concrete rather than abstract terms.
- Leave the audience with an incomplete message – something to ponder so they have to make an effort at closure.
- Ask your audience for a conclusion.
- Tell the audience the implications of their conclusion.

Source: James MacLachlan, "Making a Message Memorable and Persuasive," *Journal of Advertising Research,* vol. 23 (December 1983–January 1984), 51–59

Medium

After the message has been formulated, it must be transmitted to receivers through a channel, or communications **medium**. A voice in personal selling, the Internet, television, radio, stadium signage, billboards, blimps, newspapers, magazines, athletes' uniforms, and even athlete's bodies all serve as media for sports marketing communication. In addition to these more traditional media, new communications channels such as social media and the multitude of sports-specific cable programming (e.g., the Golf Channel) are emerging and growing in popularity.

Decisions on which medium or media to choose depend largely on the overall promotional objectives. Also, media decisions must consider the costs to reach the desired target audience, the medium's flexibility, its ability to reach a highly defined audience, its lifespan, the sports product or service complexity, and the characteristics of the intended target market. These media considerations are summarized in Table 9.2. For example, sports marketers attempting to reach the African American market may choose television as a communications medium because this market watches more television than average households. In addition, the African American market watches more WNBA, NBA, and college basketball than the average household. Furthermore, a decision to target women may include advertising specific to the NFL. American women watch the NFL more than MLB and the NBA. In the past decade, the NFL has launched several marketing and outreach programs such as coaching clinics, women's apparel, and the donning of pink during Breast Cancer Awareness Month to target the female viewing audience. This target audience has grown from 32.6 percent in 2006[12] to over 45 percent in 2018.[13]

As Table 9.3 illustrates, there was a record number of viewers for Super Bowls XLIX, XLVIII, and 50. In fact, each of these Super Bowls successfully became the most-watched television program of all time in the United States, recording 114.44, 112.19, and 111.86 million viewers, respectively.[14] As this number increased, the gap between male and female viewers shrank. Forty-six percent

---

Table 9.2 Making media decisions

- Cost to reach target audience
- Flexibility of media
- Ability to reach highly specialized, defined audience
- Lifespan of the media
- Nature of the sports product being promoted (e.g., complexity of product)
- Characteristics of the intended target market

Source: Nielsen 2019

Table 9.3 Most-watched programs in U.S. television history

No.	Show	Viewership	Date	Network
1	Super Bowl XLIX	114,442,000	February 1, 2015	NBC
2	Super Bowl XLVIII	112,191,000	February 2, 2014	Fox
3	Super Bowl 50	111,864,000	February 7, 2016	CBS
4	Super Bowl XLVI	111,346,000	February 5, 2012	NBC
5	Super Bowl LI	111,319,000	February 5, 2017	Fox
6	Super Bowl XLV	111,041,000	February 6, 2011	Fox
7	Super Bowl XLVII	108,693,000	February 3, 2013	CBS
8	Super Bowl XLIV	106,476,000	February 7, 2010	CBS
9	M*A*S*H ("Goodbye, Farewell and Amen")	105,970,000	February 28, 1983	CBS
10	Super Bowl LII	103,471,000	February 4, 2018	NBC

Source: Nielsen 2019. "Historical Super Bowl Viewership." Nielsen Media Research. February 4, 2019. Archived from the original on February 5, 2019. Retrieved July 14, 2019. https://web.archive.org/web/20190205000209/www.nielsen.com/us/en/insights/news/2019/super-bowl-liii-draws-98-2-million-tv-viewers-32-3-million-social-media-interactions.html

of the Super Bowl audience was female, while approximately 54 percent of the U.S. audience was male, and about 11 percent of the U.S. audience was African American. For Super Bowl XLIX, there was a continuation of success, as it became the most-watched program in U.S. history. This is the fourth time in five years that the Super Bowl has reached record audiences. The Super Bowl claims the top eight spots for the most-watched TV programs, the CBS series finale for M*A*S*H claims the ninth spot, and the Super Bowl reclaims the tenth spot.[15] In comparison, on an international level, it is estimated that 1 billion people tuned in to watch portions of the 2019 Women's FIFA World Cup, while a combined 3.572 billion viewers watched a portion of the 2018 Men's FIFA World Cup.[16]

Decoding

The medium carries the message to the receiver, which is where decoding takes place. **Decoding**, performed by the receiver, is the interpretation of the message sent by the source through the channel. Once again, the goal of communication is to establish a common link between sender and receiver. This can only happen if the message is received and interpreted correctly. Even if the message is received by the desired target audience, it may be interpreted differently because of the receiver's personal characteristics and past experience. In addition, the more complex the original message, the less likely it is to be successfully interpreted or decoded. As the accompanying article illustrates, decoding often varies among consumers, and sometimes proper decoding can lead to questionable interpretations of ads as well as a range of interpretations.[17]

ARTICLE 9.3
SPOTLIGHT ON SPORTS MARKETING ETHICS

The top 8 most recent controversial ads

Have you ever seen an advert that has left you scratching your head? Well, you're not the only one.

Advertising can often be very hit or miss depending on the target audience and the marketing team in charge. Sometimes marketing departments can hit the nail on the head and deliver an incredible marketing campaign to impress their client and boost sales.

Other times, marketing departments can get it completely wrong and produce terrible adverts that cause a lot of controversies, often resulting in a boycott and loss of sales.

Over the decades, there have been multiple examples of companies delivering terrible campaigns which have been talked about for all the wrong reasons. These whoopsies can affect any company no matter how big or small and have lasting impressions.

To give you an idea of terrible ad campaigns that have caused a lot of controversies, we're taking a look at some of the most memorable commercials and ads from recent memory.

In no particular order, here are the top most controversial ads from the past decade, including some controversial ads that worked!

Protein World – beach body

The Ad: Starting off our list is this beach body ad campaign by health supplement supplier Protein World. Released in 2015 across London and New York billboards, the ads pictured a bikini-clad girl with the slogan "Are you beach body ready?". The idea was to promote their supplements to users who wanted the perfect beach body for summer. However, the ad quickly received plenty of backlash via social media and even resulted in many passersby vandalizing and writing over the ad.

The Problem: The problem with this ad campaign was the fact that is promoted "body shaming". Many feminist groups noted that the wording of the ad insinuates that the body in the picture is the only "acceptable" beach body. This means that any other body type not like the one in the picture is "unready".

Despite the backlash from the public the ad received a lot of publicity and press coverage. Protein World went on to make a reported £1 million profit from the £250,000 they spent on the advertising campaign. Although it caused a lot of controversy around the world, it somehow still managed to boost the company's sales. Hopefully next time they run an ad campaign they'll be able to get the same success without offending as many people as possible.

Bud Light – #upforwhatever

The Ad: The ad in question, (that you can watch above) looks pretty harmless and normal regarding how most commercials go. A random guy gets asked to do something, and he goes along with it since he's "up for whatever". In a series of events (and short ads) he ends up playing table tennis with Arnold Schwarzenegger at a OneRepublic concert (like you do). No violence, no swearing, no nudity. What could possibly be controversial about this ad?

The Problem: If you've watched the commercial above, then it might not seem controversial, but it wasn't the TV commercial itself that was the problem. Instead, it was the overall premise of the ad campaign, especially with the hashtag #upforwhatever. The printed messages on the beers themselves actually said "the perfect beer for removing no from your vocabulary for the night".

Considering the role alcohol frequently plays in rape cases, it definitely wasn't the best idea to promote that kind of message on the side of their beers. The ad received a lot of backlash from customers who said the campaign "encouraged and promoted rape" by printing those messages on their bottles. In the end, Bud Light apologised and pulled the entire campaign. Hopefully next time they'll think twice about what their campaigns are telling customers to do.

Pepsi – live for now

The Ad: Pepsi is known for their high budget ads which usually feature famous faces such as Lionel Messi, Beyonce, Pink, Michael Jackson, and Beckham to name a few. This ad was no different and featured celebrity fashion icon, Kendall Jenner. Released in 2017, the ad (which you can watch above) shows Kendall joining a protest outside after removing her black wig and makeup. She then proceeds to give a can of Pepsi to a police officer during a stand-off who then smiles and the crowd cheers. Kendall Jenner has saved the day, all thanks to Pepsi!

The Problem: During the time the advert was released, there were many protests and riots taking place in America over the #BlackLivesMatter campaign. The ad took a lot of "inspiration" from these protests and fundamentally undermined the whole point of the protests. In addition to this, the ad also received a lot of criticism for how Pepsi was responsible for "saving the day". Within 24 hours of releasing the ad, Pepsi faced a lot of criticism from online users over the ad and had to release an official statement while also pulling the ad.

Nivea – white is purity

The Ad: Nivea is a German skincare brand that is known for manufacturing antiperspirants, face creams, and plenty of other cosmetics. To promote one of their new invisible antiperspirants, Nivea decided to use the tagline "white is purity" on their social media campaign. The ad featured a woman wearing a white top while looking out the window with the slogan in bold blue letters. This ad was just one of a number of other ads from the same campaign to promote their new product.

The Problem: As you can probably see from the advert above, the choice of words for this campaign were very poorly chosen. To make things worse, they specifically aimed the campaign at people in the Middle East which caused many people to call the advert racist. In addition to this, many right-wing groups started to promote the advert with some going as far as saying Nivea was the official alt-right antiperspirant. Eventually, Nivea released a statement about the ad and immediately withdrew it after realizing the wording and context caused offence to many viewers.

Dove – lotion ad

The Ad: Similar to Nivea, Dove is a popular skincare brand that targets numerous countries around the world with their moisturizers, deodorants and hair care products. In 2017, Dove released a social media ad on their Facebook page of a black woman "transforming" into a white woman. The advert showed a black woman removing her top to reveal a white woman underneath after using Dove's body lotion. As you can probably tell, there are many things wrong with this advert.

The Problem: The controversy caused by the advert is as clear as day. Not only is the advert racist, but it's also insulting to viewers.

The campaign was instantly removed from Facebook while the owners of the brand Unilever, released a statement apologising for the advert. The scary thing about this advert is that is must have been approved at some point during the marketing process, which makes it worrying that nobody thought it would cause offence. This also wasn't the first time Dove received backlash over their ads. In 2011 they came under fire for a similar image showing the transition of a black woman to a white woman after using their lotion. Tweets from users showed that people don't just forget about these type of ads overnight. A bad ad campaign can leave you with a negative reputation for years.

> Boykin, K. [@keithboykin]. (2020, October 8). Okay, Dove . . . One racist ad makes you suspect. Two racist ads makes you kinda guilty. Twitter.

2018 might be over, but there's still some ads we can't seem to get out of our heads. Not because they were good, but the complete opposite. Maybe you saw some articles in the news regarding these ads or perhaps this is your first time seeing them. Whatever the case, these ads caused a lot of controversy in 2018 for different reasons. Here's why.

The Ad: LUSH is a UK based handmade cosmetics manufacturer that has stores all across the UK and USA. In 2018 LUSH released their spy cops campaign across all their UK stores which raised many eyebrows. In addition to running the advert across all of their UK shops, they also produced several online articles explaining the issue. The campaign focused on "spy cops" or undercover police who infiltrate political groups and form relationships in order to gather and collect data on subjects. There have been many stories of police offers having sexual relations with these campaigners all while hiding the truth from their real families. The ad was basically a whistleblowing campaign to raise awareness of the polices tactics and the devastation it brings to families and children.

The Problem: The main issue with this campaign is that it came across as very anti-police to most of the general public. In fact, there were reports of people complaining and becoming very aggressive in the stores, resulting in LUSH having to call the police. Due to the negative reception of the ads, LUSH ended up pulling them and releasing an official statement on their website.

Nike – Colin Kaepernick

The Ad: Nike is undoubtedly one of the biggest companies when it comes to sportswear and sports brands. Known for their sports footwear, clothes and accessories, Nike regularly invests in multi-million-dollar ad campaigns featuring the likes of famous sports athletes. In 2018 Nike launched an advert featuring the American quarterback Colin Kaepernick who at the time was known for protesting over the American national anthem during football games. The ad was plastered on billboards all over America with the tag line "Believe in something. Even if it means sacrificing everything". The line being a nod to Kaepernick's previous actions of not standing for the national anthem in protest over the treatment of ethnic minorities.

The Problem: After Kaepernick refused to stand for the national anthem, many viewers became angry at him and viewed him as anti-American. The fact that Nike was using him in their ads made many people believe Nike was also anti-American. This sparked a lot of controversies online with many social media users destroying their Nike products while posting the hashtag #JustBurnIt.

However, despite the online backlash over the campaign and casting of Kaepernick, Nike reportedly made over $6 billion in sales and saw online sales grow by 31%.

Credit: Sam Carr, published Oct 10, 2019

Rightsholder: PPC Protect Limited

URL: https://ppcprotect.com/top-controversial-ads/

Receiver

The **receiver**, or the audience, is the object of the source's message. Usually, the receiver is the sports marketer's well-defined target audience. However, and as previously mentioned, the receiver's personal characteristics play an important role in whether the message is correctly decoded. For example, consumers' demographic profile (e.g., age, marital status, and gender), psychographic profile (e.g., personality, lifestyle, and values), and even where they live (geographic region) may all affect the interpretation and comprehension of the sports marketing message. In addition, noise, timing, manner received, and context of the environment can all have an impact on message delivery to the receiver.

Feedback

To determine whether the message has been received and comprehended, feedback is necessary. **Feedback** is defined as the response a target audience makes to a message. The importance of feedback as an element of the communication process cannot be overlooked. Without feedback, communication would be a one-way street, and the sender of the message would have no means of determining whether the original message should remain unchanged, be modified, or be abandoned altogether. There are several ways for the consumer or target audience to deliver feedback to the source of the message. The target market might provide feedback in the form of a purchase. In other words, if consumers are buying tickets, sporting goods, or other sports products, then the sports marketer's message must be effective. Likewise, if consumers are not willing to purchase the sports product, then feedback is also being provided to the source. Unfortunately, the feedback in this case is that the message is either not being received or being incorrectly interpreted.

When using personal communication media, such as personal selling, feedback is received instantly by verbal and nonverbal means. Consumers will respond favorably by nodding their head in approval, acting interested, or asking intelligent questions. In the case of disinterest or inattention, the source of the message should make adjustments and change the message as it is being delivered to address any perceived problems.

Another common form of feedback comes through changes in attitude about the object of the message. In other words, the consumer's attitude shifts toward a more favorable belief or feeling about the sports product, athlete, team, or sport itself. Generally, the more positive the attitude toward the message, the more positive the consumer's attitude toward the sports product. This should, in turn, lead to increases in future purchases. One of the many uses of marketing research is to gather feedback from consumers and use this feedback to create or redesign the strategic sports marketing process. The control phase of the strategic marketing process is dedicated to evaluating feedback from consumers and making adjustments to achieve marketing objectives.

Thus far, we have only examined feedback in one direction – from consumer of the product to producer of the product. However, feedback is an interactive process. That is, consumers also receive feedback from the sports organization. Organizations let consumers know they are listening to the "voice of the consumer" by reintroducing new and improved versions of sports products, changing the composition of teams and their coaches, adjusting prices, and even varying their promotional messages.

For example, when the Nets left New Jersey if the fall of 2012, there was nothing written in stone to guarantee success of the transformation to Brooklyn. The immaculate, billion-dollar, green-roofed, wood, and glass-paneled Barclays Center was not enough to distract attendees from a number of problems, one of which was that the games felt sterile.[18] In fact, fans throughout the tristate area were not convinced of the hype surrounding the team's much-anticipated move from the Prudential Center in Newark, New Jersey. Since the move, the Brooklyn Nets have struggled to attract consumers. In fact, again in 2018-2019, the Nets ranked dead last in NBA attendance. However, a strong year-ending performance and multiple free agency acquisitions, for example, Kevin Durant and Kyrie Irving, have fans and stakeholders alike believing that it was not only a better year but that the team is making strides in the right direction. According to *NetsDaily*, even before the playoffs – which offered an opportunity to boost revenue – not only was late-season attendance strong, local TV ratings were up 24 percent over the previous season, sales of Nets gear were up 40 percent, and ticket revenue was up 21 percent – perhaps reflecting future commitments to season tickets, which were up as well.[19] While offering a resounding sense of hope, marketers must understand that "you have a different cachet with the New York sports fan."[20] New York will always, unmistakably, be a Knicks city, but, if Brooklyn continues on its upward trajectory, Nets fandom may not always seem so rare.[21]

Noise

The final element in the communication process is noise. Unfortunately, there is no such thing as perfect communication because of **noise**, or interference, in the communications process. Interference may occur at any point along the channel of communication. For example, the source may be ineffective; the message may be sent through the wrong medium; or there may be too many competing messages, each "fighting" for the limited information-processing capacity of consumers.

When communicating through stadium signage, the obvious source of noise is the game itself. Noise can even be present in the form of ambush marketing techniques, where organizations attempt to confuse consumers and make them believe they are officially affiliated with a sporting event when they are not. An excellent example of how noise can affect the communication process is found in ambush marketing, which will be explored in Chapter 11.

Sports marketers must realize that noise will always be present in the communications process. By gaining a better understanding of the communications process, factors contributing to noise can be examined and eliminated to a large extent.

Promotion planning

Armed with a working knowledge of the communications process, the sports marketer is now ready to create an efficient promotion plan. Not unlike the strategic marketing process, promotional plans come in all shapes and sizes, but all share several common elements. Our **promotional planning** document consists of four basic phases: (1) identifying target market considerations,

(2) setting promotional objectives, (3) determining the promotional budget, and (4) developing the promotional mix.

Target market considerations

Promotional planning is not done in isolation. Instead, plans must rely heavily on the objectives formulated in the strategic sports marketing process. The first step to promotional planning is identifying **target market considerations**. During the planning phase, target markets have been identified, and promotion planning should reflect these previous decisions. Promotional planning depends largely on who is identified as the primary target audience. One promotional strategy is based on reaching the ultimate consumer of the sports product and is known as a pull strategy. The other strategy identifies channel members as the most important target audience. This strategic direction is termed a push strategy. These two basic strategies are dependent on the chosen target of the promotional efforts and guide subsequent planning. Let us explore the push and pull strategies in greater detail.

Push strategy

A **push strategy** is so named because of the emphasis on having channel intermediaries "push" the sports product through the channel of distribution to the final consumer. If a push strategy is used, intermediaries such as a *manufacturer* might direct initial promotional efforts at a *wholesaler*, who then promotes the sports product to the retailer. In turn, the *retailers* promote the sports product to the final user. When using a push strategy, you are literally loading goods into the distribution pipeline. The objective is to get as much product as possible into the warehouse or store. Push strategies generally ignore the consumer. A variety of promotion mix elements are still used with a push strategy, although personal selling is more prevalent when promoting to channel members closer to the manufacturer (i.e., wholesalers) than end users.

Pull strategy

The target audience for a **pull strategy** is not channel intermediaries but the ultimate consumer. The broad objective of this type of promotional strategy is to stimulate demand for the sports product – so much demand, in fact, that channel members, such as retailers, are forced to stock their shelves with the sports product. Because the end user, or ultimate consumer, is the desired target for a pull strategy, the promotion mix tends to emphasize advertising rather than personal selling. It is important to note that because sports marketing is based largely on promoting services rather than goods, pull strategies targeting the end user are more prevalent. In pull strategies, your objective is to get consumers to pull the merchandise off the shelf and out the door. Its focus is to capture, nurture, and continuously improve. For example, many sport companies use pull techniques via their web sites or use mobile apps. These strategies allow consumers to search for additional information and further explore the product or the brand. Similarly, companies like GoPro have used pull strategies that have attracted consumers to become heroes of their own adventures, which is both inspiring and memorable. They feature user-generated content from novel perspectives, which creates a revolving door, where consumers want to come back for more. They allow consumer self-interest to tell the story. By crafting the brand around the passion of the customer, they further align with the customer and further enhance the exchange.[22]

Adidas utilized YouTube in its Dugout promotion to allow fans to engage with their favorite stars. Dugout was a series of interactive interviews and shows relating to the 2014 FIFA World Cup. The promotion afforded fans from all over the world the opportunity to interact with their favorite stars. It was designed to focus on moments that can happen at any time and generated more than 1.5 billion impressions on YouTube. Other examples include a contest developed by Hill Holliday linking Dunkin' Donuts with Major League Baseball. The two entities partnered so that fans had a chance to step up to the plate every Tuesday during Major League Baseball's regular season to win prizes. Prize awards were associated with total runs scored, so if the fan's team scored, so did the fans. Additionally, Burger King signed a six-month, seven-figure agreement to become Major League Soccer's first official quick-service restaurant. Burger King offered in-store and online promotion of a $100,000 sweepstakes and also gave away Burger King- and MLS-branded soccer balls and "Have It Your Way" gift cards valued at $2.

Although pull strategies are more common in sports marketing, the most effective promotion planning integrates both push and pull components. For example, marketing giant Procter & Gamble's (P&G) objective was to stimulate consumer demand for its Sunny Delight and Hawaiian Punch brands. To do so, P&G designed a promotion featuring the late UCLA basketball coach John Wooden and one of his former star players, Bill Walton. The pull strategy offered consumers a Wooden and Walton autographed picture and coin set for $19.95 and proof of purchase. The push promotional strategy was directed at Sunny Delight and Hawaiian Punch distributors and retailers who carried the P&G brands. If the "trade" reached their performance goals during the promotion, they earned a framed picture of Walton and Wooden that was autographed and personalized for the distributor.

Participatory marketing

As the Internet, new technology, and communication channels continue to emerge, so does participatory marketing.[23] Participatory marketing is a mind shift that conceptually recognizes the emergence of the social Internet and how its outcomes produce more efficient customers. Customers turn to other customers for information. Therefore, corporations must rethink their approaches and learn how to market with consumers, identifying where consumers are likely to further solicit a higher level of peer interaction. Companies such as Red Bull, Ford, and Nike have deployed participatory marketing strategies. For example, Nike, in its "what do we play for" campaign, called on teens to share their sports stories.[24] The result was passionate, inspirational tales that further demonstrate the company's evolution by using the power of participatory marketing. On the other hand, Red Bull has a unique ability to sell their brand without pushing their product. They focus on publishing content that visualizes the brand. Whether it is through telling a story or creating memorable events and stunts, Red Bull strategies work due to their audience-first, product-second approach, further accentuating the content, delivery, and value of the brand.

Promotional objectives

After target markets have been identified, the next step in the promotion planning process is to define the **promotional objectives**. Broadly, the three goals of promotion are to inform, persuade, and remind target audiences. Consumers must first be made aware of the product and how it might satisfy their needs. The goal of providing information to consumers is usually desired when products are in the introductory phase of the product life cycle. Once consumers are aware of the sports product, promotional goals then turn to persuasion and convincing the consumer to purchase the product. After initial purchase and satisfaction with a given product, the broad promotional goal is then to remind the consumer of the sports product's availability and perceived benefits.

Informing, persuading, and reminding consumers are the broad objectives of promotion, but the ultimate promotional objective is to induce action. These consumer actions might include volunteering to help with a local 10K race, donating money to the U.S. Olympic Team, purchasing a new pair of inline skates, or just attending a sporting event they have never seen. Marketers believe promotions guide consumers through a series of steps to reach this ultimate objective – action. This series of steps is known as the hierarchy of effects (also sometimes called the hierarchy of communication effect).

The hierarchy of effects

The **hierarchy of effects** is a seven-step process by which consumers are ultimately led to action.[25]

Figure 9.2
Hierarchy of effects

Photo 9.1
Having greater knowledge of sports such as hockey moves consumers through the hierarchy of effects

Credit: Shutterstock, ID# 109773617 by Michael Pettigrew

URL: www.shutterstock.com/image-photo/ice-hockey-action-shot-forward-player-109773617

The seven steps are unawareness, awareness, knowledge, liking, preference, conviction, and action. As shown in Figure 9.2, consumers pass through each of these steps before taking action.

- **Unawareness** - During the first step, consumers are not even aware the sports product exists. Obviously, the promotional objective at this stage is to move consumers toward awareness. Awareness may occur in a variety of ways and helps expose a consumer to the products; however, it is important to note that consumption cannot occur if a consumer is unaware of the product.

- **Awareness** - The promotional objective at this early stage of the hierarchy is to make consumers in the desired target market aware of the new sports product. To reach this objective, a variety of promotional tools are used.

- **Knowledge** - Once consumers are aware of the sports product, they need to gather information about its tangible and intangible benefits. The primary promotional objective at this stage is to provide consumers with the necessary product information. For instance, the NHL initiated a program called Learn to Play (http://learntoplay.nhl.com). Learn to Play is available for children to experience hockey for the first time. Children are taught the basics of hockey by NHL alumni in a fun and safe environment. Additionally, as mentioned previously, the NBA created the NBA Junior program. Another example of creating and enhancing knowledge is the proliferation of classes called Football 101 (https://operations.nfl.com/football-101/) targeted toward women and novice fans. Football 101 educates the consumer on the basics of the game. Football 101 primers have been held at the Super Bowl Fan Experiences, various NFL and college football game day events, and even been offered in Spanish to accommodate all fans. Teams and organizers hope that once the fans become more knowledgeable, they will then move to the next level of the hierarchy – liking.

- **Liking** - Having knowledge and information about a sports product does not necessarily mean the consumer will like it. Generating positive feelings and interest regarding the sports product is the next promotional objective on the hierarchy. The promotion itself cannot cause the consumer to like the product, but research has shown the linkage between attitude toward the promotion (e.g., advertisement) and attitude toward the product.[26] The objective is to create a feeling of goodwill toward the product via the promotion.

- **Preference** - After consumers begin to like the sports product, the objective is to develop preferences. As such, sports marketers must differentiate their product from the competition through promotion. The sports product's differential advantage may be found in an enhanced image and tangible product features.

- **Conviction** - Moving up the hierarchy of effects, consumers must develop a conviction or intention to take action. Behavioral intention, however, does not guarantee action. Factors such as the consumer's economic condition (i.e., financial situation), changing needs, or availability of new alternatives may inhibit the action from ever taking place. The objective of the conviction step of the hierarchy of effects is to create a desire to act in the mind of the target audience.

- **Action** - The final stage of the hierarchy, and the ultimate objective of any promotion, is to have consumers act. As stated previously, actions may come in a variety of forms but usually include purchase or attendance.

Theoretically, the hierarchy of effects model states that consumers must pass through each stage in the hierarchy before a decision is made regarding purchase (or other behaviors). Some marketers have argued this is not always the case. Consider, for instance, purchasing season tickets to a professional sport for business purposes. The purchaser does not have to like the sport or team to take action and buy the tickets. Regardless of what the hierarchy of effects proposes to do or not do, the fact remains that it is an excellent tool to use when developing promotional objectives. Knowing where the target audience is on the hierarchy is critical to formulating the proper objectives.

Establishing promotional budgets

Global advertising expenditures continue to see steady growth. According to figures provided by Zenithmedia, global advertising expenditures are expected to grow to $636 billion in 2022.[27] Furthermore, these expenditures are expected to grow by 4.4 percent in 2019 and 4.3 percent in 2020, with Asia having the largest potential growth, 7.4 percent. Total advertising spending in the United States is predicted to reach $217 billion in 2020, accounting for over 37 percent of all global expenditures. China (15 percent), Japan (8 percent), the United Kingdom (4.7 percent), and Germany (4.0 percent) round out the top five countries in global advertising expenditures. Television is predicted to retain the second-largest share of advertising expenditures, accounting for approximately 31.2 percent, followed by Internet display (23 percent) and Internet paid search (17.9 percent). Internet classifieds are predicted to be 3.8 percent, newspapers 7.3 percent, magazines 3.8 percent, outdoor 6.4 percent, radio 5.7 percent, and cinema 1.0 percent.[28] As marketers continue to shift budgets toward targeted, digital media, Zenithmedia predicts that online advertising will increase its share of the advertising market from 20.7 percent in 2013 to 52 percent in 2021, while newspapers and magazines will continue to shrink at an average of 4–5 percent per year.[29]

Over the past several years, this growth, in part, has been attributed to a surge in digital spending and continued success across televised platforms, further enhancing opportunities surrounding events such as the Olympic Games. NBC estimated that it would generate billions in revenue for Olympic advertisement spots. Perhaps unsurprisingly, after such phenomenal success, Internet

Table 9.4 Most significant sponsorship/advertising trends over the past year

Trend	2020	2018	2015
Social media (networking, social gambling)	18%	35%	33%
Accountability/measurement (ROI, ROO, etc.)	23%	30%	38%
Digital marketing	6%	10%	15%
Mobile marketing	0%	10%	6%
Digital/streaming	12%	5%	0%
Multicultural marketing	6%	5%	4%
Cause marketing	18%	5%	4%
Radio	0%	0%	0%
Television	>5	0%	0%
E-sports	12%	0%	NA
Sustainability	5%	NA	NA

Source: Seaver, Ron & Kahler, Jim, 2020. *2020 Corporate Sponsor and Advertiser & Industry Report.* Seaver Marketing Group

advertising is facing a pushback; however, Zenith research shows there has been no retreat in the digital transformation.[30] Seaver and Kahler, in the recent *Corporate Sponsor/Advertiser & Industry Report* presented at the National Sports Forum, noted digital concerns, specifically social media and accountability measures, were the most significant trends/concerns of sport executives relative to sponsorship and advertising in the past year (see Table 9.4).[31]

In today's environment, digital screens are a critical part of the sport marketing mix. Advertisers are ramping up their spending on technology, innovation, and content to create new opportunities for their brands. Sports play a powerful role in connecting people in person as well as on social media channels. Good content is what drives followers, likes, and fans. Fans are passionate and engaged, and entities that tap into these enthusiasm streams are transforming the game and creating unique exchange opportunities for their brands.

As Frank Weishaupt, SVP of global revenue for Millennia Media, states, "if the sports vertical were an athlete, we'd accuse him of juicing with that kind of statistical improvement in just one year."[32] While some experts may emphasize that mega-sports such as the Olympics and the FIFA World Cup may have fueled much of that bump, the upward trend is projected to continue and it's more likely to be considered a by-product of the ability to watch almost every pro sport on your mobile device. Mobile has definitely changed the way we follow our favorite teams. This is not surprising, given that the largest viewership times on online videos are tilted towards sports.

Global sporting events such as the Olympics and the FIFA World Cup are big attractions for advertisers, and sport appears to be a perfect vehicle to help advertising mediums, especially the digital platforms utilizing Internet and mobile devices, to finally reach their potential. The continued growth in smartphone penetration, faster network speeds, and humanity's love of watching sport have created a perfect melting pot for sport to showcase digital marketing's true potential for marketers. According to Adam French, author of "Sport and the Mobile Marketing Revolution,"[33] this melting pot exists for three primary reasons: (1) **sport = engagement**: Marketers of sports properties are working with a market filled with fans – highly passionate, energized, and engaged people rallying around a particular team, individual, or group. French adds that fans are highly passionate and invest their emotions, time, and money in supporting a team, contending that this passion manifests itself as a disproportionate interest in everything connected to that team, including advertising. (2) Sport consists of **easily definable segments**: Leagues and competitions very neatly split markets. Sport segments consist of a group loosely defined as "people with an active interest," and there is a very clear set of large segments within that, split neatly across team loyalty. French notes that the ease of basic segmentation pairs nicely with new digital targeting techniques such as contextual and geographic targeting. (3) Value utilization in **second screening**: In today's environment, consumers utilizing a second screen while they watch sport is commonplace, and with the onslaught of 5G networks, more fans will be able to watch sports on their mobile, representing another fantastic opportunity. French adds that the statistics, player data, and social banter inherent in most sports make sport a perfect use case for second screening. Collectively, these innovative new targeting and rich media mobile platforms stand poised to offer ever-increasing, targeted value to sports fans and better returns on investment for marketers, in turn enriching fan experiences.

The NFL generates billions of dollars in revenue yearly, and these interests are tied with many other large powerful companies. Companies such as Anheuser-Busch, Pepsi Co., Verizon, and Barclays, among others, invest a significant amount of money in advertising and sponsorship. The sports sponsorship industry remains healthy, and televised sports remain a ratings behemoth, but signs of trouble maybe on the horizon. Decreases in viewership and live attendance and graying sports audiences create concerns for brand developers. Entities need to evolve and bring relationships to life. There's a lot at stake; marketers are demanding more access to content and fan experiences that only teams and leagues can provide. There is a shift from what the rights holder wants to sell to what the brand needs to buy. This translates into assessment, creativity, and engagement. The goal is to think experience first and deploy new incentive-based approaches that can resonate widely across the sporting landscape.[34] Many are concerned what their return on investment will be, and any interruption of play is a concern for all sponsors and advertisers.[35]

In addition to companies spending huge dollars on sports advertising, teams and leagues are constantly promoting the sport. For instance, the NHL released the poorly reviewed "Game On" campaign after the strike season, MLB is trying to capture young fans through "Let the Kids Play" campaign, and the NBA is still using the classic "NBA Cares" and a more recent "I'm Why" promotion. In the case of the NHL, increases in advertising were needed to make potential fans more knowledgeable about and able to appreciate hockey. Major League Baseball wanted to attract younger fans, a population that is slowly diminishing from reach. In all cases, teams and leagues are advertising to keep up with the tremendous competitive threat of other entertainment choices for the fans.

In theory, the promotional budget of the NHL or the NBA would be determined based on the many objectives set forth by the leagues' marketing strategy. In practice, **promotional budgeting** is an interactive and unscientific process by which the sports marketer determines the amount spent based on maximizing the monies available. Some of the ways promotional budgets may be established include arbitrary allocation, competitive parity, percentage of sales, and the objective and task method.

Arbitrary allocation

The simplest, yet most unsystematic, approach to determining promotional budgets is called **arbitrary allocation**. Using this method, sports marketers set the budget in isolation from other critical factors. For example, the sports marketer disregards last year's promotional budget and its effectiveness, what competitors are doing, the economy, and current strategic objectives and budgets using some subjective method. The budget is usually determined by allocating all the money the organization can afford. In other words, promotional budgets are established after the organization's other costs are considered. A sports organization that chooses this approach does not place much emphasis on promotional planning.

Competitive parity

Setting promotional budgets based on what competitors are spending (**competitive parity**) is often used for certain product categories in sports marketing. For example, the athletic shoe industry closely monitors what the competition is doing in the way of advertising efforts. adidas has an annual budget of roughly $21.915 billion,[36] of which approximately 13.6 percent is spent on advertising and marketing.[37] Under Armour's annual budget is $5.2 billion, with a marketing expense of 10.5 percent;[38] Puma's budget is $4.65 billion,[39] with approximately 10 to 12 percent being allocated to marketing, and Asics has a budget of $3.5 million.[40] Other contenders such as Brooks have budgets of less than $500 million.[41] In fact, Brooks Sports CEO Jim Weber noted that Nike will spend more by noon today than they will spend on marketing in a whole year.[42]

Competitively, these entities race to keep pace with Nike's promotional spending if they intend to increase market share. Nike, whose annual budget consists of roughly $36.4 billion in revenue, of which approximately $3.5 billion is spent on "demand creation," a marketing label used to categorize expenditures which consist of advertising, promotion, and the cost of endorsement contracts with athletes, is the current market leader,[43] at the equivalent of just under a million dollars a day.

One athletic shoe company that does not follow its competitors' huge promotional spending is New Balance. New Balance has begun to turn toward a more conventional route for advertising. New Balance is going to begin advertising with TV, print, digital advertising, online communities, and viral video content as well as in-store and event exposure. New Balance had $4.5 billion in sales in 2018.[44] Instead of using famous athletes, New Balance has paved its success by understanding its primary consumer, the 35–59-year-old baby boomer. Rather than paying celebrities to endorse their products, they prefer to invest in research, design, and domestic manufacturing. They have adopted a marketing strategy that encourages associates all over the world to do, to make mistakes, to take risks, to fail, and to learn from that. In a realm where challenge brands are the love of consumers, often companies do not take risks.[45] A common phrase that people use within the organization is that we "look, feel and act like a 110-year-old start-up," noted VP of Global Marketing Chris Davis. He explained employees are taught to act quickly but make sure everything they do is authentic to the brand.[46] Recently New Balance launched "Fearlessly Independent Since 1906" – its new global brand platform. They introduced a model called 50/30/20, where they are using 50 percent of their budget to capitalize on what they know works, 30 percent on slight evolution, and 20 percent on high-risk, uncharted, and innovative territory.

Percentage of sales

The **percentage of sales** method of promotional budget allocation is based on determining some standard percentage of promotional spending and applying this proportion to either past or forecast sales to arrive at the amount to be spent. It is common for the percentage to be used on promotional spending to be derived from some industry standard. For example, the athletic shoe industry typically allocates 5 to 10 percent of sales to promotional spending. Therefore, if a new athletic shoe company enters the market and projects sales of $1 million, then they would allocate $50,000 to the promotional budget. Likewise, if Converse, a subsidiary of Nike, Inc. since 2003, totaled $2 billion in sales in the previous year, then it might budget $1 to 2 million to next year's promotional budget.

Although the percentage of sales method of budgeting is simple to use, it has a number of shortcomings. First, if percentage of forecast sales is used to arrive at a promotional budget figure, then the sales projections must be made with a certain degree of precision and confidence. If historical sales figures (e.g., last year's numbers) are used, then promotional spending may be either too high or too low. For example, if New Balance has a poor year in sales, then the absolute promotional spending would be decreased. This, in turn, could cause sales to slide even further. With sales declining, it may be more appropriate to increase (rather than decrease) promotional spending. A second major shortcoming of using this method is the notion that budget is very loosely, if at all, tied to the promotional objectives.

Objective and task method

If arbitrary allocation is the most illogical of the budgeting methods, then the objective and task method could be characterized as the most logical and systematic. The **objective and task method** identifies the promotional objectives, defines the communications tools and tasks needed to meet those objectives, and then adds up the costs of the planned activities.

Although the objective and task method seems the most reasonable, it also assumes the objectives have been determined correctly and the proper promotional mix has been formulated to reach those objectives. For instance, suppose the Vanderbilt University women's basketball team wanted to achieve an attendance increase of 15 percent from the previous season. To this end, the director of marketing for athletics must develop a promotional mix that includes local advertising, related sales promotions, and public relations in an effort to reach all target audiences. Even if the attendance goal is achieved, it is difficult to determine whether the money required to achieve this objective was spent in the most efficient and effective fashion.

Choosing an integrated promotional mix

The final step in building an overall promotional plan is to determine the appropriate promotional mix. As stated earlier, the traditional promotional mix consists of advertising, personal selling, public relations, and sales promotions. The sports marketing manager must determine which aspects of the promotional mix will be best suited to achieve the promotional objectives at the given budget.

In choosing from among the traditional elements, the sports marketer may want to broadly explore the advantages and disadvantages of each promotional tool. For example, personal selling may be the most effective way to promote the sale of personal seat licenses, but it is limited in reaching large audiences. Table 9.5 outlines some of the considerations when deciding on the correct mix of promotional tools.

Table 9.5 Evaluating the promotional mix elements

| | Promotional Tools | | | |
	Advertising	Personal Selling	Sales Promotion	Public Relations
Sender's control over the communication	Low	High	Moderate to low	Moderate to low
Amount of Feedback	Little	Much	Little to moderate	Little
Speed of Feedback	Delayed	Immediate	Varies	Delayed
Direction of message flow	One Way	Two way	One way	One way
Speed in reaching large audiences	Fast	Slow	Fast	Typically fast
Message flexibility	None	Customized	None	Some
Mode of communication	Indirect and impersonal	Direct and face to face	Usually indirect and impersonal	Usually indirect and impersonal

Although the factors listed in Table 9.5 are important determinants of which promotional tools to use to achieve the desired objectives, there are other considerations. The stage of the life cycle for the sport product, the type of sports product, the characteristics of the target audience, and the current market environment must also be carefully studied. Whatever the promotion mix decision, it is critical that the various elements be integrated carefully.

Promotional planning for sports is becoming increasingly complex. With the rapid changes in technology, new promotional tools are being used to convey the sports marketer's message. In addition, it is becoming harder and harder to capture the attention of target audiences and move them along the hierarchy of effects. Because of the growing difficulty in reaching diverse target audiences, the clarity and coordination of integrating all marketing communications into a single theme is more important than ever.

The concept under which a sports organization carefully integrates and coordinates its many promotional mix elements to deliver a unified message about the organization and its products is known as **integrated marketing communications** (IMC). IMC should focus on nurturing the customers, content, channels, and consistency of the delivery process. By articulating and blending the delivery of the four Cs, one can further clarify brand values, enhance channel synergy, accentuate marketing relationship orientations, and enhance customer engagement opportunities. Collectively, this enables clearer development of targeting and positioning strategies. It helps to control costs, enhances ROI, and can often create unique competitive advantages, such as the adidas example previously. Think for a moment about the promotional efforts of the WNBA. The promotional goals are to increase awareness and develop excitement about the league. To accomplish this, the WNBA will combine national advertisements, sponsorships, cable and network broadcast schedules, and tie-ins with the NBA. All of these communications media must deliver a consistent message that produces a uniform image for the league to be successful. Not only must the WNBA deliver an integrated promotional mix, but the league's sponsors and the 12 teams must also transmit a unified message.

The primary advantage of integrating the promotional plan includes more effective and efficient marketing communications. Unfortunately, determining the return on investment for an integrated promotion plan is still difficult, if not impossible. Professor Don Schultz has identified four types of information that must be available to begin to measure ROI for integrated communications.[47] These factors are the following:

- **Identification of specific customers** - Identification of specific households, including information on the composition of those households to make inferences.
- **Customer valuation**-Placing a value on each household based on either annual purchases or lifetime purchases. Without this information on the purchase behavior of the household or individual, the calculation of ROI is of limited value to the marketer.
- **Track message delivery** - Understanding what media consumers or households use to make their purchase decisions and how a household receives information and messages over time. In addition, this involves measuring "brand contacts," or when and where consumers come into contact with the brand.
- **Consumer response** - To establish the best ROI, behavioral responses are captured. In other words, consumer responses such as attitudes, feelings, and memory are deemed unimportant and purchases, inquiries, and related behaviors (e.g., coupon redemption) are evaluated.

Summary

Promotional planning is one of the most important elements of the sports marketing mix. Promotion involves communicating to all types of sports consumers via one or more of the promotion mix elements. The promotion mix elements include advertising, personal selling, sales promotions, public relations, and sponsorship. Within each of these promotion mix elements are more specialized tools to communicate with consumers of sport. For example, advertising may be developed for print media (e.g., newspapers and magazines) or broadcasts (e.g., radio and television). However, regardless of the promotion mix element that is used by sports marketers, the fundamental process at work is communication.

Communication is an interactive process established between the sender and the receiver of the marketing message via some medium. The process of communication begins with the source or sender of the message. In sports marketing, the source of the message might be an athlete endorser, team members, a sports organization, or even a coach. Sometimes the source of a marketing message can be friends or family. The effectiveness of the source in influencing consumers is based largely on the concept of source credibility. Credibility is typically defined as the expertise and trustworthiness of the source. Other characteristics of the source, such as gender, attractiveness, familiarity, and likeability may also play important roles in determining the source's effectiveness.

After the source of the message is chosen, message encoding occurs. Encoding is defined as translating the sender's thoughts or ideas into a message. The most effective encoding uses multiple ways of getting the message across and always keeps the receiver of the message in mind. Once encoding takes place, the message is more completely developed. Although there are any number of ways of constructing a message, sports marketers commonly choose between emotional (e.g., humor, sex, or fear) and rational (information-based) appeals.

The message, once constructed, must be transmitted to the target audience through any number of media. The traditional media include television, radio, newspapers, magazines, outdoor billboards, and stadium signage. Nontraditional media, such as the Internet, are also emerging as powerful tools for sports marketers. When making decisions about what medium to use, marketers must consider the promotional objectives, cost, ability to reach the targeted audience, and nature of the message being communicated.

The medium relays the message to the target audience, which is where decoding occurs. Decoding is the interpretation of the message sent by the source through the medium. It is important to understand the characteristics of the target audience to ensure successful translation of the message will occur. Rarely, if ever, will perfect decoding take place, because of the presence of noise.

The final elements in the communications model are the receiver and feedback. The message is directed to the receiver, or target audience. Again, depending on the purpose of the communication, the target audience may be spectators, participants, or corporate sponsors. Regardless of the nature of the audience, the sports marketer must understand as much as possible about the characteristics of the group to ensure an effective message is produced. Sports marketers determine the effectiveness of the message through feedback from the target audience.

Understanding the communications process provides us with the basis for developing a sound promotional plan. The promotional planning process includes identifying target market considerations, setting promotional objectives, determining the promotional budget, and developing the promotional mix.

The first step in the promotional planning process is to consider the target market identified in the previous planning phase of the strategic sports marketing process. The two broad target market considerations are the final consumers of the sports product (either spectators or participants) or intermediaries, such as sponsors or distributors of sports products. When communicating to final consumers, a pull strategy is used. Conversely, push strategies are used to promote through intermediaries. After target markets are considered, promotional objectives are defined. Broadly, objectives may include informing, persuading, or reminding the target market. One model that provides a basis for establishing promotional objectives is known as the hierarchy of effects, which states that consumers must pass through a series of stages before ultimately taking action (usually defined as making a purchase decision). The steps of the hierarchy of effects are unawareness, awareness, knowledge, liking, preference, conviction, and action. Once objectives have been formulated, budgets are considered. In the ideal scenario, budgets are linked with the objectives that have been set in the previous phase of the promotion planning process. However, other common approaches to promotional budgeting include arbitrary allocation, competitive parity, and percentage of sales. Most sports organizations use some combination of these methods to arrive at budgets. The final phase in the promotion planning process is to arrive at the optimal promotion mix. The promotion mix includes advertising, personal selling, public relations, sales promotion, and sponsorship. Decisions about the most effective promotion mix must carefully consider the current marketing environment, the sports product being promoted, and the characteristics of the target audience. Ideally, the sports marketer designs an integrated promotion mix that delivers a consistent message about the organization and its products.

Key terms

- arbitrary allocation
- communication
- comparative messages
- competitive parity
- credibility
- decoding
- easily defined segments
- elements in the communications process
- emotional versus rational appeal
- encoding
- feedback
- hierarchy of effects
- integrated marketing communications
- match-up hypothesis
- medium
- message
- message characteristics
- noise

- objective and task method
- percentage of sales
- promotion
- promotion mix elements
- promotional budgeting
- promotional objectives
- promotional planning
- pull strategy
- push strategy
- receiver
- second screening
- sidedness
- source
- target market considerations

Review questions

1 Define promotion and then discuss each of the promotion mix elements.
2 Describe the elements of the communication process. Why is communication so important for sports marketers? What is the relationship between communication and promotion?
3 Define the source of a sports marketing message and provide some examples of effective sources. What is source credibility? What are the two components of source credibility?
4 What is meant by encoding? Who is responsible for encoding sports marketing messages?
5 Discuss the various message characteristics. What are the simple techniques used to create more effective messages?
6 Why is television considered the most powerful medium for sports marketing messages?
7 Define feedback. How is feedback delivered to the source of the message?
8 Outline the basic steps in promotion planning.
9 What is the fundamental difference between a push and a pull strategy?
10 Describe the three broad objectives of any type of promotion. What is the hierarchy of effect, and how is this concept related to promotional objectives?
11 What are the various ways of setting promotional budgets? Comment on the strengths and weaknesses of each.
12 Comment on how you would choose among the various promotion mix tools. Define integrated marketing communication.

Exercises

1 Evaluate the promotional mix used for the marketing of any intercollegiate women's sport at your university. Do you believe the proper blend of promotional tools are being used? What could be done to make the promotional plan more effective for this sport?

2   Find any advertisement for a sports product. Then describe and explain each of the elements in the communications process for that ad. Do the same (i.e., explain the communications process) for the following scenario: A salesperson is trying to sell stadium signage to the marketing director of a local hospital.

3   Conduct an interview with the marketing department of a local sports organization and discuss the role of each of the promotional tools in the organization's promotion mix. In addition, ask about their promotional budgeting process.

4   Describe three television advertisements for sports products that are designed to inform, persuade, and remind consumers. Do you believe the advertisements are effective in reaching their promotional objectives?

5   Locate advertisements for three different sports products. Comment on which response in the hierarchy of effects you believe each advertisement is trying to elicit from its target audience.

6   Find an example of a comparative advertisement. What do you believe are the advantages and disadvantages of this type of message?

Internet exercises

1   Using the Internet, find an example of an advertisement for a sports product and a sports-related sales promotion. For each, discuss the targeted audience, the promotional objectives, and the message characteristics.

2   How do organizations get feedback regarding their promotions via the Internet? Find several examples of ways of providing sports marketers with feedback about their promotions.

3   Consider any sports product and find evidence of advertising and sales promotion *not* on the Internet. Then locate the product's promotion on the Internet. Comment on whether this organization practices integrated marketing communications.

Notes

1   Allen Bush, "Sports Celebrity Influence on the Behavioral Intentions of Generation Y," *Journal of Advertising Research*, vol. 44, no. 1 (2004), 108–118.

2   Kurt Badenhausen, "Behind the Numbers of the Top-Paid Athletes of 2019," *Forbes* (June 11, 2019). Available from: www.forbes.com/sites/kurtbadenhausen/2019/06/11/behind-the-numbers-of-the-top-earning-athletes-2019/#22679b896bbe, accessed July 14, 2019.

3   Forbes staff and Kurt Badenhausen, "Lionel Messi Claims Top Spot on Forbes' 2019 List of The World's 100 Highest-Paid Athletes" (June 11, 2019). Available from: https://www.forbes.com/sites/forbespr/2019/06/11/lionel-messi-claims-top-spot-on-forbes-2019-list-of-the-worlds-100-highest-paid-athletes/#226c57dc7c5f, accessed July 14, 2019.

4   D. L. Andrews and S. J. Jackson, *Sport Stars: The Cultural Politics of Sporting Celebrities* (London, England: Routledge, 2001).

5   A. Manta, "The Celebrity Athlete: A Powerful Endorsement Tool in the Mass Media," *Boston College University Libraries* (2013). Available from: http://hdl.handle.net/2345/3060.

6 Kurt Badenhausen, "The NBA's Highest-Paid Players 2019: LeBron James Leads with $89 Million" (February 12, 2019). Available from: www.forbes.com/sites/kurtbadenhausen/2019/02/12/the-nbas-highest-paid-players-2019-lebron-james-leads-with-89-million/#4244814725d1, accessed July 14, 2019.

7 Christy Kilmartin, "Insights into Adidas' New 'All-in' Campaign – 'We Run All'", *Adidas Group Blog* (March 29, 2012). Available from: http://blog.adidas-oup.com/2012/03/insights-into-adidas%E2%80%99-new-all-in-campaign-we-all-run/, accessed March 9, 2014.

8 Kurt Badenhausen, "The NBA's Highest-Paid Players 2019: LeBron James Leads with $89 Million" (February 12, 2019). Available from: www.forbes.com/sites/kurtbadenhausen/2019/02/12/the-nbas-highest-paid-players-2019-lebron-james-leads-with-89-million/#4244814725d1, accessed July 14, 2019.

9 Michael Kamins, "An Investigation into the Match-Up Hypothesis in Celebrity Advertising: When Beauty May Be Only Skin Deep," *Journal of Advertising*, vol. 19, no. 1 (1990), 4–13.

10 adidas Group/Company (2019). Available from: www.adidas-group.com/en/group/strategy-overview/.

11 Michael Santo, "adidas to Launch Biggest Ever Marketing Campaign with a New Slogan," *Huliq.com* (March 15, 2011). Available from: http://www.huliq.com/3257/adidas-launch-all-adidas-2011-global-marketing-campaign-its-biggest-ever. Ibid.

12 adidas Group, "Performance Counts Sustainability Progress Report 2011." Available from: Adidas-group.com, accessed March 9, 2014.

13 adidas Group/Company, 2019. Available from: www.adidas-group.com/en/group/strategy-overview/.

14 Martha Irvin, "If Not on Point, Slang Can Make a Tight Campaign Sound Wack," *The Commercial Appeal* (November 29, 2002), C1.

15 Nielsen Newswire, "Football TV Ratings Soar: The NFL's Playbook for Success," *Nielsen Newswire* (January 28, 2011). Available from: www.nielsen.com/us/en/newswire/2011/football-tv-ratings-soar-the-nfls-playbook-for-success.html, accessed June 22, 2014.

16 FIFA, "More Than Half the World Watched Record-Breaking 2018 World Cup" (2019). Available from: www.fifa.com/worldcup/news/more-than-half-the-world-watched-record-breaking-2018-world-cup; BBC, "Women's World Cup: Record-Breaking" (2019). Available from: numberswww.bbc.com/news/world-48882465.

17 Samantha Baier, "Marketing to the Overlooked Female NFL Fan" (October 4, 2018). Available from: www.odwyerpr.com/story/public/11392/2018-10-04/marketing-overlooked-female-nfl-fan.html/.

18 Chris Almeida, "Is Brooklyn in the House? Nets Fandom Is Having Its New York Moment," *The Ringer* (April 18, 2019). Available from: www.theringer.com/nba/2019/4/18/18412811/brooklyn-nets-playoffs-new-york-city-fan-base, accessed July 14, 2019.

19 Norm Oder, "Nets Still Last in the League Attendance, but a Much Stronger Year, with Playoffs Berth and New Revenue (Plus Gambling Future)" (April 13, 2019). Available from: https://atlanticyardsreport.blogspot.com/2019/04/nets-still-last-in-league-attendance.html, accessed July 14, 2019.

20 Nielsen Newswire, "Historical Super Bowl Viewership," *Nielsen Media Research* (February 4, 2019). Archived from the original on February 5, 2019. Available

from: https://web.archive.org/web/20190205000209/www.nielsen.com/us/en/insights/news/2019/super-bowl-liii-draws-98-2-million-tv-viewers-32-3-million-social-media-interactions.html, accessed July 14, 2019.

21 Chris Almeida, "Is Brooklyn in the House? Nets Fandom Is Having Its New York Moment," *The Ringer* (April 18, 2019). Available from: www.theringer.com/nba/2019/4/18/18412811/brooklyn-nets-playoffs-new-york-city-fan-base, accessed July 14, 2019.

22 Samuel Hum, "3 Ways Go Pro Became Synonymous with Action Cameras," *Referral Candy* (July 21, 2015). Available from: www.referralcandy.com/blog/gopro-marketing-strategy/, accessed July 14, 2019.

23 Michael Della Penna, "Participatory Marketing – Pull Marketing's New Push," *Target Marketing* (October 1, 2009). Available from: www.targetmarketingmag.com/article/particpatory-marketing--pull-marketing-new-push/.

24 Ibid.

25 Radio & Television Business Report, "Looking at the Football TV Ratings Explosion," *Radio & Television Business Report* (January 28, 2011). Available from: http://rbr.com/looking-at-the-football-tv-ratings-explosion/; Robert Lavidge and Gary Steiner, "A Model for Predictive Measurements of Advertising Effectiveness," *Journal of Marketing*, vol. 24 (1961), 59–62 .

26 BBC FIFA, "More Than Half the World Watched Record-Breaking 2018 World Cup" (2019). Available from: www.fifa.com/worldcup/news/more-than-half-the-world-watched-record-breaking-2018-world-cup. And BBC, "Women's World Cup: Record-Breaking Numbers" (2019). Available from: www.bbc.com/news/world-48882465; Rajeev Batra and Michael Ray, "Affective Responses Mediating Acceptance of Advertising," *Journal of Consumer Research*, vol. 13 (September 1986), 236–239; Leon Shiffman and Leslie Kanuk, *Consumer Behavior*, 4th ed. (Upper Saddle River, NJ: Prentice Hall, 1996), 237–239.

27 Bill Sanders, "How Impact of 'Tiger Recession' Changed Athlete Marketability," *Sports Business Journal* (August 2, 2010). Available from: www.sportsbusinessdaily.com/Journal/Issues/2010/08/20100802/From-The-Field-Of/How-Impact-Of-Tiger-Recession-Changed-Athlete-Marketability.aspx.

28 Chris Almeida, "Is Brooklyn in the House? Nets Fandom Is Having Its New York Moment," *The Ringer* (April 18, 2019). Available from: www.theringer.com/nba/2019/4/18/18412811/brooklyn-nets-playoffs-new-york-city-fan-base, accessed July 14, 2019.

29 Norm Oder, "Nets Still Last in the League Attendance, but a Much Stronger Year, with Playoffs Berth and New Revenue (Plus Gambling Future)" (April 13, 2019). Available from: https://atlanticyardsreport.blogspot.com/2019/04/nets-still-last-in-league-attendance.html), accessed July 14, 2019.

30 ZenithOptimedia, "Global Intelligence," *Zenithmedia.com* (2018). Available from: www.zenithmedia.com/wp-content/uploads/2018/05/global-intelligence-05_4MB.pdf.

31 Ron Seaver and Jim Kahler, "2018 Corporate Sponsor and Advertiser & Industry Report," *Seaver Marketing Group* (2018).

32 Frank Weishaupt, "Mobile Ad Spend Increase across Verticals," *Millennial Media* (March 19, 2014). Available from: www.millennialmedia.com/blog/2014/03/mobile-ad-spend-increases-across-verticals-yoy/, accessed June 21, 2014.

33   Adam French, "Sport and the Marketing Revolution." *MarketingDive.com* (October 29, 2013). Available from: https://www.marketingdive.com/ex/mobilemarketer/cms/opinion/columns/16469.html, accessed June 21, 2014.

34   E. J. Schultz, "Marketers Demand More and More for Sport Sponsorships," *AdAge* (June 25, 2018). Available from: https://adage.com/article/cmo-strategy/marketers-demand-sports-sponsorships/314004, accessed July 14, 2019.

35   Rich Thomaselli, "Over $12 Billion at Stake If NFL Lockout Prevents 2011 Season," *Advertising Age* (January 10, 2011). Available from: http://adage.com/article/news/12b-stake-nfl-lockout-prevents-2011-season/148093/, accessed March 9, 2014; https://adage.com/article/news/12b-stake-nfl-lockout-prevents-2011-season/148093.

36   Kantar Media, "Kantar Media Reports, U.S. Advertising Expenditures Increased 3 Percent in 2012," *Kantar Media* (March 11, 2013). Available from: http://kantarmedia.us/press/kantar-media-reports-us-advertising-expenditures-increased-3-percent-2012, accessed March 9, 2014.

37   adidas Annual Report, 2018. Available from: https://report.adidas-group.com/#our-strategy.

38   Under Armour 2018 Annual Report. Available from: https://underarmourinc.gcs-web.com/static-files/17136a1a-d71e-417b-bc64-8d27a19d7511.

39   Puma 2018 Annual Report. Available from: https://annual-report-2018.puma.com/en/annual-report/.

40   Asics 2018 Annual Report. Available from: https://corp.asics.com/en/investor_relations/library/annual-reports.

41   Cynthia Boris, "Sports Goes for the Mobile Ad Gold with Near 500 Percent Growth in Spending," *MarketingPilgrim.com* (March 24, 2014). Available from: www.marketingpilgrim.com/2014/03/sports-goes-for-the-mobile-ad-gold-with-near-500-percent-growth-in-spending.html, accessed June 21, 2014.

42   Adam French, "Sport and the Marketing Revolution," *Mobile Marketer* (October 29, 2013). Available from: www.mobilemarketer.com/cms/opinion/columns/16469.html, accessed June 21, 2014.

43   Nikes 2018 Annual Report. Available from: https://investors.nike.com/investors/news-events-and-reports/?toggle=reports.

44   New Balance Annual Report. Available from: www.newbalance.com/about-new-balance-content-assets/inside-nb-overview.html.

45   The Challenger Project, "How New Balance Got Its Swagger Back: An Interview with the CEO and VP Global Marketing," *Eat Big Fish*. Available from: https://thechallengerproject.com/blog/2018/new-balance-ceo-vp-marketing-interview, accessed July 14, 2019.

46   Ibid.

47   Don Schultz, Stanley Tannenbaum, and Robert Lauterborn, *Integrated Marketing Communications: Putting It Together and Making It Work* (Lincolnwood, IL: NTC Publishing Group, 1992); Don Schultz, "Rethinking Marketing and Communications' ROI," *Marketing News* (December 2, 1996), 10; Don Schultz and Paul Wang, "Real World Results," *Marketing Tools* (April–May 1994).

Promotion mix elements

After completing this chapter, you should be able to:

- Describe each element of the promotion mix in detail.
- Understand the basic process for designing a successful advertising campaign.
- Discuss emerging forms of promotion.
- Outline the strategic selling process and explain why this is relevant for sport marketers.
- Identify the various forms of promotion.
- Specify the importance of public or community relations to sports marketers.

A very popular example of a true integrated marketing campaign is Red Bull. Started in 1987 with a single beverage energy drink, Red Bull has grown, in part, because of its association with action and extreme sports. Integrated marketing is so critical to the success of Red Bull, they have established their own media house to control their use of print, TV, online, mobile, and other channels of promotion. One of its first marketing campaigns, "Red Bull Gives You Wings," was promoted through mountain biking, snowboarding, skateboard, surfing, and other extreme sports.

More traditional sports such as Formula 1 racing and football/soccer have also been used as sponsorship vehicles to promote Red Bull. Along with those sports, athlete endorsers such as Parks Bonifay - wakeboarding, Joey Brezinski - skateboarding, and Dylan Bowman - ultrarunning are used in the integrated marketing mix. These endorsers and sports aren't mainstream or household names but present the perfect association between Red Bull and its target audience. Red Bull also uses more traditional sports like basketball and baseball to complement its marketing reach. In addition to individual athlete endorsers, Red Bull sponsors teams (e.g., Red Bull Brazil, Red Bull Sailing Team), events (Red Bull Cliff Diving World Championships, Red Bull Global Rallycross Championship), and stadiums like

DOI: 10.4324/9780429030673-13

Photo 10.1

Stadium signage – one of the first forms of promotion and still an important strategic tool

Credit: Shutterstock, ID# 1535975285 by Massimo Todaro

URL: www.shutterstock.com/image-photo/inside-emirates-stadium-known-ashburton-grove-1535975285

Red Bull Arena in New Jersey and Red Bull Arena in Leipzig. Using an integrated marketing approach with different platforms (individual athletes, teams, sports) and media (TV, social media, outdoor signage), Red Bull has emerged as the clear number one in energy drinks, selling nearly 7 billion cans in 2018.[1]

As demonstrated by the Red Bull example, sports marketers must carefully integrate the promotion mix elements to establish successful promotions to consumers and trade. In Chapter 9, we explored the importance of communication and the basic concepts of promotional planning. This chapter examines each of the **promotional mix elements** in greater detail. By doing so, sports marketers will be in a better position to choose the most effective promotional elements for the construction of the promotional plan. Let us begin by looking at one of the most widely used forms of promotion – advertising.

Advertising

Advertising remains one of the most visible and important marketing tools available to sports marketers. Although significant changes are taking place in the way sports products and services are promoted, the reasons for advertising remain the same. Advertising creates and maintains brand awareness and brand loyalty. In addition, advertising builds brand image

Figure 10.1
Designing an advertising campaign

and creates a distinct identity for sports products and services. Most importantly, advertising directly affects consumer behavior. In other words, it causes us to attend sporting events, buy that new pair of running shoes, or stream the NCAA Women's Basketball tournament on our device.

Most of us associate the development of an advertisement with the creative process. As you might imagine, advertising is more than a catchy jingle. To develop an effective advertisement, a systematic process is employed. Some of the steps in this process are very similar to the promotional planning process discussed in Chapter 9. This is not unexpected, as advertising is just another form of communication, or promotional tool, used by sports marketers.

The advertising process is commonly referred to as designing an advertising campaign. An advertising campaign is a series of related advertisements that communicate a common message to the target audience (see Figure 10.1). The advertising campaign (similar to the promotional planning process) is initiated with discussions and decisions about the objectives and budget. Next, creative decisions, such as the ad appeal and execution, are developed. Following this, the media strategy is planned, and, finally, the advertising campaign is evaluated. Let us explore each of the steps in designing an advertising campaign or the ad process in greater detail.

Advertising objectives

The first step in any advertising campaign is to examine the broader promotional objectives and marketing goals. The overall objectives of the advertising campaign should, of course, be consistent with the strategic direction of the sports organization. The specific objectives and budgeting techniques for advertising are much the same as those discussed in Chapter 9. That is, advertising is designed to inform, persuade, remind, and cause consumers in the target market to take action.[2] In addition to these broad objectives, **advertising objectives** are sometimes categorized as either direct or indirect.

The purpose of **direct objectives** in advertising is to elicit a behavioral response from the target audience. In sports marketing, this behavioral response may be in the form of purchasing tickets to a game, buying sporting goods that were advertised on the web, or even volunteering at a local event. Sometimes an advertisement asks consumers to make multiple behavioral responses – for instance, retired quarterback Tony Romo is now promoting Skechers athletic footwear and asks that we visit the Web site, feel the comfort, and buy the shoes.

Web Capture 10.1
Titleist Golf using a direct objective advertising technique

Credit: Titleist

Rightsholder: Acushnet Company

URL: www.titleist.com/golf-clubs/golf-drivers

Direct advertising objectives can be further categorized into two distinct types: advertising to end users and sales promotion advertising. However, all direct response objectives are designed to induce action.

Advertising by sports organizations to end users

In this case, the objectives of advertising are not to enhance the perceived image of the event, the team, or the league but rather to generate immediate response. With this type of objective, the sports marketer is attempting to build immediate sales and revenue. As such, the specific objective of advertising to end users is usually stated in terms of increasing sales volume.

Sales promotion advertising

It is common for contests, sweepstakes, coupons, and other forms of sales promotions to be advertised via any number of media. As such, the objectives of direct response advertisements are to have consumers participate in the contests and sweepstakes or redeem coupons. Objectives, therefore, are measured in terms of the level of participation in the sales promotion and ultimately an increase in sales.

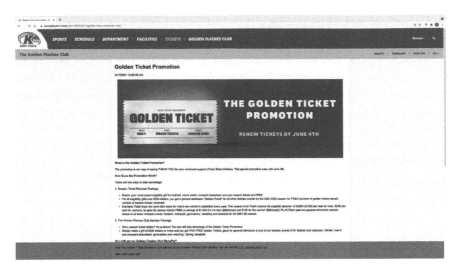

Web Capture 10.2
Kent State University Golden Flash Club recent season ticket sales promotion

Source: Kent State University Athletics

URL: https://kentstatesports.com/sports/2021/3/17/golden-ticket-promotion.aspx

Indirect objectives are based on establishing pre-behavioral (i.e., prior to action) responses to advertising, that is, accomplishing goals, such as increasing awareness, enhancing image, improving attitudes, or educating consumers. These indirect objectives should, in turn, lead to more direct behavioral responses. Consider the ad for Bank of America promoting the fact that they are the "Official Bank of Major League Baseball" and asking fans to describe their favorite MLB memories. The objective of this advertisement is to enhance the image of Bank of America through its connection with baseball, the American pastime. Ultimately, the advertisement's sponsor hopes these indirect objectives will lead to the behavior response of securing new customers and reminding existing customers to purchase more products and services from Bank of America. This strategy, based on all measures, seems to be producing ROI results beyond expectations.[3]

Indirect objectives, such as image enhancement, are always present to some extent in advertising. Sports leagues, such as the NFL, use indirect advertising (such as Play 60 - a national youth health and fitness campaign) to generate awareness of the NFL and its engagement in the community. In addition, these leagues often work with individual teams to further enhance behavioral objectives such as the handful of teams who participated in Major League Baseball's Dog Day Games. At these special events like "Pups in the Park," ticketholders and their best friends sit in a designated section and can take part in activities such as a pregame parade, a costume contest, special treats, and more. Even better, many ballparks donate a portion of these ticket proceeds to local animal charities.

Advertising budgeting

As with advertising objectives, budgeting methods for an ad campaign are largely the same as those for other forms of promotion. For example, techniques such as competitive parity, objective and task, and percentage of sales are again relevant to advertising. Whatever the methods used, it is important to remember that **advertising budgeting** should ideally stem from the objectives the advertising is attempting to achieve. However, other factors, such as monies available, competitive activity, and how the sports organization views the effectiveness of advertising in general, should be kept in mind.

Creative decisions

After the objectives and the budget have been established, the creative process becomes the focus of the advertising campaign or **creative decisions**. The **creative process** has been defined as generating the ideas and the concept of the advertisement. Advertising and sports marketing agencies hire individuals who possess a great deal of creativity, but even the most innovative people use a systematic process to harness their creativity.

To begin the creative process, most advertising agencies prepare a creative brief. The purpose of any creative brief is to understand clients' communication objectives so the creative process will be maximized. The **creative brief** is a tool used to guide the creative process toward a solution that will serve the interests of the client and their customers. When used properly, the creative brief can be thought of as a marketing-oriented approach to the design of an advertising campaign.

The three outcomes of the creative process are (1) identifying benefits of the sports product, (2) designing the advertising appeal – what to say, and (3) developing the advertising execution – how and when to say it. The importance of an effective creative brief and each of these elements in the creative decision process is discussed in the following article.

ARTICLE 10.1
6 REASONS WHY IT'S IMPORTANT TO HAVE A STRONG
CREATIVE BRIEF

Generated before the design process even begins, the creative brief is a document that organizes a client's objectives and serves as a guide throughout the process ahead. Since creative briefs tend to be short (about 1–2 pages) and because they are inward-facing, it can be easy to undervalue their importance. But these documents can serve many functions and lay the foundation for several phases of the work that will come down the road. So today we'll discuss six reasons why it's important to have a strong creative brief.

Before we get into the specific benefits of a strong creative brief, let's quickly talk about the document itself. Although every firm has their own approach to writing a creative brief, below are a few of the topics that are typically included:

- Client Information
- Technical Specifications for Deliverable Materials
- Details about the Product/Service
- Brand Elements
- Stylistic Preferences
- Project Timeline

Why is it so important to effectively capture this information and other similarly relevant information? Because . . .

1. **Gets Everyone on the Same Page:** From account managers and creative directors to designers and copywriters, the creative brief is an easy way to get all project participants on the same page. Especially because not everyone is going to be involved with every client meeting; nor, most likely, will every contributor be a part of the process from start to finish. In fact, several specialists (i.e. a character animator, a voice-over artist) are only involved in the project for a very short period of time, and the creative brief is like the baton in your relay race. So it's valuable to have a short, easy-to-read, single depot that accumulates all the relevant information.

2. **Helps Identify What You *Don't* Know:** Although the primary benefit of a creative brief is the synthesizing key information in a single place, the process of doing so often results in a subtle perk: realizing what you don't know. Or, at the least, realizing where your intel and understanding could be stronger. And by making the effort to reconcile that issue, and supplement your creative brief with additional thought or information, you'll inevitably wind up with a more comprehensive understanding of the client's objective and better determine how you can assist with that.

3. **More Than Just a Database:** Because the creative brief compiles several bits of information, it may be tempting to think of the document as something like a database. But while it does indeed include those relevant details, the creative brief must be more than just a collection of facts. It needs to capture the client's tone and their specific brand messaging. As a result, a strong creative brief doesn't just parrot quotes about the client's product or service. It needs to go the extra mile, accounting for context and objective. Simply put: there should be a vision to the document. A vision – describing what the clients wants, requires, and needs – that is clear enough to inform all stakeholders from start to finish.

4. **Conductive to Effective Messaging:** As a result of pairing vision with information, the creative brief will begin to address your overarching responsibility: messaging. By successfully tracing a starting point (the information) and the desired end point (the vision),

stakeholders reviewing the document will gain insight into the possible routes to get there. This is particularly effective when there is a strong link between product, brand and style; a trio of factors that, when combined together, can help shine a light on the best path forward.

5. **Inspiration (and Confirmation):** While we would all like to believe that every minute on the clock is fueled with an equal amount of energy and passion, the truth is that those things tend to ebb and flow. A professional, of course, will push through the ups and downs, but it never hurts to have an additional source of inspiration to help get the juices flowing. Which, when done well, is exactly what a creative brief can be. This does *not* mean that a creative brief should be filled with positive, you-can-do-it messages, but simply that a well-shaped and thoughtful document could help spark ideas. And in addition to providing a spark, it can also be helpful as a means to confirm the instincts (and provide confidence) to employees who read it. Once again, it's about getting everyone on the same page, so as to get the best out of everyone involved.

6. **A Reviewable, Recorded Document:** Even when you've completed a project, the creative brief still maintains value. Although it is no longer needed on an active basis, it can be useful when working on similar projects or working with similar clients. It can be a reminder of what we right before, and provide insight into what might be needed to ensure a similar success going forward. So even when a creative brief helps lead to a jump well done, make sure to save that document as it might come in handy down the line!

Source: 6 Reasons Why It's Important to Have a Strong Creative Brief. www.business2community.com/strategy/6-reasons-important-strong-creative-brief-01450576

Identifying benefits

Designing a distinctive advertising campaign involves identifying the key benefits of the sports product. We have briefly discussed the importance of understanding benefits in the context of segmenting consumer markets. As defined in Chapter 7, benefits describe why consumers purchase a product or service or what problem the product solves for the consumer. For advertising purposes, describing the benefits or reasons consumers should buy the sports product is a must. Marketing research is used to understand the benefits desired or perceived by consumers who might use or purchase the sports product.

Advertising appeals

Understanding benefits and developing **advertising appeals** go hand in hand. Once the desired benefits are uncovered, the advertising appeal is developed around these benefits. In short, the advertising appeal recounts *why* the consumer wants to purchase the sports product. The major advertising appeals used in sports marketing include health, emotion, fear, sex, and pleasure.

Health appeals are becoming prevalent in advertising, as the value placed on health continues to increase in the United States. Over the five years prior to 2019, the gym, health, and fitness clubs industry has experienced substantial growth in demand, and, as a result, the breakdown of the industry's markets has also changed. The aging population has encouraged health and fitness clubs to widen their target demographic beyond the traditional market of 18- to 35-year-olds. Industry operators are increasingly expanding their target market to include 35- to 50-year-olds and individuals aged over 50.

According to the Physical Activity Council, the 50+ demographic is the most likely to be inactive: 32.5 percent of individuals aged 55 to 64 and 40.7 percent of those over the age of 65 are considered inactive. However, this demographic has a relatively high participation rate in fitness sports as well as outdoor sports. Over the five years prior to 2019, the burgeoning elderly population has become increasingly health conscious, stimulating demand for industry services. In 2019, IBISWorld expects that 24.6 percent of demand will stem from this cohort.[4]

A number of **emotional appeals**, such as fear, humor, sex, pleasure, and the drama associated with athletic competition, are also used in sports marketing promotions. One of the unique aspects of sports marketing is the emotional attachment that consumers develop for the sports product. As discussed in Chapter 5, many fans have high levels of involvement and identification with their favorite athletes and teams.[5] Some fans may even view themselves as part of the team. Recognizing this strong emotional component, many advertisers of sports use emotional appeals. The infamous "Thrill of victory and agony of defeat" message used for decades for ABC's *Wide World of Sports* opening captures the essence of an emotional appeal. Emotional appeals that allow fans to relive the team's greatest moments and performances of past years are often used to encourage future attendance.

One specific type of emotional appeal is a fear appeal. **Fear appeals** are messages designed to communicate what negative consequences may occur if the sports product or service is not used or is used improperly. Scare tactics are usually inappropriate for sports products and services, but in some product categories, moderate amounts of fear in a message can be effective. Consider, for example, messages concerning exercise equipment or health club membership. Many promotional campaigns are built around consumers' fears of being physically unfit and aging. Even athletic promoters use moderate fear appeals by telling consumers that tickets will be sold out quickly and that they should not wait to purchase their seats. Effective sports marketers identify their sports products as solutions to the common fears of consumers. For example, manufacturers of bike and skateboard helmets are quick to cite the plethora of head injuries that result without the use of proper headgear. Perhaps the best recent example and often in the news are the brain injuries sustained in football. The VICIS ZERO1 football helmet claims to be the best and safest helmet in the world based on superior engineering.[6]

Another emotional appeal is sex. **Sex appeals** rely on the old adage that "sex sells." Typically, marketers who use sex appeals in their messages are selling products that are sexually related, such as perfumes, jewelry, and clothing. Danica Patrick, Ronda Rousey, and Skylar Diggins have all been cited as female athletes who have used their outer beauty to enhance their career off the field. Additionally, a recent cover of *Golf Digest*'s Fitness Edition featured a young Lexi Thompson draped in a towel, attracting immediate attention and sparking a debate about the use of sex appeals by female athletes.[7]

In sports marketing, sex appeals are sometimes used, but this is always a delicate ethical subject. Everywhere we look, we find ourselves drawn to images of scantily clad, attractive men and women that are supposed to inspire us to purchase products they endorse. Sex appeal can increase the effectiveness of an ad or a commercial because it draws the customer's attention. It's human nature to be curious about sex and though it takes more explicitness to grab our attention and arouse us than before, it can be effective; however, misuse of connotations in marketing and advertising platforms can be costly.[8]

ARTICLE 10.2
SPOTLIGHT ON SPORTS MARKETING ETHICS

This Girl Can('t)? campaign simply reworks 'sex sells' approach

Authors: Paul Harrison, Laura McVey

Sport England is to partner with VicHealth for a social marketing campaign to encourage women to participate in sport based on its This Girl Can campaign. However, beyond the campaign's initial "feel-good" nature, this news may not be as totally positive as it seems.

In its attempt to motivate and empower women, the campaign material may unintentionally work with entrenched norms of sexualising women to perpetuate their self-objectification. This is likely not only to be detrimental to their mental and physical health, but also to further their commodification in society.

The origins of This Girl Can

In 2015, Sport England launched This Girl Can to encourage women to be more active, regardless of body type or age. The mainstream and social media response was positive, and the campaign has received significant global attention for its "Just Do It" style of messaging.

The aim was to bridge the gender gap in sport participation. Two million more British men than women were playing sport or exercising regularly. Yet 75% of women say they want to be more active.

'This Girl Can' campaign ad

Many have debated the campaign's likely effect on women. But what's clear is that This Girl Can is an example of the continuing power of hegemonic discipline over women's bodies and self-conception.

Commercial marketing has always used this commodification of women. But its use in a campaign aimed at empowering women should be of concern.

What's the problem?

Nike has long traded on women 'just doing it' to sell sportswear.

The romanticisation of women who are "just doing it" has long been used to sell women's sportswear. This ideology is now reaching a crescendo. In the This Girl Can advertisement, simulated hypersexuality is posited as essential to agency and action. This turns a laudably intended campaign of empowerment into one of sexual subjectification and self-surveillance. The "male gaze" – depicting women and the world from a male point of view – has cemented itself as a staple in advertising, including sports campaigns. What is telling in the This Girl Can campaign is the way in which this male gaze has become an internalised self perception

Another point of distinction in this campaign is a shift from women's sexualized bodies presented as passive, mute objects of a male gaze to active, desiring sexual subjects. They are women who choose to present themselves in a seemingly objectified manner because it is in their (implicitly "liberated") self-interest.

The likelihood of women internalizing their agency as directly linked to their sexual capital is highly related to how normalized this is. Research has found that as group identification increases, a person becomes increasingly likely to adopt that group's behavioral norms. Considering the campaign's viral status, this is an important consideration.

The exposure of bodies is central to the campaign's intended message of body confidence and erasing fears of judgement. But, far from what many headlines would have you believe, this campaign is not revolutionary in its construction of women.

Being "confident", "carefree" and "unconcerned about one's appearance" are now central aspects of femininity – even as they exist alongside injunctions to meet impossibly high standards of beauty.

So, although we should rejoice at the portrayal of "normal" bodies in this and other campaigns, the same objectification of women is at play. Even when showing women's bodies in action, rather than focusing on the traits of health, agility and co-ordination, the campaign ad frames the female body as an object.

The focus is on women's buttocks, faces, hips and chests, the sexualized movements of twerking, "wobbling", hip shaking and heavy breathing, and taglines such as "Hot, and not bothered" and "Sweating like a pig, feeling like a fox".

Under Armour uses empowering language in its campaigns, but the imagery doesn't stray far from the norm. This approach, while seemingly empowering, could also be read as a simple re-engineering of the objectified female (in contrast to the athletic male) that we often see in sportswear advertising.

An American Psychological Association taskforce, examining the sexualization of girls in US culture, concluded that this had negative impacts on girls' cognitive functioning, physical and mental health, body dissatisfaction and appearance, anxiety, sexuality, attitudes and beliefs.

Many would contend that sexualization can act as empowerment. However, there is some danger in this proposition for selling sports involvement to women. The taskforce highlighted a negative relationship between self-objectification and girls' sports performance.

The campaign's use of the text overlay of "I kick balls. Deal with it" reminds the viewer of the traditional androcentric domination of sports. However, we suggest empowerment is not just about claiming back an insult but understanding the reality of the constricted space and physicality of women.

As Iris Young argues, there is not only a style of "throwing like a girl", but also "running like a girl", "hitting like a girl", and so on. For women in sport, a space surrounds them in imagination that they are not free to move beyond.

What would a better campaign do?

A better way forward would be to focus on "real women's" voices (in more than stylized overlays and sexualized panting) rather than bodies – highlighting the judgement women fear, as well as the pleasure they can get exercising.

It could prove empowering to take the enjoyment often reserved for men's experience of physical activity – independent of desirability – and allowing that to be the drive for women's participation.

A focus on the female voice is also prime, as the voiceover in advertising – the credible, convincing and authoritative voice of reason – is overwhelmingly likely to be male. To allow the female voice to exist free from the constraints of the gaze – that is, disembodied, omniscient, objective and empowered – could offer a route to a stronger construction of women in sports advertising.

When campaigns do use images of women participating in sport, a greater reliance should be on the highly relevant and typically untextualized body parts of hands and feet – signifiers more often used in marketing sports (and sports equipment) to men.

Involving more women in sport is significant. Sport and leisure spaces are a key setting in the primary prevention of violence against women.

The chance for sport to be a site of redefining power is monumental – the very centrality of sport in gender socialization is key to its ability to challenge traditional roles and construct new, more positive identities for both sexes.

We do applaud the campaign's success in encouraging women to participate in sport in the UK. Unfortunately, for the most part, it does little to take women away from the usual *sex sells* approach (albeit with the inclusion of more "real" women) we have come to expect of mainstream advertising.

Source: The Conversation, https://theconversation.com/this-girl-can-t-campaign-simply-reworks-sex-sells-approach-81609

Although it may be hard to argue against sex selling sport in today's society, many think enough is enough.[9] In fact, two researchers showed that women's sports gain nothing from marketing the athletes' looks. Mary Jo Kane and Heather Maxwell showed groups of people photos of sportswomen covering the spectrum from highly athletic to highly sexualized. Their initial findings showed that none of those images motivated men to attend games or buy tickets. Kane and Maxwell's research suggests that selling out women to sexist stereotypes does nothing to advance the cause of women's sports, nor does it serve the bottom line.

Pleasure or fun appeals are designed for those target audiences that participate in sports or watch sports for fun, social interaction, or enjoyment. These advertising appeals should stress the positive relationships that can be developed among family members, friends, or business associates by attending games or participating in sports. A recent advertisement by Buick captured a father watching his son play pee-wee football, only to see him magically transform into Cam Newton. The essence of the appeal was that the car pulling up to watch the game couldn't possibly be a Buick (implying it was too nice) and the father saying that if that car was a Buick, my son is Cam Newton. Another classic example of a fun appeal was a McDonald's ad featuring legends Larry Bird and Michael Jordan trying to outdo each other in a game of HORSE with a Big Mac and fries on the line to the winner.[10]

Advertising execution

The **advertising execution** should answer the appeal that the advertiser is trying to target. In other words, it is not what to say but how to say it. Let us look at some of the more common executional formats, such as message sidedness, comparative advertisements, slice of life, scientific, and testimonials.

One executional format is whether to construct the message as **one-sided versus two-sided**. A one-sided message conveys only the positive benefits of a sports product or service. Most sports organizations do not want to communicate the negative features of their products or services, but this can have its advantages. Describing the negatives along with the positives can enhance the credibility of the source by making it more trustworthy. In addition, discussing the negative aspects of the sports product can ultimately lower consumers' expectations and lead to more satisfaction. For instance, you rarely hear a coach at any level talk about how unbeatable a team or player is. Rather, the focus is on the weaknesses of the team, which reduces fan (and owner) expectations.

Comparative advertisements, another executional format, contrast one sports product with another. When doing comparative advertisements, sports advertisers stress the advantages of their sports product relative to the competition. For new sports products that possess a significant differential advantage, comparative advertisements can be especially effective. The risk involved with comparative advertisements is that consumers are exposed to your product as well as the competitor's product.

Golf ball advertisements, which typically rely on selling their technical superiority to produce longer distance and softer feel, commonly use comparative ads. Titleist promotes its Tour Soft ball in a compelling commercial narrated by golf announcer Jim Nantz, adding credibility to the claim. As Nantz talks about the Titleist ball, he cleverly compares the ball to the Bridgestone and TaylorMade tour balls without ever showing them to the consumer.[11]

Because of the unique nature of sport, many advertisements are inherently comparative. For example, boxing advertisements touted the "Fight of the Century" between Muhammad Ali and Joe Frazier. In fact, there have been many "Fight of the Century" advertisements that are strikingly similar, comparing two boxers' strengths and weaknesses. Other sporting events,

Web Capture 10.3
Easton stresses its competitive advantage

Source: Easton Sports

URL: www.easton.com/

such as the made-for-television first, which pay-per-view called "The Match: Tiger vs Phil", use a similar comparative format for promoting events. Many home teams skillfully use comparative advertisements to attract moderately involved fans interested in the success of the local team. These fans are attracted by the allure of the visiting team or one of its star athletes. For instance, many basketball advertisements promote the big-name athletes of the opposing team rather than highlighting their own stars.

Slice-of-life advertisements show a "common" athlete or consumer in a common, everyday situation in which the consumer might be using the advertised sports or non-sports product. For example, Campbell's Chunky Soups has teamed up with a number of NFL athletes and their mothers in an effort to promote their line of soups that "eat like a meal." The advertisement focuses on promoting the hearty soups, emphasizing the slice-of-life choices between a mother and her child at any age. The latest Campbell's ads feature former Dallas Cowboy turned TV analyst Jason Witten, and another features NFL star Dak Prescott.

A slight variation of this style is **lifestyle advertisements**, wherein the advertisement is intended to portray the lifestyle of the desired target audience. For example, the classic Nike "Just Do It" campaign uses a slice-of-life format that appeals to the participant in each of us. In another slice-of-life example, Wrangler has run a very effective campaign for their product using former football star and Hall of Famer Brett Favre as their "everyday" spokesperson who feels comfortable in their jeans all day long.

Another executional style that is also readily used in sports advertising is called **scientific advertisements**. Advertisers using this style feature the technological superiority of their sports product or use research or scientific studies to support their claims. Golf equipment manufacturers use scientific claims to sell their products. Callaway is touting its Chrome Soft and Chrome

Web Capture 10.4
Brett Favre creates a powerful message for Wrangler

Credit: Wrangler

URL: www.wrangler.com/worn-by-greats/brett-favre.html

Soft X balls' top performance because of the use of graphene, a one-atom-thick nanoparticle that is part of the dual-core construction. The discovery of graphene was awarded the Nobel Prize in physics in 2010, so Callaway is using technological advancement at the highest levels to improve and market their product.

One of the most prevalent executional styles for sports advertising is the use of **testimonials**. Testimonials are statements about the sports product given by endorsers. These endorsers may be the "common" athlete, professional athletes, teams, coaches and managers, owners, or even inanimate objects such as mascots. Table 10.1 highlights the 50 most popular celebrity sport endorsers in 2019.

Table 10.1 Fifty most marketable active athletes of 2019

1. Naomi Osaka	26. Katie Ledecky
2. Raheem Sterling	27. Ada Hegerberg
3. Zion Williamson	28. Odell Beckham Jr.
4. Megan Rapinoe	29. Christian Pulisic
5. Kylian Mbappe'	30. Son Heung-min
6. Giannis Antetokounmpo	31. Eliud Kipchoge
7. Brooks Koepka	32. Luka Doncic
8. Charles Leclerc	33. Aja Wilson
9. Dina Asher-Smith	34. Mohamed Salah
10. Simone Biles	35. Tyson Fury
11. Paul Pogba	36. Sloan Stephens
12. Leticia Bufoni	37. Joel Embiid
13. Harry Kane	38. Stephan Curry
14. Chloe Kim	39. Shohei Ohtani
15. Virat Kohli	40. Jofra Archer
16. Alexander Zverev	41. Lexi Thompson
17. Saquon Barkley	42. Lieke Martens
18. Anthony Joshua	43. Baker Mayfield
19. Max Verstappen	44. Cody Bellinger
20. Dominic Thiem	45. Noah Lyles
21. Adam Peaty	46. Virgil Van Dijk
22. Alex Morgan	47. Ashleigh Barty
23. JuJu Smith-Schuster	48. Auston Matthews
24. Mikaela Shiffrin	49. Egan Bernal
25. Aaron Judge	50. Ko Jin-Young

*Source:*www.sportspromedia.com/most-marketable

Why are athlete testimonials so popular among sports advertisers? The answer to this question is the ability of sports celebrities to persuade the target audience and move them toward purchase. Athletes' persuasive power stems from their credibility and, in some cases, attractiveness. **Credibility** refers to the expertise and the trustworthiness of the source of the message. **Expertise** is the knowledge, skill, or special experience possessed by the source about the sports product. Of course, successful athletes who promote products needed to participate in their sport have demonstrable expertise. Examples of the athlete-athletic product match-up include Kevin Durant and Maya Moore - basketball shoe contracts, Tiger Woods and Lydia Ko - golf equipment, Kevin Harvick and Dale Earnhardt Jr. - automotive industry, Bryce Harper and Mike Trout - baseball gloves, Ashleigh Barty and Andy Murray - tennis racquets, and Sidney Crosby and Alex Ovechkin - hockey equipment.

The other dimension of source credibility is **trustworthiness**. This refers to the honesty and believability of the athlete endorser(s). Trustworthiness is an intangible characteristic that is becoming harder and harder for professional athletes to establish. Today's consumers realize athletes with already large salaries are being paid huge sums of money for endorsements. Because of this, the athlete's believability is often suspect. Nevertheless, even some of the highest-paid athlete endorsers, such as George Foreman, the late Arnold Palmer, and Peyton Manning, seem to have established themselves as trustworthy sources of information, while

Web Capture 10.5

Under Armour using this powerful imagery of Jordan Spieth

Credit: Under Armour

URL: www.underarmour.com/en-us/sports/golf?iid=sig&iidasset=190215_SS19_GOLF_VaniishSiteSIG_DIG#kits

others, such as Tiger Woods, have tarnished their credibility and trustworthiness in the eye of the American public, only to come back and potentially regain the public's trust and admiration.

In addition to credibility, another factor that makes athletes successful endorsers is **attractiveness**. Although attractiveness is usually associated with physical beauty, it appears to have another, nonphysical dimension based on personality, lifestyle, and intellect. Attractiveness operates using the process of identification, which means that the target audience identifies with the source (athlete) in some fashion. Gatorade's classic "I wanna be like Mike" campaign, featuring Michael Jordan, is a good example of the identification process.

Athlete trustworthiness and attractiveness can change in an instance; consider the following opinion of Tiger Woods and how this view is different today and somewhat of a roller coaster with respect to public opinion. Although athlete endorsers can be extremely effective, there are risks involved. Athletes are costly, may suffer career-threatening injuries, or may just do foolish things.

The following article showcases a classic example of how an athlete's choices may or may not have a detrimental impact on endorsements as well as their career.

ARTICLE 10.3
SPOTLIGHT ON SPORTS MARKETING ETHICS

Six months after Ronaldo was accused of rape, why is the case in legal limbo?

Ronaldo was accused in September of raping an American woman in Las Vegas back in 2009. Police have since reopened the investigation.

ON A WARM October day in Las Vegas, we slip our car into a parking lot wedged between two buildings, then push open the door to the lawyer's office. My colleague, Nicole Noren, and I figure this will be simple. We are in Nevada reporting on the rape allegations against Cristiano Ronaldo, and we want to meet Ronaldo's attorneys, as well as the lawyers representing Kathryn Mayorga, the woman accusing him.

Normally, this sort of meeting is pretty straightforward for journalists. Lawyers, particularly those who do a lot of personal injury work in places with no shortage of clients like Las Vegas, almost always have a strong perspective on a case and are generally happy to tell you all about it. When those clients are celebrities and the cases are in the public eye, that chattiness – on the record or on background – is amped up even more.

We have seen news reports that a lawyer named Peter Christiansen is representing Ronaldo, though we have not confirmed this, and even if it is true, we are not sure *which* Peter Christiansen – there is a Peter J. and a Peter S. in this office. We find the Christiansen Law Offices down the street from a bail bondsman and a wedding chapel. We go inside and, seeing no receptionist or secretary, follow a sign for "Christiansen" down a hall.

We step into an office where two women and a man are sitting. We identify ourselves and ask if we can either talk to or make an appointment with one of the Christiansens. The women physically recoil.

"You have to leave right now," one of them replies. Her voice rises. "You're not allowed to be here. You have to go. You have to go."

She is frantic. I explain that there is no one at the front desk area so we'd decided to walk back. I ask if we can leave a message or even just confirm which Peter Christiansen is Ronaldo's lawyer. The woman becomes more animated. "You need to leave right now!" she says. "I can call the police if I need to."

We back away, confused. "A lawyer won't even confirm he is representing someone? That's never happened to me before," I say to Nicole as we walk to the car. She nods. "Never for me either."

The whole thing feels strange. We look over our shoulders and see the woman from the office watching us as we leave. She peers out the door as we drive away.

Even with a rape allegation dangling over its biggest star, Juventus is enjoying a Ronaldo boom.

THERE IS A lot that feels unusual about this case: the circumstances surrounding the alleged crime, the start-stop-start-again police investigation, the fallout (or lack thereof) that comes with the world's most famous athlete being accused of committing a violent sex crime.

A big part of this is the timeline. According to Mayorga, Ronaldo raped her in the early hours of June 13, 2009, after she and a friend met him at a club and spent part of the previous evening together. Mayorga, then 25, reported the assault to Las Vegas police that afternoon. She did not identify Ronaldo by name at that time, she says, because he was a public figure and she felt intimidated. She was taken to a hospital and had a rape kit examination.

In the following months, according to Mayorga's attorneys, private investigators hired by Ronaldo's European lawyers trailed her and recorded her movements. She also claims that Ronaldo's lawyers, working with private investigators and crisis consultants, pushed for an out-of-court settlement that would require her to drop all charges; they also tried, she says, to use that potential outcome to dissuade police from investigating. Ultimately, Mayorga signed a nondisclosure agreement with Ronaldo's team in January 2010. She received roughly $375,000, and police closed the investigation.

More than seven years later, in 2017, German magazine *Der Spiegel* published a story about an alleged rape committed by Ronaldo, without naming Mayorga. Much of the information for the story came from emails, memos and documents *Der Spiegel* received from a computer hacking group known as Football Leaks, a website primarily focused on exposing the murky underworld of international soccer business transactions and relationships.

Ronaldo's agent denied and discredited the report, saying that the documents were obtained illegally and claiming it was illegal for *Der Spiegel* to publish on the subject. A year and a half later, in September 2018, *Der Spiegel* published another report on the case, this time naming and interviewing Mayorga. In that story, she described, in graphic detail, how Ronaldo assaulted and anally raped her, as well as her years of suffering in the aftermath. *Der Spiegel* also unearthed a trove of documents related to the case, again obtained via Football

Leaks, including one in which Ronaldo described the encounter to his lawyer as "rude" and admitted Mayorga "said no and stop several times."

Ronaldo's European attorneys have denied the allegations and questioned the documents' authenticity. Around the same time, Las Vegas police reopened their investigation into the alleged act, eight years after closing it. (In Nevada, the statute of limitations on rape cases is 20 years.) Mayorga, meanwhile, announced later in September that she is suing Ronaldo. Her new lawyer, a man named Leslie Stovall, contends that the documents detailing what happened in the aftermath of the alleged rape show an attempted and improper cover-up. The intimidation of Mayorga by Ronaldo's private investigators and their interactions with police while the case was being investigated were designed to "prevent or delay criminal prosecution," Stovall told *Der Spiegel* in October, adding that "hiding a crime is a crime."

Stovall also told *Der Spiegel* that the original nondisclosure agreement is not valid for many reasons, including Ronaldo's failure to comply with parts of it. Most notably, Stovall believes that correspondence between Ronaldo's agents and lawyers shows that a letter Mayorga wrote to Ronaldo after the settlement was reached – in which she describes her pain and upbraids him – was never read to Ronaldo, despite that being a requirement of the agreement.

Presumably, all of this is a massive development – only it isn't. Stovall holds a news conference on Oct. 3 at his tiny offices on the outskirts of Las Vegas and livestreams it (with dodgy audio) on his firm's Facebook page. The volume of news coverage around the world is hardly overwhelming, and social media is surprisingly muted.

This dissonance is jarring, particularly when one considers the base reality: The most famous player in the world's most popular sport has been accused of doing something that, should he be convicted, could mean a life sentence in prison. (Rape is a Category A felony in Nevada.)

This is more than gossip, more than a misunderstanding. The stakes are real, and everyone waits to see what will happen next.

Except . . . nothing does.

IT'S BEEN MORE than five months since Stovall announced Mayorga's lawsuit and the police reopened their investigation. There has been no announcement about whether charges will be filed against Ronaldo, no update on whether the police have discovered anything that makes them believe officers were compromised during the initial investigation. Police did request a DNA sample from Ronaldo, which is common and, since Ronaldo's team doesn't deny that there was a sexual encounter, not necessarily that damaging.

It is a disquieting limbo. While Mayorga, according to her attorneys, is still battling depression related to the alleged assault and has spent many weeks away from home in Nevada to avoid the media crush, Ronaldo has not faced any significant fallout. He continues to score goals and post photos of his family, his team celebrations and his impeccable physique on Instagram to his 156.3 million followers. His main American sponsors – Nike and EA Sports – made statements expressing concern about the allegations but took no substantive action.

Ronaldo's club is steadfast in its support. Juventus, an Italian club looking to keep up with more popular, wealthier teams in England and Spain, broke the league transfer record to sign Ronaldo last July and, even with a rape accusation dangling over its new star, basks in his fame: Shares are up; millions of fans are latching on to the club's social platforms; ticket and jersey sales are soaring.

Initially, it seemed as though Ronaldo thought this would simply go away. In an Instagram Live post shortly after the lawsuit was announced, he casually described Mayorga's allegations as "fake news" and said it was "normal" that someone would "wanna be famous – to say my name." He added that situations like this are "part of the job."

Ronaldo kept with that theme when he released a more standard statement a few days later in which he denied raping Mayorga and said rape is "an abominable crime," adding, "I refuse to feed the media spectacle created by people seeking to promote themselves at my expense. My clear [conscience] will thereby allow me to await with tranquillity the results of any and all investigations."

That last part might be a clue to his legal team's approach: running the clock. While the criminal investigation slogs on, Mayorga's civil suit against Ronaldo has stalled as well. That is primarily because Ronaldo has still not officially been served notice of the lawsuit. Serving a lawsuit to someone who lives abroad is a tricky process that requires following rules set forth in international treaties, and Ronaldo has not authorized his American attorney to accept on his behalf. Peter S. Christiansen, who has not returned ESPN's calls and messages since the visit to his office, isn't even listed as an attorney of record in the court's digital filing of Mayorga's lawsuit. That space is blank.

Stovall and his associates have been unsuccessful serving Ronaldo in Italy. The initial 120-day period expired at the beginning of February, and Stovall has filed a motion asking the court to grant an extension and to allow service by leaving the paperwork at Juventus' training center or via public notification (publishing the lawsuit in Las Vegas and Turin newspapers in lieu of handing Ronaldo a copy). According to portions of the motion published by the *Daily Mail*, an English tabloid, the Italian process server hired by Stovall spent several months trying to serve Ronaldo but was stymied at every turn. At one point, per the motion, the server reported that Juventus players are treated "like royalty" in Turin, making it nearly impossible to access Ronaldo. From Ronaldo's perspective, that is presumably the idea.

"A rich defendant can wear down a plaintiff with lesser means," says Abed Awad, an attorney and legal commentator with experience in international law. "It's a delaying tactic, and it's a calculated strategy. Sometimes it works, sometimes it backfires."

Maybe, at some point, there will be a criminal charge. Maybe, at some point, the civil case will proceed. For now, only dribs and drabs tumble out, barely registering beneath the regular cacophony of a famous athlete's buzz: Ronaldo's mother said she believes Mayorga knew when she went to Ronaldo's hotel that it "wasn't to play cards." A former girlfriend of Ronaldo's has said she was bullied and threatened by him. (After speaking with her, Stovall says he doesn't see a helpful connection.) In January, Ronaldo had a different brush with the law, this time in Spain, where he settled a tax evasion charge stemming from his time at Real Madrid. Meanwhile, the rape case is in limbo.

This, it seems, is the reality of fame. The type of fame Ronaldo enjoys means power – the power to hide in plain sight, to appear on screens in every country every weekend yet avoid being served. Ronaldo might not be above the law, but he can surround himself with a protective layer of lawyers, private investigators and fixers so thick he can hover above it for a lot longer than most. And so, Ronaldo continues to score goals. Juventus continues to thrive. And Mayorga, with her scars now bared to all the world, continues to wait.

Source: Borden, Sam 2019. Six months after Ronaldo was accused of rape, why is the case in legal limbo? ESPN.com, March 12, 2019. Accessed September 24, 2020. www.espn.com/soccer/soccer/0/blog/post/3794488/six-months-after-ronaldo-was-accused-of-rapewhy-is-the-case-in-legal-limbo

In addition, the following narratives illustrate how adverse situations create endorsement issues for individual athlete endorsers.[12] Ryan Lochte, 12-time Olympic medalist, and three of his U.S. teammates claimed that they were robbed at gunpoint following a party in Rio. However, an investigation revealed that the swimmers had made up most of the story. They actually vandalized a gas station after having too much to drink.

Just a few short months after returning to the court following the birth of her first child, Serena Williams found herself at the center of a controversy at the U.S. Open. During the final against 20-year-old Naomi Osaka, Williams called chair umpire Carlos Ramos a "thief" and a "liar" after he deducted a point from the tennis superstar for committing three code violations, including receiving coaching from the stands and verbal abuse. After the match, Williams doubled down on her comments, accusing Ramos of sexism.[13]

The story of Shaun White's 2018 Olympics quickly went from that of comeback to scandal after a pair of controversies overshadowed the American snowboarder's gold medal run in the halfpipe event. First White was accused of mishandling the American flag after winning a competition, and then allegations of sexual harassment made by a former bandmate resurfaced.[14]

Seattle Mariners second baseman Robinson Cano was handed an 80-game suspension for violating the league's joint drug agreement, testing positive for the diuretic furosemide, often used as a masking agent for drug tests. Before the suspension, Cano, who is second all-time in home runs for second basemen, was well on his way to Cooperstown.[15]

One of the biggest controversies to rock cricket took place in Australia, where captain Steve Smith and vice-captain David Warner were involved in ball-tampering scandal during the Cape Town Test. Cameron Bancroft was caught on camera pulling a tape from his pocket and rubbing it on the ball. Furthermore, captain Steve Smith, in a press conference, admitted to devising a plan for ball tampering – by rubbing dirt on the surface, enabling it to swerve in the air, which also is considered illegal. The image of Bancroft stuffing the sandpaper back in his pocket became the iconic picture of shame for Australian cricket as the three accepted tampering with the ball to alter the ball condition.[16]

Although scandals typically involve individual athletes, an entire sport can also be involved in unethical, performance-enhancing practices. Because of the increased risk and incidence of scandal, many sports advertisers are shying away from signing megastar individual athletes to huge contracts and are instead using teams or events as their advertising platform.

ARTICLE 10.4
THE ATHLETE ENDORSEMENT MODEL IS BROKEN

Nearly two weeks after Nike revealed Colin Kaepernick as the face of its new "Just Do It" ad campaign, Nike shares hit an all-time high on Friday. Nike's online sales also saw a bump in the wake of the Kaepernick ad. The controversial campaign has, by most metrics, been an objective success.

But Nike's (NKE) Kaepernick endorsement is actually an exception to the norm, and bucks the trend: big sponsorships of a single athlete are going out of style – fast.

"The paid endorser model is simply broken," NPD Group retail analyst Matt Powell wrote in a blog post in July. "Consumers have begun to realize how phony these pay-to-wear deals are. Celebrities have no loyalty to brands, or fans. They simply will endorse whatever they are paid to wear."

NBA rookie Deandre Ayton proved Powell's point in June. After he signed a lucrative endorsement deal with Puma, Ayton told Bleacher Report straight up the decision was about money: "Nike is Nike. Adidas is Adidas . . . but now it's a business. You don't want just product. You're not a kid anymore. You're really trying to get bank. That's about it."

As Ayton alluded to, the majority of sneaker endorsement deals these days are for a small fee and free product. Steph Curry didn't get his big Under Armour (UA) contract until 2013, when he had been in the league for four seasons. Under Armour built its entire basketball sneaker line around Curry, and while it brought the brand buzz in the sport, it couldn't save things from going south when basketball performance sneakers declined as a category industrywide.

In fact, Under Armour arguably has one of the strongest stables of athletes of any apparel company, with Curry, Tom Brady, Jordan Spieth, Michael Phelps, Lindsey Vonn, and Dwayne "The Rock" Johnson – and that still couldn't prevent sales declines in North America.

Federer's staggering Uniqlo deal

That's why Powell was so baffled when Uniqlo signed Roger Federer to a new 10-year endorsement deal in July, reportedly worth $300 million. And Federer himself, sounding a lot like Deandre Ayton, told the New York Times this month, "We tried to work it out [with Nike] for a year . . . from my point of view, I thought I was being reasonable. But everybody sees it differently. And what you see as your value may be not what they see. I'm happy to be proven right, with this long-term deal with Uniqlo."

The price tag is staggering – even more so considering that Federer is 37 years old. Underscoring the risk inherent in Uniqlo's expensive signing, Federer lost in the quarterfinals of Wimbledon this summer, then lost early in the U.S. Open. Uniqlo may be biting its nails.

On the other hand, Uniqlo is likely betting on Federer's lasting fame and appeal well beyond whenever he stops competing professionally. There is a select group of athletes who clearly have enough recognition and likability that they can appear in advertising long after they retire: Peyton Manning, Charles Barkley, and Shaquille O'Neal are examples. LeBron James, Serena Williams, and Tiger Woods will all surely be in that group after they retire. Will Federer?

Powell doesn't think it's a sure thing, and doesn't think he makes sense for Uniqlo as a spokesperson. "Federer talks to wealthy boomers, and that's not who Uniqlo needs to focus on," Powell tells Yahoo Finance. "He's not talking to the millennial. And I think his appeal right now is very much the presence that he has because he's playing, not so much because of who he is. I don't know that he's ever established himself as a personality."

The same goes for New York Yankees slugger Aaron Judge. Toward the end of his rookie season, which ended with Judge winning AL Rookie of the Year, Pepsi signed Judge to an endorsement deal. Nothing shocking there: only a few years ago, all the biggest pro athletes had a Coke or Pepsi deal. But Powell says, "I don't think Judge sells product. If he did, he'd have a whole lot of product contracts already. At the end of the day, millennials and Gen-Z are the consumers who matter. And baseball as a sport doesn't speak to Gen-Z."

Apparel brands still need pros to wear their gear

Powell isn't suggesting the big sports apparel brands will stop signing contracts with athletes. Nike, Adidas, and Under Armour need to have pro athletes wearing their products because it "creates credibility and authenticity," he says. But the era in which brands would sign athletes to 10-year-long contracts (Under Armour and Spieth, Nike and Rory McIlroy, Adidas and Derrick Rose) is on its way out. "My gut is we will see fewer of these marquee deals," Powell says.

Instead, you could see more of the Kaepernick model, which is more about making a statement than forming a decade-long relationship with one athlete. The terms of Nike's deal with Kaepernick have not been made public, but Powell suggests it is a short-term deal, and not necessarily a highly lucrative one.

"It's probably your standard NFL deal, which is worse than your standard NBA deal," Powell says. "I gotta believe it's not a lot of money. I do not believe we will see a signature shoe or clothing line. I think here we are looking at a different phenomenon, which is Nike recognizing that consumers want brands to take stands on social issues."

For now, that thinking is working wonders for Nike.

Source: Daniel Roberts, Yahoo Finance, September 15, 2018 https://finance.yahoo.com/news/athlete-endorsement-model-broken-160012574.html

One promising alternative that reduces the risk of potential problems is to use athletes who are no longer alive.[17] Athletes such as the legendary Arnold Palmer still draw significant attention. Deceased athletes are more cost effective, scandal proof, and are icons in the world of sports.[18] Although there are inherent risks, athlete endorsers are still used extensively. Table 10.2 presents some guidelines for those organizations who believe athletes can be an effective tool.

Table 10.2 Guidelines for using sports celebrities as endorsers
• Sports celebrities are more effective for endorsing sports-related products. Match-up hypothesis again holds true – does not matter if consumers recognize the athlete if they cannot remember the product that is being endorsed
• Long-term relationships or associations between the product and the endorser are key – cannot be short-term or one-shot deals to be effective. Examples include Arnold Palmer with Pennzoil and Michael Jordan with Nike
• Advertisements using athlete endorsers who appear during contests or events in which the athlete is participating are less effective
• Athletes who are overexposed may lose their credibility and power to influence consumers. Tiger Woods is planning to limit his association to just five global brands to avoid overexposure

Source: Adapted from Amy Dyson and Douglas Turco, "The State of Celebrity Endorsement in Sport," *Cyber-Journal of Sport Marketing*

Photo 10.2
Opportunities for engagement are seemingly limitless. The way sports are handled over social media will certainly change in the coming years

Credit: Steve Prezant via Getty Images

Media strategy

As presented in Chapter 9, a medium or channel is the element in the communications process by which the message is transmitted. Traditional mass media, such as newspapers, television, radio, or magazines, are usually thought of as effective ways of carrying advertising messages to the target audience. However, the new king is the many forms of social media that grip today's society. The following article illustrates the growing nature of sports and social media.

Social media and other emerging platforms still demand we understand the habits and preferences of each market segment, and often these

---

ARTICLE 10.5
2019 WILL SEE A CHANGE IN HOW SPORTS ARE PROCESSED OVER SOCIAL MEDIA

This past year in the world of sports has been full of new advancements, conversations and controversies on social media.

Through social sponsorship, brands moved into the forefront and commanded the narrative on social media during major moments, from Coca-Cola capitalizing on the Boston Red Sox's triumph in the World Series to Fortnite launching a partnership with the NFL. Data privacy became an everyday conversation topic as the Cambridge Analytica story brought the topic to the front page. Esports continued to emerge as a powerful new vertical for branded activations, with new streaming stars and grander arenas for competitions seemingly popping up overnight. And that's just scratching the surface.

As social media and the way we use it continues to evolve, it's important to stay on the pulse of what's to come and prepare for the trends that will define the next year. Reading the tea leaves based on conversations we've heard this year with key decision-makers in sports and entertainment, here are predictions for sports marketing and sponsorship on social media in 2019.

Incentivizing teams and leagues for high-engagement activation

Brands and properties (teams and leagues) are quickly realizing that the old ways of measuring their sponsorship investments like impressions and logo placements simply don't add up in a digital-first world. That's why more brands will adopt incentive-based sponsorship models. These deals will include a base compensation package for the team or league paired with different tiers of rewards that are triggered by activation performance metrics.

Now it's time for brands to dive fully in and take advantage of the sky-high levels of engagement in the space.

Properties can no longer simply slap their partners' logo on social posts in order to fulfill their sponsorship requirement. This new model encourages creativity and requires verified measurement to ensure activations drive engagement and meaningful results for all involved.

Social media will move into the forefront of sponsorship deals

Social media will move into focus for all sponsorship deals as a far more impactful way to generate value for a brand outside of an event. With the leagues' vast social footprints and the cost to boost a sponsored social campaign being widely underpriced, there's plenty of valuable opportunities to create a successful branded social campaign.

Since the start of 2017, entities from the big five U.S. sports leagues (MLB, MLS, NBA, NFL, NHL) and NASCAR have posted more than 6.3 million social posts, resulting in 16.7 billion engagements. Brands realized the opportunity before them and are now more involved than ever. In the last two years, 19 percent of those 6.3 million posts were branded posts, resulting in over $2.1 billion in attributed value generated for the brands featured in the content.

Facebook and Instagram will emphasize data security

After Cambridge Analytica and Facebook's late September 2018 security breach, social media giants will continue to place importance on elevating data security. This means that they will be scrutinizing and evaluating third-party data providers on a stricter scale, tightening their grip on users' data to distance themselves from privacy concerns. Only a small handful of trusted partners will be approved to weed out players that abuse and misuse the data. The barrier for entry for leveraging Facebook's and other social platforms' data will only increase, leaving behind an elevated group of vetted and approved third-party data providers.

Brands will focus on creating intentional posts

While some traditional sponsorship activations can be seen in the background of social posts, brands are beginning to seek more strategic, intentional logo placements and mentions in social campaigns. There is a huge difference in the amount of value generated for a brand when a logo is picked up in the background of a social post compared to a creative campaign that drives fan engagement around the brand. Brands value this incidental pick up of their logo in a social post far less than intentional branded posts with meaningful engagement.

Different campaign types leveraging the moments in sports, including branded game score posts, starting line-up announcements and play-of-the-game highlights, will become more prevalent in 2019. Rate cards will reflect a higher price for such highly engaging content as properties explore new ways to drive value for brands in an authentic way.

TV viewership will continue to decline

In recent years, sports media has seen a decline in viewership on television and other traditional viewing channels, especially amongst younger audiences, which is causing leagues to leverage OTT media services like social to stream exclusive content. As a result, OTT has moved into the forefront as teams and leagues search for new ways to distribute existing and new content directly to their audiences. Look for properties to shift their focus to releasing exclusive, long-form content on these channels as the properties become much more content centric in 2019. They will heavily invest in content producers to create original content for these channels and leverage their reach to attract new audiences for their brands.

Esports will continue to grow as more brands invest in sponsorship deals

The esports industry has evolved with a lot of curiosity and skepticism from major brands in its infancy, but the time has come for brands to fully capitalize on this highly engaged audience.

In 2017–18, many brands were testing the waters, trying to find out how to work with esports gamers and streamers, publishers and events. Now it's time for brands to dive fully in and take advantage of the sky-high levels of engagement in the space. Streaming stars and the esports leagues and teams will see more of these eye-popping numbers through sponsorships in the year to come as the industry leverages third-party measurement to highlight the attention they have captured from their audience. In several cases, this level of attention is overshadowing the engagements other sports are seeing across social media platforms.

As the year progresses, we'll see which of these predictions come true. One thing is certain, though: The brands and properties that are most prepared to adapt to these trends and the evolving social media landscape will be the ones that win in the upcoming year.

Source: Kyle Nelson, December 24, 2018; www.adweek.com/brand-marketing/2019-will-see-a-change-in-how-sports-are-processed-over-social-media/

behaviors are identified using data/marketing analytics. Knowing these habits and preferences can enhance communication and marketing efforts for these audiences. For example, teens use a multitude of media each day, and technology is also an integral part of teen life. Technology influences the type of media teens use – from researching potential purchases and schoolwork to maintaining friendships. Teens often actively multi-task or let one medium influence their use on another concurrent behavior. Deciding what medium or media to use is just one aspect in developing a comprehensive media strategy. **Media strategy** addresses two basic questions about the channel of communication. First, what medium or media mix (combination of media) will be most effective in reaching the desired target audience? Second, how should this media be scheduled to meet advertising objectives?

Media decisions or media selection

The far-ranging (and growing) number of media choices makes selecting the right media a difficult task. Choosing the proper media requires the sports advertiser to be mindful of the creative decisions made earlier in the advertising process. For instance, an emotional appeal – best suited for video – would be difficult to convey using print media. It is also critical that the media planner keep the target market in mind. Understanding the profile of the target market and their media habits is essential to developing an effective advertising campaign.

Every type of media has strengths and weaknesses that must be considered when making advertising placement decisions. Table 10.3 demonstrates selected advantages and disadvantages when choosing among advertising media.

Table 10.3 Profiles of major media types

Medium	Advantages	Limitations
Internet	Allows messages to be customized; reaches specific market; interactive capabilities	Clutter; audience characteristics; hard-to-measure effectiveness
Newspapers	Flexibility; timeliness; good local market coverage; broad acceptability; high believability	Short life; poor reproduction quality; small pass-along audience
Television	Good mass market coverage; low cost per exposure; combines sight, sound, and motion; appealing to the senses	High absolute costs; high clutter; fleeting exposure; less audience selectivity
Direct mail	High audience selectivity; flexibility; no ad competition within the same medium; allows personalization	Relatively high cost per exposure; "junk mail" image
Radio	Good local acceptance; high geographic and demographic selectivity; low cost	Audio only, fleeting exposure; low attention ("the half-heard" medium); fragmented audiences
Magazines	High geographic and demographic selectivity; credibility and prestige; high-quality reproduction; long life and good pass-along readership	Long advertisement purchase lead time; high cost; no guarantee of position
Outdoor	Flexibility; high repeat exposure; low cost; low message competition; good positional selectivity	Little audience selectivity; creative limitations

Sources: Adapted from Philip Kotler and Gary Armstrong, *Marketing: An Introduction*, 4th ed. (Upper Saddle River, NJ: Prentice Hall, 1997), 471. www.thebalancesmb.com/different-types-of-advertising-methods-38548

Alternative forms of advertising

Because of the advertising clutter present in traditional advertising media, sports marketers are continually evaluating new ways of delivering their message to consumers. Alternative forms of advertising range from the more conventional stadium signage to the most creative media. Consider the following alternative form of advertising finally gaining acceptance in the NBA.

ARTICLE 10.6
NBA: BIG PAYOFF FOR A LITTLE PATCH

The NBA's jersey patch program is more than halfway through its three-season test and the results are clear: It's a slam dunk.

As the league continues to search for new revenue, the patch program has delivered, generating more than $150 million. And 20 of the 29 team patch sponsors, including Harley-Davidson and Rakuten, are doing business with NBA teams for the first time.

Now the task ahead will be how to improve and expand the patch program, including where teams are allowed to sell jerseys containing the patches.

Team, league and brand executives all feel the program has been an overwhelming success, with exposure numbers easily exceeding projections. Clubs expect new deals and renewals will be for more money and longer terms. One top team executive predicts a 20 percent to 30 percent price increase for Patch 2.0.

The patch program has produced more than $150 million in revenue. Teams could see increases of 20 percent to 30 percent on their next round of deals.

"Like most teams, we're heading towards renewal thinking these are worth substantially more, because the impression numbers have been so good," said Milwaukee Bucks President Peter Feigin, who would not disclose specific patch values.

The league would not discuss any specific increases in value, but expects new or renewed patch deals to be more lucrative. The current deals reportedly range between $5 million and $20 million annually. At press time, every NBA team but the Oklahoma City Thunder had a patch deal.

"The revenue has exceeded expectations and we think the success of the program to date will help drive value in the future," said Amy Brooks, president of the league's team marketing and business operations division and chief innovation officer for the NBA. "It has proven to be a unique asset that draws brands for different reasons."

According to Navigate Research, which has valued select jersey patch deals for NBA teams, the average exposure value has been 25 percent to 50 percent higher than the sponsor fees, with the average patch exposure at 10 to 15 minutes of highly legible visibility during game broadcasts.

"The next phase of the deals is to maximize the marketplace," said Emilio Collins, chief business officer for Excel Sports Management, which represents a handful of teams in their patch deals. "The data supports substantial increases in value. There has been phenomenal reach."

The patch program was created in 2017 after more than a year of consideration as owners debated how the deals would be structured and how revenue would be shared. Any changes to the current three-year pilot patch program, which ends in April 2020, must be approved by league owners.

As the NBA looks to extend the program, league and team officials say there is no demand to increase the size of the 2.5-by-2.5-inch patches. "There has been zero negative reaction to the size of the patch," said Alex Martins, CEO of the Orlando Magic. "Consumers have become accustomed to it."

Active discussions are focused on making NBA jerseys with ad patches the league's "authentic" on-court wear – and thus the only jerseys available at retail. Currently, NBA jerseys with patches are only sold at team-controlled stores and websites.

More preliminary and more complicated are talks between the league and its teams on whether to expand territorial rights for patches and other marketing inventory. The league emphasized the early nature of those talks and would not comment on any specific changes.

"We are discussing retail distribution first and foremost," Brooks said. "Our data has shown that fans want what the players wear on the court. Also, more flexibility in creative for a patch partner especially as we have flexibility in creative in our uniforms."

Team executives are clear in their push for expanding the patch at retail.

"You can't even buy a European soccer jersey without the sponsor on it," said Golden State Warriors President Rick Welts, who in 2008 sold the WNBA's first uniform ad, when Arizona-based LifeLock bought space on the Phoenix Mercury's jerseys.

"Fans want whatever's authentic," Welts continued. "So inevitably, that [all jerseys at retail having ad patches] is going to happen."

Predictably, Nike is far less sanguine about having an advertising patch be part of every NBA jersey at retail, preferring that decision be made by consumers. Because of the long lead times required by jersey manufacturers (six to nine months), it's already growing late for the 2019–20 season should the league want to revamp the program early.

For the first iteration of jersey advertising, the NBA prohibited categories including spirits, gambling, tobacco, media concerns, political ads, and competitors of Nike, which holds on-court uniform rights.

Said Cleveland Cavaliers CEO Len Komoroski, "There were stops and starts on the way in, but clearly it has worked even better than we hoped. As we move forward, it will be helpful to have it at a vantage point as a long-term proposition, rather than just a test."

Patching things up

The 29 brands whose logos have been visible on NBA jerseys this season have combined to generate nearly $54 million in media value since Oct. 1, according to Sport24 and Social24 data provided to Sports Business Journal by Nielsen Sports. Games that aired on national and regional networks combined to drive 70 percent of that value, with social bringing in the remainder. Shopping app Wish, whose logo adorns the Los Angeles Lakers' jerseys, has generated the most exposure.

Source: Sports Business Journal. https://www.sportsbusinessjournal.com/Journal/Issues/2019/02/25/Leagues-and-Governing-Bodies/NBA-patches.aspx

In other alternative forms of promotion, 35 public golf courses in Connecticut signed up for a program that put advertisements in the bottom of their holes. Formerly, 7-Eleven entered into a three-year $500,000 sponsorship contract with the White Sox, calling for all weekday games to start at 7:11. A company spokesperson called this a "fun way to insert our name into fans' hearts and minds." This sort of creativity could open up other areas where brands can get involved without impacting the field of play, as well as additional inventory for teams to sell.

Stadium signage

Stadium signage, or on-site advertising, is back and is an extremely popular form of promotion and sponsorship packages. For some time, nary a sign was found on the outfield wall of an MLB team or on the boards at an NHL game. Now, stadium signage prevails on every inch of available space. Not unlike other forms of advertising, stadium signage is designed to increase brand or corporate awareness, create a favorable image through associations with the team and sport, change attitudes or maintain favorable attitudes, and ultimately increase the sale of product. The Cubs have struck a three-year sponsorship deal with Under Armour to place two 7-by-12-foot signs on the Wrigley Field outfield doors, the first corporate advertising to be placed among the famed brick-and-ivy outfield wall in the stadium's then-93-year history.

Traditionally, stadium sponsors and advertisers have utilized in-stadium ads, naming rights, and banners visible on TV to capture consumer attention. However, with the advent of digital technology, attention is becoming a scarce resource. Due to consumer behaviors such as multitasking and shorter attention spans, the quality of viewer attention has eroded over the past two-and-a-half decades.[19] Therefore, marketers today must be innovative, integrating more targeted and interactive advertising strategies. Attention economics have been a scarce commodity in the age of information overload. However, in this playing field, aggregating the attention of fans and selling a portion to advertisers and sponsors is where the real riches lie.[20] For example, in the NFL, teams like the Dallas Cowboys earn in excess of $150 million from sponsorships and advertising in a single season, while the NFL's 32 teams generated

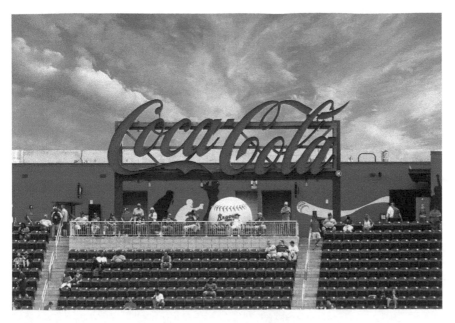

Photo 10.3
Coca-Cola creates a positive association with baseball by using stadium signage

Credit: Shutterstock, ID# 1423239606 by Darryl Brooks

$1.4 billion in revenue last season from sponsorships, ad signage, and stadium naming rights.[21]

Estimated expenditures on stadium signage and sponsorships are expected to continue to increase. Thus, given the advent of new technologies, allowing stadium billboards to be changed and customized for local markets, the use of flat panel displayers for digital out of home advertising will continue to be one of the fastest-growing industries and, with deployment of stadium signage, will appear in almost every major world market.

Although stadium signage can be an effective means of advertising, it can also be costly. The Dallas Cowboys stadium is one of the world's most modern venues, but it came with a significant price tag, $1.2 billion. The stadium features a retractable roof and a signage scheme unlike any other. Cowboys Stadium is home to the world's largest outdoor digital display. The 2,100-inch display weighs in at approximately 600 tons, spans 25,670 square feet, features back-to-back high-definition LED screens, and has two small screens at each end to accommodate the stadium end zone fans. The cost of this massive display is just a mere $40 million. However, the digital signage does not end there; apart from having the largest outdoor back-to-back HD screens, they also utilize over 3,000 small displays around the stadium to allow fans to stay abreast of the game and to inform fans of news related to the team.

Photo 10.4

Tottenham Hotspur's new stadium built at an estimated cost of $1 billion plus

Credit: Shutterstock, ID# 1368459644 by Silvi Photo

URL: www.shutterstock.com/image-photo/london-uk-april-13-2019-panoramic-1368459644

In other venues across the country, items such as rotating/digital scorers and press tables often seen at NBA and collegiate basketball games can cost between $50,000 and $250,000. How is expensive stadium signage sold and justified by sports marketers? First, research has shown that locations considered part of the game (e.g., scorer's table or on the ice) are more effective than those locations removed from the action (e.g., scoreboards).[22] Other research found that spectators had improved recognition of and attitudes toward eight courtside advertisers for an NCAA Division I men's basketball team. This finding is, of course, extremely important to sponsors considering the cost and effectiveness of this type of stadium signage.[23]

Other outdoor

A new form of outdoor advertising is also becoming popular at national sporting events. This type of outdoor promotion uses live product demonstrations or characters to attract fans' attention. For example, the following image has fans forming the brand image of Telekom at a Bayern Munich game.

Photo 10.5

Twitter utilizing live events to enhance advertising strategies

Credit: Will Dowling

URL: https://twitter.com/willdowningcomm/status/941051048797630464

Additional forms

Orlando City FC joined Major League Soccer in 2015. They needed to find a supporter base and found a creative way to put themselves on the map by organizing a scavenger hunt. For that, they first hid tickets for upcoming games around the city. After that, they posted clues about where to find them on Twitter, Instagram, and Periscope. The latter was also used to show winners' reactions and keep followers up to date. By using existing tools, the campaign proved simple, cheap, and effective.[24]

Sports marketers sometimes use variations of product placement techniques. Product placement occurs when manufacturers pay to have their products used in cooperation with sporting events, television shows, movies, and other entertainment media such as music videos and, of course, video games. Perhaps the earliest sports product placement was when James Bond, 007, used Slazenger golf balls on the links in the classic *Goldfinger*. In the ultimate product tie-in, the Anaheim Ducks of the NHL were named after the series of movies created by their then-parent company, Disney. Are these product placements effective? Even though some studies show mixed support for the effectiveness of product placement,[25] anecdotal evidence shows that product demonstrations seem to work and are certainly popular. Title Boxing Equipment, ESPN, and WBC were all promoted in the movie *Creed 2*.

Photo 10.6

MGM Grand and Bud Light are examples of partnerships in action with the UFC

Credit: Shutterstock, ID# 1730468443 by A.RICARDO

URL: www.shutterstock.com/image-photo/rio-de-janeiro-brazil-march-10-1730468443

The advantages that have been cited for alternative forms of advertising include:[26]

- **Exposure** - A large number of people go to the movies, rent movies, or could be exposed to a live-product demonstration if they are attending a sporting event or watching television.
- **Attention** - Moviegoers are generally an attentive audience. Sports spectators are also a captive audience when they are waiting for the action to begin.
- **Recall** - Research has shown that audiences have higher levels of next-day recall for products that are placed in movies than for traditional forms of promotion.
- **Source association** - For product placements, the audience may see familiar and likable stars using the sports product. As such, the product's image may be enhanced through association with the celebrity.

Another alternative form of advertising is using the athlete as a "human billboard."[27] The history of athletes wearing an advertisement can be traced back to the 1960s, when organizations began establishing relationships with stock car drivers. Soon, the practice of drivers wearing patches on their clothing spread to other sports, such as tennis and golf. The use of athletes as advertisers is much more common in individual sports because these individuals have the ability to negotiate and wear whatever they want, as opposed to the tight controls imposed on athletes in team sports by their respective leagues.

Today, the use of athletes as human billboards is part of the integrated marketing communications plan rather than a stand-alone promotion. Rickie Fowler, Ian Poulter, and Jonas Blixt of the PGA wear hats, sweaters, pants, shoes, and shirts from Puma Golf in addition to the other advertisements and promotions for the brand. The major appeal of this form of advertising is the natural association (classical conditioning) formed in consumers' minds between the athlete and the organization or product.

How much does it cost sponsors to rent advertising space on an athlete's body? An IndyCar driver's helmet might cost between $50,000 and $250,000, depending on the driver. The precious space on a professional golfer's visor would cost between $250,000 and $500,000. A logo on the front of a golfer's hat or on the left breast of his shirt could cost between $250,000 and $2 million annually.[28] Although these prices may seem outrageous, organizations are willing to pay the price for the exposure and enhanced brand equity.

In addition to these more conventional examples, boxers have used their bodies as billboards by tattooing corporate logos on their chest and

Photo 10.7
Drivers such as Ricky Stenhouse Jr., Kyle Larson, and Denny Hamlin exemplify the human billboard

Credit: Shutterstock, ID# 1330001177 by Grindstone Media Group

URL: www.shutterstock.com/image-photo/march-01-2019-las-vegas-nevada-1330001177

back. The Nevada State Athletic Commission tried to ban body billboards but ultimately lost to the state court's ruling protecting boxers' right to free speech.

Digital

Once considered non-traditional but now a mainstay in the world of advertising media is digital. As discussed in Chapter 2, the Internet has long been a valuable source of sports information for participants and fans. Figure 10.2 provides some fast facts about the size of the digital market around the world.

In addition to the figures presented in Figure 10.2, 30 percent of U.S. sports fans now stream live sports on their smartphones or tablets, and 80 percent use the Internet when watching sports to enhance their experience.[29] Especially for younger fans, digital is the norm, and digital advertising is an effective platform.

Digital platforms are fast becoming the choice of media for sports fans and are pushing the boundaries of media convergence across television, Internet, and mobile devices. The television and the Internet now outweigh other media at peak viewing times, and twice as many sports fans watch video via mobile devices compared with the average mobile device user. These individuals are also known to multitask, for results indicate that twice as many sports fans use the Internet while watching TV compared with the average user. Ultimately,

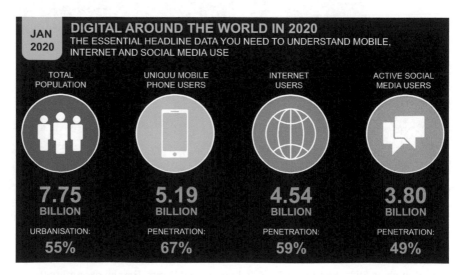

Figure 10.2
Digital around the world in 2020

Source: Hootsuite and We Are Social

URL: https://datareportal.com

sport users are more engaged and receptive than the average Internet user to online advertising, and these users are more likely to increase their sports consumption online due to its ease of use, accessibility, technology, and real-time availability.[30] Finally, the Internet is the ideal medium to target college sports fans due to greater access and usage rates among students. Generally, the Internet allows the sports advertiser to reach an extremely focused targeted market.[31]

Another distinct advantage of promotion via the web is the interactive nature of the medium. Promotions attract the attention of the target audience and then create involvement by having consumers point and click on the information they find of interest. For instance, the Major League Soccer site (www.mlssoccer.com) has advertisements asking soccer fans to download the MLS app and "live your colors." A point and click of the mouse will take fans to the DC United soccer link, which features the ability to download player screen savers and wallpapers, enter the MLS store, and, of course, watch the latest videos and sign up for the latest team news.

Other advantages of the Internet versus more traditional media include the Internet's ability to be flexible. Web promotions can be updated, and changes can be made almost instantly. This flexibility is a tremendous advantage for sports marketers, who are constantly responding to a changing environment. In fact, the Internet seems to be the perfect tool for sports marketers using the contingency framework for strategic planning. For example, the emergence of social media has supercharged an age-old consumer activity allowing consumers to chat about things like scores,

Web Capture 10.6
The Internet has become a popular medium for all forms of online purchasing

Credit: Major League Baseball trademarks and copyrights are used with permission of Major League Baseball. Visit MLB.com

URL: www.mlb.com/cardinals/tickets

stats, and other sport interests. This established consumer behavior, now enabled by new technology platforms, is driving a fundamental change in the way sport brand marketing works. Today's relationships are more explicit and must consider the engagement of the message and the consumer; these engagements make platforms much more measurable, which constantly inspires new ideas between research, media, and consumer brand perceptions.

A final benefit of promotion via the Internet is its cost effectiveness. The Internet provides organizations with a means of promoting sports to consumers around the world at a low cost. The ability to reach a geographically diverse audience at a low cost is one of the primary advantages of Internet promotion.

Although there are many advantages, promotion via the Internet can also pose potential problems. As with other forms of advertising, it is difficult to measure the effectiveness of sports promotion over the Internet. Often, marketers use the "number of hits" as a proxy for effectiveness, but this cannot be used to determine the interest level of the consumer or purchase intent.

Promotional clutter is another difficulty with Internet promotions. As the Internet becomes a more popular advertising medium, more organizations will compete for the audience and its attention. To break through the clutter, sports marketers must design new Internet promotions. Differentiating among

Web Capture 10.7
Social media continues to emerge as an interactive Web strategy

Source: Twitter, https://twitter.com/cricketcomau?lang=en

Credit: Cricket Australia

URL: www.cricketaustralia.com.au/

Web promotions will become increasingly important in gaining the attention of consumers and developing a unique position for organizations.

A final disadvantage of promotion on the Internet is its inability to reach certain groups of consumers. Although the Internet is a great medium to reach younger, college-educated, computer-literate consumers, it may be extremely inefficient in trying to promote to the mature market or, perhaps, consumers of lower socioeconomic standing. Although we have looked at some of the pros and cons of promotion via digital, the fact remains that the Internet is here to stay. The low costs, ability to target sports fans and participants, and high flexibility far outweigh the disadvantages of this medium.

Choosing a specific medium

Once the medium or media mix is chosen by the sports organization along with the advertising agency, the specific medium must be addressed. In other words, if the advertisement will appear in a magazine, then we must choose which magazine will be most effective. Do we want our advertisement to promote the NHL to appear in *Sports Illustrated, Sporting News Magazine*, the *Hockey News*, or some combination of these specific media? Should we promote Texas Motor Speedway via social media, text messaging, podcasting, or more traditional means - television, radio, magazine, and newspaper? To answer this question, we must consider our reach and frequency objectives.

Reach refers to the number of people exposed to an advertisement in a given medium. For the advertiser who wants to generate awareness and reach the largest number of people in the target audience, perhaps *Sports Illustrated*, with a print circulation of 2.75 million, would be the most effective medium. However, if the target audience is younger consumers, then the print version of *Sports Illustrated* might be reaching people who are not potential users and would prefer the digital content.

The reach of an advertisement is determined by a number of factors. First, nature of the media mix influences reach. The general rule is that the greater the number of media used, the greater the reach. For example, if the advertising campaign for the NHL were broadcast on television, printed in magazines, and also appeared in social media, reach would be increased. Second, if only one medium is to be used, increasing the number and diversity within this medium will increase the reach.

For instance, if cable television were chosen as the sole medium for the NHL campaign, reach would be increased if the commercial were aired on ESPN, Lifetime, and Fox Sports versus ESPN alone. Finally, reach can be enhanced by airing the advertisements during different times of the day or day parts. The advertisement might be shown at night after 9:00 p.m. and also in the morning to reach a greater percentage of the target audience.

Along with reach, another consideration in making specific media decisions is frequency. **Frequency** refers to the number of times the individual or household is exposed to the media vehicle. An important point is that frequency is measured by the number of exposures to the media vehicle rather than the advertisement itself. Just because an advertisement is shown on television during the Super Bowl does not mean that the target audience has seen it. Consumers might change channels, leave the room, or simply become involved in conversation. A study examined this issue using Super Bowl viewers in a bar setting.[32] It found that visual attention levels for the game are similar to attention levels for the advertisements, attention to commercials varies by their location in the cluster of advertisements and time of the game, and that Super Bowl commercials may receive more attention than commercials on other programs.

Media scheduling

Four basic **media scheduling** alternatives are considered once the medium (e.g., magazines) and specific publications (e.g., *Rugby World*) are chosen. These schedules are called continuous, flighting, pulsing, and seasonal. A **continuous schedule** recognizes that there are no breaks in the demand for the sports product. This is also called steady, or "drip," scheduling. During the advertising period, advertisements are continually run. Most sporting goods and events are seasonal and, therefore, do not require a continuous schedule. Some sporting goods, such as running shoes, have roughly equivalent demand and advertising spending throughout the year.

A **flighting schedule** is another alternative, where advertising expenditures are varied in some months and zero is spent in other months. Consider the case of the Major League Baseball. Heavy advertising expenditures are spent in March, April, and May leading up to the season. Reminder-oriented advertising is placed over the course of the rest of the season, and no advertising dollars are spent in the winter months. This type of scheduling is most prevalent in sports marketing due to the seasonal nature of most sports.

A **pulsing schedule** is a variant of the flighting schedule. Ad expenditures may vary greatly, but some level of advertising is always taking place. Although it sounds similar to a flighting schedule, remember that a flighting schedule has some months where zero is spent on advertising.

Personal selling

Now that we have looked at the advertising process in detail, let us turn to another important element in the promotion mix - personal selling.

Personal selling is used in a variety of ways in sports marketing, such as in securing corporate sponsorships, selling luxury suites or boxes in stadiums, and hawking corporate and group ticket sales. In the marketing of sporting goods, the primary applications of personal selling are to get retailers to carry products (push strategy) and consumers to purchase products (pull strategy).

Personal selling represents a unique element in the promotion mix because it involves personal interaction with the target audience rather than mass communication to thousands or millions of consumers. The definition of personal selling reflects this important distinction between personal selling and the other promotion tools. **Personal selling** is a form of person-to-person communication in which a salesperson works with prospective buyers and attempts to influence their purchase needs in the direction of their company's products or services.

All the advantages of personal selling described in Figure 10.2 make it an attractive promotional tool, so the ability to use personal selling to develop long-term relationships with consumers is becoming increasingly important to sports marketers. In fact, building long-term relationships with consumers has become one of the critical issues for marketers. More formally, **relationship marketing** is the process of creating, maintaining, and enhancing strong, value-laden relationships with customers and other stakeholders.[33]

As Kotler and Armstrong point out, the key premise of relationship marketing is that building strong economic and social ties with valued customers, distributors, dealers, and suppliers leads to long-term profitable transactions. Many sports organizations are realizing it is cheaper to foster and maintain strong relationships with existing customers rather than find new customers or fight the competition for a stagnant consumer base.

Table 10.4 Benefits of personal selling

- Personal selling allows the salesperson to immediately adapt the message they are presenting based on feedback received from the target audience.
- Personal selling allows the salesperson to communicate more information to the target audience than other forms of promotion. Moreover, complex information can be explained by the salesperson.
- Personal selling greatly increases the likelihood of the target audience paying attention to the message. It is difficult for the target audience to escape the message because communication is person to person.
- Personal selling greatly increases the chances of developing a long-term relationship with consumers, due to the frequent person-to-person communication.

The ultimate goal of developing long-lasting relationships is to create truly loyal and passionate fans who are ambassadors for the sports entity. One common sports marketing approach is to create fan loyalty programs. The Wild were one of the first NHL teams to start a fan loyalty club as part of their marketing strategy. Their "Wild Rewards" program, started in 2013, focuses on fan retention and gaining valuable fan insight. Their objective is to improve the fan experience independent of team performance. They achieve this by offering merchandise exclusive to members and customized rewards that suit the individual fan and by providing game-day purchase incentives at concessions and merchandise outlets.[34] In addition, academic research has shown these programs to have high perceived value from fans.[35] Fan loyalty programs, as Chapter 6 illustrated (see Article 6.7), can be effective if marketers understand the ins and outs of these programs and their impact on consumers.

The strategic selling process

Now that we have defined personal selling and discussed some of its major advantages, let us examine how the selling process operates in sports marketing. As previously discussed, sports marketers are generally concerned with selling an intangible service versus a tangible good. Most salespeople view the selling of services as a much more difficult process, because the benefits of the sports product are not readily observable or easily communicated to the target audience. It is much easier to sell the new and improved M6 driver from TaylorMade when the consumer can see the design, feel the weight of the club, and swing the club. In essence, the product sells itself. Contrast this with the sale of a luxury box to a corporation in a stadium that is yet to be built. Selling this sports product is dependent on communicating both the tangible and intangible benefits of the box to the prospective buyer. In addition to the problems associated with selling a service versus a good, the sale of many sports products requires several people to give their approval before the sale is complete. This factor also makes the selling process more complex.

In the ever-changing world of sports marketing, the "good ol' boy" approach to selling is no longer valid. To be more effective and efficient in today's competitive environment, a number of personal selling strategies have been developed. One process, developed by Robert Miller and Stephen Heiman, is called **strategic selling**.[36]

Miller and Heiman suggest the first step in any strategic selling process is performing an analysis of your current position. In this instance, position is described as understanding your personal strengths and weaknesses as well as the opportunities and threats that are present in the selling situation. In essence, the salesperson is constructing a mini-SWOT analysis, an analysis of strengths, weaknesses, opportunities, and threats. Questions regarding how prospective clients feel about you as a salesperson, how they feel about your products and services, who the competition is, and how they are positioned must all be addressed at the initial stages of the strategic selling process.

Good salespeople realize that they must adapt their current position for every account before they can be successful. To change this position, six elements in the strategic selling process must be considered in a systematic and interactive fashion. These elements, which must be understood for successful sales, are buying influences, red flags, response modes, win-results, the sales funnel, and the ideal customer profile. Let us take a brief look at how these elements work together in the strategic selling process.

Buying influences

A complex sale was earlier defined as one where multiple individuals are involved in the buying process. This is true of large organizations considering a sponsorship proposal or families considering the purchase of exercise equipment for a new workout facility in their home. One of the first steps in the strategic sales process is to identify all the individuals involved in the sale and to determine their buying roles.

Roles are patterns of behavior expected by people in a given position. Miller and Heiman believe there are generally four critical buying roles that must be understood in a complex sale (no matter how many people play these roles). The **economic buying role** is a position that governs final approval to buy and that can say yes to a sale when everyone else says no, and vice versa. The **user buying role** makes judgments about the potential impact of your product or service on their job performance. These individuals will also supervise or use the product, so they want to know what the product or service will do for them. The **technical buying role** screens out possible suppliers on the basis of meeting a variety of technical specifications that have been determined in advance by the organization. The technical buyers also serve as gatekeepers, who screen out potential suppliers on the basis of failing to meet the stated specifications. Finally, the **coach's role** is to act as a guide for the salesperson making the sale. The coach is a valuable source of information about the organization and can lead you to the other **buying influences**. As Miller and Heiman point out, identifying the individuals playing the various roles is the foundation of the strategic selling process.

Red flags

Once the individuals have been identified, the next step in the strategic selling process is to look for **red flags**, or things that can threaten a complex sale. Red flags symbolize those strategic areas that can require further attention to avoid mistakes in positioning. In addition, red flags can be used to capitalize on an area of strength. Some of the red flags that can threaten a complex sale include either missing or vague information, buying influences who are not contacted, or reorganization. For example, any buying influences who are not contacted are considered a threat to the sale.

Those buying influences who are not contacted are analogous to uncovered bases in baseball. Teams cannot be fielded or successful when there is no shortstop or catcher. Likewise, a sale cannot be successful until all the relevant players have been contacted.

Response modes

After the buyer(s) have been targeted and you have correctly positioned your products or services by identifying red flags, the next step in the strategic selling process is to determine the buyer's reaction to the given sales situation. These varying reactions are categorized in four **response modes**. These modes include growth mode, trouble mode, even keel mode, and overconfident mode.

Growth mode is characterized by organizations who perceive a discrepancy between their current state and their ideal state in terms of some goal (e.g., sales or profits). In other words, the organization needs to produce a higher-quality sports product or put more people in the seats in order to grow. In this situation, the probability of a sale is high.

The second response mode is known as **trouble mode**. When an organization is falling short of expectations, it is in trouble mode. Here again, there is a discrepancy between the current and ideal states. In growth mode, the organization is going to improve upon an already good situation. However, trouble mode indicates that the buyer is experiencing difficulties. In either case, the potential for a sale is high.

Even keel mode presents a more difficult case for the salesperson. As the name implies, there is no discrepancy between the ideal and current results and, therefore, the likelihood of a sale is low. The probability of a sale can be enhanced if the salesperson can demonstrate that a discrepancy actually exists, the buyer sees growth or trouble coming, or there is pressure from another buying influence.

The final response mode is **overconfident mode**. Overconfidence is generally the toughest mode to overcome from the salesperson's perspective in that the buyers believe things are too good to be true. Just think about individual athletes or teams who are overconfident. Invariably they lose because of their false sense of superiority. Organizations that are overconfident are resistant to change because they are exceeding their goals (or at least they think so), so sales are difficult. The NFL is one example of a sports league currently at the top in terms of fan popularity but subject to overconfident mode. Specifically, off-the-field issues (as noted earlier) may alienate fans and sponsors. Gene Upshaw, the former executive director of the NFL Players Association, commented that "I do not want the fans to turn us off because of off-field behavior. It has happened in other sports, and I would not want that to happen to the NFL."[37] In this stage of the strategic sales process, the response mode of the organization should be analyzed. In addition, each of the buying influences should be examined to determine their perception of the current situation. By analyzing the buying influences and their perceptions, the salesperson is in a position to successfully adapt his or her approach to meet the needs of each buying influence and each customer.

Win-results

Much of sports marketing today is based on the premise of strategic partnerships. The same is true for the strategic sales process. In strategic partnerships, the sales process produces satisfied customers, long-term relationships, repeat business, and good referrals. To achieve these outcomes, the salesperson must look at clients as partners rather than competition that must be beaten.

Miller and Heiman define the **win-results** concept in the strategic selling process as an objective result that gives one or more of the buying influences a personal win. The key to this definition is understanding the importance of both wins and results. A result is the impact of the salesperson's product or service on one or more of the client's business objectives. Results are usually tangible and quantifiable and affect the entire organization. Wins, however, are the fulfillment of a promise made to oneself. Examples of personal wins for the potential client include gaining recognition within the organization, increasing responsibility and authority, and enhancing self-esteem. It is important to realize that wins are subjective and intangible and do not benefit all the people in the organization the same way.

The sales funnel

The sales funnel is another key element in the strategic sales process. This is a tool used to organize all potential clients, as opposed to developing a means for understanding an individual client. Basically, the **sales funnel** is a model that is used to organize clients so salespeople might organize their efforts in the most efficient and effective manner. After all, allocating time and setting priorities are two of the most challenging tasks in personal selling.

The sales funnel divides clients into three basic levels – above the funnel, in the funnel, and the best few. Potential clients exist above the funnel if data (e.g., a call from the prospective client wanting information or acquiring information from personal sources) suggest there may be a possible fit between the salesperson's products or services and the needs of the potential client. The salesperson's emphasis at this level is to gather information and then develop and qualify prospects.

Potential clients are then filtered to the next level of the sales funnel. If clients are placed in the funnel (rather than above it), then the possibility of a sale has been verified. Verification occurs once a buying influence has been contacted and indicates that the organization is in either growth or trouble response mode. Remember that these two response modes represent ideal conditions for a sale to occur.

When all the buying influences have been identified, red flags have been eliminated, and win-results have been addressed, sales prospects can be moved from in the funnel to the best potential customers. At this final level of the sales funnel, the sale is expected to happen roughly 90 percent of the time.

Ideal customers

The ideal customer concept in strategic selling extends the notion of the sales funnel. In this case, all potential customers outside the funnel are evaluated against the hypothetical "ideal customer." The strategic sales process is based on the belief that every sale is not a good sale. The **ideal customer** profile is constructed to cut down on the unrealistic prospects that should not be in the sales funnel in the first place.

When constructing the ideal customer profile, the salesperson must judge each prospect with respect to organizational demographics, psychographics, and corporate culture. Current prospects can then be evaluated against the ideal customer profile to determine whether additional time and energy should be invested.

Sales promotions

Another promotion element that communicates to large audiences is sales promotions. **Sales promotions** are a variety of short-term, promotional activities that are designed to stimulate immediate product demand.

The sales promotions used in sports marketing come in all shapes and sizes. Think about some of the sales promotions with which you may be familiar. Classic examples might include Straight-A Night or all-you-can-eat at the ballpark, coupons for reduced green fees at public golf courses, a sweepstakes to win a free trip to the Super Bowl, seat upgrades to courtside recliners, or Coke's Win-a-Player Promotion.

Every professional franchise and nearly all D-I college athletics programs provide their season-long sales promotion calendars to fans. For example, the 2019 promotion calendar for the LA Galaxy of MLS includes the following: Pride Night, LA Kings Night, Fan Appreciation Night, Firefighter Appreciation Night, Lakers Night, and Military Appreciation Night. The full promotional schedule including sponsors can be found at www.lagalaxy.com/post/2019/02/28/la-galaxy-announce-2019-promotional-calendar.

Minor league baseball has always been known for its creative sales promotions. Some sales promotions are tied to pop-culture anniversaries like the West Michigan Whitecaps celebrating the release of Led Zeppelin's debut album or the 50th anniversary of Woodstock being recognized by the Potomac Nationals. The Reno Aces created a Johnny Cash Weekend promotion where the team sported black theme jerseys, gave away Johnny Cash T-shirts, and hosted musically inclined members of his family at the ballpark. While Pups in the Park has become a staple, the State College Spikes offer a Purr in the Park promotion where cats were welcomed and games like the Kitty Litter Dig were between-inning entertainment.[38] In fact, an entire Twitter feed is devoted to minor league baseball promotions at https://twitter.com/milbpromos?lang=en.

As stated in the definition, all forms of sales promotions are designed to increase short-term sales. Additional objectives may include increasing brand awareness, broadening distribution channels, reminding consumers about the offering, or inducing a trial to win new customers. To accomplish these objectives, sports marketers use a variety of sales promotion tools.

Premiums

Premiums are probably the sales promotion technique most associated with traditional sports marketing. **Premiums** are items given away with the sponsor's product as part of the sales promotion. Baseball cards, NASCAR model car replicas, water bottles, hats, refrigerator magnets, posters, bobbleheads, and almost anything else imaginable has been given away at sporting events. Although premiums are often given away to spectators at events, they can also be associated with other sport promotions. For example, both *Sports Illustrated* and *ESPN* magazines give away hats, T-shirts, and videos to induce potential consumers to subscribe. In another example, many credit card companies are giving away hats with the logo of the fan's favorite team for applying for a line of credit.

Perhaps the most effective and exciting premium over the years has been the bobblehead. The bobblehead can be traced all the way back to Buckingham Palace in 1765, but the sports craze has been credited to the San Francisco Giants in 1999 with a Willie Mays giveaway. In fact, there is even a bobblehead Hall of Fame established in 2014.[39] Who knows what the next premium craze might be in sports?

Sport marketers have traditionally used premiums to increase sales for lower-demand games. In the past, popular premiums included items such as hats and bats or low-cost items such as pens, pencils, or magnets. Today teams have developed sophisticated models to accurately measure the incremental revenue generated by premiums. They often have to integrate value components while accounting for other variables such as strength of opponent, weather, and the day of the game. Today's consumers demand a higher level of sophistication in the products, and although the premium cost is paid for by corporate sponsors, the *Sports Business Journal* reports that professional teams are now including giveaways for weekend and higher-demand games even where there are much smaller potential revenue gains from ticket sales.[40]

Although premiums can bring people to games who would not otherwise attend, they can also have negative consequences and must be carefully planned. In the now-defunct World Hockey Association (WHA), the Philadelphia Blazers handed out souvenir pucks at the first home game. Unfortunately, the game had to be postponed because the ice was deemed unfit for skating. When the Blazers' Derek Sanderson announced the game cancellation to the crowd at center ice, he was pelted with the pucks.[41] In a similar scenario, the LA Dodgers had to forfeit a game because fans began throwing baseballs (that they had been given) onto the field, endangering

Photo 10.8

Athlete signing autographs before a game as part of a sales promotion

Credit: Shutterstock, ID# 56009983 by Paul Hakimata Photography

URL: www.shutterstock.com/image-photo/new-york-may-27-phillies-ryan-56009983

players and other fans. The Dodgers can also be used to illustrate the height of premium marketing. In 1984, the Los Angeles Olympic Games created a region-wide craze for pin collecting. Sensing the "legs" of this mania, the Dodgers created six pin-giveaway nights at their stadium. They picked games that would typically have low attendance. The result was that all six of these games sold out on the strength of a $0.60 per unit collector's pin!

Contests and sweepstakes

Sweepstakes and contests are another sales promotional tool used by sports marketers to generate awareness and interest among consumers. Contests are competitions that award prizes on the basis of contestants' skills and ability, whereas sweepstakes are games of chance or luck. As with any sales promotion, the sports marketing manager must attempt to integrate the contest or sweepstakes with the other promotion mix elements and keep the target market in mind.

One of the classic contests sponsored by the NFL was the punt, pass, and kick competition. This has now been replicated in a joint effort by the Masters Tournament, USGA, and PGA as the Drive, Chip, and Putt competition designed to grow the game of golf with junior golfers. It has gained huge popularity, with the finals being televised on ESPN and held at Augusta National.

Web Capture 10.8
Chicago Bears engage the community

Credit: Chicago Bears

URL: www.chicagobears.com

As sweepstakes become more and more popular, companies are constantly looking for new ways to break through the clutter. Consider the Delta Sky Magazine–3M Open Giveaway that will award a grand prize winner a trip for two to the attend the 3M Open in Minneapolis, including accommodations, airfare, gift cards, and so on. Coca-Cola, a longtime sponsor of NASCAR, has designed a Race Day Salute Sweepstakes with seven grand prize winners receiving a VIP meet and greet with NASCAR drivers, a pit row experience, and accommodations to attend Homestead-Miami Speedway. Sleep Number has developed a sweepstakes to activate their Facebook site. The Ultimate 100th Season Sweepstakes will award one grand prize winner a trip to the Super Bowl and a Sleep Number Smart Bed.[42]

A unique sweepstakes example is the ESPN Zone Baltimore Ultimate Couch Potato Contest, which is a competition to see who can watch the most continuous television sports coverage among the four chosen finalists. Finalists were chosen based on a required 200-word essay discussing why they should be selected as a finalist. One grand prize winner received a gift certificate to Best Buy in the amount of $1,000, one XZipIt Recliner chair with a logo of the winner's choosing, payment to cover one year of cable bills, a $500 ESPN Zone game card, $500 in food and beverage certificates, and an ESPN Zone Ultimate Couch Potato Trophy.

The Philadelphia Flyers and NBCSports Philadelphia have granted fans a chance to win two tickets, a pregame live sports tour, and Flyers gear as part of the NHL Stadium Series Sweepstakes.

Photo 10.9

The Philadelphia Flyers use sweepstakes to further engage audiences

Credit: NBC Sports

URL: www.nbcsports.com/philadelphia/flyerssweepstakes

For those with a taste for horses and finish-line seats with spectacular views, the Rocket Mortgage Homestretch Sweepstakes will take 20 finalists to the Kentucky Derby. One lucky winner whose horse finishes first will be given $250,000 to assist in paying their mortgage. CEO Jay Farner captures the essence of why organizations like Quicken Loans, parent company of Rocket Mortgage, want to develop these contests and partner with iconic sporting events.

> Much like Rocket Mortgage, the Kentucky Derby is symbolized by speed and power. That is why Rocket Mortgage by Quicken Loans is the perfect fit for the most exciting two minutes in sports. We are a company that has made a name for itself by being bold, innovative and the first to do things – from the Quicken Loans Carrier Classic to the Billion Dollar Bracket – partnering with Churchill Downs and the Kentucky Derby is the next step.[43]

Sampling

One of the most effective ways of inducing customers to try new products that are being introduced is **sampling**. Unfortunately, it is very difficult to give away a small portion of a sporting event. However, sports have been known to integrate sampling into their events and contests. For example, anyone who has run in their local 10K or marathon typically enjoys samples of energy bars, healthy drinks, and new food and beverage products that might be relevant to the running demographic. Product giveaways at larger sports events prove an excellent way for brands to be recognized and, more importantly, tried for future purchase.

The NCAA has often partnered with a variety of companies to provide product samples to consumers to be distributed in conjunction with NCAA March Madness. The fan experience is full of activities for all ages and includes a number of sampling opportunities. Coca-Cola is the official fan refreshment of the NCAA and has set up flavor rooms for sampling new Orange Vanilla Coke and Orange Vanilla Coke Zero. Similarly, Buffalo Wild Wings has a sports bar and asks fans to stop by and sample their famous traditional wings.[44]

Point-of-purchase displays

Point-of-purchase or **P-O-P displays** have long been used by marketers to attract consumers' attention to a particular product or retail display area. These displays or materials, such as brochures, cut-outs, and banners, are most commonly used to communicate price reductions or other special offers to consumers. For instance, tennis racquet manufacturers, such as Prince, design huge

Photo 10.10
Official Store FC Barcelona, offering clothing, footwear, team souvenirs, and paraphernalia for fans and visitors

Credit: Shutterstock, ID# 1017876976 by Lestertair

URL: www.shutterstock.com/image-photo/barcelona-spain-12-january-2018-official-1017876976

tennis racquets, which are then displayed in the storefronts of many tennis retail shops to catch the attention of consumers. The Super Bowl, an American classic, provides a forum where many official sponsors and non-sponsors of the game utilize point-of-purchase display tie-ins to interact and attract consumers.

Companies like Heineken have been innovative with their use of point-of-purchase displays with events such as the U.S. Open. Heineken launched an upscale aluminum bottle to U.S. consumers, and the bottle, when viewed under a black light, revealed hidden patterns of stars and trails. In addition to the black light properties, the 16-ounce bottle displayed a progressive European design which further indicated the upscale style and attitude to Heineken's consumers.

Coupons

Another common sales promotion tool is the coupon. **Coupons** are certificates that generally offer reductions in price for sports products. Coupons may appear in print advertisements, be part of the product's package, be inserted within the product packaging, be mailed to consumers, be printed on or part of an admissions ticket, or be offered as part of a social media strategy. Labeled by many a new "social sport," couponing offers an inexpensive way to try something new, often with an emphasis on local business. In fact, the business has its own terminology; for example, **stacking** means using both a manufacturer's coupon and store coupon for purchase. Consumers' reasons for utilizing coupons range from critical issues like the economy to simpler reasons such as freeing up more money to spend on fun activities. The idea for many of being able to go out for a meal with friends or family at a discounted price, while also trying out a new sport venue, game, or show, is a valuable brand asset. Today many organizations utilize social media platforms to gain exposure to key demographics. Surprisingly, the demographic users are wealthier and younger than most people would expect. In many instances, it provides a business a unique opportunity to attract new customers without spending a fortune on advertising. Couponing is a great way to get people to attend an event, but the task of turning it into repeat purchase or profit lies with the business. For example, utilizing couponing to secure patrons to participate at a fitness center or bowling alley is one thing; getting them to repeat the use or purchase is another. Although coupons have been found to induce short-term sales, there are disadvantages. For instance, some marketers believe continual coupon use can detract from the image of the product in the minds of consumers, in essence reducing the perceived brand image and value. It is not a forum that should be utilized with every game or event but may be utilized several times a year and continue to attract consumers. Another concern is that couponing only affords business an opportunity to make back a portion of the profit. In addition, most coupon redemption is done by consumers who already use the product, thereby limiting the use of coupons to attract new customers.

Public relations

The final element in the promotional mix is public relations. Quite often, public relations gets confused with other promotional mix elements. Public relations often gets mistaken for publicity. This is an easy mistake to make because the goals of public relations and publicity are to provide communication that will enhance the image of the sports entity (athlete, team, or league). Before we make a distinction between public relations and publicity, let us define public relations. **Public relations** is the element of the promotional mix that identifies, establishes, and maintains mutually beneficial relationships between the sports organizations and the various publics on which its success or failure depends.

Within the definition of public relations, reference is made to the "various publics" with which the sports organization interacts. These "publics" can be divided into external publics, which are outside the immediate control of sports marketers, and internal publics, which are more directly controlled by sports marketers. External publics include the community (e.g., city and state officials, community members, corporations), sanctioning bodies (e.g., NCAA), intermediary publics (e.g., sports marketing agencies), and competition (e.g., other sports or entertainment choices). Internal publics, such as volunteers, employees, suppliers, athletes, and spectators, are associated with manufacturing, distributing, and consuming the sport itself.

Sports marketers have a variety of public relations tools they can use to communicate with internal and external publics. The choice of tools depends on the public relations objective, the targeted audience, and how public relations is being integrated into the overall promotional plan. These tools and techniques include generating publicity (news releases or press conferences), participating in community events, producing written materials (annual report or press guides), and even legislative lobbying (personal selling necessary for stadium location decisions).

One of the most important and widely used public relations tools is publicity. Publicity is the generation of news in the broadcast or print media about a sports product. The news about a sports product is most commonly disseminated to the various sports publics through news releases and press conferences. Although public relations efforts are managed by the sports organization, publicity can sometimes come from external sources. As such, publicity might not always enhance the image of the sports product. Research by Funk and Pritchard noted that less committed readers tended to recall more facts from negative articles, while committed fans tended to counter-argue with more favorable thoughts.[45] Because publicity is often outside the control of the sports organization, it is seen as a highly credible source of communication. Information that is coming from "unbiased" sources, such as magazines, newspaper articles, or the televised news, is perceived to be more trustworthy.

In addition to publicity, another powerful public relations tool used to enhance the sports organization's image is **community involvement**. A study was conducted to determine what, if anything, professional sports organizations are doing in the area of community relations. The survey specifically examined the NBA, NHL, NFL, and MLB to determine how they are involved in community relations and how important community relations are to their overall marketing program. All the responding teams indicated they were involved in some sort of community program, with the most common form of community involvement being (1) sponsoring public programs (e.g., food and toy drives, medical programs and services, auctions, and other fundraisers), (2) requiring time commitment from all of the sports organizations' employees, (3) partially funding programs, and (4) providing personnel at no charge. Interestingly, the study found no differences among the importance of community relations by type of league. In other words, the NBA, NHL, NFL, and MLB are all equally involved in community relations.[46]

To celebrate its 100th anniversary, the NFL is rolling out its **HuddleFor100** initiative. Fans are encouraged to choose a cause and contribute 100 minutes of their time to better their community. The goal of the initiative is to reach 100 million volunteer hours by bringing together fans, players, and their teams as they "Huddle" together to serve their communities. Teams will be competing for the most volunteer minutes. Each team and fans will choose their own volunteer efforts. For example, one of the volunteer opportunities hosted by the Houston Texans was at the Bridge Over Troubled Water women's shelter in Pasadena, Texas. The Texans players and the Battle Red Ladies helped beautify the area by creating an herb garden, adding flower beds, mulching, staining outdoor structures, and power-washing sidewalks.

Another example of the community involvement is with Major League Baseball and one of its important initiatives, Stand Up To Cancer (SU2C). This program was created to accelerate innovative cancer research that gets new therapies to patients quicker. Major League Baseball and its 30 clubs have donated more than $40 million to SU2C since the partnership was first formed in 2009. As a founding donor, MLB has conducted significant awareness-building efforts through public service announcements, in-stadium promotions, and various fundraising events.[47]

Although community involvement benefits any number of stakeholders in the organization, it is typically more than philanthropy alone. As suggested in the following article, sports entities like the NBA and WNBA are reaping the rewards of their goodwill.

ARTICLE 10.7

NBA MOBILIZES DURING CORONAVIRUS OUTBREAK TO GET THE MESSAGE OUT AND PROVIDE FUNDING, RELIEF ASSISTANCE

The NBA knows how to mobilize, especially in difficult times.

In the days since coronavirus (COVID-19) not only suspended the NBA season but brought everyday life to a near standstill, the league has found ways to help through its NBA Cares program – from NBA and WNBA players and teams donating money to assist out-of-work arena workers, public-service announcements from players to mental health assistance to helping kids stay active and healthy during this time.

"There's no group of people who can contribute as much as our players can in terms of getting the message out," NBA president of social responsibility and player programs Kathy Behrens told USA TODAY Sports. "Obviously, the people on the front lines, the health-care workers, the people who are essential employees who are going in every day, that's a whole other level of sacrifice.

"But everybody in the world right now has to do something, has to sacrifice something. We know that our players have a reach and have a platform and people are listening to them."

The NBA and WNBA, along with players and teams, have pledged $50 million to COVID-19 related efforts, and the NBA and National Basketball Players Associated each donated $1 million to benefit Solidarity Response Fund for the World Health Organization, Crisis Text Line, Direct Relief and Share Our Strength, among others.

The total right now is around $35 million.

"Philanthropy is going to be incredibly important especially given the economic challenges," Behrens said.

The NBPA Foundation, which helps players with their philanthropic work to maximize impact, is in the process streamlining donation process to that organizations receive money faster, especially now when getting money and goods to those in need is a necessity.

"We're seeing an influx of players calling in trying to figure out what is the right them for them to do in light of how widespread the impact of COVID-19 is going to be," NBPA Foundation executive director Sherrie Deans said.

The foundation is thinking big picture, too. It created an online resource for players called Big Hearts, Big Impact that allows to explore "areas that aren't the first things you think about around the social safety net and around thinking about long-term policies to make some of things more secure for vulnerable people," Deans said. "We're trying to find them links to those organizations that are doing that kind of work so as they think not just about the immediate response but the long-term response, they have options."

Brooklyn's Kyrie Irving on Monday donated $323,000 plus a $200,000 match from Lineage Logistics to deliver meals to families, and Philadelphia's Joel Embiid said he will donate $500,000 to COVID-19 relief.

The NBA moved quickly with its NBA Together campaign, designed for global outreach, social engagement, education and inspiration.

It started with PSAs on health and social distancing from several players, including Steph Curry, Kevin Love, Trae Young, Jayson Tatum, Damian Lillard, Victor Oladipo, Pau Gasol, Layshia Clarendon and Courtney Williams.

Those messages have been watched more than forty five million times on various platforms. And keep in mind, these aren't polished production pieces. They are players recording videos on their phones and sending them in.

It continued with a Know the Facts web page and Acts of Caring initiative aimed to inspire one million acts of kindness big and small and to share those acts on social media with the hashtag #nbatogether.

"One of the great things about the Kevin Love message was yes, we have to be socially distant but it doesn't mean we have to isolate ourselves so that's why we talked about building your community," Behrens said. "How do you connect people? How do you reach people?"

The Jr. NBA at Home program has also unveiled workout programs, exercises and basketball drills for kids to do solo in a limited space. The Jr. NBA's partners are also helping with education tools including virtual lessons for at-home learning.

The NBA also relies on Headspace, a mental health and wellness app that promotes meditation and mindfulness. It's a way that "that the stress and anxiety can be lessened because this is a stressful and anxiety-producing time as any of us have probably seen in a generation," Behrens said.

Each day the NBA is hosting NBA Together Live events on Instagram and Twitter, featuring players. Kevin Love, Dennis Scott, Miles Bridges, Bruce Bowen and Lillard have participated.

The NBA also is streaming classic games on NBA social platforms, including Facebook and YouTube. "This is a time of great sacrifice and everybody can do something," Behrens said. "We're no different in trying to figure out how we use our platform and reach and how can we be helpful in a world that needs a lot of help."

Source: NBA mobilizes during coronavirus outbreak to get the message out and provide funding, relief assistance

Credit: Jeff Zillgitt, March 24, 2020. Accessed September 24, 2020

Rightsholder: © USA TODAY Sports

URL: www.usatoday.com/story/sports/nba/2020/03/24/nba-nbpa-amp-up-coronavirus-covid-19-funding-relief-assistance/2905503001/

Summary

Chapter 10 focuses on gaining a better understanding of the various promotional mix elements. Advertising is one of the most visible and critical promotional mix elements.

Although most of us associate advertising with developing creative slogans and jingles, there is a systematic process for designing effective advertisements. Developing an advertising campaign consists of a series of five interrelated steps, formulating objectives, designing an ad budget, making creative decisions, choosing a media strategy, and evaluating the advertisement.

Advertising objectives and budgeting techniques are similar to those discussed in Chapter 9 for the broader promotion planning process. Advertising objectives are sometimes categorized as either direct or indirect. Direct advertising objectives, such as advertising by sports organizations to end users and sales promotion advertising, are designed to stimulate action among consumers of sport. Alternatively, the goal of indirect objectives is to make consumers aware, enhance the image of the sport, or provide information to consumers. After objectives have been determined, budgets for the advertising campaign are considered. Budget techniques, such as competitive parity, objective and task, arbitrary allocation, and percentage of sales, are commonly used by advertisers.

Once the objectives and budget have been established, the creative process is considered. The creative process identifies the ideas and the concept of the advertisement. To develop the concept for the advertisement, benefits of the sports product must be identified, ad appeals (e.g., health, emotional, fear, sex, and pleasure) are designed, and advertising execution decisions (e.g., comparative advertisements, slice of life, and scientific) are made. After creative decisions are crafted, the next phase of the advertising campaign is to design media strategy. Media strategy includes decisions about how the medium (e.g., radio, television, and Internet) will be most effective and how to best schedule the chosen media.

Another communications tool that is part of the promotional mix is personal selling. Personal selling is unique in that person-to-person communication is required rather than mass communication. In other words, a salesperson must deliver the message face to face to the intended target audience rather than through some medium (e.g., a magazine) that is not personal. Although there are many advantages to personal selling, perhaps none is greater than the ability to use personal selling to develop long-term relationships with customers.

In today's competitive sports marketing environment, a number of strategies have been developed to maximize personal selling effectiveness. One process, designed by Miller and Heiman, is called the strategic selling process and consists of six elements. The elements that must be considered for successful selling are buying influences, red flags, response modes, win-results, the sales funnel, and the ideal customer profile.

Sales promotions are another element in the promotional mix that are designed primarily to stimulate consumer demand for products. One of the most widely used forms of sales promotion in sports marketing includes premiums, or items that are given away with the core product being purchased. In addition, contests and sweepstakes, free samples, point-of-purchase displays, and coupons are forms of sales promotion that often are integrated into the broader promotional mix.

A final promotional mix element considered in Chapter 10 is public, or community, relations. Public relations is the element of the promotional mix that identifies, establishes, and maintains mutually beneficial relationships between the sports organization and the various publics on which its success or failure depends. These publics include the community, sanctioning bodies, intermediary publics, and competition. Other publics include employees, suppliers, participants, and spectators. The tools with which messages are communicated to the various publics include generating publicity, participating in community events, producing written materials such as annual reports and press releases, and lobbying.

Key terms

- advertising
- advertising appeals
- advertising budgeting

- advertising execution
- advertising objectives
- attractiveness
- buying influences
- coach's role
- community involvement
- comparative advertisements
- continuous schedule
- coupons
- creative brief
- creative decisions
- creative process
- credibility
- direct objectives
- economic buying role
- emotional appeals
- even keel mode
- expertise
- fear appeals
- flighting schedule
- frequency
- growth mode
- health appeals
- ideal customer
- indirect objectives
- lifestyle advertisements
- media scheduling
- media strategy
- one-sided versus two-sided
- overconfident mode
- personal selling
- pleasure or fun appeals
- P-O-P displays
- premiums
- promotional mix elements
- public relations
- pulsing schedule
- reach
- relationship marketing
- response modes
- roles
- sales funnel
- sales promotions
- sampling
- scientific advertisements

- sex appeals
- slice-of-life advertisements
- stacking
- stadium signage
- strategic selling
- sweepstakes and contests
- technical buying role
- testimonials
- trouble mode
- trustworthiness
- user buying role
- win-results

Review questions

1 What are the major steps in developing an advertising campaign?
2 Explain direct advertising objectives versus indirect advertising objectives.
3 Describe the creative decision process. What are the three outcomes of the creative process?
4 Discuss, in detail, the major advertising appeals used by sports marketers. Provide at least one example of each type of advertising appeal.
5 What are the executional formats commonly used in sports marketing advertising?
6 Comment on the advantages and disadvantages of using athlete endorsers in advertising.
7 What two decisions do advertisers make in developing a media strategy? What are the four basic media scheduling alternatives? Provide an example of each type of media scheduling.
8 Discuss the strengths and weaknesses of the alternative forms of advertising available to sports marketers.
9 When is personal selling used by sports marketers? Describe, in detail, the steps in the strategic selling process.
10 Describe the various forms of sales promotion available to sports marketers.

Exercises

1 Design a creative advertising strategy to increase participation in Little League Baseball.
2 Design a survey instrument to assess the source credibility of 10 professional athletes (of your choice) and administer the survey to 10 individuals. Which athletes have the highest levels of credibility, and why?
3 Attend a professional or collegiate sporting event and describe all the forms of advertising you observe. Which forms of advertising do you feel are particularly effective, and why?

4 Visit a sporting goods retailer and describe all the sales promotion tools that you observe. Which forms of sales promotion do you believe are particularly effective, and why?

5 Interview the director or manager of ticket sales for a professional organization or collegiate sports program to determine their sales process. How closely does their sales process follow the strategic selling process outlined in this chapter?

6 Interview the marketing department (or director of community/public relations) from a professional organization or collegiate sports program to determine the extent of their community or public relations efforts. How do sports organizations decide in which community events or activities to participate?

Internet/Social Media exercises

1 Using social media, find two examples of advertisements for sports products that use indirect objectives and two examples of advertisements that use direct objectives.

2 Find 10 advertisements on the web for sports products and describe the executional format for each advertisement. Which type of execution format is most commonly used for Internet advertising?

Notes

1   https://www.redbull.com/us-en/energydrink.
2   See, for example, Joel Evans and Barry Berman, *Marketing*, 6th ed. (New York: Macmillan, 1994), 610.
3   www.sponsorship.com/Report/2017/10/23/Bank-of-America-Banks-Success-with-MLB-Activation.aspx.
4   https://clients1.ibisworld.com/reports/us/industry/productsandmarkets.aspx?entid=1655.
5   William A. Sutton, Mark A. McDonald, George R. Milne, and John Cimperman, "Creating and Fostering Fan Identification in Professional Sports," *Sport Marketing Quarterly*, vol. 6, no. 1 (1997), 15-22.
6   Fastco Studios, "This Highly Engineered Football Helmet Wants to Put a Dent in Concussions." Available from: www.youtube.com/watch?v=SWWNHjJ35cM.
7   Golf Digest, 2015. Photos: Lexi Thompson And LPGA Stars Get Golf Strong. April. Available from: https://www.golfdigest.com/gallery/lpga-fitness-photos.
8   Nicole Fallon, "Why Sex Sells…More Than Ever," *Business News Daily* (June 25, 2021). Available from: https://www.businessnewsdaily.com/2649-sex-sells-more.html.
9   Kevin Seifert, "Enough is Enough," *Minneapolis Star Tribune* (April 11, 2007), 3C.
10 "Larry Bird vs. Michael Jordan McDonalds Commercial." Available from: www.youtube.com/watch?v=_oACRt-Qp-s.

11   Jim Nantz, Titleist Tour Soft TV Commercial, "This is Your Soft." Available from: www.ispot.tv/ad/IEEn/titleist-tour-soft-better-distance.

12   MSN.com. "34 of the Biggest Scandals in Sports" (March 11, 2020), accessed September 7, 2021. Available from: https://www.msn.com/en-ca/sports/sportsphotos/34-of-the-biggest-scandals-in-sports/ss-BB112OXH#image=2.

13   Tennisplanet.me, 2018. Available from: https://www.tennisplanet.me/blog/2018/09/page/2/.

14   The SPUN by Sports Illustrated, "Shaun White Issues Apology Over Treatment of American Flag" (February 14, 2018), accessed September 7, 2021. Available from: https://thespun.com/more/olympics/shaun-white-issues-apology-over-treatment-of-american-flag.

15   MLB.com. "Cano Suspended 80 Games for Violation of Drug Policy" (May 15, 2018), accessed September 7, 2021. Available from: https://www.mlb.com/news/robinson-cano-suspended-80-games-c276822884.

16   MSN.con. "34 of the Biggest Scandals in Sports" (March 11, 2020), accessed September 7, 2021. Available from: https://www.msn.com/en-ca/sports/sportsphotos/34-of-the-biggest-scandals-in-sports/ss-BB112OXH#image=2.

17   www.brandingstrategyinsider.com/2016/07/10748.html#.XJBUgi2ZNQY.

18   Zach O'Malley, "The Highest Paid Dead Celebrities of 2018." Available from: www.forbes.com/sites/zackomalleygreenburg/2018/10/31/the-highest-paid-dead-celebrities-of-2018/#3eccbd0a720c.

19   Thales Teixeira, "World Cup Soccer: 770 Billion Minutes of Attention," Forbes.com (June 13, 2014). Available from: www.forbes.com/sites/hbsworkingknowledge/2014/06/13/world-cup-soccer-770-billion-minutes-of-attention/, accessed June 22, 2014.

20   Ibid.

21   Kurt Badenhausen, "The Dallas Cowboys Head The Nfl's Most Valuable Teams at $4.8 Billion." Available from: www.forbes.com/sites/kurtbadenhausen/2017/09/18/the-dallas-cowboys-head-the-nfls-most-valuable-teams-at-4-8-billion/#94037a7243f8.

22   Jay Gladden, "The Ever Expanding Impact of Technology on Sport Marketing, Part II," *Sport Marketing Quarterly*, vol. 5, no. 4 (1996), 9–10.

23   Douglas Turco, "The Effects of Courtside Advertising on Product Recognition and Attitude Change," *Sport Marketing Quarterly*, vol. 5, no. 4 (1996), 11–15.

24   Nick Schaferhoof, "9 Awesome Sports Marketing Examples to Learn." Available from: www.themeboy.com/blog/sports-marketing-examples/.

25   Kaylene Williams, Alfred Petrosky, Edward H. Hernandez, Robert Page, "Product Placement Effectiveness: Revisited and Renewed," *Journal of Management & Marketing Research*, vol. 7 (2011/04/01), 132–155.

26   George Belch and Michael Belch, *Advertising and Promotion: An Integrated Marketing Communications Perspective*, 4th ed. (New York: Irwin, McGraw-Hill, 1998), 431–434.

27   Joe Layden, "Human Billboards," in *Mark McCormack's Guide to Sports Marketing*. (Largo, FL: International Sports Marketing Group, 1996), 129–136.

28   www.star-telegram.com.

29   Guest Author, "Want a Success Digital Sports Strategy? Start by Getting the Right Channel Mix." Available from: www.adweek.com/digital/want-a-successful-digital-sports-strategy-start-by-getting-the-right-channel-mix/.

30   "Sports Fans Twice as Likely to Watch Videos on Mobile Phones," *European Interactive Advertising Association* (June 2008).

31   Raechel Johns, "Sports Promotion & The Internet," *Cyber-Journal of Sport Marketing*, vol. 1, no. 4 (1997). Available from: http://fulltext.ausport.gov.au/fulltext/1997/cjsm/v1n4/johns.htm.

32   Fred Beasley, Matthew Shank, and Rebecca Ball, "Do Super Bowl Viewers Watch the Commercials?" *Sport Marketing Quarterly*, vol. 7, no. 3 (1998), 33–40.

33   Philip Kotler and Gary Armstrong, *Marketing: An Introduction*, 4th ed. (Upper Saddle River, NJ: Prentice Hall, 1997).

34   Earl Jessiman, "NHL Loyalty Programs Reward Fans & Drive Data Collection." Available from: https://thehockeywriters.com/nhl-loyalty-programs-rewards-data-collection/.

35   Masayuki Yoshida, Brian Gordon, and David Hedlund, "Professional Sport Teams and Fan Loyalty Programs: A Perceived Value Perspective," *International Journal of Sport Management*, vol. 19 (2018/07/01), 235–261. Available from: www.researchgate.net/publication/326752921_Professional_Sport_Teams_and_Fan_Loyalty_Programs_A_Perceived_Value_Perspective.

36   Robert Miller and Stephen Heiman, *Strategic Selling* (New York: Warner Books, 1985).

37   Mark Maske and Les Carpenter, "Player Arrests Put the NFL in a Defensive Mode," *WashingtonPost.com* (December 16, 2006). Available from: https://www.washingtonpost.com/wp-dyn/content/article/2006/12/15/AR2006121502134.html, accessed June 23, 2014.

38   Benjamin Hill, "Top Promotions Battle for MiLBY." Available from: https://www.milb.com/news/gcs-25003636.

39   Nick Faris, "The Greatest Gift in Sports: How the Bobblehead Became a Beloved Symbol of baseball." Available from: https://nationalpost.com/sports/baseball/mlb/the-greatest-gift-in-sports-how-the-bobblehead-became-a-classic-symbol-of-baseball-season.

40   J. Cisvk and P. Courty, "Stadium Giveaway Promotions: How Many Items to Give and the Impact on Ticket Sales in Live Sports," *The Journal of Sport Management*, vol 35 (May 2021), pp 1–15. DOI: https://doi.org/10.1123/jsm.2020-0322.

41   Ed Willes, "A Legacy of Slapstick and Slap Shots," *New York Times* (November 30, 1997), 33.

42   https://ultracontest.com/Category/Sports-Tickets-Sweepstakes/3900.

43   "Rocket Press Room, And They're Off! Rocket Mortgage Partners with Churchill Downs to Launch the 'Homestretch Sweepstakes' for The Kentucky derby Offering One Lucky Winner $250,000." Available from: www.quickenloans.com/press-room/2019/03/18/and-theyre-off-rocket-mortgage-partners-with-churchill-downs-to-launch-the-homestretch-sweepstakes-for-the-kentucky-derby-offering-one-lucky-winner-250000/#4S0GyQr4Tg5cTWs7.99.

44   www.ncaa.com/final-four/activities.

45   Daniel C. Funk and Mark P. Pritchard, "Sports Publicity: Commitment's Moderation of Message Effects," *Journal of Business Research*, vol. 59, no. 5 (2006), 613–621.

46   Denise O'Connell, "Community Relations in Professional Sports Organizations" (Unpublished master's thesis, The Ohio State University, Columbus, Ohio).

47   MLB Press Release, "Wednesday, September 1st Is "Childhood Cancer Awareness Day" Throughout MLB in Support of Stand Up to Cancer." Available from: www.mlb.com/mlb-community/stand-up-to-cancer.

Sponsorship programs

After completing this chapter, you should be able to:

- Comment on the growing importance of sports sponsorships as a promotion mix element.
- Design a sponsorship program.
- Understand the major sponsorship objectives.
- Provide examples of the various costs of sponsorship.
- Identify the levels of the sports event pyramid.
- Evaluate the effectiveness of sponsorship programs.

ARTICLE 11.1
JAY-Z'S ROC NATION ENTERING PARTNERSHIP WITH NFL

Roc Nation, the entertainment company founded by rapper and businessman Shawn "Jay-Z" Carter, is entering into a multiyear partnership with the NFL to enhance the NFL's live game experiences and to amplify the league's social justice efforts.

As part of the agreement, Roc Nation will advise on the selection of artists for major NFL performances like the Super Bowl. A major component of the partnership will be to nurture and strengthen community through football and music, including through the NFL's Inspire Change initiative.

The NFL formally launched the Inspire Change initiative in early 2019, after more than two years of work with NFL players, with the goal of creating positive change in communities across the country. Through this initiative, NFL teams and the league office work with the Players Coalition and other NFL players to support programs and initiatives that reduce barriers to opportunity, with a focus on three priority areas: education and economic advancement; police and community relations; and criminal justice reform.

DOI: 10.4324/9780429030673-14

"With its global reach, the National Football League has the platform and opportunity to inspire change across the country," Carter said in a press release. "Roc Nation has shown that entertainment and enacting change are not mutually exclusive ideas – instead, we unify them. This partnership is an opportunity to strengthen the fabric of communities across America."

Carter added during a Wednesday Q&A with select media: "I'm really into action – I'm into real work. I'm not into how it looks. How it looks only lasts for a couple months until we start doing the work. I've been in this position many times. Take Tidal as a great example from five years ago. Now, people look at it today, people have a different outlook on it. But at the time, people didn't see what was going on. So I've been in this position many times. I just show up and do the work, I'm not interested in how things look on the outside. If protesting on the field is the most effective way, then protest on the field. But, if you have a vehicle that you can inspire change and you can speak to the masses and educate at the same time."

Carter said the platform that the NFL provides speaks to the work in the community that the league and Roc Nation can do together.

"Inspire Change is already happening (with Roc Nation) and the NFL has a huge platform," he said. "We can use that huge platform, and we've seen it happen. Like with J.J. Watt, when he brought the aid to everyone in Houston, everybody forgot about the turmoil that was in the NFL. If you can use this platform to do that in different areas, that's a home run. That's how I would view a success. That's success for me."

Roc Nation also will work with the NFL to create and distribute content across multiple music streaming services for a variety of initiatives.

"Every conversation I've had with Jay has been inspiring," NFL Commissioner Roger Goodell said Wednesday. "Not just on his perspective on the process of how we do the entertainment, but what we should try to achieve. We always say we should get better and we should evolve. We think we should partner with the best, and that's why we're sitting here. We believe we're partnering with the best. So, his perspective is going to drive us."

Source: Jay-Z's Roc Nation entering partnership with NFL. Published Aug. 13, 2019, accessed September 24, 2020

Credit: NFL, 2019

URL: www.nfl.com/news/story/0ap3000001041162/article/jayzs-roc-nation-entering-partnership-with-nfl

Growth of sponsorship

The opening cause-related scenario is just one example of a sport organization activating sport partnerships to help achieve their marketing objectives. A wide variety of organizations are realizing that sports partnerships are a valuable way to reach new markets and retain an existing customer base. Sponsorships can increase sales, change attitudes, heighten awareness, and build and maintain relationships with consumers. It is no wonder that sponsorships became the promotional tool of choice for sport marketers and continue to grow in importance. Before we turn to the growth of sponsorship as a promotional tool, let us define sponsorship.

In Chapter 9, sponsorships were described as one of the elements in the promotional mix. More specifically, **sponsorship** was defined as investing in a sports entity (athlete, league, team, or event) to support overall organizational objectives, marketing goals, and promotional strategies. Sponsorship is a mutual exchange between properties that creates a commercial competitive advantage. The sponsorship investment may come in the form of monetary support and trade. For example, nonrevenue sports have been the biggest winners in the University of Kansas Athletics Department's sponsorship deal with adidas. The recent 14-year renewal runs through the 2030-31 school year and is worth $14 million annually, collectively totaling about $196 million. KU first partnered with adidas in 2005, signing an eight-year agreement. The pact was renewed in 2013 when KU executed a six-year extension. Compared to the previous six-year extension, adidas will pay the KU athletic department an average of $3.86 million more per year in base compensation ($1.68 million vs. $5.54 million per year), $4.12 million more per year in product allowance ($2.38 million vs. $6.5 million), and about $800,000 more per year for marketing.[1] adidas is sponsoring the university's athletics program to support their marketing objective of increasing awareness of their brand and to associate with a winning NCAA program. Understanding how sponsorship can help achieve marketing goals and organizational objectives is discussed when we look at the construction of a sponsorship plan or program. For now, let us turn our attention to the dramatic growth of sponsorship as a promotional tool.

In our brief discussion of sponsorship, we have alluded to the "dramatic growth" of sponsorship, but just how quickly is sponsorship growing? In 2020, prior to the coronavirus pandemic, WARC released an advertising report predicting that the global sports sponsorship market would record the strongest growth in over a decade, expected to reach $48 billion worldwide.[2] However, as sports marketing company Two Circles estimated, the pandemic impact is estimated to cause a 37 percent decline in those estimates. The following facts and figures regarding sponsorship activities help to paint a clear picture of sponsorship growth:[3]

- According to WARC, spending on sports sponsorship is expected to rise 5.0 percent this year to reach $48.4 billion worldwide – the strongest growth in a decade – according to data from specialist agency Two Circles. The market has expanded at a compound annual growth rate (CAGR) of 4.2 percent since 2011, consistently outpacing brand investment in traditional media.
- North American sports sponsorship spending reached $15.5 billion in 2020, a 3.5 percent increase from 2019, according to data analysis by Two Circles. Despite the continued growth, Two Circles analysis revealed that sports properties sponsorship assets are significantly undervalued. The

research identified $5.7 billion in unrealized value due to unsold inventory, unreported engagement, and outdated asset packaging. As noted by IEG in previous years, sponsorship sport spending accounts for approximately 68-72 percent of sponsorship spending. The remaining spending can be attributed to entertainment (10 percent), causes (9 percent), arts and festivals, fairs and annual events (4 percent), and associations and membership organizations (3 percent). The majority of investment – based on where deals are signed – is concentrated in North America; the region is expected to account for 38.8 percent of global spend this year. North America is the primary growth engine, too, expanding at a compound annual growth rate of 4.6 percent since 2011.[4]

- By 2024, global sponsorship spending is projected to reach $62 billion. According to Two Circles, growth should remain steady between 4 to 6 percent year-on-year. Brands continue to want more measurable tangible and measurable engagement opportunities. Continued optimizing of digital platforms will create a plethora of opportunities to optimize messaging and creatives that will ultimately improve value. Europe is expected to account for 26.7 percent of the global total at $12.9 billion in 2020 and Asia 23.9 percent at $11.6 billion. Latin America (5.0 percent, or $2.4 billion), Africa (4.3 percent, $2.1 billion) and ANZ (1.3 percent, $625 million) follow.[5] Comparing global spending forecasts for media and other marketing expenditures, advertising would see the largest growth, 4.6 percent compared with 4.4 percent for marketing/promotions.

- The esports industry has been growing and establishing itself as a force to reckon with. The latest global esports audience estimates show that the money spent on sponsorships is targeting millions of fans. The audience will reach 550 million by 2021, and with the average revenue per esports fan in 2018 being $5.5, projected global esports advertising and sponsorship is expected to reach $1.2 billion by 2020. In 2017, companies spent almost $500 million, with over $230 million on sponsorship deals, $140 million on advertising, and $90 million on media rights in esports. The audience is also diverse, meaning that sponsors won't only be targeting adolescent males, as some may wrongly assume. Around a third of esports fans are female, and those aged 36-50 account for nearly 7 percent of the viewership. Therefore, esports sponsorship is an effective way to leverage the appeal of events, teams, and personalities.[6]

- Continued investment in sports properties, as well as the growth and development of platform exchanges, that is, esport, will afford the industry continued growth in the next five to seven years. Two Circles notes that brands are attracted to sport by scale, and they will continue to desire the widespread media exposure that broadcast coverage provides; however, collective exchanges in the digital realm will enhance delivery, activation channels, and value. In fact, average year-on-year growth between 2020 and 2024 is projected to be 4 to 6 percent, denoting that as a marketing platform to reach on-scale audiences, sport sponsorship is unrivaled and still a valued investment for rightsholders to evolve sponsorship business.[7]

- The coronavirus pandemic had a significant impact on sponsorship properties. The estimated 37 percent decline in sales was extremely evident in the airline (61 percent), automotive (55 percent), financial services (45 percent), energy (44 percent), and retail (37 percent) categories. Not surprisingly, the technology (18 percent), alcohol (19 percent), and telecom (19 percent) categories were the least impacted.[8]

IEG noted, as it has in most years over the past two-plus decades, that sponsorship's growth rate will be ahead of the growth rate experienced by advertising and sales promotion in North America but not globally, 4 percent vs. 5.5 percent, for corporate interest in other marketing activities, particularly digital platforms, has to this point dampened enthusiasm about some forms of sponsorship spending.[9] Today, fans consume media and sports across a range of digital platforms, and sport has struggled to covert these exchanges into value for brands.[10] Brands continue to desire more tangible and measurable engagements with their audiences. As sport entities begin to comprehend how data can be used to create impactful brand activations through digital channels, sponsorship propositions, pound for pound, will outperform "regular" digital marketing strategies.[11]

Phil Stephan of Two Circles noted that much of the growth has been driven by the sustained dominance of sports broadcasting and the ability to deliver engagement through digital channels. For example, in 2018, 92 of the top 100 most-watched U.S. broadcasts were sport related, while globally, according to FIFA, 1.1 billion people tuned in to watch the 2018 World Cup. If sport properties continue to increase the integration of digital platforms and enhance value returns for their partners, sponsorship will be seen as a viable marketing alternative.

Overall, continued interest in major sports properties should make it the fastest-growing segment. For example, the NHL is expected to show the largest increase among the big four sports, recording a 10.8 percent year-on-year growth.[12] Spending on the league and its member clubs was $559.5 million, an increase of 54.5 percent compared to 2016–2017. The remaining three, NFL, MLB, and NBA, equate to $3.97 billion in spending. According to WARC, the NFL has the largest sponsorship pot ($1.53 billion in 2020, up 4.9 percent from 2019). This total is equivalent to 9.9 percent of all sports sponsorship spending in the United States. Major League Baseball deals are projected to rise 5.6 percent in value to $1.05 billion in 2020, while tie-ins with the National Basketball Association should rise 7.1 percent to $1.39 billion for the 2020/21 season.[13] Though Europe will remain the largest source of sponsorship spending apart from North America, growth in Asia and Central/South America is expected to heat up because of the growth in esport and hosting mega-events such as Tokyo 2020. However, as we have recently witnessed, the impact of pandemic events such as the coronavirus (COVID-19), identified as an emerging, rapidly evolving situation, may adversely affect these forecasts.

The esports market is growing rapidly. Data from Newzoo estimates that brand investment is expected to reach $795.1 million worldwide in 2020, a 23.1 percent rise from 2019. Approximately three-quarters of this ($584 million) is to be invested in sponsorships, while an additional $211 million is to be spent on spots during ad breaks.[14] The demographics of esports viewers make it an appealing channel for brands. In fact, according to WARC, GlobalWebIndex data show 22 percent of Internet users count themselves as esports fans, with over 70 percent aged 16 to 34. Most (64 percent) are male, and three-quarters have mid-to-high-earning incomes. Another unique factor of engaged and enthused esports fans is that approximately 85 percent either delete cookies, use private browsing windows, or block ads, providing advantages to alternative sponsorship exchanges. Nielsen reported that the majority of sponsorships were from non-endemic (60 percent), those without a direct stake in computing, vs. endemic (40 percent), those with a stake in the industry, brands. Growth has been attributed to the match-making systems, normalcy (easier to relate to), deployment of localized franchise models of esports leagues, and consumer recognition of technology. WARC Best Practice suggests brands should apply a test-and-learn approach and be ready to optimize strategies on the fly to reach these audiences.[15]

Much of the impetus behind surging sponsorship growth in Asia has been associated with the influx of mega-events. Events, both past and present, such as the Beijing Olympics (1.22 billion), the Sochi Winter Games, and Tokyo 2020 Summer Games, have had a profound impact on sponsorship offerings. For example, Olympiad sales for The Olympic Partners (TOP) and domestic sponsors for Tokyo 2020 have surpassed all sponsorship procurement records. The respective TOP (1.954 billion) and domestic (3.982 billion) totals are set to reach record highs and continue to grow. Additionally, the advent and introduction of programs such as Crickets IPL and Twenty20 (T20) campaigns has had an impact on sponsorship growth in many of the Asian regions. Twenty20 cricket, often abbreviated to T20, is a form of cricket originally introduced in England and Wales for professional intercounty competition. A Twenty20 game involves two teams; each has a single inning, batting for a maximum of 20 overs.[16] A Twenty20 game is completed in about three hours, with each inning lasting around 75-90 minutes (with a 10–20-minute interval), thus bringing the game closer to the timespan of other popular team sports. Shortening the game allows matches to be completed in a single evening, and the method of play is to score runs quickly rather than eking out a high score over a much larger period of time. The format provides a host of benefits for the game, drawing in broader audiences and securing better and more lucrative TV cricket coverage.[17] Global cricket sponsorship is now worth $405 million a year, has come about mainly because of the introduction of these expedited formats.[18] In fact, according to *Sponsorship Today* report editor Simon Rines, the profile of industries sponsoring in developing countries is, in many cases, more healthy for the sport than in developed countries.[19] Similar to Asia, much of the stimulus for growth in South

America may be attributed to the procurement and implementation of mega-events, for example, the 2014 World Cup and the 2016 Olympic Games. South America provides an opportunity for sponsors, sponsees, and the host country to begin to link and identify long-term benefits. A variety of synergies exist in hosting the two events. These relate to development (i.e., hotels, stadiums, and living communities), infrastructure (i.e., telecommunication and transportation), and the use of human resources. Brazil has the world's sixth largest economy; however, growth as of late has been less than 1 percent – a cause for concern. Traditionally, Brazil has not been an everyday stop but an exotic tourism destination. The 2016 Olympics and 2014 World Cup served as catalysts to ignite and promote long-term development of sponsorship platforms.[20]

Not unlike other forms of promotion, sponsorship marketing is also reaching its saturation point in the marketplace (see Table 11.1 for the official sponsors of NASCAR). Consumers are paying less attention to sports sponsorships as they become more the rule than the exception, and although sponsorship is still seeing steady growth, corporate interest in other marketing alternatives, particularly digital (including social and mobile) media, has altered spending habits.

Sponsorship clutter is causing businesses to design more systematic sponsorship programs that stand out in the sea of sponsorships. In addition, businesses are fighting the clutter of sponsoring mainstream sports by exploring new sponsorship opportunities (e.g., esports, X-Games, women's sports, and Paralympics) and by becoming more creative with existing sponsorship opportunities. As IEG noted, instead of viewing "new media" as competition, sponsorship properties would be wise to emphasize their role as catalysts in driving interest, engagement, and enthusiasm for these digital, social, and mobile platforms.[21] Often organizations undertake a creative sponsorship approach trying to help distinguish their brand in the minds of the consumers and offset the clutter of many traditional sports mediums, as shown in the accompanying articles.

Table 11.1 Official sponsors of NASCAR

Official partners

Series Entitlement Partners	Monster Energy – Official energy drink
	Xfinity – Official cable service provider
	Gander Outdoors – Official outdoor company
Official Partners of NASCAR	3M – Official partner
	AWS – Official cloud partner
	AMR – Official medical emergency services partner
	Bluegreen Vacations – Official vacation ownership provider

continued

Table 11.1 *continued*

Official partners

	Axalta – Official paint
	Busch Beer – Official beer
	Chevrolet – Official partner
	Coca-Cola – Official fan refreshment
	CreditOne Bank – official credit card
	Digital-Ally – Official technology partner
	Draft Kings – Official daily fantasy sports game
	Fanatics – Official trackside retailer
	FDP Friction Science – Official brakes
	Featherlite Trailers – Official trailer
	Ford – Official partner
	Geico – Official insurance partner
	Goodyear – Official tire
	Growth Energy – Official partner
	Hotels for Hope – Official hotel booking partner
	Ingersoll Rand – Official power tools
	Jacob Companies – Official construction company
	K & N – Official filter, official series sponsor
	Lilly Diabetes – Official diabetes medicine
	Lixar – Preferred technology partner
	M&M's – Official chocolate
	MACK – Official hauler
	Mobil – Official motor oil
	MOOG – Official chassis and suspension parts
	Netjets – Official private aviation partner
	Pit Boss – Official grill
	PNC – Official bank
	Peak – Official antifreeze/coolant
	Prevost – Official luxury motorcoach

*Source:*https://www.nascar.com/officialsponsors

In essence, a sports sponsorship program is just another promotion mix element to be considered along with advertising, personal selling, sales promotions, and public relations. One difference, however, between sponsorship and the other promotion mix elements is that sports marketing relies heavily on

ARTICLE 11.2
2019–20 PROMOTIONAL AND THEME NIGHT SCHEDULE

The Cleveland Cavaliers have released their 2019–20 promotional schedule and fans of all ages can look forward to a season filled with special giveaways, and exciting theme nights highlighted by the Cavs 50th Season Celebration.

The celebration begins on Opening Night *Driven by Goodyear* when the Cavs suit up in the retro black, blue and orange Classic Edition uniforms to take on the Indiana Pacers on Saturday, October 26th at 8:00 p.m. All fans attending the season home opener at the newly transformed Rocket Mortgage FieldHouse will receive an Opening Night Cavs t-shirt presented by Cleveland Clinic.

50th Season Era Nights

The centerpiece of the Cavs 50th Season Celebration will be "Era Nights," themed home games dedicated to honoring five periods of Cavaliers basketball beginning in 1970 when the Cavs joined the NBA as an expansion team. Each Era Night will feature unique content, activities and more, all to pay homage to the rich history and journey of the Cavaliers franchise.

In addition, each era will include a commemorative fan-voted bobblehead giveaway of a Cavaliers legend who represented the team on or off the court during that specific time in history.

The Early Years (1970–1983) *presented by Medical Mutual*

- Wednesday, November 27 vs. ORL – **Nick Mileti Cavalier Hat Giveaway**
- Tuesday, December 3 vs. DET – **Austin Carr Bobblehead Giveaway**
- Friday, December 6 vs. ORL – **Early Years Era Night**

Richfield Coliseum Era (1983–1993) *powered by FirstEnergy*

- Saturday, January 4 vs. OKC – **Mark Price Bobblehead Giveaway**
- Sunday, January 5 vs. MIN – **Richfield Coliseum Era Night**
- Tuesday, January 7 vs. DET – **Cavs Puzzle Cube Giveaway**

Gund Arena Era (1994–2003)

- Saturday, November 23 vs. POR – **Fanny Pack Giveaway** *presented by Mtn. Dew*
- Monday, November 25 vs. BKN – **Sword 50th Season Magazine**
- Wednesday, December 11 vs. HOU – **Gund Arena Era Night**
- Friday, December 20 vs. MEM – **Whammer Bobblehead Giveaway** *presented by Discount Drug Mart*
- Tuesday, January 28 vs. NOP – **Retro 5-Panel Hat Giveaway** *powered by FirstEnergy*
- Saturday, February 29 vs. IND – **Zydrunas Ilgauskas Bobblehead Giveaway**
- Saturday, April 11 vs. MIL – **Gund Arena Era Night**

New Wine & Gold Era (2003–2010)

- Monday, March 2 vs. UTA – **Joe Tait Talking Microphone Giveaway**
- Wednesday, March 4 vs. BOS – **Fan-Voted Bobblehead Giveaway***
- Saturday, March 7 vs. DEN – **New Wine & Gold Era Night**

Championship Era and Beyond (2011-Present)

- Thursday, March 26 vs. LAL – **Championship Era and Beyond Era Night**
- Monday, March 30 vs. PHX – **Fan-Voted Bobblehead Giveaway***

* Fans still have the opportunity to vote on who they want to see as the New Wine & Gold Era bobblehead and the Championship Era and Beyond bobblehead. Follow @Cavs on Twitter, Instagram and Facebook to be notified on when voting for each bobblehead begins.

In addition to the 50th season Era Nights, the Cavs 2019–20 season will feature *even more* exclusive giveaways and fan-favorite theme nights:

Wall of Honor Night On Sunday, November 17th at 3:00 p.m. vs. Philadelphia 76ers, all fans in attendance will receive a **retro 3D photo viewer** featuring timeless images of the inaugural class of the Cavaliers *Wall of Honor.* The new Wall of Honor, located in North Atrium area of Rocket Mortgage FieldHouse, will serve as a special tribute to former members of the Cavaliers franchise who have played a distinguished, pivotal role in Cavaliers history.

Postgame Fan Free Throws Cavs fans have the opportunity to step up to the line and shoot a free throw after these select games throughout the season:

- Saturday, October 26 vs. IND
- Sunday, November 17 vs. PHI
- Friday, December 20 vs. MEM
- Monday, January 20 vs. NYK
- Saturday, February 29 vs. IND
- Saturday, March 7 vs. DEN
- Saturday, April 11 vs. MIL

Toy Drive *driven by Lexus* & Harvest for Hunger Food Drive *presented by TrustedSec* The Cavs will continue to support community needs by donating toys and food, and encouraging their fans to join them at select games throughout the season. The annual Toy Drive *driven by Lexus* will take place over the course of six games between Saturday, November 23rd vs. Portland Trailblazers and Friday, December 6th vs. Orlando Magic.

In the spring, the Harvest for Hunger Food Drive *presented by TrustedSec* will take place on Tuesday, March 24th vs. Sacramento Kings and Thursday, March 26th vs. Los Angeles Lakers.

The Cavaliers organization will match all fan donations to each of these important community benefit drives.

Black Heritage Celebration (BHC) *presented by Crown Royal Regal Apple* The Cleveland Cavaliers 16th Annual Black Heritage Celebration (BHC) *presented by Crown Royal Regal Apple* will tip off on Martin Luther King Jr. Day – Monday, January 20th when the Cavs take on the New York Knicks. This game will begin a six-week long celebration featuring BHC theme nights on Saturday, February 1st vs. Golden State Warriors, Wednesday, February 12th vs. Atlanta Hawks and Wednesday, February 26th vs. Philadelphia 76ers.

Fit as a Pro Games *presented by Medical Mutual and in association with Giant Eagle* Every year the Cleveland Cavaliers reach thousands of students across Northeast Ohio through the team's "Fit as a Pro" program, *presented by Medical Mutual and in association with Giant Eagle*, encouraging kids to live a healthy lifestyle. Cavs fans of all ages will be able to benefit from the well-being initiative when the Cavs host Fit as a Pro Games on both Thursday, January 23rd vs. Washington Wizards and Saturday, January 25th vs. Chicago Bulls as part of the annual NBA Fit Week.

Fan Appreciation Night *presented by Discount Drug Mart* A fan-favorite tradition, the 18th Annual Fan Appreciation Night *presented by Discount Drug Mart* concludes the regular season on Monday, April 13th when the Cavs host the Brooklyn Nets at Rocket Mortgage FieldHouse. During this signature Celebration the Cavs will thank the best fans in the NBA for their season-long support by giving away over $1 MILLION in prizes!

The Cavaliers 2019–20 season also includes these exclusive giveaways:

- Wednesday, October 30 vs. CHI – Cavs Schedule Magnet
- Thursday, January 2 vs. CHA – Cavs Reusable Shopping Tote *presented by Republic Services*
- Thursday, March 26 vs. LAL – Cavs Trading Cards *presented by Panini*

In addition to the 50th Season Celebration Era Nights, fans can look forward to these fun-filled theme nights during the upcoming season:

- Wednesday, October 30 vs. CHI – **Breast Cancer Awareness Night** *presented by Cleveland Clinic & Susan G. Komen Northeast Ohio*
- Tuesday, November 5 vs. BOS – **Cavs Salute to Service** *presented by Ohio CAT*
- Sunday, November 17 vs. PHI – **Wall of Honor Night**
- Friday, December 20 vs. MEM – **Mascot Night**
- Monday, December 23 vs. ATL – **Holiday Game**
- Thursday, January 2 vs. CHA – **Recycling Night** *presented by Republic Services*
- Thursday, January 23 vs. WAS – **EveryFAN Night** *presented by Speedway*
- Saturday, January 25 vs. CHI – **Chinese New Year**
- Thursday, January 30 vs. TOR – **Pride Night**
- Sunday, February 9 vs. LAC – **Youth Night**
- Saturday, March 7 vs. DEN – **Colorectal Cancer Awareness Night** *presented by Fight Colorectal Cancer & Cleveland Clinic*
- Sunday, March 8 vs. vs. SAS – **International Women's Day**
- Tuesday, March 24 vs. SAC – **Noche Latina**
- Saturday, April 11 vs. MIL – **Autism Awareness Night** *presented by Cleveland Clinic Children's & KultureCity*

Cavs fans can view the entire 50th season promotional schedule by visiting *Cavs.com/Promos*. Great seats to any of the 41 regular season home games at the newly-transformed Rocket Mortgage FieldHouse are on sale now at *Cavs.com/Tickets*.

Cavs classic edition jerseys available for presale now

The Cavs will wear the recently announced 2019–20 Classic Edition uniforms for 15 games throughout the 50th season. Fans can pre-order their Classic Edition jerseys (with the Goodyear Wingfoot patch) **NOW** at *Cavs.com/Shop*.

A limited-edition 90s jersey & lunchbox kit will be also be available for presale. The kit will include a Classic Edition jersey (player or customized) packaged in a retro lunchbox with pennant, socks and a Whammer pin. Fans can go to ***Cavs.com/Shop*** to pre-order the exclusive set.

Single game ticket info & promotions

Cavs fans can purchase single game tickets for all home preseason games and the entire 41 regular season 2019–20 home games schedule **NOW at *Cavs.com/Tickets*** **or at any one of Discount Drug Mart's 60 northern Ohio locations**.

Fans can also take advantage of two special ticket promotions:

Family Fun Pack – Make it a family night out at Rocket Mortgage FieldHouse on Saturday and Sunday home Cavs games! The Family Fun Pack includes four (4) tickets and four (4) fan meals (Sugardale Hotdog, small Pepsi and bag of chips). Starting at just $13 per ticket, fans will score savings of over 40% off of regular ticket prices. Available in Loudville or lower level seating, while supplies last.

Buds Night Out *presented by Budweiser* – Back by popular demand, fans can enjoy any regular season Monday and Wednesday game this season with their "favorite bud" by taking advantage of the Buds Night Out ticket deal which includes two (2) Loudville tickets and two (2) Budweiser beers for only $50, while supplies last.

For more information on 2019–20 ticket promotions visit ***Cavs.com/Offers***.

NOTE: All promotional schedule giveaways and theme nights are subject to change.

Rightsholder: NBA Properties Inc.

Credit: The NBA and individual member team identifications reproduced herein are used with permission from NBA Properties, Inc. C 2020 NBA Properties, Inc. All rights reserved.

URL: www.nba.com/cavaliers/releases/promotional-schedule-2019-20. Published September 11, 2019. Accessed September 24, 2020.

ARTICLE 11.3
MLS ANNOUNCES MULTI-YEAR PARTNERSHIP WITH BODYARMOR SPORTS DRINK

Major League Soccer on Tuesday announced a multi-year partnership with BODYARMOR that makes the product the league's official sports drink partner in the United States.

As part of the agreement, BODYARMOR sports drinks will hydrate MLS players on sidelines at matches and practices, in locker rooms and in training facilities; the company's logo and branding will be featured on coolers, cups, squirt bottles and towels on MLS sidelines within the US starting in 2020. BODYARMOR and MLS will also collaborate on exclusive custom content featuring top MLS players and BODYARMOR athlete partners.

The partnership extends BODYARMOR's presence beyond MLS to the *Leagues Cup* and *Campeones Cup* competitions. Though the formal partnership doesn't kick off until January, BODYARMOR will be featured at the inaugural Leagues Cup final between Liga MX sides Cruz Azul and Tigres UANL in Las Vegas on Wednesday (10:30 pm ET | ESPN2, UniMás, TUDN, TVAS, TSN1).

"BODYARMOR is America's new leader in sports hydration and they are a great fit for Major League Soccer – the League for a new North America," said MLS senior VP of Business Development Carter Ladd in statement.

"BODYARMOR believes in the future of Major League Soccer and is committed to joining us in our ongoing efforts to elevate soccer's popularity to even higher levels in North America. BODYARMOR's rise and momentum mirrors that of MLS, and we are excited to kick off the partnership at the Leagues Cup final and look forward to working with them for many years to come."

A premium sports drink with potassium-packed electrolytes, antioxidants and coconut water made with no artificial flavors, sweeteners and no colors from artificial sources, BODYARMOR is now the No. 2 sports drink sold in US convenience stores nationwide and on track to eclipse $700 million in retail sales by the end of 2019. It is also the official sports drink of UFC and boasts an impressive athlete partner roster including Mike Trout, *Houston Dynamo* owner James Harden, Megan Rapinoe and Diana Taurasi.

Credit: MLS

URL: www.mlssoccer.com/post/2019/09/17/mls-announces-multi-year-partnership-bodyarmor-sports-drink. Published September 17, 2019. Accessed September 24, 2020.

developing successful sponsorship programs. In fact, sponsorship programs are so prevalent in sports marketing that the field is sometimes defined in these terms. Since sponsorship is so critical, let's better understand how to develop the most effective sponsorship program.

Designing a sports sponsorship program

Sports sponsorship programs come in all shapes and sizes. The following are just a few examples:

- Sponsorships in sports are also taking place at the high school level. Recently, First National Bank has developed and programmed a sponsorship opportunity called "First Hoop." This sponsorship is designed to promote team spirit and fan participation. The First Hoop program has awarded over $200,000 to participating high school athletic departments.[22]

- Nike took over for adidas as the official sponsor of uniforms for the NBA. Nike and the NBA came to an agreement and signed an eight-year deal that is worth nearly $1 billion. Not only do the Nike uniforms offer a pleasing aesthetic, they also offer a quality fit and feel that is noticed by the athletes.[23]

- FIFA and adidas formally announced an extension of their long-term partnership agreement granting adidas the official partner, supplier and licensee rights for the FIFA World Cup and all FIFA events until 2030. Already one of the longest and most successful partnerships in modern history, the sponsorship will extend their partnership beyond 60 years and provide an estimated $100 million per four-year World Cup cycle.[24]

- The LA Clippers have several community engagement partnerships that include youth basketball, mentorship, education, and community out-reach. They offer programs such as Teacher Appreciation, which recognizes outstanding teachers for their hard work and dedication; LA Clippers Activity Challenge, a fun challenge to get kids and families interacting with basketball, education, mindfulness, health and fitness activities; LA Clippers Read to Achieve Program, designed to promote a love of lifelong reading and the importance of literacy; LA Clippers Math Hoops, a fast-paced basketball board game and mobile app that allows students to learn fundamental math skills through direct engagement with the real statistics of their favorite players; and Clippers Community Heroes Program, which honors people in their community. These programs inspire children through community service, sport, mentorship, and education that includes scholarships to assist college-bound students. The LA Clippers partner with local youth organizations and schools to provide mentorship and assistance with mentor-based community initiatives. The Clippers team is active in the LA community all year long. The Clippers also utilize ticket programs and their foundation to partner with local businesses, season ticket members, and fans who want to give back and foster philanthropic exchanges aimed at making a difference in the lives of Los Angeles children.[25]

- Weston FC/AYSO 644 soccer club is a 501(c)-(3) non-profit organization located in southern Florida. Weston FC/AYSO 644 is Florida's largest soccer club. Weston FC/AYSO 644 provides both recreational and competitive soccer programs for elite, travel, and beginner soccer players between the ages of 4 and 19. Weston offers a year-long title sponsorship estimated at $50,000, a Weston Cup, and Showcase Title Sponsorship seeking $15,000 yearly web sponsorships at $350 apiece; Weston Cup and Showcase web sponsorships valued at $150 apiece; practice T-shirt sponsorships at $450; and AYSO Team and Team Plus packages.[26]

- The PGA Tour partnered with a number of today's fashion leaders. These brands include Kendra Scott, tasc Performance, and Tiffany & Co. In addition to Tiffany & Co. designing the tournament trophy and providing gifts for all Pro-Am participants, the brand also offers a high-end hospitality venue overlooking the green of the par-five 17th hole. This venue is called the Skybox and offers all-inclusive food and beverages, TVs to watch the live telecast, and finally completely branded walls with Tiffany's advertisements and campaign ideas.[27]

- The International Olympic Committee (IOC) and Samsung Electronics Co. Ltd. announced the extension of their Olympic partnership through 2028. Samsung offers strides in wireless communications equipment. With this partnership, the benefit is the ability to promote artificial intelligence, virtual reality, and augmented reality. Ultimately, the two have agreed to further engage young generations to help promote the power of sports and the true values of the Olympic games.[28]
- Six U.S. Olympic athletes signed a sponsorship deal with Coca-Cola to become their "Six Pack" of athletes. The athletes will help in Coca-Cola's marketing efforts, retail awareness, social media advertising, and more.[29]

What do each of these sponsorship examples have in common? First, they were developed as part of an integrated marketing communications approach in which sponsorship is but one element of the promotion mix. In addition, each of the sponsors has carefully chosen the best sponsorship opportunity (with individual athletes, teams, conferences, events, and/or leagues) to meet organizational objectives and marketing goals.

To carefully plan sponsorship programs, a systematic process is being used by an increasing number of organizations. The process for designing a sports sponsorship program is presented in Figure 11.1. Before explaining the process, it is important to remember that sponsorship involves a marketing exchange. The sponsor benefits by receiving the right to associate with the sports entity (e.g., team or event), and the sports entity benefits from either monetary support or products being supplied by the sponsor. Because the marketing exchange involves two parties, the sponsorship process can be explored from the perspective of the sponsor (e.g., Allstate) or the sports entity (e.g., Sugar Bowl). We look at the process from the viewpoint of the sponsor rather than the entity sponsored.

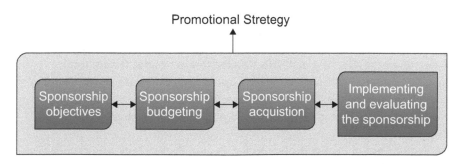

Figure 11.1
The sponsorship process

Source: Hawkins et al., *Consumer Behavior: Implications for Marketing Strategy*, 6/e © 1994 © The McGraw-Hill Companies, Inc.

ARTICLE 11.4
ESPORTS' APPEAL TO MAINSTREAM SPONSORS CONTINUES TO GROW

Credit: Sports Business Journal

URL: www.sportsbusinessdaily.com/Global/Issues/2018/05/03/Marketing-and-Sponsorship/Esports-Marketing.aspx

If you're like many marketers, you've been hearing about the esports opportunity for a couple of years now. And while the idea of competitive video gaming may seem mystifying to some, the dollars flowing in—and the number of eyeballs watching—are bound to give even the most cynical marketer pause. Esports is no longer emerging. It's here.

How fast is esports growing? In 2018, revenues shot up 38 percent to hit $905 million, per forecasts from analyst Newzoo. By 2021, global esports revenues will rocket to $1.65 billion, $1.4 billion of which will come directly from brand investment.

There are two key factors at play here. One is the age of the audience— esports fans typically fall into the coveted 18-35 demographic, significantly younger than traditional sports viewers. Second is the digital side of esports, which makes sponsorship more directly measurable.

But those aren't the only differences between esports and more traditional sports sponsorships. While brands don't have to toss out their sports sponsorship playbook, they do need to be aware of the unique attributes of esports and build out their plans accordingly. So, what does esports sponsorship look like?

The esports ecosystem is complicated (see page 6-7). There are game publishers, leagues, competitions, platforms, teams/organizations and players/influencers. All may be looking for your sponsorship dollars. But for the sake of clarity, this guide will examine the opportunity offered by esports organizations.

Sometimes improperly referred to as teams, esports organizations are essentially holding companies that field teams across a variety of different game titles and leagues. Among esports fans, these are the household names— organizations like Team SoloMid (TSM), NRG, Optic Gaming, Team Liquid and Cloud9. Each of these organizations has teams across the different leagues (like North American League of Legends, NBA2K or the Overwatch League), but they all represent the parent organization. It would be like the Yankees and Red Sox having teams in MLB as well as the NFL, NBA and NHL. This creates enormous fan equity.

When working with these organizations, brands can sponsor all the teams across all game titles. Or, they can sponsor specific titles that may have the most appropriate audiences— each league and each game can have its own fan demographics. The goal: get in on the live tournament excitement.

But there's also another option that is distinct to the gamer world. Many esports organizations also have rosters of influencers that regularly stream on channels like Twitch and/or post their videos to YouTube. Each influencer can have their own audience of fans that regularly tunes in to watch them stream. Consider this: TSM member Myth, a popular Fortnite streamer, had 250,000 followers on Twitch in January 2018. That's impressive… until you realize that just nine months later, that figure grew to 4 million.

Common Esports Sponsor Activations

JERSEY PATCH SPONSORSHIP
Just like in European soccer or in the NBA, brands appear on player jerseys when they play or practice on-camera.

TWITCH OVERLAY
Inclusion of the sponsor brand in regular Twitch influencer streaming. Teams often have accounts that stream as much as 12 hours each day.

INTEGRATED SIGNAGE
Sponsored locations like the scrimmage/ streaming room where players hang when they're not competing. Think of it as sponsoring a team's practice facility.

BRANDED CONTENT
Players are used to help tell the brand's message in a way that's authentic to the team's fans.

IN-STREAM INTEGRATIONS
These can include things like product callouts and product placements.

DON'T BE A SPONSORSHIP NOOB

For many brands, esports is such a new opportunity that there is little institutional knowledge. To get started, here are some best practices to follow:

Combine comp and influencer.

Esports competition schedules have down time throughout the year, while Twitch influencer streaming tends to be more consistent year round. Using both gives brands persistent exposure throughout the year with opportunities for lifts when there is competitive success.

Know where the fans are.

To gauge exposure and assess the value of your sponsorship, consider: competition broadcasts/live streams; regular Twitch influencer streaming; owned social media accounts; and long- tail social media highlight clips that appear on Twitch, YouTube, Instagram, Twitter and Reddit.

Be aggro across platforms.

Seek out an esports organization that activates across multiple platforms to reach a broad, diverse and engaged audience.

Don't shut out game titles.

Reduce your risk of missing out on the next hot game (e.g. Fortnite) by aligning with esports organizations that are diversified across popular titles.

Watch influencer zone-out.

Brands should examine streamer roster depth to ensure that the departure of one streamer roster won't hinder your ability to drive exposure.

Overlap can gank your value.

If your brand has multiple sponsorships across the esports ecosystem, be sure to analyze where there is audience overlap to ensure your portfolio maximizes its reach.

Brand safety can't be nerfed.

Brands should make sure that the esports organization provides media training to its players and that it enforces standards of conduct.

KPIs beyond KDAs.

Twitch streams and some live broadcasts now are using concurrent views to gauge audience, counting the number of viewers that are watching a stream at each second. This is more accurate than total viewers, a figure that GumGum Sports estimates may inflate the audience by more than 60 percent in some cases.

Push your learnings.

Remember, esports is new. Seek out experts. Listen to the community. Be authentic. Take chances. And create the playbook that shows results for your brand.

What does it take to succeed in esports?
We spoke with two of the leading experts in esports sponsorship. Brad Sive oversees partnerships as CRO of Team SoloMid, coming to esports after a two-decade career in sports and entertainment at places like ESPN and Catalysts Sports & Media. Chris DeAppolonio, VP of global partnership at esports agency Triggerfish (parent company of Optic Gaming), saw the esports boom coming a decade ago when it was the subject of his NYU master's thesis. They were interviewed by Jeff Katz, VP strategy and strategic partnerships of GumGum Sports.

ESPORTS

BY THE *NUMBERS*

The real esports rankings, based on GumGum Sports' exclusive Q3 2018 analysis of social reach for team, player and influencer accounts across Twitch, Instagram, Facebook, Twitter and YouTube.

TOP 10 OVERALL ESPORTS ORGANIZATIONS

1. Team SoloMid
2. NRG
3. Optic Gaming
4. Team Liquid
5. Cloud9
6. Fnatic
7. 100 Thieves
8. Immortals (LA Valiant/MIBR)
9. Rogue
10. Counter Logic Gaming

TOP 10 PLAYERS/ INFLUENCERS

1. Myth (Team SoloMid)
2. Lachlan (NRG)
3. Daequan (Team SoloMid)
4. MrMuselk (NRG)
5. Dakotaz (Team SoloMid)
6. LazarBeam (NRG)
7. Dr Lupo (Rogue)
8. Noahj456 (100 Thieves)
9. Scump (Optic Gaming)
10. Gotaga (Vitality)

TOP 5 ON INSTAGRAM

1. Team SoloMid
2. Optic Gaming
3. NRG
4. Rogue
5. Immortals

TOP 5 ON YOUTUBE

1. NRG
2. Team SoloMid
3. Optic Gaming
4. 100 Thieves
5. Team Liquid

TOP 5 ON TWITCH

1. Team SoloMid
2. Cloud9
3. Team Liquid
4. NRG
5. Rogue

TOP 5 ON TWITTER

1. Optic Gaming
2. Team SoloMid
3. Team Liquid
4. NRG
5. Cloud9

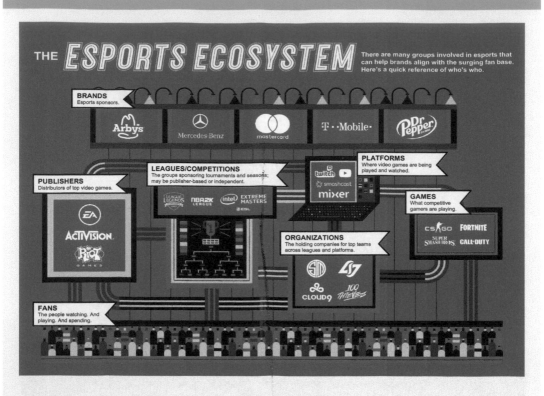

Both of you have backgrounds in traditional sports and esports sponsorships. What do you see as the differences between the two?

Brad: Esports organizations offer sponsors opportunities to drive value all year round, due to the always-on nature of esports. Players who play competitively often livestream during the "offseason" as they scrimmage to get better and prepare for upcoming tournaments.

Think of it this way: Imagine if fans were able to watch Steph Curry, who happens to be a Team SoloMid investor, practice all day, every day and ask him questions and see him get better? This is a tremendous opportunity for fans to engage directly with their favorite streamers, giving sponsors more chances to attach themselves to fan passion points. It's a level of engagement that must be valued differently than passive traditional sports TV broadcasts.

Chris: Signage-style inventory on jerseys is similar to that of the European soccer leagues where there are limited inventory spaces that provide a generous amount of impressions and exposure. Fans are excited for a new sponsor to be put on the jerseys, and they gravitate towards those announcements.

When our players are streaming on Twitch, we provide branded overlays for our partners, which allow them to be showcased to the hyperengaged fans of our individual players and content creators. For a traditional team, they are mostly selling signage in-venue rather than on any type of broadcast. Esports venues and team-specific venues are planned, but they are not the norm.

Who is the audience watching these streams? Are they that much different from people watching regular sports?

Chris: It is a much younger, digitally native and global audience. With sponsorship being quite new to esports compared to traditional sports, research studies are showing greater brand loyalty and consideration of sponsors who are supporting the teams, events and industry.

It's not like traditional sports where you are on a broadcast of an NFL game. You are showcasing the lives of esports athletes to the fans and letting them connect in a way that they don't necessarily get to do otherwise. There is a lot of shoulder content and lifestyle integration that you don't see in traditional sports.

Brad: The esports audience can be highly difficult to reach via traditional means. They have high instances of ad blocker use, and many are cord-cutters and cord-nevers. This also means that they are potentially more responsive to advertisers since they are not being bombarded with ads relative to the general population.

But you have to talk to them the right way, correct? Brands can't be tone deaf to the gamer world.

Brad: You also need to be contextually relevant within esports. If you are dealing with a Fortnite audience, you have to speak to them in a totally different way than you would a League of Legends audience. You have to be really in tune with that. A lot of times we at Team SoloMid are educating brands as consultants on ideas for how best to integrate a brand given the unique audience.

So how do you educate and engage with sponsors so they do all this right and get the return they expect?

Chris: Education is something we do often with prospective sponsors. A lot of them know that esports is somewhere they want to be, but they aren't sure what to do. We end up providing them with an overview of the industry and the ways to get involved. A lot of what we do is consulting on strategy as well, helping them understand how their brand fits the space and what type of marketing or promotions may work well for them.

Additionally, many brands are worried about games that have red blood or are realistic shooters, which is understandable. But there are lots of ways to get around that. We have a very popular Call of Duty Team, but not everyone wants to be associated with Call of Duty. We have been able to integrate brands in a way that has zero seconds of game play footage so you're talking to the audience, connecting with them, but not associated with any of the first-person shooter aspects of the game.

Brad: Let me give you an example. We work with Dr Pepper and they sponsored MLG years ago and were looking to come back into esports. They wanted to figure out where was the best place to plant a flag. We used FanAI data to make them feel comfortable that their demographic profile and overall audience align very well with the TSM audience.

It's important to provide this information to brands because many of the non- endemic brands are deciding if they should get involved with esports. We even have to use this approach with brands like Geico and Gillette who have been with us for years to help reaffirm their strategy.

Finally, we have to help them measure their sponsorship and convey performance. We work with GumGum Sports on that. Essentially, we need a very transparent measurement infrastructure so we can have an objective conversation when evaluating and negotiating a sponsorship.

Last question: Tell me about one of the successful integrations you've seen in esports.

Chris: T-Mobile was the presenting sponsor of the Houston Outlaws in Overwatch League this season. They were a jersey partner and there are facecams in the Overwatch League, and when our players came out in the new jerseys, fans started chanting "T-Mobile!" And every time we won a match, they continued to chant "T-Mobile!" and started to coopt our logo, which looks like a Longhorn skull, and with the T-Mobile "T." The affinity for T-Mobile we saw from our fans was really unprecedented.

Brad: We were talking about the growth of Fortnite with Dr Pepper and they asked if we could wrap Dr Pepper bottles with faces of Fortnite players and send it to them so they can tweet it out. It was the most engaged tweet in Dr Pepper's history with over 50K retweets. Myth, one of our big streamers, got on and did an in-stream shout out and that went viral. Little things like that have a massive impact and can really push a sponsorship forward.

READY TO TAKE THE PLUNGE WITH ESPORTS SPONSORSHIP?

GumGum Sports will help you understand the real media value of all your sports and esports sponsorships.

A division of GumGum, a computer vision company, GumGum Sports helps clients quantify previously unmeasured sponsor media value across all television, streaming and social in order to inform decision-making at all stages in the sports partnership cycle.

GumGum Sports helps brands, agencies and rights-holders go Beyond the Broadcast™ using patent-pending sports detection algorithms to analyze the millions of social photos and video clips that represent the new age of sports media consumption. GumGum Sports' accurate, timely and comprehensive media valuations enable rights-holders to retain and grow partner revenue and give sponsors the ability to track and optimize media value across a portfolio of sponsorships.

As shown in the model, decisions regarding the sponsorship program are not made in isolation. Rather, the **sponsorship program** is just one element of the broader promotional strategy. It was suggested earlier that all the elements in the promotional mix must be integrated to have the greatest and most effective promotional impact. However, sponsorship decisions influence much more than just promotion. Sponsorship decisions can affect the entire marketing mix; as the accompanying GumGum narrative articulates, the key is understanding the ecosystem.

There are two important things to consider before signing a sponsorship agreement: (1) all your organization is getting is the right to be called a sponsor, not a completed sponsorship plan, and (2) you should spend two to three times your sponsorship fee to leverage your relationship as a sponsor – if you do not have the funds to promote, do not buy the sponsorship.

When designing the sponsorship program, the initial decisions are based on sponsorship objectives and budgets. These two elements go hand in hand. Without the money, the most meaningful objectives will never be reached. Alternatively, appropriate objectives must be considered without total regard to cost. If the objectives are sound, senior-level managers will find a way to allocate the necessary monies to sponsorship.

After the objectives and budget have been agreed upon, the specific sports sponsorship opportunity is chosen from the hundreds available. For example, large corporations like Pepsi may receive as many as 500 sponsorship proposals each year with others receiving even more annually. Just what are corporations evaluating when they are considering the multiple opportunities to attach themselves to the "right" sports platform? Platform analysis allows for a corporation to effectively evaluate all incoming sponsorship opportunities and may include multiple profile factors. Questions are often asked and information obtained to fully evaluate the opportunity and risks of sponsorship.

In today's digital world, most corporate entities require the completion of an online application called generically a sponsorship request form that includes but is not limited to name and contact information; description of organization, including mission, vision, goals, and objectives; history; services provided; date of event; event timeline, including deadline for event materials; event sponsorship levels and exchanges, including marketing promo plans, fees, list of committed sponsors to date, and other sources of funding; history of previous support; description of event, including participants, volunteers, and employees and its impact on deliverables identified such as attendance and the environment; demographics of the audience; frequency with which the sponsor's name and/or logo will be seen, including in any media; community engagement opportunities; hospitality opportunities; amount of media coverage in all forms (broadcast, TV ads, print ads, social media, etc.); and whether there are competing events.

With the growth of sporting events, leagues, teams, and other platforms, there are a wealth of sponsorship opportunities available to potential sponsors. Table 11.2 illustrates how the Wyndham Golf Championship presents various tiers of information to potential sponsors.[30]

When choosing from among many sponsorship opportunities, three decisions must be addressed. The first decision is whether to sponsor a local, regional, national, or global event. Second, the organization must choose an athletic platform. For instance, will the organization sponsor an individual athlete, team, league, or stadium? Third, once the broad athletic platform is chosen, the organization must decide on a specific sports entity. For example, if a league

Table 11.2 Sponsorship opportunities for the Wyndham Championship: sponsorship levels

Corporate Hospitality

CHAMPIONS CLUB *(HOSPITALITY AT 6 LOCATIONS)*

Located in the historic Sedgefield Clubhouse overlooking the 9th Green, this package features an upscale buffet lunch, afternoon appetizers, and access to 5 on-course Viewing Platforms with complimentary beverage service.

Four Tickets – $5,000

- Four (4) Champions Club Tickets Each Day, Thursday–Sunday
- Four (4) Clubhouse Tickets Each Day, Tuesday–Wednesday
- One (1) VIP Parking Permit

Eight Tickets – $8,000

- Eight (8) Champions Club Tickets Each Day, Thursday–Sunday
- Eight (8) Clubhouse Tickets Each Day, Tuesday–Wednesday
- One (1) VIP Parking Permit

Fifteen Tickets – $13,000

- Fifteen (15) Champions Club Tickets Each Day, Thursday–Sunday
- Fifteen (15) Clubhouse Tickets Each Day, Tuesday–Wednesday
- Two (2) VIP Parking Permits & Two (2) Sponsors Event Invitations
- Exclusive opportunity to purchase dual-logoed merchandise bearing your company logo and the Wyndham Championship Logo

15TH GREEN SKYBOX – $50,000

Entertain guests in an air-conditioned Skybox with open-air seating at one of golf's most historic locations

- One (1) Skybox on the 15th Green at Sedgefield Country Club, which includes Lunch and Full, Open Bar, Thursday-Sunday
- Forty (40) Skybox Tickets each day, Thursday–Sunday
- Four (4) VIP Parking Permits & Four (4) Sponsors Event Invitations
- Two (2) Staff Badges
- Exclusive opportunity to purchase dual-logoed merchandise bearing your company logo and the Wyndham Championship Logo

Half Skybox with 20 Tickets – $27,500

Quarter Skybox with 10 Tickets – $14,500

*Source:*www.wyndhamchampionship.com/sponsorships/corporate-hospitality/

Credit: PGA Tour, Wyndham Championship

is selected as the athletic platform, will the organization sponsor the WNBA, MLS, or NFL?

The final stage of the sports sponsorship process involves implementation and evaluation. Typically, the organization wants to determine whether their desired sponsorship objectives have been achieved. Measuring the impact of sponsorship on awareness levels within a targeted audience is a relatively easy marketing research task. However, as the costs of sponsorships continue to increase, there is a heightened sense of accountability. In other words, organizations want to assess the impact of sponsorship on the bottom line – sales. The shift from philanthropy to evaluating sponsorship return on investment is also documented in the academic sport sponsorship literature. Traditional (Figure 11.2a) and modernized models as seen in Figure 11.2b and Nielsen Sports' ROI Sponsorship Model (Figure 11.3), illustrate the emerging need to understand the complexities of sponsorship return and evaluation.[31] Now that we have a rough idea of how the sponsorship process works, let us explore each stage of the sports sponsorship model in greater detail.

Sponsorship objectives

The first stage in designing a sponsorship program is to carefully consider the sponsorship objectives. Because sponsorship is just one form of promotion, the **sponsorship objectives** should be linked to the broader promotional planning process and its objectives. The promotional objectives will, in turn, help achieve the marketing goals, which should stem from the objectives of the organization. These important linkages were stated in our definition of sponsorship.

Not unlike advertising objectives, sponsorship objectives can be categorized as either direct or indirect. **Direct sponsorship objectives** have a short-term impact on consumption behavior and focus on increasing sales. **Indirect sponsorship objectives** are those that ultimately lead to the desired goal

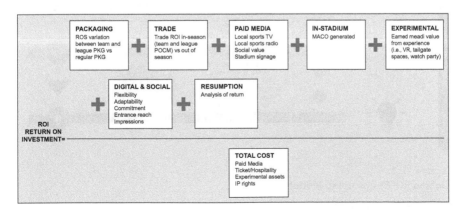

Figure 11.2a
Anheuser-Busch Property ROI Model – version 1.0

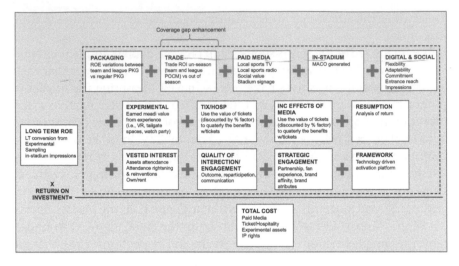

Figure 11.2b
Anheuser-Busch Property ROI Model – version 2.0

Source: IEG Strategy: Inside Anheuser-Busch's Sustainable Sponsorship Strategy, April 30, 2018. www.
sponsorship.com/Report/2018/04/30/Inside-Anheuser-Busch-s-Sustainable-Sponsorship-St.aspx

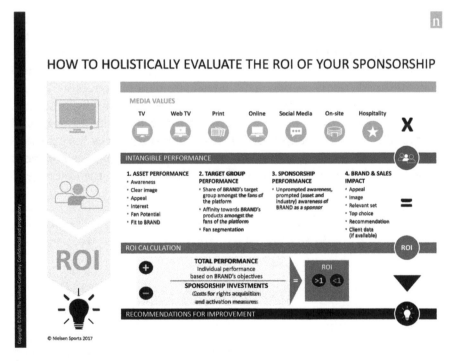

Figure 11.3
Nielsen ROI Sponsorship Model

Source: Nielson Sports, 2017

of enhancing sales. In other words, the sponsor has to generate awareness and create the desired image of the product before consumers purchase the product. The indirect sponsorship objectives include generating awareness, meeting and beating competition, reaching new target markets, building relationships, and improving image.[32] One of the reasons that sponsoring sporting events has risen in popularity is that sponsorship provides so many benefits to those involved in the partnership. In other words, both the sponsor and the sports entity (event, athlete, or league) gain from this win–win partnership. Let us look at some of the primary objectives of sponsorship from the sponsor's perspective.

Awareness

One of the most basic objectives of any sponsor is to generate **awareness** or raise levels of awareness of its products and services, product lines, or corporate name. Sponsors must understand which level to target (i.e., individual product versus company name) based on the broader promotional or marketing strategy. For an existing company or a new company or product, sponsorship is an important way to generate widespread awareness in a short period of time. For example, beginning in 2020, Nike will become the exclusive provider of Major League Baseball's on-field uniforms (which will feature a Nike Swoosh), including base layers, game-day outerwear, and training apparel.[33] As baseball commissioner Rob Manfred, noted, Nike's global brand and reputation as a leader in driving innovation make them an ideal partner. Nike continues as an official MLB sponsor, supporting league initiatives, grassroots marketing, and fan events but as part of the new agreement will partner with all 30 MLB clubs and promote its brand and products across MLB media assets, including MLB Network, MLB.com, and MLB Social. Nike currently has endorsement relation ships with more than 500 MLB and minor league players.

From the event or sports entity's perspective, having a large corporate sponsor will certainly heighten the awareness of the entity or event. The corporate sponsor will design a promotional program around the event to make consumers aware of the sponsor's relationship with the event. The corporate sponsor will also want to ensure their promotional mix elements are integrated. In other words, advertising, sponsorship of the event, and sales promotion will all work in concert to achieve the desired promotional objectives. A study conducted by Hoek, Gendall, Jeffcoat, and Orsman[34] found that sponsorship generated higher levels of awareness than did advertising. In addition, sponsorship led to the association of a wider range of attributes with the brand being promoted than did advertising.

Competition

Another primary objective of sponsorship is to stamp out or meet any competitive threats or **competition**. Many corporate sponsors claim they are not that interested in sponsorship opportunities, but they cannot afford not to be. In other words, if they do not make the sponsorship investment, their competitors will. Sponsorship is thought of as a preemptive tactic that will reduce competitive threat. For instance, Texaco sponsors virtually every national governing body of U.S. Olympic sports. They promote only a handful of these sports, but their sponsorship of the others effectively keeps other competitors out of any chance of ambushing their Olympic efforts. Another example of competitive threat comes from the fierce rivalry between Pepsi and Coke, including Pepsi's deal with the NFL, snatching that relationship away from Coke, and Coke's turnabout in securing the NCAA, which had been rival Mountain Dew's domain. More recently, PepsiCo Inc. took over league sponsorship rights for the National Basketball Association, ending a 28-year partnership that the league had with Coca-Cola Co. Coca-Cola had been the NBA's official beverage sponsor since 1986 and Sprite the league's official soda in the United States since 1994. Interestingly, Coca-Cola decided to not renew their global contract with the NBA; however, they continued their relationships with individual venues, teams, and players, The new deal with Pepsi was worth significantly more than the NBA's partnership with Coca-Cola in terms of the overall investment,

In an attempt to gain a competitive edge in the insurance industry, State Farm Insurance continues to utilize sport sponsorships to seek out and expand its market and brand presence. In the sponsorship realm, State Farm spends approximately 67 percent of its money on sports, 18 percent on causes, 14 percent on entertainment, and 1 percent on the arts. While the company may be one of the world's largest advertisers, the continued presence and expansion efforts have put the company on an entirely new playing field.[35] Recently State Farm bought naming rights for the home venues of both the Atlanta Hawks (State Farm Arena) and the Arizona Cardinals (State Farm Stadium). The increased brand presence in these two hubs that lie in two different time zones aligns them with two of the most popular sport organizations (NFL and NBA). According to Rand Harbert, State Farm's CMO, the company has recognized that as traditional media continues to change, so should their efforts to reach new customers.[36] In fact, State Farm recently announced that it would be sponsoring one of the most well-known names in esports, Benjamin Lupo (DrLupo). The deal includes a plethora of activations, provides relatability and credibility in dissemination, and further aligns with philanthropic and massive fanbases. These platform exchanges should translate into authentic brand opportunities. The esports industry has been growing and establishing itself as a force to reckon with for quite some time now, and corporations with advertising budgets running into the millions are getting interested. They require sustainability of their sponsorship activities and a wide reach. At this moment, the largest esports events can offer just that.

Unfortunately, a sponsoring company, such as State Farm Insurance, can still be harmed by competitors who use ambush marketing tactics. **Ambush marketing** is a planned effort (campaign by an organization) to associate themselves indirectly with an event to gain at least some of the recognition and benefits that are associated with being an official sponsor.[37] Ambush marketing involves a corporation or a brand associating itself with an event in an attempt to create an illusion that it is an affiliated sponsor, thereby reaping the benefits that are associated with sponsorship status.[38] Ambushing may occur in a variety of ways. Corporations may buy commercial time prior to and during event broadcasts (e.g., Amex '92 and '94 Winter Olympics), sponsor broadcasts of events rather than directly sponsoring the event (e.g., Wendy's on ABC at '88 Calgary), sponsor individual teams and athletes (e.g., Pepsi and Magic in '92 Barcelona), or use sport event tickets in consumer giveaways, sweepstakes, or contests.[39] One of the earliest examples of ambush marketing at its finest was Nike's 1984 "I Love LA" marketing campaign.[40] Although the company was not an official Olympic sponsor, this campaign inextricably tied Nike to the city and event. Most sports marketers consider this ambush campaign the catalyst for the steady rise in ambush marketing practices, and although marketers continue to employ more stringent legislation to combat ambushing tactics, such as IOC Rule 40, ambushers seem more interested in circumventing the rule.[41]

Rule 40, by-law paragraph 3, of the Olympic Charter states, "except as permitted by the IOC Executive Board, no competitor, coach, trainer or official who participates in the Olympic Games may allow his person, name, picture or sports performances to be used for advertising purposes during the Olympic Games," basically banning advertisers from using the names or images of Olympic participants during the games unless the advertiser is an Olympic sponsor.[42] Despite the onset of Rule 40 as well as other regulations, ambushing, especially when it comes to mega-events, is still prevalent today. Furthermore, events such as the Olympic Games seem to be the "sporting event of choice" for ambush marketers. In the 1984 Olympics, Fuji was the official program sponsor of the Games, at considerable cost of $40 million. Their competitors, Kodak, became the "sponsor" of the U.S. track team and of ABC television's broadcast of the Games. Its film thereby became the official film of the U.S. track team, and it also proceeded to use the network's own set of symbols to advertise its merchandise. Arguably one of the greatest ambush moments in the Olympic history occurred in 1992 when Michael Jordan (a Nike icon) covered the Reebok logo with the American flag. Likewise, the 1996 Atlanta Games are remembered for Nike's aggressive ambush marketing campaign against Reebok, the official Olympic sportswear partner. Nike bought up advertising billboards throughout the city and established "Nike Town" on the edge of the Olympic park

Other notable Olympic campaigns include American Express's cat-fight of sorts with VISA over two Winter Olympics: "The Olympics only take VISA ... "(VISA - the official sponsor) vs. "You don't need a visa to travel to Norway ... " (AMEX). Additionally, the following Olympic ambush moment occurred in Vancouver where the chief executive of the Vancouver Organizing Committee for the 2010 Winter Olympic Games used public pressure in order to get Imperial Oil/Esso, a Canadian petroleum company, to modify a marketing campaign that was accused of constituting ambush marketing. Imperial Oil/Esso formulated a "Cheer on Canada/Torino, Italy" campaign which involved a competition with prizes of tickets to attend men's and women's Olympic ice hockey games in Turin. Although the competition did not use any Olympic symbols, by referring to the Olympic Games, it created an unauthorized association with the Olympic Games in Turin and with the Canadian Olympic team. Although Imperial Oil/Esso is a sponsor of the national governing body (Hockey Canada) and the national team, it is not a sponsor of either the Olympic Games or the Canadian Olympic team.

In more recent campaigns, Nike, not an official sponsor of the London Olympics, ran a television advertising campaign "Find your greatness" celebrating athletes of all abilities competing in places called London, but, again, they were "Londons" outside of the United Kingdom, so London in Nigeria and London, USA.[43] Additionally, athletes have unwittingly been the focus of numerous ambush campaigns. For example, superstar snowboarder Shaun White was featured on a series of Times Square billboards advertising Target during the 2010 Vancouver Winter Olympics. Target was not an Olympic sponsor but got around Rule 40 restrictions by posting the billboards before the games began. By the day of the opening ceremony, Target altered the billboard by changing the image of White into a silhouette, accompanied by the message "Gone to Vancouver."[44]

Other notable ambushing examples in the realm of sport and entertainment include:

- **Bavaria beer** – Budweiser was the official beer of the 2010 World Cup, but during the Holland vs. Denmark match, 36 attractive women in bright orange mini-skirts descended upon the crowd and stole the show by standing, dancing, and waving their arms in the air. What's the problem, you might be asking? Well, they weren't exactly there for the party atmosphere. Allegedly sent by the Dutch beer company Bavaria, they ambushed the match to subtly promote the Bavaria brand. The dresses only featured a tiny outer label with the Bavaria name, but just before the World Cup, the Dutch beer company made sure the dresses had instant brand association by arranging to have one modeled by the well-known wife of Dutch midfielder Rafael van der Vaart in advertising spots.[45] Budweiser, as official beer sponsor and with tens of millions less in their coffers for the privilege, complained to FIFA, and the ladies were swiftly escorted out of the stadium. The two "alleged organizers" were arrested by South African police, and football pundit Robbie Earle, to whom the seats were originally allocated, was fired by ITV.
- **Lufthansa** – At the 2006 World Cup, Lufthansa painted a soccer ball on the nose of many of its planes, to the annoyance of FIFA and Emirates Air, which paid a substantial sum to FIFA to be an official sponsor.
- **Pringles** not only made their product look like a tennis ball canister but conveniently placed around 24,000 of these cans outside Wimbledon, and the imaginative ambush marketing stunt certainly caught a lot of attention.

- **Vodafone**, noting that publicity may be utilized to create sales, enlisted a streaker with the Vodafone logo printed across their backside to run across the field prior to an All Blacks (New Zealand Rugby) game. The game was sponsored by Telecome.
- **BMW**'s recent response to an Audi billboard advertisement in Santa Monica, California, where Audi noted "your move BMW"; their response was "Checkmate," with a billboard three times the size.

ARTICLE 11.5
AMBUSH MARKETING IN SPORTS

Ambush marketing is incredible. What's better is that when done properly, ambushers don't need to break any laws to get a positive result.

So what is ambush marketing and where does it come from?

The International Olympic Committee (IOC) has zealously guarded its trademarks for decades, but if there was one tipping point, it happened 23 years ago, during the 1996 Summer Olympics in Atlanta. On July 29, 1996, two pieces of history were made, both the athletic and marketing kind. That afternoon, sprinter Michael Johnson won gold in the 400m dash after finishing in 43.49 seconds. Tall, muscular and graceful, Johnson blew past his competitors as though they were standing still. Adding to the mesmerizing effect of his grace were the gold-colored shoes that Johnson wore, a $30,000 pair of lightweight racing spikes given to him by Nike. Not only did millions of television viewers see those Nike shoes on their screens, millions of Americans saw those same shoes slung around Johnson's neck a few days later on the cover of Time Magazine.

It's hard to imagine a more successful piece of marketing for any Olympic sponsor; except for one small problem: Nike *wasn't* an Olympic sponsor. Instead of paying for an official sponsorship, Nike decided it could advertise the brand in the 1996 games in other ways, and Johnson's gold shoes were just the beginning. The brand opened an outsized "Nike Centre" right beside the athletes' village. Nike also distributed flags to fans, guaranteeing that its "swoosh" logo would be in full view all over the property. These tactics infuriated Reebok, who had paid a reported $50 million to become an official sponsor. What Nike did in Atlanta 1996 directly resulted in the much more stringent guidelines that both the IOC and the United States Olympic Committee (USOC) have today. In this instance Nike ambushed the event but there are three main types of ambush marketing:

- **Direct ambushing**: the unauthorised use of protected symbols, logos, words or designs
- **Ambushing the event**: deliberately gaining exposure for a product or service by creating an unauthorised link or association with an event
- **Ambushing a sponsor**: deliberately undermining the marketing strategy of an official sponsor

So what's the law?

Imagine an American business tweeting "Congratulations to Usain Bolt for winning gold in the 100m at Rio 2016!" Sounds legit? Don't do it! I promise you it's not worth it!

Marketers have learned that the United States Olympic Committee (USOC) has ironclad regulations, backed by US trademark law. These laws prevent non-sponsor brands from saying anything even vaguely resembling or evoking the Olympics. For example, at London 2012 the words Games, Two Thousand and Twelve, 2012 or Twenty twelve cannot be used together or in conjunction with Gold, Silver, Bronze, London, Medals, Sponsor or Summer under s.33 and schedule 4 of the London Olympic Games & Paralympic Games Act 2006. So yes, even saying London 2012 as I just did breaks the rules . . . oops.

The biggest barrier, imposed by the IOC is Rule 40, by-law paragraph 3 of the *Olympic Charter* which states that, *"except as permitted by the IOC Executive Board, no competitor, coach, trainer or official who participates in the Olympic Games may allow his person, name, picture or sports performances to be used for advertising purposes during the Olympic Games"*. Basically, it bans advertisers from using the names or images of Olympic participants during the games unless the advertiser is an Olympic sponsor, which can cost as much as $100 million. Even a standard 30 second television ad (without superstar athletes) costs around $96,000.

These high costs are exactly why this type of ambush marketing was born; as a way for clever, risky and adventurous companies to circumvent these rules and costs, while still latching on to the bright, burning flame of the Olympic torch. Here are some other "Olympic-sized" ambush campaigns that have managed to win attention and customers through their cleverness and audacity.

Budweiser

Budweiser featured Wayne Gretzky and other hockey legends breathlessly watching a championship hockey game in its' "Let It Shine" ad campaign for the 2018 PyeongChang Winter Olympics. Everyone erupts in cheers when the home team scores the winning goal. Before the final score, bar staff are putting gold, medal-shaped coasters on beer glasses, a subliminal link to the gold medal? The brilliance of the ad is that it doesn't reference the Olympics even once. Yet the gold lighting, the gold lanterns held by the fans, the gold beer coasters, the ecstatic fans and the end caption "Bring It Home" all bring back memories of the legendary Olympic victory of the 1980 U.S. Hockey Team.

Target

PyeonChang athletes have unwittingly been the focus of ambush campaigns. For example, superstar snowboarder Shaun White, who won his third gold medal at the PyeongChang games, was featured on a series of Times Square billboards advertising Target during the 2010 Vancouver Winter Olympics. Not being an Olympic sponsor, Target got around Rule 40 restrictions by posting the billboards before the games began. By the day of the opening ceremony, Target altered the billboard by changing the image of White into a silhouette, accompanied by the message "Gone to Vancouver."

Dr. Dre's Beats

No newcomer to ambush marketing, Dr. Dre crashed the 2012 Summer Olympics in London with an amazing ambush tactic: product placement. The company sent special versions of their headphones to high-profile athletes; each set decorated with the athlete's home flag. Superstars such as U.S. swimmer Michael Phelps and British diver Tom Daley were seen (by millions of television viewers) sporting the headphones immediately before their events. Several athletes even brought social media marketing into the mix by tweeting about them. This high-profile product placement at the London games motivated consumers and companies worldwide to search online for the headphones.

Nike

Nike ambushed the 2014 Brazil World Cup by releasing an advert just before the tournament that referenced the players in Brazil leading everyone to believe they were involved with the competition despite Adidas being the official sponsors.

Paddy power

Unless claiming, or giving the impression, that the advertiser has an official link with the event, it is very difficult to prove illegality. Paddy Power circumvented the laws by sponsoring an egg and spoon race in a small pub in London, France.

Bruno Banani

Bruno Banani was a Tongan luger who was competing to be a part of the 2014 Sochi Olympic Games. Strangely enough he had the same name as his sponsor a German underwear company. Yes . . . he really did change his name as part of a marketing hoax . . .

Ultimately ambush marketing isn't for everyone; it can actually lead companies into trouble. When it's done the right way, however, companies can utilize this strategy to reach millions of new customers and bring home "advertising gold". If used correctly, brands can cash in and win big in these "marketing games".

Credit: LEX SPORTIVA

URL: https://lexsportiva.blog/2019/04/15/ambush-marketing-in-sports/. Published 15th April 2019. Accessed 24th July 2020.

Do most ambush marketing tactics work for organizations that do not want to pay the cost for official Olympic sponsorship? The answer to this question seems to be an overwhelming yes. Studies have shown that most consumers cannot correctly identify the true Olympic sponsors. Research from the

Chartered Institute of Marketing (CIM) revealed that brands that adopted ambush marketing strategies enjoyed more public recognition than the official Olympic sponsors.[46] The study, which questioned 1,000 adults regarding brands associated with the Olympics in an official or nonofficial capacity, found that 33 percent of consumers linked either adidas or Reebok with the Sydney Games despite the fact that neither were official Olympic partners.

On the positive side, Coca-Cola, an official partner of the Games, achieved the most recognition, with 22 percent of respondents associating the soft drink brand with the Olympics. However, other sponsors fared less well, with Visa International, Samsung, Panasonic, and IBM all scoring less than 5 percent in terms of public recognition. In the case of Visa, this lack of awareness was put into even more perspective by the fact that its main rival, American Express, scored higher recognition despite not being an official sponsor.

Because ambush marketing tactics are effective and consumers do not really care (only 20 percent of consumers said that they were angered by corporations engaging in ambush marketing), it appears that there is no end in sight for this highly competitive tactic. However, harsh preventive measures are taking place to protect the investments of the actual sponsors. As the accompanying article indicates, the sponsees continually try to enact measures to protect their sponsors (see Article 11.6).

ARTICLE 11.6
SPOTLIGHT ON SPORTS MARKETING ETHICS

Ambush Marketing: when sponsors cry "foul"

Ads bombard us daily – television, billboards, search engines and websites, apps, print and radio. Brands seek ways to break through this noise, to create a buzz and drive consumer demand for their products. In this pursuit, advertisers sometimes invest in sponsoring a big event, a famous individual or a team to leverage fans' excitement to promote the sponsor's brand. Events like the Olympic Games, the World Cup and the Super Bowl, to name a few, attract corporate sponsors that pay large sums, often in the hundreds of millions of dollars, to gain greater exposure for their brands. Sponsorships typically confer exclusive rights in a category to the sponsor, which can advertise itself as the official sponsor in that category, e.g., the official soft drink of the event. These marketing investments are imperiled when the sponsor's event-related advertising is ambushed by a competitor's advertising that makes that same association, even though not an official sponsor.

Direct ambushes versus indirect ambushes

The easy cases to spot are direct ambushes – ones in which the actual trademarks of the event organizer are used to create the false impression that they are associated with an event;

for example, if the use is of the distinctive symbol comprising five interlocking rings of the International Olympic Committee.

Events like the Olympic Games, the World Cup and the Super Bowl, to name a few, attract corporate sponsors that pay large sums, often in the hundreds of millions of dollars, to gain greater exposure for their brands.

The more difficult cases are indirect ambushes, ones in which the ambush marketer capitalizes on the event without misuse of the event's trademarks or without making a direct false claim of affiliation with the event. A myriad of approaches can accomplish this, from buying advertising space near the event, branding transportation to the venue, featuring individuals participating in the event, and using a color scheme and words that imply the event, to name a few.

Indirect ambush marketing is best illustrated by examples. During the London 2012 Olympic Games, Nike launched the *Find Your Greatness* campaign featuring regular individuals doing all manner of sports, filmed in locations called London, other than London, England – for example, London, Nigeria. In another example, Puma, which sponsors Usain Bolt, flooded the media with images of the athlete holding his golden Puma shoes after he won gold medals in the 2016 Rio Olympic Games and filled social media with the post "When you are @Usain Bolt, you are #ForeverFaster," which tied Usain Bolt's gold medal performance with Puma's *Forever Faster* slogan. These examples did not encroach upon any sponsor rights, notwithstanding the obvious implicit connection to the Olympic Games.

During the Winter Olympic Games in 2018 in PyeongChang, SK Telecom created a series of three broadcast ads using two South Korean Olympic athletes and the phrases "See you in PyeongChang" and "See you in 5G Korea". Although the advertisements appeared carefully crafted not to make a direct association between SK Telecom's services and the Olympic Games, the Korean Intellectual Property Office found that the campaign violated the rights of the official sponsor, KT Corporation.

Indirect ambush marketing campaigns also occur when the non-sponsored brand physically intrudes on the event. For example, Beats Electronics has executed campaigns during World Cup games and the Olympic Games in London and Rio, providing free Beats headphones to athletes who wore them in the event venue and in some cases tweeted about them. In another example, at an Indian Premier League match in 2017, Reliance Jio, a mobile network operator, engineered a daring ambush. It had certain game attendees wear black and white shirts in a pattern that spelled out JIO and was clearly visible to those in the stadium and, even more importantly, to the many viewing the match on television, thereby successfully ambushing the official sponsor, and Reliance Jio's rival, Vodafone.

The single most important step a sponsor can take in anticipation of ambush marketing is to address it as a critical part of the sponsorship negotiation.

Enforcers beware of a potential backlash

Taking action against such intrusive ambushes comes with the peril of a viral backlash. In the 2010 World Cup, 36 attractive women all wearing orange mini dresses provided by Bavaria, a beer maker without a sponsorship deal, showed up to cheer the Dutch team. The women were ejected by FIFA, which asserted that this activity ambushed the rights of the official sponsor, Budweiser. Although the sponsor won in the short run, the enforcement of these rights backfired, as studies show that press coverage effectively cemented the association between Bavaria and the World Cup in the minds of consumers.

When a sponsor has paid dearly for exclusive advertising rights, it will want an immediate solution to prevent or stop a competitor from stealing that benefit and will look to the owner of the rights, the event organizer, to step in. The organizer may be reluctant to take aggressive action for fear of setting an unfavorable precedent that could encourage others to be bold in creating ambush advertising around the event. Moreover, when the ambushes occur during an event, the organizer may have many pressing issues to address. What may be of urgent concern to a sponsor facing an ambush may be less critical to an organizer dealing with the production of the event in its entirety.

The single most important step a sponsor can take in anticipation of ambush marketing is to address it as a critical part of the sponsorship negotiation. While the business team may have other pressing concerns, the lawyer on the team needs to ensure that ambush marketing is addressed, with strict and measurable requirements, by the event organizer. The following is a list of suggestions for the sponsor, although often the facts of the event may dictate additional considerations.

Practical steps in negotiating a sponsorship deal

First, agree upon a specific set of steps that will be taken in response to ambush marketing, up to and including litigation, in what time frame and at whose expense. One of the great challenges for a sponsor is that when an ambush is effective, a cease-and-desist letter, after the fact, will not repair the damage caused. Determining in advance what steps will be taken can improve the relationship between the parties during the critical time a sponsor is demanding action. Such steps can include:

a. Pre-event publicity by the organizer stating that ambush marketing will not be tolerated; proactive sweeps of media and the physical venue, up to and during the event, for potential infringements of the sponsor's rights; designated personnel, including security and legal counsel, to address ambushes and the preparation of draft court papers.

b. Identification of competitors that the sponsor knows are likely to ambush an event. Often, a sponsor will have examples of past occurrences and even press clippings that show the ambusher was reported mistakenly as an official sponsor. Such documentation should be shared with the event organizer to support requests that the organizer issues advance warnings and prepares for immediate enforcement activity against the competitor as required.

c. Requiring the event organizer to establish clean zones around the arena or concert hall, working with the local municipality to establish a perimeter within which non-sponsor advertising is not permitted. This is often something the event organizer will have done, but nonetheless the guarantee of a clean zone should be specifically included in the agreement. A wily competitor could host a party near or on the day of the event in a building that falls within the clean zone, featuring invited guests and celebrities associated with the event, to build a subtle association with the event. A clear obligation to provide a clean zone will help the sponsor in that circumstance.

d. The sponsorship agreement should specifically impose obligations on the event organizer to ensure the organizer will have:

- adequate language on the back of tickets stating that certain actions will be grounds for ejection from the event and that tickets may not be used in promotional activities;
- rules for individual athletes or performers on how and when non-sponsor brands can be used within the venue; and
- terms in supply agreements with suppliers which haven't also obtained a sponsorship, that expressly prohibit promotional activities or advertising in conjunction with the mere fact of supplying the event.

e. Focusing on the product category and making sure it is comprehensive and anticipates future product developments in the category, if possible. Broad category definitions may make it easier to convince the organizer to take action, even against other sponsors, where there is some question about where the product of the ambusher falls. In an early ambush case, Mastercard, the official sponsor of the 1992 World Cup for "all card-based payment systems and account access devices," successfully enjoined Sprint, which was marketing pre-paid telephone calls with the event logo. However, category specificity is an issue that continues to lurk, particularly in categories where technology and social media have created new products and services.

To attract top sponsors, event organizers will often take proactive measures on behalf of all sponsors. Ensuring clean zones, as mentioned above, is one. Another is obtaining enhanced legal protections in the jurisdiction hosting the event, often as a condition of bringing the event to a specific country. Nonetheless, governmental response to enacting special legislation and needed implementing rules can be slow. Thus, sponsors should continue to raise these issues with the event organizer.

A balancing act

Of course, non-sponsors will always try to compete, despite their lack of official rights. To be fair, if there is only one sponsor per category, some – even those willing to pay the sponsorship fee – will be left out. Free speech rights, such as those defined by the First Amendment in the United States and by common law in other jurisdictions can be implicated if restrictions are too broad. Where to draw the line is not black or white, but gray. Both the event organizer and the sponsor should be sensitive to taking steps that are perceived as an over-reaction, particularly in this day of social media.

Trademark bullying, a concept that has gained traction in the United States, among other places, is shorthand for the overreaction of a big brand to an alleged encroachment by a smaller one. The assertion that one's free speech has been abridged or that one has been targeted by a bully, can be a very effective way to color public perception about the issue, and can work against the sponsor and the event. Yet, the organizer may have to weigh this concern against the fact that ambush marketing is a serious legal issue and that turning the proverbial blind eye against one ambusher may weaken a future legal action against a more serious ambush. Even more importantly, the organizer will know that a failure to act may have a negative impact on the value proposition of a sponsorship.

Despite the best efforts on the part of the sponsor and the event organizer, ambush marketers may well pull off a heist, and grab the spotlight sought by the sponsor. Planning clever marketing in advance to respond to an ambusher, or at a minimum, having a marketing team poised to take action at a moment's notice to shift attention robustly back to the sponsor, may be the best option. Lawyers can help ensure that in the tit-for-tat, the sponsor does not itself stumble into trouble, by helping it avoid infringement, unfair competition and product disparagement claims.

Credit: Kathryn Park

Rightsholder: WIPO Magazine

URL: www.wipo.int/wipo_magazine/en/2019/02/article_0004.html. Published April 2019. Accessed 24th September 2020.

Arguably the most effective means for organizers of sporting events to block out unauthorized advertising is to negotiate deals with stadium owners (which may be, for example, cities, sports clubs, or operating companies), which allow organizers to fully control advertising on the premises. For example, the organizer may demand the stadium to be handed over as a clean site so that the stadium would have to be cleared of all advertising by unofficial sponsors. The organizer may also require the stadium to be renamed for the time of the event and control access to the stadium grounds, including the airspace above. By cleverly designing the general terms and conditions of ticket sales, organizers can even impose dress codes on the spectators, enabling the exclusion of those wearing shirts or caps which display the logos of nonsponsors.

For example,[47] even though Burger King was an official sponsor of the Olympic Games of London, they launched a campaign with focus on the competition. In his official Twitter profile, Brazilian fighter Anderson Silva, who's the poster boy of the fast food chain, stated that for each medal that Brazil earned in London, Burger King would pay double French fries in the company's restaurants the next day.

Reaching target markets

Reaching new target markets is another primary objective of sponsorship programs. One of the unique features and benefits of sponsorship as a promotional medium is its ability to reach people who are attracted to sports entities because they share a common interest. Therefore, sporting events represent a natural forum for psychographic segmentation of consumers, that is, reaching consumers with similar activities, interests, and opinions. Stephen Cannon, vice president of marketing for Mercedes-Benz USA, sums up their sponsorship deal with U.S. Open Tennis, replacing Lexus as the official vehicle of the U.S. Open by saying,

> The partnership with the USTA aligns with our strategy to place Mercedes-Benz at the forefront of marquee events. The Open takes place in one of our most important markets and is an unrivaled opportunity to uniquely connect with fans and attendees.[48]

Recognizing the growth of global markets, Mercedes-Benz announced a 10-year agreement for the newly rebranded Mercedes-Benz arena in Shanghai, China. The 18,000-seat arena is the first naming rights deal for Mercedes-Benz outside of Germany and created a powerful precedent in the global sports marketplace.

YETI has established itself as an Austin icon. Austin FC president Andy Loughane said in a statement,

> YETI is an Internationally acclaimed brand with passionate supporters who lead active lifestyles and embody the creative energy often found in our sport and widely found in Austin. Austin FC is elated to begin their journey to reach new consumers in MLS alongside an Austin legend.[49]

Additionally, the Daytona 500 announced its travel packages for the 2022 racing season offering multiple lodging, ticketing and sponsorship exchanges.

> What's Included in our Daytona 500 Packages: Three, four, or five nights lodging, 2022 Daytona 500 tickets and Xfinity Series plus options for the Truck race and Dual at Daytona, full hot breakfast daily, commemorative race program and Admission to the all new Motorsports Museum! A must for Daytona Race Weekend is a Sprint Fan Zone pass. Walk on Pit Road and watch the Driver Introductions from the infield![50]

Consider the following examples of how sponsors have attempted to reach new and sometimes difficult-to-capture audiences: The X-Games represent a perfect opportunity to reach Generation Xers, a target market that is "difficult to reach through traditional media." Another target market that has been neglected includes the millions of disabled Americans. With the growth of the Paralympic Games and programs such as A Sporting Chance, which provide opportunities for people with disabilities to participate in sports, marketers are now addressing this market. Originating in 1960 as an event "parallel" to the Olympics, the Paralympics have blossomed into a major competition of their own. The Paralympic Games are a multisport, multidisability competition of elite, world-class athletes held approximately two weeks after the regular Olympics in the same host city. "The Paralympic Games have truly come home and found

Web Capture 11.1
Disabled athletes compete in Paralympic games

*Source:*www.paralympic.org

their pathway to the future here in London," Sir Philip Craven declared to the 80,000 in attendance. Just consider some of the impressive numbers. More than 4,000 athletes from 164 teams competed. The London Paralympics sold more tickets than any previous Games and were broadcast to more people in more countries. More than 2.7 million tickets were sold for the London Games, which is 900,000 more than in Beijing.[51]

Perhaps the fastest-growing target market for many marketers interested in sports sponsorship opportunities is women, and the growth of women's sports is taking place at all levels. More and more women are participating in sports and watching sports, which has created opportunities for equipment and apparel manufacturers as well as for broadcast media. In addition, marketing to women through the athletic medium has become an interesting and valuable tool for corporate America. In short, women are becoming the target market of choice for sports marketers.

Although women are growing in importance to sports marketers, relatively little is known about sponsorship decisions relative to women's sport. What are the women's sports that are experiencing the most growth, and does sponsorship growth align? As seen in Table 11.3a and 11.3b, according to NCAA research, lacrosse and bowling have had the most significant growth in the last 10 years, while at the collegiate level, soccer, golf, lacrosse, cross country, and softball have all grown in sponsorship spending at a rate of over 100 percent in the last 25 years. Additionally, only two sports (field hockey and gymnastics) have shown a decrease in sponsorship spending, and interestingly, both are negative in terms of participation at the high school level. A study by Nancy Lough and Richard Irwin was designed to better understand corporate sponsorship of women's sport.[52] The study questioned whether corporate sport sponsorship decision makers differ with respect to why they sponsor women's sport versus more "traditional" sponsorship opportunities. The authors found that corporate decision makers are more concerned with meeting objectives related to image building and increasing target market awareness, as opposed to building sales and market share. Summarized results of the research are shown in Table 11.4.

Table 11.3a High school and NCAA women's sports growth		
Ten-year percentage change in women's sports participation in high school and NCAA college sports		
	High school	NCAA
Lacrosse	54%	72%
Bowling	19%	61%
Track and field (indoor)	18%	33%
Water polo	18%	5%
Ice hockey	17%	28%
Golf	15%	26%
Fencing	15%	4%
Soccer	14%	21%
Rifle	14%	13%
Volleyball	12%	20%
Cross country	11%	11%
Rowing	10%	0%
Swimming and diving	9%	12%
Track and field (outdoor)	7%	32%
Tennis	7%	–1%
Gymnastics	–1%	6%
Softball	–2%	17%
Field hockey	–6%	9%
Basketball	–10%	7%

Notes: Percentage change from 2008–09 to 2018–19. High school numbers calculated using data from the National Federation of State High School Associations. College numbers derived from the NCAA Sports Sponsorship and Participation Rates Report.

Credit: © National Collegiate Athletic Association

Table 11.3b NCAA women's sports sponsorship growth

Sport	% growth over 25 years
Soccer	1,041%
Golf	286%
Lacrosse	151%
Cross country	125%
Softball	119%
Outdoor track	65%
Volleyball	63%
Basketball	45%
Tennis	44%
Swimming	41%
Field hockey	–1%
Gymnastics	–35%

Credit: © National Collegiate Athletic Association

Table 11.4 Importance of corporate sports sponsorship objectives by sports sponsorship type

Mean ratings (1–7) objective	General	Women's
Increase sales/market share	5.94	5.72
Increase target market awareness	5.88	5.89
Enhance general company image	5.81	5.94
Increase public awareness of company	5.56	5.53
Demonstrate community involvement	4.75	4.88
Build trade relations	4.50	4.29
Build trade goodwill	4.31	4.24
Demonstrate social responsibility	4.19	4.57
Block/preempt the competition	4.19	4.00
Enhance employee relations	3.76	3.78
Demonstrate corporate philanthropy	3.13	3.71

Relationship marketing

As discussed in Chapter 10, **relationship marketing**, building long-term relationships with customers, is one of the most important issues for sports marketers in today's competitive marketing environment. Building relationships with clients or putting the principles of relationship marketing to work is another sponsorship objective. Corporate hospitality managers see to it that sponsors are given ample space to "wine and dine" current or prospective clients.

Companies began throwing more lavish sports-related parties at the Super Bowl during the mid-1980s. Fans shifted from individuals and families attending their favorite sporting event to corporate clients using sporting events for business purposes. As such, the whole sports hospitality business has blossomed as companies are trying to generate new business and keep current clients as well.

When Bank of America became the sponsor of the BAC Colonial Tournament, the company wanted to create a touring hospitality program that would further enhance the bank's "Higher Standards" brand statement and give them a fitting opportunity to socialize with a large number of current and prospective customers.

The result was Hogan's Alley, an environment that resembled more of a leather-clad country club than simply a tent serving hot dogs and cold beverages. The area included a library filled with golf magazines and books on legendary golfer Ben Hogan, a conversation area, a large bar and dining area, and cocktail tables.

To measure the business impact of Hogan's Alley and determine the tangible results of its investment from their attendees after their experience, Bank of America established a database for all their guests. The company offered high-end door prizes for guests who completed detailed surveys querying them about the event and their banking activities. According to company research,[53] Bank of America determined that 96 percent of attendees were satisfied with the experience, 73 percent said it was the best corporate hospitality they had ever experienced, and 84 percent said it strengthened their relationship with the bank. More than 88 percent of attendees stated that they were more likely to consider using the bank because of the experience.

Very few academic studies have explored company attitudes toward corporate hospitality or the effectiveness of this activity, but recently Bennett looked at this growing sports marketing function. He found that two-thirds of the companies he surveyed believed that "highly formal" procedures were applied to the management of corporate hospitality and that one-third of the expenses were incorporated into marketing budgets. Additionally, two-thirds of the companies responding to the survey said that the decision on choice of events for corporate hospitality was based on "the in-house assessment of the goodness of the match between corporate hospitality activities and specific clients." Two-thirds of the companies felt that corporate hospitality was a vital element of the marketing mix and even if faced with a recession would not cut their budget in this area. Finally, companies stated that the greatest benefit of corporate hospitality activities was retaining profitable customers.[54]

Table 11.5 Athlete endorsements gone bad

Athlete endorser	Endorsements lost	Financial impact to athlete	Issue/scandal
Lance Armstrong	Trek, Easton-Bell Sports, 24 Hour Fitness, Nike, Anheuser-Busch, Oakley, Honey Stinger, FRS	~$150 million	Banned from cycling for doping
Tiger Woods	Accenture, AT&T, Gatorade, Buick	$22 million	Car crash and marital issues
Mike Tyson	Pepsi, Toyota, Kodak, Suntory Beer, USA Today, Nintendo	~$11million	Car accidents, rumors of suicide attempts, fights, and police encounters
Oscar Pistorius	Nike, Oakley, Thierry Mugler	$2 million	Found guilty of murder
Michael Vick	Nike, Reebok, AirTran Airways, Rawlings, Donruss, Upper Deck	Unknown	Illegal dogfighting ring
Ray Rice	Nike, Vertimax, Electronic Arts, Dick's Sporting Goods	$1.6 million	Domestic violence
Barry Bonds	Potential endorsements never achieved	$10 million	Alleged steroid use
Adrian Peterson	Radisson, Castrol, Nike	$4 million	Child abuse
Magic Johnson	KFC, Target, Converse	~$25 million in future earnings	HIV positive announcement
Gilbert Arenas	adidas	$40 million	Unregistered firearms

Source: Andrew Lisa, 24 Athletes Who Lost Their Huge Endorsement Deals, published August 14, 2019. Accessed September 24, 2020

URL: www.gobankingrates.com/net-worth/sports/athletes-lost-huge-endorsement-deals/amp/

Corporations choose to participate to generate new business, retain key clients, celebrate top-performing employees, and align with marquee events in the community. Often these sponsorship and hospitality programs feature several levels of participation designed to meet the needs and budgets of companies both large and small. How much are organizations willing to pay to retain and gain customers? Figure 11.2 provides a glimpse at the prices for hospitality areas at the U.S. Open, hosted at Torrey Pines Golf Course in San Diego, California. Incidentally, almost all of these areas were sold out more than a year in advance to the event.

Course Map and Pricing

The following outlines the amenities and pricing of the tent, suite and table packages along with the location of each venue on the championship course.

Hospitality Option	Location on the Golf Course	Hospitality Tickets Per Day	Option Tickets for Purchase Per Day	Pre-Open Outing Participants	VIP Parking Per Day	Cost Plus all applicable taxes
300 Ticket Tent	14th Green	300	25	13	150	$425,000
100 Ticket Tent	17th Green(Left)	100	20	4	50	$290,000
50 Ticket Tent	17th Green(Right)	50	10	2	25	$165,000
Open-Air Luxury Suites	16th Green 15th Green	30	2	N/A	15	$101,750*
Daily Open-Air Luxury Suites	16th Green 15th Green	30	2	N/A	15	$26,550* - Wednesday $39,050* - Thu. or Fri. $29,050* - Sat. or Sun.
Champions Pavilion Table	1st Fairway	12	1	N/A	5	$40,800* - Weekly $9,820* - Wednesday $12,820* - Thu. or Fri. $10,820* - Sat. or Sun.

*Cost includes food & beverage.

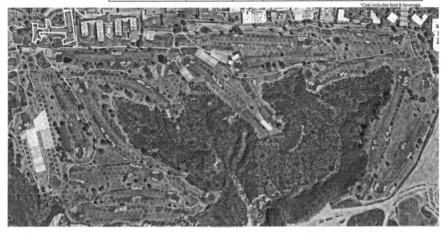

Web Capture 11.2
U.S. Open

Credit: MSG Promotions

URL: https://www.msgpromotions.com/us-open-hospitality/2022-u-s-open-championship/

Although corporate sponsors and their clients live and die by the relationships they forge, the community is another public with which sponsors want to build relationships. Many corporate sponsors believe returning something to the community is an important part of sponsoring a sporting event. For example, the coronavirus (COVID-19) pandemic had a substantial, prolonged impact on everyday life – and not just in sports. In particular, the issue of food insecurity skyrocketed due to necessitated quarantining and social distancing guidelines. That's why Michael Rubin, part owner of the 76ers and founder of Fanatics, created the "All In Challenge," a digital fundraising effort that incentivizes donations by offering "once-in-a-lifetime experiences" from sports, music, and entertainment figures as potential prizes. The All In Challenge "aims to be the world's largest digital fundraiser in history by raising tens of millions of dollars," with hopes to battle food insecurity brought on or exacerbated by COVID-19. According to the site, 100 percent of the proceeds will go to Feeding America, Meals On Wheels, World Central Kitchen, and No Kid Hungry.

Another example aligns with the Houston Open, which enriches the lives of Houstonians and empowers the community through the game of golf and has raised more than $69 million in charity contributions since its inception in 1946. In fact, the PGA Tour and its tournaments have surpassed the $3 billion mark in all-time giving. The PGA Tour's charitable total, which included a record $204.3 million in 2019 to bring the all-time total to $3.05 billion, includes donations made by tournaments on the PGA Tour, PGA Tour Champions, Korn Ferry Tour, Mackenzie Tour-PGA Tour Canada, PGA Tour Latinoamérica, and PGA Tour Series-China.[55]

> The outstanding work that is done by our tournaments, players, volunteers and sponsors is an integral part of what the PGA TOUR is all about, and our "Together, anything's possible" platform will enable us to tell that story in a more compelling way,

PGA Tour Commissioner Tim Finchem said.

> Their charitable efforts too often are underappreciated on a national scale, so we want to tell the stories of how they are changing people's lives and provide a means by which individuals can support their favorite causes through "Together, anything's possible."[56]

Image building

Perhaps the most important reason for sponsorship of a sports entity at any level is to maintain or build an image. **Image building** is a two-way street for both the sponsoring organization and the sports entity. The sponsoring organization associates itself and/or its brands with the positive images generated by the unique personality of the sporting event. Ferrand and Pages describe the process of finding a congruence between event and sponsor as "looking for the perfect wedding."[57] The researchers also point out that "any action toward sponsoring an event should begin with an analysis of the common and unique attributes of the event and the brand or product." Waste Management showcased their "green" initiatives through title sponsorship of the Waste Management Phoenix Open. As the following link illustrates, Waste Management utilizes the sponsorship platform to show people ways to better understand and "green up" their businesses: www.wm.com/us/en/inside-wm/phoenix-open/sustainability-report.

Exposure is not the only reason for sponsorship exchanges. Slazenger provided its first donation of hand-sewn balls to Wimbledon in 1902, and more than 100 years later, its balls can still be seen on court.[58] The sponsorship between Wimbledon and Slazenger is reportedly the longest running at over 114 years. There are many benefits of partnering with iconic global events such as Wimbledon. The enduring long-term sponsorship reflects alignment of organizational and event values, heritage, performance, and quality. This is so true, in fact, that others, such as Robinson's Barley Water, which instituted its relationship in 1935 and has appeared by the umpire's chair ever since, have followed suit.

In 1925, Ford made the decision to sponsor Australia's Geelong Football Club, and 91 years later, the automobile company is still the club's main sponsor.[59] Through the good times and bad, Ford has been key partner in providing support to the club. Slazenger, Robinson's, and Ford aren't the only companies with long-standing sponsorship relationships. From Coca-Cola and the Olympic Games to Canon and the World Cup tournaments, sponsorships are spanning decades with no end in sight.[60] Here are a few other notable examples:

Carlsberg will remain the official beer of Liverpool until the end of the 2023/24 season, ensuring the pair's partnership will continue to be the Premier League's longest standing, now going up to a record 31 years after first partnering in 1992. This is the longest-serving partnership of any Barclays Premier League club. The Danish beer was the club's main shirt sponsor for 17 years before becoming their official beer partner in 2010.[61] As *Clipper Around the World* noted, the link between Carlsberg has enhanced their marketing and commercial returns as well as capitalizing on football's ever-growing following to maintain their position at the top of the world of beer's premier league.

Consider an event like the Summer Extreme Games (X-Games), which possesses a well-defined image that includes characteristics such as aggressiveness, hipness, cool, no fear, and no rules. The image of extreme sports such as sky-surfing, street luge, or the adventure race will certainly "rub off" or become associated with the sponsoring organization. Taco Bell, Nike, and Mountain Dew will take on the characteristics of the extreme sports, and the image of their products will be maintained or enhanced. "Sponsorship is an opportunity to directly touch consumers and be true to the lifestyle of the brand," explains Chris Fuentes, former VP-marketing at Nautica. "It lets you have a conversation with consumers."

In Chapter 9, the **match-up hypothesis** was described as the more congruent the image of the endorser with the image of the product being promoted, the more effective the message. This simple principle also holds true for sponsorship. However, the image of the sports entity (remember, this may be an event, individual athlete, group of athletes, or team) should be congruent with the actual or desired image of the sponsor's organization or the product being sponsored. In Figure 11.4, we can see how the image of Taco Bell has shifted toward the X-Games and how the image of the X-Games also shifts toward the sponsor.

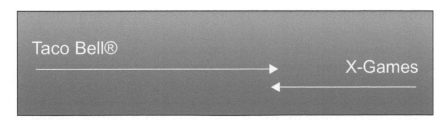

Figure 11.4
Sponsorship match-up

Sometimes the "match-up" between sponsor and sports entity is not seen as appropriate. Gatorade joined AT&T and Accenture in denouncing its relationship with Tiger Woods following his extra marital affairs. Nike recently cut ties with Antonio Brown in the wake of multiple sexual assault allegations and also historically broke ties with Lance Armstrong after his debacle regarding the use of illegal supplements. As Table 11.5 illustrates, an array of athletes have encountered adverse impacts related to sponsorship endorsement deals.

In another alcohol-related example, full-page ads in college newspapers called on university leaders, athletic conferences, and the NCAA to "stop the madness" by banning alcohol marketing from college sports. The ads, tied to March Madness and sponsored by the American Medical Association (AMA), ran in college papers in six cities in advance of the NCAA men's basketball tournament: in the *Chronicle of Higher Education* and student newspapers at Georgia Tech, University of Iowa, University of Wisconsin, Indiana University, University of Mississippi, and DePaul University. "The truly insane thing about March basketball is all the money universities get from alcohol advertising," the ads read. An illustration showed cheering sports fans holding signs reading: "Stop the Madness." The ad claimed that the alcohol industry spent more than $52 million to advertise its products during televised college sports in a recent year. Spokesman Bob Williams said the NCAA limits alcohol ads to one minute per hour of broadcast, won't allow ads for hard liquor, and encourages "responsibility themes and messages" in the ads.[62] The AMA has campaigned to the NCAA for years to ban alcohol-related ads.

Philip Morris USA and Philip Morris International (both subsidiaries of Altria) claim they are changed, responsible companies that do not market to kids and are concerned about the health risks of their products. But the companies' actions tell a different story. In the latest example, Philip Morris International is the only tobacco company that continues to sponsor Formula One auto races, which exposes spectators and tens of millions of television viewers worldwide – including millions of children – to the name, logo, and red-and-white colors of the company's best-selling Marlboro cigarettes. Arguably, no responsible company would continue to associate deadly and addictive cigarettes with the excitement and glamour of auto racing, thereby increasing their appeal to children.

Sales increases

The eventual objective for nearly all organizations involved in sponsorship programs is **sales increases**. Although sometimes there is an indirect route to sales (i.e., the hierarchy of effects model of promotional objectives, which states that awareness must come before action or sales), the major objective of sponsorship is to increase the bottom line. Organizations certainly would not spend millions of dollars to lend their names to stadiums or events if they did not feel comfortable about the return on investment. Likewise, the events are developed, in some cases (e.g., the Skins Game and the World's Strongest Man Competition), for the sole purpose of making a profit. Without sponsorship, the event would lose the ability to do so. Additionally, events such as The Match: Champions for Charity, which saw Phil Mickelson and Tom Brady team up versus Tiger Woods and Peyton Manning at Medalist Golf Club in Florida during the recent COVID-19 pandemic, are established to generate money. Serving audiences starved of live sport during the ongoing coronavirus pandemic, The Match II drew 6.3 million viewers to become U.S. cable TV's most-watched golf event. Turner-owned Bleacher Report recorded 38 million video views, more than 5 million social engagements, and 172 million social impressions for related content up to and during the event. The event raised US$20 million for the U.S. COVID-19 relief fund. When organizations are considering a sponsorship program, the first step is to determine the organizational objectives and marketing goals that might be achieved most effectively through sponsorship. However, the primary motivation for organizations participating in sports sponsorships is still unclear. Historically, organizations entered into sponsorships to create awareness and enhance the image of their brands, product lines, or corporations. Numerous studies examining the primary reasons for engaging in sponsorship found increasing awareness and enhancing company image to be the most important objectives.[63] More recently, studies have shown that increasing sales and market share are the primary motives of sponsorship (see Table 11.6).

Regardless of the relative importance of the various sponsorship objectives, organizations must carefully evaluate how the sponsorship will help them achieve their own unique marketing objectives. Along with examining the sponsorship objectives, the organization must find a sponsorship opportunity that fits within the existing promotion budget. Let us look briefly at the basic budgeting considerations, the next step in the sponsorship model.

Sponsorship budgeting

As with the promotional budget, determining the **sponsorship budgeting methods** includes competitive parity, arbitrary allocation, percentage of sales, and the objective and task method. Because the fundamentals of these budgeting methods have already been discussed, let us examine the sponsorship budgeting process at several organizations.

The only generality to be made about the budgeting process is that decision making varies widely based on the size of the company and its history and commitment to the practice of sponsorship.[64] Larger organizations that have used sponsorship as a form of communication for many years tend to have highly complex structures and those new to sponsorship tend to keep it simpler.

Table 11.6 Importance of sponsorship objectives

Objectives	Mean importance rating
Increase sales and market share	6.14
Increase target market awareness	6.07
Enhance general public awareness	5.88
Enhance general company image	5.47
Enhance trade relations	4.60
Enhance trade goodwill	4.55
Involve community	4.48
Alter public perception	4.15
Enhance employee relations	3.84
Block competition	3.68
Develop social responsibility	3.13
Develop corporate philanthropy	3.12

Source: Doug Morris and Richard L. Irwin, "The Data-Driven Approach to Sponsorship Acquisition," *Sport Marketing Quarterly*, vol. 5, no. 2 (1996), 9

Consider, for example, the budgeting process at Anheuser-Busch. Anheuser-Busch's budgeting process begins with determining the corporate-wide marketing budget. This is usually anywhere from 3 to 5 percent of the previous year's sales (percentage of sales method discussed in Chapter 10). The total budget is then divided among the company's more than 30 brands with Budweiser, the flagship brand, receiving the largest share of the budget. The final decision on budget allocation is made by two high-level management teams, who receive and review potential sponsorships. The first team looks at how the managers plan on supporting their sponsorships with additional promotional mix elements such as point-of-sale merchandising. The second team hears the brand managers present their case and defend their budget.

Although Anheuser-Busch's budgeting process represents a more complex and structured approach, Marriott uses a simpler technique. Marriott, a relative newcomer to sports sponsorship, leaves the whole business to its corporation's hotel and timeshare properties. The same practice holds true for Procter & Gamble, where managers of individual brands like Tide decide which sponsorship opportunities to pursue and how much money to allocate.

Once specific budgets are allocated, the organization must look for sponsorship opportunities that will meet objectives and still be affordable. To accommodate budgetary constraints, most sports entities offer different levels of sponsorship over a range of sponsorship fees. For example, as Table 11.2 illustrated, the cost of sponsorship and the tangible benefits received by the sponsor do vary, often significantly. Sponsorship packages are presented in a variety of areas such as hospitality, branding, pro-am, advertising, and tickets. A variety of sponsorship opportunities within each of these categories exists.

It is important to note that the sponsorship fee is not the only expense that should be considered. As Brant Wansley of BrandMarketing Services, Ltd., points out,

> Buying the rights [to the sponsorship] is one thing, capitalizing on them to get a good return on investment is another.... Purchasing a sponsorship is like buying an expensive sports car. In addition to the initial cost, you must invest in the maintenance of the car to ensure its performance.[65]

Sponsorship must be integrated with other forms of promotion to maximize its effectiveness. Rod Taylor, senior vice president of the CoActive Marketing Group, adds, "The only thing that you get as a sponsor is a piece of paper saying you've paid to belong. It is up to you as the marketer to convince consumers that you do, in fact, belong!" Bill Chipps, of the IEG Sponsorship Report, says that "the rule of thumb is that for every dollar a company spends on a rights fee, to maximize the sponsorship, they spend another $2 to $3 on leverage."

The average sponsor spends $1.60 to leverage its deals for every $1 it pays in rights fees, according to the IEG/Performance Research Sponsorship Decision-Makers Survey. According to IEG, the survey's high-water mark for activation spending was 1.9-to-1. Thirty-five percent of the sponsors said they would increase activation spending over the previous year. Forty-eight percent of these respondents said they would retain the same levels of expenditure, while only 18 percent projected a decrease in their expenditures. Over the past few years, 50 percent of the respondents identified an increase in their return on investment from sponsorship, while only 6 percent identified a decrease on their return on investment.[66]

An excellent example of an organization leveraging its Olympic sponsorship is Coca-Cola. In addition to print and broadcast advertisements, Coca-Cola produced themed collectible Olympic cans and accompanying P-O-P displays to stimulate sales at the retail level. According to Katie Bayne, chief marketing officer of Coca-Cola North America,

> The dedication to active living and amazing athletic performances of our Six-Pack of athletes served as an inspiration for these Coca-Cola Olympic Games-themed collectible cans. Our special packaging and overall Coca-Cola Olympic Games program are a great way to celebrate the Games and open a little happiness while enjoying the exciting competition with your friends and family.[67]

Choosing the sponsorship opportunity

Once sponsorship objectives have been carefully studied and financial resources have been allocated, organizations must make decisions regarding the appropriate sponsorship opportunity. Whatever the choices, thoughtful consideration must be given to the potential opportunities.

Endemic and non-endemic sponsors

The sponsorship industry has been growing and establishing itself as a force to reckon with for quite some time now. As corporations both large and small continue to garner interest, they require sustainability in deployment, methods and engagement of their sponsorship activities. Traditional platforms, for example, leagues, teams and athletes, as well a variety of developing platforms, such as esports, along with the advancement of technology, offer a plethora of engagement opportunities. As Nathan Lindberg, senior director of global sponsorships for Twitch, noted, sponsorship investment is no longer a passive marketplace but in fact a race to capture as much real estate for your brand as possible.[68]

The race for sponsorship is driven between those who have an endemic and non-endemic relation to the correlated activity, and both, if applied strategically, can have successful outcomes. An endemic sponsor would be a sponsor that is highly associated with sport, such as the likes of Wilson in tennis and football, Nike in baseball, or HyperX or Intel in esports. Many endemic brands (companies that sell products used in their respective sports) have well-established sponsorship contracts with top athletes, teams, and leagues. In fact, in a study conducted by IEG, endemic brands in the consumer electronics category were 13.4 times more likely to sponsor events affiliated with esports properties than the average of all sponsors.[69] Not only does the endemic relation seem logical, it often proves a wise investment, as sponsors have been able to increase their market share and brand recognition among fans and, therefore, boost sales of their products.

A non-endemic sponsor is a sponsor that offers products and services that are not directly related to the production or execution of a sport's activities. Examples of companies such as McDonald's, Geico, Amazon, or Home Depot would fit into the non-endemic realm. Since 2017, we have clearly seen an uptick in sponsorships from the non-endemic community as notable brands recognize the appeal and affiliated benefits. Many large non-endemic brands are getting their foot in the door to appeal to fans, and although these corporations sell products and services that are not vital to the respective industries, they recognize the affiliated value exchange opportunities. For example, in 2018, Tinder, the world-famous dating app, decided to expand its footprint with the younger audience and attract esports fans by supporting the relaunched Made in Brazil (MIBR) team. This is a great example of great marketing combined with esports' prowess that has the potential to push other small and medium-sized non-endemic sponsors to make their first but essential steps into esports and sport sponsorships.[70]

Choosing the most effective sponsorship opportunity for your organization necessitates a detailed decision-making process. Several researchers have examined the organizational decision-making process in attempts to understand the evaluation and selection of sponsorship opportunities. A conceptual model of the corporate decision-making process of **sport sponsorship acquisition** developed by Arthur, Scott, and Woods is shown in Figure 11.5.

The process begins with the acquisition of sponsorship proposals. Generally, this is a reactive process in which organizations receive a multitude of sponsorship possibilities from sports entities wanting to secure sponsors. Within the sponsorship proposal, potential sponsors commonly look for the following information to assist in decision making:

- Fan attendance and demographic profile of fans at the event
- Cost or cost per number of people reached
- Length of contract
- Media coverage
- Value-added promotions
- Sponsorship benefits

After the proposals have been acquired, the next step is to form the buying center. The buying center is the group of individuals within the organization responsible for **sponsorship evaluation** and choice. The buying center

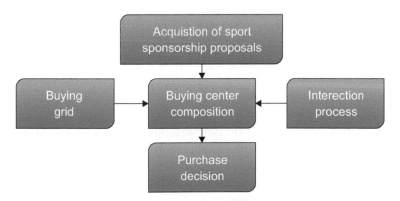

Figure 11.5
Sports sponsorship acquisition model

Source: Reprinted by permission from D. Arthur, D. Scott, and T. Woods. "A Conceptual Model of the Corporate Decision-Making Process of Sport Sponsorship Acquisition, *Journal of Sport Management*, vol. 11, no. 3 (1997), 229

usually consists of four to five individuals who each play a unique role in the purchase. Typically, these roles are described as gatekeepers, influencers, decision makers, and purchasers. These roles were previously discussed in the context of personal selling. You will recall that one of the sales activities was to identify the individuals within the organization who performed these roles. Similarly, the sponsorship requester must learn who these individuals are before submitting the proposal. Hopefully, the proposal can then be tailored to meet the unique needs of the individuals who make up the buying center.

Gatekeepers control the flow of information to the other members of the buying center. They are able to pass on the relevant proposals to other group members and act as an initial filtering device. The **influencers** are individuals who can impact the decision-making process. These individuals often have information regarding the sports entity that is requesting the sponsorship. The influencers have acquired this information through contacts they have in the community or industry. The **decision maker** is the individual within the buying center who has the ultimate responsibility to accept or reject proposals. In our earlier examples, describing the budgeting process for Proctor & Gamble, the brand managers were the ultimate decision makers in the sponsorship acquisition process. Finally, the **purchasers** are responsible for negotiating contracts and formally carrying out the terms of the sponsorship.

The composition of the buying center, in terms of the number of individuals and the interaction between these individuals, is a function of the type of sponsorship decision. The buying grid refers to the organization's previous experience and involvement in sponsorship purchases. If this is the first time the organization has engaged in sport sponsorship, then more information will be needed from the sponsorship requester. In addition, the buying center will have additional members with greater interaction. However, if the sponsorship is simply being renewed (also known as a straight sponsorship rebuy), the buying center will play a less significant role in the decision-making process.

The next step in the sponsorship acquisition model is to make the purchase decision. Typically, it takes an organization three to six weeks to make a final sponsorship decision. While this may seem slow, purchasing a sponsorship is a complex decision that requires the coordination and interaction of all the members in the buying center.

The purchase decision consists of three interrelated steps. In the first step, the organization must consider the desired scope of the sponsorship (e.g., international versus local). To do this, a simple scheme for categorizing sponsorship opportunities has been developed, called the Sport Event Pyramid. The second interrelated step requires the organization to select the appropriate athletic platform for the sponsorship. Does the organization want to sponsor an event, a team, a league, or an individual athlete? Finally, after the organization has chosen the scope of sponsorship and the athletic platform, it specifies the particular sports entity. After the final decision is made, a quick audit can be conducted to determine whether the organization has made the appropriate choice of sponsorship. Let us examine the three steps in the purchase decision-making process in greater detail.

Determining the scope of the sponsorship

The first step in the purchase decision phase of sponsorship acquisition is to determine the desired scope of the sponsorship. David Shani and Dennis Sandler have developed a way to categorize various sponsorship opportunities called the **Sports Event Pyramid**.[71] The Sports Event Pyramid is an excellent first step in reducing the number of sponsorship proposals to a smaller subset.

The Sports Event Pyramid consists of five levels: global events, international events, national events, regional events, and local events. Each level of the Sports Event Pyramid classifies events on the basis of the width and depth of interest in the event. Shani and Sandler describe the width as the geographic reach of the event via the various communications media, and the depth of the event refers to the level of interest among consumers.

Global events are at the apex of the pyramid. As the name implies, global events have the broadest coverage and are covered extensively around the world. In addition to their wide coverage, global events generate a great deal of interest among consumers. Shani and Sandler suggest that the World Cup and the Olympic Games are the only examples of truly global events. Corporations that want to position themselves in the global market should be prepared to pay top dollar for sponsorship of these events due to the tremendous reach and interest in the events.

International events are the next level in the hierarchy. For any event to be considered international in scope, it might (1) have a high level of interest in a broad, but not global, geographic region, or (2) be truly global in scope but have a lower level of interest in some of the countries reached. Examples of international events include Wimbledon, European Cup Soccer, America's Cup (yachting), the Rugby Union World Cup, and the Pan-American Games. Sponsoring these types of events is useful for corporations that have more narrowly targeted global markets.

Extremely high interest levels among consumers in a single country or two countries is categorized in the Sports Event Pyramid as a **national event**. National events, such as the World Series, the NCAA Final Four, and the Super Bowl, attract huge audiences in the United States. Although many of these events attract an international media audience, the focus is still on national consumers.

Regional events have a narrow geographic focus and are also characterized by high interest levels within the region. The Big East conference tournament in basketball and the Boston Marathon are considered good examples of regional events.

In the lowest level of the pyramid are **local events**. Local events have the narrowest geographic focus, such as a city or community, and attract a small

Photo 11.1
Little League (Youth Baseball League)
Credit: Shutterstock, ID# 503982 by Timothy Kosheba
URL: www.shutterstock.com/image-photo/youth-baseball-league-503982

segment of consumers that have a high level of interest in the event. High school sports, local races, and golf scrambles are examples of local events.

The primary purpose of the pyramid is to have marketers first develop an understanding of what level of sponsorship is consistent with corporate sponsorship objectives and budgets. Next, the corporation can decide which specific sporting events at the correct level present the best match. The organization may start small and choose to sponsor local events at the beginning. The larger the organization gets, the more likely it will be involved in sponsorship at each of the five levels of the pyramid. For example, Coca-Cola is deeply involved in sponsorships at all five levels.

Although the Sports Event Pyramid is a great tool for marketers developing a sponsorship program, it does have some potential flaws. First, local events are shown at the base of the pyramid. To some, this may imply the broadest geographic focus, whereas, in fact, local events have the most narrow focus. Second, it may be extremely difficult to categorize certain events. For example, the Super Bowl is cited as a national event that, by definition, has a one- or two-country focus with a high level of interest. The Super Bowl, of course, is broadcast in hundreds of countries but may have limited interest levels in most. Therefore, it is uncertain as to whether the event should be categorized as a national event, an international event, or both.

Determining the athletic platform

After the general level of sponsorship reach is considered via the sponsorship pyramid, a more specific sponsorship issue must be considered, namely choosing the appropriate athletic platform. Professor Christine Brooks defines the **athletic platform** for sponsorship as being either the team, the sport, the event, or the athlete.[72] In addition, choice of athletic platform could be further subdivided on the basis of level of competition. For instance, common levels of competition include professional, collegiate, high school, and recreational.

The choice of athletic platform (or, in some instances, platforms) is based on sponsorship objectives, budget, and geographic scope. More specifically, when selecting the athletic platform, several factors should be considered.

- What is the sponsorship budget? What type of athletic platform is feasible given the budget?
- What is the desired geographic scope? How does the athletic platform complement the choice made in the sports sponsorship pyramid?
- How does the athletic platform complement the sponsorship objectives?

Let us take a closer look at each of the broad choices of athletic platform for sponsorship. These include athletes, teams, sports/leagues, and events.

ARTICLE 11.7
SPONSORSHIP INFORMATION

Business/corporate sponsorship opportunities

Bishop Montgomery High School offers several opportunities for business/corporate partnership. These comprehensive sponsorships afford the donor visibility in school publications and at events throughout the year. Proceeds from corporate sponsorships benefit all students at Bishop Montgomery.

Benefits of partnering with Bishop Montgomery

- Companies benefit from association with a local, prominent non-profit educational organization. *Bishop Montgomery has approximately 1,000 students each year and over 16,500 alumni.*
- Increase company exposure through print media, banner signage and event acknowledgment.
- Show support for the mission of Bishop Montgomery, which is to provide quality Catholic education primarily to college-bound students of varied academic abilities
- Donations may be tax-deductible.

Corporate sponsorship benefit levels

Bishop Montgomery offers several levels at which businesses can partner with the school. Below is an explanation of the levels and benefits that come with each level.

Bronze $1,500

- business logo and website link on BMHS' website (corporate sponsor page) (1 year)
- Monthly recognition on BMHS' social media sites (Facebook, Twitter, Instagram) (1 year)

Silver $2,500

- business logo and website link on BMHS' website (corporate sponsor page) (1 year)
- monthly recognition on BMHS' social media sites (Facebook, Twitter, Instagram) (1 year)
- business logo and website link or flyer in BMHS' monthly parent newsletter & alumni e-newsletter (1 year)

Gold $5,000

- business logo and website link on BMHS' website (corporate sponsor page) (1 year)
- monthly recognition on BMHS' social media sites (Facebook, Twitter, Instagram) (1 year)
- business logo and website link or flyer in BMHS' monthly parent newsletter & alumni e-newsletter (1 year)
- ½ page, full-color ad in *Veritas* Magazine (1 issue per year) and Annual Report (1 issue per year)

Platinum $10,000

- business logo and website link on BMHS' website (corporate sponsor page) (1 year)
- monthly recognition on BMHS' social media sites (Facebook, Twitter, Instagram) (1 year)
- business logo and website link or flyer in BMHS' monthly parent newsletter & alumni e-newsletter (1 year)
- Full page, full-color ad in *Veritas* Magazine (1 issue per year) & Annual Report (1 issue per year)
- banner display at athletic events (football, baseball, soccer) (1 year)

Explanation of Bishop Montgomery website, social media, & publications

- Bishop Montgomery's website, www.bmhs-la.org, receives approximately 4,000–5,000 hits per day
- Facebook – @BMHSKnights has approximately 5,000 followers
- Twitter – @BMHSKnights has over 1,000 followers
- Instagram – @BMHSKnights has over 1,000 followers

- Monthly parent newsletter is received, digitally, by over 900 current families
- Monthly alumni e-newsletter is sent to over 6,000 alumni
- *Veritas*, the official magazine of Bishop Montgomery, is sent once a year to approximately 14,500 members of the school community

Sponsor a Bishop Montgomery event

Each year BMHS hosts a number of events for the parents, alumni, and greater school community. Contact the Advancement Office to learn how your company can underwrite any of the following events:

Freshman family BBQ

- An annual event at the start of each school year that brings together our newest members of the BMHS community

Athletic Hall of Fame

- Annual event held in September in conjunction with a home football game. This event brings together past and present members of the community. Each year, honorees are inducted into the BMHS Athletic Hall of Fame in a ceremony held in the gymnasium and at halftime of that night's football game

Homecoming event & football game

- Each year, Bishop Montgomery's homecoming event and football game is one of the most well-attended and popular celebrations. Prior to the game, BMHS hosts food trucks from around Los Angeles. The event and game is attended by current students, parents, faculty, alumni, and friends of BMHS.

Spring fundraising event

- The spring fundraising event varies from year-to-year. Events range from the Black & Gold Gala held off campus to a craft beer festival held on campus. This event is a 21 & over event and attracts current and past parents, alumni, and friends of the school.

Athletic event banners

- The school offers opportunities for corporations, organizations, and community members to purchase a banner for display at all home football, soccer, and/or baseball games.
- Football Banner/$600 per year
- Boys' & Girls' Soccer Banner/$500 per year

- Baseball Banner/$500 per year
- All Season Banner/$1300 per year

Credit: Bishop Montgomery High School

URL: www.bmhs-la.org/apps/pages/index.jsp?uREC_ID=289317&type=d&pREC_ID=665662

Athletes

We have previously examined the opportunities and risks of athletes as endorsers in Chapters 9 and 10. To summarize, athletes can have tremendous credibility with the target audience and can create an immediate association with a product in the consumer's mind. For example, NASCAR fans talk about Kyle Busch driving the "M & M" car or Denny Hamlin the "FedEx" car. Interestingly, when it comes to athletes as sponsors, golfers have always been at the head of the pack. In fact, most believe the entire sports marketing industry was built on the backs of professional golfers, such as Arnold Palmer, Jack Nicklaus, and Gary Player. While Tiger Woods's fall from global sports icon to tabloid fodder was stunning, losing Accenture, AT&T, Gatorade, and Pepsi as sponsors, he still carries the flag and remains one of the highest-paid athletes in the world thanks to huge deals with Nike, Electronic Arts, and Upper Deck. Woods has earned $1.5 billion from endorsements, appearances, and course design fees.

As Bleacher Report noted, controversy is no stranger to sports: if success is measured by wins and losses, stats and superlatives, then no possible point of contention goes unnoticed. Like politics and cafeteria lunch specials, everything has two "sides" in sports.[73] So, if controversy is synonymous with sports, then divisive issues are everywhere and all around. Many athletes have dominated the sport headlines, some spanning years rather than news cycles for all the wrong reasons. Whether it be the likes of O.J. Simpson, Lance Armstrong, Mike Tyson, or Tonya Harding, to name a few, often sports + athletes = controversy.

One athlete who is always surrounded by controversy and seems to exemplify the bad-boy image is former NFL QB Michael Vick. Sonya Elliot filed a civil lawsuit against Vick alleging that she contracted genital herpes from Vick and that he failed to inform her that he had the disease. Elliot further alleged that Vick had visited clinics under the alias "Ron Mexico" to get treatments and thus he knew of his condition. In another incident with a former team, the Atlanta Falcons, Vick made an obscene gesture at Atlanta fans, holding up two middle fingers during a game against the New Orleans Saints in the Georgia Dome on November 26, 2006. To add fuel to the fire, Vick surrendered a water bottle to security at Miami International Airport. Due to Vick's reluctance to leave the bottle behind, it was later retrieved from a trash receptacle. The bottle was found to have a hidden compartment that contained a small amount of dark particulate and a pungent aroma closely associated with marijuana. On April 24, 2007, Vick was scheduled to lobby on Capitol Hill, hoping to persuade lawmakers to increase funding for after-school programs. Vick missed a connecting flight in Atlanta and failed to show for his morning appearance.[74] In his most publicized and scandalous act yet, Vick pleaded guilty to a federal dog-fighting conspiracy charge on August 27, 2007, in U.S. District Court and served 21 months in prison, followed by 2 months in home confinement. With the loss of his NFL salary and product endorsement deals, combined with previous financial mismanagement, Vick filed for Chapter 11 bankruptcy in July 2008. Most recently, Vick has been accused of using steroids, but he denies these allegations. Currently, Vick continues to rebuild his broken reputation and regain the trust of the public.

Teams

Teams at any level of competition (Little League, high school, college, and professional) can serve as the athletic platform. The accompanying article illustrates how companies are finding creative ways to solidify sport sponsorship exchanges not only with professional sport teams but at all levels, including college athletic departments and amateur sports.

ARTICLE 11.8
THE FAST-CHANGING WORLD OF SPORTS SPONSORSHIPS

From Stadium walls and 2.5-inch patches to Olympic runners arms, and controversial basketball shoes, sponsorship deals have taken a wild turn over the last few years. Just take a look at any Major League Baseball stadium outfield if you need a little proof with sign after sign sharing brand after brand. Before you even step inside, a majority of these stadiums have naming rights tied to the property turning, for instance, the home of the New York Mets into Citi Field, a plug for Citigroup, the New York financial services company.

You could say this sign of the times has grown into a very lucrative and creative enterprise in the sports marketing world. While companies will still obviously purchase premium advertising space at stadiums, today companies are getting even more creative in the ways they are sharing and placing their brands. It is evolving in ways no one could have easily predicted.

According to sport.nsw.gov.au, the definition of a sponsorship is when a business provides funds, resources or services to a club, in return for some form of rights and/or association with the club to help the business commercially. The sponsorship could be placing a logo on a football, signs at an oval or with advertising in the team's newsletter. The reason is simple. It is all about increasing brand awareness in an industry that is never at a loss for fans or customers. When a fan is in the stands cheering on their favorite professional sports team and they see a product or brand, it becomes ingrained, maybe even subconsciously, in their brains. It increases awareness and could ultimately change the way a person sees that specific brand or product.

I've been to more than a few professional sporting events over the past few years and personally when I see a brand or product displayed at the stadium, I take note. Because a brand is willing to put their messaging at such a large venue, it elevates the product. Whether real or imagined, it increases the reputation of that brand.

Companies spend a considerable amount of money trying to pinpoint their target audience. So, there's little doubt that those companies who shell out some of the highest advertising dollars in the nation to align themselves with a sports team, did a little research on the fans who sit in the seats. After all, they want to make sure they are getting the best bang for their buck if they choose to add a banner, a multimedia message, a real-time internet stream, a digital ad on a mobile app or share sponsorship collectibles during a game. If they have the right target, the audience is captive, spending upwards of three hours to take in a game with a sponsor's message front and center before them.

In order to land a sponsorship deal, each party must have an agreement set in place that outlines each side's role. This sponsorship proposal outlines the rules and regulations for each sponsorship. It makes sure both sides move forward without violating any of the terms or conditions of the sponsorship.

Fast forward to 2019, and the sponsorship mentality has completely shifted. Instead of just adding your logo to a sign or banner, companies' logos are being emblazoned on the athlete's jerseys. If your favorite player is sporting the logo of a prominent company, that sponsorship tie just might increase not only awareness but brand loyalty as well. With every broadcast showing incredible plays and highlighting the players behind them, companies are taking note and are slowly shifting from the stadium placement to having their logos, literally, on the players.

Look back to 2006 and you'll find a brief history about jersey sponsorships and how they began. According to mentalfloss.com, Major League Soccer's Real Salt Lake became the first major professional team in the United States to embrace jersey-front sponsorship when it announced a deal with XanGo, which produces nutritional supplement products. Shortly after the MLS broke the jersey sponsorship ice in the United States, the WNBA authorized its teams to feature sponsors' logos on their uniforms. The Phoenix Mercury was the first team to take the bait, replacing its logo with that of LifeLock, which specializes in identity-theft protection. The NBA Development League wasn't far behind. In 2010, the league champion Rio Grande Valley Vipers forged a partnership with Lone Star National Bank, agreeing to feature the bank's logo on the front of its jerseys. Around the same time, the NBDL's Erie BayHawks announced a sponsorship agreement with the Lake Erie College of Osteopathic Medicine (LECOM). In 2009, the NFL allowed teams to sell sponsorship patches for their practice jerseys and several teams took advantage during training camp. Teams were, however, prohibited from partnering with alcohol brands. The New Jersey Nets became the first NBA team to feature sponsorship on its practice jerseys as part of a deal with PNY Technologies later that year. Shortly after the New Jersey Nets, many other NBA teams started participating in sponsorship deals that involved very small 2.5 inch patches on the front of their jerseys. This little patch was placed on the opposite side of the Nike Swoosh. According to Forbes and GumGum Sports, the 2.5 by 2.5-inch patches are generating more than $350 million worth of revenue for the NBA. The only other signage in the NBA that generates that much revenue is the Nike logo stitched on the other side of the NBA's jerseys. Not only are teams advertising the NBA sponsor on one side of the jersey, but teams are selling the other side to a company that aligns with their team's mentality as well. There are now 20 NBA teams that have inked deals with large companies that allow that company the rights to a small patch on the jerseys of the players.

Jumping on the jersey sponsorship opportunity, the Boston Celtics agreed to a multi-year partnership with General Electric (GE). This little patch on the Jerseys cost GE $24 million over three years. GE could have easily purchased some signage at TD Garden which is the home of the Boston Celtics, but they chose this different route. GE, a company that prides itself on being an innovator decided not to call the move a sponsorship. Instead, it took to social media and referred to the deal as an innovative partnership. It's an innovative deal that allows GE to have their logo on each member of the Boston Celtics team. Each time the cameras zoom to catch a tip-off, a player at the free throw line or a team during a time out, GE's logo is right there in the thick of things, generating some very good brand placement for the company.

There was another notable jersey patch that generated quite the buzz. It involved Bumble and the Los Angeles Clippers. Before the deal was signed, not many had heard of this female-centric dating app. In fact, many dating apps haven't been allowed to even play in the sports sponsorship arena. They've been denied advertising. When the Clippers partnered with Bumble for space on their jerseys, they were sending the message that this team was one of the most progressive organizations in sports and entertainment. It claimed that it signed the deal to honor the NBA's largest female leadership team which includes Gillian Zucker, the only female to hold the title of the president among NBA teams. Since the Clippers empower women in their front office, it would make sense that they partnered with a dating company that empowers and even requires that women make the first move. The Clippers management stated this sponsorship was a way to highlight how that diversity and gender equality in the workplace is essential to organizational excellence.

To date, 20 out of 30 NBA teams participate in a jersey sponsorship partnership. With 66% participating, it's proven itself as a profitable enterprise for not only business but the NBA as well. In the next 3–5 years, it's predicted that every single NBA team will have some sort of jersey sponsor partnership.

Which professional league will follow in the NBA's footsteps? Let's jump to the NFL. It all started in 2009 when the NFL allowed teams to sell sponsorship patches for their practice jerseys and several teams took advantage during training camp. Even though one of the major sponsors of the NFL is Anheuser-Busch, the league decided not to allow sponsorships for any companies that sell alcohol. These sponsorships aren't allowed on game days but are allowed during the summer months when NFL teams participate in organized team activities, also known as OTAs.

This is when the team starts to gel. Players and coaches are focused on building the best strategy in the offseason and conditioning the best team. When a sports broadcaster tries to get a glimpse into a bit of that team's strategy, the spotlight falls on the star players of each team. This is how the practice jersey sponsorship came to fruition. By placing a large patch on the jerseys, companies were able to make their mark on the NFL. Take AT&T, for instance. They currently have the naming rights to the home of the Dallas Cowboys with AT&T Stadium. Once the NFL gave the approval of a practice jersey sponsorship, AT&T jumped right on it and placed their logo on the Dallas Cowboys practice jersey to further their sponsorship ties with the team.

With the NBA cashing in on a whopping $350 million annually, the big question now is will the NFL jump on board and make the move to regular season sponsorships, allowing companies to display their logo on the chests of players each game day. Many feel because of the NFL's leadership, it's not going to be an easy sell. The NBA's Commissioner, Adam Silver, is known for trying new things to increase the revenue of the NBA. The NFL's Commissioner, Roger Goodell, however, has been called a reactive leader, acting mainly when a problem arises that affects the league's bottom line. Because the NBA has a proven track record that jersey sponsorship can be a new stream of revenue for the organization, the NFL will likely jump on board and allow teams to partner with companies sometime within the next 5 years.

The NFL has a 4-week preseason that runs throughout August. During that time, each NFL team plays 4 games to help them solidify their 53-man rosters. This would be an excellent time for the NFL to test the waters on jersey sponsorships, allowing teams to partner with companies in the preseason to see if this venture would be profitable. It would also be prime time to test a sponsor's placement on a jersey. Would a logo go on the sleeve? Or, would a sponsor use the open space at the top? The preseason would be the perfect time to test how a company patch might look on game day and what spot might garner the most visibility.

Major League Baseball, 'America's Favorite Pastime,' has been drawing in large crowds and establishing team loyalty since the sport was formed in Cincinnati, Ohio back in 1869. That's when the Cincinnati Red Stockings first took to the diamond. With 150 years of history under its belt, there's little doubt this sport is ripe for the sports sponsorship pickings.

A couple of weeks ago, I was able to sit in the stands at a Seattle Mariners game during the opening weekend of the 2019–2020 MLB season. When you walk in, you see people eating hot dogs and drinking ice cold beer. Even though I'm young and have only been to a few games in my life, there is such a nostalgic and traditional feel when going to a baseball game. Even still, you'll find dozens of sponsorship ads displayed from edge to edge of the outfield. One area of "advertising real estate," that, for now, sits vacant is on the MLB jersey with its traditional feel and traditional stitched design. While there is a ton of room on most MLB jerseys, they stay plain to tie in with tradition and the nostalgic aspect of professional baseball. Out of the major sports leagues that America has, I could very well see the MLB being the last of the leagues to implement a jersey sponsorship because of how traditional the MLB has kept baseball over the last 150 years.

There are a whole host of reasons why jersey sponsorships might not be the best fit for the sport.

Each team already seems to have a plethora of corporations backing them. Jersey sponsorship would be difficult because when a fan is at the game, it's pretty hard to see a player closeup. Sure, there are jumbotrons, but the game is explosive. Many times fans are focused on a player's movement and not on the player himself or, better yet, what is on his jersey. In an NBA arena, the atmosphere feels smaller. Fans feel closer to the action and if a fan isn't in the stands, the broadcast of an NBA game is also wildly different. A camera can pan and zoom on individual players moving the ball up and down the court. A baseball broadcast isn't nearly as up close and personal.

Would you get an ad tattooed on your arm for $20,000? Nick Symmonds did. In 2012, this professional men's runner, a 6-time US National 800 meter champion, auctioned off space on his left shoulder, basically selling space on his skin to a corporate sponsor. A marketing firm paid him $11,100 to publicize their Twitter handle. The second time, John Legere, the CEO of T-Mobile put in the winning eBay bid of $21,800 for nine inches on the Olympian's right shoulder.

One of the runner's latest tattoos shows off his own company called Run Gum. This gum is specifically marketed toward runners. It's a so-called energy gum designed to deliver that burst of energy fast by letting the active ingredients of caffeine and vitamins be absorbed quickly through the tissues in a runner's mouth. Because this is Symmonds' company, whenever he wins a race, it's not only a win for him but a win for his company.

Aside from teams and arenas, sponsorships are shifting their focus and investing in players more now than ever before. In 2015, Nike signed an endorsement agreement with LeBron James for $1 billion for life. James had been a Nike athlete since the global sportswear giant offered him a seven-year contract worth $90 million before he even entered the 2003 NBA draft lottery.

Fellow NBA All-Stars have also witnessed shoe endorsements, allowing the player to design their own shoe and literally put their name on it. Players like Kobe Bryant, Michael Jordan, Kyrie Irving and Paul George are all NBA players that Nike has enlisted to market their own custom basketball shoe.

The Jordan shoe deal was one of Nike's first. Since signing that deal, Jordan was able to go down as one of the best NBA players of all time. Back in the 1980s, having a colored basketball shoe was unheard of. To put it simply, the shoes were white. When Nike came in and helped design Jordan's signature red and black shoes, it sparked controversy. The NBA put Jordan and the Chicago Bulls on notice and fined Jordan every time he wore the shoes during a game. While Nike picked up the tab for the fines, Jordan cashed the endorsement checks helping the shoes to gain popularity each time he laced them up before a game.

When it comes to sports sponsorships, gone are the days of simple signage. Today, companies are finding far more creative ways for people to see their brand image. Who would have thought that a small 2.5-inch patch would shake up the sports sponsorship world, helping the NBA land a brand new $350 million revenue stream? Who would've thought that changing a shoe from white to black and red would cause such an uproar? Who would've thought that a shoe company would pay someone $1 billion dollars for life? It's just a part of the sports sponsorship evolution. With these wild twists and turns, it's fair to say we should expect a few more in the years to come.

Credit: Calvin Koerber, published April 2019. Accessed 24th September 2020.

URL: https://medium.com/@14ideas/the-fast-changing-world-of-sports-sponsorships-7bffdd9bd7ff

The marketing of collegiate sports has skyrocketed in recent years. According to Kantar Media (2020), the NCAA men's basketball tournament has generated more than $4.5 billion of national TV ad spending over the past five years. The 21-day March Madness event provides an opportunity for marketers to connect with consumers over an extended period. In 2019, the nearly month-long tournament generated $910 million in national TV ad revenue, a number that may see an uptick this year, with CBS and Turner Sports reportedly selling out linear TV ad inventory in record time for the 2020 games.

Though ad spend was down in 2019, the number of advertisers and sponsors during the tournament has steadily grown year after year, with 2019 having the highest level we have seen since 2008. (With advertisers often placing ads for multiple brands, the number of brands differs from the number of advertisers during a given year.)

According to Kantar, in addition to a wide linear TV opportunity, some brands use March Madness as a cornerstone for wider sponsorship activations. The NCAA has 18 approved corporate marketing partners, many of whom create integrated programs with multiple consumer touchpoints coinciding with the tournament. TV spots in the games are often a core element and are supplemented by things like sweepstakes, contests, in-store events, and on-site experiential marketing at tournament sites – especially during the Final Four weekend.[75]

In 2019, corporate sponsor AT&T utilized a number of deployment opportunities to connect with consumers throughout the tournament. AT&T offered, at the Final Four in Minneapolis, enhanced wireless experience at the games and other events like concerts and fan fests. They also livestreamed concerts to fans across NCAA and AT&T social and digital channels. They created a branded Fan Zone at the Final Four to create a *Game of Thrones*-themed shot contest, which was tracked through an online leaderboard.

Kantar reported that another sponsor, Pizza Hut, leveraged the opportunity as a platform to relaunch its P'Zone offering, a menu favorite from the early 2000s. Pizza Hut used its sponsorship to promote its Book It! literacy initiative, the brand's global commitment to enabling access to books and educational resources to empower teachers and inspiring readers.[76]

In an additional example, Buffalo Wild Wings deployed multiple activations that included a bracket challenge, the creation of options if the game headed into overtime, and an on-site tool specifically designed for men who had just had vasectomies. Lee noted that this was implemented as a result of learning that instances of the procedure increase 30 percent during the first round of the tournament.[77]

Many sponsors and advertisers are loyal to the event. Two-thirds are consistently returnees from the prior year, and 23 marketers have appeared in the event for the last 10 consecutive years. This is a very high loyalty rate as compared to other major sporting events like the Super Bowl, which has a typical turnover rate among its advertisers of around 40 percent.

Apparel and footwear companies have also spent large sums of money to become the official outfitter for university athletic teams. This not only gives the company tremendous exposure via multiple media outlets but also targets a very involved and loyal alumni base. For the universities, it has also become a consistent source of athletic revenue to offset huge cost structures to run numerous programs that typically run a deficit. Many of the terms of these multimillion dollar deals are not disclosed, but some have been and give a good idea of the amount of money being invested. In 2015, Nike reportedly set a record at the time when it extended its partnership with Ohio State University for 15 years in a contract valued at $252 million. The Wall Street Journal estimated that Nike will contribute $112 million in product and at least $103 million in cash, including royalty income, to the university. That deal surpassed, by nearly $100 million, Nike's $169 million contract with the University of Michigan in July 2015. Before that, Under Armour Inc. reportedly made a $90 million-plus bid to take Notre Dame from 17-year sponsor adidas in 2014.

That's a lot of money (in cash and product) to outfit a college team. Which begs the question, why are leading brands so willing to invest millions in college sports? Three main reasons can be related to merchandising opportunity, partnering with a winning team, and securing the long-term buy-in of athletes (see Table 11.7 for a list of universities with the highest revenues from licensed merchandise sales).

Anheuser-Busch is a corporation that has chosen an integrated approach in sponsoring a number of teams. They sponsor 26 MLB teams and 25 NBA teams, and Bud Light also signed on as the official beer of the NHL in 1988 and currently sponsors 20 domestic teams.[78] In total, Anheuser-Busch sponsorships include 95 local teams across the four major sports leagues and dozens of local running and cycling events nationwide, as well as the Busch and Budweiser sponsorship affiliations with Richard Childress Racing and NASCAR.

adidas sponsors numerous teams and clubs in a variety of sports. Notably, their partnership alliances in soccer stand out and include the likes of Fulham, Manchester United, Bayern Munich, Juventus, Benfica, Real Madrid, and Valencia, to name a few. Additionally, adidas has a number of alliances with baseball, basketball, rugby, cricket, and football teams.

Table 11.7 University licensing leaders	
Rank	University
1	The University of Texas at Austin
2	The University of Alabama
3	University of Kentucky
4	University of Michigan
5	University of Tennessee

Note: Schools not under contract with the CLC (Collegiate Licensing Company) were not included on the list. This includes schools such as Notre Dame, Southern California, Stanford, and Iowa, many of which handle licensing in house.

Credit: Collegiate Licensing Company

Rightsholder: © National Collegiate Athletic Association

However, sponsoring athletic teams, just like athletes and leagues, can have a level of risk. For example, Radisson Hotels suspended its sponsorship with the Minnesota Vikings when its coach explained in front of media advertising that the team would reinstate running back Adrian Peterson. Peterson faced child-abuse charges for what he called disciplining his child with a switch. Additionally, related to the controversy, Anheuser-Busch aired its unhappiness and Nike pulled Peterson jerseys off store shelves.[79]

Sport or league

In addition to sponsoring teams, some companies choose to sponsor sports or leagues. For example, the smoothie retailer Jamba Juice made its first investment in a national sports league by signing a multi-year deal to sponsor the WNBA. The deal will be part of a national marketing campaign promoting health and wellness as well as promotional materials for Jamba Juice stores in WNBA markets. The league also worked with the retailer to promote a program known as Jamba Jump, a fitness routine that uses jump ropes. The goal was to reach 1 million children through the partnership.[80] One advantage to sponsoring women's sports and the WNBA is that there is less sponsorship clutter. Fewer companies are sponsoring women's sports or leagues, and those that do are creating a unique position and differentiating themselves.

For example, cosmetics brand CoverGirl was the presenting sponsor of the WNBA's new marketing campaign WNBA Pride, aimed at the lesbian, gay, bisexual, and transgender community. WNBA Pride is the league's platform celebrating inclusion and equality while combating anti-LGBT bias. The global consumer products company Procter & Gamble owns CoverGirl. The program would not have seen the light of day without the support and acceptance of other league marketing partners, which include Boost Mobile, adidas, American Express, BBVA, Anheuser-Busch, Coca-Cola, EA Sports, Gatorade, Nike, Spalding, and State Farm. While the WNBA welcomes all fans, athletes, and partners to the game, the value of marketing partners should not be underestimated in matters where social responsibility conforms to or conflicts with business strategies, especially when those conflicts become public knowledge.[81] For example, NFL sponsor CoverGirl was drawn into a national discussion about domestic violence after someone on social media doctored the brand's "Get Your Game Face On!" campaign to show a fan of the Baltimore Ravens with a black eye; the Ravens cut Ray Rice after a video surfaced of him punching his then-fiancée and now wife in the face in an elevator.

Notably, Budweiser became the first official beer sponsor of the National Women's Soccer League (NWSL). The multi-year partnership is built on Budweiser's year-round commitment to continue supporting women's soccer. As Monica Rustgi, vice president of marketing for Budweiser, noted,

> Budweiser has supported the U.S. Women's National team for three decades, and we realize there is so much more Budweiser can do. Becoming the official beer sponsor of the NWSL is our way of not just supporting the U.S. Women's Team once every four years, but also supporting women's soccer every single day.[82]

The deal makes Budweiser one of the biggest sponsors of the NWSL, with naming rights to the playoffs, the championship, the MVP trophy, and a newly created "Most Valuable Supporter" award for the league's biggest fan. Budweiser will activate the sponsorship locally, with support of the teams and stadiums. Budweiser's commitment will deploy an innovative off-season program that includes training on the business side of sports from Budweiser executives. Amanda Duffy, president of the National Women's Soccer League, stated that the support will amplify the visibility and influence of the league, players, and avid supporters. The continuation to the #WontStopWatching movement, which encouraged attention all season, not only during high-profile events like the World Cup, and the "Future Official" campaign, which calls on businesses to become the next sponsors of the league, together with their long-term commitments will help grow the game. As U.S. soccer legend Brandi Chastain indicated, Budweiser's sponsorship of the NWSL shows that they aren't just a champion of women's soccer abroad but that they are invested in the further development of the sport in their own backyard.[83] Surveys in other sports routinely show fans are more loyal to league partners than their competitor brands. Keeping that in mind, Anheuser-Busch pledges support to secure fans and sponsors as well as the league.

Anheuser-Busch is a corporation that has chosen an integrated approach in sponsoring a number of sports or leagues. Anheuser-Busch became the official beer of Major League Baseball in 1996 and became the official beer of the NBA in 1998. Bud Light began its sponsorship of Team Seebold in 1982, sponsors the ChampBoat Racing Series team, and became a founding partner of the

Professional Bull Riders in 1993. Anheuser-Busch's sports sponsorship portfolio includes beer sponsorships with the NFL and UFC (Bud Light); MLB and NBA (Budweiser); PGA, LPGA, and Champion's Tours (Michelob ULTRA); and the Kentucky Derby (Stella Artois). The makers of Budweiser and Bud Light are the official beer sponsors of 28 NFL teams, the exclusive alcohol and non-alcohol malt-based beverage sponsor of the Super Bowl, and the official beer of the entire NFL. It has been the official alcoholic beverage of Major League Lacrosse, which also recently added Bud Light as the official sponsor of the MLL All Star Game. Anheuser-Busch has been affiliated with MLL since the league started in 2001 and has sponsored the sport since 2004. They have also been actively engaged in surfing, snowboarding, and sponsorship of the AVP Tour. Blaise D'Sylva, vice president of media, sports, and entertainment marketing for Anheuser-Busch, noted,

> Successful sports marketing execution at Anheuser-Busch is more than purchasing a 30-second spot or signage in a stadium, it is the collective effort of hundreds of people inside the organization, our partners and our wholesalers, working together every day to leverage sports and beer in exciting and innovative ways to connect with our consumers.[84]

Leagues constantly look at sponsorship exchanges that enhance engagement opportunities. For example, throughout the NHL regular season, Stanley Cup Playoffs, and Stanley Cup Final, Truly Hard Seltzer will receive exposure to NHL fans in numerous ways, including the opportunity to try new flavors as they are released. An additional benefit of the sponsorship with the NHL will provide Truly Hard Seltzer with the title sponsorship to the Truly Hard Seltzer NHL PreGame fan festival at the 2020 Bridgestone NHL Winter Classic at Cotton Bowl Stadium and the 2020 NHL Stadium Series at the U.S. Air Force Academy's Falcon Stadium.[85]

Leagues also seek initiatives that drive innovation and grassroots efforts. For example, Major League Baseball and Nike have entered into a 10-year partnership starting in 2020 that will allow Nike to be named the Official Uniform and Footwear Supplier of MLB. In this huge deal, Nike will brand all the uniforms, other outerwear, and training gear. An additional benefit will be a strategic alliance with Fanatics, a global leader in licensed sports merchandise, that will allow MLB branded gear to be made readily available to fans everywhere. "Nike's global brand and reputation as a leader in marketing and driving innovation makes them an ideal partner," said MLB commissioner Rob Manfred. "In addition, Fanatics is a valuable partner who has proven to serve our fans with speed, agility and quality service. We're very excited about the possibilities this unique arrangement provides us over the next decade."[86]

The Ben Hogan Tour was established in 1990 as a breeding ground for golf professionals who have not cracked the PGA. In 1993, Nike sponsored the tour, followed by Buy.com, which ended its sponsorship in 2002. In 2014, Web.com became the fifth title sponsor in the history of the PGA Tour's developmental

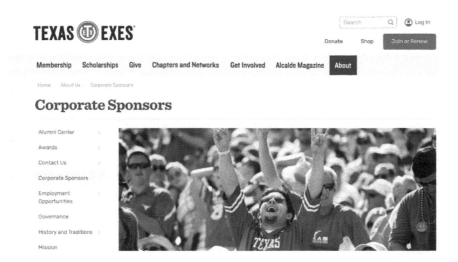

Web Capture 11.3
University of Texas's corporate partner program

Credit: The Texas Exes, the alumni association for UT Austin

URL: www.texasexes.org/about-us/corporate-sponsors

circuit, replacing Nationwide. According to the PGA, the 10-year agreement comes four months after the tour also renewed its deal for the FedExCup, a $35-million bonus series.[87] In 2013, the tour negotiated a nine-year television deal with NBC Sports and CBS Sports, establishing television contracts through 2021. The Web.com Tour serves to become the primary path for players to reach the PGA Tour.

Nike elevated its sponsorship with its addition as a title sponsor of the Winter Dew Tour's season opener, the Nike 6.0 Open. The event, hosted at Breckenridge Ski Resort, provides a platform for Nike to engage in the growing winter action sports scene. Nike, originally an associate-level partner, will receive tourwide exclusivity in the footwear, athletic and casual apparel, and outerwear categories as well as receiving fully integrated marketing benefits that include television ads and online exposure. Nike's linkage with an event such as the Winter Dew Tour illustrates the strength of the property and the brand's commitment to the industry. Lately, a variety of action sports properties have been trying to organize themselves to become more attractive to sponsors. Partnerships across these platforms provide benefits to enhance the involvement and further leverage sponsorship offerings thereby enhancing the procurement of the ultimate dollar.[88]

Action sports were not the first property to think about how best to serve the interests of sponsors. NFL Properties was designed in 1963 primarily to meet and beat the competition posed by Major League Baseball. The league, in attempting to offer a competitive advantage to sponsors, built a system whereby potential sponsors receive collective and individual team rights. That is, sponsors can create opportunities or promotions that feature all NFL teams and local teams in a local market.[89]

Sponsors choose to use the power of the league and its recognizable league logo and therefore support all the teams. From the sponsors' perspective, this represents easy and less expensive one-stop shopping. As Burton points out, "If an NFL corporate partner had to design individual local contracts to secure key markets, the collective local team fees would quickly surpass the single sponsorship fee." By allowing sponsors the opportunity to receive collective team rights, the league gains enhanced exposure. As an example, Bose, Inc. (already the official home audio sponsor of the NFL) and the National Football League announced an extension for Bose to replace Motorola to put its corporate logo on the headsets worn by all coaches during games.

Events

An athletic platform that is most commonly associated with sports marketing is the event. In a world where place-marketing is seen as essential to the success of urban centers large and small, garnering attention is imperative to the cause, implementation, and success of these events.[90] Sports stars and brands attract people, but, often more importantly, they attract the media. These events serve to showcase cities worldwide. Cities such as Tokyo, Paris, Los Angeles, Budapest, Rio de Janeiro, New York, and Doha are often front runners in the list of hosting events. In fact, according to Sportcal's data-driven Global Sports Impact (GSI) Nations Index, which analyzed 718 world championships and multisport games in 83 cities over a rolling 14-year period (excluding U.S. cities), Tokyo, Japan, was identified as the number-one city worldwide. The GSI Nations and Cities Index is based on in-depth analysis of major multisport games and world championships and in total includes 90 nations and 641 cities. GSI ratings are calculated using the latest event data across a range of indicators that measure the size, scale, and impact of an event.[91]

The advantages of using an event as an athletic platform are similar to those benefits gained by using other athletic platforms. For instance, the event will hopefully increase awareness and enhance the image of the sponsor. Investing in staging sport is ultimately a matter of turning the entire host environment into a stage, and although attracting sport tourists to the event is the immediate aim, the event is intended to lodge appealing imagery of place with a wider audience for a much longer period.[92] In addition, consumers have a forum in which to use and purchase the sponsor's products. For example, Top Golf hosted an interactive swing simulator open to all ticket holders at its vehicle display trailer. Fans were afforded the opportunity to take shots on computer-generated courses aligned with major PGA tournaments (see Photo 11.2). Additionally, to honor the new partnership between Ford and the Kentucky Derby, Ford hosted on-site activations throughout Derby Week, including special access for FordPass Rewards members, plus celebrations for veterans and active duty military personnel. In another example, Cincinnati Reds fans received refrigerator and car magnet season schedules courtesy of PNC, who were also sponsors of many other promotions at the ballpark.

Examples of sporting events sponsorship are plentiful, as are the opportunities to sponsor sporting events. However, sometimes the number of events far outweighs the number of "potentially available" corporate sponsors. In fact, research has shown that "showcase justification," which conceives the sport as less intrinsically important than its holistic, picturesque location, must be strategic and long term. As Rowe noted, hosting sporting events "does advocate looking closely at the hyperbole, concealed self-interest, confected populism and voodoo economics that try to submerge the enduring question: 'cui bono' (who benefits)?"[93] In fact, if not, the result can be catastrophic (e.g., Rio de Janeiro), for affected communities, including forced and permanent displacement, corrupt and unethical conduct by government and business, and shoddy work requiring subsequent rectification.[94]

Event planners often spend millions of dollars, whether it be of youth or professional orientation, to turn communities into tourist attractions, to impact quality of life with respect to physical, social, psychological, and environmental health for all participants during the course of the event. However,

Photo 11.2a
Companies such as TopGolf and CDW utilize athletic platforms to increase awareness and enhance networking opportunities

Source: Lyberger/Wend

Photo 11.2b *continued*

as research often demonstrates, these outcomes often produce significant challenges.[95] For example, the city of Winnipeg staged two national and international sporting events over the space of 16 months. In a city that ranks as the eighth largest in Canada and has a population of only around 680,000, the challenge was to find enough corporate sponsors. In response to this challenge, event organizers were forced to be more creative in designing sponsorship packages that appealed to organizations of all sizes.[96]

As with the other athletic platforms, one of the primary disadvantages of using events as an athletic platform is sponsorship clutter. For example, the 2020 Super Bowl had a record $435 million in game-day advertising with over 44 official NFL Super Bowl sponsors and another 44-plus sponsors of the Miami planning committee.[97] In other words, sponsors are competing with other sponsors for the attention of the target audience. One popular way to combat this clutter is to become the title sponsor or presenting sponsor of an event. Every college football bowl game now has a title sponsor. For example, Northwestern Mutual has been the presenting sponsor of the Rose Bowl Game since 2014. Northwestern Mutual annually places a floral float in the Rose Parade and has supported other Tournament of Roses-related events. The Rose Bowl Parade has 37 million viewers nationally, 28 million viewers internationally, and an estimated live attendance of 700,000. The Rose Bowl game has approximately 18.2 million viewers nationally and an estimated attendance of 91,853.[98]

Choosing the specific athletic platform

The choice of a particular athletic platform follows the selection of the general platform. At this stage of the sponsorship process, the organization makes a decision regarding the exact athlete(s), team, event, or sports entity. For instance, if the organization decides to sponsor a professional women's tennis player, who will be chosen – Serena or Venus Williams or Maria Sharapova? As with the previous decisions regarding sponsorship, the choice of a specific sponsor is based largely on finding the right "fit" for the organization and its products.

A recent trend is for sports marketers to ensure and control the fit by manufacturing their own sporting events. For example, Nike has created a division to create and acquire global sporting events. By creating their own events, Nike will be able to control every aspect of how each event is marketed. Moreover, Nike will be able to develop events that are the perfect fit for their multiple target markets.[99] Other organizations, including sponsors and sponsees such as NFL and Honda, are pursuing similar strategies. Honda has put pressure on their advertising agency to develop sporting events that will be the ideal match for the Honda target market. For example, Honda is jumping into the esports arena as a major sponsor of the NHL. They are sponsoring an esports gaming challenging featuring players from all NHL teams playing EA Sports NHL20 against one another.[100]

Once the decision regarding the general level of sponsorship and the specific athletic platform has been addressed, it may be useful to review carefully the choice(s) of sponsorship before taking the final step. To do so, Brant Wansley of BrandMarketing Services, Ltd., offers the following suggestions for choosing a sponsorship.[101]

- Does the sponsorship offer the right positioning?
- Does the sponsorship provide a link to the brand image?
- Is the sponsorship hard for competitors to copy?
- Does the sponsorship target the right audience?
- Does the sponsorship appeal to the target audiences' lifestyle, personality, and values?
- How does the sponsorship dovetail into current corporate goals and strategies?

- Can the sponsorship be used for hospitality to court important potential and current customers?
- Is there a way to involve employees in the sponsorship?
- How will you measure the impact of the sponsorship?
- Can you afford the sponsorship?
- How easy will it be to plan the sponsorship year after year?
- Does the sponsorship complement your current promotion mix?

Sponsorship implementation and evaluation

Once the sponsorship decisions are finalized, plans are put into action and then evaluated to determine their effectiveness. Do sponsorships really work? The findings to this million-dollar question are somewhat mixed. In Chapter 13, we discuss the techniques organizations use to determine whether the sponsorship has met their objectives. For now, let us look at the results of several studies that were conducted to determine consumer response to sponsorship. In a poll conducted by Performance Research, more than half of the respondents indicated they would be "not very likely" or "not at all likely" to purchase a company's products because it was an Olympic sponsor.[102]

Most studies report that sponsorship is having a positive impact on their organizations. For example, Visa reported that since its affiliation with the Olympic Games, its market share in the United States increased by one-third, but the number of consumers who considered it the best overall card doubled to 61 percent.[103] Delta Air Lines also increased awareness levels from 38 percent to 70 percent due to its Olympic sponsorship. A recent study by the International Olympic Committee found that 22 percent of respondents would be more likely to buy a product if it were an Olympic sponsor's product.[104] In another study, roughly 60 percent of consumers indicated that they "try to buy a company's product if they support the Olympic Games."[105] In addition, 57 percent of consumers around the world agreed that "they look favorably towards a company if it is associated with the Olympics."

However, some researchers found that the majority of consumers say sponsorship makes no difference to them and their purchase behavior. For example, Quester and Lardinoit conducted a study and found that Olympic sponsors could not expect to find higher levels of brand recognition or loyalty.[106] Additionally, a study by Pitts and Slattery found that over 60 percent of respondents said they would not be more likely to purchase a product, but 40 percent were, just because they knew it was a sponsor's product.[107] One potential reason for these less-than-encouraging findings is the amount of sponsorship clutter. For example, Ohio-based Wendy's, which had been an OSU sponsor for "more than two decades," decided to drop its sponsorship with the school "under pressure from activist investors to reduce costs and improve its financial performance."[108] The company has also ended its sponsorships of a local LPGA tournament and the Columbus Blue Jackets. Other reasons that sponsorships are dropped or fail are highlighted in Table 11.8.

A study by Krugler noted sponsorship confusion is material to about half of consumers.[109] Well-devised sponsorships are more than just a pure presence tool to increase brand awareness. Fox noted, as more organizations strive to develop multi-faceted relationships with their customers and other publics, sponsorships and events have emerged as an excellent conduit to potentially reach and impact consumers.[110] Evaluating and calculating sponsorship success should be strategic. Measurement and ROI don't end when the sponsorship concludes; one must take time and include a plan for (continued) post-event measurement in the sponsorship strategy. Often, we ask: What did we get in return for the dollars invested? If you just measure progress once, there is a strong likelihood that you're missing out on some meaningful data. Analysis should be standardized from event to event and sponsorship to sponsorship to meet objective measures. While often the notion of increased sales would be welcomed, there are a variety of outcomes in addition to sales.

The most important metrics likely depend on desired outcomes not just for your event sponsorship but also your organization (see Figure 11.6). Successful events are those that cultivate the desired outcomes among target publics and yield a good ROI.[111] According to Fox, research can provide an objective, quantitative evaluation of its impact on your target public.[112] Leadership should insist that the "normal course of business" include using research to develop and evaluate events. The research should be consistent and accountable, because, when done correctly, it can help enhance creativity and develop on-target sponsorships and events with a high likelihood of success, The ROI you can show will strengthen exchange values – and can positively impact sponsorship and event planning in the future.

Other reasons that sponsorships are dropped or fail are highlighted in Table 11.8.

Summary

The element of the promotional mix that is linked with sports marketing to the highest degree is sponsorship. A sponsorship is an investment in a sports entity (athlete, league, team, or event) to support overall organizational goals, marketing objectives, and/or promotional objectives. Sports sponsorships are growing in popularity as a promotional tool for sports and nonsports products (and organizations). For example, it is projected that $62 billion will be spent globally on sport sponsorships in 2024.[113] Because so much emphasis is placed on sponsorship, an organization must understand how to develop the most effective sponsorship program.

ARTICLE 11.9
CAREER SPOTLIGHT

Lesa Ukman

Lesa Ukman is a thought-leading entrepreneur, writer and speaker renowned as a pioneer in assigning value to marketing collaborations. She has propelled sponsorship from a promotional sideline to a vital discipline by creating the methodology to value and measure investments in sports, arts, entertainment and nonprofits. Her analytics have been adopted throughout the world.

While working for the City of Chicago Mayor's Office of Special Events in 1980, Lesa devised the first-ever public/private partnership programs, which still serve as the blueprint for municipal marketing.

Driven by the then-radical idea that businesses that partner with the things people love – sports, music, festivals and nonprofit causes – vastly outperform competitors, she founded IEG (sponsorship.com) in 1982. Her ideas caught the imagination of the business world, giving rise to an industry now worth more than $85 billion. In 2006 she sold IEG to WPP, the world's largest advertising, marketing and communications services group.

Lesa is an avid champion of the industry and a keen observer of sponsorship's broader impact on society. This includes expanding the notion of ROI to incorporate social as well as financial outcomes. For over three decades she has piloted the annual IEG Conference, which remains a must-attend event for professionals seeking to make the most of their sponsorship relationships.

She coined the term "Corporate Social Opportunity" to supplant "Corporate Social Responsibility", reflecting her belief that value is created when "doing good" is embedded in a company's DNA rather than limited to departments designated for philanthropy or community affairs.

In May 2016, Lesa launched a new venture, Lesa Ukman Partnerships. Its first offering is the ProSocial Valuation Service® (prosocialvaluation.com), an innovative methodology to bring social capital into partnership valuation. This situates sponsorship relationships in our current dynamic environment – a marketplace in which purpose, passion and community are in high demand. Unlike ROI analytics, which calculate financial return for the sponsor, her new service will measure the social value generated by partnership activations.

"Brands and rightsholders need to understand the social value created by their partnerships in the same way they measure profits generated. This enables employees to determine what initiatives they want to volunteer for, and for brands to understand where to invest their dollars for the biggest social impact and what to avoid as inauthentic to their customers."

Lesa is a sought-after keynote speaker, serves on various boards and she is a professor at Northwestern University's School of Professional Studies, where she teaches Sponsorship, Sports & Entertainment Marketing.

Credit: Lesa Ukman Partnerships

URL: www.lesaukman.com/about/

FOUR STEPS OF DATA BASED SPONSORSHIP ANALYSIS

01 FAN-SEGMENTATION	02 TAILORED COMMUNICATION	03 HOLISTIC EVALUATION	04 SMART OPTIMISATION
Understand your sponsorship target group (FANDNA™)	Develop data-driven activation concepts for your target groups (FANSTORIES™)	Evaluate your sponsorship activities holistically (ROSI)	Improve your Return on Sponsorship Invest continuously (ROSI CONSULTING)

Figure 11.6

Source: Nielsen Sports

Table 11.8 Why sponsorships fail

No Budget for Activation – Be prepared to spend several times your rights fees to leverage the property.

Not Long-Term – One-year commitments generally don't work. It takes time to build the association.

No Measurable Objectives – Must have internal agreement on sponsorship goals.

Too Brand-Centric – Sponsorship should be based on the needs of consumers not brands.

Overlook Ambush and Due Diligence – Knowing what you are not getting is as important is as what you are getting.

Too Much Competition for Trade Participation – When products sold through the same distribution channel sponsor the same property, the impact is diluted.

Failure to Excite the Sales Chain – A sponsorship program will not work unless the concept is sold throughout the entire distribution channel.

Insufficient Staffing – Additional staffing is needed to meet the time demands of sponsoring an event.

Buying at the Wrong Level – Higher sponsorship levels equate to more benefits. Make sure you are reaping all the benefits or buy at a lower level.

No Local Extensions – National brands must create localized execution overlays for a sponsorship to truly reach their audiences.

No Communication of Added Value – For maximum impact, sponsors must be viewed as bringing something to the event. The activity should be "provided by" the brand rather than "sponsored by" it.

The systematic process for designing a sponsorship program consists of four sequential steps, setting sponsorship objectives, determining the sponsorship budget, acquiring a sponsorship, and implementing and evaluating the sponsorship. Because sponsorship is one of the promotional mix elements, it is important to remember the relationship it has with the broader promotional strategy. As suggested in Chapters 9 and 10, all the elements of the promotional mix must be integrated to achieve maximum effectiveness.

The sponsorship process begins by setting objectives. These objectives, not unlike advertising objectives, can be categorized as either direct or indirect. Direct sponsorship objectives focus on stimulating consumer demand for the sponsoring organization and its products. The sponsoring company benefits by attaching their product to the sports entity. The sports entity also benefits by increased exposure given by the sponsor. As such, both parties in the sponsorship agreement benefit through the association. Indirect objectives may also be set for the sponsorship program. These objectives include generating awareness, meeting and beating the competition, reaching new target markets (e.g., disabled) or specialized target markets (e.g., mature market), building relationships with customers, and enhancing the company's image.

After objectives have been formulated, the sponsorship budget is considered. The techniques for setting sponsorship budgets are also in accord with the promotional budgeting methods discussed in the previous chapter. Generally, sponsorship of sporting events is not an inexpensive proposition, especially given the threat of ambush marketing. Ambush marketing is the planned effort by an organization to associate themselves indirectly with an event to gain at least some of the recognition and benefits that are associated with being an official sponsor. In past years, the Olympics have been a playground for ambush marketing techniques. For example, Nike, not an official sponsor of the 1996 Summer Olympics, constructed a building overlooking the Olympic Park to associate themselves with the festivities of the Olympic Games. Today, more stringent policing and regulation of ambush marketing is occurring by sporting event organizers to protect the heavy financial outlay of official sponsors.

The third step of the sponsorship process is to choose the sponsorship opportunity or acquire the sponsorship. This means making decisions about the scope of the sponsorship, choosing the general athletic platform, and then choosing the specific athletic platform. The scope of the sponsorship refers to the geographic reach of the sports entity, as well as the interest in the entity. Shani and Sandler describe the scope of athletic events using a tool called the Sports Event Pyramid. The Sports Event Pyramid is a hierarchy of events based on geographic scope and level of interest among spectators. The five-tiered hierarchy ranges from international events, such as the Olympic Games, to local events, such as a Little League tournament in your community. Once the scope of the sponsorship has been chosen, the athletic platform must be determined. The athletic platform for a sponsorship is generally a team, sport, event, or athlete. In addition, the athletic platform could be further categorized on the basis of level of competition (i.e., professional, collegiate, high school, or recreational). Decisions regarding the choice of athletic platform should be linked to the objectives set in the previous stages of sponsorship planning. After choosing the general athletic platform, the potential sponsor must select the specific platform. For example, if a collegiate sporting event is to be the general platform, then the specific athletic platform may be the Rose Bowl, the Championship Game of the Final Four, or a regular season baseball game against an in-state rival.

The final phase of the sponsorship process is to implement and evaluate the sponsorship plans. Organizing a sponsorship and integrating a sponsorship program with the other promotional mix elements requires careful coordination. Once the sponsorship plan is put into action, the most critical question for decision makers is, "Did the program deliver, or have we met our sponsorship objectives?" The implementation and evaluation of the strategic sports marketing process and, more specifically, sponsorships are considered in Chapter 13.

Key terms

- ambush marketing
- athletic platform
- awareness
- competition
- decision maker
- direct sponsorship objectives
- gatekeepers
- global events
- image building
- indirect sponsorship objectives
- influencers
- international events
- local events
- national event
- match-up hypothesis
- purchasers
- reaching new target markets
- regional events
- relationship marketing
- sales increases
- sponsorship
- sponsorship budgeting methods

- sponsorship evaluation
- sponsorship objectives
- sponsorship program
- sport sponsorship acquisition
- sports event pyramid

Review questions

1 Define sponsorship and discuss how sponsorship is used as a promotional mix tool by sports marketers. Provide evidence to support the growth of sports sponsorships worldwide.
2 Outline the steps for designing a sports sponsorship program.
3 Discuss, in detail, the major objectives of sports sponsorship from the perspective of the sponsoring organization.
4 What is ambush marketing, and why is it such a threat to legitimate sponsors? What defense would you take against ambush marketing tactics as a sports marketer?
5 In your opinion, why are sports sponsorships so successful in reaching a specific target market?
6 How are sponsorship budgets established within an organization?
7 Describe the various levels of the sponsorship pyramid. What is the Sports Event Pyramid used for, and what are some potential problems with the pyramid?
8 Define an athletic platform. In determining what athletic platform to use for a sponsorship, what factors should be considered?
9 What questions or issues might an organization raise when choosing among sponsorship opportunities?
10 Describe the different ways that sports sponsorships might be evaluated. Which evaluation tool is the most effective?

Exercises

1 Design a proposed sponsorship plan for a local youth athletic association.
2 Provide five examples of extremely good or effective match-ups between sporting events and their sponsors. In addition, suggest five examples of extremely poor or ineffective match-ups between sporting events and their sponsors.
3 Find at least one example of sponsorship for each of the following athletic platforms: individual athlete, team, and league.
4 Contact an organization that sponsors any sport or sporting event and discuss how sponsorship decisions are made and by whom. Also, ask about how the organization evaluates sponsorship.
5 Design a survey to determine the influence of NASCAR sponsorships on consumers' purchase behaviors. Ask 10 consumers to complete the survey and summarize the findings. Suggest how NASCAR might use these findings.

Internet exercises

1   Search the Internet and find an example of a sponsorship opportunity at each level of the Sports Event Pyramid.

2   Locate at least three sports marketing companies on the Internet that specialize in the marketing of sponsorship opportunities. What products or services are these organizations offering potential clients?

Notes

1   J. Newell, "KU Athletics, Undeterred by FBI Probe, Signs Lucrative Contract Extension with adidas," *Kansas City Star* (April 24, 2019). Available from: www.kansascity.com/sports/college/big-12/university-of-kansas/article229625079.html, accessed January 22, 2020.

2   The Repo, "Global Sports Sponsorship Market to Record Strongest Growth in a Decade Reaching $48bn in 2020" (January 30, 2020).

3   IEG Sponsorship Report, "Sponsorship Spending Growth Slows in North America as Marketers Eye Newer Media and Marketing Options" (January 7, 2014). Available from: www.sponsorship.com/iegsr/2014/01/07/Sponsorship-Spending-Growth-Slows-In-North-America.aspx, accessed May 9, 2014.

4   WARC Data, "Global Ad Trends" (2020). Available from: http://content.warc.com/rs/809-PJV-078/images/WARC_Global_Ad_Trends_Sports_Sponsorship_SAMPLE.pdf.

5   Ibid.

6   DreamTeam Token, "Sponsorships Market in Competitive Esports: Up and Running," *DreamTeam* (November 20, 2018). Available from: https://medium.com/dreamteam-gg/sponsorships-market-in-competitive-esports-up-and-running-32878447073f, accessed May 27, 2020.

7   Phil Stephan, "Data, Digital and Sponsorship's Future," *TwoCircle.com* (May 2019). Available from: https://twocircles.com/us-en/articles/digital-data-and-sponsorships-future/, accessed February 24, 2020.

8   Pat Evans, Fundamentals 2020, "Sports Sponsorships to Drop 37%," *Front Office Sports* (May 19, 2020). Available from: https://frontofficesports.com/sports-sponsorships-2020-projection/.

9   Ibid.

10   Ibid.

11   Ibid.

12   E. Jessiman, "NHL Sponsorships: Richer Than They Think," *The Hockey News* (2019). Available from: https://thehockeynews.com/news/article/nhl-sponsorships-richer-than-they-think, accessed March 9, 2020.

13   WARC Data, "Global Ad Trends" (2020). Available from: http://content.warc.com/rs/809-PJV-078/images/WARC_Global_Ad_Trends_Sports_Sponsorship_SAMPLE.pdf.

14   Ibid.

15   Ibid.

16   Twenty20 (2014). Available from: http://en.wikipedia.org/wiki/Twenty20, accessed June 29, 2014.

17   Ibid.

18 "Global Cricket Sponsorship Spend Hits $405 Million US. The Sponsorship Award 2022." Available from: https://www.sponsorship-awards.co.uk/news/global-cricket-sponsorship-spend-hits-us405-million.

19 Ibid.

20 Mark Lyberger, "Responses Submitted to Editor John Kiernan, 2014 FIFA World Cup by the Numbers," *Wallethub.com* (June 9, 2014). Available from: http://wallethub.com/blog/world-cup-by-the-numbers/4433/#ask-the-experts, accessed June 29, 2014.

21 IEG Sponsorship Report, "Sponsorship Spending Growth Slows in North America as Marketers Eye Newer Media and Marketing Options" (January, 7, 2014). Available from: www.sponsorship.com/iegsr/2014/01/07/Sponsorship-Spending-Growth-Slows-In-North-America.aspx, accessed May 9, 2014.

22 "First Hoop Is a Slam Dunk for 10 High School Athletic Departments for Its 15th Season – By First National Bank" (n.d.). Available from: https://waldo.villagesoup.com/p/first-hoop-is-a-slam-dunk-for-10-high-school-athletic-departments-for-its-15th-season/1852017.

23 S. Axson, "Nike, NBA Reveal New Game Uniforms" (July 18, 2017). Available from: www.si.com/nba/2017/07/18/nike-new-nba-uniforms.

24 "FIFA and adidas Extend Partnership until 2030." Available from: https://www.adidas-group.com/en/media/news-archive/press-releases/2013/adidas-and-fifa-extend-partnership-until-2030/ (January 21, 2013).

25 LA Clippers (2020). Available from: www.nba.com/clippers/community?query=community%20engagement&utm_source=website&utm_medium=&utm_campaign=default, accessed May 13, 2020.

26 "About Us" (n.d.). Available from: http://westonfc.org/about-us/, accessed May 18, 2020.

27 Pgatour.com, "From Runways to Fairways: Our 2018 Fashion Experience" (July 11, 2018). Available from: www.pgatour.com/tournaments/the-northern-trust/news/2018/07/11/runways-fairways-the-northern-trust-golf-fashion.html.

28 IOC, "IOC and Samsung Extend Partnership through to 2028 – Olympic News" (April 20, 2020). Available from: www.olympic.org/news/ioc-and-samsung-extend-partnership-through-to-2028.

29 "Cola Six Pack of Olympic Games Tokyo 2020 – News & Articles" (n.d.). Available from: www.coca-colacompany.com/news/coca-cola-six-pack-of-olympic-games-tokyo-2020.

30 "Sponsorships – Corporate Hospitality," *Wyndhamchampionship.com* (2014). Available from: www.wyndhamchampionship.com/sponsorships/corporate-hospitality/, accessed June 29, 2014.

31 David Stotlar, "Sponsorship Evaluation: Moving from Theory to Practice," *Sport Marketing Quarterly*, vol. 13, no. 1 (2004), 61–64.

32 See, for example, Nigel Pope, "Overview of Current Sponsorship Thought." Available from: www.cad.gu.edu.au/cjsm/pope21.htm; R. Abratt, B. Clayton, and L. Pitt, "Corporate Objectives in Sports Sponsorship," *International Journal of Advertising*, vol. 6 (1987), 299–311; Christine Brooks, *Sports Marketing: Competitive Business Strategies for Sports* (Englewood Cliffs, NJ: Prentice Hall, 1994).

33 Nike News, "Nike Enters 10-Year Partnership with Major League Baseball" (January 15, 2019). Available from: https://news.nike.com/news/nike-major-league-baseball.

34 Janet Hoek, Philip Gendall, Michelle Jeffcoat, and David Orsman, "Sponsorship and Advertising: A Comparison of Their Effects," *Journal of Marketing Communications*, vol. 3, no. 1 (1997), 21–32.

35 K. Kuchefski, "State Farm Enters the Sports Sponsorship Marketplace," *Instant Sponsor* (February 27, 2019). Available from: https://medium.com/instant-sponsor/state-farm-enters-the-sports-sponsorship-marketplace-48fda4e138f, accessed May 26, 2020.

36 Ibid.

37 Dennis M. Sandler and David Shani, "Ambush Marketing: Who Gets the Gold?" *Journal of Advertising Research*, vol. 29 (1989), 9–14; M. R. Lyberger and L. McCarthy, "An Assessment of Consumer Knowledge of Interest in and Perceptions of Ambush Marketing Strategies," *Sport Management Review*, vol. 10, no. 2 (2001), 130–137.

38 Ibid.

39 A. Choi, "Ambush Marketing – Sport Marketing," *USF Sport Management Class Power Point Presentation* (2010).

40 Robert Passikoff, "Ambush Marketing: An Olympic Competition. And Nike Goes for Gold," *Forbes* (August 7, 2012).

41 Asli Pelit, "Revised IOC Sponsor Rules Can't Stop Doritos Ambush and Athlete Ire" (July 23, 2021). Available from: https://www.sportico.com/business/sponsorship/2021/ioc-rule-40-ambush-marketing-1234635038/.

42 A. M. Rodés Portelles, "Ambush Marketing in Sports," *Lexasportiva.com* (April 15, 2019). Available from: https://lexsportiva.blog/2019/04/15/ambush-marketing-in-sports/, accessed May 27, 2020.

43 Robert Passikoff, "Ambush Marketing: An Olympic Competition. And Nike Goes for Gold," *Forbes* (August 7, 2012).

44 Ibid.

45 John Kalogiannides, "Ambush Marketing and the World Cup," *The Sponsorship Place* (June 15, 2014). Available from: www.thesponsorshipspace.com/#!Ambush-Marketing-and-The-World-Cup-/c61r/19361BB8-A4B3-4FDF-A79F-F35F25686904, accessed June 29, 2014.

46 "Brands Set Sponsor Ambush," *Sports Marketing* (November 2000), 2.

47 "In a Risky Action Burger King Uses Anderson Silva to Gain Profit with the Olympic Games" (2012). Available from: www.carlezzo.com.br/en/ler-noticia.php?id=83.

48 Alina Dumitrache, "Mercedes-Benz to Sponsor US Open, Replaces Lexus," *Auto-evolution.com* (October 2009).

49 MLS Staff, "Austin FC Enter Multi-Year Deal with YETI to be Official Jersey Sponsor." Available from: www.mlssoccer.com/post/2020/02/10/austin-fc-enter-multi-year-deal-yeti-be-official-jersey-sponsor.

50 "Title: Daytona 500." Available from: https://www.sportstraveler.net/sports-events/nascar/daytona-500.html.

51 "Paralympic Ticket Sales Smash Records" (September 6, 2012). Available from: https://www.aljazeera.com/sports/2012/9/6/paralympic-ticket-sales-smash-records.

52 Nancy Lough and Richard Irwin, "A Comparative Analysis of Sponsorship Objectives for U.S. Women's Sport and Traditional Sport Sponsorship," *Sport Marketing Quarterly*, vol. 10, no. 4 (2001), 202–211.

53 Dan Migala, "Be a Good Host: How to Increase Revenue Through Non-Traditional Hospitality Outings," *The Migala Report* (June 2, 2004). Available from: http://migalareport.com/node/66, accessed June 24, 2014.

54 Roger Bennett, "Corporate Hospitality: Executive Indulgence or Vital Corporate Communications Weapon," *Corporate Communications: An International Journal*, vol. 8, no. 4 (2003), 229–240.

55 "PGA Tour, Its Tournaments Surpass $3 Billion in All-Time Charitable Giving" (2020). Available from: www.pgatour.com/tournaments/tour-championship/news/2020/01/28/pga-tour-surpasses--3-billion-in-all-time-charitable-giving.html, accessed May 27, 2020.

56 "PGA Tour's Final Charity Total for 2009 Hits $108 Million," *Pgatour.com* (January 2010).

57 Alain Ferrand and Monique Pages, "Image Sponsoring: A Methodology to Match Event and Sponsor," *Journal of Sport Management*, vol. 10, no. 3 (July 1996), 278–291.

58 Clipper Around the World, "No Letting Go: Why the Sponsorship Game Is a Long One" (2020). Available from: www.clipperroundtheworld.com/partnerships/insight/no-letting-go-why-the-sponsorship-game-is-a-long-one#:~:text=Slazenger%20provided%20its%20first%20hand,longest%20running%20at%20114%20years, accessed May 31, 2020.

59 Ibid.

60 Ibid.

61 Ibid.

62 Jennifer C. Kerr, "Consumer Group Wants College Sports to Nix the Beer Ads," *Associated Press* (November 12, 2003).

63 Robert Copeland, Wendy Frisby, and Ronald McCarville, "Understanding the Sport Sponsorship Process from a Corporate Perspective," *Journal of Sport Management*, vol. 10, no. 1 (1996), 32–48. A. Edwards, "Sports Marketing: How Corporations Select Sports Sponsorships," *The Coaching Director*, vol. 6, no. 3 (1991), 44–47. Jeff Jensen, "Sports Marketing Links Need Nurturing," *Advertising Age*, vol. 65, no. 13 (1994), 30. Stephen Kindel, "Anatomy of a Sports Promotion," *Financial World*, vol. 162, no. 8 (1993), 48. P. Lucas, "Card Marketers Go for the Gold," *Credit Card Management*, vol. 9, no. 2 (1996), 22–26. James H. Martin, "Using a Perceptual Map of the Consumer's Sport Schema to Help Make Sponsorship Decisions," *Sport Marketing Quarterly*, vol. 3, no. 3 (1994), 27–31. Douglas W. Nelms, "Going for the Gold," *Air Transport World*, vol. 33, no. 11 (1996), 71–74. Nigel K. Pope and Kevin E. Voges, "An Exploration of Sponsorship Awareness by Product Category and Message Location in Televised Sporting Events," *Cyber-Journal of Sport Marketing*, vol. 1, no. 1 (1997), 16–27. David K. Stotlar and David A. Johnson, "Assessing the Impact and Effectiveness of Stadium Advertising on Sport Spectators at Division I Institutions," *Journal of Sport Management*, vol. 3, no. 2 (1989), 90–102. Douglas M. Turco, "Event Sponsorship: Effects on Consumer Brand Loyalty and Consumption," *Sport Marketing Quarterly*, vol. 3, no. 3 (1994), 35–37.

64 Roger Williams, "Making the Decision and Paying for It," in *Mark McCormack's Guide to Sports Marketing* (Cleveland, OH: International Sports Marketing Group, 1996), 166–168.

65 Brant Wansley, "Best Practices Will Help Sponsorships Succeed," *Marketing News* (September 1, 1997), 8.

66 "11th Annual IEG/Performance Research: Sponsorship Decision-Makers Survey," *IEG* (March 2011).

67 "Coca-Cola Launches 'Open The Games. Open Happiness' Campaign for the Vancouver 2010 Olympic Winter Games," *Official Press Release – The Coca-Cola Company* (January 2010).

68 IEG, "IEG Esport Sector Update 2018" (2018).

69 Ibid.

70 DreamTeam, "Sponsorships Market in Competitive Esports: Up and Running" (November 20, 2018). Available from: https://medium.com/dreamteam-gg/sponsorships-market-in-competitive-esports-up-and-running-32878447073f, accessed May 30, 2020.

71 David Shani and Dennis Sandler, "Climbing the Sports Event Pyramid," *Marketing News* (August 26, 1996), 6.

72 Christine Brooks, *Sports Marketing* (Benjamin Cummings, University of Michigan Press, 1994).

73 A. Lee, "15 Most Divisive Issues in Sports Right Now," *Bleacher Report* (January 24, 2015). Available from: https://bleacherreport.com/articles/2339584-15-most-divisive-issues-in-sports-right-now, accessed May 31, 2020.

74 Jeremy Mullman, "Is Nike Next? ATA Drops Scandal-Prone Vick; Football Pitchman Faces Indictment for His Alleged Role in Dog-Fighting Ring," *Advertising Age* (June 4, 2007), 6.

75 Ibid.

76 Ibid.

77 Ibid.

78 Bryan McWilliam, "Anheuser-Busch a Sports Sponsorship Heavyweight," *SportsNetworker.com* (May 24, 2013). Available from: www.sportsnetworker.com/2013/05/24/anheuser-busch-a-sports-sponsorship-heavyweight/, accessed May 9, 2014.

79 M. Hall, "NFL Draws Rebukes from Anheuser-Busch, Nike, CoverGirl," *San Diego Union-Tribune* (September 26, 2014). Available from: www.sandiegouniontribune.com/opinion/the-conversation/sdut-covergirl-nfl-game-face-2014sep16-htmlstory.html, accessed May 31, 2020.

80 Katie Thomas, "WNBA Signs Jamba Juice as New Sponsor," *Nytimes.com* (August 2010).

81 Barry Janoff, "WNBA Scores Points in Diversity Marketing," *Mediapost.com* (May 27, 2014). Available from: www.mediapost.com/publications/article/226619/wnba-scores-points-in-diversity-marketing.html, accessed July 1, 2014.

82 Anheuser-Busch, "Budweiser Becomes First Official Beer Sponsor of the National Women's Soccer League" (July 7, 2019). Available from: https://www.anheuser-busch.com/newsroom/2019/07/budweiser-becomes-first-official-beer-sponsor-of-the-national-wo.html, accessed May 30, 2020.

83 Ibid.

84 Ibid.

85 Boston Beer Company Inc., "The Boston Beer Company and NHL Announce Multiyear U.S. Partnership Making Truly Hard Seltzer the Official Hard Seltzer of the NHL" (2019). Available from: www.prnewswire.com/news-releases/the-boston-beer-company-and-nhl-announce-multiyear-us-partnership-making-truly-hard-seltzer-the-official-hard-seltzer-of-the-nhl-300922964.html.

86 M. Brown, "MLB Officially Partners with Nike and Fanatics; To Be Official Uniform and Footwear Provider," *Forbes Inc.* (January 25, 2019). Available from: www.forbes.com/sites/maurybrown/2019/01/25/mlb-officially-partners-with-nike-and-fanatics-nike-to-be-official-uniform-and-footwear-prov ider/#3207807572d2, accessed May 31, 2020.

87 Doug Ferguson, "Web.com Takes Over as Title Sponsor of Nationwide Tour, Starting Right Now," *PGA.com* (2014). Available from: www.pga.com/news/nationwide-tour/webcom-takes-over-title-sponsor-nationwide-tour-starting-right-now, accessed July 1, 2014.

88 "Nike 6.0 Increases Winter Dew Tour Sponsorship with Namesake Breckenridge Stop," *www.theskichannel.com* (September 2010).

89 Rick Burton, "A Case Study on Sports Property Servicing Excellence: National Football League Properties," *Sport Marketing Quarterly*, vol. 5, no. 3 (1996), 23–30.

90 D. Rowe, "For Cities, Hosting Major Sporting Events Is a Double-Edged Sword," *The Conversation* (May 4, 2017). Available from: https://theconversation.com/for-cities-hosting-major-sporting-events-is-a-double-edged-sword-76929, accessed May 30, 2020.

91 Colin Stewart, "GSI Cities Index 2019: Tokyo Retain 'Global Sports City' Title for Second Consecutive Year Ahead of Paris and Budapest" (April 30, 2019). Available from: https://sportcal.com/Insight/Features/125571.

92 D. Rowe, "For Cities, Hosting Major Sporting Events Is a Double-Edged Sword," *The Conversation* (May 4, 2017). Available from: https://theconversation.com/for-cities-hosting-major-sporting-events-is-a-double-edged-sword-76929, accessed May 30, 2020.

93 Ibid.

94 Ibid.

95 R. Pfitzner and J. Koenigstorfer, "Quality of Life of Residents Living in a City Hosting Mega-Sport Events: A Longitudinal Study," *BMC Public Health*, vol. 16, no. 1102 (2016). https://doi.org/10.1186/s12889-016-3777-3.

96 Nancy Boomer, "Winnipeg's Next Flood." Available from: www.marketingmag.ca/Content/1.98/special.html.

97 Richard Collings, "Super Bowl 54 Sets Record with $435 Million In-game Ad Spend, Adweek" (February 3, 2020). Available from: https://www.adweek.com/brand-marketing/super-bowl-54-sets-record-with-435-million-in-game-ad-spend/.

98 Rose Bowl, "Sponsorship Opportunities" (2020). Available from: https://tournamentofroses.com/wp-content/uploads/2019/10/2019-Sponsorship-Oppor tunities.pdf.

99 Jeff Jenson, "Nike Creates New Division to Stage Global Events," *Advertising Age* (September 30, 1996), 2.

100 Dianne Christie, "Honda Sponsors Esports Matchups Between NHL Players," *Marketing Dive* (April 24, 2020). Available from: https://www.marketingdive.com/news/honda-sponsors-esports-matchups-between-nhl-players/576709/.

101 Brant Wansley, "Best Practices Will Help Sponsorships Succeed," *Marketing News* (September 1, 1997), 8.

102 Carol Emert, "Olympic Seal of Approval," *The San Francisco Chronicle* (September 2, 2000), D1.

103 Ibid.

104 Pascale Quester and Thierry Lardinoit, "Sponsors' Impact on Attitude and Purchase Intentions: Longitudinal Study of the 2000 Olympic Games" (December
2001). Available from: https://digital.library.adelaide.edu.au/dspace/handle/
2440/29424.

105 Stuart Elliott, "After $5 Billion Is Bet, Marketers Are Racing to Be Noticed Amid
the Clutter of the Summer Games," *The New York Times* (July 16, 1996), D6.

106 Pascale Quester and Thierry Lardinoit, "Sponsors' Impact on Attitude and Purchase Intentions: Longitudinal Study of the 2000 Olympic Games" (December
2001). Available from: https://digital.library.adelaide.edu.au/dspace/handle/2440/
29424.

107 Brenda Pitts and Jennifer Slattery, "An Examination of the Effects of Time on
Sponsorship Awareness Levels," *Sport Marketing Quarterly*, vol. 13, no. 1 (2004),
43–54.

108 "McDonald's to Sponsor Ohio State Athletics" (March 13, 2007). Available from:
www.bizjournals.com/columbus/stories/2007/03/12/daily9.html?from_
msnbc=1, accessed May 8, 2014.

109 Matthew B. Kugler, "The Materiality of Sponsorship Confusion (January
20, 2016)," *UC Davis Law Review*, vol. 50, no. 1911 (2017); Northwestern Public Law Research Paper No. 16–22. Available from SSRN: https://ssrn.com/
abstract=2628522 or http://doi.org/10.2139/ssrn.2628522.

110 B. Fox, "A Guide to Measuring Event Sponsorships," *Institute for PR* (2005). Available from: www.instituteforpr.org//wp-content/uploads/2005_EventSpon
sorships-Bruce-Jeffries-Fox.pdf, accessed May 31, 2020.

111 Ibid.

112 Ibid.

113 WARC Data, "Global Ad Trends" (2020). Available from: http://content.warc.
com/rs/809-PJV-078/images/WARC_Global_Ad_Trends_Sports_Sponsor
ship_SAMPLE.pdf.

2 Pricing concepts and strategies

After completing this chapter, you should be able to:

- Explain the relationship among price, value, and benefits.
- Understand the relationship between price and the other marketing mix elements.
- Describe how costs and organizational objectives affect pricing decisions.
- Explain how the competitive environment influences pricing decisions.
- Describe how and when price adjustments should be made in the final stage of pricing.

If you were an executive of a sports franchise, what price would you charge your fans? What factors would you consider when making your pricing decision in a continually changing marketing environment? How would you estimate the demand for tickets? Will the financial benefit of increasing prices offset the negative fan relations?

In this chapter, we explore the subjective nature of pricing sports products. More specifically, we consider how factors such as consumer demand, organizational objectives, competition, and technology impact pricing. Also, we examine how pricing interacts with the other elements of the marketing mix and how effective pricing adjustments are made. Let us begin by developing a basic understanding of pricing.

What is price?

Price is a statement of value for a sports product. For example, the money we pay for being entertained by the Boston Celtics is price. The money that we pay for shorts featuring the Notre Dame logo is price. The money we pay for

DOI: 10.4324/9780429030673-15

Photo 12.1
To some, golf lessons may be priceless

Credit: Shutterstock, ID# 812018 by Cindy Hughes

URL: www.shutterstock.com/image-photo/golf-swings-practice-range-812018

a personal seat license, which gives us the right to purchase a season ticket, is price. The money we pay for concessions is price. So is the money we pay to experience the Richard Petty Driving School. In all these examples, the price paid is a function of the value placed on the sports product by consumers.

The essence of pricing is the exchange process discussed in Chapter 1. Price is simply a way to quantify the value of the objects being exchanged. Typically, money is exchanged for the sports product. We pay $26 in exchange for admission to the sporting event. However, the object of value that is being exchanged does not always have to be money. For instance, Play It Again Sports, a new and used sporting goods retailer, allows consumers to trade their previously owned sports equipment for the store's used or new equipment. This form of pricing is more commonly referred to as barter or trade. It is common for kids who exchange baseball cards to use this form of trade. Many golf courses hire retirees and pay them very low wages in exchange for free rounds of golf.

Regardless of how pricing is defined, value is the central tenet of pricing. The value placed on a ticket to a sporting event is based on the relationship of the perceived benefits to the price paid. Stated simply,

$$\text{Value} = \frac{\text{Perceived benefits of sports product}}{\text{Price of sports product}}$$

The perceived benefits of the sports product, or what the product does for the user, are based on its tangible and intangible features. The tangible benefits are important in determining price because these are the features of the product that a consumer can actually see, touch, or feel. For example, the comfort of the seats, the quality of the concessions, and the appearance of the stadium are all tangible aspects of a sporting event. The intangible benefits of going to a sporting event may include spending time with friends and family, feelings of association with the team when they win (e.g., BIRGing), or "being seen" at the game.[1]

The perceived benefit of attending a St. Louis Cardinals game is a subjective experience based on each individual's perception of the event, the sport, and the team. One consumer may pay a huge amount to see the game because of the perceived benefits of the product (mostly intangible), whereas another consumer may attend the game only if given a ticket. In either case, the perceived benefits either meet or exceed the price, resulting in "perceived value."

For the high-involvement sports fan, the Cardinals ticket represents a chance to be able to tell his grandchildren that he saw former star MVP players such as Stan Musial (1943, 1946, 1948), Bob Gibson (1968), Willie McGee (1985), or 2001 Rookie of the Year and 2005, 2008, and 2009 MVP Albert Pujols. To the no- or low-involvement individual, recognition of the historic achievement or the game itself may appear to be a complete waste of time. Again, it is important to recognize that the value placed on attending the sporting event is unique to each individual, even though they are consuming the same product (in this case, a Cardinals game). As researcher Valerie Zeithaml points out, "What constitutes value - even in a single product category - appears to be highly personal and idiosyncratic."[2]

Using a different example, a Honus Wagner baseball card in mint condition may be realized for millions of dollars. At an auction in August 2021, a mint card was purchased for $6.6 million.[3] A collector or baseball enthusiast may see this as a value because the perceived benefits outweigh the price. However, the non-collector (or the mom or dad who threw our cards away) may perceive the card as having barely more value than the cost of the paper on which it is printed.

In yet another example, professional sports franchises are assigned monetary values based on tangibles such as gate receipts, media revenues, venue revenues (e.g., concessions, stadium advertising, and naming), players' costs, and operating expenses. Further consideration in the value of a professional sports franchise is brand equity, a highly intangible characteristic. Table 12.1 provides a list of the franchises with the highest values in each sport and the respective percentage change from the previous year.

The combination of revenue growth and investments in new, revenue-rich ballparks (for example, the New York Yankees and the Dallas Cowboys moved into their new homes in 2010), fueled a significant valuation increase in MLB average team values from an average of $491 million in 2009 to over $1.3 billion.

Table 12.1 Top professional sports franchise values in 2019/2020[5]		
Major League Baseball	Current in millions	1-year change
Yankees	$5,000	+09%
LA Dodgers	$3,400	+03%
Boston Red Sox	$3,300	+03%
Chicago Cubs	$3,200	+ 03%
National Football League	Current in millions	1-year change
Cowboys	$5,500	+10%
Patriots	$4,100	+ 08%
New York Giants	$3,900	+18%
National Basketball Association	Current in millions	1-year change
Knicks	$4,600	+15%
Lakers	$4,400	+19%
Golden State Warriors	$4,301	+23%
National Hockey League	Current in millions	1-year change
Rangers	$1,650	+06%
Maple Leafs	$1,500	+ 03%
Canadiens	$1,340	+03%
Soccer teams worldwide	Current in millions	1-year change
Manchester United	$3,810	–08%
Real Madrid	$4,240	+04%
Barcelona	$4,020	–01%

Source: Forbes.com

The average NFL team is now worth over $2.5 billion. The average hockey team increased their worth to approximately $594 million, while the average NBA teams are worth $1.65 billion, almost a five-fold increase from 2009.[4]

Two important points emerge from the previous examples of value. First, value varies greatly from consumer to consumer because the perceived benefits of any sports product will depend on personal experience. Second, pricing is based on perceived value and perceived benefits. As such, consumers' subjective perceptions of the sports product's benefits and image are fundamental to setting the right price. In this case, image really is everything. All too often, price is equated incorrectly with the objective costs of producing the sports product. Because many sports products are intangible services, setting prices based on the costs of producing the product alone becomes problematic. For instance, how do you quantify the cost of spending time with your friends at a sporting event or having the television rights to broadcast NFL games? How do sports organizations provide a quality experience for fans so they feel they are getting their money's worth?

Many event promoters believe the solution is to add more value via interactive experiences to supplement the core product. For example, the San Diego Padres' Petco Park is spectacular in combining aesthetic sightlines with architectural and natural beauty. The contemporary integration of concourses and seating, collectively with an array of modern amenities, are woven right into the ballpark, which is located in the center of downtown San Diego. Petco offers consumers a variety of choices, including dozens of local food merchants and craft beer. The stadium "beach," a.k.a. kid play area, terrace, park, and upper deck afford a vast array of experiences. Collectively, these choices, blended with the proximal location and access to bars, restaurants, and parking, provide an incredible consumer experience. In a similar vein, the NCAA created Hoop City for the men's and women's Final Four. The interactive experience provides basketball fans a chance to participate in a number of hoop skills contests, get autographs, and share the excitement of the national championship.[6]

Historically, professional and collegiate teams have chosen fans right from the audience to participate in promotions on court or on-field during breaks in play. These interactive experiences allow for multiple exchanges. Whether it is allowing fans to set foot on the playing surface or providing virtual audience experiences, teams continue to explore ways to package inventory and enhance benefits to further enhance entertainment offerings. Deployment of items such as virtual reality to enhance individual game offerings, such as from the San Francisco Giants and Golden State Warriors, as well as virtual season ticket offerings, has become a reality. Teams that create a unique proprietary service/product offering will be able to create new exchanges and revenue. Furthermore, those that use social media to elevate and enhance the level of interaction with their fans will prosper. Utilization of portable smartphones enables teams to provide fans with an interactive experience, thereby enhancing value.

The ultimate question is whether these "extras" create value and add benefits for the fans. For example, Atlanta's Mercedes-Benz Stadium recently opened, affording fans numerous unique features, a retractable roof, the world's largest video board, a three-sided mega column, over 2,500 TVs, 4,000 miles of lightning-fast fiber optics, a giant bird statue, unique sideline suites, incredible views, over 15 local food options, and over 1,260 beer taps. However, it may be the Fan First Menu (see Photo 12.2), which offers reduced food pricing, that may have the ultimate impact.[7] Sport Marketing Research Institute (SMRI) research has found that 9 out of 10 fans attend sporting events out of a love for the game or team. So are these extras creating real fans or trying to buy their way into fans' hearts? Do stadiums and arenas pay more for the interactive fan elements and end up receiving much less in the end – a fan that attends for the extras, not for the love of sports, the competitive element, the rivalry, the action; in other words: the game?

Photo 12.2
Fan First Menu pricing

Credit: Morgan Moriarty

URL: www.sbnation.com/2017/8/26/16141026/new-atlanta-falcons-mercedes-benz-stadium-peach-bowl-sec-championship-playoff

The determinants of pricing

Now that we have discussed the core concept of price, let us look at some of the factors that affect the pricing decisions of sporting marketers. Pricing decisions can be influenced by internal and external factors, in much the same way that the contingency framework for sports marketing contains both internal and external considerations. **Internal factors**, which are controlled by the organization, include the other marketing mix elements, costs, and organizational objectives. **External (or environmental) factors** that influence pricing are beyond the control of the organization. These include consumer demand, competition, legal issues, the economy, and technology. Figure 12.1

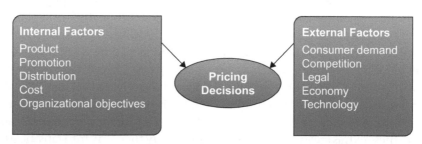

Figure 12.1
Internal and external influences on pricing

Source: Gary Armstrong and Philip Kotler, *Marketing: An Introduction*, 7th ed. 2005. Credit: Kotler, Philip R; Armstrong, Gary, *Marketing: An Introduction*, 4th Edition, © 1997, pp. 471,312

illustrates the influence of the internal and external forces on pricing decisions. Let us look at each of these forces in greater detail.

ARTICLE 12.1
SPORTS MARKETING HALL OF FAME

Pete Rozelle

Pete Rozelle was born in 1926 in a town named South Gate, California. He started his professional football career in public relations with the Los Angeles Rams. From there, Rozelle joined an international public relations firm that had been assigned to promote and raise awareness for the 1956 Summer Olympics in Australia. A year later, Rozelle found himself back with the Rams, but as the general manager this time. After a few unexpected twists and turns, Rozelle found himself being elected as the new NFL commissioner by the time he was 33 years old.

Pete Rozelle led the National Football League for nearly three decades, helping it survive bidding wars with three rival leagues and three players' strikes, before retiring unexpectedly in 1989.

Rozelle's pioneering sports marketing accomplishments include Monday Night Football and the Super Bowl, which blossomed into America's most-watched sporting event. The "Father of the Super Bowl" put the NFL on television just about everywhere and transformed the way Americans spend Sunday afternoons.

Rozelle arrived at about the time as the rival American Football League, a development that created competition for players and television ratings. In 1962, Rozelle negotiated a $9.3 million television contract with CBS, a deal that earned him reelection as commissioner and a $10,000 bonus that pushed his salary to $60,000. By 1966, the two warring leagues, weary of the battle for player talent, merged, creating a single professional football league, with Rozelle as commissioner. The merger also produced a world championship game, which would eventually come to be known as the Super Bowl.

It was Rozelle who brought sports into 10 figures when he negotiated a landmark five-year, $2.1 billion contract with television's three major network in 1982. Then he expanded to cable, selling a Sunday night series to ESPN in 1986. The current television contract, for which Rozelle set the groundwork, is more than 2,000 times what Rozelle got in his first contract with CBS in 1962.

Along with these accomplishments, Rozelle's biggest contribution may have been introducing revenue sharing in pro football 30 years before it created havoc in other sports. Doing so allowed teams in minor markets like Green Bay to equally share TV revenues-the biggest part of the NFL pie-with teams in New York, Chicago, and Los Angeles.

Rozelle is also credited, along with Roone Arledge, for creating Monday Night Football, now the nation's longest-running sports series. Because the NFL had an agreement not to televise on Friday night or Saturday in competition with high school and college football, he decided Monday night would be the obvious time to showcase a single game nationally. Overall, Rozelle's impact was as much social as it was financial. He changed the nation's leisure habits and lifestyle by making Sunday afternoons and Monday nights sacred during football seasons.

For his courageous acts and significant strides made during his tenure as the Commissioner, Pete Rozelle was inducted into the Hall of Fame in 1985. Rozelle passed away 11 years later in December of 1996. It is no question that Pete Rozelle helped shaped the NFL and his efforts will never be forgotten.

Sources: "Innovator Rozelle Dies at 70," *Cincinnati Enquirer* (December 7, 1996), C1, C5 used with permission of Bloomberg L.P. Copyright 2014. All rights reserved

Pete Rozelle's legacy. (2005, January 1). Retrieved from www.profootballhof.com/news/pete-rozelle-s-legacy/

Internal factors
Other marketing mix variables

Price is the element of the marketing mix that has been called a "pressure point" for consumers. That is, price can make or break a consumer's decision to purchase a sports product. Although price is critical, the other **marketing mix** variables must be carefully considered when determining the price of a sports product. Pricing must be consistent with product, distribution, and promotional planning. For marketing goals to be reached, all the marketing mix elements must work in concert with one another.

How is price connected to other marketing mix variables? Let us begin by examining the relationship between price and promotional planning. Each of the promotional mix elements discussed in Chapter 9 (advertising, public relations, personal selling, sales promotions, and sponsorships) is related to price. Broadly, the promotion function communicates the price of the sports product to consumers. For example, advertisements often inform consumers about the price of a sports product. In comparative advertisements, the price of a sports product versus its competition may be the central focus of the message.

Many forms of sales promotion are directly related to price. For example, price reductions are price discounts designed to encourage immediate purchase of the sports product. Coupons and rebates are simply another way for consumers to get money back from the original purchase price. Moreover, premiums are sometimes offered for reduced prices (or for free) to build long-term relationships with consumers. For instance, kids can join the Pittsburgh Pirates Bucaroos Kids Club for just $30 gold membership (silver membership is free) for the entire season. For this, kids receive the following benefits: ticket vouchers, Web-based newsletters and e-mails about other Pirates/Bucaroos special events,

Pirates apparel, invitation to one autograph session, Front-of-the-Line privileges for Kids-Run-the-Bases, and an opportunity to be chosen to participate in select Kids Take the Field events.

The relationship between pricing and promotion also extends to personal selling. Depending on the sports product, sales personnel sometimes negotiate prices. Although not the case for most sports products, some prices are negotiable. The sale of boats, golf clubs, squash lessons, scalped tickets, and luxury boxes each represents an example of a sports product that has the potential for flexible pricing.

The public relations component of the promotional mix is also related to pricing in several ways. First, publicity and public relations (PR) personnel often stress the value of their ticket prices to potential consumers. For example, the Arizona Coyotes public relations department may provide fans information about how the Coyotes have the lowest cost in the NHL for a family of four to attend a game. The Kansas City Royals may emphasize that they have the lowest average ticket prices in baseball compared with other major league sports and teams.

Second, public relations are important in the launch of a new sports product. For example, the Dayton Dragons initiated a PR campaign to engage the public prior to naming the team and the onset of their first season. This PR strategy has helped the Dragons achieve record-setting attendance standards that consist of being the first and only team in minor league baseball history to sell out a season before it began. They continue their record-setting run, having sold out every season since their inception in 2000. Media releases that alert the public to the features of the new product, as well as the pricing, are an important aspect of creating awareness. In addition, sources not only inside but also outside of the sports organization play roles in providing information about changes to the product. For instance, when a professional sports team raises its ticket price, you can bet that the story will generate "negative public relations."

A final link between price and promotion is the cost of the promotion itself. The price of running a promotion may influence potential consumers. The price of a Super Bowl advertisement (upward of a record $5 million for a 30-second spot in 2019), upon becoming public knowledge, may shape consumers' expectations and perceptions of not only the advertisement but also the product and the company. Consumers' expectations for advertisements featured during the Super Bowl are generally higher because of the hype and the advertisement's high price tag. At the same time, the high levels of free publicity generated by Super Bowl advertisements, both prior to and after the event itself, can offset the exorbitant expense and render the advertisements cost effective.

The distribution element of the marketing mix is also related to pricing. The price of a sports product is certainly dictated (in part) by the choice of distribution channel(s). In a traditional channel (manufacturer of the sporting good to wholesaler to retailer to consumer), the costs of covering the various functions of the channel members are reflected in the ultimate price charged to consumers. In a more nontraditional channel, such as purchasing a product over the Internet, prices are generally reduced. For example, the Titleist T2 driver may cost $500 in a golf specialty store but is sold for hundreds of dollars less via the Internet.

The retailer is also a common member of the distribution channel that shapes pricing decisions. More specifically, the type of retailer selling the sporting good or facility where the sporting event takes place will affect price perceptions. For instance, consumers expect to pay more for golf equipment in a country club pro shop than they do at a local golf discount outlet. Likewise, consumers who attended a football game at Dallas's new AT&T Stadium paid an average ticket price of $285 on the secondary market last season, and one would expect to pay higher ticket prices for a newer state-of-the-art facility than do consumers at an aging facility such as Arrowhead Stadium in Kansas City (built in 1972). A concern facing professional sports is that the new sports palaces being built around the country may drive the common fan out of professional sports markets.

A final element of the marketing mix related to price is the sports product itself. The price of attending a sporting event is related to expectations of service quality. The higher the ticket price being purchased, the higher fan expectations of value and customer service. Likewise, the higher the price of the sporting goods, the higher the consumer's expectations of product quality. In this way, price is used to signal quality to consumers, especially to those who have little or no previous experience using the sports product.

Pricing is also used to differentiate product lines within the sports organization. An organization will offer product lines with different price ranges to attract different target markets. For example, Converse still offers a canvas basketball shoe at a low price for traditionalists who prefer canvas over the more popular - and more expensive - leather style.

The product life cycle also suggests the strength of the price-product relationship. As illustrated in Chapter 8, pricing strategies vary throughout the stages of the product life cycle. For example, during the introductory phase, products are typically priced either low to gain widespread acceptance or high to appeal to a specific target market and to signal quality. Product prices are slashed during the decline phase of the life cycle to eliminate inventory and related overhead costs.

The design of sports products is the final factor that demonstrates the close relationship between product and price. Product design and pricing are interdependent. Sometimes, product design is altered during the manufacturing process to achieve a target price. For instance, a number of championship teams have dramatically dropped payroll in the year following winning the championship, causing fan dissatisfaction and poor performance on the field or court. In this case, the product design refers to the quality of the team; the manufacturing process is the team's performance on the field. Unfortunately, the team and its fans may suffer from this move to achieve target price. Other times, prices must be adjusted (usually upward) to achieve the desired product design. New York Yankees late owner George Steinbrenner historically spent large sums of money to build a winning team, with success, as the team appeared in the World Series Championships seven times between 1996 and 2010.

Research has been conducted to examine the relationship between team payroll and team performance in Major League Baseball from 1985 to 2002. The results indicated that the relationship has changed over time. Unlike the early years, there is now a much clearer relationship between payroll and performance. Specifically, in the latter part of the 1990s and continuing into the 21st century, the greater the team payroll and the more equally this payroll is distributed among team members, the better the on-field performance of the team. This is a problem of particular concern because of the growing disparity in team payrolls, which, in turn, affects the competitive balance of the sport.

Clearly, price is closely associated with the rest of the marketing mix. Usually, there are two ways of coordinating the element of price with the rest of the marketing mix variables: nonprice and price competition. Let us look at these two distinctly different pricing strategies in greater detail.

Nonprice versus price competition

Nonprice competition is defined as creating a unique sports product through the packaging, product design, promotion, distribution, or any marketing variable other than price. This approach permits a firm to charge higher prices than its competitors because its product has achieved a competitive advantage. In turn, consumers are often willing to pay more for these products because the perceived benefits derived from the product are believed to be greater. Nevertheless, an element of risk is attached to using this nonprice competition approach.

Consider a commodity like a golf ball. Titleist may adopt a nonprice competition strategy for its brand of golf balls (Pro V1) by featuring the packaging, the product design, or something other than price. This can be a risky strategy for Titleist. What if consumers fail to recognize the superiority of the Pro V1 golf ball? They may instead purchase a competitor's lower-priced golf ball that offers the same benefits.

When adopting the distinctly different **price competition** strategy, sellers primarily stimulate consumer demand by offering consumers lower prices. For example, minor league franchises successfully use price competition to attract dissatisfied fans unable or unwilling to spend large sums of money to attend major league sporting events. In response to a price competition strategy, and to offset its own higher ticket costs, a major league franchise is likely to stress the greater intangible benefits associated with attending its more prestigious events. These benefits include the higher quality of competition, the more exciting atmosphere, and the greater athletic abilities of the stars.

Costs

Costs are those factors associated with producing, promoting, and distributing the sports product. Consider the cost of owning a minor league hockey franchise. To produce the competition or event, players are necessary. These players require salaries and equipment in order to perform. In addition, these players require support personnel such as coaches, trainers, equipment managers, and so on. Also, these players need a place to play, which includes the costs of rent, utilities, cleaning, and maintenance. These represent some of the basic costs for producing a hockey game. However, they do not tell the entire story.

In addition to these core costs, other costs can include advertising, game promotions, and the salaries of front-office personnel (secretaries, general managers, and scouts). Team transportation is another cost. All these costs, or the **total cost** of owning a minor league hockey franchise, can be expressed as the sum of the variable and fixed costs, as shown:

$$TC = FC + VC$$

where
TC = total cost
FC = fixed cost
VC = variable costs

Fixed costs are the sum of the producer's expenses that are stable and do not change with the quantity of the product consumed. Almost all costs associated with the minor league hockey team in the preceding example would be considered fixed. For example, rent on the arena, salaries, and transportation are all fixed costs. They do not vary at all with the amount of the product consumed (or, in this case, the team's attendance). The bulk of the game promotions are determined prior to the season and, as a result, are also considered fixed costs.

Variable costs are the sum of the producer's expenses that vary and change as a result of the quantity of the product being consumed. Advertising may represent a variable cost for the minor league hockey franchise. If advertising expenditures increase from one month to the next because the team is doing poorly at the box office, then the dollar amount spent varies. Similarly, advertising could represent a variable cost if additional advertising or promotions are used because attendance is higher than expected.

Although an athletic team experiences very few variable costs in the total cost equation, a manufacturer of pure sporting goods would encounter a significantly greater number of variable costs. Usually, variable costs for manufacturing a sporting good range between 60 and 90 percent of the total costs. For example, the cost of the packaging and materials for producing the good varies by the number of units sold.

Costs are considered an internal factor that influences the pricing decision because they are largely under the control of the sports organization. The minor league hockey team management makes decisions on player salaries, how much money to spend on advertising and promoting the team, and how the team travels. These costs loom large in the sport franchise because they affect the prices charged to the fans.

Obviously, the most visible and controversial costs incurred by professional sports organizations are player salaries. The Spotlight on Sports Marketing Ethics box discusses whether any athletes are worth the huge payday they are receiving.

ARTICLE 12.2
SPOTLIGHT ON SPORTS MARKETING ETHICS

Astronomical athlete salaries: are they worth it?

It is a great day to take in a ball game, do not you think? With our hustling, bustling jaunt through the economy, we probably deserve a relaxing afternoon of hot dogs and peanuts with my favorite baseball team – the Shady Valley Primadonnas. Of course, the hot dogs and peanuts are overpriced, and you might need a second mortgage on your house to buy the ticket, but the expense is worth watching the finest athletes in the world display their world-class athletic abilities. We might even coax an autograph from the Primadonnas' all-star centerfielder – Harold "Hair Doo" Dueterman.

Are these guys worth it?

Although we thoroughly enjoy the game – the Primadonnas come from behind to win in the bottom of the ninth – our favorite player, Hair Doo, strikes out four times and commits an error in center field. This raises a really, really important question in the grand scheme of the universe: Is Hair Doo worth his $10 gadzillion salary? Should Hair Doo get 100 times the salary of an average, overworked, underappreciated member of the third estate?

Hair Doo's salary really raises another more general question: Why does anyone get paid what they get paid? Any questions we ask about Hair Doo Dueterman's salary could also be asked about the wage of any average, overworked underappreciated member of the third estate – Hair Doo's numbers just happen to be bigger. Because wages and salaries are nothing more than prices, the best place to look for answers is the market.

The market says yes!

Let us first ponder the supply side of the market. Hair Doo performs his athletic prowess before thousands of adoring fans – supplies his labor – because he is willing and able to take on his designated duties for a mere $10 gadzillion. If Hair Doo was not willing and able to play baseball for $10 gadzillion, then he would do something else.

Hair Doo's willingness and ability to play our nation's pastime depends on his opportunity cost of other activities, such as deep sea diving, coal mining, ballet dancing, or game show hosting. By selecting baseball, Hair Doo has given up a paycheck plus any other job-related satisfaction that could have been had from those pursuits. He has decided that his $10 gadzillion salary and the nonmonetary enjoyment of playing baseball outweigh his next best alternative. We should have little problem with this decision by Hair Doo, because we all make a similar choice. We pursue a job or career that gives us the most benefits.

But ... (this is a good place for a dramatic pause) ... someone also must be willing to pay Hair Doo Dueterman $10 gadzillion to do what he does so well. This is the demand side of the process, which we affectionately call the market. It deserves a little more thought.

The someone who's willing to pay Hair Doo's enormous salary, the guy who signs Hair Doo's paycheck, is the owner of Shady Valley Primadonnas – D. J. Goodluck. You might remember D. J.'s grandfather from Fact 3, "Our Unfair Lives," a wheat farmer on the Kansas plains who had the good fortune of homesteading 160 acres with a BIG pool of crude oil beneath. (The Goodlucks still visit the toilet each morning in a new Cadillac. They did, however, sell their ownership in Houston, Texas, and bought South Carolina.)

Why on earth would D. J. and his Shady Valley Primadonnas baseball organization pay Hair Doo this astronomical $10 gadzillion salary? D. J. must have a pretty good reason. Let us consider D. J.'s position.

Hair Doo's statistics are pretty impressive. In the past five years, he has led the league in umpire arguments, souvenir foul balls for adoring fans, product endorsements for nonbaseball-related items, and instigation of bench-clearing fights. All these have made Hair Doo an all-star, number-one fan attraction.

While Hair Doo may or may not help the Shady Valley Primadonnas win the championship, he does pack fans into the stands. And he has packed fans into the stands for the past five years.

Fans in the stands translate into tickets for the Shady Valley Primadonnas, national television broadcasts, and revenue for D. J. Goodluck. D. J. is willing to pay Hair Doo $10 gadzillion to perform his derring-do, because Hair Doo generates at least $10 gadzillion in revenue for the team. If Hair Doo failed to generate revenue equal to or greater than his $10 gadzillion salary, then D. J. would trade him to the Oak Town Sludge Puppies (the perennial last-place cellar-dwellers in the league), send him to the minor leagues, or just release him from the team.

The bottom line on Hair Doo's salary is the same for any average, overworked, underappreciated member of the third estate – an employer is willing and able to pay a wage up to the employee's contribution to production. If your job is making $20 worth of Hot Mamma Fudge Bananarama Sundaes each day, then your boss – Hot Mamma Fudge – would be willing to pay you $20 per day.

Many are worth even more

As entertainers, athletes are paid for fan satisfaction. The more fans who want to see an athlete perform, the more an athlete is paid. In fact, most athletes – even those who make gadzillions of dollars for each flubbed fly ball, dropped pass, and missed free throw – probably deserve even higher salaries. The reason is competition. The degree of competition on each side of the market can make the price too high or too low. If suppliers have little or no competition, then the price tends to be too high. If buyers have little or no competition, then the price tends to be too low.

In the market for athletes, competition is usually less on the demand side than on the supply side. The supply of athletes tends to be pretty darn competitive. Of course, Hair Doo is an all-star player, but he faces competition from hundreds of others who can argue with umpires and hit foul balls into the stands.

The demand side, however, is less competitive. In most cases, a particular team, like the Shady Valley Primadonnas, has exclusive rights to a player. They can trade those rights to another team, like the Oak Town Sludge Puppies, but the two teams usually do not compete with each other for a player's services. There are a few circumstances – one example is "free agency" where two or more teams try to hire the same player, but that is the exception rather than the rule.

With little competition among buyers, the price tends to be on the low side. This means that Hair Doo Dueterman's $10 gadzillion salary could be even higher. It means that the Shady Valley Primadonnas probably get more, much more, than $10 gadzillion from ticket sales and television revenue. It means that D. J. Goodluck would probably be willing and able to pay more, much more, than $10 gadzillion for Hair Doo Dueterman's athletic services. The only way to find out how much Hair Doo is worth to the Shady Valley Primadonnas is to force them to compete for Hair Doo's services with other teams.

This is a good place to insert a little note on the three estates. Most owners of professional sports teams, almost by definition if not by heritage, tend to be full-fledged members of the second estate. The players, in contrast, usually spring from the ranks of the third. The idea that one team owns the "rights" of a player stems from the perverse, although changing notion, that the third estate exists for little reason other than to provide second-class servants for the first two estates.

Colleges are worse

If professional athletes who get gadzillions of dollars to play are underpaid, how do college athletes, who get almost nothing, compare? It depends on the sport.

Big-time college sports, especially football and basketball, are highly profitable entertainment industries. Millions of spectators spend tons of money each year for entertainment provided by their favorite college teams. Star college athletes can pack the fans into the stands as well as star professional athletes. With packed stands come overflowing bank accounts for the colleges.

What do the athletes get out of this? What are their "salaries"? Being amateurs, college athletes are not paid an "official" salary. They are, however, compensated for their efforts with a college education, including tuition, books, living accommodations, and a small monthly stipend. Although a college education is not small potatoes – $100,000-plus at many places – this compensation tends to fall far short of the revenue generated for the school. The bottom line is that bigtime college athletes, like the pros, are usually underpaid.

The reason is very similar to that of the professional athletes. College athletics have limited competition among the "employers" but a great deal of competition among the "employees." Many more high-school athletes hope to play big-time college ball than ever realize that dream. While different colleges may try to hire – oops, I mean recruit – the same athlete, the collegiate governing bodies, most notably the National Collegiate Athletic Association, limit the degree of competition and fix the "wage" athletes can receive. You often hear about the NCAA penalizing a college because it went "too far" in its recruiting efforts. This translates into the charge that a college paid an athlete "too much" to play, such as new cars, bogus summer jobs with high wages, and cash payments from alumni.

Underpayment is most often a problem for big-time football and basketball revenue-generating sports. Athletes in sports with less spectator interest, such as tennis, gymnastics, or lacrosse, actually may be overpaid based on their contribution to their colleges' entertainment revenue.

Here's a tip to keep in mind in the high-priced world of athletics: Athletes are paid based on their contribution to fan satisfaction. If you think athletes are paid too much, then do not contribute to their salaries by attending games or watching them on television. If, however, you enjoy their performance and are willing to pay the price of admission, then worry not about their pay.

Credit: Orley Amos

URL: www.amosweb.com/cgi-bin/awb_nav.pl?s=pdg&c=dsp&k=9

Do you agree or disagree? Whether you agree or disagree with escalating player contracts, there is no dispute that the increasing cost of player salaries has been passed on, in part, to the fans. Table 12.2 shows an example of the Fan Cost Index (FCI) for the MLB. The FCI represents the total dollar amount that a family of four would have to pay to attend a home game. This total cost includes the price of four tickets, two small beers, four sodas, four hot dogs, parking, and two twill caps. The other costs indicate the pricing of one unit. In other words, based on the FCI, the cost of one beer at the Chicago Cubs game is $9.50, while at an Arizona Diamondbacks game, it is $4.00. The major league average for a family of four was $234.38 in 2019. The highest cost was associated with visiting a Chicago Cubs game ($370.12), while the lowest was an Arizona Diamondbacks game ($142.42). The Team Marketing Report FCIs are calculated for all major professional sports leagues.

Although cost is usually considered an internal, controllable factor for organizations, it can have an uncontrollable component. For instance, the league may impose a minimum salary level for a player that is beyond the control of the individual team or owner. The costs of raw materials for producing sporting goods may rise, representing a cost increase that is beyond the control of the manufacturer. Players' unions for professional teams may set minimum standards for travel that are not under the individual team's control. All these examples describe the uncontrollable side of costs that must be continually monitored by the sports marketer.

Organizational objectives

The costs associated with producing a good or service are just one factor in determining the final price. Cost considerations may determine the "price floor" for the sport product. In other words, what will be the minimum price that an organization might charge to cover the cost of producing the sports

Table 12.2 An example of the Fan Cost Index for the MLB

2019 MLB Fan Cost Index	Avg. ticket	AT$ change	Avg. prem.	Beer	Oz	$/Oz	Soft drink	Oz	$/Oz	Hot dog	Parking	Cap	FCI	FCI change
Chicago Cubs	$ 59.49	1.6%	$ 241.99	$ 9.50	16	$ 0.59	$ 5.25	20	$ 0.26	$ 6.50	$ 26.16	$ 20.00	$ 370.12	0.5%
Boston Red Sox	$ 59.32	4.1%	$ 189.81	$ 8.50	12	$ 0.71	$ 5.25	16	$ 0.33	$ 5.25	$ 14.28	$ 21.99	$ 354.54	2.5%
Houston Astros	$ 49.85	23.9%	$ 145.00	$ 6.50	14	$ 0.46	$ 5.00	21	$ 0.24	$ 5.50	$ 15.00	$ 21.99	$ 313.38	19.2%
Washington Nationals	$ 44.12	5.0%	$ 232.67	$ 9.20	16	$ 0.56	$ 6.00	22	$ 0.27	$ 7.00	$ 20.00	$ 15.00	$ 296.48	2.9%
New York Yankees	$ 47.62	0.0%	$ 346.63	$ 6.00	12	$ 0.50	$ 3.00	12	$ 0.25	$ 3.00	$ 27.50	$ 19.99	$ 293.96	-2.5%
San Francisco Giants	$ 38.32	0.1%	$ 110.93	$ 8.25	14	$ 0.59	$ 5.50	16	$ 0.34	$ 6.50	$ 20.42	$ 20.00	$ 278.20	2.4%
Los Angeles Dodgers	$ 42.62	3.6%	$ 164.75	$ 6.25	16	$ 0.39	$ 6.00	20	$ 0.30	$ 6.75	$ 5.00	$ 18.00	$ 274.98	2.6%
Seattle Mariners	$ 37.77	1.2%	$ 138.84	$ 5.00	12	$ 0.42	$ 5.25	16	$ 0.33	$ 6.50	$ 10.00	$ 19.99	$ 258.06	2.7%
St. Louis Cardinals	$ 35.54	0.0%	$ 87.56	$ 5.00	12	$ 0.42	$ 6.25	21	$ 0.30	$ 5.00	$ 17.30	$ 20.00	$ 254.46	-1.0%
Philadelphia Phillies	$ 36.04	0.0%	$ 91.37	$ 6.00	12	$ 0.50	$ 5.00	20	$ 0.25	$ 4.00	$ 18.00	$ 20.00	$ 250.16	0.0%
New York Mets	$ 27.60	0.0%	$ 91.43	$ 11.00	20	$ 0.55	$ 5.75	20	$ 0.29	$ 6.75	$ 25.00	$ 19.99	$ 247.38	1.2%
Kansas City Royals	$ 32.84	-2.2%	$ 134.61	$ 4.00	12	$ 0.33	$ 4.00	16	$ 0.25	$ 5.75	$ 12.00	$ 19.99	$ 230.34	-1.3%
Chicago White Sox	$ 28.38	6.2%	$ 95.32	$ 7.00	16	$ 0.44	$ 5.50	24	$ 0.23	$ 4.50	$ 20.00	$ 17.99	$ 223.50	3.0%
Atlanta Braves	$ 29.44	2.6%	$ 169.05	$ 5.00	12	$ 0.42	$ 5.50	22	$ 0.25	$ 4.25	$ 16.00	$ 19.99	$ 222.74	6.2%
Texas Rangers	$ 25.75	0.0%	$ 66.55	$ 6.00	16	$ 0.38	$ 5.50	20	$ 0.28	$ 6.00	$ 20.00	$ 19.99	$ 220.98	3.7%
Cleveland Indians	$ 31.16	3.7%	$ 76.26	$ 5.00	12	$ 0.42	$ 3.75	12	$ 0.31	$ 4.25	$ 13.00	$ 20.00	$ 219.64	4.5%
Toronto Blue Jays ($)	$ 29.69	14.6%	$ 72.21	$ 5.63	16	$ 0.35	$ 3.94	20	$ 0.20	$ 4.13	$ 15.17	$ 19.52	$ 216.51	1.9%
Colorado Rockies	$ 27.29	4.9%	$ 54.01	$ 3.00	12	$ 0.25	$ 4.50	26	$ 0.17	$ 5.50	$ 19.50	$ 19.99	$ 214.64	8.4%
Detroit Tigers	$ 28.31	0.6%	$ 79.04	$ 5.00	12	$ 0.42	$ 4.75	16	$ 0.30	$ 5.00	$ 10.00	$ 19.99	$ 212.22	5.3%
Oakland Athletics	$ 24.30	0.7%	$ 62.94	$ 6.00	12	$ 0.50	$ 5.00	16	$ 0.31	$ 5.75	$ 20.00	$ 19.95	$ 212.10	6.3%

continued

Table 12.2 continued

2019 MLB Fan Cost Index	Avg. ticket	AT$ change	Avg. prem.	Beer	Oz	$/Oz	Soft drink	Oz	$/Oz	Hot dog	Parking	Cap	FCI	FCI change
Minnesota Twins	$ 32.68	0.2%	$ 74.50	$ 5.00	12	$ 0.42	$ 2.00	16	$ 0.13	$ 4.00	$ 6.00	$ 20.00	$ 210.72	−11.3%
Milwaukee Brewers	$ 28.44	9.0%	$ 51.35	$ 5.00	12	$ 0.42	$ 5.00	24	$ 0.21	$ 6.00	$ 12.00	$ 15.00	$ 209.76	−0.3%
Cincinnati Reds	$ 21.14	0.0%	$ 77.16	$ 6.50	14	$ 0.46	$ 6.25	24	$ 0.26	$ 5.50	$ 10.00	$ 25.00	$ 204.56	7.6%
Los Angeles Angels	$ 30.92	2.2%	$ 162.44	$ 5.00	12	$ 0.42	$ 3.50	16	$ 0.22	$ 5.00	$ 10.00	$ 9.99	$ 197.66	1.9%
San Diego Padres	$ 22.22	2.0%	$ 94.97	$ 6.00	12	$ 0.50	$ 5.50	20	$ 0.28	$ 5.25	$ 16.00	$ 18.00	$ 195.88	2.0%
Baltimore Orioles	$ 29.95	0.0%	$ 51.87	$ 4.00	12	$ 0.33	$ 1.50	12	$ 0.13	$ 1.50	$ 8.00	$ 20.00	$ 187.80	0.0%
Pittsburgh Pirates	$ 22.81	−3.0%	$ 70.87	$ 6.00	16	$ 0.38	$ 3.50	16	$ 0.22	$ 3.50	$ 11.20	$ 19.99	$ 182.42	1.9%
Miami Marlins	$ 22.55	−28.6%	$ 178.36	$ 5.00	12	$ 0.42	$ 3.00	24	$ 0.13	$ 3.00	$ 11.50	$ 19.99	$ 175.68	−23.0%
Tampa Bay Rays	$ 22.53	4.3%	$ 98.55	$ 5.00	12	$ 0.42	$ 5.00	22	$ 0.23	$ 5.00	$ –	$ 10.00	$ 160.12	2.4%
Arizona Diamondbacks	$ 20.86	6.2%	$ 59.76	$ 4.00	14	$ 0.29	$ 2.00	12	$ 0.17	$ 2.00	$ 15.00	$ 9.99	$ 142.42	3.5%
MLB FCI league avg.	$ 32.99	2.1%	$ 119.03	$ 5.97	13.5	$ 0.44	$ 4.60	18.7	$ 0.25	$ 4.95	$ 14.80	$ 18.74	$ 234.38	1.8%

The TEAM MARKETING REPORT
FAN COST INDEX®

*Published March 20, 2019

The Team Marketing Report Fan Cost Index is composed of the prices of four adult average-price tickets, parking for one car, and the least expensive ballpark-available pricing for: two draft beers, four soft drinks, four hot dogs, and two (adult-size) adjustable caps. Costs are determined through calls, emails, and online research with teams, venues, concessionaires, and season ticket holders. Identical questions are asked of all sources. TMR reserves the right to update FCI numbers when additional information is presented and verified.

Average ticket represents a weighted average of season ticket prices for general seating categories. This is determined by factoring the full-season ticket cost for each category as a percentage of the total number of seats in each venue. This takes into account variable pricing. Premium seating (tickets that come with at least one added amenity or classified by team as premium) are not included in the survey to calculate average ticket price. Average premium ticket prices are listed separately. Luxury suites are excluded. Season ticket pricing is used for any team that offers some or all tickets at lower prices for customers who buy season seats. When a seat category is not offered as a season ticket, we use the weighted average price sold by the team. Teams have a say in what seats are considered general or premium.

Beer ounces and soft drink ounces denote size of lowest-priced beverage in ounces.

($) Prices for Toronto tickets and game costs are converted to US dollars using Bank of Canada monthly average exchange rates for the first three months of each year. Note: For year-over-year percentage changes, we compare the team's CAD prices, not the converted USD prices listed in the FCI.

Credit: Fan Cost Index

Rightsholder: Team Marketing Report

URL: www.teammarketing.com

product? Covering costs, however, may be insufficient from the organization's perspective. This depends largely on the organization's objectives. As we have stressed throughout this text, marketing mix decisions – including pricing – must consider the broader marketing goals. Effective marketing goals should be consistent with the organizational objectives.

There are four categories of **organizational objectives** that influence pricing decisions. These are income, sales, competition, and social concerns. **Income objectives** include achieving maximum profits or simply organizational survival. In the long term, all professional sports organizations are concerned with maximizing their profits and having good returns on investment. Alternatively, amateur athletic events and associations are in sports not necessarily to maximize profits but to "stay afloat." Their organizational objectives center on providing athletes with a place to compete and covering costs.

Sales objectives are concerned with maintaining or enhancing market share and encouraging sales growth. If increasing sales is the basic organizational objective, then a sporting goods manufacturer or team may want to set lower prices to encourage more purchases by existing consumers. In addition, setting lower prices or offering price discounts may encourage new groups of consumers to try the sports product. By doing so, the team may increase fan identification and, ultimately, fan loyalty. This will, in turn, lead to repeat purchases.

Another broad organizational objective may be to compete in a given sports market. An organization may want to meet competition, avoid competition, or even undercut competitive pricing. These **competitive objectives** are directly linked to final pricing decisions. Traditionally, professional sports franchises are the "only game in town," and competitive threats are less likely to dictate pricing than they would in other industries.

A final organizational objective that influences pricing is referred to as a **social concern**. Many sports organizations, particularly amateur athletic associations, determine the pricing of their sporting events based on social concerns. For example, consider a local road race through downtown St. Louis on St. Patrick's Day. The organizational objective of this race is to encourage as many people as possible to participate in the community and the festivities of the day. As such, the cost to enter the race is minimal and designed only to offset the expense of having the event.

Regardless of which organizational objective is established, each has a large role in setting prices for sports products. In practice, more than one objective is typically set by the sports organization. However, prices can be determined more efficiently and effectively if the organization clearly understands its objectives. Let us look at an example of how the original MLS mission statement provided direction for pricing.

Major League Soccer's mission statement:

> To create a profitable Division I professional outdoor soccer league with players and teams that are competitive on an international level, and to provide affordable family entertainment. MLS brings the spirit and

intensity of the world's most popular sport to the United States. Featuring competitive ticket prices and family oriented promotions such as "Soccer Celebration" at the stadium, MLS appeals to the children who play and the families who support soccer. MLS players are also involved with a variety of community events.

As indicated in the mission statement, MLS is concerned with profitability for its league and teams. Moreover, the pricing of MLS games should be affordable, so families who support soccer will be financially able to purchase tickets, reflecting a social concern. Finally, the mission statement reflects the competitive nature of pricing. The interaction of the organizational objectives of the MLS should exert a great influence on the price that fans pay to see U.S. professional soccer

External factors

Thus far, we have described the internal, or controllable, determinants of pricing and factors believed to be under the control of the sports marketer. The uncontrollable or external factors also play an important role in pricing decisions. The uncontrollable factors that influence pricing include consumer demand, competition, legal issues, the economy, and technology. Let us turn our discussion to each of these major external factors.

Consumer demand

One of the most critical factors in determining the price of a sports product is **consumer demand**. Demand is the quantity of a sports product that consumers are willing to purchase at a given price. Generally, consumers are more likely to purchase products at a lower price than a higher price. More formally, economists refer to this principle as the law of demand. To better understand the nature of the **law of demand** and its impact on any given sports product, let us examine the price elasticity of demand.

Price elasticity explains consumer reactions to changes in price. **Price elasticity** or **price inelasticity** measures the extent to which consumer purchasing patterns are sensitive to fluctuations in price. For example, if the St. Louis Cardinals raise their Coca-Cola Scoreboard Patio ticket prices from $70.00 to $80.00, will the demand for seats decline? Similarly, if the ticket prices are reduced by a given amount, will the demand increase?

Mathematically, price elasticity is stated as:

$$e = \frac{DQ/Q}{DP/P}$$

where e = price elasticity
DQ/Q = percentage change in the quantity demanded
DP/P = percentage change in the price

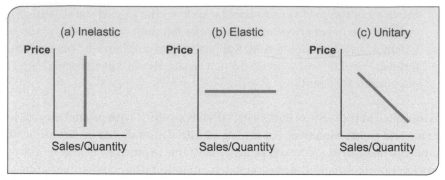

Figure 12.2
Price elasticity of demand

Consumer price elasticity may be described in one of three ways: elastic demand, inelastic demand, or **unitary demand**. Inelastic demand states that changes in price have little or no impact on sales. In the previous example, demand probably would have been inelastic, because even relatively large increases in the ticket prices would have had little impact on the number of fans attending each game. If demand is inelastic, then *e* is less than or equal to 1 (see Figure 12.2a). Because of the great demand for tickets, the Green Bay Packers, who have been sold out on season tickets since 1960, could probably raise their minimum ticket price to $300 and still sell out all their games.

    Elastic demand refers to small changes in price producing large changes in quantity demanded. For example, if the average price of a ticket to a Miami Heat game is reduced from $58.55 to $48.00, and if the number of units sold increases dramatically, then demand is considered elastic, because *e* is greater than 1 (see Figure 12.2b).

    Finally, **unitary demand** is defined as a situation where price changes are offset exactly by changes in demand. In other words, price and demand are perfectly related. A small change in price produces an equally small change in the number of units sold. Similarly, a large change in price causes an equally large change in the number of units sold. In a situation where demand is unitary, *e* is equal to 1 (see Figure 12.2c).

Estimating demand

The basic notion of demand allows sports marketers to explore the relationship between price and the amount of sports product that is sold. In practice, a sports marketer cannot continually change the price of a product and then determine the impact of this price change. Rather, the sports marketer must develop estimates of demand. The three basic factors that are used in **estimating demand** are consumer trends and tastes, availability of substitute sports products, and the consumer's income. Let us briefly explore the three demand factors.

Consumer tastes

Consumer tastes, both as participants and spectators, play an influential role in estimating demand. For example, consumer demand (as spectators) for football is at an all-time high, which influences ticket prices (and the price of rights to televise football). In addition, as reflected in the 2018 NSGA Sports Participation trends can often affect value exchange components. Table 12.3 illustrates a decrease in participation in water sports (-1.6%) and an increase in fitness (6.2%), outdoor (2.3%), team ((1.4%), racquet (0.4%) and winter (1.0%) sports over the six year period. Fluctuation in participation often affects demand of "popular" sports, which will also affect pricing of equipment to consumers.

With sophisticated statistical techniques, sports marketers can understand what, when, and how factors are influencing consumer tastes and the likelihood of purchasing products. For example, demand for a new design of inline skates in any given market may be expressed as a function of a number of factors other than price. These factors can include the number of consumers currently participating in this recreational activity, the desire of recreational skaters to have more technologically advanced skates, the amount that the new skates have been advertised or promoted, or the availability of the skates.

Today, successful players in the sport and entertainment industry look to create innovative solutions utilizing marketing research. **Marketing research**, as defined by the American Marketing Association, is:[8]

> the function that links the consumer, customer, and public to the marketer through information – information used to identify and define marketing opportunities and problems; generate, refine, and evaluate marketing actions; monitor marketing performance; and improve understanding of marketing as a process. Marketing research specifies the information required to address these issues, designs the method for collecting information, manages and implements the data collection process, analyzes the results, and communicates the findings and their implications.

Plain and simple, marketing research is the process of objectively listening to the voice of the marketplace and then utilizing and conveying the information in an ascertainable manner. In the words of David Ogilvy,[9] "if you're trying to

Table 12.3 Sports and fitness activities participated in by U.S. population 6-year trend, ages 6+						
Sport category	2014	2015	2016	2017	2018	2019
Fitness sports	61.3%	61.9%	63.9%	65.5%	66.0%	67.3%
Outdoor sports	48.4%	48.4%	48.8%	49.0%	50.5%	50.7%
Individual sports	45.0%	47.7%	46.8%	46.2%	45.3%	45.0%
Team sports	22.0%	22.6%	23.2%	22.6%	22.8%	23.4%
Water sports	14.0%	14.5%	14.3%	13.8%	13.7%	13.6%
Racquet sports	12.6%	13.1%	13.4%	13.3%	13.2%	13.0%
Winter sports	7.2%	7.8%	8.0%	8.3%	8.2%	8.2%

Source: National Sporting Goods Association

URL: www.nsga.org/

persuade people to do something, or buy something, it seems you should use their language, the language in which they think." Whether it is simple customer comment cards or complex feasibility assessments, the research process affords one the opportunity to enhance the fundamental **marketing** process, the process or function for creating, communicating and delivering value to customers and for managing customer relationships in ways that benefit the organization and its stakeholders.

Marketing research (as discussed in Chapter 3) allows us to estimate demand for new and existing sports products. Firms conduct research to determine consumers' past purchase behavior and the likelihood of their buying a new product. In addition, businesses rely on environmental scanning to monitor changes in the demographic profile of a market, changes in technology, shifts in popular culture, and other issues that may affect the size or tastes of the consumer market.

Environmental scanning and marketing research assist sports marketers in understanding what consumers expect and are willing to pay for sports products. Let us look at how consumers evaluate price (see Figure 12.3).

Figure 12.3
Consumer pricing evaluation process

In the **consumer pricing evaluation process**, acceptable price ranges are determined by consumers' expectations. These expectations are influenced by communicating with other consumers (i.e., word of mouth), promotions or advertising, and, to some extent, past experience in purchasing the products. If the gap between expectations and the actual price is too large, a problem arises for the sports organization. If prices are much higher than expected, the consumer will be much less likely to purchase. However, if prices are much lower, then the quality of the sports product may be called into question.

The sport of professional boxing provides an excellent example of the role past experience plays in determining an acceptable price range for consumers. Fan satisfaction with professional boxing has reached an all-time low because of the short length of heavyweight fights and the heavyweight prices paid by pay-per-view (PPV) customers to watch these fights. To combat this problem of short telecasts, Cablevision introduced a controversial pricing strategy. Consumers who wanted to view the historic title fight between Evander Holyfield and Mike Tyson paid a $10-a-round price with a $50 cap. This innovative strategy apparently sparked a 200 percent jump in sales in Cablevision's 1.99 million PPV homes (a PPV record). Equally important, the product quality was not called into question. Cablevision paid a flat fee (roughly $4 million) for the rights to the fight, and the boxers did not receive any additional money based on the fight's length.[10] The fight still ranks sixth on the all-time PPV list, while the 2015 Mayweather v. Pacquiao fight ranks number one, with 4.6 million PPV viewers.[11]

Along with previous experience with pricing, expectations of future pricing also influence the acceptable range of prices a consumer is willing to pay. For example, when an innovative sports product, such as the Power Block Dumbbell System, is in the introductory phase of the product life cycle, little competition exists and start-up costs are high. Most consumers would expect the price of this product to drop over time, and some may be willing to wait for this to occur. However, sports fans may expect prices to continually rise in the future and purchase the new product immediately rather than waiting for the inevitable higher prices.

Along with expectations of current and future prices, a number of other individual consumer judgments will also play a role in determining the acceptable price range for any given sports product. As shown in Figure 12.3, these variables include consumer income, situational factors, price of substitutes, cost of information search, and perceptions of value.

Consumer income, one of the three demand factors, refers to the consumer's ability to pay the price. Generally, the higher the consumer's income, the wider the range of acceptable prices. For example, a sports fan who has an annual income of $100,000 might perceive a $10 increase in ticket prices as still within his or her price range. However, the same $10 increase in price may be unaffordable to the fan earning $30,000 per year. Significantly, both fans may find the increase in ticket prices unacceptable, but only the latter finds it unaffordable.

The **situational factors** that may affect a consumer's acceptable range of prices include the presence or absence of time, the usage situation, and social factors. Consider the following situations and how each might affect the price you would be willing to pay. First, you are getting ready for a much-anticipated round of golf when you discover you only have one ball left in your bag. Typically, you purchase golf balls at your local discount store for roughly $6 a sleeve (package of three). Given the situation (absence of time), you are forced to "cough up" $12 at the pro shop for the three balls needed to get you through the round. This absence of time to shop for less expensive golf balls caused the acceptable price range to double in this situation.

The next scenario illustrates how your usage situation influences the range of acceptable prices. Imagine you are purchasing a new set of golf clubs that will be used only once or twice a month at the local public course. In this situation, the acceptable price range for this set of clubs might be from $250 to $400. It is likely that you may even purchase less expensive, previously owned clubs. However, if you are planning to use the clubs once or twice a week and are more concerned about their quality and your image, the acceptable range of prices would increase.

The final situation places you in the position of purchasing tickets for the Daytona 500. The cost of purchasing one ticket is approximately $220. You are not a huge car racing fan, and the thought of spending $220 for a ticket seems disagreeable. However, a group of your best friends are attending the event and encourage you to "go along for the ride." You agree and purchase the ticket because of the social situational influence.

Another interesting social situational influence is referred to as the "mob effect." The **mob effect** (or the crowd effect) describes a situation in which consumers believe it is socially desirable to attend "special" sporting events, such as the NBA Finals, bowl games, or the World Series. Because these events constitute unique situations that can never be duplicated, consumers are willing to pay more than usual for the "right" to be a part of the mob (or crowd).

An additional consumer determinant of acceptable prices is the **expected price range of substitute products**. The prices of competitive products will have a major influence on what you deem acceptable. If a sports organization's pricing becomes out of line (higher) versus competition, for example, when a manufacturer like CIME Industries brought 3D printing to the mass production of snowboards, then consumers will no longer pay the higher price.

The **cost of information search** also determines what a consumer considers acceptable. A consumer wanting to purchase a series of tennis lessons has a relatively low cost of information search because information is easily obtained from friends or by calling various tennis professionals. In this case, the cost of the search is less than the benefit of finding the best value. Interestingly, in purchasing a sports product, the cost of information search may be negligible because fans may find the search itself intriguing.

Finally, as discussed previously, **perception of value** will dictate acceptable price ranges for sports products. Remember, perceptions of value will vary from individual to individual and are based on the perceived benefits. The greater the perceived benefits of the sports product, the higher the range of acceptable prices. Most people would consider $400 an outrageous price to attend a single pro football game. However, that cost might look like the bargain of a lifetime if that single game were the Super Bowl.

Availability of substitute products

Another demand factor, other than price alone, that may affect demand is the **availability of substitute products**. Generally, as the number of substitute products for any given sports product increases, demand for the product will decrease. Consider the case of almost any professional sports franchise and substitute products. Typically, there is no substitute product for the professional sports team. Therefore, demand remains relatively unchanged, even when ticket prices are increased (in other words, demand is highly inelastic). For example, there is no substitute product for the St. Louis Cardinals, although baseball is played in St. Louis at the collegiate, high school, and amateur levels. However, consumers may choose to spend their sports dollars on purchasing televised broadcasts of the Cardinals rather than paying the price increase.

Consumer's income

The final demand factor that influences the consumer's ability to purchase the sports product is the consumer's income. Simply stated, the more income a consumer realizes, the higher the demand for various sports products. This "income-related" demand factor is related to the cost of the sports product under consideration. That is, the higher the cost of the sports product, the more "consumer income" matters. Consider the case of New York Knicks courtside seats that are priced at $2,500–$3,600 per seat. For this "paltry" sum, fans get a small TV display and as much food and drink as they can ingest. Not to mention the fact that they will be sitting next to celebrities (most likely). Obviously, these are not seats that most middle-income consumers would be able to afford.[12]

The potential consumer's personal income and ability to purchase products is also highly related to the state of the economy in general. The economy is one of the "other external factors" that influence pricing, which is discussed in the next section.

Economy

The current economic cycle, or **economy**, also influences pricing decisions. A recessionary period, for instance, is characterized by reduced economic activity. During these times, there is a reduced demand for goods and services. In addition, unemployment rates are typically higher. Although this sounds grim for consumers and sports fans, imaginative sports marketers might be able to take advantage of these slowdowns in the economy by holding or slightly reducing prices while stressing the continued value of the sports product.

Periods of inflation also require a pricing review. During inflationary periods, the cost of inputs (e.g., supplies or raw materials) necessary to produce the sports product will rise and ultimately increase prices to consumers. Rather than increase prices, sports marketers may adopt a cost reduction strategy during inflation. Such a strategy necessitates reducing or stabilizing costs of producing the product so consumer prices need not be increased.

Whatever the phase of the economic cycle, it is important to understand the direct relationship between pricing and the economy. In the preceding discussion, prices were adjusted due to changes in the economy. The prices set by manufacturers and sports organizations equally have a tremendous impact on the demand for these products and services and, in turn, affect the economy.

Competition

As stated earlier, competition is one of the most critical factors in determining prices. Every sports organization must closely monitor the pricing structure of competing firms to successfully implement prices for its own products. One key to understanding the relationship between price and competition is exploring the sports organization's competitive environment. These four competitive environments are pure monopolies, oligopoly, monopolistic competition, and pure competition.

Most professional sports organizations operate in a **pure monopoly**, which means they are the only seller who sets the price for a unique product. With the exception of New York, Chicago, and California, there are few areas large enough to support two professional sports franchises in the same sport (e.g., the Cubs and White Sox). As such, most professional sports teams are free to manipulate prices as they want. The same would hold true for many college athletic programs, where college sports may be "the only show in town."

An **oligopoly** is where a small number of firms control a market. Conditions for an oligopoly exist when no one seller controls the market, but each of the few sellers has an impact on the market. In the sports industry, an example of an oligopoly is the sports news networks, where ESPN and Fox have dominant control over the market. In the case of many sporting goods, **monopolistic competition** is the norm. There are dozens of brands with identical products to sell. This competitive environment requires both price competition and nonprice competition. For example, all tennis balls are designed the same, but the many different brands compete based on lower prices and/or other marketing mix elements (promotions, product image, and sponsorships). The same holds true for golf balls, basketballs, and so on.

Pure competition is a market structure that has so many competitors that none can singularly influence the market price. The market conditions that must exist for pure competition include homogeneous products and ease of entry into the market. Although pure competition exists in industries selling uniform commodities such as agricultural products, it does not exist in the sports industry.

Legal issues

In addition to the other external factors, sports marketers must consider **legal issues**, such as constraints imposed on pricing. Several key laws that affect sports marketers were presented in Chapter 2. Table 12.4 presents U.S. legislation that specifically affects the pricing of sports products. One of the most notable legal issues that the sports industry has been wrestling with for years is the secondary ticket market, or, as it is more commonly known, ticket scalping (see the following article).

Table 12.4 Laws influencing the price of sports products

- Sherman Act, 1890 – Establishes legality of restraint/price of trade and fixing. It also restricts the practice of predatory pricing to drive competition from the marketplace through pricing.
- Clayton Act, 1914 – Restricts price discrimination.
- Robinson-Patman Act, 1936 – Limits the ability of firms to sell the same product at different prices to different customers.
- Wheeler-Lea Act, 1938   Ensures pricing practices are not deceiving to consumers.
- Consumer Goods Pricing Act, 1975 – Eliminates some control over retail pricing by wholesalers and manufacturers. It allows retailers to establish final retail prices in most instances.

ARTICLE 12.3
THE ECONOMICS OF TICKET SCALPING

Event promoters are underpricing and undersupplying tickets.

Allegations that tickets to recent AFL and NRL finals matches were being resold for up to three times their initial price raises questions of why ticket scalping happens, and whether anything can be done about it.

To an economist, the existence of a secondary market – where tickets are resold – is a sign that they have been undersupplied, underpriced or a combination of the two.

Event promoters, for example, are incentivized to sell as many tickets as possible so they can profit off sales of food, drinks and other concession stand items. This leads them to price tickets low.

Scalpers thrive off such conditions as it presents them with an arbitrage opportunity (the chance to make a profit from buying and selling the same thing) that would never have existed in a world where tickets were plentiful and priced in line with demand.

Online reselling platforms also put upward pressure on prices by making tickets easier to re-sell, while simultaneously allowing ticketing companies to double dip on commissions and booking fees. The Australian Competition and Consumer Commission is taking ticket re-seller Viagogo to the Federal Court, alleging the company engaged in deceptive pricing.

While some Australian states have introduced legislation to limit the amount that tickets can be resold for, promoters and policymakers are struggling to keep up with advances in technology that make scalping tickets easier than ever.

Why is there scalping?

The continued existence of scalping and resale markets is puzzling to economists. If tickets to major events are consistently undervalued, to the point that there is an entire industry based on resale, why do promoters continue to price tickets so low?

One argument is that event promoters are risk averse, preferring the certainty of a guaranteed sell-out over the uncertainty of potentially over-valuing tickets.

This fits with research that suggests people prefer to attend events in a packed-out venue, as opposed to a sparsely attended one. This incentivizes event promoters to sell out venues as people's demand for tickets depends, to some extent, on the demands of others.

There is also the somewhat idealistic idea that fairness stops event promoters from setting prices too high. This is the idea, often voiced in the media, that tickets should end up in the hands of "true fans".

The pros and cons of scalping and reselling

But there is an argument that ticket scalping actually enhances the total welfare of concert goers and sports fans. Scalpers act to distribute tickets to those who value them the most, or, as economists would say, they increase the allocative efficiency of the market.

Secondary markets for tickets allow potential buyers to indicate how much they want to go to the event – their "willingness to pay". If tickets can only be bought at a single price on a first come first serve basis, then some people who really want to go will be left out. Secondary markets permit these mutually beneficial exchanges to take place.

Online platforms for buying and selling tickets actually increase this allocative efficiency. These platforms arm buyers and sellers with ever increasing amounts of information, and the time and expenses associated with the purchase of each resold ticket (known as "transaction costs") are greatly reduced.

But scalping and secondary ticket markets are not without their downsides. Enterprising scalpers may be encouraged to buy up large proportions of available tickets in order to maximize their profits.

This is called "rent seeking" and has been shown to potentially reduce (or even eliminate) any gains in allocative efficiency.

There is also the issue of fairness, and whether "true fans" will be priced out of going to see their favorite performer or team. And then there is the issue that scalpers take away profits that could have instead accrued to the very artists, entertainers or sporting personalities on show.

Can anything be done about scalping?

As demonstrated by the likes of Taxi competitor Uber (and soon to be found in some Australian cinemas), "pricing bots" can adjust prices in real time based on demand or other consumer characteristics.

Such technology could reduce ticket scalping by putting pricing power in the hands of event promoters. But as previously noted, there is a reluctance to increase prices, and so some artists and groups have begun a series of blunt measures designed to tackle the problem.

Kid Rock, for example, has embarked on a number of "US$20 Best Night Ever" tours. As the name suggests, almost all tickets are sold for US$20 at supermarkets and venue box offices. Making the ticket price clear and transparent up front is a rather neat trick to try and stop tickets from being sold above face value.

Kid Rock also tends to perform many shows at the same venue. This increases the total supply of tickets on offer in a single city, reducing the premium that can be placed on a ticket in the secondary market.

The Glastonbury music festival has begun printing pictures of the ticket purchaser on every ticket. This may ensure the purchaser of the ticket and the attendee are the same person. However, the high cost of administering such tight controls make them viable to only the most profitable of events.

A similar system will be in place when former 1-Directioner, Harry Styles, plays Sydney's Enmore Theatre later this year. Ticket holders will be required to attend a "check-in" before entering the venue.

Meanwhile Taylor Swift has announced that fans can "boost" their place in the virtual ticketing queue by participating in a range of Swift related activities such as watching music videos and purchasing her music.

While Swift's stated goal of "getting tickets into the hands of fans ... NOT scalpers or bots" is admirable, this has been viewed by many as nothing more than an opportunistic cash grab from her most loyal fans.

Measures such as these are more likely to inconvenience ardent ticket scalpers rather than deter them. As long as tickets to major events are being systematically under-priced, scalpers have an incentive to bypass tighter controls and headlines bemoaning "inflated" prices will continue.

Credit: Paul Crosby, Macquarie University, Australia and Jordi McKenzie, Macquarie University, Australia

Rightsholder: The Conversation

URL: www.theconversation.com/the-economics-of-ticket-scalping-83434

Technology

Without a doubt, all sports products are becoming more and more technologi-cally advanced. The trend toward **technology** can have an indirect or direct influence on pricing decisions. Experience tells us that greater technology costs money. The high cost of research and development, as well as the higher costs for production and materials, drive up the price of the sports product. For example, if our stadiums are equipped with mini-screen monitors at every seat, the consumer would be expected to pay the price for this technology in the form of higher ticket prices. In this case, an advance in technology has a direct impact on the pricing.

ARTICLE 12.4
NEW ERA TICKETS USES IOVATION TO KEEP SCALPERS AND FRAUDSTERS OUT OF THE ARENA

About New Era Tickets

Created by Comcast-Spectator in 2004, New Era Tickets brings a new way of doing business to the entertainment industry through its full-service ticketing and database marketing solutions. Making use of the latest technology, New Era Tickets provides a variety of services including internet ticket sales, order fulfillment, customer service, access control and print-at-home technology, up-selling and cross-selling, stored value technology, online ticket exchange, ticket auctions, client training and support team, and database marketing.

In addition to offering a comprehensive list of services, New Era Tickets also makes its solutions highly customizable, offering clients complete control over their ticket prices, branding, and marketing data. By allowing clients to leverage their own brands, and their unique understanding of their customers and markets, New Era Tickets helps its clients realize increased ticket sales and overall revenue growth.

Based out of Exton, Pennsylvania, New Era Tickets serves over 60 clients through the US and Canada, from sports organizations to entertainment companies, including the Philadelphia 76ers, the General Motors Centre, The Rose Quarter, Dover Motorsports and Pocono Raceway.

Handling 11–12 million ticket sales annually, New Era Tickets processes $400–450 million in business transactions each year. Additionally, the company manages 30 different customer databases, with each database containing up to 2 million records.

The fraud challenge

In the time that New Era Tickets has been in business, the company has seen a significant shift in people's buying habits. "Five years ago, if we could sell 40–50% of the tickets online, that was considered a success. Now, we sell 90% of the tickets online," observes Steve Geib, Vice President of Client Services for New Era Tickets. However, despite the benefit of increased online sales, the down side is that criminals making purchases online can much more easily use stolen or illegitimate credit cards, due to the card-not-present buying environment.

While the challenge of fraudsters using stolen credit cards is common among most online retail sites, the online sale of tickets, as opposed to other "hard goods," presents its own unique challenges. With the advent of new technologies like print-at-home tickets that make the transfer of the good being purchased almost immediate, the review time on transactions is extremely limited. "In our business, catching the bad guys can be really difficult. Since there's nothing being shipped, we've got to stop them upfront. Our real challenge is trying to find them fast and reject the order out-right," says Geib. If the fraudulent behavior isn't caught at the time of purchase, New Era Tickets – who processes the transactions for its clients – faces the potential increase of its chargeback rate at the same time its clients are stuck with the loss of the ticket price.

Another challenge is that online fraud, in all industries, is becoming increasingly dominated by organized individuals with well-planned strategies for taking advantage of the system. With many sporting events and music concerts commanding enormous ticket prices – such as $180 for an NHL ticket, or $750 for an Eagles ticket – fraudsters can make significant profits by fraudulently purchasing multiple tickets online and then quickly reselling them. Obviously, the more demand there is for a ticket, and the closer it is to the time of the event, the easier it will be for a fraudster to turn the tickets around, and thus the more susceptible the event is to fraud.

In one particular case Geib recalls, someone purchased a single ticket to a Rolling Stones concert online, then, using the print-at-home feature, printed the ticket multiple times and sold all of the illegitimate copies for over $1,000 each. The result? Not only did all of the unsuspecting victims who purchased the illegitimate tickets lose their money – as well as their faith in the security of online sales – but since the original ticket was purchased with a stolen credit card, the venue lost as well. In order to combat these kinds of situations and protect both event-goers and the venues, New Era Tickets had to find an effective fraud solution that could catch fraudsters quickly and keep them from coming back.

The iovation solution

When New Era Tickets began looking for fraud solutions, iovation was immediately recommended by multiple merchant services companies in the industry. And, as New Era Tickets began seriously comparing its various options, iovation Reputation Manager 360 emerged as the best fit. "Everything iovation does just fit for us. It was quick, it was easy, it was up and running on the first day – and the return was almost immediate," says Geib.

Part of what makes iovation so effective for New Era Tickets is that it gives the company quick visibility into the activity on its sites by focusing on the computers being used to submit transactions, rather than on the personally identifiable information being submitted. Without this device-based information, organized fraud rings and repeat offenders are extremely hard to identify since they can set up multiple accounts with different information every time. This is partly the reason that government efforts to mitigate scalping and regulate ticket sales have been largely ineffective. "The reality is that device recognition is one of the only ways to really stop scalping and unfair ticket sales," says Geib. "Every time someone puts in a new address, a new name, etcetera – you can't tell if it's really a different person. But with iovation, I can tell that someone at one machine just bought 80 tickets."

When New Era Tickets sees fraudulent activity originating from a computer, using iovation Reputation Manager, that device can be tagged so that the client site can simply deny any future transactions originating from it. This kind of visibility gives New Era Tickets a powerful advantage. "We know who our scalpers are and where they're coming from," says Geib. "They think they're fooling us, but we can see them moving around."

Results

By using iovation Reputation Manager 360, New Era Tickets gained the ability to protect its clients from fraud at the same time as regulating ticket sales and keeping the marketplace fair for event-goers. What started out as a significant fraud problem – resulting in nearly six-figure losses from one client alone – turned into an almost non-existent issue, with Geib estimating a 98% reduction on the company's fraud losses, thanks to iovation. The company has been so effective at stopping fraud, in fact, that Geib notices many fraudsters have gotten the hint and simply started avoiding its sites. "There's almost no fraud anymore," says Geib. "Now it's a matter of someone not liking their seat. Can you imagine? Now that's our biggest problem."

Another huge benefit for New Era Tickets has been the savings on operational costs that iovation has made possible. With iovation, the fraud management process is so efficient that New Era Tickets needs only one dedicated full time person. This saved the company from hiring a whole team of people – as many as 12 more full time employees – that would have been required for tracking the fraud without the use of iovation. "When you're talking about manual reviews, the man hours are huge. With iovation, we're so much more efficient. Thanks to this technology, we know exactly who we're dealing with and we can tie it all together quickly. That knowledge is priceless."

Credit: Iovation Inc. (2013), www.iovation.com.

URL: https://content.iovation.com/resources/iovation-case-study-newera-ticketing.pdf?mtime=2019110 4174016

Although technology and higher prices are typically believed to go hand in hand, as illustrated in the following article on dynamic pricing, technology does not always have to increase pricing. A consumer may be able to buy a Taylormade M4 titanium driver for $350 using ecommerce sites versus $429 if purchased in a traditional retail outlet. In this case, technology is having an indirect influence on pricing, happily reducing the price of goods to consumers.

Price adjustments

As we discussed in the preceding sections, initial prices are determined by a variety of internal and external issues that are continually changing with new market conditions. For instance, more or less competition may provide the impetus for price changes.

ARTICLE 12.5
DYNAMIC TICKET PRICING USE TAKES OFF, AND TEAMS HOPE IT'LL LURE FANS BACK INTO SPORTS STADIUMS

Adjusting sports ticket prices according to supply, demand and other factors is becoming more popular as a tool to fill stadiums.

"Dynamic pricing" makes tickets act "just like a stock," according to one market observer.

Jacob Young, special to CNBC.com
Published 1:00 PM ET Sun, 3 Dec 2017
CNBC.com

Many sports fanatics seem content to watch their favorite teams in a bar or in the comfort of their own homes.

It's easy to understand why, as pro sports ticket prices often run in the hundreds or even thousands of dollars, depending on the game and location. According to Statista.com, the average ticket price for a National Football League game during the 2015–2016 season was $92.98 – well above other sports and almost triple the average Major League Baseball ticket at $31.

To combat this, franchises and secondary market sites are ramping up their use of dynamic ticket pricing, currently in use by at least a quarter of NFL teams, as well as in other sports. It means prices are modified in real time to account for the current market, a team's opponent, weather conditions, and other factors determined by supply and demand.

"It is a supply-demand-driven commodity, just like a stock," said Jesse Lawrence, founder of TicketIQ, an event ticket search aggregator. "The price should reflect the fair market value."

'Worthy of consumer dollars and attention'

The move to get more spectators into stadiums comes at a challenging time for professional football. Although negative attention from on-field protests has taken a toll on television ratings, NFL stadium attendance is actually up slightly this season when compared with last, according to data from Pro Football Reference, which crunches the numbers on fan attendance at stadiums.

This strategy seems to be making headway in attracting devoted fans away from the big screen and back to the stadium. "At the end of the day, there is more competition, demands for consumers' attention," Lawrence said. "That's always going to be challenging."

Waning TV ratings raise the stakes for teams, who "have to make sure the product is worthy of consumer dollars and attention," Lawrence added. "It raises the bar in terms of the quality of experience consumers expect."

Ultimately, dynamic pricing allows teams to use potentially cheaper ticket prices to encourage buying and create loyalty. Beyond the professional level, variable pricing seems to be a trend with big-time NCAA football programs as well, with some programs betting that lower prices will help fill the bleachers.

Ohio State University has one of the nation's most storied and popular college football programs, which a Wall Street Journal analysis recently valued at $1.5 billion. Recently, Ohio State's Board of Trustees announced a plan to return some of that value to ticket buyers, cutting next season's ticket prices by more than $50.

"Ticket pricing is evaluated and potentially changed each year, with the primary driving factor being the overall athletic department budgetary needs," Brett Scarbrough, associate athletic director and head of ticketing, told CNBC in an email. "Pricing each individual opponent separately creates this season-to-season fluctuation."

Ohio State introduced premier-game pricing in 2013, and has built on that by offering different prices per opponent and percentage discounts for season-ticket holders. Next season reserved seats will cost $195 when the Buckeyes host rival Michigan, but only $67 against Tulane.

Like some other universities, Ohio State relies on verified resale sites to assist with ticket distribution, such as Ohio State Ticket Exchange. "We see this as a benefit to our season- and single-game ticket buyers to have flexibility in managing their ticket investment," he said.

Also see: www.researchgate.net/publication/313568208_Dynamic_Pricing_in_Major_League_Baseball_Tickets_Issues_and_Challenges

Credit: Jacob Young

URL: www.cnbc.com/2017/12/01/dynamic-ticket-pricing-use-takes-off-and-teams-hope-itll-lure-fans-back-into-sports-stadiums.html

Also, **price adjustments** may be made to stimulate demand for sports products when sales expectations are not currently being met. Finally, prices might be adjusted to help meet the objectives that have been developed. The

next section explores some of the ways in which price adjustments are implemented by sports marketers, and, as the accompanying article illustrates, there
may be new approaches to pricing of traditionally priced products, like season
ticket packages.

Price increases and reductions

As with most things in sports marketing, prices are dynamic, and decisions are
continually being made about whether prices should be increased or decreased
based on a number of internal and external factors.

Price increases represent an important adjustment made to established
prices. In recent years, many sports organizations have had to increase prices
for a variety of reasons, even though consumers, retailers, and employees dis-
courage such actions. One of the primary reasons for increasing prices is to keep
up with cost inflation. In other words, as the cost of materials or of running
a sports organization increases, prices must be increased to achieve the same
profit objectives. Another reason for implementing a price increase is because
there is excess demand for the sports product. For example, if thousands of fans
join the season-ticket waiting list in the week that a Hall of Fame coach returns
to a team, then slight increases to these ticket prices may be acceptable.

A winning season may have a huge impact on the decision to raise prices.
After winning their first Super Bowl ever, Philadelphia Eagles ticket values
soared to an average of $368.00. The sum is more than double the $177 valuation of tickets at Lincoln Field in 2011, up $53 from a previous high for the
2017 season. In addition, tickets to the 2018 Eagles v Jaguars game in London
trended on the secondary market at $1,000.00.[13]

Because of the negative consequences of raising prices, sports organizations
may consider potential alternatives to straight price increases. These alternatives include eliminating any planned price reductions, lessening the number
of product features, or unbundling items formerly "bundled" into a low price.

If there are no viable alternatives to increasing prices, it is important to
communicate these changes to fans and consumers in a straightforward fashion to avoid potential negative consequences. Remember, much of pricing
is based on consumer psychology. If fans or consumers of sporting goods are
told why prices are being increased, they may believe price increases are justified. Typically, **price reductions** are efforts to enhance sales and achieve
greater market share by directly lowering the original price. In addition to
the direct reductions in price, rebates or bundling products are other types of
price breaks commonly employed. After a mediocre 2017 season, the New York
Jets announced a restructured ticket pricing program for 2018 and 2019 that
included a reduction of ticket prices by an average of more than 11 percent.
Jets President Neil Glat noted that more than 50 percent of the seating options
would decrease, while the rest would stay flat. Those who opted for the renewal
plan by the established March deadline would see a price freeze through the

2019 season. In addition, the team offered more choices for seats that did not require a PSL but continued to provide PSL owners with added benefits.[14]

Numerous factors impact the pricing rates of sports teams. Factors such as location, profile, ownership, distribution of TV rights, facility contracts, and management philosophy all impact pricing parameters. However, not all teams or leagues operate using the same strategy. For example, the English Premier League made a considerable effort after obtaining a new TV rights deal with Sky Sports to make family attendance at soccer matches realistic and cost affordable. The effort resulted in impressive 34 percent reduction for the 2016-2017 season.[15]

In another example, in 2020, the Charlotte Hornets elected to drop ticket prices of lower level seats and have also not increased ticket prices over the past three years. This is clearly an attempt to stimulate demand through pricing and also monitoring external threats like the Panthers and the new MLS team.[16]

Although teams commonly reduce or increase prices after the season, sports organizations rarely reduce or increase the price charged to consumers during the course of the season to stimulate demand. However, exceptions do exist. For example, MLB.TV reduced their subscription price from $79.99 to $39.99 after the All-Star break. It is much more common, however, for marketers of sporting goods to reduce and increase prices. Simply said, the Los Angeles Dodgers will probably never have an end-of-the-season sale of tickets. You will, however, be able to find any number of sales of baseball equipment at the end of the summer.

Whatever the form of price reductions, they are frequently risky for sports organizations for a number of reasons. First, consumers may associate multiple price reductions with inferior product quality. Second, consumers may associate price reductions with price gouging (always selling products at a discount, so the initial price must be unreasonably high). Third, price reductions may wake a sleeping dog and cause competition to counter with its own price decreases. Finally, frequent price changes make it more difficult for the consumer to establish a frame of reference for the true price of sports products. If tennis balls regularly sell for $4.99 for a package of three, and I conduct three sales over the season that offer the balls for $2.99, then what is the perceived "real" price?

An important concept when making price adjustments (either up or down) is known as the **just noticeable difference** (JND).[17] The just noticeable difference is the point at which consumers detect a difference between two stimuli. In pricing, the two stimuli are the original price and the adjusted price. In other words, do consumers perceive (notice) a difference when prices are increased or decreased? The following examples illustrate the importance of the just noticeable difference.

Dick's Sporting Goods may sell Wilson softball gloves at a regular price of $49.99 (note the psychological price strategy of odd pricing being used). With softball season right around the corner, Dick's decides to reduce prices and sell the gloves for $44.99. Does this $5 reduction surpass the difference threshold? In other words, does the consumer believe there is a noticeable difference between the regular price and the sale price? If not, then the price reduction will not be successful at stimulating demand.

Suppose that because of the increasing cost of raw materials needed to produce the gloves, the price has to be increased from $49.99 to $54.99. Again, the sports marketer has to determine whether consumers will notice this increase in price. If not, then the price increase may not have negative consequences for the sale of Wilson softball gloves.

Price discounts

Combined with straight price decreases, **price discounts** are other incentives offered to buyers to stimulate demand or reward behaviors that are favorable to the seller. The two major types of price discounts that are common in sports marketing are quantity discounts and seasonal discounts.

Quantity discounts reward buyers for purchasing large quantities of a sports product. This type of discounting may occur at all different levels of the channel of distribution. Using the previous softball glove example, Wilson may offer a quantity discount to Dick's Sporting Goods for sending in a large purchase order. Consumers hope that Dick's Sporting Goods will pass the savings on to them in the form of price reductions. The purchase of group ticket sales is another common example of quantity discounts in sports marketing.

Seasonal discounts are also prevalent in sports marketing because of the nature of sports. Most sports have defined seasons observed by both participants and spectators. Seasonal discounts are intended to stimulate demand in

Web Capture 12.1
Loveland Ski may use bundled as well as seasonal discounting

Credit: Loveland Ski Area

URL: www.skiloveland.com

off-peak periods. For example, ski equipment may be discounted in the summer months to encourage consumer demand and increase traffic in skiing specialty stores. Ski resorts also frequently offer seasonal deals. For instance, the Loveland Ski Area in Colorado offers multiple value passes each season. From March 1–May 2, they offer a discount package, while full-season packages purchased in September provide unlimited skiing and riding and membership to the Powder Alliance, which includes bonus access to 19 resorts spanning four countries and two hemispheres.[18]

In addition to sporting goods, seasonal discounts are often offered for ticket prices to sporting events. Timing discounts are often part of fan strategies to get the best price possible. For example, ticket sales to NBA games were 25 percent less if purchased the week of the game versus buying tickets well in advance. Golf tee times are also often cheaper when purchasing the day of play due to supply and demand issues.

Summary

The pricing of sports products is becoming an increasingly important element of the sports marketing mix. Price is a statement of value for a sports product, and understanding consumers' perceptions of value is a critical determinant of pricing. Value is defined as the sum of the perceived benefits of the sports product minus the sum of the perceived costs. The perceived benefits of the sports product, or what the product does for the user, are based on its tangible and intangible features. Each consumer's perception of value is based on his or her own unique set of experiences with the sports product.

A variety of factors influence the pricing decisions for any sports product. Similar to the internal and external contingencies that affect the strategic sports marketing process, pricing influences can be categorized as internal or external factors. Internal factors are those under the control of the sports organization, such as the other marketing mix elements, cost, and organizational objectives. External factors are those factors beyond the control of the sports organization that influence pricing. These include consumer demand, competition, legal issues, the economy, and technology.

Marketing mix elements other than price must be carefully considered when determining the price of the sports product. Promotional mix elements (e.g., advertising and sales promotions) often communicate the price (or price reductions) of the sports product to consumers. The channel of distribution that is selected influences the price of sports products. For instance, consumers expect to pay higher prices (and are charged higher prices) when purchasing tennis equipment from a pro shop versus directly from the manufacturer. Product decisions are also highly related to pricing. Simply, price is used to signal product quality. Generally, the higher the price charged, the greater the perceived quality of the product.

Two distinct pricing strategies that emerge based on the emphasis of marketing mix elements are price and nonprice competition. As the name suggests, nonprice competition tries to establish demand for the sports product using marketing mix elements other than price. Price competition, however, attempts to stimulate demand by offering lower prices.

In addition to other marketing mix variables, costs play a major role in pricing decisions. Costs are those factors that are associated with producing, promoting, and distributing the sports product. The total cost of producing and marketing a sports product is equal to the sum of the total fixed costs and the total variable costs. The fixed costs, such as players' salaries, do not change with the quantity of the product consumed, whereas variable costs change as a result of the quantity of the product being consumed. Today, the costs of running a professional sports franchise are skyrocketing because of players' salaries.

A final internal factor that influences pricing is organizational objectives. The four types of pricing objectives are income, sales, competitive, and social objectives. Typically, a combination of these four objectives is used to guide pricing decisions.

External factors, which are beyond the control of the organization, include consumer demand, competition, legal issues, the economy, and technology. Demand is the quantity of a sports product that consumers are willing to purchase at a given price. Price elasticity measures the extent to which consumer purchasing patterns are sensitive to fluctuations in price. For some sports products, such as a ticket to the Super Bowl, demand is relatively inelastic, which means that changes in price have little impact on game attendance. However, when demand is elastic, small changes in price may produce large changes in quantity demanded. Sports marketers try to estimate the demand for products by examining consumer trends and tastes, determining the number of substitute products, and looking at the income of the target market.

One of the most critical factors in determining pricing for sports products is to examine the prices charged for similar products by competing firms. Most professional sports franchises operate in a monopolistic environment in which no direct competitors exist. Because of this market condition, the price of attending professional sporting events is continually increasing. In fact, many "average" fans believe they are being priced out of the market and can no longer afford the cost of admission. In addition to competition, laws influence the pricing structure for sports products. For example, the Sherman Act was designed to protect freedom of competition, thereby freeing prices to fluctuate subject to market forces. The phase of the economic cycle is another important consideration in pricing. During periods of inflation, prices may rise to cover the higher costs, and during periods of recession, prices may be lowered. Finally, advances in technology are related to pricing decisions. Typically, consumers are willing to, and expect to, pay more for "high-tech" sports products. However, this is not always the case, as sometimes technological change can reduce pricing by facilitating marketing of the sports product.

Once the price of the sports product has been determined, adjustments are constantly necessary as market conditions, such as consumer demand, change.

Price reductions or increases are used to reach pricing objectives that have been determined. Generally, price reductions are used to help achieve sales and market share objectives, whereas increases are used to keep up with rising costs. Regardless of whether adjustments are made to raise prices or lower prices, an important consideration in pricing is the concept known as the JND, or just noticeable difference. The JND is the point at which consumers can detect a "noticeable" difference between two stimuli: the initial price and the adjusted price. Depending on the rationale for price adjustments, sports marketers sometimes want the change to be above the difference threshold (i.e., consumers will notice the difference), and sometimes it will be below the difference threshold (i.e., consumers will not notice the difference).

Key terms

- availability of substitute products
- competition
- competitive objectives
- consumer demand
- consumer income
- consumer pricing evaluation process
- consumer tastes
- cost of information search
- costs
- economy
- elastic demand
- estimating demand
- expected price range of substitute products
- external (or environmental) factors fixed costs
- income objectives
- inelastic demand
- internal factors
- just noticeable difference (JND)
- law of demand
- legal issues
- marketing mix variables
- mob effect
- monopolistic competition
- nonprice competition
- oligopoly
- organizational objectives
- perception of value
- price
- price adjustments

- price competition
- price discounts
- price elasticity
- price increases
- price inelasticity
- price reductions
- pure competition
- pure monopoly
- sales objectives
- situational factors
- social concern
- technology
- total cost
- unitary demand
- variable costs
- quantity discounts
- seasonal discounts

Review questions

1 Define price, perceived value, and perceived benefits. What is the relationship among price, value, and benefits?
2 Discuss the advantages and disadvantages of personal seat licenses from the consumer's perspective and the sports organization's perspective.
3 Outline the internal and external factors that affect pricing decisions. What is the primary difference between the internal and external factors?
4 Provide examples of how the marketing mix variables (other than price) influence pricing decisions.
5 Define fixed costs and variable costs and then provide several examples of each type of cost in operating a sports franchise. Do you believe costs should be considered controllable or uncontrollable factors with respect to pricing?
6 What are the four organizational objectives, and how does each influence pricing? Which organizational objective has the greatest impact on pricing?
7 What is meant by the law of consumer demand? Explain the difference between elastic and inelastic demand.
8 Describe, in detail, how sports marketers estimate the demand for new and existing sports products. What are the three demand factors, and which do you believe is the most critical in estimating demand?
9 What laws have a direct impact on pricing? Briefly describe each law.
10 How do advances in technology influence pricing? How does the economy influence pricing decisions?

11 Describe the different types of competitive environments. Why is competition considered one of the most critical factors influencing pricing?

12 What are the risks associated with reducing the price of sports products? Describe two common types of price discounting.

Exercises

1 Interview five consumers and ask them, "If a new athletic complex was built for your college or university basketball team, would you be willing to pay higher seat prices?" Summarize your results and discuss the findings in terms of perceived value and perceived benefits.

2 Interview five consumers and ask them to describe a sports product they consider of extremely high value and one they consider of extremely poor value. Why do they feel this way?

3 Find two examples of sports products you consider to compete solely on the basis of price. Provide support for your answer.

4 For any professional sports franchise, provide examples of how the rest of its marketing mix is consistent with its pricing.

5 Provide two examples of sports organizations that have (either in whole or in part) a social concern pricing objective.

6 Interview five people to determine whether demand could be characterized as elastic or inelastic for the following sports products: season tickets to your favorite basketball team's games, golf lessons from Tiger Woods, and Nike Air Jordans.

7 Provide examples of how technology has increased the ticket prices of professional sporting events. Support your examples from a cost perspective.

8 Interview the organizer of a local or neighborhood road race (e.g., 5K or 10K) and determine the costs of staging such an event. Categorize the costs as either fixed or variable. Assess the role of cost in the price of the entry fee for participants.

Internet exercises

1 Using the Internet, find three examples of promotion for sport products that provide consumers with pricing information.

2 Find an example of a sports product that is being sold via the Internet for a lower price than offered via other outlets. How much cheaper is the sports product? What does the consumer have to give up to purchase the product at a lower price over the Internet?

3 Using the Internet, find an example of price bundling sports products.

4 Using the Internet, find an example of product line pricing for the pricing of a sponsorship package (i.e., sponsorship levels at different prices).

5 Searching the Internet, find an example of a sports product that uses prestige pricing. Comment on the construction of the Web site itself. Is it consistent with the prestige pricing?

Notes

1   Robert B. Cialdini, Richard J. Borden, Avril Thorne, Marcus R. Walker, Stephen Freeman, and Lloyd R. Sloan, "Basking in Reflected Glory: Three (Football) Field Studies," *Journal of Personality and Social Psychology*, vol. 34, no. 3 (1976), 366–375.

2   Valarie Zeithaml, "Consumer Perceptions of Price, Quality, and Value: A Means-End Chain Model and Synthesis of Evidence," *Journal of Marketing*, vol. 52 (1988), 2–21.

3   Liz Roscher, "Honus Wagner Card Sells for $6.6M, Obliterating Record for Most Expensive Card" (August 16, 2021). Available from: https://sports.yahoo. com/honus-wagner-card-obliterates-record-with-66-million-sale-mike-trout-mickey-mantle-131824566.html?guccounter=1&guce_referrer=aHR0cHM 6Ly93d3cuZ29vZ2xlLmNvbS8&guce_referrer_sig=AQAAAHXAfbfVWl_ QRnSnmUm3nNVrUvFD5CARbtkvKR2yAm-YUOTqCkWBMqWhCM6z4Z SD6LNSAPAuyusljg-SlT_MSalu05bqeZjBGxi_XVyewqJdnYpw8MvXXP1p1f-1ZUGa77twwMBH1oXc9Wql8lJYkDfaQzM6VktZX-nHoxnkD9Mk5.

4   www.forbes.com/sites/mikeozanian/2013/11/25/the-nhls-most-valuable-teams/; www.forbes.com/sites/mikeozanian/2013/08/14/the-most-valuable-nfl-teams/.
www.forbes.com/sites/kurtbadenhausen/2017/09/18/the-dallas-cowboys-head-the-nfls-most-valuable-teams-at-4-8-billion/#7a53421b243f.
www.forbes.com/sites/kurtbadenhausen/2018/02/07/nba-team-values-2018-every-club-now-worth-at-least-1-billion/#3711ebd27155.
www.forbes.com/sites/mikeozanian/2017/12/05/the-nhls-most-valuable-teams-4/#7604130617c7.
www.forbes.com/pictures/mlm45gdfgj/baseballs-most-valuable/#75501 47092bc.

5   www.forbes.com/mlb-valuations/list/#tab:overall; www.forbes.com/nfl-valuations/ list/#tab:overall;
www.forbes.com/nhl-valuations/list/#tab:overall;
www.forbes.com/nba-valuations/list/#tab:overall; www.forbes.com/soccer-valuations/list/#tab:overall.

6   Kurt Foss, "NCAA March Madness 2004: PDF Hoop Dreams," *Planetpdf.com* (April 14, 2004). Available from: https://planetpdf.com/ncaa-march-madness-2004-pdf-hoop-dreams/.

7   Amy Wenk, "Mercedes-Benz Stadium Set to Wow" (August 18, 2017). Available from: https://www.bizjournals.com/atlanta/news/2017/08/18/mercedes-benz-stadium-set-to-wow-atlanta.html.

8   "2021 Physical Activity Council's Overview: Report on U.S. Participation." Available from: https://eb6d91a4-d249-47b8-a5cb-933f7971db54.filesusr.com/ ugd/286de6_610088e5e73d497185ac181a240833a9.pdf.

9   American Marketing Association, "Definition of Marketing Research." Available from: https://www.ama.org/the-definition-of-marketing-what-is-marketing/.

10 GoodreadsInc (2021). Available from: www.goodreads.com/author/quotes/ 25181.David_Ogilvy.

11 www.businessinsider.com/the-50-best-selling-pay-per-view-events-boxing-ufc-wrestling-tv-history-2017-8#1-floyd-mayweather-v-manny-pacquiao-46-million-ppv-buys-51.

12 Rudy Martzke, "SET Expects Pay-Per-View Recordbreaker," *USA Today* (1996), 2C; Ana Kieu, "The Sportster, Here's How Much a Courtside Seat Costs in Every NBA Arena" (September 10, 2018). Available from: https://www.thesportster. com/basketball/how-much-a-courtside-seat-costs-in-every-nba-arena/.

13 www.ticketIQ.com.
    https://theeagleswire.usatoday.com/2018/08/08/eagles-2018-nfl-season-tickets/.

14 www.usatoday.com/story/sports/nfl/2018/01/16/jets-reducing-ticket-prices-on-average-11-percent-for-2018/109509276/.

15 www.forbes.com/sites/andrewbrennan/2017/01/31/the-american-big-four-need-to-stop-pushing-up-ticket-prices-like-english-football-has/#43dd33064b1e.

16 "Press Release: Mets Reduce Ticket Prices for 2011," *New York Mets* (November 3, 2010). Available from: http://newyork.mets.mlb.com/news/press_releases/ press_release.jsp?ymd=20101103&content_id=15970796&vkey=pr_ nym&fext=.jsp&c_id=nym, accessed June 25, 2014.

17 Erik Spanberg, "The Strategy Behind the Hornets' Decision to Drop Some Ticket Prices," *Charlotte Business Journal* (January 22, 2020). Available from: https:// www.bizjournals.com/charlotte/news/2020/01/22/whats-leading-hornets-to-drop-certain-season.html.

18 Business Wire, "Atlanta Hawks, Atlanta Thrashers, Houston Rockets and Utah Jazz Select Qcue to Power Dynamic Ticket Pricing," *Businesswire.com* (August 16, 2010). Available from: www.businesswire.com/news/home/20100816005210/ en/Atlanta-Hawks-Atlanta-Thrashers-Houston-Rockets-Utah.

PART IV

Implementing and controlling the strategic sports marketing process

Implementing and controlling the strategic sports marketing process

After completing this chapter, you should be able to:

- Describe how the implementation phase of the strategic sports marketing process "fits" with the planning phase.

- Explain the organizational design elements that affect the implementation phase.

- Identify the general competencies and the most important skills that effective sports marketing managers possess.

- Describe the basic characteristics of total quality management (TQM) programs and how TQM might be implemented in sports organizations.

- Identify some of the guidelines for designing reward systems.

- Define strategic control and how the control phase of the strategic sports marketing process "fits" with the implementation phase.

- Explain the differences among planning assumption control, process control, and contingency control.

ARTICLE 13.1

INSIDE THE GEORGETOWN HOYAS BASKETBALL MARKETING STRATEGY

The program is known for its unique promotions.

With 347 division one basketball programs, many marketing departments are pushing new ideas, but it is the work of one college hoops brand that is standing out amongst the rest.

Being at the forefront of the latest ideas and technology to make it possible has allowed the Georgetown Hoyas, led by Assistant AD of Marketing Chris Grosse, to take the initiative to be creative and push the envelope for the Hoyas basketball team and its fans. Joining the Hoyas in 2014, Grosse arrived at a time of transition for the Big East Conference. Luckily, he saw a unique opportunity in that.

"I came to Georgetown at a very unique time. The BIG EAST Conference had just undergone realignment, which saw several of our traditional rivals move out of the yearly schedule. We also play in a huge arena. I believe it is the seventh biggest in the country, so there are a lot of seats to fill. We couldn't stick to the status quo of just releasing our schedule and watching tickets sales soar, we had to be more strategic about things, and come up with creative ways to bring extra attention to some of our lower demand games," said Grosse.

Like many conferences today, there's a struggle to attract the fan base for certain games and Grosse has found that this trend can change with activities and themes off the floor.

"Since I took over, I think we have tried to add more to the experience for both our students and our general fanbase. We have tried to be creative, to offer the fans something different from other experiences in the area. We have introduced more themed nights for our student body (Denim Night, Fashion Faux Pas Night, Winter Onesieland), to create some buzz on campus and give the students something to rally around. We have really adopted more of a minor league promotional/creative approach to the way we do things. As the team is improving and getting better over these next few seasons, that will only add to the experience," said Grosse.

Grosse knows that being creative is a big part of developing the brand, and that it takes support from the administration for an idea to see the light of day. Thankfully, this is something the Hoyas possess.

"There are a TON of amazingly creative people in this industry, both college athletics marketing and sports marketing in general. I think we are lucky to have an administration that enjoys pushing the envelope with a lot of what we do. They understand that we are a small marketing staff with limited resources, as compared to a lot of schools, so they see the value in being creative and trying to grab headlines," said Grosse.

It is easy to overthink, but sometimes it's just the simple plans that work best for basketball marketing departments when students are away from campus throughout the season on breaks.

"A lot of these promotions really help bring attention to some of our less-hyped games. We try to do the most creative stuff during our non-conference schedule, so we can drive people to our games in hopes they enjoy the experience and come back." – Chris Grosse

"Some promotion's results are easy to measure; you can count tickets sold through promo codes or increases in overall attendance. We have been running our 'Student for a Day' promotion, which fills our student section with general fans over break games, for four years now, and every year the section is packed with fans. It's easy to measure those results. A lot of what we do, though, is to raise awareness of our events, our department, and the great things our student-athletes are doing, and that is a little tougher to measure. We see increases in social media engagement, earned media and coverage of our games, but sometimes we might not have tangible attendance increases to count," said Grosse.

As for us as fans, we see the final product and continue to have fun with the ideas that marketing brings to the table, but it may just be what we do not see that's just as vital.

"It's quite the process and, sometimes, depending on the trending topics, a lot has to be done in a short amount of time. . . . As we develop the idea, we always have to keep in mind how we are actually going to execute the plan on game day. We have to be creative and work within our budgets to make a lot of the things we come up with happen. A big part of our plan is making sure our promotional announcements on social media are done correctly . . . the

initial announcement is important, especially on Twitter, because the initial tweet will get the most views if the promotion goes viral," said Grosse.

Not everyone can make it out to every Georgetown hoops game, but the marketing team, putting together so many great theme nights, gives fans a reason to come out to the games.

> "Almost all of our 'viral' ideas come from out-of-the-box thinking . . . the ideas that get the most attention come from when we break the mold and take some risks. . . . We try to be the first to do something, or we try to be different than other promos that have already been done and take them to the next level. . . . Our coach was in Space Jam, and we wanted to do a theme around that. We didn't just do a Space Jam Night, we called it Monstars Night and had some fun with it," said Grosse.

One thing is for sure, the Hoyas, behind Grosse's leadership, are using their platform to the best of their ability and the results speak for themselves. Being first to the idea is not just a passion for Grosse, it's in his DNA, and that has the Hoyas set up for success for years to come.

Credit: Jeremy Fitch

Rightsholder: Front Office Sports, published 3/16/18

URL: www.frntofficesport.com/inside-the-georgetown-hoyas-basketball-marketing-strategy/

The opening scenario presents an excellent example of how sports organizations operate in uncertain and competitive conditions. The Hoyas' marketing strategy also stresses elements of creativity, the power of strong leadership, and the control or assessment of these actions. Moreover, sports organizations must consider the internal and external environments and formulate a plan that achieves a "fit" with these environments. The strategic sports marketing process is ultimately directed toward the achievement of the organization's mission, goals, and objectives. As we have learned, the contingency theory of sports marketing suggests that there are a variety of marketing plans that can achieve these goals. However, not all these plans are equally effective. Likewise, organizations have a variety of ways to implement and control the strategic sports marketing plan they have developed, not all of which are equally useful for putting the plan into action. Thus, sports marketers, like those in the Georgetown example, should allocate the time and effort necessary to develop a program that will lead to the desired outcomes and most effectively implement and control the planning process.

The remainder of this chapter looks at the last two phases of the strategic marketing process – implementation and control. We begin by examining a model of the implementation process and the organizational design elements that facilitate or impede the execution of the marketing plan. Then, we shift our focus to the control phase and look at some of the common forms of strategic control.

Implementation

Implementation can be described as putting strategy into action, or executing the plan. As illustrated in the opening scenario, Georgetown University's goal of enhancing the brand can be achieved with proper planning. However, none of these plans matter unless the Hoyas continually monitor the implementation process to make sure plans are being carried out in the correct manner.

To successfully manage the implementation process, the sports marketer must consider a number of organizational design elements. These organizational design elements include communication, staffing, skills, coordination, rewards, information, creativity, and budgeting. Implementation must begin with **communication**. Effective communication requires a leadership style that allows and encourages an understanding of the marketing plan by all members of the sports marketing team. A second critical element involves **staffing** and developing the **skills** in those people who are responsible for carrying out the plan. These people must also be placed within the organization so they can work together to implement the plan; thus, a third critical design element is **coordination**. **Rewards** that are congruent to the plan can provide the motivation and incentives necessary for people to work effectively toward the achievement of the goals and objectives outlined within the plan. **Information** must be available to those people who will carry out the plan so effective decisions can be made throughout the implementation phase. Effective work environments also allow for and encourage **creativity** from individuals who are expected to find ways to carry out the strategic marketing plan. Finally, a supportive **budgeting** system is critical to the successful achievement of strategic goals and objectives. These seven organizational design elements of implementation and their relationship to the strategic sports marketing process are outlined in Figure 13.1.

Each of these seven elements must be carefully considered within the strategic marketing process by the sports marketing manager. The implementation design must be appropriate for the plan. In other words, a "fit" between the planning phase and the implementation phase is required. Thus, a change in the strategic marketing plan of a sports organization could lead to the need to make changes in one or more of these design elements. As you read the accompanying article on the critical issues impacting Major League Baseball,[1] think about how each of the design elements would have to be addressed to enhance the league.

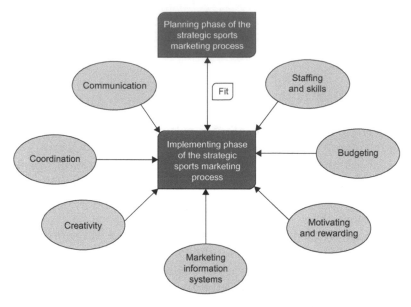

Figure 13.1
Implementation phase of the strategic sports marketing process

ARTICLE 13.2
HOW MAJOR LEAGUE BASEBALL CAN FIX ITS ATTENDANCE PROBLEM

Where have all the people gone?

In case you haven't heard, Major League Baseball attendance is down. It is down 8.6% overall and 2018 is seeing the worst attendance start since 2003. Is a less than 10% drop in fans actually showing up at the ballpark reason to panic? Consider this: MLB has not seen more than a 2% change in attendance since 1995, a season that followed a World Series cancelling strike. The real reason to sound the alarm is that there is no apparent cause for the drop.

The NFL is suffering a similar fate, but at least it can be tied to the overt disrespect for the National Anthem by players (despite the NFL using everything from presidential debates to weather to try and sugarcoat the reality). Baseball actually did see some very baseball unfriendly weather at the start of the 2018, with games being called for snow. But, unlike the NFL, MLB is not tone deaf enough to blame the entire attendance slump on mother nature.

The most likely cause is the ever increasing cost of attending an MLB game. What was once a spectator sport for the masses has rapidly become an event for the upper middle class. The average cost of a game for a family of four in 2017 was $219, a 176% increase from 1991 when it was a reasonable $79 (adjusted for inflation, that $79 would equate to $142). When a service continually outpaces inflation, it is only a matter of time before certain segments of society are fiscally excluded from being able to use that service; or in this case entertainment.

Then there is the question of value of product. It is one thing to spend a ton of cash to see a contender play, but if your home team is one of those that is 20 games out of first place by the all-star break, it is hard to justify the expenditure. In the last decade or so, there have been some powerhouse teams that were exciting to see play, and a lot of substandard teams that had fans shunning the ballpark. If the trend continues, the sport of curling with have more fans by the time the 22nd century rolls around.

These times are changin' (or they need to)

What can MLB do to fix falling attendance? Here is a laundry list of actions baseball can take to bolster putting butts in the seats:

While it is up to individual teams set ticket prices, there has to be a path for even below average wage earners to attend a game. Take a look at any game on television. With a few exceptions of rivalries or post-season games, a very large portion of the upper decks are empty. Teams like the Washington Nationals and Colorado Rockies have figured out that you can pack in more fans by offering up those normally empty seats for a very low ticket price. The Nationals have $5 tickets and when the Braves played at Turner Field they made several thousand tickets available for $1. Filling up the upper decks with cheap tickets makes sense for fans and teams alike. A filled $5 seat will earn a team five bucks. An empty seat earns them nothing. And fans in cheap seats get just as hungry as the field level fans. Ballparks make a killing on concessions, and even letting fans in the upper decks for free would prove profitable with the extra concessions sales. Make super cheap tickets available for the less desirable seats and watch frugal fans pour in.

Baseball has been working on ways to decrease the length of a game. Ballgames have slowly creeped up in length until it exceeded the three hour mark. While fans like me love long games (extra inning for me means free baseball), most do not. Many take their youngsters to the game and three hours in a hard plastic seat for a 8 year old is an eternity. The pace of play rules implemented by the MLB have helped some. Batters must now keep one foot in the batter's box (instead of spending 90 seconds adjusting their cup and batting gloves), have a clock to keep the time between innings reasonable, and have the instantaneous intentional walk that shaves a minute or two off of each game, and limiting manager/catcher trips to the mound. Baseball needs to do better, setting a goal of two hours and thirty minutes for an average game. A pitch clock would be helpful, as would demanding that relief pitchers be ready to pitch as soon as they exit the bullpen and do away with the on-mound warm up tosses during pitching changes (injury related changes exempt).

Many parking lots for MLB stadiums are run by a company other than the team or stadium owner. Those entities are out to make money, and lots of it in a short period of time. Nothing is more disheartening for a hard working parent to rack his brain figuring out if he can afford to take his family to the ballpark, and when he finally scrapes enough together, gets hit with a $15 parking fee (or more for many parks). It is the equivalent to charging shoppers to park at the mall.

Teams with downtown ballparks should work with the city and run express busses from existing park and rides directly to and from the ballpark. This would alleviate fans from having to fight attendance killing traffic and make it much more convenient for fans to get to the game. Baseball teams could tout it as their effort to reduce carbon emissions.

While teams should expect to make a profit, in addition to curbing ticket prices there should be an effort to make it affordable to eat at the game as well. Teams could continue to offer the $12 monstrosity hot dog with 30 toppings, but why not offer a $2 plain hot dog as well. If fans can attend a game for cheap and eat for a reasonable price, they would flock to the ballpark.

It is hard for me to say this but, it might be time for the MLB to contract. I am a huge fan of expansion actually, and I would like to see the addition of at least four other teams. But I also remember when EVERYONE in the southeast was a Braves fan. It was a rite of passage every summer for a family to make a pilgrimage to Atlanta to see a game. That was when Florida had no team of their own. Now, the Sunshine State has two teams and both have abysmal attendance records. More teams also mean dilution of talent, with smaller markets never being able to afford fan-attracting superstars. Ditching both Florida teams, the San Diego Padres and either the Pirates or Phillies would be a good start. I know, I hate the idea too, but I also hate going to the dentist yet I do it because I know it is good for me. Think of league contraction as an MLB trip to the dentist.

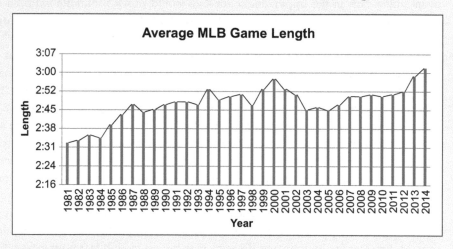

Figure 13.2
Games have gotten longer in recent years

*Source*https://images.saymedia-content.com/.image/t_share/MTc1NDU0MzUwMDMyOTcwOTQ2/
how-major-league-baseball-can-fix-its-attendance-problem.png

Reeling in free agency would do wonders to keep the insane salaries to a minimum. No one should keep players from being paid fairly, but giving a pitcher that plays every fifth game 20 million a year is not healthy for anyone. It would also help build a more loyal fanbase, and loyal fans are more likely to attend a game. Before free agency madness, team rosters remained relatively consistent year to year. Now, the highest bidder can scoop up talent from other teams once a player's contract comes to an end. A more reasonable approach is for MLB to put a cap on player salary and allow for a little extra based on incentives. A max salary of ten million per year plus the possibility of an extra two million for incentive based performance would allow players to still make bank, and only be enticed to switch teams if they wanted to play for a contender or a change of scenery. Salary caps would also help teams reduce ticket prices.

Get rid of dynamic ticket pricing. Charging more for weekend games or rivalry games only makes fans feel like they are getting fleeced. It is the baseball equivalent of charging more for gasoline when a hurricane evacuation is in progress. Just stop it. The only people who think it is a good idea are team accountants.

It's not too late

Implementing these changes are paramount if baseball want to curb the decline in game attendance. Enticing fans to the ballpark with good entertainment at a good value is the only solution to an issue that will only get worse if not addressed. Baseball faces the same challenges as movie theaters. With high definition big screen TVs becoming the norm in most living rooms, coupled with the ability to stream EVERY MLB game with a $120 MLBTV subscription, fans, like movie goers, are doing the math. For what it costs to take a family to an MLB game, sacrificing a few trips to the ballpark could pay for a nice TV and an MLBTV subscription. Just as potential movie customers have discovered, the baseball viewing experience can be just as good in the living room as it is at the ballpark; without the traffic.

It cuts me to the quick to see baseball suffering the malaise of fans and their lack of motivation to get out to see their team. I am one of those guys that would put a cot up on the main concourse and live at the ballpark all summer if they would let me. But as much as I love baseball, the sport has created its own quandary when it comes to attendance. It is not over-the-top kid's zones or two foot long hot dogs that fans want, it is an affordable, hassle-free, pure baseball experience. To sort of quote one of the more famous baseball movies: change it and they will come.

Credit: Tom Lohr

URL: www.howtheyplay.com/team-sports/How-Major-League-Baseball-Can-Fix-Its-Attendance-Problem

Communication

Effective communication is critical to the successful implementation of the strategic sports marketing plan. Before we discuss the issues involved in effective communication, we must understand the importance of having a leader who is committed to the strategic sports marketing plan. Without such commitment, the best communication efforts will be ineffective. The values of the marketing leader and the president/CEO of the organization not only affect the strategic sports marketing process but also the way the plan will be implemented. Strategic leadership requires a "champion," someone who believes so strongly in the strategic marketing plan that he or she can share the "what," "why," and "how" with those who will be responsible for its implementation.

The commitment of the leader to the plan usually dictates the level of commitment among those who will carry it out. In addition, different strategies require different skills, even among leaders. Therefore, when strategy changes, a change in leadership often follows. That relationship may also be reversed. A change in leadership will often lead to a change, or at least an adjustment, to the strategy. There is obviously a close relationship between strategy and leadership, and it is sometimes necessary to bring in outside sports marketers to implement a changed or new strategy. Organizations will also often bring in someone new when they believe a new marketing strategy is needed to enhance performance of a team, event, or league.

Photo 13.1
Sports organizations, such as this trailer produced by The All England Lawn Tennis Club for The Championships, to link Wimbledon to important moments in history, often utilizing creative marketing strategies to illustrate their global proposition to fans

Credit: The All England Lawn Tennis Club

URL: www.wimbledon.com

Just how important is communication? Just think about the impact the various strategic actions and communication styles of the commissioners have had on the success of the major sports leagues discussed in the following article.[2]

ARTICLE 13.3
POLL: WHO IS THE BEST PROFESSIONAL SPORTS COMMISSIONER?

Recently, we have seen news of Adam Silver getting a contract extension as commissioner of the NBA, and Gary Bettman getting into the Hockey Hall of Fame. Usually, however, commissioners are in the news for bad things, such as making contentious rules in the league, or deciding to suspend players when they did not deserve it. Overall, commissioners are very controversial.

Roger Goodell is probably the most controversial when it comes to commissioners. Goodell just came out with the newest rule on the national anthem, requiring all players to stand or just stand in the locker room during the anthem. He also has cracked down on the marijuana policies that the NFL has for repeat offenders. The ratings have also dropped with the NFL as of late. But, Goodell's crowning achievement is bringing football back to Los Angeles, with the Rams and Chargers. He has also tried to make the NFL a more international brand, rather than just a national brand.

Adam Silver got a six-year extension recently, meaning that he will be the face of the NBA front office for years to come. He is known for being the most player-friendly commissioner. He tries to make the league more fun for the players, and allow for player mobility. But, the one big criticism was allowing the Kevin Durant move to the Warriors, as the NBA has been overinflated with a lot of money from TV deals.

Rob Manfred, the MLB commissioner, has been able to improve the relationships between owners and players, along with expanding how people can see games all around the country. He is one of the quieter commissioners, but still is making moves with the league as a whole. The most controversial move he made was trying to speed up the pace of the game. He implemented a clock in between innings, and limited the amount of visits a manager can have on a specific game. They said if the average game length is not under three hours, they will implement a pitch clock for all major league games.

The NHL commissioner, Gary Bettman, was the first commissioner in the entire league after a long labor battle between the owners and players in 1993. He has grown the NHL into what we've seen it today and they have had a huge revenue growth. The franchises are worth way more than they used to be, and the NHL is not as unwatchable and boring as it used to be. However, his public perception is absolutely horrendous. You know Bettman is entering an arena just by the sound of the boo's around the stadium. He has a bad relationship with players, and has botched many projects along the way that could have destroyed the NHL.

Credit: William Boyd, published 28th June 2018

Rightsholder: The Daily Caller

URL: www.dailycaller.com/2018/06/28/best-sports-commissioner/

Clearly, the organizational leadership sets the tone for communication within the sports organization. Communication may be formal or informal and may use a number of different channels. For example, some organizations may require that all communications be written and meetings be scheduled and documented. Other organizational leaders may have an informal, open-door policy and allow for more "spur of the moment" meetings and "hallway" discussions. Either policy can be effective when it comes to implementing strategy within the sports organization, as long as the necessary information is clearly and accurately communicated.

Strategy was once considered a "top-down"-only process, where those who had a "big-picture" view of the organization were considered the best candidates for formulating strategy. This often led to huge communication requirements as organizational leaders attempted to inform those who had to carry out the strategy about not only the strategy but also the rationale for strategic choices made by the top management. Experience and research have shown that the communication process is easier when those who are expected to implement the plan are involved throughout the process. Thus, involving the entire sports marketing team throughout the strategic sports marketing process can usually be more effective than attempting to communicate the plan after it has been developed.

Even when everyone responsible for implementing the plan is involved in its development, strategic sports marketing plans should be communicated often. Due to the contingent nature of the strategic sports marketing process, plans and circumstances can change, and people can forget the original plan and the premise on which the plan was formulated. Employees can learn about or be reminded about the content and purpose of the plans in a variety of ways. This information can be communicated in regularly scheduled meetings or at gatherings where the strategic plan is the primary agenda item. Printed material can also be useful. Some sports organizations may give employees desk items, such as calendars or paperweights, with keywords that remind them of the strategy. They may even program screen savers on computers with words that will remind employees of the strategic thrust of the marketing plan. Promotional literature that can be displayed around the office or sent to employees through e-mail is also useful. In essence, sports marketing organizations that can provide daily reminders of the strategy are more likely to keep everyone involved on the same strategic path. Many forms of internal promotion can be used to achieve this goal.

Communication with groups and individuals outside the marketing department is also important. Many such individuals and groups, both within the organization and outside the organization, have a stake in the marketing strategy and can have an impact on the implementation of the plan. Therefore, it is important to inform other departments within the sports organization who affect or are affected by the strategy of the strategic marketing direction.

For example, many teams and leagues are in the process of trying to develop long-term relationships with their fans. One of the ways to build these relationships is to allow fans more access and contact with the players. At the collegiate level, almost all universities have implemented Kid's Clubs offering such benefits as free admission to events, pizza parties, T-shirts, and access to special events and clinics. This creative plan can only be executed by communicating its importance to coaches, members of the teams, and the athletic department as a whole. In addition, the NCAA does a tremendous job of engaging fans at its sports championships. Obviously, the Men's D-I Final Four basketball

Table 13.1 NCAA enhancing the fan experience

2019 NCAA Wrestling Fan Festival Schedule

Thursday, March 21

Time	Event	Location
TBA	NCAA Wrestling Fan Festival Open	TBA
TBA	WIN Magazine Memorabilia Show	TBA
TBA	USA Wrestling Practice	Fan Festival Stadium Mats
TBA	USA Wrestling Feature Match	Fan Festival Stadium Mats
TBA	NWHOF and Pro Football Hall of Fame Presentation	Fan Festival Main Stage
TBA	NWHOF and Pro Football Hall of Fame Autograph Session	Fan Festival Main Stage

Friday, March 22

Time	Event	Location
TBA	NCAA Wrestling Fan Festival Open	TBA
TBA	WIN Magazine Memorabilia Show	TBA
TBA	USA Wrestling Practice	Fan Festival Stadium Mats
TBA	USA Wrestling Feature Matches	Fan Festival Stadium Mats
TBA	USA Wrestling Autograph Session	Fan Festival Stadium Mats
TBA	Semifinals Preview Show	Fan Festival Main Stage

*Source:*www.ncaa.com/championships/wrestling/d1/fan-fest

championships holds fan fests to engage fans and activate sponsorships. How-ever, even less popular sports like wrestling are joining the fold to create a bet-ter fan experience, as shown in Table 13.1.

On the professional front, many teams hold an annual fan appreciation day and preseason fan fests to enhance fan relations. The Portland Trailblazers, for example, hold an annual fan fest event prior to the beginning of the basket-ball season. Highlights of the event include player meet and greets with auto-graphs, intrasquad scrimmage, and even asking the Trailblazer rookies to show off their dancing skills in front of the entire arena.[3] Taking it one step further, many college and professional teams have developed fan advisory councils. The councils, typically composed of groups of 12 to 14 season ticket holders, meet once to discuss anything and everything related to improving the fan experience. Of course, the ownership hopes this will help engage fans, create more loyal and satisfied fans, and ultimately increase ticket sales.

Even venues such as the Richmond Raceway have established fan advisory councils to promote a better "stadium" experience. The Raceway not only has a regular advisory group but has established a youth advisory board to engage fans at an earlier age and create loyalty for a lifetime.[4] All of these activities contribute to strengthening the team/venue-fan relationship, but, as shown in Table 13.2, some stadium experiences are historically aspirational benchmarks for others to try to emulate.

As with internal promotion, external promotion and communication of the strategic sports marketing plan can take many forms. Some channels for these communications include social media and the utilization of web sites,

Table 13.2 Top 10 stadium experience rankings
1. Wrigley Field – Chicago Cubs
2. Fenway Park – Boston Red Sox
3. AT&T Park – San Francisco Giants
4. Oriole Park at Camden Yards – Baltimore Orioles
5. Lucas Oil Stadium – Indianapolis Colts
6. Lambeau Field – Green Bay Packers
7. PNC Park – Pittsburgh Pirates
8. CenturyLink Field – Seattle Seahawks
9. Dodger Stadium – Los Angeles Dodgers
10. Memorial Stadium – Clemson University Tigers
11. Folsom Field – Colorado University Buffaloes
12. Rose Bowl – The Rose Bowl Game
13. Heinz Field – Pittsburgh Steelers
14. Coors Field – Colorado Rockies
15. Kyle Field – Texas A&M University Aggies

Source: Paul Swaney, Top 100 Stadium Experiences of 2017, https://stadiumjourney.com/news/top-100-stadium-experiences-of-2017/

annual reports, mailers, marketing specialties such as calendars, or meetings. Again, the key to effectively communicating to outside or inside groups is committed and competent leadership. It is with this leadership and effective communication efforts that the foundation for successful implementation of the strategic sports marketing plan is provided.

ARTICLE 13.4
SPORTS MARKETING HALL OF FAME

Gary Davidson

Gary Davidson was once called the man who has had the greatest impact on professional sports in America. A former lawyer, Davidson founded and served as president of the American Basketball Association (ABA), the World Hockey Association (WHA), and the World Football League (WFL) in the late 1960s and early 1970s.

These leagues, of course, offered alternatives for professional athletes that would have never existed otherwise. By breaking the virtual monopoly held on talent by the existing NBA, NHL, and NFL franchises, Davidson attracted stars such as Wayne Gretzky, Bobby Hull, "Dr. J." Julius Erving, and Rick Barry to play in his rebel leagues. Davidson and his leagues are also credited with some major rule changes that subsequently were adopted by the existing professional leagues. For instance, the three-point shot was created to add excitement to the ABA and has changed the entire course of modern basketball.

In addition to his ambush marketing tactics, Gary Davidson broadened the scope of professional sports. He placed professional franchises in cities that were previously considered too small to support major league sports. For example, San Antonio and Indianapolis were two of his original ABA teams that are now successful NBA franchises. Davidson's leagues have benefited the fans, the players, and major league sports.

Sources: Steve Rushin, "Gary Davidson," *Sports Illustrated* (September 19, 1994), 145. Courtesy of Time, Inc.; https://www.latimes.com/archives/la-xpm-2008-apr-14-sp-crowe14-story.html; www.si.com/more-sports/2014/08/05/si-60-how-we-got-here-gary-davidson-steve-rushin-1994

Staffing and skills

As we just discussed, it is critical to the success of the strategic sports marketing plan to have a leader who can "champion" and communicate the strategy. As important as the leader is to effective implementation, it is equally important to have a staff that cares about and is capable of implementing the strategy. A group of individuals must be assembled who have the appropriate mix of backgrounds, experiences, know-how, beliefs, values, work and managerial styles, and personalities.

It is important to consider strategy prior to hiring and training new employees and in retraining those who are already with the marketing team. This is especially vital in managerial or other key positions. However, staffing for the implementation of strategic sports marketing plans must go much deeper into the organizational ranks. In fact, putting together an effective marketing team is one of the cornerstones of the implementation process.

A few studies have examined the relationship between types of strategy and staff characteristics. One study of corporate executives and their perceptions regarding the relationship between managerial characteristics and strategy offered two interesting findings.[5] First, experience and exposure to a particular type of strategy have been viewed by corporate executives as essential for managers. Previous experience and exposure to a strategy can provide an opportunity for these experienced individuals to provide important input into the implementation of the plan. However, the second finding suggests that a "perfect match" between managerial characteristics and strategy is likely to result in an overcommitment to a particular strategy. In other words, managers may not be able to change strategic direction when contingencies change if they are perfectly matched in education, training, experience, and personality to one particular strategy. These findings may be particularly relevant and of importance for sports organizations who often operate in unpredictable, uncertain and rapidly changing environments.

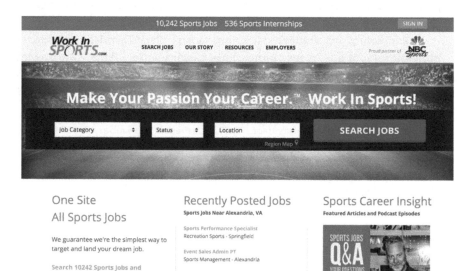

Web Capture 13.1
Sports careers on the Web

Credit: Work In Sports

URL: www.workinsports.com

To develop a staff capable of implementing the strategy, three categories of characteristics must be considered: education, training, and ability; experience and previous track record; and personality and temperament. With any team-building activity, it is important to consider the compatibility of the individuals who will work together to implement the strategic sports plan.

Just what skills are necessary to land and keep your dream job in sports marketing? The answer to this question is best addressed in two parts. First, what knowledge is required for an individual to be successful in all sports management positions? In other words, what are the foundational skills for a successful career? Second, what are the marketing-specific core competencies of the sports marketing manager?

In addressing the first question, the general competencies necessary for all sports marketing management careers include being able to:[6]

- Direct the work effort of people or groups of people.
- Interrelate with the community.
- Negotiate to arrive at a solution to a problem.
- Function within a specified budget.
- Use supervision techniques.
- Evaluate the results of your decisions in light of work objectives.
- Evaluate employees' job performance.
- Use problem-solving techniques.
- Interpret basic statistical data.
- Speak before large audiences.
- Apply the knowledge of the history and evolution of sport into the structure of today's society.
- Appreciate the psychological factors that pertain to an athlete's performance and attitude on the playing field.

The University of Florida recently published a list of skills for sport marketers that included task management, big-picture thinking, initiative and leadership building, and writing skills.[7] You might be thinking these skills would be applicable to any industry, and this is probably true. It is important to point out that many of these competencies are gained outside of classes in sport management or business. So what about more specific sport marketing skills? This question was posed to sports marketing professionals employed in sports marketing firms, amateur sports organizations, professional sports organization, and college athletics. The results of this study are presented in Table 13.3 and, although over 20 years old, still ring true today. What skills might be added to this list if the study were replicated today?

Remember, changes in strategy may lead to modification of the staff and skill base. Thus, employee training and retraining is often an important part of the implementation process. As strategy is developed and the implementation plan formulated, sports marketers must consider not only new staffing needs

Table 13.3 Most important skills for sports marketing managers

Presented in rank order, where 1 is the most important skill and 20 is the least important skill

1. Establish a positive image for your sporting organization.
2. Achieve sponsors' promotional goals.
3. Stimulate ticket sales.
4. Maximize media exposure for events, athletes, and sponsors.
5. Acquire sponsors through personal contacts.
6. Maintain good relations with community, authorities, and partners.
7. Acquire sponsors by formal presentations.
8. Develop special promotions.
9. Improve budget construction.
10. Negotiate promotion contracts.
11. Evaluate sports marketing opportunities and performance.
12. Design and coordinate content of events.
13. Coordinate press coverage of events.
14. Create contracts.
15. Provide corporate hospitality of events.
16. Build public image and awareness of athletes.
17. Schedule events and facilities.
18. Establish event safety factors.
19. Build rapport with editors, reporters, and other media reps.
20. Buy and resell media rights.

Source: Peter Smolianov and David Shillbury, "An Investigation of Sport Marketing Competencies," *Sport Marketing Quarterly,* vol. 5, no. 4 (1996), 27–36

but also new skill needs. Training and retraining programs should be designed and included in the implementation plans so the staff is prepared to implement the new or modified strategy. Until all the staff and skills are in place, it is unlikely that the sports organization can proceed with the successful implementation of the marketing plan.

Coordination

Successful implementation of the marketing plan depends not only on capable and committed leadership who can effectively communicate internally and externally and a staff with the necessary skills but also on the effective organization of those people and their tasks. Structure helps to define the key activities and the manner in which they will be coordinated to achieve the strategy. A fit between strategy and structure has been shown to be critical to the successful achievement of strategy and the performance of organizations. According to one important study of organizations, when a new strategy was chosen, a decline in performance was observed and administrative problems occurred until a new method of organizing people and activities was put into place. Once the new method was implemented, organizational performance began to improve, and the strategy was more likely to be achieved.[8] Thus, the strategic marketing plan must dictate how people and tasks are organized.

One way of coordinating people and tasks in a sports organization is by practicing some form of **Total Quality Management**. Quality improvement programs and practices have long become an important and powerful tool for organizations, including sports organizations.[9] Nearly all major corporations and industries in the United States have adopted some type of quality initiative to meet competitive challenges. Traditionally, TQM programs have been focused on manufacturing quality. To manufacturers of sporting goods, quality is likely to mean an excellent consistency of goods and deliveries made by their suppliers. In a manufacturing environment, TQM has been primarily concerned with both the counting and reduction of defects and reducing the cycle time taken to complete any given process.

Even though TQM philosophies originally were used in manufacturing companies, a large number (69 percent) of service organizations are also using the principles of TQM. Although the nature of services is vastly different from those of manufactured products (see Chapter 7), Roberts and Sergesketter argue that the fundamental quality issues are similar.[10] A service organization, like a manufacturing organization, must concentrate on the reduction of defects and cycle times for important processes. As such, the philosophies of TQM are just as applicable for sports services as they are for manufacturing. Even more specifically, an article authored by Rexhepi, Ramadani, and Ratten[11] argues that the principles of TQM are very applicable to driving performance in sport organizations.

Although TQM represents a quality philosophy, there is little agreement as to what TQM (or quality) actually is and how best to manage the TQM process in an organization.[12] Evans and Lindsay define TQM as an integrative management concept for continuously improving the quality of goods and services delivered through the participation of all levels and functions of the organization.[13] In addition, TQM is described as incorporating design, control, and quality improvement, with the customer as the driving force behind the process.

Although the definitions of TQM may vary on the basis of wording and relative emphasis, all quality improvement programs share a common set of features or characteristics.[14] These characteristics include, but are not limited to, the following:

1. *Customer-driven quality* - Quality is defined by customers, and all TQM practices are implemented to please the customer.
2. *Visible leadership* - Top management is responsible for leading the quality charge and places quality above all else.

3. ***Data-driven processes*** - All TQM processes are driven by data collection, use of measurement, and the scientific method.
4. ***Continuous improvement philosophy*** - It is always possible to do a better job, and continual, small changes in improvement are just as critical as an occasional major breakthrough.

Rewards

As we discussed previously, the execution of strategy ultimately depends on individual members of the organization. Effective communication, staffing, skill development and enhancement, and coordination are vital to implementation efforts and should be planned for and considered throughout the strategic sports marketing process. Another critical component in the design of an implementation plan is to provide for motivating and rewarding behavior that is strategy supportive. Thus, a reward system is a key ingredient in effective strategy implementation.

There is no one "correct" reward system. From a strategic perspective, rewards must be aligned with the strategy; therefore, the best reward system is contingent upon the strategic circumstances. These rewards and incentives represent another choice for management. Thus, reward systems will reflect the beliefs and values of the individuals who design them. However, to successfully motivate desired behavior, reward systems must consider the needs, values, and beliefs of those who will be motivated by and receiving the rewards.

Management can choose from several types of motivators, which can be classified on the basis of three types of criteria. Motivators can be positive or negative, monetary or nonmonetary, and long run or short run. Some examples include compensation (salary or commission), bonuses, raises, stock options, benefits, promotions, demotions, recognition, praise, criticism, more (or less) responsibility, performance appraisals, and fear or tension.

Experience has shown that positive rewards tend to motivate best in most circumstances; however, negative motivators are also frequently used by organizations. Many organizations assume that only financial motivators will lead to desired behaviors. However, many organizations have obtained great success with nonfinancial rewards. Typically, a combination of both provides optimal results. Timing is also an important consideration in motivating performance with reward systems. Reward systems should be based on both short- and long-term achievements so that employees can both receive immediate feedback and yet be motivated to strive for the longer-term strategic goals. An excellent review of reward systems in general can be found in *Managing Employee Performance and Rewards: Concepts, Practices, and Strategies* by Shields, et. al.[15] More specific performance management strategies for sport are discussed in Taylor, Doherty, and McGraw's book, *Managing People in Sport Organizations*.[16]

In some sports, like professional golf and tennis, a pay-for-performance system could not be more pronounced. The athletes bear the cost of expenses but reap all the reward based on their performance. In other sports realms, the system structure is quite the opposite and often controversial, for example, collegiate sports and paying college players. As the accompanying article (13.5) illustrates, in the college environment, there are a number of considerations. Interestingly, some sports owners would like to link their teams' on-field performance to salaries. David Gill, former chief executive of Manchester United, English football's biggest brand, said he "would like to see players' salaries more variable, where they win rewards if we are winning." His model is not new to some industry executives, like bankers, but sports is arguably different. Athletes risk injury and the end of their career every time they run out to play and also have a short career span. Unsurprisingly, sports stars prefer a guaranteed salary to a performance-related payout.[17]

One debate that is currently raging, and has a surprisingly long history,[18] is whether college athletes should be paid. Aside from the ethical and values-based arguments that are presented, one question that remains to be answered is how pay would impact team or athlete performance. The following article addresses some of the questions that need to be resolved before play for pay at the college level is implemented.

ARTICLE 13.5
THE CASE FOR PAYING COLLEGE ATHLETES

These past few months, the American sporting landscape has turned upside down. The NBA and NHL are now navigating postseasons in bubbles, keeping players from their families for months. Professional athletes have committed to the new normal, their difficulties cushioned by a love for their sports and by their exorbitant paychecks. But what about the college athletes who have no such financial benefits?

College players are beginning to use their leverage against the multi-billion dollar college sports industry that can't survive without them. They're calling for eligibility extensions, campus support services and access to medical treatment. But given this priceless opportunity for reform, they should go further and demand an end to bans on player compensation. And the NCAA should listen.

In 2018, the Department of Education reported that college sports programs collected $14 billion in revenue. Historically, student athletes have only received the crumbs of that massive income. According to a 2019 report, NCAA schools spent $986 million on athletic scholarships every year – averaging out to about $22,000 for each of the 45,000 athletes represented. Conversely, $1.2 billion was divided among 4,400 coaches, coming out to an average annual salary of $273,000.

Worse than this, the NCAA bars students from accepting endorsement deals. For daring to use their own name, image and likeness to their advantage, athletes risk being deemed ineligible for play. Meanwhile, experts predict that the most recognizable college stars could make up to $250,000 per national ad campaign, with five-figure deals available to less popular, but locally known, players.

So what's the hang-up?

The NCAA is somehow deluded that its athletes are still students first, ignoring the "big-timeazation" of college sports that's taken place in the past few decades. Academic requirements supposedly separate college athletes from professional players, but college athletes simply don't have time to attend class, given their constant training, workouts and travel to out-of-state games. Scandals have rocked athletic programs again and again and again as players try to stay academically eligible, bringing shame to schools and teams alike.

That's hardly surprising, given our mistaken view that college athletes can have it both ways. Josh Rosen, UCLA quarterback and a first-round NFL draft pick in 2018, rightfully said, "Look, football and school don't go together. . . . Trying to do both is like trying to do two full-time jobs."

Indeed, the average Division 1 athlete devoted 34 hours per week on athletically related activities during the season, according to a 2016 NCAA study. Though the NCAA says athletes can't spend more than 20 hours per week on athletics, there's no enforcement mechanism.

And perhaps there shouldn't be. It's clear that the NCAA's collegiate model is failing athletes academically, but what it could do is provide an opportunity to train for a professional sporting career.

Critics cry that under 2% of college athletes will go pro. This, they say, proves the need for academics. But academic programs are clearly inadequate. Payment would be more helpful. Players could face the slim odds of going pro with a monetary promise to soften their risk – and if they found that the trade-off wasn't worth it, they could choose academics over athletics.

Thankfully, legislative efforts are already in the works. On Aug. 13, a group of senators announced their "College Athletes Bill of Rights," which would revolutionize athlete pay. And last year, California passed landmark legislation that would allow college athletes to profit from their name, image or likeness. Set to take effect in 2023, California's bill has inspired New York, Colorado, South Carolina and Michigan to consider similar measures.

The tide is turning – two-thirds of Americans surveyed this year supported endorsement money for college players. We've finally begun to see these athletes as quasi-professionals. The NCAA needs to follow suit. As the association entertains new regulations for the COVID-19 era of college sports, it can finally do right by the people who keep the system alive.

In summary, reward systems are critical to the successful achievement of the strategic sports marketing plan. To be effective, these systems must motivate behavior that "fits" with and ensures adequate attention to the strategic plan. Although reward systems are contingent upon the internal and external contingencies and the specific circumstances around which a sports marketing group must operate, there are some important general guidelines for developing effective reward systems (see Table 13.4).

Information

Accurate information is essential for decision making and action and necessary for all phases of the strategic sports marketing process. Execution of the

Table 13.4 Guidelines for designing reward systems
1. Rewards must be tightly linked to the strategic plan.
2. Use variable incentives and make them part of the compensation plan for everyone involved in strategy
3. Rewards should be linked to outcomes that the individual can personally affect.
4. Performance and relationship to the success of the strategy should be rewarded rather than the position held by the individual.
5. Be sensitive to the discrepancies between top and bottom of the organization.
6. Give everyone the opportunity to be rewarded.
7. Being fair and open can lead to more effective reward systems.
8. Reward success generously – make the reward enough to matter and motivate.
9. Do not underestimate the value of nonfinancial rewards.
10. Be willing and open to adapting the reward system to people and situation changes.

Source: John Pearce and Richard Robinson, *Formulation, Implementation, and Control of Competitive Strategy*, 5th ed. (Boston: Irwin, 1994)

sports marketing plan depends on effective information systems. These systems should provide the necessary information but should not offer more than is needed to give a reliable picture of issues critical to the implementation of the strategy.

Reports of information must be timely. The flow of information should be simple, including all the critical data being reported only to the people who need it. In other words, reports do not necessarily need wide distribution.

To aid strategy implementation, information reports should be designed to make it easy to flag variances from the strategic plan. In designing these reports, the critical questions to ask are as follows:

1. Who is going to need this information?
2. For what purpose will they need it?
3. When do they need it?

Today's sport organizations are not unlike other industries that are trying to harness the power of informatics and big data and analytics. Before even considering the application of big data, it is useful to define the term. One description of big data is just large amounts of data that an organization produces, collects, and stores in its day-to-day operations. Examples of big data in other industries may include the online choices made daily by consumers of Netflix or Amazon. Perhaps it's all the data collected on patients in a health care system or all the information collected by your own university to track the amount of time students are logging on to the system in an online class.[19] In sports organizations, we see nearly every team investing in systems to collect big data and people who ultimately need to make sure of the information.

Sports organizations, who are sometimes notorious for being slow to adopt trends in other industries, are playing catch-up, but some teams, like the New England Patriots, have been in the "big data" business for over a decade, and the results have paid off. One successful outcome for the Pats was to use analytics to design a T-shirt printed with the slogan, "Do Your Job," and sold only at the team store at Gillette Stadium. According to Kraft Analytics Group CEO Jessica Gelman, "That product line became a million-dollar business. "It all started with this very small piece of data and testing and analytics, and thinking about your customer and what they want, and it became something much bigger."[20]

Big data and analytics are here to stay in sports (and all industries), and teams and leagues are investing to assist in implementing organizational and marketing strategies. The following article presents a wonderful framework that illustrates various perspectives on analytical applications in the context of professional sports.

ARTICLE 13.6
THE ROLE OF ANALYTICS IN PROFESSIONAL SPORTS

In advance of the current European Soccer Championship, there was a controversial debate about the role of technology in professional sports – especially regarding the use of goal-line technology that helps the referee to decide if a goal was an actual goal. Despite many doubts, the "Hawk Eye" goal-line technology is now in use and already has proved itself in some tricky situations. This discussion was somehow surprising, since technology is already ubiquitous in the modern sports and there has always been a strong connection between professional sports and the idea of data analytics.

However, in the past most analytics happened intuitively (e.g. in the brain of the coach) and were usually based on rather general empirical data, like winning/losing a match or the subjective feeling about the performance of an athlete. With the rise of information technology, there are new possibilities to collect and process data in sports. Coaches can now make decisions based on tons of detailed data. Furthermore, there are a lot of technologies and algorithms that help them to make sense of the data.

One game changer in this context is the Internet of Things where information technology becomes ubiquitous. Wearable technologies that enable a continuous monitoring of vital data (or other KPIs that are essential for professional athletes) have gained a lot of attention recently. Wearables not only refer to well-known fitness wristbands popular in private use, such as the Fitbit, but rather to smart clothing with accurate (and invisible) sensors [2].

In the context of professional sports, not only vital data of the athletes are relevant, but also environmental data. It is therefore not surprising that all other physical objects (e.g., bats, gloves, balls or even the floor) are increasingly enriched with sensors that collect data and provide insights to players, coaches, fans and regulators.

Operational analytics

The operational use of analytics is probably the most obvious application in professional sports. Gathering more data during training and competitions enables athletes and coaches to optimize training programs. With real-time performance data, for instance, a coach can monitor the health and performance of his or her athletes and can adjust training programs accordingly. In the last years, smart sport utilities, such as smart bats or balls that analyze player technique (e.g. swing angle, strength) and give instant feedback [3, 4, 5], became a big market. These tools help athletes to bring their technique to perfection.

Strategic analytics

Despite operational uses, analytics can also be of use in the strategic area. If you've seen the movie "Moneyball", you know that mathematical methods can help a team to identify the right players to acquire. Data Scientists analyze the collected data of a team to identify weaknesses and then screen the available athletes with matching skillsets.

This shift to more data-centric decisions also holds new business opportunities. College teams can for instance sell their collected player information to talent scouts that then can choose on a mathematical basis which teams to visit and which players to investigate closer.

Regulation

The new analytics technology is not only useful for athletes and teams, but also for leagues, referees or regulators. Exact tracking via "Hawk Eye" type technology (see above) can help referees make right decisions. If you push this idea to the limit, one can imagine that in perhaps 15 years there are no human referees and matches are supervised by autonomous machines.

In relation to this, sensors and smart objects can also be used to identify cheating and doping in sports. Smart Chemical Sensors could for instance enable a real-time doping control, which would eliminate manipulation during today's doping control processes or fraud inside doping labs. Besides that, monitoring of vital data could also increase safety and help to prevent injuries or serious overexertion of athletes [6].

When talking about safety, the security in stadiums is also a big topic. There is a lot of research about "Real Time Crowd Tracking" that monitor crowds and identifies possible threats. Current approaches are mostly based on video feeds or cellphone data.

Fan insights & experience

Another interesting and more commercial application are fan insights. The main goal here is to identify what fans want and how a team or league can transform that into revenue. The methods here are very similar to classical customer intelligence. Sentiment analyses can help teams mine social media networks to discover what fans think or identify potential candidates for season-tickets.

Another important aspect here is customer experience: New technology enables a real-time interaction with fans. This might allow TV hosts and merchandising manager to react to the mood of the audience to deliver a better experience and have the right articles in the stores. Despite of security matters, additional sensors in seats and Crowd Tracking (see above) can also help to improve fan experience. After a match the stadium manager can see at which position how many people are leaving the stadium and can control visitor streams by motivating people to stay a few minutes longer (e.g. with showing highlights on certain screens or intelligent couponing, like free parking if you stay 10 minutes longer or get a beer at half price) [7].

This article shows that analytics is becoming an integral part of sports. We will probably see many developments in this sector in the near future. However, there are also concerns that too much technology will ruin the competition and thrill of sport, but this is a philosophical topic for another discussion.

Article 13.6 – The role of analytics in professional sports

Credit: Julian Ereth, published 22nd June 2016

Rightsholder: Eckerson Group

URL: www.eckerson.com/articles/sports-intelligence-the-role-of-technology-in-professional-sports

Creativity

The design of the strategic sports marketing plan's implementation phase is concerned with putting in place an effective system for executing marketing programs that will lead to the achievement of goals and objectives developed by the organization. The premise of this book is that the changing and uncertain environments in which sports organizations operate often require the need to adjust or change plans based on changing internal and external contingencies. Innovative plans and processes are vital to finding a fit with those contingencies. Thus, innovation, in the context of the strategic sports marketing process, is concerned with converting ideas and opportunities into a more effective or efficient system.

The **creative process** is the source of those ideas and, therefore, becomes an important component in the successful formulation and implementation of strategic sports marketing plans. Without creative endeavors, innovation is unlikely, if not impossible. An increase in creative efforts should likewise lead to an increase in innovative plans and processes.

When we talk about creativity, it is important to consider both the creative process and the people who engage in that process. The creative process can be learned and used by virtually anyone. However, some people have more experience with being creative and more confidence in their ability to be creative than others.

Many organizations can encourage creativity in their employees. This process of creating and innovating within an organization has been referred to as **intrapreneurship**, or corporate entrepreneurship. Intrapreneurial efforts have become popular as organizations have acknowledged the value of innovation in changing and uncertain environments. The watchword of today's businesses, sports organizations included, is change. As we discussed, innovation is vital to an organization's ability to change and adapt to internal and external contingencies. There are two general steps that can lead to an increase in the number of creative efforts and the resulting innovations: education and training regarding the creative process and establishing an organizational culture and internal environment that encourage creativity.

The creative process

Although creativity is usually associated with promotion, it is important for all elements of the marketing mix. To be competitive, sports organizations must be creative in their pricing, in developing new products and services, and in getting new sports products to the consumer. The first step in increasing creative efforts within a sports organization is educating employees about the creative process. Creativity is a capability that can be learned and practiced. It is a distinctive way of looking at the world and involves seeking relationships between things that others have not seen.

Although they are referred to by different names, there are four commonly agreed-upon steps in the creative process. They are knowledge accumulation, incubation, idea generation, and evaluation and implementation.

The **knowledge accumulation phase** is an often-overlooked, but absolutely vital, stage in the process of creating. Extensive exploration and investigation must precede successful creations. Because creations are simply putting together two existing ideas or tangibles in a new way, it is necessary to have an understanding of a variety of related and unrelated topics. This information gathering provides the creator with many different perspectives on the subject under consideration. Information can be gathered through reading, communication with other people, travel, and journal keeping. Simply devoting time to natural curiosities can be useful in this stage. The key is that the more the creator can learn about a broad range of topics, the more there is to choose from as the new creation is being developed.

In phase two, **the incubation period**, the creative individual allows his or her subconscious to mull over the information gathered in the previous stage by engaging in other activities. The creative effort is dropped for other pursuits. Routine activities, play, rest, and relaxation can often induce the incubation process. "Getting away" from the creative endeavor allows the subconscious mind to consider all the information gathered.

Often, when the creator least expects it, solutions will come. The next stage, **idea generation**, is the stage that is often portrayed as the "lightbulb" coming on in one's mind. The opportunity for this has been set, however, in the first two phases. As the body rests from the research and exploration, the subconscious mind sees the creative opportunity or the "light."

The last stage, **evaluation and implementation**, is often the most difficult. It requires a great deal of self-discipline and perseverance to evaluate the idea and determine whether it will lead to a useful innovation. Following through with that implementation is even more challenging. This is especially true because those individuals who are able to generate creative ideas are often not the ones who can turn those ideas into innovations. Creators may fail numerous times as they attempt to implement creative efforts. And, as the accompanying article illustrates, sometimes the innovative ideas that do reach the marketplace aren't the most welcomed, especially by fans.[21]

ARTICLE 13.7
WORST SPORTS INNOVATIONS

1. Performance-enhancing drugs

Steroids, human growth hormone, greenies and God-knows-what else. Have sports gotten more exciting since these products flooded the market? No. Everyone gets better at pretty much the same rate (just wait – soon the pitchers will catch up to the hitters, and the old 20 strikeout mark will be obliterated). In the meantime, records become meaningless, and athletes get all kinds of gruesome side effects. Lyle Alzado was a harbinger. More, inevitably, will die young.

2. Artificial turf

Dick Allen said in 1970, "If a horse can't eat it, I don't want to play on it." Norman Mailer said, "The injuries are brutal and the fields stink; at the end of the game they smell of vomit and spit and blood because it doesn't go into the earth. All the odors just cook there on this plastic turf." There you have it: Players hate it, fans hate it. Now that test tube strains of green blades can flourish in all kinds of climates, and real grass fields can be cultivated outdoors and slid indoors when it's time to play, it's time for the plastic stuff to go.

3. BCS

Bowl Championship Series? No. Bad College System. Bowls make big bucks, but the BCS is just a lousy idea that's eventually going to give way to college football playoffs. As the Atlanta Journal Constitution's Tim Tucker wrote last December, "By putting Nebraska – last seen giving up 62 points and losing by 26 to Colorado – in the national championship game, the BCS surrendered all credibility and exposed itself as even worse than we thought, which was plenty bad enough.

4. Aluminum bats

Politicians often do the wrong things, and sometimes say the right things. So we'll just quote from a speech given by Illinois representative Richard H. Durbin in 1989: "Designated hitters, plastic grass, uniforms that look like pajamas, chicken clowns dancing on the baselines, and of course the most heinous sacrilege, lights in Wrigley Field. Are we willing to hear the crack of a bat replaced by the dinky ping? Are we ready to see the Louisville slugger replaced by the aluminum ping dinger? Is nothing sacred?"

5. Enormous tennis rackets, grooved golf club heads, liquid centered golf balls and titanium

Equipment on steroids. Big, titanium rackets result in 150 mph serves, which lead to lots of aces. Yippee. Big titanium clubs result in 350-yard drives, which lead, inevitably, to longer golf courses. What fun. Altogether, this new equipment has changed the whole balance of power in these sports, and have changed the meaning of records and history.

6. Contraction

Bud Selig does the math and figures that MLB lost $232 million. Forbes magazine does the math and finds that MLB racked up $75 million in profits. As Twins outfielder Denny Hocking put it, "Gee, should I believe a magazine that spends 365 days a year researching finances?

Or a guy who has zero credibility?" Can one former used-car dealer from Milwaukee ruin the national pastime? Twenty-nine other owners are hoping to find out. Proof that making a bundle of money doesn't make you an economic genius.

7. Indoor football (NFL domes)

Another strategy masher, for a sport that needs to encourage more innovation, not more sameness. Last year's great Patriots-Raiders playoff game in the snow was a tantalizing glimpse of all we've lost to climate control.

8. Naming rights

We have no beef with Campbell Soup Field, the home of the Camden (N.J.) Riversharks. But think about it. Enron. PSInet. TWA. Fruit of the Loom. What do these companies have in common? They all went bankrupt. What else? They all bought stadium naming rights. Fans don't benefit, and what ballclub benefits by association with the losers of the business world?

9. Off-track betting

OTB seemed like a spiffy idea when it was launched in New York City on April 8, 1971 – state-sanctioned gambling for days when a player couldn't get out to the track. But over the years, it's proved a losing proposition. OTB has ruined racing in New York and in lots of other places all over the country – the tracks have become wastelands, with attendance falling precipitously almost everywhere. Major stakes races have disappeared, purses have dropped, fields have gotten smaller, racing has gotten worse, as the state drains much-needed money away from a dying sport without giving much back. The sport of kings is becoming largely a studio sport, with little to differentiate it from state lottery gimmicks, except it's a lot slower.

10. Olympic hockey shootout

Although numerous pundits clamored for the NHL to adopt many of the international rules showcased in Salt Lake City, there's no disputing the NHL's sudden-death, let-'em-play-until-somebody-scores overtime method is the best way to determine a winner. Penalty shots are a nice skills showcase, but it's like having a free throw or slam dunk contest to decide a winning team in basketball.

Also receiving votes

> The save statistic in baseball
> NHL's glowing puck
> Penalty kicks to decide a winner in soccer
> Publicly funded ballparks
> Body armor for hitters

Zone defenses in the NBA
3-pointers
Personal seat licenses

Credit: ESPN

URL: www.espn.com/page2/s/list/innovations/worst.html

Encouraging intrapreneurship

Creative efforts and the innovations within organizations are a function of both individual and organizational factors. Entrepreneurial employees add value to the organization and enhance implementation by finding creative ways to achieve the strategic plan. However, these efforts can flourish only if organizational features foster creativity. To encourage an intrapreneurial environment, staff members must be rewarded for entrepreneurial thinking and must be allowed and even encouraged to take risks. Failure and mistakes must be allowed and even valued as a means to creative and innovative expression.

The key to successfully creating a climate that encourages creativity and innovation is to understand the components of such an atmosphere. Those components include management support, worker autonomy, rewards, time availability, and flexible organizational boundaries. To understand these components, consider the following guidelines used at 3M Company:[22]

- *Do not kill a project* - If an idea does not seem to find a home in one of 3M's divisions at first, a 3M staff member can devote 15 percent of their time to proving it is workable. In addition, grant money is often provided for these pursuits.
- *Tolerate failure and encourage risk* - Divisions at 3M have goals of 25-30 percent of sales from products introduced within the last five years.
- *Keep divisions small* - This will encourage teamwork and close relationships.
- *Motivate champions*- Financial and nonfinancial rewards are tied to creative output.
- *Stay close to the customer* - Frequent contact with the customer can offer opportunities to brainstorm new ideas with them.
- *Share the wealth*- Innovations, when developed, belong to everyone.

Sports marketers are always looking for new and innovative approaches to all elements of the marketing mix, and technology and social media are transforming the delivery of these marketing experiences. Advances in technology have made information more accessible and put spectators in the heart of the action. Whether the enhancement of promotional delivery systems, broadcast, venue management, sportscape, logistics, or safety and security, people want technology to enhance their sporting lives. Spectators, governing bodies, and event planners are demanding more from their sporting events; therefore, real-time information utilizing multimedia solutions must be integrated into planning and promotion. For instance, the NHL is set to implement Smart Puck technology in the 2019-2020 season. The technology will allow the league to track movement on the ice at a rate of around 200 times a second and hopefully enhance the fan and broadcast experience.[23]

On the promotion side, and as talked about in Chapter 9, the use of social media as an innovative force to engage fans is here to stay, although the tools and techniques are changing constantly. Just think, it was over a decade ago that the Portland Trailblazers became one of the first teams to adopt a social media strategy, and now they have over 1 million Instagram followers. Brian Clapp has put forward some unique strategies for the use of social media in sports marketing.[24] Several keys include prioritizing the right social network for your audience, creating a distinct story and voice, leveraging players, and collecting and using feedback from users.

On the product side, one area of constant innovation is sports facility design. With so many new stadiums emerging all over the world, there is an arms race to see who can design the best in-stadium technology and capture the attention of fans. Trends in design may include "high density" Wi-Fi that allows huge numbers of users to access information in their devices in a quick and seamless fashion. In addition, stadia will be turning to 5G mobile device service and in-seat charging capabilities. We'll also see a trend in designing venues for esports, as we see the trend in esports participation and viewing grow exponentially.[25]

In other examples of technological influence, Nike has developed a new line of "smart clothing" for the NBA, placing an embedded sensor in fan jerseys. This will allow wearers to access team videos, player music playlists, and other information through their smartphones.[26] Shifting to athlete performance, uniforms are now becoming much more than a promotion piece for team and sponsor logos. Uniform technology is having a huge impact on athletic performance itself, with manufacturers all competing to have the most breathable, lightest, most comfortable, and most fashionable uniforms. Perhaps the best example is the work done for the Olympic games.

In a classic example, Speedo produced a swim suit that was so aerodynamic, it was actually banned from competition and deemed the equivalent of using a performance-enhancing drug. Nike has manufactured new Zoom Vaporfly shoes that are engineered with proprietary foam that requires long-distance runners to exert less effort over the course of a marathon. Under Armour produced a new fabric called ColdGear Infrared for bobsledding teams who, in Korea, had to be particularly concerned about the cold and the drag. These types of new technologies are especially important in sports, where the difference between first and second place may be milliseconds.[27]

Budgeting

Budgets are often used as a means of controlling organizational plans. However, the budgeting process can be an important part of the implementation plan if budget development is closely linked to the sports marketing strategy. In fact, the allocation of financial resources can either promote or impede the strategic implementation process.

Marketers within the sports organization must typically deal with two types of budgetary tasks. First, they must obtain the resources necessary for the marketing group to achieve the marketing plan goals. Second, they must make allocation decisions among the marketing activities and functions. These two types of activities require working with individuals and groups internal and external to the sports marketing function.

To develop strategy-supportive budgets, those individuals responsible should have a clear understanding of how to use the financial resources of the organization most effectively to encourage the implementation of the sports marketing strategy. In general, strategy-supportive activities should receive priority budgeting. Depriving strategy-supportive areas of the funds necessary to operate effectively can undermine the implementation process. However, over-allocation of funds wastes resources and decreases organizational performance. In addition, just like the rest of the strategic sports marketing process, the budgeting process is subject to changing and often unpredictable changes that may necessitate changes in the marketing budget. A change in strategy nearly always calls for budget reallocation. Thus, those individuals who are responsible for developing budgets must be willing to shift resources when strategy changes.

Control

In the uncertain and changing environments in which sports organizations operate, it is critical to consider four questions throughout the strategic sports marketing process.

1. Are the assumptions on which the strategic marketing plan was developed still true?
2. Are there any unexpected changes in the internal or external environment that will affect our plan?
3. Is the marketing strategy being implemented as planned?
4. Are the results produced by the strategy the ones that were intended?

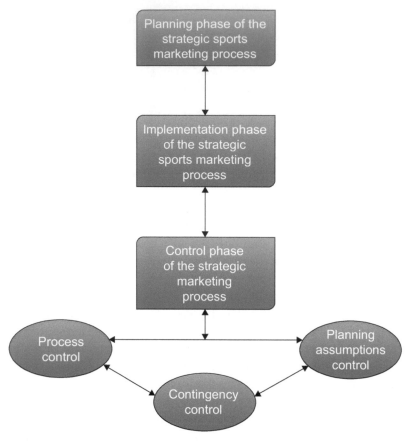

Figure 13.3
Control phase of the strategic sports marketing process

These questions are considered the basis of strategic control and the fundamental issues to be considered in the **control** phase of the strategic sports planning process model. **Strategic control** is defined as the critical evaluation of
plans, activities, and results – thereby providing information for future action.
As illustrated in Figure 13.3, the control phase of the model is the third step to
be considered. However, it is important to note that the arrows allow for "feed-
forward." In other words, even though control is the third phase of the model,
we consider it as we develop earlier phases of the process. Once the initial plan is
developed, the assumptions on which the plan was developed and the internal
and external contingencies must be examined and monitored. As the implementation process is set in place and as the plan is executed, strategic control
reviews the process as well as the outcomes. Variances from the original assumptions, plans, and processes are noted and changes are made as needed.

     The three types of strategic control that sports marketers must consider are
planning assumptions control, process control, and contingency control. The
following sections outline each of these three types of control.

Planning assumptions control

As we have discussed throughout this text, it is vital to understand internal and external contingencies and formulate strategic sports marketing plans that establish a fit with those contingencies. During the planning phase, it is often necessary to make assumptions concerning future events or contingencies about which we do not have complete information. In addition, individual planners may perceive and interpret data differently. In other words, the strategic sports marketing plan is based on a number of situation-specific premises and assumptions. This level of control attempts to monitor the continuing validity of these assumptions. Thus, in **planning assumptions control**, the sports marketer asks the question: "Are the premises or assumptions used to develop the marketing plan still valid?" To fully evaluate the responses to this question, the assumptions used during the development of the marketing plan must be listed. This step is vital to the success of this control mechanism so those individuals who are responsible can monitor them throughout the process. In essence, being able to shift gears quickly is at the heart of any contingency model of sport marketing strategy where adjustments need to be made continually as new data emerge. Teams that are expected to win games, series, or championships lose. NCAA conferences continually shift as teams move from one conference to another. Attendance figures rise and fall, and sports marketers are expected to adjust strategies.

Another example of a planning control assumption has been associated with the marketing and endorsement of players, teams, and leagues. Scandals such as the Russian doping, Cristiano Ronaldo rape allegations, Australian cricket ball tampering, and the NCAA basketball payoffs, to name a few,[28] have made corporate partners rethink their plans and uses.

Because of the complexity of the decision-making process, it may be impossible to monitor all the assumptions or premises used to formulate the strategic sports marketing plan. Therefore, it is often practical not only to list the premises but also to prioritize them based on those that may most likely effect a change in the marketing plan.

Although all assumptions should be considered in this form of control, two categories of premises are most likely to be of concern to the sports marketer: external environmental factors and sports industry factors. As we discussed earlier, strategic sports marketing plans are usually based on key premises about many of these variables. Some examples of external environmental factors include technology, inflation, interest rates, regulation, and demographic and social changes. The relevant sports industry in which a sports organization operates is also usually a key premise aspect in designing a marketing plan. Competitors, suppliers, league regulations, and leadership are among the industry-specific issues that need to be considered when identifying the critical assumptions used to develop the strategic plan.

Monitoring the premises or assumptions used to develop the strategic sports marketing plan is vital to the control phase of the strategic sports marketing process, but it is not sufficient. In other words, this form of control does not measure how well the actual plan is progressing, nor is it able to take into account the aspects of the internal and external environment that could not be detected during the planning phase when the premises were developed. Thus, effective control must consider two additional forms of evaluation: process control and contingency control.

Process control

Process control monitors the process to determine whether it is unfolding as expected and as desired. This type of control measures and evaluates the effects of actions that have already been taken in an effort to execute the plan.

Because of changes in premises and contingencies, the realized strategic marketing plan is often not the intended strategic marketing plan. Changes and modifications to the plan usually occur as a result of the process control activities carried out by marketers. In other words, during this stage of control, sports marketers attempt to review the plan and the implementation process to determine whether both remain appropriate to the contingencies. Either the marketing plan or the implementation process put in place to execute the plan may not proceed as intended. These variances may lead to a need to change the plan or the process or both. Thus, the key question asked by this form of control is: "Should either the strategic plan or the implementation process be changed in light of events and actions that have occurred during the implementation of the plan?" It is important to note that to change or modify the marketing plan or implementation process is not necessarily a decision to avoid. The benefit of this form of control is that sports marketers can minimize the allocation of resources into a strategic plan or implementation process that is not leading to achievement of the objectives and goals they deem important. To answer the preceding question, two measures are typically used: **monitoring strategic thrusts** and **reviewing milestones**. As we discussed earlier, the strategic sports marketing plan is a means of achieving strategic and financial organizational goals and marketing objectives. An important part of evaluating the plan and process is to review the achievement of these objectives and goals during the execution of the plan. Because objectives are not time specific or time bound (as discussed in Chapter 2), strategic thrusts can be examined to evaluate progress in the direction of strategic and financial objectives. On the other hand, reviewing milestones typically examines achievement of marketing objectives. Let us look at each of these two forms of process control more closely.

Monitoring strategic thrusts

Monitoring strategic thrusts attempts to evaluate or monitor the strategic direction of the plan. As a part of the overall strategic plan, smaller projects are usually planned that will lead to the achievement of the planned strategy. Successful pursuit of these smaller projects can provide evidence that the strategic thrust is the intended one. However, if these projects are getting lost to other "nonstrategic" projects, it could mean that the overall strategy is not progressing as planned.

One strategic thrust of special interest to sports organizations and organizations marketing their products through sports is, of course, sponsorship. Determining the effectiveness of a sponsorship program is becoming increasingly more important as the costs of sponsorship continue to rise. A 2017 Sponsorship Decision-Makers Survey found the most valuable service a property can provide to its partners is help in evaluating whether the sponsorship is meeting its goals. In addition, half of the survey respondents rated assistance measuring ROI a 9 or 10 on a 10-point scale of value, up from 41 percent in 2016.[29]

Just how, then, do we measure or determine whether we are seeing a return on our marketing investment? ESP Properties describes five foundational techniques for the measurement of sponsorship ROI.[30] These are:

- Sponsors and properties should have a conversation about the importance of establishing a good measurement process.
- Measurable goals should be set.
- Goals should be as specific as possible.
- Sponsors should use established processes for developing measurement plans.
- Compare results to multiple mileposts.

Sponsorship return can be measured. The key lies in defining objectives, establishing a pre-sponsorship benchmark against which to measure, and maintaining consistent levels of advertising and promotion so that it is possible to isolate the effect of sponsorship.

The lack of a universal yardstick for measuring sponsorship is a problem, but it is also an opportunity. The problem is that sponsorships often are dropped not because they don't have measurement value but because no one has actually measured the value.

The lack of a single, standardized measurement is also an opportunity because it means sponsors can tailor their measurement systems to gauge their specific objectives.

Since there are no universal measures, companies struggle with finding the resources and determining what the right things to measure are. In the sporting world, it is not uncommon for companies not to measure return from sponsorship. In fact, in 2017, when IEG asked the question, "Does your company actively measure return from its sponsorship?" nearly one-third of the sponsors said no, and nearly half only spend less than 1 percent of sponsorship budget on measurement. Companies often choose the easiest method of assessment, focusing on awareness of products, attitudes, and brands. The more challenging methods that focus on the harder-to-determine effectiveness measures are further down the purchase funnel. Marketers also continue to rely on their property partners for evaluation assistance, with half of survey respondents ranking their dependence on rightsholders to help them measure return as a 9 or 10 on a 10-point scale.[31] Table 13.5 shows a few of the more popular ways of measuring sponsorship effectiveness and brand impact against common sponsorship objectives.[32]

As mentioned in previous chapters, generating awareness is always step one toward creating powerful brand equity. Awareness is sometimes assessed through "media equivalencies," that is, determining how much "free" time the sponsor has accumulated through television, streaming, and social media coverage. For example, Joyce Julius & Associates calculated all the interview times and mentions of NASCAR drivers to determine how much this coverage would have otherwise cost, if paid. In another example, the former Utah

Table 13.5 Measuring sponsorship effectiveness	
Brand visibility	Value of visibility (media)
	Media mentions (PR)
Get your brand or product known	Awareness with target audience
	Knowledge of products and services
Improve brand image	Opinion of the brand
	Reputation of the company
	Brand associations
	Brand equity
Brand affinity	Participant comments
	Appreciation of the activation
	Relevance of the property/brand
	Identification with the brand
Sales	Purchase intent/unsubscribe intent
	Changes in sales vs. comparable period
	Percentage of coupon use
	Direct revenue
	Conversion rate
Keep or motivate employees	Participation
	Engagement rate

Source: Elevent, https://en.elevent.co/blogs/sponsorship/19077697-six-essential-tools-for-effi cient-sponsorship-measurement

Web Capture 13.2
Joyce Julius & Associates measure marketing, sponsorship and brand metrics across all forms of media

Credit: Joyce Julius & Associates, published 3rd October 2018

URL: https://twitter.com/joyce_julius?lang=en

State University quarterback Jordan Love was estimated to bring $18 million in media equivalence – just on draft day – to a school that rarely gets exposure on the national stage.[71]

Milestone review

The second form of process control is **milestone review**. Marketing managers at sports organizations usually establish milestones that will be reached during the execution of the marketing plan. These milestones may be critical events, major allocations, achievements, or even the passage of a certain amount of time. They are often an integral part of a program evaluation and/or network analysis strategy. Critical path or milestone reviews help market planners to prioritize goals and objectives and define time lines, as well as the sequence, order, and thresholds of market strategies. As these milestones are reviewed on a continuous basis, an evaluation of the advisability of continuing with the plan and the process is afforded.

Financial analysis

Financial information can be used to understand and control the process of strategic marketing plan implementation, that is, to perform **financial analyses**. It is important for any sports organization to have a good accounting

Photo 13.2

Sponsors such as Kia must design controls to evaluate sponsorship effectiveness

Credit: Gabriel Roux photography

Rightsholder: Kia Classic

URL: www.thedrum.com/news/2017/03/14/kia-builds-womens-sports-sponsorship-portfolio-with-ladies-pga-deal

system. In terms of process control, the accounting system can provide the following:

- A ready comparison of present financial performance with past performance, industry standards, and budgeted goals.
- Reports and financial statements that can be used to make appropriate strategic decisions.
- A way of collecting and processing information that can be used in the strategic sports marketing process.

Two important components of a good accounting system are the **income statement** and **balance sheet**. The balance sheet and income statement are the traditional financial statements that have been required in annual reports for many years.

Income statements provide a summary of operating performance. These documents summarize both money coming into and going out of the sports organization and the marketing department or division. Because income statements are a good measure of customer satisfaction and operating efficiency, they should be prepared frequently – at least every three months, if not monthly. Balance sheets provide a summary of the financial health of the sports organization at a distinct point in time. The balance sheet provides the sports marketer with a summary of what the organization is worth; what has been

Table 13.6a Rich Creek Rockers income statement

Income statement for the year ended December 31, 2012

Revenues:		
Single game admissions	$140,000	
Season ticket holders	275,000	
Concessions	250,000	
Advertising revenue	95,000	760,000
Expenses:		
Cost of concessions sold	100,000	
Salary expense – players	235,000	
Salary and wages – staff	130,000	
Rent	150,000	615,000
Profits before taxes		145,000
Income tax		33,000
Income after taxes		$112,000

Table 13.6b Rich Creek Rockers balance sheet

Balance sheet at December 31, 2012

Assets		Liabilities and owner's equity	
Cash	$ 10,000	Accounts payable	$ 20,000
Accounts receivable	82,000	Capital stock	50,000
Equipment	40,000	Retained earnings	62,000
Total assets	$ 132,000	Total liabilities and owner's equity	$132,000

invested in assets, such as inventories, land, and equipment; how the assets were financed; and who has claims against the assets. Tables 13.6a and 13.6b provide simple examples of the information typically found on income statements and balance sheets. In contrast, the statement of cash flow, which replaced the statement of changes in the late 1980s, shows the sources and uses of a firm's cash. The statement of cash flows details where the resources of cash come from and how they are used. It provides more valuable information about liquidity than can be obtained from the balance sheet and income statements.

One of the more useful method of financial analysis for control purposes is known as **ratio analysis**. Financial ratios are computed from income statements and balance sheets. These ratios can tell the sports marketing manager a lot about the progress and success of the strategic sports marketing plan. In other words, using financial ratios can help a sports marketing manager assess whether the marketing strategy continues to provide an appropriate fit with internal and external contingencies. There are several types of financial ratios that can be categorized as follows:

- **Profitability ratios** - Provide an indication of how profitable the organization or division is during a period of time.
- **Liquidity ratios** - Indicate the ability of the organization to pay off short-term obligations without selling off assets.
- **Leverage ratios** - Measure the extent to which creditors finance the organization.
- **Activity ratios** - Measure the sales productivity and utilization of assets.
- **Other ratios** - Determine such things as return to owners in dividends, the percentage of profits paid out in dividends, and discretionary funds.

Table 13.7 lists some of the more commonly used ratios, how each is calculated, and what each can tell the sports marketing manager. Examples of how these ratios are applied and interpreted are shown in Table 13.8.

Table 13.7 Summary of selected key financial ratios

Ratio	Calculation	Question(s) answered
Gross profit margin	*Sales – cost of goods sold* / *Sales*	What is the total margin available to cover operating expenses and provide profit?
Net profit margin	*Profit after taxes* / *Sales*	Are profits high enough given the level of sales? Are we operating efficiently?
Return on total assets	*Profit after taxes* / *Total assets*	How wisely has management employed assets?
Asset turnover	*Sales* / *Average total assets*	How well are assets being used to generate sales revenue?
Current ratio	*Current assets* / *Current liabilities*	Does our organization have enough cash or other liquid assets to cover liabilities?
Debt-to-assets load	*Total debt* / *Total assets*	Is the organization's debt excessive?
Inventory turnover	*Cost of goods sold* / *Average inventory*	Is too much cash tied up in inventories?
Accounts receivable turnover	*Annual credit sales* / *Accounts receivable*	What is the average length of time it takes our firm to collect for sale? Made on credit?

Table 13.8 Examples of key financial ratios

Net profit margin

$$\frac{112,000}{760,000} = 14.7\%$$

Interpretation – Approximately 15 percent of sales is yielding profits. This percentage should be compared with industry (similar sports organizations) averages and examined over a period of several years. Declining or subpar percent could mean expenses are too high, prices are too low, or both.

Return on assets

$$\frac{112,000}{132,000} = 84.8\%$$

Interpretation – This is a measure of the productivity of the assets in the sports organization. Once again, this number should be compared with similar sports organizations and examined over several years. If this number is declining, it may indicate that assets are not being used as effectively or efficiently as they were in previous years.

Inventory turnover

$$\frac{2,500,000}{100,000} = 25 \text{ times}$$

Interpretation – Inventory turnover is a measure of the number of times inventory is sold during a period of time. Assuming an average inventory of $100,000 (beginning inventory + ending inventory/2) the inventory (in this example concessions) was sold 25 times. If this number is higher than the average for this type of sports organization, then ordering costs may be too high and stockouts may be occurring. If the number is lower, it may mean too much inventory is being stored, tying up money unnecessarily, and the products (in this case, food) may lack freshness.

The third form of control, **contingency control**, is based on the assumption that sports marketers operate in an uncertain and unpredictable environment and that the changing nature of the internal and external environments may lead to the need to reassess strategic choices. Although it is included as a part of the control phase, this form of control should be of concern throughout the strategic sports marketing process.

The goal of contingency control is to constantly scan the relevant environments for internal and external contingencies that could affect the marketing planning process. Foreseeability, the ability to anticipate the future events, outcomes, or results of an action based on the circumstances, past experiences, apparent riders, or reasonable sense expected of a human being, is critical to the success of contingency control. Unlike planning assumptions control, the goal here is to remain unfocused so any unanticipated events will not be missed. In other words, the "big picture" is of most concern in this phase of control. The primary question to be addressed here is: "How can we protect our marketing strategy from unexpected events or crises that could affect our ability to pursue the chosen strategic direction?" Attempts to control without a prestructured list of variables of concern may not seem to make sense at first. However, it is easier to understand this form of control if one thinks in terms of how a crisis usually occurs. The daily events leading up to an unpredicted event lead to a focus in the form of a crisis. Previously unimportant or unnoticed events become more problematic until an actual crisis requires some action. Learning to notice and interpret signals thus becomes an important way to circumvent crises. Thus, the goal of contingency control is to learn to notice these signals and to have a plan of action in place to cope with a crisis if it occurs.

Sports scandals and crises are not infrequent. Anyone who reads a newspaper sports section has observed situations that could lead to a public relations nightmare for a sports organization or individual athlete. More research is now being conducted on better understanding the defining characteristics of scandal and attempting to quantify the magnitude of a specific scandal. Hughes and Shank found that media and corporate sponsors generally identified four consistent characteristics that make an event in athletics scandalous or not.[34] These characteristics included an action that was either illegal or unethical, involved multiple parties over a sustained period of time, and whose impact affected the integrity of the sport with which they were associated.[35]

Although there are new scandals emerging daily that might subjectively make this list, the top five worldwide sports scandals of all time are presented in Table 13.9.[36] Also, let's not forget the crisis that has impacted all industries, including sport - COVID.

Although crises such as these are unpredictable, it is useful to plan so the chosen response can be not only faster but also more effective. A **crisis plan** should include elements of the following:[37]

- Well-defined organizational response strategies
- Specific procedures that will lead to a more efficient and effective response
- Steps that will deal effectively with potential media impact and will enhance image
- Efficient ways to deal with a variety of problems that could occur

Moreover, sports organizations may benefit from an informal and a formal crisis response plan. The key is that any crisis plan should offer priorities for proactive and reactive response under a variety of circumstances. It should have the capacity to both alert and calm people during an unexpected event that could have the potential for major consequences.

Table 13.9 Top 5 Sporting Scandals that Shocked the World

Lance Armstrong

Probably the biggest scandal to hit modern sport is the revelation of doping by 7-time Tour winner, Lance Armstrong. Whilst allegations had swirled for years, Armstrong was strong in his denial of any wrong doing, even swearing under oath that he was clean.

Armstrong was eventually forced to come clean in an infamous interview with Oprah Winfrey, after the US Anti-Doping Agency applied pressure suggesting he was behind the "most sophisticated, professionalized and successful doping program" sport had ever seen. This story held extra sting given Armstrong's comeback following testicular cancer, and the wave of hope that was provided by the narrative. However Lance's achievements were stripped from him, and he now has a lifetime ban on competition.

Tiger Woods

Tiger Woods was the golden boy of golf, the greatest of all time, and one of the most marketable sportsmen of our era. Then came 2009. A car crash was the straw that broke the camels back, leading to the revelation of over a dozen affairs, and a bitter divorce. The personal troubles had a significant impact on his golf, and Tiger is only now on the way to getting his golf game back on track, although his legacy will unlikely live up to the potential it held back in the day.

OJ Simpson

While not strictly sport related, many forget that OJ Simpson was an NFL star before his acting days, and of course the time of his infamous Bronco highway chase. The chase overshadowed the NBA final being played at the time, as Simpson hit the road to run from police following a horrific double murder. Simpson was later acquitted of the charges in one of the most watched trials of all time. OJ was jailed years later however on robbery charges.

Tonya Harding

Now the subject of hit movie *I, Tonya*, the scandal surrounding the lead up to the 1994 Winter Olympics saw Tonya Harding and her co-conspirators attack rival Nancy Kerrigan with a club, injuring her leg. Following training, Kerrigan was struck with the intention of ending her season on the ice, paving the way for Harding's Olympic triumph. The attack didn't go according to plan however, with Harding finishing 8th, and Kerrigan taking silver, despite the injury.

Oscar Pistorius

On Valentine's Day 2013, Paralympic athletic champion Pistorius (aka "Bladerunner") opened fire on his girlfriend, model Reeva Steenkamp, in what he claimed was self-defense. According to Pistorius, he had thought Steenkamp was an intruder, however after a lengthy trial, and subsequent appeal in 2015, he was found guilty of murder, and is currently serving a 13-year jail sentence.

Source: https://www.menshealth.com.au/top-5-sporting-scandals-that-shocked-the-world

Credit: Scott Henderson, published 26th March 2018

Rightsholder: Australian Men's Health

Summary

Implementing and controlling the strategic sports marketing process is the emphasis of Chapter 13. After the planning phase of the strategic marketing process is completed, the implementation and control phases are considered. Implementation is described as an action step where strategic marketing plans are executed. Without the proper execution, the best plans in the world would be useless. To facilitate the implementation process, seven organizational design elements must be addressed. The organizational design elements include communication, staffing and skills, coordination, rewards, information, creativity, and budgeting. To begin, the organization must effectively communicate the plan and its rationale to all the members of the sports marketing team who will play a role in executing the plan. In terms of staffing and skills, there must be enough people, and they must have the necessary skills and expertise to successfully implement the strategic marketing plan. Research has shown that the skills deemed most important for sports marketing managers include establishing a positive image for your sports organization; achieving sponsors' promotional goals; stimulating ticket sales; maximizing media exposure for events, athletes, and sponsors; and acquiring sponsors through personal contacts.

Coordination is another of the organizational design elements that influences implementation. Coordination involves determining the best structure for the organization to achieve the desired strategy. Research has shown the importance of good fit between structure and successful implementation. One way of coordinating people and tasks that has received considerable attention over the last decade is through total quality management. TQM philosophies are based on aligning the organizational structure to best meet the needs of the customers.

Another important organizational design element that affects implementation is the rewards structure of the sports organization. With proper pay and incentives, employees may be motivated to carry out the strategic plan. Some guidelines for designing effective rewards systems include linking rewards to the strategic plan using a variety of incentives: link performance with rewards, give everyone the opportunity to be rewarded, and be willing to adapt the rewards system.

Information is one of the most essential elements of effective implementation. To aid in the gathering and dissemination of information for strategic decision making, organizations must design information systems. Before gathering information, consider: Who is going to need this information, for what purpose is the information needed, and when do they need it?

Fostering creativity, another organizational design element, is yet another important aspect of implementation. Creativity and innovation within the organization is called intrapreneurship or corporate entrepreneurship and is developed through education and training. To enhance employee creativity, the creative process, consisting of four steps, is used by organizations. These steps are knowledge accumulation, idea generation, evaluation, and implementation. Efforts to encourage intrapreneurship are also enhanced by creating an organizational environment that cultivates such thinking.

The final organizational design element that has a direct impact on implementation is budgeting. Without proper monies, the strategic sports marketing plan cannot be properly implemented or carried out. Budgets must be secured for all marketing efforts within the larger organization. Once these monies are obtained, they must then be allocated within marketing to achieve specific marketing goals that have been prioritized.

After plans have been implemented, the control phase of the strategic sports marketing process is considered. Strategic control is defined as the critical evaluation of plans, activities, and results, thereby providing information for future action. In other words, the control phase explores how well the plan is meeting objectives and makes suggestions for adapting the plan to achieve the desired results. Three types of strategic control considered by sports marketers are planning assumptions control, process control, and contingency control.

Planning assumptions control asks whether the premises or assumptions used to develop the marketing plan are still valid. Two categories of assumptions that should receive special consideration from sports marketers are those concerned with the external contingencies and the sports industry. Because plans are typically developed by carefully considering the external environment and the sports industry, assumptions with respect to these two issues are critical.

Process control considers whether the plan and processes used to carry out the plan are being executed as desired. The key issue addressed by process control is whether the planning or implementation processes should be altered in light of events and actions that have occurred during the implementation of the plan. To make decisions about whether plans or the implementation process should be changed, sports organizations review milestones that have been set or monitor strategic thrust. Milestones such as financial performance are more specific objectives that can be examined, while strategic thrust evaluates whether the organization is moving toward its intended goals.

Key terms

- activity ratios
- budgeting
- communication
- contingency control
- control
- coordination
- creative process
- creativity
- crisis plan
- financial analyses

- implementation
- information
- intrapreneurship
- leverage ratios
- liquidity ratios
- milestone review
- monitoring strategic thrust
- planning assumptions control
- process control
- profitability ratios
- ratio analysis
- rewards
- staffing and skills
- strategic control
- total quality management (TQM)

Review questions

1 What are the organizational design elements that must be managed for effective implementation?
2 Why must there be a fit between the planning and implementation phases of the strategic sports marketing process?
3 What are some of the common ways of communicating with groups both inside and outside the sports organization?
4 What are the marketing-specific core competencies of the sports marketing manager?
5 Define TQM. What are the common characteristics of any TQM program? Why is it important for sports organizations to practice a TQM philosophy?
6 What are the guidelines for designing rewards systems?
7 What is intrapreneurship? What are the four steps in the creative process? How can sports organizations encourage intrapreneurship?
8 Define strategic control. What are the three types of strategic control that sports marketers must consider?
9 What two measures are typically used during process control?
10 How can we evaluate sponsorship effectiveness?
11 Describe the different financial ratios that can be calculated to assess whether a sports organization's financial objectives are being met.
12 What are the fundamental components of a crisis plan?

Exercises

1 Describe three sports organizations that have a strong leader who communicates well outside the sports organization. What are the common

characteristics of these leaders, and why do these leaders communicate effectively?

2   How does the education that you are receiving complement the marketing-specific skills required of sports marketing managers?

3   Locate the organizational charts for the marketing department of two professional sports organizations. How will this structure facilitate or impede the implementation of their strategic marketing effort?

4   Design a reward system to encourage intrapreneurship.

5   Discuss the last three major "crises" in sport (at any level). How did the organizations or individuals handle these crises?

6   Discuss how being the quarterback of a football team is similar to being a marketer responsible for implementing and controlling the strategic sports marketing process.

7   Interview three marketing managers who are responsible for sponsorship decisions in their organization. Determine how each evaluates the effectiveness of their sponsorship.

Internet exercises

1   Browse the Web site of the Sports & Fitness Industry Association (SFIA) (www.sfia.org) and discuss how the information found on this site might be useful for developing a strategic marketing plan for a new professional lacrosse league.

2   Find two web sites that would provide sports marketing managers with information about whether their planning assumptions regarding the demographics of the U.S. population remain valid.

3   Find examples of three nonsports organizations that advertise on ESPN's Web site (www.espn.com). How might these companies evaluate the effectiveness of their Web-based advertising?

Notes

1   https://howtheyplay.com/team-sports/How-Major-League-Baseball-Can-Fix-Its-Attendance-Problem.

2   Source: http://dailycaller.com/2018/06/28/best-sports-commissioner/.

3   www.blazersedge.com/2018/9/30/17922484/portland-trail-blazers-rookie-dance-leonard-mvp-fanfest-2018.

4   www.richmondraceway.com/Articles/2017/12/FAB.aspx.

5   Anil K. Gupta and V. Govindarajan, "Build, Hold or Harvest: Converting Strategic Intentions into Reality," *Journal of Business Strategy* (Winter 1984), 41.

6   Peter Smolianov and David Shilbury, "An Investigation of Sport Marketing Competencies," *Sport Marketing Quarterly*, vol. 5, no. 4 (1996), 27–36.

7   https://sm.hhp.ufl.edu/news/what-does-a-sports-marketer-do/.

8   Alfred D. Chandler, *Strategy and Structure* (Cambridge, MA: MIT Press, 1963).

9   Barbara Aquilani Cecilia Silvestri, Alessandro Ruggieri, and Corrado Gatti, "A Systematic Literature Review on Total Quality Management Critical Success Factors and the Identification of New Avenues of Research," *The TQM Journal*, vol. 29, no. 1 (2017), 184–213. https://doi.org/10.1108/TQM-01-2016-0003.

10 Harry Roberts and Bernard Sergesketter, *Quality Is Personal* (New York: Free Press, 1993).

11 G. Rexhepi, V. Ramadani, and V. Ratten, "TQM Techniques as an Innovative Approach in Sport Organisations Management: Toward a Conceptual Framework," *International Journal of Business and Globalisation*, vol. 20, no. 1 (January 2018), 18–29.

12 George Easton and Sherry Jarrell, "The Effects of Total Quality Management on Corporate Performance: An Empirical Investigation," *Journal of Business*, vol. 71, no. 2 (1998), 253–261.

13 James Evans and William Lindsay, *The Management and Control of Quality*, 2nd ed. (St. Paul, MN: West, 1993).

14 Ibid.

15 John Shields, Michelle Brown, Sarah Kaine, Catherine Dolle-Samuel, Andrea North-Samardzic, Peter McLean, Robyn Johns, Patrick O'Leary, Jack Robinson, and Geoff Plimmer, *Managing Employee Performance & Reward: Concepts, Practices, Strategies*, 2nd ed. (Cambridge: Cambridge University Press, 2016).

16 Tracy Taylor, Alison Doherty, and Peter McGraw, *Managing People in Sport Organizations: A Strategic Human Resource Management Perspective* (London: Routledge, January 2015).

17 "Pay for Performances: Why Footballers Are Not Remunerated Like Investment Bankers," *Financial Times*, London (January 27, 2007), 10.

18 www.aspeninstitute.org/blog-posts/history-behind-debate-paying-ncaa-athletes/.

19 https://www.simplilearn.com/tutorials/big-data-tutorial/big-data-applications.

20 www.sportsbusinessdaily.com/Daily/Issues/2017/10/12/Sports-Facilities-and-Franchises/Fan-Identity.aspx?hl=information%20systems.

21 Source: www.espn.com/page2/s/list/innovations/worst.html.

22 R. Mitchell, "Masters of Innovation," *Business Week* (April 10, 1989), 58–63.

23 www.si.com/nhl/2018/05/22/nhl-smart-puck-technology-introduction.

24 www.workinsports.com/blog/unique-strategies-for-using-social-media-in-sports-marketing/.

25 www.sporttechie.com/4-trends-stadium-technology-infrastructure-watch-2018/.

26 https://www.wareable.com/sport/nike-connected-nba-jerseys-5092.

27 https://www.popsci.com/olympics-clothing-performance-impact.

28 https://www.theguardian.com/sport/russia-doping-scandal; www.thetimes.co.uk/edition/sport/cristiano-ronaldo-notes-on-a-scandal-fjsp6tjgz; www.abc.net.au/news/2018-10-05/cricket-australia-seeks-forgiveness-after-ball-tampering-scandal/10339174; https://www.cbssports.com/college-basketball/news/college-basketball-trial-documents-allege-collin-sexton-paid-5000-while-at-alabama-had-monthly-salary/.

29 https://www.sponsorship.com/User/Login.aspx?ReturnUrl=%2fReport%2f2018%2f01%2f29%2fMeasurement-Essentials-Part-1.aspx&Access=0&Reason=NoUser.

30 https://www.sponsorship.com/Report/2018/01/29/Measurement-Essentials-Part-1.aspx.

31 https://www.sponsorship.com/IEG/files/f3/f3cfac41-2983-49be-8df6-3546345e27de.pdf.

32 https://en.elevent.co/blogs/sponsorship/19077697-six-essential-tools-for-efficient-sponsorship-measurement.

33 David Ching, "Jordan Love's First-Round Draft Status Worth $18 Million in Draft-Day Exposure for Utah State" (April 27, 2020). Available from: https://www.forbes.com/sites/davidching/2020/04/27/jordan-loves-first-round-status-worth-18-million-in-draft-day-exposure-for-utah-state/?sh=4364812ced32.

34 Stephanie Hughes and Matt D. Shank, "Defining Scandal in Sport: Media and Corporate Sponsor Perspectives," *Sport Marketing Quarterly*, vol. 14, no. 4 (2005), 207–216.

35 Ibid.

36 https://www.menshealth.com.au/top-5-sporting-scandals-that-shocked-the-world.

37 Emre Belli, Orcan Mizrak, and Yagiz Saracoglu, "Crisis Management in Sports Organizations: The Case of Covid-19," *Journal of Physical Education and Sports Management*, vol. 7, no. 1 (June 2020), 55–65.

Appendix A

Career Opportunities in Sports Marketing

Many of us have dreamed of becoming a professional athlete. Unfortunately, reality sets in rather quickly. We discover that we cannot throw a 95-mile-per-hour fastball or even touch the rim – much less slam dunk. However, there are many other opportunities for careers in sports. In fact, there are a wide variety of sports careers in sports marketing. In this appendix, we will explore some of the career options in sports marketing and present some interview and résumé-writing tips for landing that dream job. Finally, we will examine some additional sources of information on careers in sports marketing.

Before we look at some of the career alternatives in sports marketing, it is useful to think about how the concepts discussed in this text can be useful in your job search. As you know, the strategic marketing process begins by conducting a SWOT analysis. You should build a SWOT into your career planning. First, ask questions about your own strengths and weaknesses. You can be sure the organizations you interview with will be asking similar questions. Next, try to identify the opportunities that exist in the marketplace. What sports are hot? What level of sport is growing (e.g., high school, college, youth sports)? Where are the growth areas in sports marketing?

The next step of your strategic career search should be to gather information and conduct research on prospective employers. Research should not only be conducted through a comprehensive online review but by talking to people within the industry and organization to gain a better understanding of the culture. In addition, observation might take place both before and certainly during the interview.

Next, you need to consider your target market. Of course, you won't apply for all of the sports marketing jobs in the world. Target the job opportunities based on location, type of position, and how the position or organization fits with your current and potential strengths. You also need to position yourself, as you would any sport product. Remember, careers in sports marketing are in demand, and you need to find a way to market yourself and stand out from the competition.

The marketing mix variables should also be considered in your job search. The product, in this case, is you. You are the bundle of benefits that is being offered to the prospective organization. You should also enter into the strategic career search with some understanding of price. What is the value you attach to the service and expertise that you will provide? Are the salary and benefits package being offered a satisfactory exchange?

Your résumé, cover letter, interviewing skills, and ability to sell yourself are the elements of the promotion mix. These elements communicate something about you to prospective employers. Finally, the place element of the marketing mix is the location in which you are willing to work. In the case of distribution or place, you have to understand where the work will be performed - in person or virtually.

From this brief discussion, you can begin to understand that finding the right job for yourself in sports marketing can and should be done in a systematic, organized fashion. By using the basic principles of the strategic marketing process, you will be in a better position to land your dream job. Let us turn our attention to some of the job opportunities that exist in the field of sports marketing.

Job opportunities in sports marketing

There are a wide variety of jobs in sports marketing that may be of interest to you. Here are just a few of the opportunities that exist. As you look through this section, pay special attention to the sample advertisements and the qualifications that are stressed for each position. In addition, remember not to suffer from marketing myopia when you look for your first job. Have a broad perspective and think of your first job as an entrée into the sports industry and a foundation from which you can build a career.

Internships

Nearly 70 percent of sports marketing executives began their careers serving as an intern for a sports organization, and 90 percent of sports organizations offer some type of internship. Many sports marketing students believe they will secure high-paying, glamorous, executive-level positions upon completion of their degree. The truth is, jobs in sports marketing are so competitive that internships are usually the only route to gaining the experience needed for a permanent position. By working as an intern, you become familiar with the organization and learn about the sports industry. In turn, the organization learns about you and reduces its risk in hiring you for a permanent position.

Sample advertisements

- **Sales and Marketing Manager** - Interns will assist the marketing department in the following areas:

  Sponsorship fulfillment, lead qualification, sampling/couponing programs, health and fitness expo at the Los Angeles Convention Center, and race day festival. Must be hardworking, detail oriented, friendly, energetic, and computer literate and have good communication skills. Hours would be flexible to fit interns' schedule.

- **Marketing Intern** - We have an opening for a sports marketing intern to assist in marketing programs designed to facilitate the growth of our products and services. Ideal person should have a sports marketing or sports management background. Computer, organization, and strong communication skills are essential. Internet experience preferred.

Facilities management

Whatever the sport, there must be a place to play. From brand-new multimillion-dollar sports complexes such as Globe Life Field in Arlington, Texas, to community centers used for recreational sports, facilities management is an important function. Although facilities management positions are more managerial in nature, they do include a strong marketing emphasis. For example, facilities managers are expected to perform public and community relations tasks, as well as having a strong promotion management background. Two of the largest facility management companies in the United States that you may want to explore are Spectra (www.spectraexperiences.com) and SMG (www.smgworld.com).

Sample advertisements

- **Advertising and Public Relations Manager** - Opportunity for a creative, energetic, hands-on individual to develop and implement advertising and PR programs for an established golf course facility. Minimum of five years' experience in advertising, design, broadcast production, and media planning.
- **Facility Manager** - The Special Events Center is seeking candidates for the position of facility manager. Candidates should be sales and marketing driven with experience in event planning, marketing and promotions, and facility management. Bachelor's degree with three years' related experience required. Primary liaison between users and facility staff. Provide leadership in event planning, onsite event management, and customer service.

Professional services

As the sports industry grows, the need for more and more business professionals in all areas is increasing. Today, sports careers are automatically associated with being a sports agent because of the Jerry Maguire "show me the money" phenomenon of the mid-90s. However, professional services are also needed in sports law, advertising, accounting, information systems, marketing research, finance, and sports medicine. Having the appropriate educational background before attempting to secure sports industry experience is a must. Salaries for professional services positions vary greatly depending on the job type and responsibilities.

Sample advertisements

- **Director of Special Olympics** – Seeking persons with excellent communication, fundraising, and management skills. Special Olympics is a year-round program of sports training and competition for children and adults with intellectual disabilities. Responsibilities include planning and organizing competitive events, training programs, public awareness campaigns, and fundraising activities. Candidates for position must possess excellent communication and fundraising skills as well as administrative, organizational, and volunteer management experience. Previous Special Olympics experience not required but helpful.
- **Global Advertising/Merchandising Manager** – Multinational manufacturer of cycling components. Responsible for leading the creation and execution of global advertising, athlete and event sponsorship, media planning and communication, global product merchandising, and global cost center management. This position requires an analytical thinker with excellent leadership and execution skills. A successful candidate is an MBA who has in-depth knowledge of ad strategy, planning, and production.

Health and fitness services

As the sports-participant market continues to grow, so will jobs in the health and fitness segment of the sports industry. Numerous jobs are available in management and sales for health clubs. Additionally, health and fitness counseling or instruction (personal trainer or aerobics instruction) represents another viable job market in health and fitness. Careers in sports training and sports medicine are also increasing. In addition to working for sports organizations as a trainer or physical therapist, a number of sports medicine clinics (usually affiliated with hospitals) are targeting the recreational participant and creating a host of new jobs in the prevention or rehabilitation of sports injuries.

Sample advertisements

- **Director of Campus Recreation** – Major responsibilities: provide opportunities to enhance participant fitness, personal skills, and enjoyment for a variety of student recreational activities; supervise, coordinate, and evaluate the activities of the department; prepare operating and capital expenditure budgets; develop goals, objectives, policies, and procedures; and perform personnel administration within the department. Qualifications: Master's degree and three years' experience in recreation or a similar field, two years' experience in administrative position, and current CPR and first aid certification required.
- **Fitness Club Operations Director** – Oversee all pool and tennis associates. Duties include hiring, training, supervising, and reviewing the performance of staff; administering weekly payroll; designing employees' work schedules; and overseeing maintenance/cleanliness

of facilities and inventory. Bachelor's degree; minimum two years' experience in athletic club/resort and one year in club management; basic knowledge of tennis, fitness, and aquatics; excellent communication skills. Sales and marketing experience with a strong member services background and experience developing/implementing member retention programs preferred.

Sports associations

Nearly every sport has a governing body or association that is responsible for maintaining the integrity and furthering the efforts of the sport and its constituents. Examples of sports associations include Federation International Football Association (FIFA), National Sporting Goods Association, United States Tennis Association (USTA), and the National Thoroughbred Racing Association (NTRA). Each sports association has executive directors, membership coordinators, and other jobs to help satisfy the members' needs.

Sample advertisements

- **U.S. Tennis Association** – Assist director of marketing in sponsorship, donations, and ad sales. Professional tournament operations for one tournament and booth promotions at all Northern California tournaments.
- **Research Associate** – A nonprofit golf association. Duties include survey research, statistical analysis, report writing, and database management. Knowledge of SAS and related bachelor's degree a must. Proficiency required in mapping, spreadsheet, and word processing software. Position requires demonstrated experience in technical writing and good verbal communication skills. Knowledge of the golf industry a plus. Entry-level position.

Professional teams and leagues

Along with being a sports agent, the types of jobs most commonly associated with sports marketing are in the professional sports industry segment. Working as the director of marketing for one of the "big four" sports leagues (NBA, MLB, NHL, or NFL) or one of the major league teams requires extensive experience with a minor league franchise or college athletic program and a master's degree. Job responsibilities include sales, designing advertising and social media campaigns to generate interest in the team, and supervision of game promotions and public relations.

Sample advertisements

- **Assistant Marketing Director** – Develops season ticket campaign strategies, negotiates advertising and media tradeouts, directs promotion coordinator, sales representative. Master's degree preferred; bachelor's degree required, preferably in marketing. Excellent communication skills a must. Should have extensive experience in working with corporate sponsors and developing a client base to support athletic sales.

- **Advertising Sales** – Major sports league seeks account executive to sell print advertising for event publications. The ideal candidate will possess two to four years' consumer or trade publication sales experience, excellent written and verbal communication skills, a proven track record of increasing sales volume, the ability to work in a fast-paced environment, and the flexibility to travel.

College athletic programs

If your ultimate career objective is to secure a position with a professional team or league, college athletic departments are a great place to start. Nearly all Division I and Division II athletic programs have marketing, sales, and public relations functions. This is now also true for DIII programs. In fact, larger Division I programs have an entire marketing department that is larger than those of most minor league franchises.

Sample advertisements

- **Coordinator of the Goal Club** – Responsibilities include identifying, cultivating, soliciting, and stewarding donors together with managing special events and direct mail programs. Candidates must possess a bachelor's degree and 2 or 3 years of fundraising experience.
- **Athletic Recruiting Coordinator** – Responsibilities include developing and organizing a vigorous recruiting program for eight sports within the guidelines of NCAA Division III, representing the athletics department at college fairs, and coordinating all recruiting activities with the admissions department.

Sporting goods industry

Sporting goods is a $40+ billion industry in the United States alone that is growing and presents career choices in all of the more traditional marketing or retailing functions. Opportunities include working for sporting goods manufacturers (e.g., Nike, adidas, Callaway, or Wilson) or retailers such as Dick's Sporting Goods, Bass Pro Shops, or Foot Locker.

Sample advertisements

- **Associate Buyer** – Lady Foot Locker is looking for a professional. To qualify, you will need chain store buying experience. Sporting goods exposure a plus.
- **General Manager/Catalog Division** – An outdoor recreation equipment retailer in the burgeoning backpacking/mountaineering/climbing industry is looking for a hands-on GM with full responsibility for its

fast-growing catalog division. Responsibilities include bottom-line profitability, strategic planning/execution, financial planning, marketing, prospecting, circulation and database management, catalog development and production, purchasing and inventory control, and systems coordination. Qualifications include five-plus years' management in e-commerce.

Event planning and marketing

Rather than work for a specific team or league, some sports marketers pursue a career in events marketing. Major sporting events such as the World Series, All-Star games, or the Olympics do not happen without the careful planning of an events management organization. The largest and most well-known events management company is the International Management Group (www.imgworld.com), with offices worldwide. Event marketers are responsible for promoting the event and selling and marketing sponsorships for the event.

Sample advertisements

- **Event Management Leader** – A service management association serving the bowling industry. Candidates will have a bachelor's degree in business or hotel management along with a proven track record of professional event production.
- **Event Planner** – National sports marketing firm organizing sports leagues and special events for young professionals is seeking an entry-level candidate to assist with operations and promotions of sports leagues, parties, and special events. Should be sports minded, extremely outgoing, and organized for this very hands-on position.

Researching companies

The previous section gives you a good idea of the types of job opportunities in sports marketing. Having considered your options, it is now time to get serious about finding that first job that will launch an exciting career. You will soon send out cover letters and résumés tailored to each position and organization. If they are not, the prospective employer will sense you have not done your homework. Your research efforts should include the following types of information: age of the organization, services or product lines, competitors within the industry, growth patterns of the organization and of the industry, reputation and corporate culture, number of employees, and financial situation. Today, most of the organizational information can be obtained quickly and easily via the Web.

Cover letters and résumés

Once you have researched prospective employers, you are ready to communicate with the organizations that you wish to pursue. Let us look at how to construct simple, yet persuasive, cover letters and résumés. Remember, these documents are within your complete control (think of this as an internal contingency); use this to your advantage and present yourself in the best possible light. Let us begin with the fundamentals of cover letter preparation.

Cover letters

The major objective of any cover letter is to pique the interest of the prospective employer. First impressions are everything, and the cover letter is the employer's first glimpse of you. A cover letter is a vital tool in marketing yourself to prospective employers for several reasons: An effective cover letter will draw attention to your qualifications and experiences that are most relevant to the position for which you are applying. Employers often use letters to assess the written communication skills that you will need for any position. A letter provides you the opportunity to convey to a potential employer your interest, enthusiasm, and other personal attributes that are not easily expressed in a résumé alone. There are a few basic guidelines that you can follow to make your cover letters more effective.

In the first paragraph, state the letter's purpose and how you found out about the position. Follow this with an overview of your most impressive job-related attributes such as skills, knowledge, and expertise. Obviously, the attributes you choose should relate to the position in mind. The third part of the cover letter should stem from all the research previously gathered on the organization. Show off your knowledge of the company and their current needs. Finally, let the organization know how you can help solve their current needs. Stress the fit between your background and values and the organization's culture.

Résumés

Now that your cover letter has been constructed, you are ready to begin work on an effective résumé. Here are seven tips for writing a résumé that are guaranteed to tell your story.

1 **Be thorough** - A good résumé should give the employer an indication of your potential based on your previous accomplishments. Include things such as job-related skills, previous work experience, educational background, volunteer experiences, special achievements, and personal data.

    Activities that you might deem unimportant could provide a great deal of insight into your ability to succeed on the job. For example, how about the student who has coached a Little League team throughout his or her collegiate career?

    Some candidates might view this as totally unrelated to the job. However, wise candidates will see how this activity could be used to demonstrate unique aspects of their personality such as patience, leadership, and good organizational skills.

2   **Be creative** - Most students are under the false impression that there is a right way and a wrong way to organize their résumé. In fact, most career development centers use a boilerplate format, making every student's résumé standard and neglecting the job and the industry.

All résumés should include topical areas such as job objectives, skills, knowledge, accomplishments, personal data, education, employment history, observations of superiors, and awards. Organizing and writing these sections is limited only by your imagination. The most important thing to remember is that the format should reflect both you and the job you are seeking.

3   **Use quotations** - A powerful tool that is not widely used in résumé preparation is the use of quotations. These quotes can be found in old performance evaluations or letters of recommendation. Here is an example of a quote that was used to reinforce the strength of an application.

Mr. Gamble has contributed in a positive manner to the success of the athletic department at WPU by organizing and implementing an effective game day promotional plan.

Melissa Luekke, promotions manager, athletic department, WPU

Quotes like this can provide further evidence of your abilities while relieving you of having to toot your own horn.

4   **Make the résumé visually appealing** - Looks are everything. In one study, 60 percent of employers indicated that they formed an opinion about the candidate on the basis of the résumé's appearance. The résumé that looks good will be given more consideration than one that does not. The résumé that is badly written and produced will be tossed, regardless of the applicant's qualifications. A few things to think about when designing your résumé include length (keep it to one page), paper (high-quality stock in white or off-white), spelling, grammar, and neatness (any error is unacceptable).

5   **Include a career objective** - Most employers consider the career objective the most important part of the résumé. Why? A specific career objective indicates that you know what you want in a job. This type of goal-directed behavior is what employers want to see in a candidate. Narrate to demonstrate to the reader what you have helped the organizations accomplish.

On the other hand, some résumé preparation experts strongly disagree with this line of reasoning. They argue that by placing an objective on your résumé, you are limiting the potential position. In other words, if you leave your options open, the employer will direct your résumé to the job that best suits your qualifications.

The best advice is to have multiple résumés prepared and ready to go with multiple career objectives. Most people have multiple career interests and do not have to settle for just one job. If you are truly practicing target marketing, you should have several different résumés ready. You should try to make the career objective sound like the description of the job you are targeting.

Here is a sample career objective for a student who wishes to pursue a public/community relations position at a major university or professional sports franchise:

Public Relations Assistant - Interested in copywriting, editing, writing speeches and news releases, photography, graphics, and so on. Desire experience in organization's internal and external publications. Good writing and speaking skills with communications background should assist in advancement to a management position within the athletic department of a major university or professional sports organization.

6 **Honesty is the best policy** - Employers are checking prospective candidates' qualifications more than ever before, due to a wave of people falsifying their credentials. Obviously, deceiving the employer about what you have done, or what you are able to do, is no way to start a positive relationship.

7 **Spread the word** - You should seek feedback and constructive criticism about your résumé by showing it to everyone you know. Ask for comments from other students, your professors, and career development specialists at school. In addition, you should circulate it among people in the sports industry. Résumé writing is a dynamic process that requires constant changes and improvement.

Interviewing

Most jobs in sports marketing require a high degree of interpersonal communication; therefore, the interview becomes a place to showcase your talents. Each person should have his or her own interview style, but here are some tips that should assist all job candidates with their interviewing skills.

1 **Be mentally prepared** - As with athletes, mental preparation is the name of the game for job seekers. Most job candidates do not come to the interview fully prepared. To get ready, you should have thoroughly researched the sports organization. Next, you need to learn as much

as possible about the person or people who will be conducting the interview. Being mentally prepared means being able to ask intelligent questions. Naturally, the types of questions you ask will vary by the position of the interviewer. Here are just a few of the potential questions that you might ask of the personnel manager or human resource representative:

- What do employees like best about the company? What do employees like least about the company?
- How large is the department in which the opening exists? How is it organized?
- Why is this position open?
- How much travel would normally be expected?
- What type of training program does a new employee receive? What type of professional development programs are offered? Who conducts them?
- How often are performance reviews given, and how are they conducted?
- How are raises and promotions determined? What is the salary range of the position?
- What are the employee benefits offered by the company?
  Possible questions for your potential supervisor include:
- What are the major responsibilities of the department?
- What are the major responsibilities of the job?
- What would the new employee be expected to accomplish in the first six months or year of the job?
- What are the special projects now ongoing in the department? What are some that are coming in the future?
- How much contact with management is there? How much exposure?
- What is the path to management in this department? How long does it typically take to get there, and how long do people typically stay there?

Here are some questions that might be asked of would-be colleagues:

- What do you like most or least about working in this company? What do you like most or least about working in this department?
- Describe a typical workday.
- Do you feel free to express your ideas and concerns? Does everyone in this department?
- What are the possibilities here for professional growth and promotion?
- How much interaction is there with supervisors, colleagues, external customers?
- How much independent work is there?
- How long have you been with the company? How does it compare with other companies where you have worked?

2 **Be physically prepared** - Image is important to all organizations, and a large part of the image that you project is largely a function of your physical appearance.

In other words, if you look the part, the chances of getting the job increase exponentially. The key to dressing for an interview is not only to be professionally dressed but to convey an image that is consistent with the company and the position. An interview is not the time to redefine the meaning of professional dress. Make sure you feel comfortable in the clothes that you choose to wear to the interview. If you look good and feel good, you will undoubtedly convey these positive feelings throughout the interview.

3 **Practice makes perfect** - Many marketing experts have discussed the similarities between finding a job and personal selling. When you are job hunting, you are, in essence, marketing or selling yourself. If you were selling a product, you would strive to become as familiar as possible with that product. You would not only learn the positive features and benefits of the product but understand the limitations of the product. In this case, you have to know everything the interviewer could conceivably ask about you. This should not be difficult, but you have to be prepared. The best way to prepare is through practice and repetition so that you feel confident answering questions about yourself.

The following is a list of questions regarding school, work, and personal experiences that are often asked during interviews. The more you have thought about these questions prior to the interview, the better your responses. Questions pertaining to school experiences might include:

- Which courses did you like most? Why?
- Which courses did you like least? Why?
- Why did you choose your particular major?
- Why did you choose to go to the school you attended? What did you like most or least about this school?
- If you could start college again, what would you do differently?

Questions pertaining to work experiences might include:

- What did you like most or least about the job?
- What did you like most or least about your immediate supervisor?
- Why did you leave the job?
- What were your major accomplishments during this job?
- Of all the jobs you have had, which did you like the most and why? Of all the supervisors you have had, which did you like the most and why?

Questions pertaining to personal experiences might include:

- Of all the things that you have done, what would you consider your greatest accomplishment and why?
- What do you consider your major strengths? What do you consider to be your major weaknesses?
- What kind of person do you have the most difficulty dealing with? Assuming that you had to work with such a person, how would you do it?
- What do you think are the most valuable skills you would bring to the position for which you are applying?
- What are your short-term goals (within the next five years), and what are your long-term goals?

4   **Maintaining a proper balance** - A good interviewee will know when to talk and when to listen. Your job is to present a complete picture of yourself without dominating the conversation. The best strategy for success is adapting to the interviewer and following his or her lead. When you are answering questions, do not let your mouth get ahead of your mind. Take a moment to think and construct your answers before rushing into a vague and senseless reply.

5   **The interview process does not end with the interview** - After the interview, be sure to write a letter expressing your thanks and desire for future consideration. It is a good idea to mention something in the body of the letter that will trigger the memory of the interviewer. Look for unique things that happened or were said during the interview and write about these. Too often, students neglect writing this simple letter and lose the opportunity to present their professionalism one more time.

Where to look for additional information

Sports career books

Wong, Glenn. *The Comprehensive Guide to Careers in Sports, 2nd Edition*
Hoffman, Shirl. *Careers in Sport, Fitness, and Exercise*
Schmidt, Debra. *Careers in Sports and Fitness (Exploring Careers)*

Sports career web sites

www.globalsportsjobs.com/
www.indeed.com/q-Sports-Management-jobs.html
www.linkedin.com/jobs/sports-industry-jobs/
www.jobsinsports.com/
www.sportscareerfinder.com/
www.sportsmanagementworldwide.com/courses
www.teamworkonline.com/
www.workinsports.com/

General career preparation resources

National Career Development Association
www.ncda.org/aws/NCDA/pt/sp/resources

Career Planner
www.careerplanner.com/

Cover letter writing resources

www.thebalancecareers.com/cover-letter-writing-resources-2071847
https://novoresume.com/career-blog/how-to-write-a-cover-letter-guide

Résumé writing resources

www.cnet.com/news/best-resume-writing-service/
www.themuse.com/advice/10-resume-resources-thatll-make-it-almost-
    impossible-for-a-hiring-manager-to-pass

Appendix B

Category	URL	Annotation
Professional sports	www.nfl.com	Official site of NFL
	www.nhl.com	Official site of NHL
	www.nba.com	Official site of NBA
	www.mlb.com	Official site of MLB
	www.pgatour.com	Official site of PGA tour
	www.pba.com	Official site of PBA
	www.afl.com.au	Official site of AFL
	www.clevelandindians.com	Official site of Indians
	www.clevelandcavaliers.com	Official site of Cavs
	www.clevelandbrowns.com	Official site of Browns
	www.nascar.com	Official site of NASCAR
	www.MLSsoccer.com	Official site of MLS
	www.fifa.com	Official site of FIFA
	www.indycar.com	Official site of Indy Car
	www.atpworldtour.com	Official site of ATP
	www.milb.com	Official site of MiLB
	www.formula1.com	Formula One Racing
	www.theahl.com	Official site of AHL
	www.avp.com	Official site of AVP
Women in sports	www.lpga.com	Official site of LPGA
	www.wnba.com	Official site of WNBA
	www.profastpitch.com	Women's fastpitch
	www.aagpbl.org	Women's baseball
	www.womenssportsfoundation.org/	Women's sports
	www.womenssportsjobs.com/default.htm	Women's sports jobs
	www.aahperd.org	Women's sports

continued

continued		
Category	URL	Annotation
	www.womenssportscareers.com	Women's sports careers
International sports	www.sportcal.com	Database of International Sports
	www.ausport.gov.au	Australian Sports Directory
	www.ismhome.com	Institute of Sports Management
	www.sportaccord.com	International sports federations
	www.nbcolympics.com	NBC Olympics
	www.ontariohockeyleague.com	Official site of OHL
	www.cfl.ca	Official site of CFL
	www.uefa.com	Official site of UEFA
	www.irb.com	International Rugby Board
	www.rugbyworldcup.com	Rugby World Cup
	www.olympic.org	Olympics
	www.olympic.org/london-2012-summer-olympics	2012 Olympics
	www.paralympic.org/index.html	Paralympics
	www.olympic.org/beijing-2008-summer-olympics	2008 Olympics
	www.fiba.com/	Official site of FIBA
Other sports	www.soccerlinks.net	Soccer links
	www.uslacrosse.org	U.S. Lacrosse
	www.usagym.org	Gymnastics
	www.churchilldowns.com	Horse racing
	www.ntra.com	Horse racing
	www.baseballprospectus.com	Baseball links
	www.tennis.com	Tennis links
	www.golflink.com	Golf links
	www.ngf.org/	Golf links
	www.hockeyzoneplus.com	Hockey links
	www.esports.com	Esports links
	www.littleleague.org	Baseball links

continued

Category	URL	Annotation
	www.ssbl1.com	Baseball links
	www.glbl.org	Baseball links
	www.usabasketball.com	Baseball links
	www.usatf.org	T&F links
	www.itftennis.com/	Tennis links
	http://home.nra.org/#/home	Rifle links
College sports	www.ncaa.com	Official site of NCAA
	www.ncaafootball.com	Official site of NCAAFB
	www.collegefootball.org	College football
	www.ohiostatebuckeyes.com	Official site of Ohio State Athletics
	www.cfbstats.com	CFB stats
	www.njcaa.org	Official site of NJCAA
	www.bigten.org	Official site of Big Ten
	www.cosida.com/	College sports information
High school sports	www.maxpreps.com	High school sports
	www.fridaynightohio.com	High school football
	www.cantonmckinley.com	High school sports
	www.nfhs.org/	High school association
Sports media	www.sports-media.org	Sports Media
	www.espn.com	ESPN
	www.awsmonline.org	Women in sports media
	www.sportsmedianews.com	Sports media news
	www.sportsmediajournal.com	Sports Media Journal
	www.bleacherreport.com	Sports media
	www.cbssports.com	CBS
	www.foxsports.com	Fox
	www.nbcsports.com	NBC
	www.goal.com	Soccer media
	www.aljazeera.com/sport/	Aljazeera sports
	www.eteamz.com	Active Network
	www.msnbc.msn.com/	Microsoft news
	www.yahoosports.com	Yahoo Sports

continued

| continued | | |
Category	URL	Annotation
	www.espn.go.com/	ESPN GO
	www.octagon.com/	Sports & Entertainment
	www.iaaf.org/	World Athletic
	www.mlive.com/sports	Michigan sports
	www.about.com/sports	Sports
	www.comcast.net/sports	Comcast sports
	www.nflindex.com	NFL index
	www.databasesports.com	Sports Database
	www.aussiesportsinfo.com	Australian sports info
	www.sportingnews.com	Sporting News
	www.sportsillustrated.com	Sports Illustrated
	www.tidesports.org/	Tide sports
Research and education	topendsports.com	Fitness, nutrition, and science
	www.scarborough.com	Scarborough Research
	www.nielsen.com	Nielsen Research
	www.kantamedia.com	Media Research
	www.kff.org	Henry J. Kaiser Foundation
	www.joycejulius.com	Joyce Julius Sponsorship
	www.sponsorship.com	IEG
	www.bankofamerica.com/sponsorships/	Sponsorship
	www.anythingresearch.com	Research index
	www.refdesk.com/sports.html	Index for general sports
	www.el.com/elinks/sports	Index for general sports
	www.sizes.com/sports	Index for Sports & Rec
	www.firsttee.org	Golf links
	www.ohahperd.org	Ohio Association for HPERD
	www.humankinetics.com	Physical Activity & Health Publisher
	www.asep.com	Coach Education Center

continued

continued

Category	URL	Annotation
	www.issaonline.com	Personal Trainer & Fitness
	www.afca.com	American Football Coaches Association
	www.iabc.com/	Business Communication
	www.prsa.org/	Public Relations
	www.licensing.org/	Licensing International
	http://whatcanidowiththismajor.com/major/sport-management	Management Programs
Careers in sports	jobsinsports.com	Job opportunities
	www.teamworkonline.com/	Job opportunities
	www.sfia.org	Job opportunities
	www.usgolfjobs.com	Job opportunities
	www.sportsdiversityrecruiting.com	Job opportunities
	www.sportscareersinstitute.com	Job opportunities
	www.sportscareers.com	Job opportunities
	www.workinsports.com	Job opportunities
	www.collegesportscareers.com	Job opportunities
	www.sportsmanagementworldwide.com	Job opportunities
	www.gamefacesportsjobs.com	Job opportunities
	www.sportscastingcareers.com	Job opportunities
	www.sportscareerfinder.com	Job opportunities
	www.teammarketing.com/	Job opportunities
	www.ifma.org/default.htm	Job opportunities
Recreation	www.ihrsa.org/	Keeping clubs open
	www.nsca-lift.org/	Strength and conditioning
	www.ymca.net/	YMCA of the USA
	www.ideafit.com/	Health and fitness
	www.acacamps.org/	American Camp Association
	www.nps.gov/index.htm	National Park Service
	www.nrpa.org/	National Recreation & Park Association

continued

continued

Category	URL	Annotation
Sporting goods	www.rawlings.com	Sports gear
	www.nsga.org	Sporting goods
	www.sporting-goods-industry.com	Sporting goods industry
	www.fesi-sport.org	European sporting goods
Sport marketing/ management	www.sportsmarketingnetwork.com	National Sports Marketing Network
	www.sportsbusinessdaily.com	Sports Business Daily
	www.sportbusiness.com	Sport business insight
	www.cmaa.org/	Management
	www.smaanz.org/	Sports management
	www.nacda.com	Collegiate Directors of Athletics
	www.nassm.com	Sport Management
Facilities/stadia	www.ezfacility.com	Club management software
	www.recmanagement.com	Recreation management
	http://sportsfac.ucsd.edu/	UCSD recreation
	www.sportsfacilitymanagement.com	Sports facility management

Illustration credits

Disclaimer

The publishers have made every effort to contact authors/copyright holders of works reprinted in *Sports Marketing* and to obtain permission to publish extracts. This has not been possible in every case, however, and we would welcome correspondence from those individuals/companies whom we have been unable to trace. Any omissions brought to our attention will be remedied in future editions.

Chapter 1

Ad 1.1 - E-sports blurring the line between spectator and participant
Credit: NEA (National Esports Association)
URL: www.nea.gg

Article 1.1 - Consumer fitness survey finds post COVID-19, billions in spend will be lost or reallocated in massive industry transformation
Credit: Rich Myers, 2020
Accessed August 20, 2020
Rightsholder: Businesswire
URL: www.businesswire.com/news/home/20200526005202/en/Consumer-Fitness-Survey-Finds-Post-COVID-19-Billions

Article 1.2 - Career Spotlight: Louise Waxler, Executive Director, Mclean Youth Soccer
Credit: Louise Waxler, interviewee

Article 1.3 - Technology in sport: inside the stadium of the future
Credit: Mark Samuels, 2019. Used with permission of Adweek Copyright© 2021. All rights reserved
Accessed August 20, 2020
Rightsholder: ZD Net
URL: www.zdnet.com/article/technology-in-sport-inside-the-stadium-of-the-future/

Article 1.5 - What can be done to close the merchandise gap?
What can be done to close the merchandise gap? The perpetual dispar-
ity between the availability - and marketing - of men's and women's
apparel is symbolic of how female fans are viewed
Credit: Shira Springer, 2019
Accessed August 20, 2020
Rightsholder: Sports Business Journal
URL: www.sportsbusinessjournal.com/Journal/Issues/2019/05/06/Opin-
ion/Springer.aspx

Photo 1.1 - The sports collector's dream - the Baseball Hall of Fame
Credit: Shutterstock, ID# 247304224 by Nagel Photography
URL: www.shutterstock.com/image-photo/cooperstown-new-york-
january-15-2015-247304224

Table 1.1 - Grand Rapids: built to last
Credit: David Broughton, 2019. Sports Business Daily
Accessed August 20, 2000
Rightsholder: Sports Business Journal
URL: www.sportsbusinessdaily.com/Journal/Issues/2019/09/23/In-Depth.
aspx

Web Capture 1.1 - The growth of sports information on the World
Wide Web
Credit: Sports Business Journal
URL: www.sportsbusinessjournal.com/Daily.aspx

Web Capture 1.2 - Ski.com provides information for ski enthusiasts
Credit: Ski.com
URL: www.ski.com

Web Capture 1.3 - NCAA: one of the most powerful sanctioning bodies
Credit: © 2020 National Collegiate Athletic Association
URL: www.ncaa.com

Chapter 2

Ad 2.1 - Cobra stresses an improved performance based on its technologi-
cal product improvements
Credit: Cobra Golf
URL: www.cobragolf.com/

Article 2.1 - Future of marketing - a sneak peek into 2020 and beyond

Credit: Aditya Kathotia
Rightsholder: Business 2 Community
URL: www.business2community.com/marketing/future-of-marketing-a-sneak-peek-into-2020-and-beyond-02190399

Article 2.2 – On the industry's radar
Globalisation to take TV sports rights past $85BN by 2024
Article Author: Joseph O'Halloran
Rightsholder: Rapid TV News, published 9/29/19
URL: www.rapidtvnews.com/2019092957428/globalisation-to-take-tv-sports-rights-past-85bn-by-2024.html#ixzz61hZuWeXx

Article 2.3 – Sports and politics: world of uncertainty
The NBA's China crisis is not a foreign situation for American sports – and it promises to come up again
Credit: Ben Fischer
Rightsholder: Sports Business Journal
URL: www.sportsbusinessdaily.com/Journal/Issues/2019/10/14/Sports-and-Society/NBA-China.aspx

Article 2.4 – Report: NBA still leads men's pro sports in diversity hiring
Credit: NBC Sports
Rightsholder: Front Office Sports (sports business publisher)
URL: https://nba.nbcsports.com/2018/06/26/report-nba-still-leads-mens-pro-sports-in-diversity-hiring/

Photo 2.1 – The mature market: staying young and having fun in record numbers
Credit: Shutterstock, ID# 696624586 by Ruslan Huzau
URL: www.shutterstock.com/image-photo/couple-playing-tennis-696624586

Photo 2.2 – As the controversy unfolded, workers in Shanghai took down a sign promoting the Oct. 10 game between the Los Angeles Lakers and the Brooklyn Nets
Credit: Bloomberg via Getty Images (Image #: 1174673698)
URL: www.gettyimages.co.uk/detail/news-photo/workers-pull-down-a-banner-advertising-a-national-news-photo/1174673698?adppopup=true

Web Capture 2.1 – FIFA's new model accenting its vision
Credit: FIFA
URL: www.fifa.com/about-fifa/who-we-are/explore-fifa.html?intcmp=fifacom_hp_module_corporate

Web Capture 2.2 – The Myrtle Beach Pelicans use a low-cost market niche strategy
Credit: Myrtle Beach Pelicans
URL: www.milb.com/myrtle-beach/tickets/ticket-information

Web Capture 2.3 – SportingNews.com providing sports information via the Internet
Credit: Sporting News
URL: www.sportingnews.com

Web Capture 2.4 – STX showing its latest advances in lacrosse technology
Credit: STX, LLC
URL: www.stx.com/womens-lacrosse

Web Capture 2.5 – NCAA capitalizes on the new opportunities based on the growth in women's sports
Credit: © 2020 National Collegiate Athletic Association
URL: www.ncaa.com/sports/basketball-women/d1

Chapter 3

Article 3.1 – We are wrong about millennial sports fans
Credit: Dan Singer, 2017
Accessed September 24, 2020
Rightsholder: Sports Business Journal
URL: www.sportsbusinessdaily.com/Journal/Issues/2017/09/18/Opinion/Singer.aspx

Article 3.2 – Case study: a sponsorship measurement solution
Case Study: A Sponsorship Measurement Solution from A Sponsorship Measurement Solution, Credit: Ukman, L & Krasts, M, October 2011
Rightsholder: IEG
URL: www.sponsorship.com/ieg/files/07/07903e35-98d1-4f1c-b318-7524b3104222.pdf

Article 3.3 – Structural representation in American sport: factors of race and socioeconomic status in football
Credit: White, K., Wilson, K., Yim, B., Donnelly, M., Mulrooney, A., Lyberger, M., & Walton-Fisette, T. (2017, November). Blind side: High school economics and becoming an NFL player. Paper presented at North American Society for the Sociology of Sport, Windsor, Canada

Photo 3.1 - The growing number of women's sport participants is being monitored through secondary marketing research
Credit: Elissa Unger

Web Capture 3.1 - Sport market analytics is an excellent source of primary and secondary data
Credit: Sports Market Analytics
URL: www.sportsmarketanalytics.com

Chapter 4

Ad 4.1 - Titleist highlighting the latest technology in their driver lines
Credit: Titleist
Rightsholder: Acushnet Company
URL: www.titleist.com/golf-clubs/golf-drivers

Article 4.1 - Marketing and promotion of the Olympic Games
Credit: Lee, Johnny, K., 2005. The Sport Journal, Volume 21, U.S. Sport Academy. ISSN 1543-9518
Rightsholder: The Sports Journal
URL: www.olympic.org/uk/organisation/facts/introduction/index_uk.asp

Article 4.2 - Sports Marketing Hall of Fame: Babe Didrikson Zaharias
Credit: Elizabeth Lynn, *Babe Didrikson Zaharias: Champion Athlete* (New York, Chelsea House, 1989). 1-55546-684-2 © 1989 by Chelsea House Publishers an imprint of Infobase Learning
Rightsholder: Infobase

Article 4.3 - High school sports participation increases for 28th straight year, nears 8 million mark
Credit: National Federation of State High Schools Associations
URL: www.nfhs.org/articles/high-school-sports-participation-increases-for-28th-straight-year-nears-8-million-mark/

Article 4.4 - The most popular 2019 New Year's resolutions
Rightsholder: Vitagene, Blog published December, 2019
www.vitagene.com/blog/most-popular-2019-new-years-resolution/

Figure 4.1 - Participation rates segmented by generations, U.S. population, age 6+

Credit: 2018 Physical Activity Council Participation Report
Rightsholder: Sports Marketing Surveys
URL: www.sportsmarketingsurveysusa.com

Photo 4.1 – Father and son fishing together by the ocean
Credit: Shutterstock, ID# 57789094 by BlueOrange Studio
URL:www.shutterstock.com/image-photo/father-son-fishing-together-by-
    ocean-57789094

Photo 4.2 – Many consumers see a discrepancy between the "ideal" and
    "actual" body
Credit: Shutterstock, ID# 106274624 by Diego Cervo
URL: www.shutterstock.com/image-photo/sports-activity-young-man-
    woman-exercising-106274624

Photo 4.3 – A growing number of consumers participate in high-risk
    sports
Credit: Shutterstock, ID# 107616701 by Vitalii Nesterchuk
URL: www.shutterstock.com/image-photo/jumping-rope-rock-107616701

Photo 4.4 – Sports participants fulfilling the need for self-actualization
Credit: Shutterstock, ID# 97358237 by Dudarev Mikhail
URL: www.shutterstock.com/image-photo/young-tourists-backpacks-
    enjoying-valley-view-97358237

Photo 4.5 – The high involvement cyclist
Credit: Shutterstock, ID# 107083253 by Ljupco Smokovski
URL: www.shutterstock.com/image-photo/view-biker-riding-mountain-
    bike-on-107083253

Photo 4.6 – Girls' sport participation is eroding traditional gender roles
Credit: Shutterstock, ID# 59662453 by Lipik Stock Media
www.shutterstock.com/image-photo/man-woman-white-
    taekwondo-kimono-training-59662453

Photo 4.7 – Marathon
Credit: Credit: Shutterstock, ID# 162584165 Suzanne Tucker
URL: www.shutterstock.com/image-photo/marathon-starting-line-
    shallow-depth-field-162584165

Table 4.2 – Why people participate in sports
Credit: George Milne, William Sutton, and Mark McDonald, "Niche
    Analysis: A Strategic Measurement Tool for Managers," *Sport Marketing
    Quarterly*, vol. 5, no. 3 (1996), 17–21
Rightsholder: Sport Marketing Quarterly

Table 4.3 - Segmentation of runners by motives
Credit: Andrew J. Rohm, George R. Milne, and Mark A. McDonald, "A Mixed-Method Approach for Developing Market Segmentation Typologies in the Sports Industry," *Sport Marketing Quarterly*, 2006, 15, 29–39, © West Virginia University
Rightsholder: Sport Marketing Quarterly

Table 4.5 - Household income for select sports and activities
Credit: Sports & Fitness Industry Association
URL: www.sfia.org

Web Capture 4.1 - Explore the Resort, online information source
Credit: Vail Resorts
URL: www.vail.com/

Chapter 5

Article 5.1 - MLB eyes increasing pace of play with new rule changes this season
Credit: Street and Smith's Sport Business Daily, February 13, 2020. Accessed July 24, 2020
Rightsholder: Sports Business Journal
URL:www.sportsbusinessdaily.com/Daily/Issues/2020/02/13/Leagues-and-Governing-Bodies/MLB.aspx?hl=pace+of+play&sc=2

Article 5.2 - Another year of declining attendance: how worried should MLB be?
Credit: Eddie Moran, 2019. Fan Experience, October 7
Accessed September 24, 2020
Rightsholder: Front Office Sports (sports business publisher)
URL: www.frntofficesport.com/mlb-attendance-2019-2/

Article 5.4 - Global sports betting market expected to reach nearly $155.49 B by 2024
Credit: Yogonet Gaming News
URL: www.yogonet.com/international/noticias/2020/06/24/53713-global-sports-betting-market-expected-to-reach-nearly-15549-b-by-2024

Figure 5.2 - Who's a sports fan?
Credit: © 2006 Pew Research Center, Social and Demographic Trends Project. Americans to Rest of World: Soccer Not Really Our Thing
URL: www.pewresearch.org/social-trends/2006/06/14/americans-to-rest-of-world-soccer-not-really-our-thing/
[https://pewresearch.org/assets/social/pdf/Sports.pdf]

Figure 5.4 - Model for fan identification
Credit: William A. Sutton, *Sport Marketing Quarterly. Reproduced with permission of Fitness Information Technology, Inc., via Copyright Clearance Center*
Rightsholder: Sports Marketing Quarterly

Photo 5.1 - Soccer crowd. Group of happy Brazilian soccer fans commemorating victory, with the flag of Brazil swinging in the air
Credit: Shutterstock, ID# 160923683
URL: www.shutterstock.com/image-photo/group-happy-brazilian-soccer-fans-commemorating-160923683

Photo 5.2 - The sport of bullfighting depicts a "lack of overlap" between sports participants and sports spectators, for very few have the courage and/or the skills to master the ring
Credit: Shutterstock, ID# 155340746 by Matej Kastelic
URL: www.shutterstock.com/image-photo/traditional-corrida-bullfighting-spain-bulfighting-has-155340746

Photo 5.3 - New sports facilities such as AT&T Stadium in Dallas influence attendance
Credit: Dallas Cowboys
URL: www.dallascowboys.com

Table 5.3 - What's your favorite sport? Favorite sports to watch by interest in sports news
Credit: © 2006 Pew Research Center, Social and Demographic Trends Project. Americans to Rest of World: Soccer Not Really Our Thing
URL: www.pewresearch.org/social-trends/2006/06/14/americans-to-rest-of-world-soccer-not-really-our-thing/
[https://pewresearch.org/assets/social/pdf/Sports.pdf]

Web Capture 5.1 - Mario Andretti Driving Experience: allowing fans to feel racing thrills
Credit: Mario Andretti Driving Experience
URL: www.andrettiracing.com/

Chapter 6

Ad 6.1 - Pygmy's segmentation on the basis of the family life cycle
Credit: Pygmy
URL: www.pygmyboats.com

Ad 6.2 – Crucial Catch positions itself as the official licensee of the National Football League
Credit: Lids
URL: www.lids.com

Article 6.1 – Technical report – Sport England market segmentation
Credit: Technical Report – Sport England Market Segmentation (2010), Sport England
URL: www.segments.sportengland.org/

Article 6.2 – Here to stay: generation Z's impact on sports content strategy
Credit: Pat Evans, 2019
Accessed September 24, 2020
Rightsholder: Front Office Sport (sports business publisher), published 14th March 2019
URL: www.frntofficesport.com/generation-z-sports/

Article 6.3 – Women in sports: are brands keeping up?
Credit: Olivia Atkins, 2019
Accessed September 24, 2020
Rightsholder: The Drum
URL: www.thedrum.com/news/2019/11/05/women-sports-are-brands-keeping-up

Article 6.4 – Women at the forefront of U.S. Olympic Movement
Credit: Ben Fischer, 2019
Accessed September 24, 2020
Rightsholder: Sports Business Journal
URL: www.sportsbusinessdaily.com/Journal/Issues/2019/01/07/Olympics/USOC-women.aspx?hl=women%27s+participation+in+sport&sc=0

Article 6.5 – Colts unveil family-friendly activities, benefits for 2019 game days
Credit: Reprinted by permission of Indianapolis Colts, Inc.
Accessed September 24, 2020
URL: www.colts.com/news/colts-unveil-family-friendly-activities-benefits-for-2019-game-days

Article 6.6 – The NBA's China crisis is not a foreign situation for American sports – and it promises to come up again
Sports and politics: World of uncertainty
Credit: Ben Fischer, 2019
Rightsholder: Sports Business Journal

URL: www.sportsbusinessdaily.com/Journal/Issues/2019/10/14/Sports-and-Society/NBA-China.aspx?hl=china+nba+&sc=0

Article 6.8 – The online reputation of athletes
Credit: Reputation VIP
URL: www.reputationvip.com/blog/online-reputation-of-athletes

Photo 6.1 – Professional sports are realizing the importance of the kids' market to their long-term success
Credit: Shutterstock, ID# 1240253 by Christopher Penler
URL: www.shutterstock.com/image-photo/young-boy-watching-baseball-game-1240253

Photo 6.2 – Polo is a sport that has typically appealed to the upper class
Credit: Shutterstock, ID# 63037606 by fritz16
URL: www.shutterstock.com/image-photo/ebreichsdorf-austria-september-10-polo-european-63037606

Photo 6.3 – Events that occurred some years before and their digital footprints are still present on the first Google page of Lance Armstrong

Table 6.2 – Core participation in select sports
Credit: Project Play, Aspen Institute
Rightsholder: Sports and Fitness Industry Association (SFIA)
URL: www.aspenprojectplay.org/youth-sports-facts/participation-rates

Table 6.3 – Top 25 sports/activities by participants in 2019, ages 6+
Credit: Sports and Fitness Industry Association (SFIA)
URL: www.physicalactivitycouncil.com/pdfs/current.pdf

Table 6.5 – Claritas PRIZM premier social groups
Source: Claritas
Credit: © Claritas LLC, 2018

Table 6.8 – Six dimensions or attributes of sports
Credit: James H. Martin, "Using a Perceptual Map of the Consumer's Sport Schema to Help Make Sponsorship Decisions," *Sport Marketing Quarterly*, vol. 3, no. 3 (1994), 27–33
Rightsholder: Sport Marketing Quarterly/Fitness Information Technology

Web Capture 6.1 – A wide array of youth football programs exist that target participation in youth football and cheerleading
Credit: Reprinted with permission of Cleveland Browns Inc. (2020)
URL: www.twitter.com/browns/status/1005166083794489345

Web Capture 6.2 - Build-a-Bear
Credit: Build-a-Bear
URL: www.buildabear.com/collections/sports/mlb – baseball

Web Capture 6.3 - Demographic segmentation of NBA Jr. creating a new, loyal fan base
Credit: NBA
URL: https://jr.nba.com/

Web Capture 6.4 - Cincinnati Reds targeting the mature market through Senior Days
Credit: Major League Baseball trademarks and copyrights are used with permission of Major League Baseball. Visit MLB.com
URL: www.mlb.com/reds/tickets/specials/seniors

Web Capture 6.5 - Women's Football Alliance promoting inequality and opportunity
Still sweating inequality? Together, we're changing the game
Credit: Women's Football Alliance
URL: www.wfaprofootball.com

Web Capture 6.6 - Reaching women's sports fans on the Web
Credit: Washington Spirit
URL: www.washingtonspirit.com

Chapter 7

Article 7.2 - Spotlight on international sports marketing
Excerpted from *The Stupidest Sports Book of All Time*
Copyright © 2017 by Kathryn and Ross Petras
Used by permission of Workman Publishing Co., Inc., New York
All Rights Reserved
URL: https://blog.workman.com/2017/10/the-weirdest-wackiest-worst-sports-endorsements-of-all-time/

Article 7.3 - These pro sports teams are running out of fans
Credit: Grant Suneson, 2019
Rightsholder: 24/7 Wall Street, published 7/24/19
URL: https://247wallst.com/special-report/2019/07/09/sports-teams-running-out-of-fans-3/

Photo 7.1 - This baseball, glove and bat represent pure goods
Credit: Shutterstock, ID# 62893237 by David Lee
URL: www.shutterstock.com/image-photo/baseball-glove-bat-62893237

Photo 7.3 - Bike manufacturers must stress the importance of product design and technology
Credit: Shutterstock, ID# 81690598 by Dudarev Mikhail
URL: www.shutterstock.com/image-photo/set-pictures-bicycle-theme-81690598

Table 7.4 - Quality dimensions of goods
Source: Adapted from D. A. Garvin, "Competing on the Eight Dimensions of Quality," Harvard Business Review (November - December 1987), 101-109
Rightsholder: Harvard Business School Press

Web Capture 7.1 - TaylorMade's split from Adidas Golf provided "freedom and independence" according to TaylorMade CEO David Abeles
Source: © 2019 TaylorMade Golf Company, Inc.
URL: www.taylormadegolf.com/

Web Capture 7.2 - Sources on the Internet provide a definitive gallery of sports logos
Credit: Fanning Creative (https://fanningcreative.carbonmade.com/)
URL: www.mentalfloss.com/article/53219/logo-mashups-all-teams-each-city

Web Capture 7.3 - Licensed merchandise on the web
Source: FansEdge, Incorporated
URL: www.fansedge.com

Chapter 8

Article 8.1 - The defining innovations and products of 2018
Credit: Nike News
URL: https://news.nike.com/news/defining-innovations-products-2018

Article 8.3 - Why American universities sponsor commercial sports
Credit: Allen Sanderson and John Siegfried, published July 31, 2018
Rightsholder: Milken Institute Review
URL: www.milkenreview.org/articles/why-american-universities-sponsor-commercial-sports

Article 8.4 - Under Armour feels the pressure of the U.S. sports retail sector
Credit: Andria Cheng, October 31, 2017

Rightsholder: emarketer retail

URL: https://retail.emarketer.com/article/under-armour-feels-pressure-of-struggling-us-sports-retail-sector/59f8f1a4ebd4000aa48d8eb6/

Infographic 8.1 - Fantasy sports becoming big business as popularity continues to rise

Source: Fantasy Sports & Gaming Association (FSGA)

URL: https://thefsga.org/wp-content/uploads/2020/05/2020-Press-Kit.pdf

Infographic 8.2 - Global broadcast and audience summary, FIFA World Cup Russia 2018

Source: FIFA

Photo 8.1 - Concept testing is used to understand consumer reactions to sports such as whitewater rafting

Credit: Shutterstock, ID# 102918779 by Ammit Jack

URL: www.shutterstock.com/image-photo/raft-water-white-whitewater-river-adventure-102918779

Photo 8.2 - Extending the product life cycle of the waterbike

Credit: Shutterstock, ID# 158192810 by EpicStockMedia

URL: www.shutterstock.com/image-photo/young-man-on-jet-ski-tropical-158192810

Web Capture 8.1 - The new sport of Bossaball combines volleyball, football, gymnastics, and capoeira and now draws large crowds

Credit: Bossaball International

URL: www.bossaballsports.com/

Chapter 9

Article 9.2 - How brands should use celebrities for endorsements

Credit: Steve Olenski Contributor, CMO Network, published July 20, 2016

Rightsholder: From Forbes. © 2016 Forbes. All rights reserved. Used under license

URL: www.forbes.com/sites/steveolenski/2016/07/20/how-brands-should-use-celebrities-for-endorsements/#5f485ac25593

Article 9.3 - The top 8 most recent controversial ads

Credit: Sam Carr, published Oct 10, 2019

Rightsholder: PPC Protect Limited

URL: https://ppcprotect.com/top-controversial-ads/

Photo 9.1 – Having greater knowledge of sports such as hockey moves consumers through the hierarchy of effects
Credit: Shutterstock, ID# 109773617 by Michael Pettigrew
URL: www.shutterstock.com/image-photo/ice-hockey-action-shot-forward-player-109773617

Chapter 10

Article 10.1-6 reasons why it's important to have a strong creative brief
Credit: Claude Harrington, February 12, 2016
Rightsholder: Business 2 Community
URL: www.business2community.com/strategy/6-reasons-important-strong-creative-brief-01450576

Article 10.2 – Spotlight on sports marketing ethics: This Girl Can('t)? campaign simply reworks 'sex sells' approach
Credit: Paul Harrison and Laura McVey
Rightsholder: The Conversation
URL: https://theconversation.com/this-girl-can-t-campaign-simply-reworks-sex-sells-approach-81609
Republished under a Creative Commons (Attribution/No derivatives) license

Article 10.3 – Six months after Ronaldo was accused of rape, why is the case in legal limbo?
Credit: Sam Borden, March 12, 2019. Accessed September 24, 2020
Rightsholder: ESPN
URL: www.espn.com/soccer/soccer/0/blog/post/3794488/six-months-after-ronaldo-was-accused-of-rapewhy-is-the-case-in-legal-limbo

Article 10.4 – The athlete endorsement model is broken
Credit: Daniel Roberts: Yahoo Finance; https://finance.yahoo.com/news/athleteendorsement-
model-broken-160012574.html

Article 10.5 – 2019 will see a change in how sports are processed over social media
Credit: Kyle Nelson, December 24, 2018
Rightsholder: Adweek via YSG Group
URL: www.adweek.com/brand-marketing/2019-will-see-a-change-in-how-sports-are-processed-over-social-media/

Article 10.6 – NBA: big payoff for a little patch
Credit: Sports Business Journal
URL: www.sportsbusinessdaily.com/Journal/Issues/2019/02/25/Leagues-
and-Governing-Bodies/NBA-patches.aspx

Article 10.7 – NBA mobilizes during coronavirus outbreak to get the
message out and provide funding, relief assistance
Credit: Jeff Zillgitt, March 24, 2020. Accessed September 24, 2020
Rightsholder: © USA TODAY Sports
URL: www.usatoday.com/story/sports/nba/2020/03/24/nba-nbpa-amp-
up-coronavirus-covid-19-funding-relief-assistance/2905503001/

Figure 10.2 – Digital around the world in 2020
Source: Hootsuite and We Are Social
URL: https://datareportal.com

Photo 10.1 – Stadium signage – one of the first forms of promotion and
still an important strategic tool
Credit: Shutterstock, ID# 1535975285 by Massimo Todaro
URL: www.shutterstock.com/image-photo/inside-emirates-stadium-known-
ashburton-grove-1535975285

Photo 10.2 – Opportunities for engagement are seemingly limitless. The
way sports are handled over social media will certainly change in the
coming years
Credit: Steve Prezant via Getty Images
URL: www.gettyimages.co.uk/detail/photo/hands-of-woman-photograph-
ing-baseball-game-with-royalty-free-image/764779057?adppopup=true

Photo 10.3 – Coca-Cola creates a positive association with baseball by
using stadium signage
Credit: Shutterstock, ID# 1423239506 by Darryl Brooks
URL: www.shutterstock.com/image-photo/atlanta-georgia-september-5-
2018-braves-1423239506

Photo 10.4 – Tottenham Hotspur new stadium built at an estimated cost
of $1 billion plus
Credit: Shutterstock, ID# 1368459644 by Silvi Photo
URL: www.shutterstock.com/image-photo/london-uk-april-13-2019-
panoramic-1368459644

Photo 10.5 – Twitter utilizing live events to enhance marketing strategies
Credit: Will Dowling
URL: https://twitter.com/willdowningcomm/status/941051048797630464

Photo 10.6 – MGM Grand and Bud Light are examples of partnerships in action with the UFC
Credit: Shutterstock, ID# 1730468443 by A. Ricardo
URL: www.shutterstock.com/image-photo/rio-de-janeiro-brazil-march-10-1730468443

Photo 10.7 – Drivers such as Ricky Stenhouse Jr., Kyle Larson, and Denny Hamlin exemplify the human billboard
Credit: Shutterstock, ID# 1330001177 by Grindstone Media Group
URL: www.shutterstock.com/image-photo/march-01-2019-las-vegas-nevada-1330001177

Photo 10.8 – Athlete signing autographs before games as part of sales promotion
Credit: Shutterstock, ID# 56009983 by Paul Hakimata Photography
URL: www.shutterstock.com/image-photo/new-york-may-27-phillies-ryan-56009983

Photo 10.9 – The Philadelphia Flyers use sweepstakes to further engage the audience
Credit: NBC Sports
URL: www.nbcsports.com/philadelphia/flyerssweepstakes

Photo 10.10 – Official Store FC Barcelona, offering clothing, footwear, team souvenirs, and paraphernalia for fans and visitors
Credit: Shutterstock, ID# 1017876976 by Lestertair
URL: www.shutterstock.com/image-photo/barcelona-spain-12-january-2018-official-1017876976

Web Capture 10.1 – Titleist Golf using direct objective
Credit: Titleist
Rightsholder: Acushnet Company
URL: www.titleist.com/golf-clubs/golf-drivers

Web Capture 10.3 – Easton stresses its competitive advantage
Source: Easton Sports
URL: www.easton.com/

Web Capture 10.4 – Brett Favre creates a powerful message for Wrangler
Credit: Wrangler
URL: www.wrangler.com/worn-by-greats/brett-favre.html

Web Capture 10.5 - Under Armour using this powerful imagery of Jordan Spieth
Credit: Under Armour
URL: www.underarmour.com/en-us/sports/golf?iid=sig&iidasset=190215_SS19_GOLF_VaniishSiteSIG_DIG#kits

Web Capture 10.6 - The Internet has become a popular medium for all lines of online purchasing
Credit: Major League Baseball trademarks and copyrights are used with permission of Major League Baseball. Visit MLB.com
URL: www.mlb.com/cardinals/tickets

Web Capture 10.7 - Social media continues to emerge as an interactive web strategy
Source: Twitter, https://twitter.com/cricketcomau?lang=en
Credit: Cricket Australia
URL: www.cricketaustralia.com.au/

Web Capture 10.8 - Chicago Bears engage the community
Credit: Chicago Bears
URL: www.chicagobears.com

Chapter 11

Article 11.1 - Jay-Z's Roc Nation entering partnership with NFL
Source: Jay-Z's Roc Nation entering partnership with NFL. Published Aug. 13, 2019, accessed September 24, 2020
Credit: NFL, 2019
URL: www.nfl.com/news/story/0ap3000001041162/article/jayzs-roc-nation-entering-partnership-with-nfl

Article 11.2 - 2019-20 Promotional and Theme Night Schedule
Rightsholder: NBA Properties Inc.
Credit: The NBA and individual member team identifications reproduced herein are used with permission from NBA Properties, Inc. © 2020 NBA Properties, Inc. All rights reserved
URL: www.nba.com/cavaliers/releases/promotional-schedule-2019-20. Published September 11, 2019. Accessed September 24, 2020

Article 11.3 - MLS announces multi-year partnership with BODYARMOR sports drink
Credit: MLS

URL: www.mlssoccer.com/post/2019/09/17/mls-announces-multi-year-partnership-bodyarmor-sports-drink. Published September 17, 2019. Accessed September 24, 2020

Article 11.4 - Esports' appeal to mainstream sponsors continues to grow
Credit: Sports Business Journal
URL: www.sportsbusinessdaily.com/Global/Issues/2018/05/03/Marketing-and-Sponsorship/Esports-Marketing.aspx

Article 11.5 - Ambush marketing in sports
Credit: Lex Sportiva
URL: https://lexsportiva.blog/2019/04/15/ambush-marketing-in-sports/. Published 15th April 2019. Accessed 24th July 2020

Article 11.6 - Spotlight on sports marketing ethics
Credit: Kathryn Park
Rightsholder: WIPO Magazine
URL: www.wipo.int/wipo_magazine/en/2019/02/article_0004.html. Published April 2019. Accessed 24th September 2020
Republished under a Creative Commons (Attribution 3.0 IGO (CC BY 3.0 IGO)) license

Article 11.7 - Sponsorship information
Credit: Bishop Montgomery High School
URL: www.bmhs-la.org/apps/pages/index.jsp?uREC_ID=289317&type=d&pREC_ID=665662

Article 11.8 - The fast-changing world of sports sponsorships
Credit: Calvin Koerber, published April 2019. Accessed 24th September 2020
URL: https://medium.com/@14ideas/the-fast-changing-world-of-sports-sponsorships-7bffdd9bd7ff

Article 11.9 - Career Spotlight: Lesa Ukman
Credit: Lesa Ukman Partnerships
URL: www.lesaukman.com/about/

Figure 11.6 - Four steps of data-based sponsorship analysis
Credit: Nielsen Sports

Photo 11.1 - Little League (Youth Baseball League)
Credit: Shutterstock, ID# 503982 by Timothy Kosheba
URL: www.shutterstock.com/image-photo/youth-baseball-league-503982

Table 11.2 - Sponsorship opportunities for the Wyndham Championship: sponsorship levels
Corporate Hospitality
Credit: PGA Tour, Wyndham Championship
URL: www.wyndhamchampionship.com/sponsorships/corporate-hospitality/

Table 11.3a - High school and NCAA women's sports growth
Credit: © National Collegiate Athletic Association

Table 11.3b - NCAA women's sports sponsorship growth
Credit: © National Collegiate Athletic Association

Table 11.6 - Importance of sponsorship objectives
Source: Doug Morris and Richard L. Irwin, "The Data-Driven Approach to Sponsorship Acquisition," Sport Marketing Quarterly, vol. 5, no. 2 (1996), 9
Credit: Sport Marketing Quarterly, Fitness Information Technology

Table 11.7 - University licensing leaders
Credit: Collegiate Licensing Company
Rightsholder: © National Collegiate Athletic Association
Web Capture 11.1 - Disabled athletes compete in Paralympic games
Credit: International Paralympic Committee
URL: www.paralympic.org

Web Capture 11.2 U.S. Open
Credit: MSG Promotions
URL: www.msgpromotions.com/us-open-hospitality/2021-u-s-open-championship/

Web Capture 11.3 - University of Texas's corporate partner program
Credit: The Texas Exes, the alumni association for UT Austin
URL: www.texasexes.org/about-us/corporate-sponsors

Chapter 12

Article 12.2 - Spotlight on sports marketing ethics - astronomical athlete salaries: are they worth it?
Credit: Orley Amos
URL: www.amosweb.com/cgi-bin/awb_nav.pl?s=pdg&c=dsp&k=9

Article 12.3 - The economics of ticket scalping
Credit: Paul Crosby, Macquarie University, Australia and Jordi McKenzie, Macquarie University, Australia

Article 12.4 – New Era Tickets uses iovation to keep scalpers and fraudsters out of the arena

Credit: iovation Inc. (2013), www.iovation.com

URL: www.iovation.com/images/uploads/case-studies/PDF/iovation-newera-ticketing-case-study.pdf

Article 12.5 – Dynamic ticket pricing use takes off, and teams hope it'll lure fans back into sports stadiums

Credit: Jacob Young

URL: www.cnbc.com/2017/12/01/dynamic-ticket-pricing-use-takes-off-and-teams-hope-itll-lure-fans-back-into-sports-stadiums.html

Photo 12.1 – To some, golf lessons may be priceless

Credit: Shutterstock, ID# 812018 by Cindy Hughes

URL: www.shutterstock.com/image-photo/golf-swings-practice-range-812018

Photo 12.2 – Fan First Menu pricing

Credit: Morgan Moriarty

URL: www.sbnation.com/2017/8/26/16141026/new-atlanta-falcons-mercedes-benz-stadium-peach-bowl-sec-championship-playoff

Table 12.2 – An example of the Fan Cost Index for the MLB

Credit: Fan Cost Index

Rightsholder: Team Marketing Report

URL: www.teammarketing.com

Table 12.3 – Sports and fitness activities participated in by U.S. population 6-year trend, ages 6+

Credit: National Sporting Goods Association

URL: www.nsga.org/

Web Capture 12.1 – Loveland Ski may use bundled as well as seasonal discounting

Credit: Loveland Ski Area

URL: www.skiloveland.com

Chapter 13

Article 13.1 - Inside the Georgetown Hoyas basketball marketing strategy
Credit: Jeremy Fitch
Rightsholder: Front Office Sports, published 16th March 2018
URL: www.frntofficesport.com/inside-the-georgetown-hoyas-basketball-marketing-strategy/

Article 13.2 - How Major League Baseball can fix its attendance problem
Credit: Tom Lohr, published 22nd March 2019
URL: www.howtheyplay.com/team-sports/How-Major-League-Baseball-Can-Fix-Its-Attendance-Problem

Article 13.3 - Poll: who is the best professional sports commissioner?
Credit: William Boyd, published 28th June 2018
Rightsholder: The Daily Caller
URL: www.dailycaller.com/2018/06/28/best-sports-commissioner/

Article 13.5 - The case for paying college athletes
Credit: Fiona Harrigan, 2020. Accessed September 3, 2020
Rightsholder: The Detroit News
URL: https://eu.detroitnews.com/story/opinion/2020/08/31/opinion-case-paying-college-athletes/5658183002/

Article 13.6 - The role of analytics in professional sports
Credit: Julian Ereth, published 22nd June 2016
Rightsholder: Eckerson Group
URL: www.eckerson.com/articles/sports-intelligence-the-role-of-technology-in-professional-sports

Article 13.7 - Worst sports innovations
Credit: ESPN
URL: www.espn.com/page2/s/list/innovations/worst.html

Photo 13.1 - Sports organizations, such as this trailer produced by The All England Lawn Tennis Club for The Championships, Wimbledon, tying the history of the event to important moments in history, often utilize creative marketing strategies to illustrate their global proposition to fans
Credit: The All England Lawn Tennis Club
URL: www.wimbledon.com

Photo 13.2 - Sponsors such as Kia must design controls to evaluate sponsorship effectiveness
Credit: Gabriel Roux photography

Rightsholder: Kia Classic
URL: www.thedrum.com/news/2017/03/14/kia-builds-womens-sports-sponsorship-portfolio-with-ladies-pga-deal

Table 13.9 - Top 5 sporting scandals that shocked the world
Credit: Scott Henderson, published 26th March 2018
Rightsholder: Australian Men's Health
URL: www.menshealth.com.au/top-5-sporting-scandals-that-shocked-the-world

Web Capture 13.1 - Sports careers on the Web
Credit: Work In Sports
URL: www.workinsports.com

Web Capture 13.2 - Sponsorship ROI evaluations
Credit: Joyce Julius & Associates, published 3rd October 2018
URL: https://twitter.com/joyce_julius?lang=en

Index

Page numbers in *italics* indicate figures and page numbers in **bold** indicate tables.

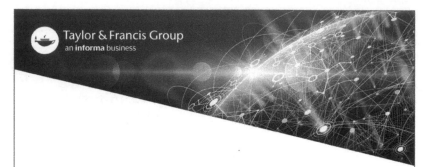